DATE DUE			
Nov 12'74			
Dec 18'7			
Jan 21'75			
Feb 17'75			
Apr 12'76			
Apr 25'80			

Edited by

A MODERN

HARLAN HATCHER • University of Michigan

REPERTORY

HARCOURT, BRACE & COMPANY

New York

Calligraphy by Lili Cassel

The author records his thanks for the use of the selections reprinted in this book by permission of the following publishers and copyright holders:

Dodd, Mead & Company, for *Candida* by Bernard Shaw. Reprinted by permission of Dodd, Mead & Company. Copyright, 1898, by Herbert S. Stone & Co. Copyright renewed 1926 by Bernard Shaw.

Harcourt, Brace and Company, Inc., for *Murder in the Cathedral* by T. S. Eliot. Copyright, 1935, by Harcourt, Brace and Company, Inc.

New Directions Books, for *Summer and Smoke* by Tennessee Williams. Reprinted by permission of New Directions Books, published by James Laughlin, 333 Sixth Avenue, New York City. Copyright, 1948, by Tennessee Williams.

Oxford University Press, Inc., for *Venus Observed* by Christopher Fry. Copyright 1949 by Christopher Fry. Reprinted by permission of the Oxford University Press, Inc.

Princeton University Press, for *Billy Budd* by Louis O. Coxe and Robert Chapman. Reprinted by permission of the publishers. Copyright, 1951, by Princeton University Press.

Random House, Inc., for *The Madwoman of Chaillot* by Jean Giraudoux, copyright, 1947, by Maurice Valency; for *Detective Story* by Sidney Kingsley, copyright, 1948, 1949, as an unpublished work by Sidney Kingsley and Madge Evans; copyright, 1949, by Sidney Kingsley; for *Ah, Wilderness!* by Eugene O'Neill, copyright, 1933, by Eugene O'Neill. All reprinted by permission of Random House, Inc.

The Macmillan Company and Macmillan & Co., Ltd., for *Juno and the Paycock* from *Two Plays* by Sean O'Casey. Reprinted by permission of the publishers. Copyright, 1927, by The Macmillan Company.

CONTENTS

CONTENTS

INTRODUCTION

▶ Dramas have been designed, almost without exception, not for private reading but for production before an audience in some kind of theatre. Shakespeare clearly had no thought of writing his plays for publication, and no premonition that they would become a part of world literature. They were brought to life in his day by the voice and movement of living actors on the boards of an empty stage. But what an audience sees and hears in the theatre is the product of the originating mind of the author, of the careful study and imaginative projection of the play by the director and producer, and of the equally careful study and interpretation of every detail of the various parts by the actors themselves. All this precedes the moment when the curtain rises and the audience gets its first look at the finished theatre product. That is to say, the people who create the drama as a living spectacle have first *read* the play.

The reader of these plays may share through the printed text the exhilarating experience of producing the drama in his own imagination. This is creative reading in its most challenging form. It finds its own adequate substitute for the supporting arts of stage design, costume, lighting, music, and the human voice. These allied arts are not to be deprecated in the least. They have grown in importance with the development of the modern theatre, and they are generally agreeable to the spectator; but the play may be enjoyed without them. Indeed, we remember that in some of the greatest periods of drama and the theatre —the classic Greek and the Shakespearean, for example—most of these subsidiary arts gave scant support, if any, and yet the force of the play was not in the slightest degree damaged. And today the play is still the thing.

We need not argue the value of the private reading, study, and classroom discussion of drama. As a literary form, drama has been one of the most favored mediums of expression from the golden age of Greece to the present. (It is significant that nine of the recipients of the Nobel prize for literature since 1901 have been dramatists.) And while no form of literature asks more from the reader, few forms, if any, give richer rewards in return. Because of the limitations of the theatre, for which it is ultimately designed, a drama must be compact and concentrated. Its playing time is usually little more than two hours. Yet in its brief compass it manages to convey as much as a novel which requires hours and hours of reading time. A novelist may ramble; a dramatist cannot—he must make every word do double duty. A novelist may consume several pages in character description or in analysis of thought and motive. A dramatist has but a few moments at his disposal, and even then he must convey his meanings through spoken words, while the central action of the play drives steadily forward. The burden of understanding and interpretation, therefore, is laid upon the reader himself. In his imagination he must catch the inflection of the character's voice, and detect the nuances of expression which reveal his nature. He must create and furnish the scene (a novelist like Hardy or Conrad would do this for him in dozens of pages). He must give the action its proper pace, and manipulate the entrances and exits of the characters.

These are the requirements for the creative reading of plays. A little conscious practice will master the art, and the rewards will be great. Since every word counts and signals to the creative imagination, the savoring of phrases and the stimulus of interpretation may be fully indulged. If the reader will take diligent care with all details of the first act of a play, the rest will unfold with mounting satisfaction and effect. And the experience of creation will be matched only by some of the highest forms of poetry.

Fortunately the printing and reading of plays is a significant part of our literary life today. The initial failure of Bernard Shaw's plays on the stage led him to publish them with elaborate and lively prefaces. In book form his plays became literary events and were more often read than they were seen. The plays of Barrie and Galsworthy, though quite successful on the stage, also enjoyed wide reading in book form. By the time O'Neill began making theatrical history in America, it had become customary to publish plays to coincide with their presentation on the stage. Today very few plays that are presented on Broadway fail to appear shortly thereafter in book form. The plays of Christopher Fry and T. S. Eliot, for example, have probably won more customers in the bookstores than at the box office. In short, many plays have become as much a part of contemporary literature as the novels of Faulkner and Hemingway, or the poetry of T. S. Eliot and Carl Sandburg.

The theatre has been in a lively state of health during most of the past seventy-five years. In all the European countries, in England and Ireland, and in America, thousands of plays have been written and produced. Many have been ephemeral, many unimportant, many merely topical; but a few have risen high above the passing interests of the moment to speak to later audiences on subjects of permanent concern to mankind. The passing of time imposes new standards of judgment on all literary works. A gay comedy by Noel Coward may engage and delight the fancy of one generation and yet utterly fail to attract the interest of a later generation. Conversely, a comedy by Bernard Shaw may be based on aspects of human life which are relatively unaffected by the changing mores and surface trappings of life. It speaks across the transitory to the persistent truths of life.

It is always the responsibility of any generation to preserve the old and to create the new. This is what is happening today in the drama. The giants of the past have had their say and have left their bequests to future generations. Those bequests which are found good are now placed in the growing treasury of the modern theatre. But in paying the giants tribute we must not forget to listen to the newer voices. Indeed, it is one of the purposes of this collection of nine plays to present some of the newer work that has enriched our theatre and our perception of life.

These nine plays are offered not to represent historically the extraordinary scope, versatility, and richness of modern English, American, and Continental drama, but to represent, to a fair degree at least, some of the more recent achievements and the present character of drama. They are good and rewarding both as independent works of art and as expressions of the times and conditions of which they are a part. It has long been conventional, of course, to begin a collection of modern dramas with a play by Henrik Ibsen. The convention is supported by the logic of history, for Ibsen is a dominating landmark. If he did not originate the modern version of the thesis or problem play, he was at least its first major exponent. He was a dramatist of such genius that his plays were a stunning experience to the audiences of his day. Clamorous and even bitter controversy raged round them. By some they were pronounced foul, disgusting, repulsive, degrading, and vulgar; by others they were received as a liberating influence, honest, thoughtful, and sincere, a breath of fresh air in a musty room. The controversy made Ibsen a rallying point for the young moderns of the 1880's and 1890's, some of the new theatres were organized to perform his works, and he became by natural selection the foundation for a study of "modern" drama.

No injustice or lack of recognition is implied by failing to follow this now rigorous convention, and giving to Bernard Shaw's amiable and winsome comedy *Candida* preference over the heavy and somewhat dated theses of *A Doll's House, Ghosts,* or *Hedda Gabler.* Shaw, who was profoundly stirred by the great Norwegian, has had more of an impact on our own life and culture than Ibsen himself. And *Candida,* in thesis, tone, and philosophy, seems more representative of our contemporary views than any of Ibsen's earlier classics. It merits its first place in this modern repertory.

The Irish theatre has made a rich contribution to modern drama, and the plays of William Butler Yeats, Lady Gregory, J. M. Synge, Lord Dunsany, Lennox Robinson, and Paul Vincent Carroll have become a part of world theatrical literature. In this, or any other company, by any standard, the plays of Sean O'Casey arrest attention. The passing of three decades has only sharpened the portraits and the rich humanity of his masterly *Juno and the Paycock*. It has been continuously successful on the stages of the world, and it is powerful and moving in the printed word. It almost selects itself for this collection.

The plays of Eugene O'Neill coincide with the resurgence of American drama. No other dramatist in America, and few on the Continent, has written with more powerful effect during the last thirty-five years than O'Neill. Most of his plays have dealt symbolically with the deep emotional problems and the psychological disturbances of contemporary men and women. They are still great dramas, though they have faded a little with the passing of the dominant vogue of Sigmund Freud. Time, however, has in no way touched his one fine comedy, *Ah, Wilderness!*, which recreates so accurately and sympathetically a by-gone era in America. In its gentle realism it shows a quality of O'Neill's genius that might have been given fuller expression in a more sympathetic and generous age than the post-World War I decades. It seems all the more welcome now.

Poetry has never been far removed from the theatre. During the classic periods it was central. And Ibsen's *Peer Gynt*, Hauptmann's *The Sunken Bell*, Rostand's *Cyrano de Bergerac* are samples of the persistence of the tradition in a period overwhelmingly devoted to the new realism. Dramatists are constantly striving to enlarge the dimensions of their art in order to probe more deeply and to suggest more richly the elusive meanings of life and the majesty of the soul. Poetry is the ideal language for such expression, and in the hands of an artist like T. S. Eliot plays in poetic form also have life in the theatre. *Murder in the Cathedral* is a natural selection for this repertory because of its superb artistry and because it exalts the purpose of the theatre by touching the eternal problems within the soul of man in any age.

Another recent English dramatist who has made notable use of the poetic form is Christopher Fry. Fry too has reached back into the great tradition of British poetic drama and brought verse to life again on the contemporary stage. His *Venus Observed* commands recognition.

American drama since World War I has been rich and varied. Its energy has been concentrated largely on realistic reproduction on the stage of the turbulent life in our restless nation. Sidney Kingsley has had the sharpest ears for our speech, a clear picture of the spectacle of life as it flows by, and an unusual gift for reproducing it in the script of a play. His recent *Detective Story* is an especially vivid "slice of life" in the dramatic form.

There have been several greatly talented younger men who have contributed to modern American drama and have made their voices heard—dramatists like Tennessee Williams and Arthur Miller and William Saroyan. We have chosen the first because he seems to catch the tender overtones which lend some dignity to a basic, often sordid, realism. His *Summer and Smoke* shows his special talents at their best.

We have also included Herman Melville's *Billy Budd,* as dramatized by Louis O. Coxe and Robert Chapman. This is an unusual play in contemporary America because it deals successfully, in an almost stylized form, with the persistent mystery of good and evil. It points up our renewed concern for moral principles in a period besieged by doubts.

The great European centers of culture were blighted by the catastrophe of World War II, and they have been slow to recover their strength. Compared with the fertile creative period between the two World Wars, the past decade has seemed weary, frustrated, or silent, and Jean Paul Sartre has been a spokesman for its gloom. The human spirit, however, is resilient, and never given permanently to despair. Jean Giraudoux expresses this enduring zest for life, and maintains a broad perspective on our troublesome problems in his urbane comedy, *The Madwoman of Chaillot.* We include it here for these reasons, and because it is a delight as a unique work of art.

This repertory, as we have said, is not meant to be representative of all types and trends of modern drama. Each selection is self-contained, and derives its primary interest from its intrinsic merits. All the selections have stood the test of production in the theatre; they have also stood the still more demanding test of close reading in printed form. Taken together, we believe, they offer to the imaginative reader some of the best individual works of art from the contemporary theatre.

A MODERN
REPERTORY

George Bernard Shaw

▶ Shaw towered high above all other dramatists writing in English during the first half of the twentieth century. He was an international personality as well as a man of letters. Age did not tarnish his lustre; although he had become venerable in his nineties, he still spoke with vivacity and wit to a world audience which still regarded him with attention. The deferential attitude, which had become habitual and touched with awe, was revealed by the title of John Mason Brown's tribute at the time of Shaw's death: "GBS, Headmaster to the Universe." And the almost worshipful student-master relationship is expressed in the closing paragraph of Brown's tribute: "It is something to have lived on this planet as the contemporary of such a titan as George Bernard Shaw."

The generation now in college has difficulty in sharing this extreme adulation. Shaw was born in 1856, while Franklin Pierce was still President of the United States, and before Lincoln was a public figure. He was nearing eighty when the college students now reading his plays were born. The backdrop of Queen Victoria's world, against which Shaw's intellect and dramatic talent scintillated so devastatingly, has faded almost beyond restoration. Many of the ideas with which he dealt, and which then seemed so fresh and new, so bold and even breath-taking, are now outmoded, or are absorbed into our present intellectual world and become commonplace.

In all, Shaw wrote more than two score plays, many volumes of essays and criticisms, several novels, and enough miscellaneous pieces to constitute a fair-sized library. He had something to say on every topic of any concern to his epoch, and he said it brightly, forcefully, and provocatively. He wrote about military heroes and militarism, slum-landlordism, marriage, prostitution, vegetarianism, evolution, the Life Force, censorship, poverty, general stupidity, and scores of other social problems.

It is inevitable that much of this writing was topical and parochial. But it is also true that through the cumulative force of his writings, and of his personality, Shaw made such a decisive impact upon the world in the early years of the twentieth century that he altered its attitudes and helped to reset the course of its thinking. Like any good schoolmaster, he did his work so well that he freed his students from dependence upon him.

Seldom in our literary history has one man commanded such devoted attention over so long a period. On that account, present-day readers of Shaw must guard against doing an injustice to his genius. We have reached the point where more objective critical appraisal is possible. Without in the least detracting from his importance to his contemporaries, we may well consider the setting of his work and ask about the survival value of his plays, and which of them seem to have permanence in the developing body of English drama.

Although Shaw's life actually was not eventful, he made the most of it. He was clever and boastful about his unique genius and made copy of it throughout his life, in the spirit of his oft-quoted statement, "things have not happened to me: on the contrary it is I who have happened to them." An early cartoon shows young Shaw standing on his head at a busy street corner to attract attention to himself. He was a master of self-advertising. From his earliest school days he exhibited the tendency of the physically unaggressive but mentally alert boy to overassert his intellectual superiority. In the Dublin society of his boyhood he was troubled also by the loss of position brought on his proud family by an alcoholic father. He felt his outcast status keenly in his early years, though he spoke brightly and humorously of it in the period of his success, calling himself the "upstart son of a down-start father."

His education was desultory and unplanned. He was encouraged in his study of music by a gifted mother who followed this art in London. When he was twenty Shaw went to London to be near her. He studied at the British Museum without thought of a literary career, and formed a youthful enthusiasm for Wagner and Ibsen. During the 1890's he wrote critical books about both. He tried his hand at five novels without satisfaction or success. Between the years 1885 and 1898 he became successively an art critic on the *World,* a music critic for the *Star,* and dramatic critic for *The Saturday Review.*

It was an exhilarating period for the then younger generation. The Age of Victoria was already stolid and in decline, ready for the eager iconoclasm of Wilde, Shaw, and the reformers. The dramas of Ibsen, Strindberg, Hauptmann, and the realistic exponents of the useful theatre had reached sedate London. So, too, had Henry George, the Webbs, and the Fabian Society, which Shaw joined in 1884. At their free-for-all meetings, where arguments about social evils were spirited, Shaw learned to speak with cleverness, clarity, and precision, and grew in confidence as he sensed his peculiar gifts for dramatizing ideas and making talk exciting.

In the midst of all this end-of-the-century ferment, Shaw tried his hand at writing a play in the "modern" thesis manner. It was called *Widowers' Houses.* According to Shaw himself it was "a grotesquely realistic exposure of slum landlordism, municipal jobbery, and the pecuniary and matrimonial ties between it and the pleasant people of 'independent' incomes who imagine that such sordid matters do not touch their own lives." It was produced in 1892 at J. T. Grein's new Independent Theatre—the London counterpart of the Free Theatres of Paris and Berlin created to produce the controversial plays of Ibsen and his contemporaries. The play was no dramatic success, but it was sensationally attacked and reviled, and Shaw, somewhat like Byron, awoke to find himself famous. He had caught the attention of the public, and he had learned how to keep it and use it. He retained the secret for nearly sixty active years.

The stupendous verve and energy and audacity of the young playwright astonished and intrigued the age. Shaw later referred to himself in this period as "a young tiger, fearing neither God nor man." He wrote *The Philanderer* in 1893, satirizing the "new woman," the marriage compact, and the medical profession. The following year he wrote *Mrs. Warren's Profession* on the economic basis of prostitution and related themes. It was forbidden by the Censor in London, and was later raided by the police in New York when performed there.

Shaw had thus far written three plays with no stage success whatever. But he had revealed to himself and a widening public a unique genius for dialogue and for witty criticism and an ability to cause an uproar with his pen, in what he called his "most energetically egotistic fighting style." Since there was no outlet for his product through the theatre, he hit upon the idea of publishing his plays—"though the Stage is bound, the Press is free." With calculated provocativeness, he titled them *Unpleasant* plays because, he said, "their dramatic power is used to force the spectator to face unpleasant facts." He followed up with four more plays and prefaces which he labeled *Pleasant,* among them *Candida,* and then with three more published as *Three Plays for Puritans,* which included *Caesar and Cleopatra.* He continued the practice of publishing his plays with prefaces, epilogues, and commentaries throughout his long career.

The plays and prefaces were a literary success. The clean, sparkling expository style was reminiscent of Jonathan Swift. The wit and the lively comic spirit linked these productions to the great classic tradition of English comedy at its best.

Shaw found that a delighted public first granted him outrageous liberties, then expected him to use them, and paid him handsomely for his gibes and insults. What he could not say forthrightly as his own opinions he could put into the mouths of the characters in his plays. He relished as fully as his bitterest critics the paradox of his becoming a privileged millionaire while castigating the curse of poverty and extolling the virtues of socialism and equality of income. He did not relish the day when, in a final burst of irony, the tax gatherer whom he had encouraged took his doctrine realistically and redistributed his wealth.

A surprisingly large number of Shaw's plays have survived the passing years and are already a permanent portion of English dramatic literature. Considering the massiveness of the output, the level of the writing was very high, and, at its best, the equal of anything of its kind in the language. It seems fairly certain that the portion of it which later generations, detached from the original setting, will find good will be generous. Critical and reader judgment are now nearly unanimous in the selection of *Candida, Caesar and Cleopatra, Man and Superman, Androcles and the Lion, Saint Joan,* and portions of *Back to Methuselah,* with *Pygmalion,* and, perhaps, *The Devil's Disciple* making strong claims for audience. In selecting this distinguished list, to keep the perspective clear, we must observe and remind ourselves that enough good drama is left over to support several reputations at a level higher than that attained by the author of *The Second Mrs. Tanqueray* or *The Case of Rebellious Susan.*

Man and Superman is a good case in point. Much of it seems dated, belonging to the turn-of-the-century era when Spencer, Darwin, and Bergson's creative evolution furnished ideas for debate. It was, however, something of a surprise to audiences of the 1950's to find how engaging the neglected Don Juan section of the old play still is. Without benefit of stage trappings, lighting, costumes, or music, with simply a bare lecture platform and four good voices, the brilliant and coruscating talk became a gripping drama of ideas.

A triumph of the same magnitude in a totally different vein is achieved in Scene IV of *Saint Joan*. The theatre holds few instances of such a dramatic tour de force where so long a scene is carried as effectively as the talk of Warwick and Cauchon sitting immobile in a tent.

Candida remains a representative favorite among Shaw's plays, for it is a masterpiece of its kind. It always comes to life on the stage. Its successful presentation on the New York stage by Arnold Daly in the season of 1903-4 was Shaw's introduction to American audiences and the beginning of his vogue. It has been revived season after season, reaching its most artistic production in recent years with Katharine Cornell as Candida, Raymond Massey as Morell, and Burgess Meredith as Marchbanks.

The triumph is in the dramatic writing, not in the theme itself. On the surface it belongs with the long series of plays about the "new woman." Between Ibsen's *A Doll's House* and Maugham's *The Constant Wife,* scores of plays about the feminist movement, and the rise of women from their Victorian quiet of the home to full, even dominant, citizenship, were written and produced. Almost without exception they are forgotten, dated, or else remembered only as museum period pieces.

Candida remains a fresh example of high comedy, lively and timeless as recurring spring. The situation of a maturing woman choosing on the basis of their need between her Christian Socialist clergyman husband and her moonstruck young poet lover might easily have called out Shaw's thrusts of satire and biting irony. Instead he has treated it with grace, tolerance, sympathy, and wit, and evoked the illusion of reality amidst an artificial setting. Candida is a rounded portrait, engaging in spirit and timeless in discerning on stage what she would have subconsciously assumed in real life. Her discernment is summed up in the final curtain lines, which never fail to delight. And Shaw, never quite able to still his restless mind, gives a final fillip to the printed version: Candida and Morell embrace, "But they do not know the secret in the poet's heart." And the author, with a Shavian chuckle, refrains from specifying.

CANDIDA

	MISS PROSERPINE GARNETT
	THE REVEREND JAMES MAVOR MORELL
Characters	THE REVEREND ALEXANDER MILL
	MR. BURGESS
	CANDIDA MORELL
	EUGENE MARCHBANKS

ACT ONE

*A fine morning in October 1894 in the north east quarter of London,
a vast district miles away from the London of Mayfair and St
James's, and much less narrow, squalid, fetid and airless in its
slums. It is strong in unfashionable middle class life: wide-
streeted; myriad-populated; well served with ugly iron urinals,
Radical clubs, and tram lines carrying a perpetual stream of yellow cars; enjoying in its main thoroughfares the luxury of grass-
grown "front gardens" untrodden by the foot of man save as to
the path from the gate to the hall door; blighted by a callously
endured monotony of miles and miles of unlovely brick houses,
black iron railings, stony pavements, slated roofs, and respectably
ill dressed or disreputably worse dressed people, quite accustomed
to the place, and mostly plodding uninterestedly about somebody
else's work. The little energy and eagerness that crop up shew
themselves in cockney cupidity and business "push." Even the*

policemen and the chapels are not infrequent enough to break the monotony. The sun is shining cheerfully: there is no fog; and though the smoke effectually prevents anything, whether faces and hands or bricks and mortar, from looking fresh and clean, it is not hanging heavily enough to trouble a Londoner.

This desert of unattractiveness has its oasis. Near the outer end of the Hackney Road is a park of 217 acres, fenced in, not by railings, but by a wooden paling, and containing plenty of greensward, trees, a lake for bathers, flower beds which are triumphs of the admired cockney art of carpet gardening, and a sandpit, originally imported from the seaside for the delight of children, but speedily deserted on its becoming a natural vermin preserve for all the petty fauna of Kingsland, Hackney, and Hoxton. A bandstand, an unfurnished forum for religious, anti-religious, and political orators, cricket pitches, a gymnasium, and an old fashioned stone kiosk are among its attractions. Wherever the prospect is bounded by trees or rising green grounds, it is a pleasant place. Where the ground stretches flat to the grey palings, with bricks and mortar, sky signs, crowded chimneys and smoke beyond, the prospect makes it desolate and sordid.

The best view of Victoria Park is commanded by the front window of St Dominic's Parsonage, from which not a brick is visible. The parsonage is semi-detached, with a front garden and a porch. Visitors go up the flight of steps to the porch: tradespeople and members of the family go down by a door under the steps to the basement, with a breakfast room, used for all meals, in front, and the kitchen at the back. Upstairs, on the level of the hall door, is the drawingroom, with its large plate glass window looking out on the park. In this, the only sitting room that can be spared from the children and the family meals, the parson, the REVEREND JAMES MAVOR MORELL, *does his work. He is sitting in a strong round backed revolving chair at the end of a long table, which stands across the window, so that he can cheer himself with a view of the park over his left shoulder. At the opposite end of the table, adjoining it, is a little table only half as wide as the other, with a typewriter on it. His typist is sitting at this machine, with her back* to the window. The large table is littered with pamphlets, journals, letters, nests of drawers, an office diary, postage scales and the like. A spare chair for visitors having business with the parson is in the middle, turned to his end. Within reach of his hand is a stationery case, and a photograph in a frame. The wall behind him is fitted with bookshelves, on which an adept eye can measure the parson's casuistry and divinity by Maurice's Theological Essays and a complete set of Browning's poems, and the reformer's politics by a yellow backed Progress and Poverty, Fabian Essays, A Dream of John Ball, Marx's Capital, and half a dozen other literary landmarks in Socialism. Facing him on the other side of the room, near the typewriter, is the door. Further down opposite the fireplace, a bookcase stands on a cellaret, with a sofa near it. There is a generous fire burning; and the hearth, with a comfortable armchair and a black japanned flower-painted coal scuttle at one side, a miniature chair for children on the other, a varnished wooden mantelpiece, with neatly moulded shelves, tiny bits of mirror let into the panels, a travelling clock in a leather case (the inevitable wedding present), and on the wall above a large autotype of the chief figure in Titian's "Assumption of the Virgin," is very inviting. Altogether the room is the room of a good housekeeper, vanquished, as far as the table is concerned, by an untidy man, but elsewhere mistress of the situation. The furniture, in its ornamental aspect, betrays the style of the advertised "drawing-room suite" of the pushing suburban furniture dealer; but there is nothing useless or pretentious in the room, money being too scarce in the house of an east end parson to be wasted on snobbish trimmings.

THE REVEREND JAMES MAVOR MORELL is a Christian Socialist clergyman of the Church of England, and an active member of the Guild of St Matthew and the Christian Social Union. A vigorous, genial, popular man of forty, robust and goodlooking, full of energy, with pleasant, hearty, considerate manners, and a sound unaffected voice, which he uses with the clean athletic articulation of a practised orator, and with a wide range and perfect command of expression. He is a first rate clergyman, able to say what he likes *to whom he likes, to lecture people without setting himself up against them, to impose his authority on them without humiliating them, and, on occasion, to interfere in their business without impertinence. His well-spring of enthusiasm and sympathetic emotion has never run dry for a moment: he still eats and sleeps heartily enough to win the daily battle between exhaustion and recuperation triumphantly. Withal, a great baby, pardonably vain of his powers and unconsciously pleased with himself. He has a healthy complexion: good forehead, with the brows somewhat blunt, and the eyes bright and eager, mouth resolute but not particularly well cut, and a substantial nose, with the mobile spreading nostrils of the dramatic orator, void, like all his features, of subtlety.*

The typist, MISS PROSERPINE GARNETT, *is a brisk little woman of about 30, of the lower middle class, neatly but cheaply dressed in a black merino skirt and a blouse, notably pert and quick of speech, and not very civil in her manner, but sensitive and affectionate. She is clattering away busily at her machine whilst* MORELL *opens the last of his morning's letters. He realizes its contents with a comic groan of despair.*

PROS. Another lecture?

MOR. Yes. The Hoxton Freedom Group want me to address them on Sunday morning. (*He lays great emphasis on Sunday, this being the unreasonable part of the business.*) What are they?

PROS. Communist Anarchists, I think.

MOR. Just like Anarchists not to know that they cant have a parson on Sunday! Tell them to come to church if they want to hear me: it will do them good. Say I can come on Mondays and Thursdays only. Have you the diary there?

PROS. (*taking up the diary*). Yes.

MOR. Have I any lecture on for next Monday?

PROS. (*referring to diary*). Tower Hamlets Radical Club.

MOR. Well, Thursday then?

PROS. English Land Restoration League.

MOR. What next?

PROS. Guild of St Matthew on Monday. Independent Labor Party, Greenwich Branch, on Thursday. Monday, Social-Democratic Federation, Mile End Branch. Thursday, first Confirmation class. (*Impatiently.*) Oh, I'd better tell them you cant come. Theyre only half a dozen ignorant and conceited costermongers without five shillings between them.

MOR. (*amused*). Ah; but you see theyre near relatives of mine.

PROS. (*staring at him*). Relatives of yours!

MOR. Yes: we have the same father—in Heaven.

PROS. (*relieved*). Oh, is that all?

MOR. (*with a sadness which is a luxury to a man whose voice expresses it so finely*). Ah, you dont believe it. Everybody says it: nobody believes it: nobody. (*Briskly, getting back to business.*) Well, well! Come, Miss Proserpine: cant you find a date for the costers? What about the 25th? That was vacant the day before yesterday.

PROS. (*referring to diary*). Engaged. The Fabian Society.

MOR. Bother the Fabian Society! Is the 28th gone too?

PROS. City dinner. Youre invited to dine with the Founders' Company.

MOR. Thatll do: I'll go to the Hoxton Group of Freedom instead. (*She enters the engagement in silence, with implacable disparagement of the Hoxton Anarchists in every line of her face.* MORELL *bursts open the cover of a copy of* The Church Reformer, *which has come by post, and glances through Mr Stewart Headlam's leader and the Guild of St Matthew news. These proceedings are presently enlivened by the appearance of* MORELL'S *curate,* THE REVEREND ALEXANDER MILL, *a young gentleman gathered by* MORELL *from the nearest University settlement, whither he had come from Oxford to give the east end of London the benefit of his university training. He is a conceitedly well intentioned, enthusiastic, immature novice, with nothing positively unbearable about him except a habit of speaking with his lips carefully closed a full half inch from each corner for the sake of a finicking articulation and a set of university vowels, this being his chief means so far of bringing his Oxford refinement [as he calls his habits] to bear on Hackney vulgarity.* MORELL, *whom he has won over by a doglike devotion,*

looks up indulgently from The Church Reformer, *and remarks.*)
Well, Lexy? Late again, as usual!

LEXY. I'm afraid so. I wish I could get up in the morning.

MOR. (*exulting in his own energy*). Ha! Ha! (*Whimsically.*) Watch and pray, Lexy: watch and pray.

LEXY. I know. (*Rising wittily to the occasion.*) But how can I watch and pray when I am asleep? Isnt that so, Miss Prossy? (*He makes for the warmth of the fire.*)

PROS. (*sharply*). Miss Garnett, if you please.

LEXY. I beg your pardon. Miss Garnett.

PROS. Youve got to do all the work today.

LEXY (*on the hearth*). Why?

PROS. Never mind why. It will do you good to earn your supper before you eat it, for once in a way, as I do. Come! dont dawdle. You should have been off on your rounds half an hour ago.

LEXY (*perplexed*). Is she in earnest, Morell?

MOR. (*in the highest spirits: his eyes dancing*). Yes. *I* am going to dawdle today.

LEXY. You! You dont know how.

MOR. (*rising*). Ha! ha! Dont I? I'm going to have this morning all to myself. My wife's coming back: she's due here at 11.45.

LEXY (*surprised*). Coming back already! with the children? I thought they were to stay to the end of the month.

MOR. So they are: she's only coming up for two days, to get some flannel things for Jimmy, and to see how we're getting on without her.

LEXY (*anxiously*). But, my dear Morell, if what Jimmy and Fluffy had was scarlatina, do you think it wise—

MOR. Scarlatina! Rubbish! it was German measles. I brought it into the house myself from the Pycroft Street school. A parson is like a doctor, my boy: he must face infection as a soldier must face bullets. (*He claps* LEXY *manfully on the shoulders.*) Catch the measles if you can, Lexy: she'll nurse you; and what a piece of luck that will be for you! Eh?

LEXY (*smiling uneasily*). It's so hard to understand you about Mrs Morell—

MOR. (*tenderly*). Ah, my boy, get married: get married to a good woman; and then youll understand. Thats a foretaste of what will be best in the Kingdom of Heaven we are trying to establish on earth. That will cure you of dawdling. An honest man feels that he must pay Heaven for every hour of happiness with a good spell of hard unselfish work to make others happy. We have no more right to consume happiness without producing it than to consume wealth without producing it. Get a wife like my Candida; and youll always be in arrear with your repayment. (*He pats* LEXY *affectionately and moves to leave the room.*)

LEXY. Oh, wait a bit: I forgot. (MORELL *halts and turns with the door knob in his hand.*) Your father-in-law is coming round to see you.

(MORELL, *surprised and not pleased, shuts the door again, with a complete change of manner.*)

MOR. Mr Burgess?

LEXY. Yes. I passed him in the park, arguing with somebody. He asked me to let you know that he was coming.

MOR. (*half incredulous*). But he hasnt called here for three years. Are you sure, Lexy? Youre not joking, are you?

LEXY (*earnestly*). No sir, really.

MOR. (*thoughtfully*). Hm! Time for him to take another look at Candida before she grows out of his knowledge. (*He resigns himself to the inevitable, and goes out.*)

(LEXY *looks after him with beaming worship.* MISS GARNETT, *not being able to shake* LEXY, *relieves her feelings by worrying the typewriter.*)

LEXY. What a good man! What a thorough loving soul he is! (*He takes* MORELL's *place at the table, making himself very comfortable as he takes out a cigaret.*)

PROS. (*impatiently, pulling the letter she has been working at off the typewriter and folding it*). Oh, a man ought to be able to be fond of his wife without making a fool of himself about her.

LEXY (*shocked*). Oh, Miss Prossy!

PROS. (*snatching at the stationery case for an envelope, in which she encloses the letter as she speaks*). Candida here, and Candida there, and Candida everywhere! (*She licks the envelope.*) It's enough to drive anyone out of their senses (*thumping the en-*

velope to make it stick) to hear a woman raved about in that absurd manner merely because she's got good hair and a tolerable figure.

LEXY (*with reproachful gravity*). I think her extremely beautiful, Miss Garnett. (*He takes the photograph up; looks at it; and adds, with even greater impressiveness*) extremely beautiful. How fine her eyes are!

PROS. Her eyes are not a bit better than mine: now! (*He puts down the photograph and stares austerely at her.*) And you know very well you think me dowdy and second rate enough.

LEXY (*rising majestically*). Heaven forbid that I should think of any of God's creatures in such a way! (*He moves stiffly away from her across the room to the neighborhood of the bookcase.*)

PROS. (*sarcastically*). Thank you. Thats very nice and comforting.

LEXY (*saddened by her depravity*). I had no idea you had any feeling against Mrs Morell.

PROS. (*indignantly*). I have no feeling against her. She's very nice, very good-hearted: I'm very fond of her, and can appreciate her real qualities far better than any man can. (*He shakes his head sadly. She rises and comes at him with intense pepperiness.*) You dont believe me? You think I'm jealous? Oh, what a knowledge of the human heart you have, Mr Lexy Mill! How well you know the weaknesses of Woman, dont you? It must be so nice to be a man and have a fine penetrating intellect instead of mere emotions like us, and to know that the reason we dont share your amorous delusions is that we're all jealous of one another! (*She abandons him with a toss of her shoulders, and crosses to the fire to warm her hands.*)

LEXY. Ah, if you women only had the same clue to Man's strength that you have to his weakness, Miss Prossy, there would be no Woman Question.

PROS. (*over her shoulder, as she stoops, holding her hands to the blaze*). Where did you hear Morell say that? You didnt invent it yourself: youre not clever enough.

LEXY. Thats quite true. I am not ashamed of owing him that, as I owe him so many other spiritual truths. He said it at the annual conference of the Women's Liberal Federation. Allow me to add that though they didnt appreciate it, I, a mere man, did. (*He turns to the bookcase again, hoping that this may leave her crushed.*)

PROS. (*putting her hair straight at a panel of mirror in the mantelpiece*). Well, when you talk to me, give me your own ideas, such as they are, and not his. You never cut a poorer figure than when you are trying to imitate him.

LEXY (*stung*). I try to follow his example, not to imitate him.

PROS. (*coming at him again on her way back to her work*). Yes, you do: you imitate him. Why do you tuck your umbrella under your left arm instead of carrying it in your hand like anyone else? Why do you walk with your chin stuck out before you, hurrying along with that eager look in our eyes? you! who never get up before half past nine in the morning. Why do you say "knoaledge" in church, though you always say "knolledge" in private conversation! Bah! do you think I dont know? (*She goes back to the typewriter.*) Here! come and set about your work: weve wasted enough time for one morning. Here's a copy of the diary for today. (*She hands him a memorandum.*)

LEXY (*deeply offended*). Thank you. (*He takes it and stands at the table with his back to her, reading it. She begins to transcribe her short-hand notes on the typewriter without troubling herself about his feelings.*)

(*The door opens; and* MR BURGESS *enters unannounced. He is a man of sixty, made coarse and sordid by the compulsory selfishness of petty commerce, and later on softened into sluggish bumptious-ness by overfeeding and commercial success. A vulgar ignorant guzzling man, offensive and contemptuous to people whose labor is cheap, respectful to wealth and rank, and quite sincere and without rancor or envy in both attitudes. The world has offered him no decently paid work except that of a sweater; and he has become, in consequence, somewhat hoggish. But he has no suspicion of this himself, and honestly regards his commercial prosperity as the inevitable and socially wholesome triumph of the ability, industry, shrewdness, and experience in business of a man who in private is easygoing, affectionate, and humorously convivial to a fault. Corporeally he is podgy, with a snoutish nose in the centre of a flat square face, a dust colored beard with a patch of grey in the centre under his chin, and small watery blue eyes with a plaintively sentimental expression, which he transfers easily to his voice by his habit of pompously intoning his sentences.)*

BUR. *(stopping on the threshold, and looking round).* They told me Mr Morell was here.

PROS. *(rising).* I'll fetch him for you.

BUR. *(staring disappointedly at her).* Youre not the same young lady as hused to typewrite for him?

PROS. No.

BUR. *(grumbling on his way to the hearthrug).* No: she was young-er. *(MISS GARNETT stares at him; then goes out, slamming the door.)* Startin on your rounds, Mr Mill?

LEXY *(folding his memorandum and pocketing it).* Yes: I must be off presently.

BUR. *(momentously).* Dont let me detain you, Mr Mill. What I come about is private between me and Mr Morell.

LEXY *(huffily).* I have no intention of intruding, I am sure, Mr Burgess. Good morning.

BUR. *(patronizingly).* Oh, good morning to you.

(MORELL returns as LEXY is making for the door.)

MOR. *(to LEXY).* Off to work?

LEXY. Yes, sir.

MOR. Take my silk handkerchief and wrap your throat up. Theres a cold wind. Away with you.

(LEXY, more than consoled for BURGESS's rudeness, brightens up and goes out.)

BUR. Spoilin your korates as usu'l, James. Good mornin. When I pay a man, an' 'is livin depens on me, I keep him in 'is place.

MOR. *(rather shortly).* I always keep my curates in their places as my helpers and comrades. If you get as much work out of your clerks and warehousemen as I do out of my curates, you must be getting rich pretty fast. Will you take your old chair. *(He points with curt authority to the armchair beside the fireplace; then takes the spare chair from the table and sits down at an unfamiliar distance from his visitor.*)

BUR. (*without moving*). Just the same as hever, James!

MOR. When you last called—it was about three years ago, I think—you said the same thing a little more frankly. Your exact words then were "Just as big a fool as ever, James!"

BUR. (*soothingly*). Well, praps I did; but (*with conciliatory cheerfulness*) I meant no hoffence by it. A clorgyman is privileged to be a bit of a fool, you know: it's ony becomin in 'is profession that he should. Anyhow, I come here, not to rake up hold differences, but to let bygones be bygones. (*Suddenly becoming very solemn, and approaching* MORELL.) James: three years ago, you done me a hil turn. You done me hout of a contrac; an when I gev you arsh words in my natral disappointment, you turned my daughrter again me. Well, Ive come to hact the part of a Kerischin. (*Offering his hand.*) I forgive you, James.

MOR. (*starting up*). Confound your impudence!

BUR. (*retreating, with almost lachrymose deprecation of this treatment*). Is that becomin language for a clorgyman, James? And you so particlar, too!

MOR. (*hotly*). No, sir: it is not becoming language for a clergyman. I used the wrong word. I should have said damn your impudence: thats what St Paul or any honest priest would have said to you. Do you think I have forgotten that tender of yours for the contract to supply clothing to the workhouse?

BUR. (*in a paroxysm of public spirit*). I hacted in the hinterest of the ratepayers, James. It was the lowest tender: you carnt deny that.

MOR. Yes, the lowest, because you paid worse wages than any other employer—starvation wages—aye, worse than starvation wages— to the women who made the clothing. Your wages would have driven them to the streets to keep body and soul together. (*Getting angrier and angrier.*) Those women were my parishioners. I shamed the Guardians out of accepting your tender: I shamed the ratepayers out of letting them do it: I shamed everybody but you. (*Boiling over.*) How dare you, sir, come here and offer to forgive me, and talk about your daughter, and—

BUR. Heasy, James! heasy! heasy! Dont git hinto a fluster about nothink. Ive howned I was wrong.

MOR. Have you? I didnt hear you.

BUR. Of course I did. I hown it now. Come: I harsk your pardon for the letter I wrote you. Is that enough?

MOR. (*snapping his fingers*). Thats nothing. Have you raised the wages?

BUR. (*triumphantly*). Yes.

MOR. What!

BUR. (*unctuously*). Ive turned a moddle hemployer. I dont hemploy no women now: theyre all sacked; and the work is done by machinery. Not a man 'as less than sixpence a *h*our; and the skilled ands gits the Trade Union rate. (*Proudly.*) What ave you to say to me now?

MOR. (*overwhelmed*). Is it possible! Well, theres more joy in heaven over one sinner that repenteth!—(*Going to* BURGESS *with an explosion of apologetic cordiality.*) My dear Burgess: how splendid of you! I most heartily beg your pardon for my hard thoughts. (*Grasping his hand.*) And now, dont you feel the better for the change? Come! confess! youre happier. You look happier.

BUR. (*ruefully*). Well, praps I do. I spose I must, since you notice it. At all events, I git my contrax assepted by the County Council. (*Savagely.*) They dussent ave nothink to do with me unless I paid fair wages: curse em for a parcel o meddlin fools!

MOR. (*dropping his hand, utterly discouraged*). So that was why you raised the wages! (*He sits down moodily.*)

BUR. (*severely, in spreading, mounting tones*). Woy helse should I do it? What does it lead to but drink and huppishness in workin men? (*He seats himself magisterially in the easy chair.*) It's hall very well for you, James: it gits you hinto the papers and makes a great man of you; but you never think of the arm you do, puttin money into the pockets of workin men that they dunno ow to spend, and takin it from people that might be making a good huse on it.

MOR. (*with a heavy sigh, speaking with cold politeness*). What is your business with me this morning? I shall not pretend to believe that you are here merely out of family sentiment.

BUR. (*obstinately*). Yes I ham: just family sentiment and nothink helse.

MOR. (*with weary calm*). I dont believe you.

BUR. (*rising threateningly*). Dont say that to me again, James Mavor Morell.

MOR. (*unmoved*). I'll say it just as often as may be necessary to convince you that it's true. I dont believe you.

BUR. (*collapsing into an abyss of wounded feeling*). Oh, well, if youre detormined to be hunfriendly, I spose I'd better go. (*He moves reluctantly towards the door.* MORELL *makes no sign. He lingers.*) I didnt hexpect to find a hunforgivin spirit in you, James. (MORELL *still not responding, he takes a few more reluctant steps door-wards. Then he comes back, whining.*) We huseter git on well enough, spite of our different hopinions. Woy are you so changed to me? I give you my word I come here in peeorr (pure) frenli-ness, not wishin to be hon bad terms with my hown daughrter's usban. Come, James: be a Kerischin, and shake ands. (*He puts his hand sentimentally on* MORELL's *shoulder.*)

MOR. (*looking up at him thoughtfully*). Look here, Burgess. Do you want to be as welcome here as you were before you lost that con-tract?

BUR. I do, James. I do—*h*onest.

MOR. Then why dont you behave as you did then?

BUR. (*cautiously removing his hand*). Ow d'y' mean?

MOR. I'll tell you. You thought me a young fool then.

BUR. (*coaxingly*). No I didnt, James. I—

MOR. (*cutting him short*). Yes, you did. And I thought you an old scoundrel.

BUR. (*most vehemently deprecating this gross self-accusation on* MORELL's *part*). No you didnt, James. Now you do yourself a hinjustice.

MOR. Yes I did. Well, that did not prevent our getting on very well together. God made you what I call a scoundrel as He made me what you call a fool. (*The effect of this observation on* BURGESS *is to remove the keystone of his moral arch. He becomes bodily weak, and, with his eyes fixed on* MORELL *in a helpless stare, puts out his hand apprehensively to balance himself, as if the floor had sud-denly sloped under him.* MORELL *proceeds, in the same tone of quiet conviction.*) It was not for me to quarrel with His handi-work in the one case more than in the other. So long as you come here honestly as a self-respecting, thorough, convinced scoundrel, justifying your scoundrelism and proud of it, you are welcome. But (*and now* MORELL's *tone becomes formidable; and he rises and strikes the back of the chair for greater emphasis*) I wont have you here snivelling about being a model employer and a converted man when youre only an apostate with your coat turned for the sake of a County Council contract. (*He nods at him to enforce the point; then goes to the hearthrug, where he takes up a comfortably commanding position with his back to the fire, and continues.*) No: I like a man to be true to himself, even in wickedness. Come now: either take your hat and go; or else sit down and give me a good scoundrelly reason for wanting to be friends with me. (BURGESS, *whose emotions have subsided sufficiently to be expressed by a dazed grin, is relieved by this concrete proposition. He ponders it for a moment, and then, slowly and very modestly, sits down in the chair* MORELL *has just left.*) Thats right. Now out with it.

BUR. (*chuckling in spite of himself*). Well, you orr a queer bird, James, and no mistake. But (*almost enthusiastically*) one carnt elp likin you: besides, as I said afore, of course one dont take hall a clorgyman says seriously, or the world couldnt go on. Could it now? (*He composes himself for graver discourse, and, turning his eyes on* MORELL, *proceeds with dull seriousness.*) Well, I dont mind tellin you, since it's your wish we should be free with one another, that I did think you a bit of a fool once; but I'm beginnin to think that praps I was be'ind the times a bit.

MOR. (*exultant*). Aha! Youre finding that out at last, are you?

BUR. (*portentously*). Yes: times 'as changed mor'n I could a believed. Five yorr (year) ago, no sensible man would a thought o takin hup with your hideas. I hused to wonder you was let preach at all. Why, I know a clorgyman what 'as bin kep hout of his job for yorrs by the Bishop o London, although the pore feller's not a bit more religious than you are. But today, if hennyone was to horffer to bet me a thousan poud that youll hend by bein a bishop yourself, I dussent take the bet. (*Very impressively.*) You and your crew are gittin hinfluential: I can see that. Theyll ave to give you somethink someday, if it's honly to stop your mouth. You ad the right instinc arter all, James: the line you took is the payin line in the long run for a man o your sort.

MOR. (*offering his hand with thorough decision*). Shake hands, Burgess. Now youre talking honestly. I dont think theyll make me a bishop; but if they do, I'll introduce you to the biggest jobbers I can get to come to my dinner parties.

BUR. (*who has risen with a sheepish grin and accepted the hand of friendship*). You will ave your joke, James. Our quarrel's made up now, ain it?

A WOMAN'S VOICE. Say yes, James.

(*Startled, they turn quickly and find that* CANDIDA *has just come in, and is looking at them with an amused maternal indulgence which is her characteristic expression. She is a woman of 33, well built, well nourished, likely, one guesses, to become matronly later on, but now quite at her best, with the double charm of youth and motherhood. Her ways are those of a woman who has found that she can always manage people by engaging their affection, and who does so frankly and instinctively without the smallest scruple. So far, she is like any other pretty woman who is just clever enough to make the most of her sexual attractions for trivially selfish ends; but* CANDIDA'S *serene brow, courageous eyes, and well set mouth and chin signify largeness of mind and dignity of character to ennoble her cunning in the affections. A wise-hearted observer, looking at her, would at once guess that whoever had placed the Virgin of the Assumption over her hearth did so because he fancied some spiritual resemblance between them, and yet would not suspect either her husband or herself of any such idea, or indeed of any concern with the art of Titian.*)

(*Just now she is in bonnet and mantle, carrying a strapped rug with her umbrella stuck through it, a handbag, and a supply of illustrated papers.*)

MOR. (*shocked at his remissness*). Candida! Why— (*He looks at his watch, and is horrified to find it so late.*) My darling! (*Hurrying to her and seizing the rug strap, pouring forth his remorseful re-grets all the time.*) I intended to meet you at the train. I let the time slip. (*Flinging the rug on the sofa.*) I was so engrossed by— (*returning to her*) —I forgot—oh! (*He embraces her with peni-tent emotion.*)

BUR. (*a little shamefaced and doubtful of his reception*). How orr you, Candy? (*She, still in* MORELL'*s arms, offers him her cheek, which he kisses.*) James and me is come to a nunnerstannin. A *h*onorable unnerstannin. Ain we, James?

MOR. (*impetuously*). Oh bother your understanding! youve kept me late for Candida. (*With compassionate fervor.*) My poor love: how did you manage about the luggage? How—

CAND. (*stopping him and disengaging herself*). There! there! there! I wasnt alone. Eugene has been down with us; and we travelled together.

MOR. (*pleased*). Eugene!

CAND. Yes: he's struggling with my luggage, poor boy. Go out, dear, at once; or he'll pay for the cab; and I dont want that. (MORELL *hur-ries out.* CANDIDA *puts down her handbag; then takes off her mantle and bonnet and puts them on the sofa with the rug, chat-ting meanwhile.*) Well, papa: how are you getting on at home?

BUR. The ouse aint worth livin in since you left it, Candy. I wish youd come round and give the gurl a talkin to. Who's this Eugene thats come with you?

CAND. Oh, Eugene's one of James discoveries. He found him sleeping on the Embankment last June. Havnt you noticed our new picture (*pointing to the Virgin*)? He gave us that.

BUR. (*incredulously*). Garn! D'you mean to tell me—your hown father! —that cab touts or such like, orf the Embankment, buys pictures like that? (*Severely.*) Dont deceive me, Candy: it's a 'Igh Church picture; and James chose it hisself.

CAND. Guess again. Eugene isnt a cab tout.

BUR. Then what is he? (*Sarcastically.*) A nobleman, I spose.

CAND. (*nodding delightedly*). Yes. His uncle's a peer! A real live earl.

BUR. (*not daring to believe such good news*). No!

CAND. Yes. He had a seven day bill for £55 in his pocket when James found him on the Embankment. He thought he couldnt get any money for it until the seven days were up; and he was too shy to ask for credit. Oh, he's a dear boy! We are very fond of him.

BUR. (*pretending to belittle the aristocracy, but with his eyes gleaming*). Hm! I thort you wouldnt git a hearl's nevvy visitin in Victawriar Pawrk unless he were a bit of a flat. (*Looking again at the picture.*) Of course I dont old with that picture, Candy; but still it's a 'igh class fust rate work of ort: I can see that. Be sure you hintrodooce me to im, Candy. (*He looks at his watch anxiously.*) I can ony stay about two minutes.

(MORELL *comes back with* EUGENE, *whom* BURGESS *contemplates moist-eyed with enthusiasm. He is a strange, shy youth of eighteen, slight, effeminate, with a delicate childish voice, and a hunted tormented expression and shrinking manner that shew the painful sensitiveness of very swift and acute apprehensiveness in youth, before the character has grown to its full strength. Miserably irresolute, he does not know where to stand or what to do. He is afraid of* BURGESS, *and would run away into solitude if he dared; but the very intensity with which he feels a perfectly commonplace position comes from excessive nervous force; and his nostrils, mouth, and eyes betray a fiercely petulant wilfulness, as to the bent of which his brow, already lined with pity, is reassuring. He is so uncommon as to be almost unearthly; and to prosaic people there is something noxious in this unearthliness, just as to poetic people there is something angelic in it. His dress is anarchic. He wears an old blue serge jacket, unbuttoned, over a woollen lawn tennis shirt, with a silk handkerchief for a cravat, trousers matching the jacket, and brown canvas shoes. In these garments he has apparently lain in the heather and waded through the waters; and there is no evidence of his having ever brushed them.*

(*As he catches sight of a stranger on entering, he stops, and edges along the wall on the opposite side of the room.*)

MOR. (*as he enters*). Come along: you can spare us quarter of an hour at all events. This is my father-in-law. Mr Burgess—Mr Marchbanks.

MARCH. (*nervously backing against the bookcase*). Glad to meet you, sir.

BUR. (*crossing to him with great heartiness, whilst* MORELL *joins* CANDIDA *at the fire*). Glad to meet you, I'm shore, Mr Morchbanks. (*Forcing him to shake hands.*) Ow do you find yoreself this weather? Ope you aint lettin James put no foolish ideas into your ed?

MARCH. Foolish ideas? Oh, you mean Socialism? No.

BUR. Thats right. (*Again looking at his watch.*) Well, I must go now: theres no elp for it. Yore not comin my way, orr you, Mr Morchbanks?

MARCH. Which way is that?

BUR. Victawriar Pawrk Station. Theres a city train at 12.25.

MOR. Nonsense. Eugene will stay to lunch with us, I expect.

MARCH. (*anxiously excusing himself*). No—I—I—

BUR. Well, well, I shornt press you: I bet youd rather lunch with Candy. Some night, I ope, youll come and dine with me at my club, the Freeman Founders in Nortn Folgit. Come: say you will!

MARCH. Thank you, Mr Burgess. Where is Norton Folgate? Down in Surrey, isnt it?

(BURGESS, *inexpressibly tickled, begins to splutter with laughter.*)

CAND. (*coming to the rescue*). Youll lose your train, papa, if you dont go at once. Come back in the afternoon and tell Mr Marchbanks where to find the club.

BUR. (*roaring with glee*). Down in Surrey! Har, har! thats not a bad one. Well, I never met a man as didnt know Nortn Folgit afore. (*Abashed at his own noisiness.*) Goodbye, Mr Morchbanks: I know yore too ighbred to take my pleasantry in bad part. (*He again offers his hand.*)

MARCH. (*taking it with a nervous jerk*). Not at all.

BUR. Bye, bye, Candy. I'll look in again later on. So long, James.

MOR. Must you go?

BUR. Dont stir. (*He goes out with unabated heartiness.*)

MOR. Oh, I'll see you off. (*He follows him.*)

(EUGENE *stares after them apprehensively, holding his breath until* BURGESS *disappears.*)

CAND. (*laughing*). Well, Eugene? (*He turns with a start, and comes eagerly towards her, but stops irresolutely as he meets her amused look.*) What do you think of my father?

MARCH. I—I hardly know him yet. He seems to be a very nice old gentleman.

CAND. (*with gentle irony*). And youll go to the Freeman Founders to dine with him, wont you?

MARCH. (*miserably, taking it quite seriously*). Yes, if it will please you.

CAND. (*touched*). Do you know, you are a very nice boy, Eugene, with all your queerness. If you had laughed at my father I shouldnt have minded; but I like you ever so much better for being nice to him.

MARCH. Ought I to have laughed? I noticed that he said something funny; but I am so ill at ease with strangers; and I never can see a joke. I'm very sorry. (*He sits down on the sofa, his elbows on his knees and his temples between his fists, with an expression of hopeless suffering.*)

CAND. (*bustling him goodnaturedly*). Oh come! You great baby, you! You are worse than usual this morning. Why were you so melancholy as we came along in the cab?

MARCH. Oh, that was nothing. I was wondering how much I ought to give the cabman. I know it's utterly silly; but you dont know how dreadful such things are to me—how I shrink from having to deal with strange people. (*Quickly and reassuringly.*) But it's all right. He beamed all over and touched his hat when Morell gave him two shillings. I was on the point of offering him ten.

(MORELL *comes back with a few letters and newspapers which have come by the midday post.*)

CAND. Oh, James dear, he was going to give the cabman ten shillings! ten shillings for a three minutes drive! Oh dear!

MOR. (*at the table, glancing through the letters*). Never mind her, Marchbanks. The overpaying instinct is a generous one: better than the underpaying instinct, and not so common.

MARCH. (*relapsing into dejection*). No: cowardice, incompetence. Mrs Morell's quite right.

CAND. Of course she is. (*She takes up her handbag.*) And now I must leave you to James for the present. I suppose you are too much of a poet to know the state a woman finds her house in when she's been away for three weeks. Give me my rug. (EUGENE *takes the strapped rug from the couch, and gives it to her. She takes it in her left hand, having the bag in her right.*) Now hang my cloak across my arm. (*He obeys.*) Now my hat. (*He puts it into the hand which has the bag.*) Now open the door for me. (*He hurries before her and opens the door.*) Thanks. (*She goes out; and* MARCHBANKS *shuts the door.*)

MOR. (*still busy at the table*). Youll stay to lunch, Marchbanks, of course.

MARCH. (*scared*). I mustnt. (*He glances quickly at* MORELL, *but at once avoids his frank look, and adds, with obvious disingenuousness.*) I mean I cant.

MOR. You mean you wont.

MARCH. (*earnestly*). No: I should like to, indeed. Thank you very much. But—but—

MOR. But—but—but—but—Bosh! If youd like to stay, stay. If youre shy, go and take a turn in the park and write poetry until half past one; and then come in and have a good feed.

MARCH. Thank you, I should like that very much. But I really mustnt. The truth is, Mrs Morell told me not to. She said she didnt think youd ask me to stay to lunch, but that I was to remember, if you did, that you didnt really want me to. (*Plaintively.*) She said I'd understand; but I dont. Please dont tell her I told you.

MOR. (*drolly*). Oh, is that all? Wont my suggestion that you should take a turn in the park meet the difficulty?

MARCH. How?

MOR. (*exploding good-humoredly*). Why, you duffer— (*But this boisterousness jars himself as well as* EUGENE. *He checks himself.*) No: I wont put it in that way. (*He comes to* EUGENE *with affectionate seriousness.*) My dear lad: in a happy marriage like ours, there is something very sacred in the return of the wife to her home. (MARCHBANKS *looks quickly at him, half anticipating his meaning.*) An old friend or a truly noble and sympathetic soul is not in the way on such occasions; but a chance visitor is. (*The hunted horror-stricken expression comes out with sudden vividness in* EUGENE'S *face as he understands.* MORELL, *occupied with his own thoughts, goes on without noticing this.*) Candida thought I would rather not have you here; but she was wrong. I'm very fond of you, my boy; and I should like you to see for yourself what a happy thing it is to be married as I am.

MARCH. Happy! Your marriage! You think that! You believe that!

MOR. (*buoyantly*). I know it, my lad. La Rochefoucauld said that there are convenient marriages but no delightful ones. You dont know the comfort of seeing through and through a thundering liar and rotten cynic like that fellow. Ha! ha! Now, off with you to the park, and write your poem. Half past one, sharp, mind: we never wait for anybody.

MARCH. (*wildly*). No: stop: you shant. I'll force it into the light.

MOR. (*puzzled*). Eh? Force what?

MARCH. I must speak to you. There is something that must be settled between us.

MOR. (*with a whimsical glance at his watch*). Now?

MARCH. (*passionately*). Now. Before you leave this room. (*He retreats a few steps, and stands as if to bar* MORELL's *way to the door.*)

MOR. (*without moving, and gravely, perceiving now that there is something serious the matter*). I'm not going to leave it, my dear boy: I thought you were. (EUGENE, *baffled by his firm tone, turns his back on him, writhing with anger.* MORELL *goes to him and puts his hand on his shoulder strongly and kindly, disregarding his attempt to shake it off.*) Come: sit down quietly; and tell me what it is. And remember: we are friends, and need not fear that either of us will be anything but patient and kind to the other, whatever we may have to say.

MARCH. (*twisting himself round on him*). Oh, I am not forgetting myself: I am only (*covering his face desperately with his hands*) full of horror. (*Then, dropping his hands, and thrusting his face forward fiercely at* MORELL, *he goes on threateningly.*) You shall see whether this is a time for patience and kindness. (MORELL, *firm as a rock, looks indulgently at him.*) Dont look at me in that self-complacent way. You think yourself stronger than I am; but I shall stagger you if you have a heart in your breast.

MOR. (*powerfully confident*). Stagger me, my boy. Out with it.

MARCH. First—

MOR. First?

MARCH. I love your wife.

(MORELL *recoils, and, after staring at him for a moment in utter amazement, bursts into uncontrollable laughter.* EUGENE *is taken aback, but not disconcerted; and he soon becomes indignant and contemptuous.*)

MOR. (*sitting down to have his laugh out*). Why, my dear child, of course you do. Everybody loves her: they cant help it. I like it. But (*looking up jocosely at him*) I say, Eugene: do you think yours is a case to be talked about? Youre under twenty: she's over thirty. Doesnt it look rather too like a case of calf love?

MARCH. (*vehemently*). You dare say that of her! You think that way of the love she inspires! It is an insult to her!

MOR. (*rising quickly, in an altered tone*). To her! Eugene: take care. I have been patient. I hope to remain patient. But there are some things I wont allow. Dont force me to shew you the indulgence I should shew to a child. Be a man.

MARCH. (*with a gesture as if sweeping something behind him*). Oh, let us put aside all that cant. It horrifies me when I think of the doses of it she has had to endure in all the weary years during which you have selfishly and blindly sacrificed her to minister to your self-sufficiency: you! (*turning on him*) who have not one thought—one sense—in common with her.

MOR. (*philosophically*). She seems to bear it pretty well. (*Looking him straight in the face.*) Eugene, my boy: you are making a fool of yourself: a very great fool of yourself. Theres a piece of wholesome plain speaking for you. (*He knocks in the lesson with a nod in his old way, and posts himself on the hearthrug, holding his hands behind him to warm them.*)

MARCH. Oh, do you think I dont know all that? Do you think that the things people make fools of themselves about are any less real and true than the things they behave sensibly about? (MORELL'S *gaze wavers for the first time. He forgets to warm his hands, and stands listening, startled and thoughtful.*) They are more true: they are the only things that are true. You are very calm and sensible and moderate with me because you can see that I am a fool about your wife; just as no doubt that old man who was here just now is very wise over your Socialism, because he sees that you are a fool about it. (MORELL's *perplexity deepens markedly.* EUGENE *follows up his advantage, plying him fiercely with questions.*) Does that prove you wrong? Does your complacent superiority to me prove that *I* am wrong?

MOR. Marchbanks: some devil is putting these words into your mouth. It is easy—terribly easy—to shake a man's faith in himself. To take advantage of that to break a man's spirit is devil's work. Take care of what you are doing. Take care.

MARCH. (*ruthlessly*). I know. I'm doing it on purpose. I told you I should stagger you. (*They confront one another threateningly for a moment. Then* MORELL *recovers his dignity.*)

MOR. (*with noble tenderness*). Eugene: listen to me. Some day, I hope and trust, you will be a happy man like me. (EUGENE *chafes intolerantly, repudiating the worth of his happiness.* MORELL, *deeply insulted, controls himself with fine forbearance, and continues steadily, with great artistic beauty of delivery.*) You will be married; and you will be working with all your might and valor to make every spot on earth as happy as your own home. You will be one of the makers of the Kingdom of Heaven on earth; and— who knows?—you may be a master builder where I am only a humble journeyman; for dont think, my boy, that I cannot see in you, young as you are, promise of higher powers than I can ever pretend to. I well know that it is in the poet that the holy spirit of man—the god within him—is most godlike. It should make you tremble to think of that—to think that the heavy burthen and great gift of a poet may be laid upon you.

MARCH. (*unimpressed and remorseless, his boyish crudity of assertion telling sharply against* MORELL's *oratory*). It does not make me tremble. It is the want of it in others that makes me tremble.

MOR. (*redoubling his force of style under the stimulus of his genuine feeling and* EUGENE's *obduracy*). Then help to kindle it in them— in me—not to extinguish it. In the future, when you are as happy as I am, I will be your true brother in the faith. I will help you to believe that God has given us a world that nothing but our own folly keeps from being a paradise. I will help you to believe that every stroke of your work is sowing happiness for the great harvest that all—even the humblest—shall one day reap. And last, but trust me, not least, I will help you to believe that your wife loves you and is happy in her home. We need such help, Marchbanks: we need it greatly and always. There are so many things to make us doubt, if once we let our understanding be troubled. Even at home, we sit as if in camp, encompassed by a hostile army of doubts. Will you play the traitor and let them in on me?

MARCH. (*looking round wildly*). Is it like this for her here always? A woman, with a great soul, craving for reality, truth, freedom; and being fed on metaphors, sermons, stale perorations, mere rhetoric. Do you think a woman's soul can live on your talent for preaching?

MOR. (*stung*). Marchbanks: you make it hard for me to control myself. My talent is like yours insofar as it has any real worth at all. It is the gift of finding words for divine truth.

MARCH. (*impetuously*). It's the gift of the gab, nothing more and nothing less. What has your knack of fine talking to do with the truth, any more than playing the organ has? Ive never been in your church; but Ive been to your political meetings; and Ive seen you do whats called rousing the meeting to enthusiasm: that is, you excited them until they behaved exactly as if they were drunk. And their wives looked on and saw what fools they were. Oh, it's an old story: youll find it in the Bible. I imagine King David, in his fits of enthusiasm, was very like you. (*Stabbing him with the words.*) "But his wife despised him in her heart."

MOR. (*wrathfully*). Leave my house. Do you hear? (*He advances on him threateningly.*)

MARCH. (*shrinking back against the couch*). Let me alone. Dont touch me. (MORELL *grasps him powerfully by the lapel of his coat: he cowers down on the sofa and screams passionately.*) Stop, Morell: if you strike me, I'll kill myself: I wont bear it. (*Almost in hysterics.*) Let me go. Take your hand away.

MOR. (*with slow emphatic scorn*). You little snivelling cowardly whelp. (*He releases him.*) Go, before you frighten yourself into a fit.

MARCH. (*on the sofa, gasping, but relieved by the withdrawal of* MORELL's *hand*). I'm not afraid of you: it's you who are afraid of me.

MOR. (*quietly, as he stands over him*). It looks like it, doesnt it?

MARCH. (*with petulant vehemence*). Yes, it does. (MORELL *turns away contemptuously.* EUGENE *scrambles to his feet and follows him.*) You think because I shrink from being brutally handled—because (*with tears in his voice*) I can do nothing but cry with rage when I am met with violence—because I cant lift a heavy trunk down from the top of a cab like you—because I cant fight you for your wife as a drunken navvy would: all that makes you think I'm afraid of you. But youre wrong. If I havnt got what you call British pluck, I havnt British cowardice either: I'm not afraid of a clergyman's ideas. I'll fight your ideas. I'll rescue her from her slavery to them. I'll pit my own ideas against them. You are driving me out of the house because you darent let her choose between your ideas and mine. You are afraid to let me see her again. (MORELL, *angered, turns suddenly on him. He flies to the door in involuntary dread.*) Let me alone, I say. I'm going.

MOR. (*with cold scorn*). Wait a moment: I am not going to touch you: dont be afraid. When my wife comes back she will want to know why you have gone. And when she finds that you are never going to cross our threshold again, she will want to have that explained too. Now I dont wish to distress her by telling her that you have behaved like a blackguard.

MARCH. (*coming back with renewed vehemence*). You shall. You must. If you give any explanation but the true one, you are a liar and a coward. Tell her what I said; and how you were strong and manly, and shook me as a terrier shakes a rat; and how I shrank and was terrified; and how you called me a snivelling little whelp and put me out of the house. If you dont tell her, I will: I'll write it to her.

MOR. (*puzzled*). Why do you want her to know this?

MARCH. (*with lyric rapture*). Because she will understand me, and know that I understand her. If you keep back one word of it from her— if you are not ready to lay the truth at her feet as I am—then you will know to the end of your days that she really belongs to me and not to you. Goodbye. (*Going.*)

MOR. (*terribly disquieted*). Stop: I will not tell her.

MARCH. (*turning near the door*). Either the truth or a lie you must tell her, if I go.

MOR. (*temporizing*). Marchbanks: it is sometimes justifiable—

MARCH. (*cutting him short*). I know: to lie. It will be useless. Goodbye, Mr Clergyman.

(*As he turns finally to the door, it opens and* CANDIDA *enters in her housekeeping dress.*)

CAND. Are you going, Eugene? (*Looking more observantly at him.*) Well, dear me, just look at you, going out into the street in that state! You are a poet, certainly. Look at him, James! (*She takes him by the coat, and brings him forward, shewing him to* MORELL.) Look at his collar! look at his tie! look at his hair! One would think somebody had been throttling you. (EUGENE *instinctively tries to look round at* MORELL; *but she pulls him back.*) Here! Stand still. (*She buttons his collar; ties his neckerchief in a bow; and arranges his hair.*) There! Now you look so nice that I think youd better stay to lunch after all, though I told you you mustnt. It will be ready in half an hour. (*She puts a final touch to the bow. He kisses her hand.*) Dont be silly.

MARCH. I want to stay, of course; unless the reverend gentleman your husband has anything to advance to the contrary.

CAND. Shall he stay, James, if he promises to be a good boy and help me to lay the table?

MOR. (*shortly*). Oh yes, certainly: he had better. (*He goes to the table and pretends to busy himself with his papers there.*)

MARCH. (*offering his arm to* CANDIDA). Come and lay the table. (*She takes it. They go to the door together. As they pass out he adds*) I am the happiest of mortals.

MOR. So was I—an hour ago.

ACT TWO

The same day later in the afternoon. The same room. The chair for visitors has been replaced at the table. MARCHBANKS, *alone and idle, is trying to find out how the typewriter works. Hearing someone at the door, he steals guiltily away to the window and pretends to be absorbed in the view.* MISS GARNETT, *carrying the notebook in which she takes down* MORELL'S *letters in shorthand from his dictation, sits down at the typewriter and sets to work transcribing them, much too busy to notice* EUGENE. *When she begins the second line she stops and stares at the machine. Something wrong evidently.*

PROS. Bother! Youve been meddling with my typewriter, Mr Marchbanks; and theres not the least use in your trying to look as if you hadnt.

MARCH. (*timidly*). I'm very sorry, Miss Garnett. I only tried to make it write. (*Plaintively.*) But it wouldnt.

PROS. Well, youve altered the spacing.

MARCH. (*earnestly*). I assure you I didnt. I didnt indeed. I only turned a little wheel. It gave a sort of click.

PROS. Oh, now I understand. (*She restores the spacing, talking volubly all the time.*) I suppose you thought it was a sort of barrel-organ. Nothing to do but turn the handle, and it would write a beautiful love letter for you straight off, eh?

MARCH. (*seriously*). I suppose a machine could be made to write love letters. Theyre all the same, arnt they?

PROS. (*somewhat indignantly: any such discussion, except by way of pleasantry, being outside her code of manners*). How do I know? Why do you ask me?

MARCH. I beg your pardon. I thought clever people—people who can do business and write letters and that sort of thing—always had to have love affairs to keep them from going mad.

PROS. (*rising, outraged*). Mr Marchbanks! (*She looks severely at him, and marches majestically to the bookcase.*)

MARCH. (*approaching her humbly*). I hope I havnt offended you. Perhaps I shouldnt have alluded to your love affairs.

PROS. (*plucking a blue book from the shelf and turning sharply on him*). I havnt any love affairs. How dare you say such a thing? The idea! (*She tucks the book under her arm, and is flouncing back to her machine when he addresses her with awakened interest and sympathy.*)

MARCH. Really! Oh, then you are shy, like me.

PROS. Certainly I am not shy. What do you mean?

MARCH. (*secretly*). You must be: that is the reason there are so few love affairs in the world. We all go about longing for love: it is the first need of our natures, the first prayer of our hearts; but we dare not utter our longing: we are too shy. (*Very earnestly.*) Oh, Miss Garnett, what would you not give to be without fear, without shame—

PROS. (*scandalized*). Well, upon my word!

MARCH. (*with petulant impatience*). Ah, dont say those stupid things to me: they dont deceive me: what use are they? Why are you afraid to be your real self with me? I am just like you.

PROS. Like me! Pray are you flattering me or flattering yourself? I dont feel quite sure which. (*She again tries to get back to her work.*)

MARCH. (*stopping her mysteriously*). Hush! I go about in search of love; and I find it in unmeasured stores in the bosoms of others. But when I try to ask for it, this horrible shyness strangles me; and I stand dumb, or worse than dumb, saying meaningless things: foolish lies. And I see the affection I am longing for given to dogs and cats and pet birds, because they come and ask for it. (*Almost whispering.*) It must be asked for: it is like a ghost: it cannot speak unless it is first spoken to. (*At his usual pitch, but with deep melancholy.*) All the love in the world is longing to speak; only it dare not, because it is shy! shy! shy! That is the world's tragedy. (*With a deep sigh he sits in the visitors' chair and buries his face in his hands.*)

PROS. (*amazed, but keeping her wits about her: her point of honor in encounters with strange young men*). Wicked people get over that shyness occasionally, dont they?

MARCH. (*scrambling up almost fiercely*). Wicked people means people who have no love: therefore they have no shame. They have the power to ask love because they dont need it: they have the power to offer it because they have none to give. (*He collapses into his seat, and adds, mournfully*) But we, who have love, and long to mingle it with the love of others: we cannot utter a word. (*Timidly.*) You find that, dont you?

PROS. Look here: if you dont stop talking like this, I'll leave the room, Mr Marchbanks: I really will. It's not proper. (*She resumes her seat at the typewriter, opening the blue book and preparing to copy a passage from it.*)

MARCH. (*hopelessly*). Nothing thats worth saying is proper. (*He rises, and wanders about the room in his lost way.*) I cant understand you, Miss Garnett. What am I to talk about?

PROS. (*snubbing him*). Talk about indifferent things. Talk about the weather.

MARCH. Would you talk about indifferent things if a child were by, crying bitterly with hunger?

PROS. I suppose not.

MARCH. Well: *I* cant talk about indifferent things with my heart crying out bitterly in its hunger.

PROS. Then hold your tongue.

MARCH. Yes: that is what it always comes to. We hold our tongues. Does that stop the cry of your heart? for it does cry: doesnt it? It must, if you have a heart.

PROS. (*suddenly rising with her hand pressed on her heart*). Oh, it's no use trying to work while you talk like that. (*She leaves her little table and sits on the sofa. Her feelings are keenly stirred.*) It's no business of yours whether my heart cries or not; but I have a mind to tell you, for all that.

MARCH. You neednt. I know already that it must.

PROS. But mind! if you ever say I said so, I'll deny it.

MARCH. (*compassionately*). Yes, I know. And so you havnt the courage to tell him?

PROS. (*bouncing up*). Him! Who?

MARCH. Whoever he is. The man you love. It might be anybody. The curate, Mr Mill, perhaps.

PROS. (*with disdain*). Mr Mill!!! A fine man to break my heart about, indeed! I'd rather have you than Mr Mill.

MARCH. (*recoiling*). No, really: I'm very sorry; but you mustnt think of that. I—

PROS. (*testily, going to the fire-place and standing at it with her back to him*). Oh, dont be frightened: it's not you. It's not any one particular person.

MARCH. I know. You feel that you could love anybody that offered—

PROS. (*turning, exasperated*). Anybody that offered! No, I do not. What do you take me for?

MARCH. (*discouraged*). No use. You wont make me real answers: only those things that everybody says. (*He strays to the sofa and sits down disconsolately.*)

PROS. (*nettled at what she takes to be a disparagement of her manners by an aristocrat*). Oh well, if you want original conversation, youd better go and talk to yourself.

MARCH. That is what all poets do: they talk to themselves out loud; and the world overhears them. But it's horribly lonely not to hear someone else talk sometimes.

PROS. Wait until Mr Morell comes. He'll talk to you. (MARCHBANKS *shudders.*) Oh, you neednt make wry faces over him: he can talk better than you. (*With temper.*) He'd talk your little head off. (*She is going back angrily to her place, when he, suddenly enlightened, springs up and stops her.*)

MARCH. Ah! I understand now.

PROS. (*reddening*). What do you understand?

MARCH. Your secret. Tell me: is it really and truly possible for a woman to love him?

PROS. (*as if this were beyond all bounds*). Well!!

MARCH. (*passionately*). No: answer me. I want to know: I must know. *I* cant understand it. I can see nothing in him but words, pious resolutions, what people call goodness. You cant love that.

PROS. (*attempting to snub him by an air of cool propriety*). I simply dont know what youre talking about. I dont understand you.

MARCH. (*vehemently*). You do. You lie.

PROS. Oh!

MARCH. You do understand; and you know. (*Determined to have an answer.*) Is it possible for a woman to love him?

PROS. (*looking him straight in the face*). Yes. (*He covers his face with his hands.*) Whatever is the matter with you! (*He takes down his hands. Frightened at the tragic mask presented to her, she hurries past him at the utmost possible distance, keeping her eyes on his face until he turns from her and goes to the child's chair beside the hearth, where he sits in the deepest dejection. As she approaches the door, it opens and BURGESS enters. Seeing him, she ejaculates*) Praise heaven! here's somebody (*and feels safe enough to resume her place at her table. She puts a fresh sheet of paper into the typewriter as BURGESS crosses to EUGENE.*)

BUR. (*bent on taking care of the distinguished visitor*). Well: so this is the way they leave you to yoreself, Mr Morchbanks. Ive come to keep you company. (MARCHBANKS *looks up at him in consternation, which is quite lost on him.*) James is receivin a deppitation in the dinin room; and Candy is hupstairs heducating of a young stitcher gurl she's hinterested in. (*Condolingly.*) You must find it lonesome here with no one but the typist to talk to. (*He pulls round the easy chair, and sits down.*)

PROS. (*highly incensed*). He'll be all right now that he has the advantage of your polished conversation: thats one comfort, anyhow. (*She begins to typewrite with clattering asperity.*)

BUR. (*amazed at her audacity*). Hi was not addressin myself to you, young woman, that I'm awerr of.

PROS. Did you ever see worse manners, Mr Marchbanks?

BUR. (*with pompous severity*). Mr Morchbanks is a gentleman, and knows his place, which is more than some people do.

PROS. (*fretfully*). It's well you and I are not ladies and gentlemen: I'd talk to you pretty straight if Mr Marchbanks wasnt here. (*She pulls the letter out of the machine so crossly that it tears.*) There! now I've spoiled this letter! have to be done all over again! Oh, I cant contain myself: silly old fathead!

BUR. (*rising, breathless with indignation*). Ho! I'm a silly ole fat'ead, am I? Ho, indeed (*gasping*)! Hall right, my gurl! Hall right. You just wait till I tell that to yore hemployer. Youll see. I'll teach you: see if I dont.

PROS. (*conscious of having gone too far*). I—

BUR. (*cutting her short*). No: youve done it now. No huse a-talkin to me. I'll let you know who I am. (PROSERPINE *shifts her paper carriage with a defiant bang, and disdainfully goes on with her work.*) Dont you take no notice of her, Mr Morchbanks. She's beneath it. (*He loftily sits down again.*)

MARCH. (*miserably nervous and disconcerted*). Hadnt we better change the subject? I—I dont think Miss Garnett meant anything.

PROS. (*with intense conviction*). Oh, didnt I though, just!

BUR. I wouldnt demean myself to take notice on her.

(*An electric bell rings twice.*)

PROS. (*gathering up her notebook and papers*). Thats for me. (*She hurries out.*)

BUR. (*calling after her*). Oh, we can spare you. (*Somewhat relieved by the triumph of having the last word, and yet half inclined to try to improve on it, he looks after her for a moment; then subsides into his seat by* EUGENE, *and addresses him very confidentially.*) Now we're alone, Mr Morchbanks, let me give you a friendly int that I wouldnt give to heverybody. Ow long ave you known my son-in-law James ere?

MARCH. I dont know. I never can remember dates. A few months, perhaps.

BUR. Ever notice hennythink queer about him?

MARCH. I dont think so.

BUR. (*impressively*). No more you wouldnt. Thats the danger on it. Well, he's mad.

MARCH. Mad!

BUR. Mad as a Morch 'are. You take notice on him and youll see.

MARCH. (*uneasily*). But surely that is only because his opinions—

BUR. (*touching him on the knee with his forefinger, and pressing it to hold his attention*). Thats the same what I hused to think, Mr Morchbanks. Hi thought long enough that it was ony his opinions; though, mind you, hopinions becomes vurry serious things

when people takes to hactin on em as e does. But thats not what
I go on. (*He looks round to make sure that they are alone, and
bends over to* EUGENE's *ear.*) What do you think he sez to me this
mornin in this very room?

MARCH. What?

BUR. He sez to me—this is as sure as we're settin here now—he sez "I'm
a fool," he sez; "and yore a scounderl." Me a scounderl, mind you!
And then shook ands with me on it, as if it was to my credit! Do
you mean to tell me as that man's sane?

MOR. (*outside, calling to* PROSERPINE *as he opens the door*). Get all their
names and addresses, Miss Garnett.

PROS. (*in the distance*). Yes, Mr Morell.

(MORELL *comes in, with the deputation's documents in his hands.*)

BUR. (*aside to* MARCHBANKS). Yorr he is. Just you keep your heye on im
and see. (*Rising momentously.*) I'm sorry, James, to ave to make
a complaint to you. I dont want to do it; but I feel I oughter, as
a matter o right and dooty.

MOR. Whats the matter?

BUR. Mr Morchbanks will bear me hout: he was a witness. (*Very solemnly.*) Yore young woman so far forgot herself as to call me a
silly ole fat'ead.

MOR. (*with tremendous heartiness*). Oh, now, isnt that exactly like
Prossy? She's so frank: she cant contain herself! Poor Prossy! Ha!
ha!

BUR. (*trembling with rage*). And do you hexpec me to put up with it
from the like of er?

MOR. Pooh, nonsense! you cant take any notice of it. Never mind. (*He
goes to the cellaret and puts the papers into one of the drawers.*)

BUR. Oh, Hi dont mind. Hi'm above it. But is it right? thats what I
want to know. Is it right?

MOR. Thats a question for the Church, not for the laity. Has it done you
any harm? thats the question for you, eh? Of course it hasnt.
Think no more of it. (*He dismisses the subject by going to his
place at the table and setting to work at his correspondence.*)

BUR. (*aside to* MARCHBANKS). What did I tell you? Mad as a atter. (*He *goes to the table and asks, with the sickly civility of a hungry man.*) When's dinner, James?

MOR. Not for a couple of hours yet.

BUR. (*with plaintive resignation*). Gimme a nice book to read over the fire, will you, James: thur's a good chap.

MOR. What sort of book? A good one?

BUR. (*with almost a yell of remonstrance*). Nah-oo! Summat pleasant, just to pass the time. (MORELL *takes an illustrated paper from the table and offers it. He accepts it humbly.*) Thank yer, James. (*He goes back to the big chair at the fire, and sits there at his ease, reading.*)

MOR. (*as he writes*). Candida will come to entertain you presently. She has got rid of her pupil. She is filling the lamps.

MARCH. (*starting up in the wildest consternation*). But that will soil her hands. I cant bear that, Morell: it's a shame. I'll go and fill them. (*He makes for the door.*)

MOR. Youd better not. (MARCHBANKS *stops irresolutely.*) She'd only set you to clean my boots, to save me the trouble of doing it myself in the morning.

BUR. (*with grave disapproval*). Dont you keep a servant now, James?

MOR. Yes; but she isnt a slave; and the house looks as if I kept three. That means that everyone has to lend a hand. It's not a bad plan: Prossy and I can talk business after breakfast while we're washing up. Washing up's no trouble when there are two people to do it.

MARCH. (*tormentedly*). Do you think every woman is as coarsegrained as Miss Garnett?

BUR. (*emphatically*). Thats quite right, Mr Morchbanks: thats quite right. She is corsegrained.

MOR. (*quietly and significantly*). Marchbanks!

MARCH. Yes?

MOR. How many servants does your father keep?

MARCH. (*pettishly*). Oh, I dont know. (*He moves to the sofa, as if to get as far as possible from* MORELL's *questioning, and sits down in great agony of spirit, thinking of the paraffin.*)

MOR. (*very gravely*). So many that you dont know! (*More aggres-*

sively.) When theres anything coarsegrained to be done, you just ring the bell and throw it on to somebody else; eh?

MARCH. Oh, dont torture me. You dont even ring the bell. But your wife's beautiful fingers are dabbling in paraffin oil while you sit here comfortably preaching about it: everlasting preaching! preaching! words! words! words!

BUR. (*intensely appreciating this retort*). Har, har! Devil a better! (*Radiantly.*) Ad you there, James, straight.

(CANDIDA *comes in, well aproned, with a reading lamp trimmed, filled, and ready for lighting. She places it on the table near* MORELL, *ready for use.*)

CAND. (*brushing her finger tips together with a slight twitch of her nose*). If you stay with us, Eugene, I think I will hand over the lamps to you.

MARCH. I will stay on condition that you hand over all the rough work to me.

CAND. Thats very gallant; but I think I should like to see how you do it first. (*Turning to* MORELL.) James: youve not been looking after the house properly.

MOR. What have I done—or not done—my love?

CAND. (*with serious vexation*). My own particular pet scrubbing brush has been used for blackleading. (*A heartbreaking wail bursts from* MARCHBANKS. BURGESS *looks round, amazed.* CANDIDA *hurries to the sofa.*) Whats the matter? Are you ill, Eugene?

MARCH. No: not ill. Only horror! horror! horror! (*He bows his head on his hands.*)

BUR. (*shocked*). What! Got the orrors, Mr Morchbanks! Oh, thats bad, at your age. You must leave it off grajally.

CAND. (*reassured*). Nonsense, papa! It's only poetic horror, isnt it, Eugene (*petting him*)?

BUR. (*abashed*). Oh, poetic orror, is it? I beg your pordon, I'm shore. (*He turns to the fire again, deprecating his hasty conclusion.*)

CAND. What is it, Eugene? the scrubbing brush? (*He shudders.*) Well, there! never mind. (*She sits down beside him.*) Wouldnt you like to present me with a nice new one, with an ivory back inlaid with mother-of-pearl?

MARCH. (*softly and musically, but sadly and longingly*). No, not a scrubbing brush, but a boat: a tiny shallop to sail away in, far from the world, where the marble floors are washed by the rain and dried by the sun; where the south wind dusts the beautiful green and purple carpets. Or a chariot! to carry us up into the sky, where the lamps are stars, and dont need to be filled with paraffin oil every day.

MOR. (*harshly*). And where there is nothing to do but to be idle, selfish, and useless.

CAND. (*jarred*). Oh, James! how could you spoil it all?

MARCH. (*firing up*). Yes, to be idle, selfish, and useless: that is, to be beautiful and free and happy: hasnt every man desired that with all his soul for the woman he loves? Thats my ideal: whats yours, and that of all the dreadful people who live in these hideous rows of houses? Sermons and scrubbing brushes! With you to preach the sermon and your wife to scrub.

CAND. (*quaintly*). He cleans the boots, Eugene. You will have to clean them tomorrow for saying that about him.

MARCH. Oh, dont talk about boots! Your feet should be beautiful on the mountains.

CAND. My feet would not be beautiful on the Hackney Road without boots.

BUR. (*scandalized*). Come, Candy! dont be vulgar. Mr Morchbanks aint accustomed to it. Youre givin him the orrors again. I mean the poetic ones.

(MORELL *is silent. Apparently he is busy with his letters: really he is puzzling with misgiving over his new and alarming experience that the surer he is of his moral thrusts, the more swiftly and effectively* EUGENE *parries them. To find himself beginning to fear a man whom he does not respect afflicts him bitterly.*)

(MISS GARNETT *comes in with a telegram.*)

PROS. (*handing the telegram to* MORELL). Reply paid. The boy's waiting. (*To* CANDIDA, *coming back to her machine and sitting down.*) Maria is ready for you now in the kitchen, Mrs Morell. (CANDIDA *rises.*) The onions have come.

MARCH. (*convulsively*). Onions!

CAND. Yes, onions. Not even Spanish ones: nasty little red onions. You shall help me to slice them. Come along. (*She catches him by the wrist and runs out, pulling him after her.* BURGESS *rises in consternation, and stands aghast on the hearthrug, staring after them.*)

BUR. Candy didnt oughter andle a hearl's nevvy like that. It's goin too fur with it. Lookee ere, James: do e often git taken queer like that?

MOR. (*shortly, writing a telegram*). I dont know.

BUR. (*sentimentally*). He talks very pretty. I awlus had a turn for a bit of poetry. Candy takes arter me that-a-way. Huseter make me tell er fairy stories when she was ony a little kiddy not that igh (*indicating a stature of two feet or thereabouts*).

MOR. (*preoccupied*). Ah, indeed. (*He blots the telegram and goes out.*)

PROS. Used you to make the fairy stories up out of your own head?

(BURGESS, *not deigning to reply, strikes an attitude of the haughtiest disdain on the hearthrug.*)

PROS. (*calmly*). I should never have supposed you had it in you. By the way, I'd better warn you, since youve taken such a fancy to Mr Marchbanks. He's mad.

BUR. Mad! What! Im too!!

PROS. Mad as a March hare. He did frighten me, I can tell you, just before you came in that time. Havent you noticed the queer things he says?

BUR. So thats what the poetic orrors means. Blame me if it didnt come into my ed once or twyst that he was a bit horff 'is chump! (*He crosses the room to the door, lifting up his voice as he goes.*) Well, this is a pretty sort of asylum for a man to be in, with no one but you to take care of him!

PROS. (*as he passes her*). Yes, what a dreadful thing it would be if anything happened to you!

BUR. (*loftily*). Dont you haddress no remarks to me. Tell your hemployer that Ive gone into the gorden for a smoke.

PROS. (*mocking*). Oh!

(*Before* BURGESS *can retort,* MORELL *comes back.*)

BUR. (*sentimentally*). Goin for a turn in the gording to smoke, James.

MOR. (*brusquely*). Oh, all right, all right. (BURGESS *goes out pathetically in the character of a weary old man.* MORELL *stands at the table, turning over his papers, and adding, across to* PROSERPINE, *half humorously, half absently.*) Well, Miss Prossy, why have you been calling my father-in-law names?

PROS. (*blushing fiery red, and looking quickly up at him, half scared, half reproachful*). I— (*She bursts into tears.*)

MOR. (*with tender gaiety, leaning across the table towards her, and consoling her*). Oh, come! come! come! Never mind, Pross: he is a silly old fathead, isnt he? (*With an explosive sob, she makes a dash at the door, and vanishes, banging it.* MORELL, *shaking his head resignedly, sighs, and goes wearily to his chair, where he sits down and sets to work, looking old and careworn.*)

(CANDIDA *comes in. She has finished her household work and taken off the apron. She at once notices his dejected appearance, and posts herself quietly at the visitors' chair, looking down at him attentively. She says nothing.*)

MOR. (*looking up, but with his pen raised ready to resume his work*). Well? Where is Eugene?

CAND. Washing his hands in the scullery under the tap. He will make an excellent cook if he can only get over his dread of Maria.

MOR. (*shortly*). Ha! No doubt. (*He begins writing again.*)

CAND. (*going nearer, and putting her hand down softly on his to stop him as she says*). Come here, dear. Let me look at you. (*He drops his pen and yields himself to her disposal. She makes him rise, and brings him a little away from the table, looking at him critically all the time.*) Turn your face to the light. (*She places him facing the window.*) My boy is not looking well. Has he been overworking?

MOR. Nothing more than usual.

CAND. He looks very pale, and grey, and wrinkled, and old. (*His melancholy deepens; and she attacks it with wilful gaiety.*) Here: (*pulling him towards the easy chair*) youve done enough writing for today. Leave Prossy to finish it. Come and talk to me.

MOR. But—

CAND. (*insisting*). Yes, I must be talked to. (*She makes him sit down, and seats herself on the carpet beside his knee.*) Now (*patting his hand*) youre beginning to look better already. Why must you go out every night lecturing and talking? I hardly have one evening a week with you. Of course what you say is all very true; but it does no good: they dont mind what you say to them one little bit. They think they agree with you; but whats the use of their agreeing with you if they go and do just the opposite of what you tell them the moment your back is turned? Look at our congregation at St Dominic's! Why do they come to hear you talking about Christianity every Sunday? Why, just because theyve been so full of business and money-making for six days that they want to forget all about it and have a rest on the seventh; so that they can go back fresh and make money harder than ever! You positively help them at it instead of hindering them.

MOR. (*with energetic seriousness*). You know very well, Candida, that I often blow them up soundly for that. And if there is nothing in their churchgoing but rest and diversion, why dont they try something more amusing? more self-indulgent? There must be some good in the fact that they prefer St Dominic's to worse places on Sundays.

CAND. Oh, the worse places arnt open; and even if they were, they darent be seen going to them. Besides, James dear, you preach so splendidly that it's as good as a play for them. Why do you think the women are so enthusiastic?

MOR. (*shocked*). Candida!

CAND. Oh, *I* know. You silly boy: you think it's your Socialism and your religion; but if it were that, theyd do what you tell them instead of only coming to look at you. They all have Prossy's complaint.

MOR. Prossy's complaint! What do you mean, Candida?

CAND. Yes, Prossy, and all the other secretaries you ever had. Why does Prossy condescend to wash up the things, and to peel potatoes and abase herself in all manner of ways for six shillings a week less than she used to get in a city office? She's in love with you, James: thats the reason. Theyre all in love with you. And you are in love with preaching because you do it so beautifully. And you think it's all enthusiasm for the kingdom of Heaven on earth; and so do they. You dear silly!

MOR. Candida: what dreadful! what soul-destroying cynicism! Are you jesting? Or—can it be?—are you jealous?

CAND. (*with curious thoughtfulness*). Yes, I feel a little jealous sometimes.

MOR. (*incredulously*). Of Prossy?

CAND. (*laughing*). No, no, no, no. Not jealous of anybody. Jealous for somebody else, who is not loved as he ought to be.

MOR. Me?

CAND. You! Why, youre spoiled with love and worship: you get far more than is good for you. No: I mean Eugene.

MOR. (*startled*). Eugene!

CAND. It seems unfair that all the love should go to you, and none to him; although he needs it so much more than you do. (*A convulsive movement shakes him in spite of himself.*) Whats the matter? Am I worrying you?

MOR. (*hastily*). Not at all. (*Looking at her with troubled intensity.*) You know that I have perfect confidence in you, Candida.

CAND. You vain thing! Are you so sure of your irresistible attractions?

MOR. Candida; you are shocking me. I never thought of my attractions. I thought of your goodness, of your purity. That is what I confide in.

CAND. What a nasty uncomfortable thing to say to me! Oh, you are a clergyman, James: a thorough clergyman!

MOR. (*turning away from her, heart-stricken*). So Eugene says.

CAND. (*with lively interest, leaning over to him with her arms on his knee*). Eugene's always right. He's a wonderful boy: I have grown fonder and fonder of him all the time I was away. Do you know, James, that though he has not the least suspicion of it himself, he is ready to fall madly in love with me?

MOR. (*grimly*). Oh, he has no suspicion of it himself, hasnt he?

CAND. Not a bit. (*She takes her arms from his knee, and turns thoughtfully, sinking into a more restful attitude with her hands in her lap.*) Some day he will know: when he is grown up and experienced, like you. And he will know that I must have known. I wonder what he will think of me then.

MOR. No evil, Candida. I hope and trust, no evil.

CAND. (*dubiously*). That will depend.

MOR. (*bewildered*). Depend!

CAND. (*looking at him*). Yes: it will depend on what happens to him. (*He looks vacantly at her.*) Dont you see? It will depend on how he comes to learn what love really is. I mean on the sort of woman who will teach it to him.

MOR. (*quite at a loss*). Yes. No. I dont know what you mean.

CAND. (*explaining*). If he learns it from a good woman, then it will be all right: he will forgive me.

MOR. Forgive?

CAND. But suppose he learns it from a bad woman, as so many men do, especially poetic men, who imagine all women are angels! Suppose he only discovers the value of love when he has thrown it away and degraded himself in his ignorance! Will he forgive me then, do you think?

MOR. Forgive you for what?

CAND. (*realizing how stupid he is, and a little disappointed, though quite tenderly so*). Dont you understand? (*He shakes his head. She turns to him again, so as to explain with the fondest intimacy.*) I mean, will he forgive me for not teaching him myself? For abandoning him to the bad women for the sake of my goodness, of my purity, as you call it? Ah, James, how little you understand me, to talk of your confidence in my goodness and purity! I would give them both to poor Eugene as willingly as I would give my shawl to a beggar dying of cold, if there were nothing else to restrain me. Put your trust in my love for you, James; for if that went, I should care very little for your sermons: mere phrases that you cheat yourself and others with every day. (*She is about to rise.*)

MOR. His words!

CAND. (*checking herself quickly in the act of getting up*). Whose words?

MOR. Eugene's.

CAND. (*delighted*). He is always right. He understands you; he understands me; he understands Prossy; and you, darling, you understand nothing. (*She laughs, and kisses him to console him. He recoils as if stabbed, and springs up.*)

MOR. How can you bear to do that when—Oh, Candida (*with anguish in his voice*) I had rather you had plunged a grappling iron into my heart than given me that kiss.

CAND. (*amazed*). My dear: whats the matter?

MOR. (*frantically waving her off*). Dont touch me.

CAND. James!!!

(*They are interrupted by the entrance of* MARCHBANKS *with* BURGESS, *who stop near the door, staring.*)

MARCH. Is anything the matter?

MOR. (*deadly white, putting an iron constraint on himself*). Nothing but this: that either you were right this morning, or Candida is mad.

BUR. (*in loudest protest*). What! Candy mad too! Oh, come! come! come! (*He crosses the room to the fireplace, protesting as he goes, and knocks the ashes out of his pipe on the bars.*)

(MORELL *sits down at his table desperately, leaning forward to hide his face, and interlacing his fingers rigidly to keep them steady.*)

CAND. (*to* MORELL, *relieved and laughing*). Oh, youre only shocked! Is that all? How conventional all you unconventional people are! (*She sits gaily on the arm of the chair.*)

BUR. Come: be'ave yourself, Candy. Whatll Mr Morchbanks think of you?

CAND. This comes of James teaching me to think for myself, and never to hold back out of fear of what other people may think of me. It works beautifully as long as I think the same things as he does. But now! because I have just thought something different! look at him! Just look! (*She points to* MORELL, *greatly amused.*)

(EUGENE *looks, and instantly presses his hand on his heart, as if some pain had shot through it. He sits down on the sofa like a man witnessing a tragedy.*)

BUR. (*on the hearthrug*). Well, James, you certnly haint as himpressive lookin as usu'l.

MOR. (*with a laugh which is half a sob*). I suppose not. I beg all your pardons: I was not conscious of making a fuss. (*Pulling himself together.*) Well, well, well, well, well! (*He sets to work at his papers again with resolute cheerfulness.*)

CAND. (*going to the sofa and sitting beside* MARCHBANKS, *still in a bantering humor*). Well, Eugene: why are you so sad? Did the onions make you cry?

MARCH. (*aside to her*). It is your cruelty. I hate cruelty. It is a horrible thing to see one person make another suffer.

CAND. (*petting him ironically*). Poor boy! have I been cruel? Did I make it slice nasty little red onions?

MARCH. (*earnestly*). Oh, stop, stop: I dont mean myself. You have made him suffer frightfully. I feel his pain in my own heart. I know that it is not your fault: it is something that must happen; but dont make light of it. I shudder when you torture him and laugh.

CAND. (*incredulously*). *I* torture James! Nonsense, Eugene: how you exaggerate! Silly! (*She rises and goes to the table, a little troubled*.) Dont work any more, dear. Come and talk to us.

MOR. (*affectionately but bitterly*). Ah no: *I* cant talk. I can only preach.

CAND. (*caressing his hand*). Well, come and preach.

BUR. (*strongly remonstrating*). Aw no, Candy. 'Ang it all!

(LEXY MILL *comes in, anxious and important*.)

LEXY (*hastening to shake hands with* CANDIDA). How do you do, Mrs Morell? So glad to see you back again.

CAND. Thank you, Lexy. You know Eugene, dont you?

LEXY. Oh yes. How do you do, Marchbanks?

MARCH. Quite well, thanks.

LEXY (*to* MORELL). Ive just come from the Guild of St Matthew. They are in the greatest consternation about your telegram.

CAND. What did you telegraph about, James?

LEXY (*to* CANDIDA). He was to have spoken for them tonight. Theyve taken the large hall in Mare Street and spent a lot of money on posters. Morell's telegram was to say he couldnt come. It came on them like a thunderbolt.

CAND. (*surprised, and beginning to suspect something wrong*). Given up an engagement to speak!

BUR. Fust time in his life, I'll bet. Ain it, Candy?

LEXY (*to* MORELL). They decided to send an urgent telegram to you asking whether you could not change your mind. Have you received it?

MOR. (*with restrained impatience*). Yes, yes: I got it.

LEXY. It was reply paid.

MOR. Yes, I know. I answered it. I cant go.

CAND. But why, James?

MOR. (*almost fiercely*). Because I dont choose. These people forget that I am a man: they think I am a talking machine to be turned on for their pleasure every evening of my life. May I not have one night at home, with my wife, and my friends?

(*They are all amazed at this outburst, except* EUGENE. *His expression remains unchanged.*)

CAND. Oh, James, you mustnt mind what I said about that. And if you dont go youll have an attack of bad conscience tomorrow.

LEXY (*intimidated, but urgent*). I know, of course, that they make the most unreasonable demands on you. But they have been telegraphing all over the place for another speaker; and they can get nobody but the President of the Agnostic League.

MOR. (*promptly*). Well, an excellent man. What better do they want?

LEXY. But he always insists so powerfully on the divorce of Socialism from Christianity. He will undo all the good we have been doing. Of course you know best; but—(*he shrugs his shoulders and wanders to the hearth beside* BURGESS.)

CAND. (*coaxingly*). Oh, do go, James. We'll all go.

BUR. (*grumblingly*). Look 'ere, Candy! I say! Let's stay at home by the fire, comfortable. He wont need to be more'n a couple-o-hour away.

CAND. Youll be just as comfortable at the meeting. We'll all sit on the platform and be great people.

EUG. (*terrified*). Oh please dont let us go on the platform. No: everyone will stare at us: I couldnt. I'll sit at the back of the room.

CAND. Dont be afraid. Theyll be too busy looking at James to notice you.

MOR. Prossy's complaint, Candida! Eh?

CAND. (*gaily*). Yes: Prossy's complaint.

BUR. (*mystified*). Prossy's complaint! What are you talkin about, James?

MOR. (*not heeding him, rises; goes to the door; and holds it open, calling in a commanding tone*). Miss Garnett.

PROS. (*in the distance*). Yes, Mr Morell. Coming.

(*They all wait, except* BURGESS, *who turns stealthily to* LEXY.)

BUR. Listen ere, Mr Mill. Whats Prossy's complaint? Whats wrong with er?

LEXY (*confidentially*). Well, I dont exactly know; but she spoke very strangely to me this morning. I'm afraid she's a little out of her mind sometimes.

BUR. (*overwhelmed*). Why, it must be catchin! Four in the same ouse!

PROS. (*appearing on the threshold*). What is it, Mr Morell?

MOR. Telegraph to the Guild of St Matthew that I am coming.

PROS. (*surprised*). Dont they expect you?

MOR. (*peremptorily*). Do as I tell you.

(PROSERPINE, *frightened, sits down at her typewriter, and obeys.* MORELL, *now unaccountably resolute and forceful, goes across to* BURGESS. CANDIDA *watches his movements with growing wonder and misgiving.*)

MOR. Burgess: you dont want to come.

BUR. Oh, dont put it like that, James. It's ony that it aint Sunday, you know.

MOR. I'm sorry. I thought you might like to be introduced to the chairman. He's on the Works Committee of the County Council, and has some influence in the matter of contracts. (BURGESS *wakes up at once.*) Youll come?

BUR. (*with enthusiasm*). Cawrse I'll come, James. Aint it awlus a pleasure to ear you!

MOR. (*turning to* PROSSY). I shall want you to take some notes at the meeting, Miss Garnett, if you have no other engagement. (*She nods, afraid to speak.*) You are coming, Lexy, I suppose?

LEXY. Certainly.

CAND. We're all coming, James.

MOR. No: you are not coming; and Eugene is not coming. You will stay here and entertain him—to celebrate your return home. (EUGENE *rises, breathless.*)

CAND. But, James—

MOR. (*authoritatively*). I insist. You do not want to come; and he does not want to come. (CANDIDA *is about to protest.*) Oh, dont concern yourselves: I shall have plenty of people without you: your chairs will be wanted by unconverted people who have never heard me before.

CAND. (*troubled*). Eugene: wouldnt you like to come?

MOR. I should be afraid to let myself go before Eugene: he is so critical of sermons. (*Looking at him.*) He knows I am afraid of him: he told me as much this morning. Well, I shall shew him how much afraid I am by leaving him here in your custody, Candida.

MARCH. (*to himself, with vivid feeling*). Thats brave. Thats beautiful.

CAND. (*with anxious misgiving*). But—but— Is anything the matter, James? (*Greatly troubled.*) I cant understand—

MOR. (*taking her tenderly in his arms and kissing her on the forehead*). Ah, I thought it was *I* who couldnt understand, dear.

ACT THREE

Past ten in the evening. The curtains are drawn, and the lamps lighted. The typewriter is in its case: the large table has been cleared and tidied: everything indicates that the day's work is over.

CANDIDA *and* MARCHBANKS *are sitting by the fire. The reading lamp is on the mantelshelf above* MARCHBANKS, *who is in the small chair, reading aloud. A little pile of manuscripts and a couple of volumes of poetry are on the carpet beside him.* CANDIDA *is in the easy chair. The poker, a light brass one, is upright in her hand. Leaning back and looking intently at the point of it, with her feet stretched towards the blaze, she is in a waking dream, miles away from her surroundings and completely oblivious of* EUGENE.

MARCH. (*breaking off in his recitation*). Every poet that ever lived has put that thought into a sonnet. He must: he cant help it. (*He looks to her for assent, and notices her absorption in the poker.*) Havnt you been listening? (*No response.*) Mrs Morell!

CAND. (*starting*). Eh?

MARCH. Havnt you been listening?

CAND. (*with a guilty excess of politeness*). Oh yes. It's very nice. Go on, Eugene. I'm longing to hear what happens to the angel.

MARCH. (*letting the manuscript drop from his hand to the floor*). I beg your pardon for boring you.

CAND. But you are not boring me, I assure you. Please go on. Do, Eugene.

MARCH. I finished the poem about the angel quarter of an hour ago. Ive read you several things since.

CAND. (*remorsefully*). I'm so sorry, Eugene. I think the poker must have hypnotized me. (*She puts it down.*)

MARCH. It made me horribly uneasy.

CAND. Why didnt you tell me? I'd have put it down at once.

MARCH. I was afraid of making you uneasy too. It looked as if it were a weapon. If I were a hero of old I should have laid my drawn sword between us. If Morell had come in he would have thought you had taken up the poker because there was no sword between us.

CAND. (*wondering*). What? (*With a puzzled glance at him.*) I cant quite follow that. Those sonnets of yours have perfectly addled me. Why should there be a sword between us?

MARCH. (*evasively*). Oh, never mind. (*He stoops to pick up the manuscript.*)

CAND. Put that down again, Eugene. There are limits to my appetite for poetry: even your poetry. Youve been reading to me for more than two hours, ever since James went out. I want to talk.

MARCH. (*rising, scared*). No: I mustnt talk. (*He looks round him in his lost way, and adds, suddenly.*) I think I'll go out and take a walk in the park. (*He makes for the door.*)

CAND. Nonsense: it's closed long ago. Come and sit down on the hearth-rug, and talk moonshine as you usually do. I want to be amused. Dont you want to?

MARCH. (*half in terror, half enraptured*). Yes.

CAND. Then come along. (*She moves her chair back a little to make room.*)

(*He hesitates; then timidly stretches himself on the hearthrug, face upwards, and throws back his head across her knees, looking up at her.*)

MARCH. Oh, Ive been so miserable all the evening, because I was doing right. Now I'm doing wrong; and I'm happy.

CAND. (*tenderly amused at him*). Yes: I'm sure you feel a great grown-up wicked deceiver. Quite proud of yourself, arnt you?

MARCH. (*raising his head quickly and turning a little to look round at her*). Take care. I'm ever so much older than you, if you only knew. (*He turns quite over on his knees, with his hands clasped and his arms on her lap, and speaks with growing impulse, his blood beginning to stir.*) May I say some wicked things to you?

CAND. (*without the least fear or coldness, and with perfect respect for his passion, but with a touch of her wise-hearted maternal humor*). No. But you may say anything you really and truly feel. Anything at all, no matter what it is. I am not afraid, so long as it is your real self that speaks, and not a mere attitude: a gallant attitude, or a wicked attitude, or even a poetic attitude. I put you on your honor and truth. Now say whatever you want to.

MARCH. (*the eager expression vanishing utterly from his lips and nostrils as his eyes light up with pathetic spirituality*). Oh, now I cant say anything: all the words I know belong to some attitude or other— all except one.

CAND. What one is that?

MARCH. (*softly, losing himself in the music of the name*). Candida, Candida, Candida, Candida, Candida. I must say that now, because you have put me on my honor and truth; and I never think or feel Mrs Morell: it is always Candida.

CAND. Of course. And what have you to say to Candida?

MARCH. Nothing but to repeat your name a thousand times. Dont you feel that every time is a prayer to you?

CAND. Doesnt it make you happy to be able to pray?

MARCH. Yes, very happy.

CAND. Well, that happiness is the answer to your prayer. Do you want anything more?

MARCH. No: I have come into heaven, where want is unknown.

(MORELL *comes in. He halts on the threshold, and takes in the scene at a glance.*)

MOR. (*grave and self-contained*). I hope I dont disturb you.

(CANDIDA *starts up violently, but without the smallest embarrassment, laughing at herself.* EUGENE, *capsized by her sudden movement, recovers himself without rising, and sits on the rug hugging his ankles, also quite unembarrassed.*)

CAND. Oh, James, how you startled me! I was so taken up with Eugene that I didnt hear your latchkey. How did the meeting go off? Did you speak well?

MOR. I have never spoken better in my life.

CAND. That was first rate! How much was the collection?

MOR. I forgot to ask.

CAND. (*to* EUGENE). He must have spoken splendidly, or he would never have forgotten that. (*To* MORELL.) Where are all the others?

MOR. They left long before I could get away: I thought I should never escape. I believe they are having supper somewhere.

CAND. (*in her domestic business tone*). Oh, in that case, Maria may go to bed. I'll tell her. (*She goes out to the kitchen.*)

MOR. (*looking sternly down at* MARCHBANKS). Well?

MARCH. (*squatting grotesquely on the hearthrug, and actually at ease with* MORELL: *even impishly humorous*). Well?

MOR. Have you anything to tell me?

MARCH. Only that I have been making a fool of myself here in private whilst you have been making a fool of yourself in public.

MOR. Hardly in the same way, I think.

MARCH. (*eagerly, scrambling up*). The very, very very same way. I have been playing the Good Man. Just like you. When you began your heroics about leaving me here with Candida-

MOR. (*involuntarily*). Candida!

MARCH. Oh yes: Ive got that far. But dont be afraid. Heroics are infectious: I caught the disease from you. I swore not to say a word in your absence that I would not have said a month ago in your presence.

MOR. Did you keep your oath?

MARCH. (*suddenly perching himself on the back of the easy chair*). It kept itself somehow until about ten minutes ago. Up to that moment I went on desperately reading to her—reading my own poems—anybody's poems—to stave off a conversation. I was standing outside the gate of Heaven, and refusing to go in. Oh, you cant think how heroic it was, and how uncomfortable! Then—

MOR. (*steadily controlling his suspense*). Then?

MARCH. (*prosaically slipping down into a quite ordinary attitude on the seat of the chair*). Then she couldnt bear being read to any longer.

MOR. And you approached the gate of Heaven at last?

MARCH. Yes.

MOR. Well? (*Fiercely.*) Speak, man: have you no feeling for me?

MARCH. (*softly and musically*). Then she became an angel; and there was a flaming sword that turned every way, so that I couldnt go in; for I saw that that gate was really the gate of Hell.

MOR. (*triumphantly*). She repulsed you!

MARCH. (*rising in wild scorn*). No, you fool: if she had done that I should never have seen that I was in Heaven already. Repulsed me! You think that would have saved us! virtuous indignation! Oh, you are not worthy to live in the same world with her. (*He turns away contemptuously to the other side of the room.*)

MOR. (*who has watched him quietly without changing his place*). Do you think you make yourself more worthy by reviling me, Eugene?

MARCH. Here endeth the thousand and first lesson. Morell: I dont think much of your preaching after all: I believe I could do it better myself. The man I want to meet is the man that Candida married.

MOR. The man that—? Do you mean me?

MARCH. I dont mean the Reverend James Mavor Morell, moralist and windbag. I mean the real man that the Reverend James must have hidden somewhere inside his black coat: the man that Candida loved. You cant make a woman like Candida love you by merely buttoning your collar at the back instead of in front.

MOR. (*boldly and steadily*). When Candida promised to marry me, I was the same moralist and windbag you now see. I wore my black coat; and my collar was buttoned behind instead of in front. Do you think she would have loved me any the better for being insincere in my profession?

MARCH. (*on the sofa, hugging his ankles*). Oh, she forgave you, just as she forgives me for being a coward, and a weakling, and what you call a snivelling little whelp and all the rest of it. (*Dreamily.*) A woman like that has divine insight: she loves our souls, and not our follies and vanities and illusions, nor our collars and coats, nor any other of the rags and tatters we are rolled up in. (*He reflects on this for an instant; then turns intently to question* MORELL.) What I want to know is how you got past the flaming sword that stopped me.

MOR. Perhaps because I was not interrupted at the end of ten minutes.

MARCH. (*taken aback*). What!

MOR. Man can climb to the highest summits; but he cannot dwell there long.

MARCH. (*springing up*). It's false: there can he dwell for ever, and there only. It's in the other moments that he can find no rest, no sense of the silent glory of life. Where would you have me spend my moments, if not on the summits?

MOR. In the scullery, slicing onions and filling lamps.

MARCH. Or in the pulpit, scrubbing cheap earthenware souls?

MOR. Yes, that too. It was there that I earned my golden moment, and the right, in that moment, to ask her to love me. *I* did not take the moment on credit; nor did I use it to steal another man's happiness.

MARCH. (*rather disgustedly, trotting back towards the fireplace*). I have no doubt you conducted the transaction as honestly as if you were buying a pound of cheese. (*He stops on the brink of the hearth-rug, and adds, thoughtfully, to himself, with his back turned to* MORELL.) *I* could only go to her as a beggar.

MOR. (*starting*). A beggar dying of cold! asking for her shawl!

MARCH. (*turning, surprised*). Thank you for touching up my poetry. Yes, if you like: a beggar dying of cold, asking for her shawl.

MOR. (*excitedly*). And she refused. Shall I tell you why she refused? I can tell you, on her own authority. It was because of—

MARCH. She didnt refuse.

MOR. Not!

MARCH. She offered me all I chose to ask for: her shawl, her wings, the wreath of stars on her head, the lilies in her hand, the crescent moon beneath her feet—

MOR. (*seizing him*). Out with the truth, man: my wife is my wife: I want no more of your poetic fripperies. I know well that if I have lost her love and you have gained it, no law will bind her.

MARCH. (*quaintly, without fear or resistance*). Catch me by the shirt collar, Morell: she will arrange it for me afterwards as she did this morning. (*With quiet rapture.*) I shall feel her hands touch me.

MOR. You young imp, do you know how dangerous it is to say that to me? Or (*with a sudden misgiving*) has something made you brave?

MARCH. I'm not afraid now. I disliked you before: that was why I shrank from your touch. But I saw today—when she tortured you—that you love her. Since then I have been your friend: you may strangle me if you like.

MOR. (*releasing him*). Eugene: if that is not a heartless lie—if you have a spark of human feeling left in you—will you tell me what has happened during my absence?

MARCH. What happened! Why, the flaming sword. (MORELL *stamps with impatience.*)—Well, in plain prose, I loved her so exquisitely that I wanted nothing more than the happiness of being in such love. And before I had time to come down from the highest summits, you came in.

MOR. (*suffering deeply*). So it is still unsettled. Still the misery of doubt.

MARCH. Misery! I am the happiest of men. I desire nothing now but her happiness. (*In a passion of sentiment.*) Oh, Morell, let us both give her up. Why should she have to choose between a wretched little nervous disease like me, and a pig-headed parson like you? Let us go on a pilgrimage, you to the east and I to the west, in search of a worthy lover for her: some beautiful archangel with purple wings—

MOR. Some fiddlestick! Oh, if she is mad enough to leave me for you, who will protect her? who will help her? who will work for her? who will be a father to her children? (*He sits down distractedly on the sofa, with his elbows on his knees and his head propped on his clenched fists.*)

MARCH. (*snapping his fingers wildly*). She does not ask those silly questions. It is she who wants somebody to protect, to help, to work for: somebody to give her children to protect, to help and to work for. Some grown up man who has become as a little child again. Oh, you fool, you fool, you triple fool! I am the man, Morell: I am the man. (*He dances about excitedly, crying.*) You dont understand what a woman is. Send for her, Morell: send for her and let her choose between— (*The door opens and* CANDIDA *enters. He stops as if petrified.*)

CAND. (*amazed, on the threshold*). What on earth are you at, Eugene?

MARCH. (*oddly*). James and I are having a preaching match; and he is getting the worst of it.

(CANDIDA *looks quickly round at* MORELL. *Seeing that he is distressed, she hurries down to him, greatly vexed.*)

CAND. You have been annoying him. Now I wont have it, Eugene: do you hear? (*She puts her hand on* MORELL's *shoulder, and quite forgets her wifely tact in her anger.*) My boy shall not be worried: I will protect him.

MOR. (*rising proudly*). Protect!

CAND. (*not heeding him: to* EUGENE). What have you been saying?

MARCH. (*appalled*). Nothing. I—

CAND. Eugene! Nothing?

MARCH. (*piteously*). I mean—I—I'm very sorry. I wont do it again: indeed I wont. I'll let him alone.

MOR. (*indignantly, with an aggressive movement towards* EUGENE). Let me alone! You young—

CAND. (*stopping him*). Sh!—no: let me deal with him, James.

MARCH. Oh, youre not angry with me, are you?

CAND. (*severely*). Yes I am: very angry. I have a good mind to pack you out of the house.

MOR. (*taken aback by* CANDIDA's *vigor, and by no means relishing the position of being rescued by her from another man*). Gently, Candida, gently. I am able to take care of myself.

CAND. (*petting him*). Yes, dear: of course you are. But you mustnt be annoyed and made miserable.

MARCH. (*almost in tears, turning to the door*). I'll go.

CAND. Oh, you neednt go: I cant turn you out at this time of night. (*Vehemently.*) Shame on you! For shame!

MARCH. (*desperately*). But what have I done?

CAND. I know what you have done: as well as if I had been here all the time. Oh, it was unworthy! You are like a child: you cannot hold your tongue.

MARCH. I would die ten times over sooner than give you a moment's pain.

CAND. (*with infinite contempt for this puerility*). Much good your dying would do me!

MOR. Candida, my dear: this altercation is hardly quite seemly. It is a matter between two men; and I am the right person to settle it.

CAND. Two men! Do you call that a man? (*To* EUGENE.) You bad boy!

MARCH. (*gathering a whimsically affectionate courage from the scolding*). If I am to be scolded like a boy, I must make a boy's excuse. He began it. And he's bigger than I am.

CAND. (*losing confidence a little as her concern for* MORELL's *dignity takes the alarm*). That cant be true. (*To* MORELL.) You didnt begin it, James, did you?

MOR. (*contemptuously*). No.

MARCH. (*indignant*). Oh!

MOR. (*to* EUGENE). You began it: this morning. (CANDIDA, *instantly connecting this with his mysterious allusion in the afternoon to something told him by* EUGENE *in the morning, looks at him with quick suspicion.* MORELL *proceeds, with the emphasis of offended superiority.*) But your other point is true. I am certainly the bigger of the two, and, I hope, the stronger, Candida. So you had better leave the matter in my hands.

CAND. (*again soothing him*). Yes, dear; but— (*troubled*) I dont understand about this morning.

MOR. (*gently snubbing her*). You need not understand, my dear.

CAND. But James, I (*the street bell rings*)—Oh bother! Here they all come. (*She goes out to let them in.*)

MARCH. (*running to* MORELL). Oh, Morell, isnt it dreadful? She's angry with us: she hates me. What shall I do?

MOR. (*with quaint desperation, walking up and down the middle of the room*). Eugene: my head is spinning round. I shall begin to laugh presently.

MARCH. (*following him anxiously*). No, no: she'll think Ive thrown you into hysterics. Dont laugh.

(*Boisterous voices and laughter are heard approaching.* LEXY MILL, *his eyes sparkling, and his bearing denoting unwonted elevation of spirit, enters with* BURGESS, *who is greasy and self-complacent, but has all his wits about him.* MISS GARNETT, *with her smartest hat and jacket on, follows them; but though her eyes are brighter than before, she is evidently a prey to misgiving. She places herself with her back to her typewriting table, with one hand on it to steady herself, passing the other across her forehead as if she were a little tired and giddy.* MARCHBANKS *relapses into shyness and edges away into the corner near the window, where* MORELL'S *books are.*)

LEXY (*exhilarated*). Morell: I must congratulate you. (*Grasping his hand.*) What a noble, splendid, inspired address you gave us! You surpassed yourself.

BUR. So you did, James. It fair kep me awake to the lars' word. Didnt it, Miss Gornett?

PROS. (*worriedly*). Oh, I wasnt minding you: I was trying to make notes. (*She takes out her notebook, and looks at her stenography, which nearly makes her cry.*)

MOR. Did I go too fast, Pross?

PROS. Much too fast. You know I cant do more than ninety words a minute. (*She relieves her feelings by throwing her notebook angrily beside her machine, ready for use next morning.*)

MOR. (*soothingly*). Oh well, well, never mind, never mind, never mind. Have you all had supper?

LEXY. Mr Burgess has been kind enough to give us a really splendid supper at the Belgrave.

BUR. (*with effusive magnanimity*). Dont mention it, Mr Mill. (*Modestly.*) Youre arty welcome to my little treat.

PROS. We had champagne. I never tasted it before. I feel quite giddy.

MOR. (*surprised*). A champagne supper! That was very handsome. Was it my eloquence that produced all this extravagance?

LEXY (*rhetorically*). Your eloquence, and Mr Burgess's goodness of heart. (*With a fresh burst of exhilaration.*) And what a very fine fellow the chairman is, Morell! He came to supper with us.

MOR. (*with long drawn significance, looking at* BURGESS). O-o-o-h! the chairman. Now I understand.

(BURGESS *covers with a deprecatory cough a lively satisfaction with his own diplomatic cunning.* LEXY *folds his arms and leans against the head of the sofa in a high-spirited attitude after nearly losing his balance.* CANDIDA *comes in with glasses, lemons, and a jug of hot water on a tray.*)

CAND. Who will have some lemonade? You know our rules: total abstinence. (*She puts the tray on the table, and takes up the lemon squeezer, looking enquiringly round at them.*)

MOR. No use, dear. Theyve all had champagne. Pross has broken her pledge.

CAND. (*to* PROS.). You dont mean to say youve been drinking champagne!

PROS. (*stubbornly*). Yes I do. I'm only a beer teetotaller, not a champagne teetotaller. I dont like beer. Are there any letters for me to answer, Mr Morell?

MOR. No more tonight.

PROS. Very well. Goodnight, everybody.

LEXY (*gallantly*). Had I not better see you home, Miss Garnett?

PROS. No thank you. I shant trust myself with anybody tonight. I wish I hadnt taken any of that stuff. (*She takes uncertain aim at the door; dashes at it; and barely escapes without disaster.*)

BUR. (*indignantly*). Stuff indeed! That gurl dunno what champagne is! Pommery and Greeno at twelve and six a bottle. She took two glasses amost straight horff.

MOR. (*anxious about her*). Go and look after her, Lexy.

LEXY (*alarmed*). But if she should really be— Suppose she began to sing in the street, or anything of that sort.

MOR. Just so: she may. Thats why youd better see her safely home.

CAND. Do, Lexy: theres a good fellow. (*She shakes his hand and pushes him gently to the door.*)

LEXY. It's evidently my duty to go. I hope it may not be necessary. Goodnight, Mrs Morell. (*To the rest.*) Goodnight. (*He goes.* CANDIDA *shuts the door.*)

BUR. He was gushin with hextra piety hisself arter two sips. People carnt drink like they huseter. (*Bustling across to the hearth.*) Well, James: it's time to lock up. Mr Morchbanks: shall I ave the pleasure of your company for a bit o the way ome?

MARCH. (*affrightedly*). Yes: I'd better go. (*He hurries towards the door; but* CANDIDA *places herself before it, barring his way.*)

CAND. (*with quiet authority*). You sit down. Youre not going yet.

MARCH. (*quailing*). No: I—I didnt mean to. (*He sits down abjectly on the sofa.*)

CAND. Mr Marchbanks will stay the night with us, papa.

BUR. Oh well, I'll say goodnight. So long, James. (*He shakes hands with* MORELL, *and goes over to* EUGENE.) Make em give you a nightlight by your bed, Mr Morchbanks: itll comfort you if you wake up in the night with a touch of that complaint of yores. Goodnight.

MARCH. Thank you: I will. Goodnight, Mr Burgess. (*They shake hands.* BURGESS *goes to the door.*)

CAND. (*intercepting* MORELL, *who is following* BURGESS). Stay here, dear: I'll put on papa's coat for him. (*She goes out with* BURGESS.)

MARCH. (*rising and stealing over to* MORELL). Morell: theres going to be a terrible scene. Arnt you afraid?

MOR. Not in the least.

MARCH. I never envied you your courage before. (*He puts his hand appealingly on* MORELL's *forearm.*) Stand by me, wont you?

MOR. (*casting him off resolutely*). Each for himself, Eugene. She must choose between us now.

(CANDIDA *returns.* EUGENE *creeps back to the sofa like a guilty schoolboy.*)

CAND. (*between them, addressing* EUGENE). Are you sorry?

MARCH. (*earnestly*). Yes. Heartbroken.

CAND. Well then, you are forgiven. Now go off to bed like a good little boy: I want to talk to James about you.

MARCH. (*rising in great consternation*). Oh, I cant do that, Morell. I must be here. I'll not go away. Tell her.

CAND. (*her suspicions confirmed*). Tell me what? (*His eyes avoid hers furtively. She turns and mutely transfers the question to* MORELL.)

MOR. (*bracing himself for the catastrophe*). I have nothing to tell her, except (*here his voice deepens to a measured and mournful tenderness*) that she is my greatest treasure on earth—if she is really mine.

CAND. (*coldly, offended by his yielding to his orator's instinct and treating her as if she were the audience at the Guild of St Matthew*). I am sure Eugene can say no less, if that is all.

MARCH. (*discouraged*). Morell: she's laughing at us.

MOR. (*with a quick touch of temper*). There is nothing to laugh at. Are you laughing at us, Candida?

CAND. (*with quiet anger*). Eugene is very quick-witted, James. I hope I am going to laugh; but I am not sure that I am not going to be very angry. (*She goes to the fireplace, and stands there leaning with her arms on the mantelpiece, and her foot on the fender, whilst* EUGENE *steals to* MORELL *and plucks him by the sleeve.*)

MARCH. (*whispering*). Stop, Morell. Dont let us say anything.

MOR. (*pushing* EUGENE *away without deigning to look at him*). I hope you dont mean that as a threat, Candida.

CAND. (*with emphatic warning*). Take care, James. Eugene: I asked you to go. Are you going?

MOR. (*putting his foot down*). He shall not go. I wish him to remain.

MARCH. I'll go. I'll do whatever you want. (*He turns to the door.*)

CAND. Stop! (*He obeys.*) Didnt you hear James say he wished you to stay? James is master here. Dont you know that?

MARCH. (*flushing with a young poet's rage against tyranny*). By what right is he master?

CAND. (*quietly*). Tell him, James.

MOR. (*taken aback*). My dear: I dont know of any right that makes me master. I assert no such right.

CAND. (*with infinite reproach*). You dont know! Oh, James! James! (*To* EUGENE, *musingly.*) I wonder do you understand, Eugene! (*He shakes his head helplessly, not daring to look at her.*) No: youre too young. Well, I give you leave to stay: to stay and learn. (*She comes away from the hearth and places herself between them.*) Now, James! whats the matter? Come: tell me.

MARCH. (*whispering tremulously across to him*). Dont.

CAND. Come. Out with it!

MOR. (*slowly*). I meant to prepare your mind carefully, Candida, so as to prevent misunderstanding.

CAND. Yes, dear: I am sure you did. But never mind: I shant misunderstand.

MOR. Well—er— (*He hesitates, unable to find the long explanation which he supposed to be available.*)

CAND. Well?

MOR. (*blurting it out baldly*). Eugene declares that you are in love with him.

MARCH. (*frantically*). No, no, no, no, never. I did not, Mrs Morell: it's not true. I said I loved you. I said I understood you, and that he couldnt. And it was not after what passed there before the fire that I spoke: it was not, on my word. It was this morning.

CAND. (*enlightened*). This morning!

MARCH. Yes. (*He looks at her, pleading for credence, and then adds simply.*) That was what was the matter with my collar.

CAND. Your collar? (*Suddenly taking in his meaning she turns to* MORELL, *shocked.*) Oh, James: did you—? (*She stops.*)

MOR. (*ashamed*). You know, Candida, that I have a temper to struggle with. And he said (*shuddering*) that you despised me in your heart.

CAND. (*turning quickly on* EUGENE). Did you say that?

MARCH. (*terrified*). No.

CAND. (*almost fiercely*). Then James has just told me a falsehood. Is that what you mean?

MARCH. No, no: I—I—(*desperately*) it was David's wife. And it wasnt at home: it was when she saw him dancing before all the people.

MOR. (*taking the cue with a debater's adroitness*). Dancing before all the people, Candida; and thinking he was moving their hearts by his mission when they were only suffering from—Prossy's complaint. (*She is about to protest: he raises his hand to silence her.*) Dont try to look indignant, Candida—

CAND. Try!

MOR. (*continuing*). Eugene was right. As you told me a few hours after, he is always right. He said nothing that you did not say far better yourself. He is the poet, who sees everything; and I am the poor parson, who understands nothing.

CAND. (*remorsefully*). Do you mind what is said by a foolish boy, because I said something like it in jest?

MOR. That foolish boy can speak with the inspiration of a child and the cunning of a serpent. He has claimed that you belong to him and not to me; and, rightly or wrongly, I have come to fear that it may be true. I will not go about tortured with doubts and suspicions. I will not live with you and keep a secret from you. I will not suffer the intolerable degradation of jealousy. We have agreed —he and I—that you shall choose between us now. I await your decision.

CAND. (*slowly recoiling a step, her heart hardened by his rhetoric in spite of the sincere feeling behind it*). Oh! I am to choose, am I? I suppose it is quite settled that I must belong to one or the other.

MOR. (*firmly*). Quite. You must choose definitely.

MARCH. (*anxiously*). Morell: you dont understand. She means that she belongs to herself.

CAND. (*turning on him*). I mean that, and a good deal more, Master Eugene, as you will both find out presently. And pray, my lords and masters, what have you to offer for my choice? I am up for auction, it seems. What do you bid, James?

MOR. (*reproachfully*). Cand— (*He breaks down: his eyes and throat fill with tears: the orator becomes a wounded animal.*) I cant speak—

CAND. (*impulsively going to him*). Ah, dearest—

MARCH. (*in wild alarm*). Stop: it's not fair. You mustnt shew her that you suffer, Morell. I am on the rack too; but I am not crying.

MOR. (*rallying all his forces*). Yes: you are right. It is not for pity that I am bidding. (*He disengages himself from* CANDIDA.)

CAND. (*retreating, chilled*). I beg your pardon, James: I did not mean to touch you. I am waiting to hear your bid.

MOR. (*with proud humility*). I have nothing to offer you but my strength for your defence, my honesty for your surety, my ability and industry for your livelihood, and my authority and position for your dignity. That is all it becomes a man to offer to a woman.

CAND. (*quite quietly*). And you, Eugene? What do you offer?

MARCH. My weakness. My desolation. My heart's need.

CAND. (*impressed*). Thats a good bid, Eugene. Now I know how to make my choice. (*She pauses and looks curiously from one to the other, as if weighing them.* MORELL, *whose lofty confidence has changed into heartbreaking dread at* EUGENE's *bid, loses all power of concealing his anxiety.* EUGENE, *strung to the highest tension, does not move a muscle.*)

MOR. (*in a suffocated voice: the appeal bursting from the depths of his anguish*). Candida!

MARCH. (*aside, in a flash of contempt*). Coward!

CAND. (*significantly*). I give myself to the weaker of the two.

(EUGENE *divines her meaning at once: his face whitens like steel in a furnace.*)

MOR. (*bowing his head with the calm of collapse*). I accept your sentence, Candida.

CAND. Do you understand, Eugene?

MARCH. Oh, I feel I'm lost. He cannot bear the burden.

MOR. (*incredulously, raising his head and voice with comic abruptness*). Do you mean me, Candida?

CAND. (*smiling a little*). Let us sit and talk comfortably over it like three friends. (*To* MORELL.) Sit down, dear. (MORELL, *quite lost, takes the chair from the fireside: the children's chair.*) Bring me that chair, Eugene. (*She indicates the easy chair. He fetches it silently, even with something like cold strength, and places it next* MORELL, *a little behind him. She sits down. He takes the visitors' chair himself, and sits, inscrutable. When they are all settled she begins, throwing a spell of quietness on them by her calm, sane, tender tone.*) You remember what you told me about yourself, Eugene: how nobody has cared for you since your old nurse died: how those clever fashionable sisters and successful brothers of yours were your mother's and father's pets: how miserable you were at Eton: how your father is trying to starve you into returning to Oxford: how you have had to live without comfort or welcome or refuge: always lonely, and nearly always disliked and misunderstood, poor boy!

MARCH. (*faithful to the nobility of his lot*). I had my books. I had Nature. And at last I met you.

CAND. Never mind that just at present. Now I want you to look at this other boy here: my boy! spoiled from his cradle. We go once a fortnight to see his parents. You should come with us, Eugene, to see the pictures of the hero of that household. James as a baby! the most wonderful of all babies. James holding his first school prize, won at the ripe age of eight! James as the captain of his eleven! James in his first frock coat! James under all sorts of glorious circumstances! You know how strong he is (I hope he didnt hurt you): how clever he is: how happy. (*With deepening gravity.*) Ask James's mother and his three sisters what it cost to save James the trouble of doing anything but be strong and clever and happy. Ask me what it costs to be James's mother and three sisters and wife and mother to his children all in one. Ask Prossy and Maria how troublesome the house is even when we have no visitors to help us to slice the onions. Ask the tradesmen who want to worry James and spoil his beautiful sermons who it is that puts them off. When there is money to give, he gives it: when there is money to refuse, I refuse it. I build a castle of comfort and indulgence and love for him, and stand sentinel always to keep little vulgar cares out. I make him master here, though he does not know it, and could not tell you a moment ago how it came to be so. (*With sweet irony.*) And when he thought I might go away with you, his only anxiety was—what should become of me! And to tempt me to stay he offered me (*leaning forward to stroke his hair caressingly at each phrase*) his strength for my defence! his industry for my livelihood! his dignity for my position! his—(*relenting*) ah, I am mixing up your beautiful cadences and spoiling them, am I not, darling? (*She lays her cheek fondly against his.*)

MOR. (*quite overcome, kneeling beside her chair and embracing her with boyish ingenuousness*). It's all true, every word. What I am you have made me with the labor of your hands and the love of your heart. You are my wife, my mother, my sisters: you are the sum of all loving care to me.

CAND. (*in his arms, smiling, to* EUGENE). Am I your mother and sisters to you, Eugene?

MARCH. (*rising with a fierce gesture of disgust*). Ah, never. Out, then, into the night with me!

CAND. (*rising quickly*). You are not going like that, Eugene?

MARCH. (*with the ring of a man's voice—no longer a boy's—in the words*). I know the hour when it strikes. I am impatient to do what must be done.

MOR. (*who has also risen*). Candida: dont let him do anything rash.

CAND. (*confident, smiling at* EUGENE). Oh, there is no fear. He has learnt to live without happiness.

MARCH. I no longer desire happiness: life is nobler than that. Parson James: I give you my happiness with both hands: I love you because you have filled the heart of the woman I loved. Goodbye. (*He goes towards the door.*)

CAND. One last word. (*He stops, but without turning to her. She goes to him.*) How old are you, Eugene?

MARCH. As old as the world now. This morning I was eighteen.

CAND. Eighteen! Will you, for my sake, make a little poem out of the two sentences I am going to say to you? And will you promise to repeat it to yourself whenever you think of me?

MARCH. (*without moving*). Say the sentences.

CAND. When I am thirty, she will be forty-five. When I am sixty, she will be seventy-five.

MARCH. (*turning to her*). In a hundred years, we shall be the same age. But I have a better secret than that in my heart. Let me go now. The night outside grows impatient.

CAND. Goodbye. (*She takes his face in her hands; and as he divines her intention and falls on his knees, she kisses his forehead. Then he flies out into the night. She turns to* MORELL, *holding out her arms to him.*) Ah, James!

(*They embrace. But they do not know the secret in the poet's heart.*)

Sean O'Casey

▶ The rebirth of Irish letters centering around William Butler Yeats, Lady Gregory, J. M. Synge, and other members of that lyric generation not only created the modern Irish drama but led to the organization of the Irish National Theatre Society in 1902, and the Abbey Theatre in Dublin in 1904. The existence of this theatre, with the new school of actors which gathered around it, was an immense stimulus to the writing of plays. Without it, it is quite possible that Synge might not have written *The Playboy of the Western World* or the short classic masterpiece, *Riders to the Sea*.

The creative force of this Irish literary revival was so great that Irish drama took a proud place in company with the Russian drama of the Moscow Art Theatre, the French drama of Antoine's Theatre, and the German drama of the Free Theatre of Berlin. And it was the immediate incentive for a new dramatic genius who arrived on the scene immediately following World War I and who gave new life and interest to Irish drama and to the Abbey Theatre.

He was Sean O'Casey, born in 1884, who produced in rapid succession in 1923, 1924, and 1926 three plays which carried his fame throughout the world—*The Shadow of a Gunman, Juno and the Paycock,* and *The Plough and the Stars.*

O'Casey had emerged from the tenements and the poverty of Dublin. His father had died when Sean was three. During his early years, his family lacked bread. He worked as a laborer at various jobs. He had almost no formal education and he was scornful of what he had. After teaching himself to read at the age of fourteen, he began to saturate himself with Shakespeare and the Greek dramatists. He was fascinated by the Abbey Theatre and attended its performances often. He became a familiar figure in the pit as he came week after week to see the artists on this stage bring to glowing life through natural acting and beautifully articulated speech the creations of the Irish dramatists. It is impossible to overestimate the stimulating effect of such a living medium for expression on such a retiring and unschooled genius as O'Casey.

O'Casey had absorbed the turbulent life about him with a sensitiveness and an understanding shared by few men. He had for its flavor, its color, and its dramatic heartbeats an instinctive feeling that had not been influenced or channelized by years of formal education. His lack of professional dramaturgy was more than compensated for by the full-blooded verisimilitude of his characters. And though these characters were the local folk whom he knew so intimately, under his pen they glowed with universality and spoke to all men of understanding. For here were brought together in one harmonious whole the baffling mixture of comedy and tragedy, reverence and wit, anger and love, hope and despair, courage and cowardice that are in the character and the actions of men and women.

The immediate setting of these plays is the tense, strife-torn Dublin of the World War I period when nationalism was at fierce heights, and clashes between the Irish insurgent guerillas and the British Black and Tans who were trying to suppress them kept the city in a state of war. This political conflict is present in all these plays and it takes the spotlight at frequent intervals; but it is not the dominant interest. In the total performance, it becomes a backdrop against which is seen the individual personalities and the struggle of memorable characters. And when the final curtain is drawn, it is the flesh and blood people and not the political problems in which they are embroiled that linger permanently in the minds of the audience and the readers.

It is a tribute to O'Casey's art and human understanding that these plays do soar above their historical setting, and appeal to audiences who are quite ignorant of this incident of local strife between the Irish and the British. The audiences at the Abbey Theatre who first saw them did not make this separation. The productions of both *The Shadow of a Gunman* and *Juno and the Paycock* revived the tensions of the conflict but did not produce an outbreak. *The Plough and the Stars,* however, touched off the flame and threw the theatre into a violent uproar. As the second act ended and the third, dealing with the Easter Week insurrection of 1916, began, riot broke loose in the audience, dividing the house according to political and religious sympathies. The play was stopped by the furor, which created more drama in the audience than was enacted on the stage. In a memorable scene, W. B. Yeats, a Senator and a director of the theatre, stepped out on the stage to try to quell the riot. He was booed and hissed, but he made the following speech as reported in the *Manchester Guardian:*

"I thought you had got tired of this. It commenced fifteen years ago. You have disgraced yourselves again. Is this to be an ever-recurring celebration of the arrival of Irish genius? Once more you have rocked the cradle of genius. The news of this will go from country to country. You have once more rocked the cradle of a reputation. The fame of O'Casey is born tonight. This is apotheosis."

Some shouted, "We want the play!" while others cried, "Up with the Republic!" Some women chanted the "Soldier's Song," a widow of Easter Week spoke bitterly about the play and stalked out of the theatre, the police restored order, and the play finally went on.

The Irish theatre was, indeed, a potent force in the life of Dublin, and the very violence of the reaction publicized its plays and helped to create an international audience for its playwrights. Yeats was right about O'Casey. His reputation and his fame were born in the tumult.

Juno and the Paycock continues to be the choice among O'Casey's plays as a representation of his work and on its own singular merits as a work of art. As presented with the mature artistry of the Abbey Theatre company it was a triumphant production in Dublin and in London, and their success with it was repeated in New York during the company's visit to this country in 1927-28.

The play is bursting and bubbling over with life and character from the moment the curtain rises on the Boyle family in their two rooms in a Dublin tenement until it falls on the incoherent babblings of a drunken Paycock and Joxer as life flows on past the heartbreak and the tragedy of the Boyles. In "Captain" Jack Boyle, O'Casey has caught in classic mold a facet of Irish character and life representing its loud and ribald humor, its carefree acceptance of things, and its uninhibited sentimentality. The "Captain" marches boldly and humorously through the play only dimly aware of or concerned with the deep and bitter tragedy of his long-suffering wife Juno.

Juno herself provides the strength and much of the impact of the play. At the age of forty-five her hard struggle with life, with Boyle, and for the upbringing of her children has given her once handsome face "that look which ultimately settles down upon the faces of the women of the working-class: a look of listless monotony and harassed anxiety, blending with an expression of mechanical resistance." Like the great earth-mother herself, she is caught up by forces which she cannot control and can only partially understand. She can only accept and suffer, and cry out great words ritualistically in her moments of anguish.

The words that she cries in her last speech, touched with Biblical eloquence and solemnity, are the echo of the words of her neighbor whose son was also destroyed by the uncontrollable strife: "Mother o' God, Mother o' God, have pity on us all! Blessed Virgin, where were you when me darlin' son was riddled with bullets, when me darlin' son was riddled with bullets? Sacred Heart o' Jesus, take away our hearts o' stone, and give us hearts o' flesh! Take away this murdherin' hate, an' give us Thine own eternal love!"

JUNO AND THE PAYCOCK

C.W. in Ireland

Characters

"CAPTAIN" JACK BOYLE

JUNO BOYLE, *his wife*

JOHNNY BOYLE ⎫
MARY BOYLE ⎬ *their children* *Residents in the Tenement*

"JOXER" DALY

MRS. MAISIE MADIGAN

"NEEDLE" NUGENT, *a tailor*

MRS. TANCRED

JERRY DEVINE

CHARLES BENTHAM, *a school teacher*

AN IRREGULAR MOBILIZER

TWO IRREGULARS

A COAL-BLOCK VENDOR

A SEWING MACHINE MAN

TWO FURNITURE REMOVAL MEN

TWO NEIGHBOURS

Scenes

ACT I: The living apartment of a two-room tenancy of the Boyle family, in a tenement house in Dublin.

ACT II: The same.

ACT III: The same.

A few days elapse between Acts I and II, and two months between Acts II and III.

During Act III the curtain is lowered for a few minutes to denote the lapse of one hour.

Period of the play, 1922.

ACT ONE

The living-room of a two-room tenancy occupied by the BOYLE *family in a tenement house in Dublin. Left, a door leading to another part of the house; left of door a window looking into the street; at back a dresser; farther to right at back, a window looking into the back of the house. Between the window and the dresser is a picture of the Virgin; below the picture, on a bracket, is a crimson bowl in which a floating votive light is burning. Farther to the right is a small bed partly concealed by cretonne hangings strung on a twine. To the right is the fireplace; near the fireplace is a door leading to the other room. Beside the fireplace is a box containing coal. On the mantelshelf is an alarm clock lying on its face. In a corner near the window looking into the back is a galvanized bath. A table and some chairs. On the table are breakfast things for one. A teapot is on the hob and a frying-pan stands inside the fender. There are a few books on the dresser and one on the table. Leaning against the dresser is a long-handled shovel—the kind invariably used by labourers when turning concrete or mixing mortar.* JOHNNY BOYLE *is sitting crouched beside the fire.* MARY *with her jumper off—it is lying on the back of a chair—is arranging her hair before a tiny mirror perched on the table. Beside the mirror is stretched out the morning paper, which she looks at when she isn't gazing into the mirror. She is a well-made and good-looking girl of twenty-two. Two forces are working in her mind—one, through the circumstances of her life, pulling her back; the other, through the influence of books she has read, pushing her forward. The opposing forces are apparent in her speech and her manners, both of which are degraded by her environment, and improved by her acquaintance—slight though it be—with literature. The time is early forenoon.*

MARY (*looking at the paper*). On a little bye-road, out beyant Finglas, he was found.

(MRS. BOYLE *enters by door on right; she has been shopping and carries a small parcel in her hand. She is forty-five years of age, and twenty years ago she must have been a pretty woman; but her face has now assumed that look which ultimately settles down upon the faces of the women of the working-class; a look of listless monotony and harassed anxiety, blending with an expression of mechanical resistance. Were circumstances favourable, she would probably be a handsome, active and clever woman.*)

MRS. B. Isn't he come in yet?

MARY. No, mother.

MRS. B. Oh, he'll come in when he likes; struttin' about the town like a paycock with Joxer, I suppose. I hear all about Mrs. Tancred's son is in this mornin's paper.

MARY. The full details are in it this mornin'; seven wounds he had—one entherin' the neck, with an exit wound beneath the left shoulder-blade; another in the left breast penethratin' the heart, an' . . .

JOHN. (*springing up from the fire*). Oh, quit that readin', for God's sake! Are yous losin' all your feelin's? It'll soon be that none of you'll read anythin' that's not about butcherin'!

(*He goes quickly into the room on left.*)

MARY. He's gettin' very sensitive, all of a sudden!

MRS. B. I'll read it myself, Mary, by an' by, when I come home. Everybody's sayin' that he was a Die-hard—thanks be to God that Johnny had nothin' to do with him this long time. . . . (*Opening the parcel and taking out some sausages, which she places on a plate.*) Ah, then, if that father o' yours doesn't come in soon for his breakfast, he may go without any; I'll not wait much longer for him.

MARY. Can't you let him get it himself when he comes in?

MRS. B. Yes, an' let him bring in Joxer Daly along with him? Ay, that's what he'd like, an' that's what he's waitin' for—till he thinks I'm gone to work, an' then sail in with the boul' Joxer, to burn all the coal an' dhrink all the tea in the place, to show them what a good Samaritan he is! But I'll stop here till he comes in, if I have to wait till tomorrow mornin'.

VOICE OF JOHN. (*inside*). Mother!

MRS. B. Yis?

VOICE OF JOHN. Bring us in a dhrink o' wather.

MRS. B. Bring in that fella a dhrink o' wather, for God's sake, Mary.

MARY. Isn't he big an' able enough to come out an' get it himself?

MRS. B. If you weren't well yourself you'd like somebody to bring you in a dhrink o' wather.

(*She brings in drink and returns.*)

MRS. B. Isn't it terrible to have to be waitin' this way! You'd think he was bringin' twenty poun's a week into the house the way he's going on. He wore out the Health Insurance long ago, he's afther wearin' out the unemployment dole, an', now, he's thryin' to wear out me! An' constantly singin', no less, when he ought always to be on his knees offerin' up a Novena for a job!

MARY (*tying a ribbon fillet-wise around her head*). I don't like this ribbon, ma; I think I'll wear the green—it looks betther than the blue.

MRS. B. Ah, wear whatever ribbon you like, girl, only don't be botherin' me. I don't know what a girl on strike wants to be wearin' a ribbon round her head for, or silk stockins on her legs either; it's wearin' them things that make the employers think they're givin' yous too much money.

MARY. The hour is past now when we'll ask the employers' permission to wear what we like.

MRS. B. I don't know why you wanted to walk out for Jennie Claffey; up to this you never had a good word for her.

MARY. What's the use of belongin' to a Trades Union if you won't stand up for your principles? Why did they sack her? It was a clear case of victimization. We couldn't let her walk the streets, could we?

MRS. B. No, of course yous couldn't—yous wanted to keep her company. Wan victim wasn't enough. When the employers sacrifice wan victim, the Trades Unions go wan betther be sacrificin' a hundred.

MARY. It doesn't matther what you say, ma—a principle's a principle.

MRS. B. Yis; an' when I go into oul' Murphy's tomorrow, an' he gets to know that, instead o' payin' all, I'm goin' to borry more, what'll he say when I tell him a principle's a principle? What'll we do if he refuses to give us any more on tick?

MARY. He daren't refuse—if he does, can't you tell him he's paid?

MRS. B. It's lookin' as if he was paid, whether he refuses or no.

(JOHNNY *appears at the door on left. He can be plainly seen now; he is a thin, delicate fellow, something younger than* MARY. *He has evidently gone through a rough time. His face is pale and drawn; there is a tremulous look of indefinite fear in his eyes. The left sleeve of his coat is empty, and he walks with a slight halt.*)

JOHN. I was lyin' down; I thought yous were gone. Oul' Simon Mackay is thrampin' about like a horse over me head, an' I can't sleep with him—they're like thunder-claps in me brain! The curse o'— God forgive me for goin' to curse!

MRS. B. There, now; go back an' lie down again, an' I'll bring you in a nice cup o' tay.

JOHN. Tay, tay, tay! You're always thinkin' o' tay. If a man was dyin', you'd thry to make him swally a cup o' tay!   (*He goes back.*)

MRS. B. I don't know what's goin' to be done with him. The bullet he got in the hip in Easter Week was bad enough, but the bomb that shatthered his arm in the fight in O'Connell Street put the finishin' touch on him. I knew he was makin' a fool of himself. God knows I went down on me bended knees to him not to go agen the Free State.

MARY. He stuck to his principles, an', no matther how you may argue, ma, a principle's a principle.

VOICE OF JOHN. Is Mary goin' to stay here?

MARY. No, I'm not goin' to stay here; you can't expect me to be always at your beck an' call, can you?

VOICE OF JOHN. I won't stop here be meself!

MRS. B. Amn't I nicely handicapped with the whole o' yous! I don't know what any o' yous ud do without your ma. (*To* JOHNNY.) Your father'll be here in a minute, an' if you want anythin', he'll get it for you.

JOHN. I hate assin' him for anythin'. . . . He hates to be assed to stir. . . . Is the light lightin' before the picture o' the Virgin?

MRS. B. Yis, yis! The wan inside to St. Anthony isn't enough, but he must have another wan to the Virgin here!

(JERRY DEVINE *enters hastily. He is about twenty-five, well set, active and earnest. He is a type, becoming very common now in the Labour Movement, of a mind knowing enough to make the mass of his associates, who know less, a power, and too little to broaden that power for the benefit of all.* MARY *seizes her jumper and runs hastily into room left.*)

JER. (*breathless*). Where's the Captain, Mrs. Boyle, where's the Captain?

MRS. B. You may well ass a body that: he's wherever Joxer Daly is—dhrinkin' in some snug or another.

JER. Father Farrell is just afther stoppin' to tell me to run up an' get him to go to the new job that's goin' on in Rathmines; his cousin is foreman o' the job, an' Father Farrell was speakin' to him about poor Johnny an' his father bein' idle so long, an' the foreman told Father Farrell to send the Captain up an' he'd give him a start—I wondher where I'd find him?

MRS. B. You'll find he's ayther in Ryan's or Foley's.

JER. I'll run round to Ryan's—I know it's a great house o' Joxer's.

(*He rushes out.*)

MRS. B. (*piteously*). There now, he'll miss that job, or I know for what! If he gets win' o' the word, he'll not come back till evenin', so that it'll be too late. There'll never be any good out o' him so long as he goes with that shouldher-shruggin' Joxer. I killin' meself workin', an' he shthruttin' about from mornin' till night like a paycock!

(*The steps of two persons are heard coming up a flight of stairs. They are the footsteps of* CAPTAIN BOYLE *and* JOXER. CAPTAIN BOYLE *is singing in a deep, sonorous, self-honouring voice.*)

THE CAPT. Sweet Spirit, hear me prayer! Hear . . . oh . . . hear . . . me prayer . . . hear, oh, hear . . . Oh, he . . . ar . . . oh, he . . . ar . . . me . . . pray . . . er!

JOX. (*outside*). Ah, that's a darlin' song, a daaarlin' song!

MRS. B. (*viciously*). Sweet spirit hear his prayer! Ah, then, I'll take me solemn affeydavey, it's not for a job he's prayin'!

(*She sits down on the bed so that the cretonne hangings hide her from the view of those entering.* THE CAPTAIN *comes slowly in. He is a man of about sixty; stout, grey-haired and stocky. His neck is short, and his head looks like a stone ball that one sometimes sees on top of a gate-post. His cheeks, reddish-purple, are puffed out, as if he were always repressing an almost irrepressible ejaculation.*

On his upper lip is a crisp, tightly cropped moustache; he carries himself with the upper part of his body slightly thrown back, and his stomach slightly thrust forward. His walk is a slow, consequential strut. His clothes are dingy, and he wears a faded seaman's-cap with a glazed peak.)

BOYLE (*to* JOXER, *who is still outside*). Come on, come on in, Joxer; she's gone out long ago, man. If there's nothing else to be got, we'll furrage out a cup o' tay, anyway. It's the only bit I get in comfort when she's away. 'Tisn't Juno should be her pet name at all, but Deirdre of the Sorras, for she's always grousin'.

(JOXER *steps cautiously into the room. He may be younger than* THE CAPTAIN *but he looks a lot older. His face is like a bundle of crinkled paper; his eyes have a cunning twinkle; he is spare and loosely built; he has a habit of constantly shrugging his shoulders with a peculiar twitching movement, meant to be ingratiating. His face is invariably ornamented with a grin.)*

JOX. It's a terrible thing to be tied to a woman that's always grousin'. I don't know how you stick it—it ud put years on me. It's a good job she has to be so ofen away, for (*with a shrug*) when the cat's away, the mice can play!

BOYLE (*with a commanding and complacent gesture*). Pull over to the fire, Joxer, an' we'll have a cup o' tay in a minute.

JOX. Ah, a cup o' tay's a darlin' thing, a daaarlin' thing—the cup that cheers but doesn't . . .

(JOXER's *rhapsody is cut short by the sight of* JUNO *coming forward and confronting the two cronies. Both are stupefied.)*

MRS. B. (*with sweet irony—poking the fire, and turning her head to glare at* JOXER). Pull over to the fire, Joxer Daly, an' we'll have a cup o' tay in a minute! Are you sure, now, you wouldn't like an egg?

JOX. I can't stop, Mrs. Boyle; I'm in a desperate hurry, a desperate hurry.

MRS. B. Pull over to the fire, Joxer Daly; people is always far more comfortabler here than they are in their own place.

(JOXER *makes hastily for the door.* BOYLE *stirs to follow him; thinks of*

something to relieve the situation—stops, and says suddenly.)
Joxer!

JOX. (*at door ready to bolt*). Yis?

BOYLE. You know the foreman o' that job that's goin' on down in Killesther, don't you, Joxer?

JOX. (*puzzled*). Foreman—Killesther?

BOYLE (*with a meaning look*). He's a butty o' yours, isn't he?

JOX. (*the truth dawning on him*). The foreman at Killesther—oh yis, yis. He's an oul' butty o' mine—oh, he's a darlin' man, a daarlin' man.

BOYLE. Oh, then, it's a sure thing. It's a pity we didn't go down at breakfast first thing this mornin'—we might ha' been working now; but you didn't know it then.

JOX. (*with a shrug*). It's betther late than never.

BOYLE. It's nearly time we got a start, anyhow; I'm fed up knockin' round, doin' nothin'. He promised you—gave you the straight tip?

JOX. Yis. "Come down on the blow o' dinner," says he, "an' I'll start you, an' any friend you like to brin' with you." "Ah," says I, "you're a darlin' man, a daaarlin' man."

BOYLE. Well, it couldn't come at a betther time—we're a long time waitin' for it.

JOX. Indeed we were; but it's a long lane that has no turnin'.

BOYLE. The blow up for dinner is at one—wait till I see what time it 'tis. (*He goes over to the mantelpiece, and gingerly lifts the clock.*)

MRS. B. Min' now, how you go on fiddlin' with that clock—you know the least little thing sets it asthray.

BOYLE. The job couldn't come at a betther time; I'm feelin' in great fettle, Joxer. I'd hardly believe I ever had a pain in me legs, an' last week I was nearly crippled with them.

JOX. That's betther an' betther; ah, God never shut wan door but He opened another!

BOYLE. It's only eleven o'clock; we've lashins o' time. I'll slip on me oul' moleskins afther breakfast, an' we can saunter down at our ayse. (*Putting his hand on the shovel.*) I think, Joxer, we'd betther bring our shovels?

JOX. Yis, Captain, yis; it's betther to go fully prepared an' ready for all eventualities. You bring your long-tailed shovel, an' I'll bring me navvy. We mighten' want them, an', then agen, we might: for want of a nail the shoe was lost, for want of a shoe the horse was lost, an' for want of a horse the man was lost—aw, that's a darlin' proverb, a daarlin' . . .

(*As* JOXER *is finishing his sentence,* MRS. BOYLE *approaches the door and* JOXER *retreats hurriedly. She shuts the door with a bang.*)

BOYLE (*suggestively*). We won't be long pullin' ourselves together agen when I'm working for a few weeks.

(MRS. B. *takes no notice.*)

BOYLE. The foreman on the job is an oul' butty o' Joxer's; I have an idea that I know him meself. (*Silence.*) . . . There's a button off the back o' me moleskin trousers. . . . If you leave out a needle an' thread I'll sew it on meself. . . . Thanks be to God, the pains in me legs is gone, anyhow!

MRS. B. (*with a burst*). Look here, Mr. Jacky Boyle, them yarns won't go down with Juno. I know you an' Joxer Daly of an oul' date, an' if you think you're able to come it over me with them fairy tales, you're in the wrong shop.

BOYLE (*coughing subduedly to relieve the tenseness of the situation*). U-u-u-ugh!

MRS. B. Butty o' Joxer's! Oh, you'll do a lot o' good as long as you continue to be a butty o' Joxer's!

BOYLE. U-u-u-ugh!

MRS. B. Shovel! Ah, then, me boyo, you'd do far more work with a knife an' fork than ever you'll do with a shovel! If there was e'er a genuine job goin' you'd be dh'other way about—not able to lift your arms with the pains in your legs! Your poor wife slavin' to keep the bit in your mouth, an' you gallivantin' about all the day like a paycock!

BOYLE. It ud be betther for a man to be dead, betther for a man to be dead.

MRS. B. (*ignoring the interruption*). Everybody callin' you "Captain," an' you only wanst on the wather, in an oul' collier from here to Liverpool, when anybody, to listen or look at you, ud take you for a second Christo For Columbus!

BOYLE. Are you never goin' to give us a rest?

MRS. B. Oh, you're never tired o' lookin' for a rest.

BOYLE. D'ye want to dhrive me out o' the house?

MRS. B. It ud be easier to dhrive you out o' the house than to dhrive you into a job. Here, sit down an' take your breakfast—it may be the last you'll get, for I don't know where the next is goin' to come from.

BOYLE. If I get this job we'll be all right.

MRS. B. Did ye see Jerry Devine?

BOYLE (*testily*). No, I didn't see him.

MRS. B. No, but you seen Joxer. Well, he was here lookin' for you.

BOYLE. Well, let him look!

MRS. B. Oh, indeed, he may well look, for it ud be hard for him to see you, an' you stuck in Ryan's snug.

BOYLE. I wasn't in Ryan's snug—I don't go into Ryan's.

MRS. B. Oh, is there a mad dog there? Well, if you weren't in Ryan's you were in Foley's.

BOYLE. I'm telling you for the last three weeks I haven't tasted a dhrop of intoxicatin' liquor. I wasn't in ayther wan snug or dh'other— I could swear that on a prayer-book—I'm as innocent as the child unborn!

MRS. B. Well, if you'd been in for your breakfast you'd ha' seen him.

BOYLE (*suspiciously*). What does he want me for?

MRS. B. He'll be back any minute an' then you'll soon know.

BOYLE. I'll dhrop out an' see if I can meet him.

MRS. B. You'll sit down an' take your breakfast, an' let me go to me work, for I'm an hour late already waitin' for you.

BOYLE. You needn't ha' waited, for I'll take no breakfast—I've a little spirit left in me still!

MRS. B. Are you goin' to have your breakfast—yes or no?

BOYLE (*too proud to yield*). I'll have no breakfast—yous can keep your breakfast. (*Plaintively.*) I'll knock out a bit somewhere, never fear.

MRS. B. Nobody's goin' to coax you—don't think that. (*She vigorously replaces the pan and the sausages in the press.*)

BOYLE. I've a little spirit left in me still.

(JERRY DEVINE *enters hastily.*)

JER. Oh, here you are at last! I've been searchin' for you everywhere. The foreman in Foley's told me you hadn't left the snug with Joxer ten minutes before I went in.

MRS. B. An' he swearin' on the holy prayer-book that he wasn't in no snug!

BOYLE (*to* JERRY). What business is it o' yours whether I was in a snug or no? What do you want to be gallopin' about afther me for? Is a man not to be allowed to leave his house for a minute without havin' a pack o' spies, pimps an' informers cantherin' at his heels?

JER. Oh, you're takin' a wrong view of it, Mr. Boyle; I simply was anxious to do you a good turn. I have a message for you from Father Farrell: he says that if you go to the job that's on in Rathmines, an' ask for Foreman Managan, you'll get a start.

BOYLE. That's all right, but I don't want the motions of me body to be watched the way an asthronomer ud watch a star. If you're folleyin' Mary aself, you've no pereeogative to be folleyin' me. (*Suddenly catching his thigh.*) U-ugh, I'm afther gettin' a terrible twinge in me right leg!

MRS. B. Oh, it won't be very long now till it travels into your left wan. It's miraculous that whenever he scents a job in front of him, his legs begin to fail him! Then, me bucko, if you lose this chance, you may go an' furrage for yourself!

JER. This job'll last for some time too, Captain, an' as soon as the foundations are in, it'll be cushy enough.

BOYLE. Won't it be a climbin' job? How d'ye expect me to be able to go up a ladder with these legs? An', if I get up aself, how am I goin' to get down agen?

MRS. B. (*viciously*). Get wan o' the labourers to carry you down in a hod! You can't climb a laddher, but you can skip like a goat into a snug!

JER. I wouldn't let myself be let down that easy, Mr. Boyle; a little exercise, now, might do you all the good in the world.

BOYLE. It's a docthor you should have been, Devine—maybe you know more about the pains in me legs than meself that has them?

JER. (*irritated*). Oh, I know nothin' about the pains in your legs; I've brought the message that Father Farrell gave me, an' that's all I can do.

MRS. B. Here, sit down an' take your breakfast, an' go an' get ready; an' don't be actin' as if you couldn't pull a wing out of a dead bee.

BOYLE. I want no breakfast, I tell you; it ud choke me afther all that's been said. I've a little spirit left in me still.

MRS. B. Well, let's see your spirit, then, an' go in at wanst an' put on your moleskin trousers!

BOYLE (*moving towards the door on left*). It ud be betther for a man to be dead! U-ugh! There's another twinge in me other leg! Nobody but meself knows the sufferin' I'm goin' through with the pains in these legs o' mine! (*He goes into the room on left as* MARY *comes out with her hat in her hand.*)

MRS. B. I'll have to push off now, for I'm terrible late already, but I was determined to stay an' hunt that Joxer this time. (*She goes off.*)

JER. Are you going out, Mary?

MARY. It looks like it when I'm putting on my hat, doesn't it?

JER. The bitther word agen, Mary.

MARY. You won't allow me to be friendly with you; if I thry, you deliberately misundherstand it.

JER. I didn't always misundherstand it; you were often delighted to have the arms of Jerry around you.

MARY. If you go on talkin' like this, Jerry Devine, you'll make me hate you!

JER. Well, let it be either a weddin' or a wake! Listen, Mary, I'm standin' for the Secretaryship of our Union. There's only one opposin' me; I'm popular with all the men, an' a good speaker—all are sayin' that I'll get elected.

MARY. Well?

JER. The job's worth three hundred an' fifty pounds a year, Mary. You an' I could live nice an' cosily on that; it would lift you out o' this place an' . . .

MARY. I haven't time to listen to you now—I have to go.

(*She is going out, when* JERRY *bars the way.*)

JER. (*appealingly*). Mary, what's come over you with me for the last few weeks? You hardly speak to me, an' then only a word with a face o' bittherness on it. Have you forgotten, Mary, all the happy evenins that were as sweet as the scented hawthorn that sheltered the sides o' the road as we sauntered through the country?

MARY. That's all over now. When you get your new job, Jerry, you won't be long findin' a girl far betther than I am for your sweetheart.

JER. Never, never, Mary! No matther what happens, you'll always be the same to me.

MARY. I must be off; please let me go, Jerry.

JER. I'll go a bit o' the way with you.

MARY. You needn't, thanks; I want to be by meself.

JER. (*catching her arm*). You're goin' to meet another fella; you've clicked with someone else, me lady!

MARY. That's no concern o' yours, Jerry Devine; let me go!

JER. I saw yous comin' out o' the Cornflower Dance Class, an' you hangin' on his arm—a thin, lanky strip of a Micky Dazzler, with a walkin'-stick an' gloves!

VOICE OF JOHN. (*loudly*). What are you doin' there—pullin' about everything!

VOICE OF BOYLE (*loudly and viciously*). I'm puttin' on me moleskin trousers!

MARY. You're hurtin' me arm! Let me go, or I'll scream, an' then you'll have the oul' fella out on top of us!

JER. Don't be so hard on a fella, Mary, don't be so hard.

BOYLE (*appearing at the door*). What's the meanin' of all this hillabaloo?

MARY. Let me go, let me go!

BOYLE. D'ye hear me—what's all this hillabaloo about?

JER. (*plaintively*). Will you not give us one kind word, one kind word, Mary?

BOYLE. D'ye hear me talkin' to yous? What's all this hillabaloo for?

JER. Let me kiss your hand, your little, tiny, white hand!

BOYLE. Your little, tiny, white hand—are you takin' leave o' your senses, man?   (MARY *breaks away and rushes out.*)

BOYLE. This is nice goins on in front of her father!

JER. Ah, dhry up, for God's sake!   (*He follows* MARY.)

BOYLE. Chiselurs don't care a damn now about their parents, they're bringin' their fathers' grey hairs down with sorra to the grave, an' laughin' at it, laughin' at it. Ah, I suppose it's just the same everywhere—the whole worl's in a state o' chassis! (*He sits by the fire.*) Breakfast! Well, they can keep their breakfast for me. Not if they were down on their bended knees would I take it—I'll show them I've a little spirit left in me still! (*He goes over to the press, takes out a plate and looks at it.*) Sassige! Well, let her keep her sassige. (*He returns to the fire, takes up the teapot and gives it a gentle shake.*) The tea's wet right enough.

(*A pause; he rises, goes to the press, takes out the sausage, puts it on the pan, and puts both on the fire. He attends the sausage with a fork.*)

BOYLE (*singing*).

"When the robins nest agen,
    And the flowers are in bloom,
    When the Springtime's sunny smile seems to banish all
        sorrow an' gloom;
    Then me bonny blue-ey'd lad, if me heart be true till then—
    He's promised he'll come back to me,
    When the robins nest agen!"

(*He lifts his head at the high note, and then drops his eyes to the pan.*)

BOYLE (*singing*). "When the . . ." (*Steps are heard approaching; he whips the pan off the fire and puts it under the bed, then sits down at the fire. The door opens and a bearded man looking in says.*) You don't happen to want a sewin' machine?

BOYLE (*furiously*). No, I don't want e'er a sewin' machine!

(*He returns the pan to the fire, and commences to sing again.*)

BOYLE (*singing*).

"When the robins nest agen,
    And the flowers they are in bloom,
    He's . . ."

(*A thundering knock is heard at the street door.*)

BOYLE. There's a terrible tatheraraa—that's a stranger—that's nobody belongin' to the house.

(*Another loud knock.*)

JOX. (*sticking his head in at the door*). Did ye hear them tatherarahs?

BOYLE. Well, Joxer, I'm not deaf.

JOHN. (*appearing in his shirt and trousers at the door on left; his face is anxious and his voice is tremulous*). Who's that at the door; who's that at the door? Who gave that knock—d'ye yous hear me—are yous deaf or dhrunk or what?

BOYLE (*to* JOHNNY). How the hell do I know who 'tis? Joxer, stick your head out o' the window an' see.

JOX. An' mebbe get a bullet in the kisser? Ah, none o' them thricks for Joxer! It's betther to be a coward than a corpse!

BOYLE (*looking cautiously out of the window*). It's a fella in a thrench coat.

JOHN. Holy Mary, Mother o' God, I . . .

BOYLE. He's goin' away—he must ha' got tired knockin'.

(JOHNNY *returns to the room on left.*)

BOYLE. Sit down an' have a cup o' tay, Joxer.

JOX. I'm afraid the missus ud pop in on us agen before we'd know where we are. Somethin's tellin' me to go at wanst.

BOYLE. Don't be superstitious, man; we're Dublin men, an' not boyos that's only afther comin' up from the bog o' Allen—though if she did come in, right enough, we'd be caught like rats in a thrap.

JOX. An' you know the sort she is—she wouldn't listen to reason—an' wanse bitten twice shy.

BOYLE (*going over to the window at back*). If the worst came to the worst, you could dart out here, Joxer; it's only a dhrop of a few feet to the roof of the return room, an' the first minute she goes into dh'other room I'll give you the bend, an' you can slip in an' away.

JOX. (*yielding to the temptation*). Ah, I won't stop very long anyhow. (*Picking up a book from the table.*) Whose is the buk?

BOYLE. Aw, one o' Mary's; she's always readin' lately—nothin' but thrash, too. There's one I was lookin' at dh'other day: three stories, *The Doll's House, Ghosts,* an' *The Wild Duck*—buks only fit for chiselurs!

JOX. Didja ever rade *Elizabeth, or Th' Exile o' Sibayria?* . . . Ah, it's a darlin' story, a daarlin' story!

BOYLE. You eat your sassige, an' never min' *Th' Exile o' Sibayria.*

(*Both sit down;* BOYLE *fills out tea, pours gravy on* JOXER'S *plate, and keeps the sausage for himself.*)

JOX. What are you wearin' your moleskin trousers for?

BOYLE. I have to go to a job, Joxer. Just afther you'd gone, Devine kem runnin' in to tell us that Father Farrell said if I went down to the job that's goin' on in Rathmines I'd get a start.

JOX. Be the holy, that's good news!

BOYLE. How is it good news? I wondher if you were in my condition, would you call it good news?

JOX. I thought . . .

BOYLE. You thought! You think too sudden sometimes, Joxer. D'ye know, I'm hardly able to crawl with the pains in me legs!

JOX. Yis, yis; I forgot the pains in your legs. I know you can do nothin' while they're at you.

BOYLE. You forgot; I don't think any of yous realize the state I'm in with the pains in me legs. What ud happen if I had to carry a bag o' cement?

JOX. Ah, any man havin' the like of them pains id be down an' out, down an' out.

BOYLE. I wouldn't mind if he had said it to meself; but, no, oh no, he rushes in an' shouts it out in front o' Juno, an' you know what Juno is, Joxer. We all know Devine knows a little more than the rest of us, but he doesn't act as if he did; he's a good boy, sober, able to talk an' all that, but still . . .

JOX. Oh ay; able to argufy, but still . . .

BOYLE. If he's runnin' afther Mary, aself, he's not goin' to be runnin' afther me. Captain Boyle's able to take care of himself. Afther all, I'm not gettin' brought up on Virol. I never heard him usin' a curse; I don't believe he was ever dhrunk in his life—sure he's not like a Christian at all!

JOX. You're afther takin' the word out o' me mouth—afther all, a Christian's natural, but he's unnatural.

BOYLE. His oul' fella was just the same—a Wicklow man.

JOX. A Wicklow man! That explains the whole thing. I've met many a

Wicklow man in me time, but I never met wan that was any
good.

BOYLE. "Father Farrell," says he, "sent me down to tell you." Father
Farrell! . . . D'ye know, Joxer, I never like to be beholden to any
o' the clergy.

JOX. It's dangerous, right enough.

BOYLE. If they do anything for you, they'd want you to be livin' in the
Chapel. . . . I'm goin' to tell you somethin', Joxer, that I wouldn't
tell to anybody else—the clergy always had too much power over
the people in this unfortunate country.

JOX. You could sing that if you had an air to it!

BOYLE (*becoming enthusiastic*). Didn't they prevent the people in '47
from seizin' the corn, an' they starvin'; didn't they down Parnell;
didn't they say that hell wasn't hot enough nor eternity long
enough to punish the Fenians? We don't forget, we don't forget
them things, Joxer. If they've taken everything else from us, Joxer,
they've left us our memory.

JOX. (*emotionally*). For mem'ry's the only friend that grief can call its
own, that grief . . . can . . . call . . . its own!

BOYLE. Father Farrell's beginnin' to take a great intherest in Captain
Boyle; because of what Johnny did for his country, says he to me
wan day. It's a curious way to reward Johnny be makin' his poor
oul' father work. But that's what the clergy want, Joxer—work,
work, work for me an' you; havin' us mulin' from mornin' till
night, so that they may be in betther fettle when they come hop-
pin' round for their dues! Job! Well, let him give his job to wan
of his hymn-singin', prayer-spoutin', craw-thumpin' Confraternity
men!

(*The voice of a* COAL-BLOCK VENDOR *is heard chanting in the street.*)

VOICE OF COAL VENDOR. Blocks . . . coal-blocks! Blocks . . . coal-blocks!

JOX. God be with the young days when you were steppin' the deck of a
manly ship, with the win' blowin' a hurricane through the masts,
an' the only sound you'd hear was, "Port your helm!" an' the only
answer, "Port it is, sir!"

BOYLE. Them was days, Joxer, them was days. Nothin' was too hot or
too heavy for me then. Sailin' from the Gulf o' Mexico to the

Antanartic Ocean. I seen things, I seen things, Joxer, that no mortal man should speak about that knows his Catechism. Ofen, an' ofen, when I was fixed to the wheel with a marlin-spike, an' the twins blowin' fierce an' the waves lashin' an' lashin', till you'd think every minute was goin' to be your last, an' it blowed, an' blowed—blew is the right word, Joxer, but blowed is what the sailors use. . . .

JOX. Aw, it's a darlin' word, a daarlin' word.

BOYLE. An', as it blowed an' blowed, I ofen looked up at the sky an' assed meself the question—what is the stars, what is the stars?

VOICE OF COAL VENDOR. Any blocks, coal-blocks; blocks, coal-blocks!

JOX. Ah, that's the question, that's the question—what is the stars?

BOYLE. An' then, I'd have another look, an' I'd ass meself—what is the moon?

JOX. Ah, that's the question—what is the moon, what is the moon?

(*Rapid steps are heard coming towards the door.* BOYLE *makes desperate efforts to hide everything;* JOXER *rushes to the window in a frantic effort to get out;* BOYLE *begins to innocently lilt* "Oh, me darlin' Jennie, I will be thrue to thee," *when the door is opened, and the black face of the* COAL VENDOR *appears.*)

COAL VEND. D'yes want any blocks?

BOYLE (*with a roar*). No, we don't want any blocks!

JOX. (*coming back with a sigh of relief*). That's afther puttin' the heart across me—I could ha' sworn it was Juno. I'd bether be goin', Captain; you couldn't tell the minute Juno'd hop in on us.

BOYLE. Let her hop in; we may as well have it out first as at last. I've made up me mind—I'm not goin' to do only what she damn well likes.

JOX. Them sentiments does you credit, Captain; I don't like to say anything as between man an' wife, but I say as a butty, as a butty, Captain, that you've stuck it too long, an' that it's about time you showed a little spunk.

"How can a man die bether than facin' fearful odds,
   For th' ashes of his fathers an' the temples of his gods?"

BOYLE. She has her rights—there's no one denyin' it, but haven't I me rights too?

JOX. Of course you have—the sacred rights o' man!

BOYLE. Today, Joxer, there's goin' to be issued a proclamation be me, establishin' an independent Republic, an' Juno'll have to take an oath of allegiance.

JOX. Be firm, be firm, Captain; the first few minutes'll be the worst:—if you gently touch a nettle it'll sting you for your pains; grasp it like a lad of mettle, an' as soft as silk remains!

VOICE OF JUNO (*outside*). Can't stop, Mrs. Madigan—I haven't a minute!

JOX. (*flying out of the window*). Holy God, here she is!

BOYLE (*packing the things away with a rush in the press*). I knew that fella ud stop till she was in on top of us! (*He sits down by the fire.*)

(JUNO *enters hastily; she is flurried and excited.*)

JUNO. Oh, you're in—you must have been only afther comin' in?

BOYLE. No, I never went out.

JUNO. It's curious, then, you never heard the knockin'. (*She puts her coat and hat on bed.*)

BOYLE. Knockin'? Of course I heard the knockin'.

JUNO. An' why didn't you open the door, then? I suppose you were so busy with Joxer that you hadn't time.

BOYLE. I haven't seen Joxer since I seen him before. Joxer! What ud bring Joxer here?

JUNO. D'ye mean to tell me that the pair of yous wasn't collogin' together here when me back was turned?

BOYLE. What ud we be collogin' together about? I have somethin' else to think of besides collogin' with Joxer. I can swear on all the holy prayer-books . . .

MRS. B. That you weren't in no snug! Go on in at wanst now, an' take off that moleskin trousers o' yours, an' put on a collar an' tie to smarten yourself up a bit. There's a visitor comin' with Mary in a minute, an' he has great news for you.

BOYLE. A job, I suppose; let us get wan first before we start lookin' for another.

MRS. B. That's the thing that's able to put the win' up you. Well, it's no job, but news that'll give you the chance o' your life.

BOYLE. What's all the mysthery about?

MRS. B. G'win an' take off the moleskin trousers when you're told!

(BOYLE *goes into room on left.*)

(MRS. BOYLE *tidies up the room, puts the shovel under the bed, and goes to the press.*)

MRS. B. Oh, God bless us, looka the way everything's thrun about! Oh, Joxer was here, Joxer was here!

(MARY *enters with* CHARLIE BENTHAM; *he is a young man of twenty-five, tall, good-looking, with a very high opinion of himself generally. He is dressed in a brown coat, brown knee-breeches, grey stockings, a brown sweater, with a deep blue tie; he carries gloves and a walking-stick.*)

MRS. B. (*fussing round*). Come in, Mr. Bentham; sit down, Mr. Bentham, in this chair; it's more comfortabler than that, Mr. Bentham. Himself'll be here in a minute; he's just takin' off his trousers.

MARY. Mother!

BENT. Please don't put yourself to any trouble, Mrs. Boyle—I'm quite all right here, thank you.

MRS. B. An' to think of you knowin' Mary, an' she knowin' the news you had for us, an' wouldn't let on; but it's all the more welcomer now, for we were on our last lap!

VOICE OF JOHN. (*inside*). What are you kickin' up all the racket for?

BOYLE (*roughly*). I'm takin' off me moleskin trousers!

JOHN. Can't you do it, then, without lettin' th' whole house know you're takin' off your trousers? What d'ye want puttin' them on an' takin' them off again?

BOYLE. Will you let me alone, will you let me alone? Am I never goin' to be done thryin' to please th' whole o' yous?

MRS. B. (*to* BENTHAM). You must excuse th' state o' th' place, Mr. Bentham; th' minute I turn me back that man o' mine always makes a litther o' th' place, a litther o' th' place.

BENT. Don't worry, Mrs. Boyle; it's all right, I assure . . .

BOYLE (*inside*). Where's me braces; where in th' name o' God did I leave me braces? . . . Ay, did you see where I put me braces?

JOHN. (*inside, calling out*). Ma, will you come in here an' take da away ou' o' this or he'll dhrive me mad.

MRS. B. (*going towards the door*). Dear, dear, dear, that man'll be lookin' for somethin' on th' day o' Judgement. (*Looking into room and calling to* BOYLE.) Look at your braces, man, hangin' round your neck!

BOYLE (*inside*). Aw, Holy God!

MRS. B. (*calling*). Johnny, Johnny, come out here for a minute.

JOHN. Ah, leave Johnny alone, an' don't be annoyin' him!

MRS. B. Come on, Johnny, till I inthroduce you to Mr. Bentham. (*To* BENTHAM.) My son, Mr. Bentham; he's afther goin' through the mill. He was only a chiselur of a Boy Scout in Easter Week, when he got hit in the hip; and his arm was blew off in the fight in O'Connell Street. (JOHNNY *comes in*.) Here he is, Mr. Bentham; Mr. Bentham, Johnny. None can deny he done his bit for Irelan', if that's goin' to do him any good.

JOHN. (*boastfully*). I'd do it agen, ma, I'd do it agen; for a principle's a principle.

MRS. B. Ah, you lost your best principle, me boy, when you lost your arm; them's the only sort o' principles that's any good to a workin' man.

JOHN. Ireland only half free'll never be at peace while she has a son left to pull a trigger.

MRS. B. To be sure, to be sure—no bread's a lot betther than half a loaf. (*Calling loudly in to* BOYLE.) Will you hurry up there?

(BOYLE *enters in his best trousers, which aren't too good, and looks very uncomfortable in his collar and tie.*)

MRS. B. This is me husband; Mr. Boyle, Mr. Bentham.

BENT. Ah, very glad to know you, Mr. Boyle. How are you?

BOYLE. Ah, I'm not too well at all; I suffer terrible with pains in me legs. Juno can tell you there what . . .

MRS. B. You won't have many pains in your legs when you hear what Mr. Bentham has to tell you.

BENT. Juno! What an interesting name! It reminds one of Homer's glorious story of ancient gods and heroes.

BOYLE. Yis, doesn't it? You see, Juno was born an' christened in June; I met her in June; we were married in June, an' Johnny was born in June, so wan day I says to her, "You should ha' been called Juno," an' the name stuck to her ever since.

MRS. B. Here, we can talk o' them things agen; let Mr. Bentham say what he has to say now.

BENT. Well, Mr. Boyle, I suppose you'll remember a Mr. Ellison of Santry—he's a relative of yours, I think.

BOYLE (*viciously*). Is it that prognosticator an' procrastinator! Of course I remember him.

BENT. Well, he's dead, Mr. Boyle . . .

BOYLE. Sorra many'll go into mournin' for him.

MRS. B. Wait till you hear what Mr. Bentham has to say, an' then, maybe, you'll change your opinion.

BENT. A week before he died he sent for me to write his will for him. He told me that there were two only that he wished to leave his property to: his second cousin, Michael Finnegan of Santry, and John Boyle, his first cousin, of Dublin.

BOYLE (*excitedly*). Me, is it me, me?

BENT. You, Mr. Boyle; I'll read a copy of the will that I have here with me, which has been duly filed in the Court of Probate.

(*He takes a paper from his pocket and reads.*)

6th February 1922

This is the last Will and Testament of William Ellison, of Santry, in the County of Dublin. I hereby order and wish my property to be sold and divided as follows:—

£20 to the St. Vincent de Paul Society.

£60 for Masses for the repose of my soul (5s. for each Mass).

The rest of my property to be divided between my first and second cousins.

I hereby appoint Timothy Buckly, of Santry, and Hugh Brierly, of Coolock, to be my Executors.

> (*Signed*)   WILLIAM ELLISON.
> HUGH BRIERLY.
> TIMOTHY BUCKLY.
> CHARLES BENTHAM, N.T.

BOYLE (*eagerly*). An' how much'll be comin' out of it, Mr. Bentham?

BENT. The Executors told me that half of the property would be anything between £1500 and £2000.

MARY. A fortune, father, a fortune!

JOHN. We'll be able to get out o' this place now, an' go somewhere we're not known.

MRS. B. You won't have to trouble about a job for awhile, Jack.

BOYLE (*fervently*). I'll never doubt the goodness o' God agen.

BENT. I congratulate you, Mr. Boyle. (*They shake hands.*)

BOYLE. An' now, Mr. Bentham, you'll have to have a wet.

BENT. A wet?

BOYLE. A wet—a jar—a boul!

MRS. B. Jack, you're speakin' to Mr. Bentham, an' not to Joxer.

BOYLE (*solemnly*). Juno . . . Mary . . . Johnny . . . we'll have to go into mournin' at wanst. . . . I never expected that poor Bill ud die so sudden. . . . Well, we all have to die some day . . . you, Juno, today . . . an' me, maybe, tomorrow. . . . It's sad, but it can't be helped. . . . Requiescat in pace . . . or, usin' our oul' tongue like St. Patrick or St. Bridget, Guh sayeree jeea ayera!

MARY. Oh, father, that's not Rest in Peace; that's God save Ireland!

BOYLE. U-u-ugh, it's all the same—isn't it a prayer? . . . Juno, I'm done with Joxer; he's nothin' but a prognosticator an' a . . .

JOX. (*climbing angrily through the window and bounding into the room*). You're done with Joxer, are you? Maybe you thought I'd stop on the roof all the night for you! Joxer out on the roof with the win' blowin' through him was nothin' to you an' your friend with the collar an' tie!

MRS. B. What in the name o' God brought you out on the roof; what were you doin' there?

JOX. (*ironically*). I was dhreamin' I was standin' on the bridge of a ship, an' she sailin' the Antartic Ocean, an' it blowed, an' blowed, an' I lookin' up at the sky an' sayin', what is the stars, what is the stars?

MRS. B. (*opening the door and standing at it*). Here, get ou' o' this, Joxer Daly; I was always thinkin' you had a slate off.

JOX. (*moving to the door*). I have to laugh every time I look at the deep-sea sailor; an' a row on a river ud make him sea-sick!

BOYLE. Get ou' o' this before I take the law into me own hands!

JOX. (*going out*). Say aw rewaeawr, but not good-bye. Lookin' for work, an' prayin' to God he won't get it!   (*He goes.*)

MRS. B. I'm tired tellin' you what Joxer was; maybe now you see yourself the kind he is.

BOYLE. He'll never blow the froth off a pint o' mine agen, that's a sure thing. Johnny . . . Mary . . . you're to keep yourselves to yourselves for the future. Juno, I'm done with Joxer. . . . I'm a new man from this out. . . . (*Clasping* JUNO's *hand, and singing emotionally.*)

"O, me darlin' Juno, I will be thrue to thee;
Me own, me darlin' Juno, you're all the world to me."

(CURTAIN)

ACT TWO

The same, but the furniture is more plentiful, and of a vulgar nature. A glaringly upholstered armchair and lounge; cheap pictures and photos everywhere. Every available spot is ornamented with huge vases filled with artificial flowers. Crossed festoons of coloured paper chains stretch from end to end of ceiling. On the table is an old attaché case. It is about six in the evening, and two days after the First Act. BOYLE, *in his shirt-sleeves, is voluptuously stretched on the sofa; he is smoking a clay pipe. He is half asleep. A lamp is lighting on the table. After a few moments' pause the voice of* JOXER *is heard singing softly outside at the door*—"Me pipe I'll smoke, as I dhrive me moke—are you there, Mor . . . ee . . . ar . . . i . . . teee!"*

BOYLE (*leaping up, takes a pen in his hand and busies himself with papers*). Come along, Joxer, me son, come along.

JOX. (*putting his head in*). Are you be yourself?

BOYLE. Come on, come on; that doesn't matther; I'm masther now, an' I'm goin' to remain masther. (JOXER *comes in.*)

JOX. How d'ye feel now, as a man o' money?

BOYLE (*solemnly*). It's a responsibility, Joxer, a great responsibility.

JOX. I suppose 'tis now, though you wouldn't think it.

BOYLE. Joxer, han' me over that attackey case on the table there. (JOXER *hands the case.*) Ever since the Will was passed I've run hundhreds o' dockyments through me hans—I tell you, you have to keep your wits about you. (*He busies himself with papers.*)

JOX. Well, I won't disturb you; I'll dhrop in when . . .

BOYLE (*hastily*). It's all right, Joxer, this is the last one to be signed today. (*He signs a paper, puts it into the case, which he shuts with a snap, and sits back pompously in the chair.*) Now, Joxer, you want to see me; I'm at your service—what can I do for you, me man?

JOX. I've just dhropped in with the £3 . 5s. that Mrs. Madigan riz on the blankets an' table for you, an' she says you're to be in no hurry payin' it back.

BOYLE. She won't be long without it; I expect the first cheque for a couple o' hundhred any day. There's the five bob for yourself—go on, take it, man; it'll not be the last you'll get from the Captain. Now an' agen we have our differ, but we're there together all the time.

JOX. Me for you, an' you for me, like the two Musketeers.

BOYLE. Father Farrell stopped me today an' tole me how glad he was I fell in for the money.

JOX. He'll be stoppin' you ofen enough now; I suppose it was "Mr." Boyle with him?

BOYLE. He shuk me be the han' . . .

JOX. (*ironically*). I met with Napper Tandy, an' he shuk me be the han'!

BOYLE. You're seldom asthray, Joxer, but you're wrong shipped this time. What you're sayin' of Father Farrell is very near to blasfeemey. I don't like any one to talk disrespectful of Father Farrell.

JOX. You're takin' me up wrong, Captain; I wouldn't let a word be said agen Father Farrell—the heart o' the rowl, that's what he is; I always said he was a darlin' man, a daarlin' man.

BOYLE. Comin' up the stairs who did I meet but that bummer, Nugent.

"I seen you talkin' to Father Farrell," says he, with a grin on him. "He'll be folleyin' you," says he, "like a Guardian Angel from this out"—all the time the oul' grin on him, Joxer.

JOX. I never seen him yet but he had that oul' grin on him!

BOYLE. "Mr. Nugent," says I, "Father Farrell is a man o' the people, an', as far as I know the History o' me country, the priests was always in the van of the fight for Irelan's freedom."

JOX. (*fervently*).

"Who was it led the van, Soggart Aroon?
Since the fight first began, Soggart Aroon?"

BOYLE. "Who are you tellin'?" says he. "Didn't they let down the Fenians, an' didn't they do in Parnell? An' now . . ." "You ought to be ashamed o' yourself," says I, interruptin' him, "not to know the History o' your country." An' I left him gawkin' where he was.

JOX. Where ignorance 's bliss 'tis folly to be wise; I wondher did he ever read the *Story o' Irelan'*.

BOYLE. Be J. L. Sullivan? Don't you know he didn't.

JOX. Ah, it's a darlin' buk, a daarlin' buk!

BOYLE. You'd betther be goin', now, Joxer; his Majesty, Bentham, 'll be here any minute, now.

JOX. Be the way things is lookin', it'll be a match between him an' Mary. She's thrun over Jerry altogether. Well, I hope it will, for he's a darlin' man.

BOYLE. I'm glad you think so—I don't. (*Irritably.*) What's darlin' about him?

JOX. (*nonplussed*). I only seen him twiced; if you want to know me, come an' live with me.

BOYLE. He's too dignified for me—to hear him talk you'd think he knew as much as a Boney's Oraculum. He's given up his job as teacher, an' is goin' to become a solicitor in Dublin—he's been studyin' law. I suppose he thinks I'll set him up, but he's wrong shipped. An' th' other fella—Jerry's as bad. The two o' them ud give you a pain in your face, listenin' to them; Jerry believin' in nothin', an' Bentham believin' in everythin'. One that says all is God an' no man; an' th' other that says all is man an' no God!

JOX. Well, I'll be off now.

BOYLE. Don't forget to dhrop down afther awhile; we'll have a quiet jar, an' a song or two.

JOX. Never fear.

BOYLE. An' tell Mrs. Madigan that I hope we'll have the pleasure of her organization at our little enthertainment.

JOX. Righto; we'll come down together. (*He goes out.*)

(*JOHNNY comes from room on left, and sits down moodily at the fire. BOYLE looks at him for a few moments, and shakes his head. He fills his pipe.*)

VOICE OF JUNO (*at the door*). Open the door, Jack; this thing has me nearly kilt with the weight.

(*BOYLE opens the door. JUNO enters carrying the box of a gramophone, followed by MARY carrying the horn and some parcels. JUNO leaves the box on the table and flops into a chair.*)

JUNO. Carryin' that from Henry Street was no joke.

BOYLE. U-u-ugh, that's a grand-lookin' insthrument—how much was it?

JUNO. Pound down, an' five to be paid at two shillins a week.

BOYLE. That's reasonable enough.

JUNO. I'm afraid we're runnin' into too much debt; first the furniture, an' now this.

BOYLE. The whole lot won't be much out of £2000.

MARY. I don't know what you wanted a gramophone for—I know Charlie hates them; he says they're destructive of real music.

BOYLE. Desthructive of music—that fella ud give you a pain in your face. All a gramophone wants is to be properly played; its thrue wondher is only felt when everythin's quiet—what a gramophone wants is dead silence!

MARY. But, father, Jerry says the same; afther all, you can only appreciate music when your ear is properly trained.

BOYLE. That's another fella ud give you a pain in your face. Properly thrained! I suppose you couldn't appreciate football unless your fut was properly thrained.

MRS. B. (*to* MARY). Go on in ower that an' dress, or Charlie'll be in on you, an' tea nor nothing'll be ready. (*MARY goes into room left.*)

MRS. B. (*arranging table for tea*). You didn't look at our new gramophone, Johnny?

JOHN. 'Tisn't gramophones I'm thinking of.

MRS. B. An' what is it you're thinkin' of, allanna?

JOHN. Nothin', nothin', nothin'.

MRS. B. Sure, you must be thinkin' of somethin'; it's yourself that has yourself the way y'are; sleepin' wan night in me sisther's, an' the nex' in your father's brother's—you'll get no rest goin' on that way.

JOHN. I can rest nowhere, nowhere, nowhere.

MRS. B. Sure, you're not thryin' to rest anywhere.

JOHN. Let me alone, let me alone, let me alone, for God's sake.

(*A knock at street door.*)

MRS. B. (*in a flutter*). Here he is; here's Mr. Bentham!

BOYLE. Well, there's room for him; it's a pity there's not a brass band to play him in.

MRS. B. We'll han' the tea round, an' not be clusthered round the table, as if we never seen nothin'.

(*Steps are heard approaching, and* JUNO, *opening the door, allows* BENTHAM *to enter.*)

JUNO. Give your hat an' stick to Jack, there . . . sit down, Mr. Bentham . . . no, not there . . . in th' easy chair be the fire . . . there, that's betther. Mary'll be out to you in a minute.

BOYLE (*solemnly*). I seen be the paper this mornin' that Consols was down half per cent. That's serious, min' you, an' shows the whole counthry's in a state o' chassis.

MRS. B. What's Consols, Jack?

BOYLE. Consols? Oh, Consols is—oh, there's no use tellin' women what Consols is—th' wouldn't undherstand.

BENT. It's just as you were saying, Mr. Boyle . . .

(MARY *enters, charmingly dressed.*)

BENT. Oh, good evening, Mary; how pretty you're looking!

MARY (*archly*). Am I?

BOYLE. We were just talkin' when you kem in, Mary; I was tellin' Mr. Bentham that the whole counthry's in a state o' chassis.

MARY (*to* BENTHAM). Would you prefer the green or the blue ribbon round me hair, Charlie?

MRS. B. Mary, your father's speakin'.

BOYLE (*rapidly*). I was jus' tellin' Mr. Bentham that the whole counthry's in a state o' chassis.

MARY. I'm sure you're frettin', da, whether it is or no.

MRS. B. With all our churches an' religions, the worl's not a bit the betther.

BOYLE (*with a commanding gesture*). Tay!

(MARY *and* MRS. BOYLE *dispense the tea.*)

MRS. B. An' Irelan's takin' a leaf out o' the worl's buk; when we got the makin' of our own laws I thought we'd never stop to look behind us, but instead of that we never stopped to look before us! If the people ud folley up their religion betther there'd be a betther chance for us—what do you think, Mr. Bentham?

BENT. I'm afraid I can't venture to express an opinion on that point, Mrs. Boyle; dogma has no attraction for me.

MRS. B. I forgot you didn't hold with us: what's this you said you were?

BENT. A Theosophist, Mrs. Boyle.

MRS. B. An' what in the name o' God's a Theosophist?

BOYLE. A Theosophist, Juno, 's a—tell her, Mr. Bentham, tell her.

BENT. It's hard to explain in a few words: Theosophy's founded on The Vedas, the religious books of the East. Its central theme is the existence of an all-pervading Spirit—the Life-Breath. Nothing really exists but this one Universal Life-Breath. And whatever even seems to exist separately from this Life-Breath, doesn't really exist at all. It is all vital force in man, in all animals, and in all vegetation. This Life-Breath is called the Prawna.

MRS. B. The Prawna! What a comical name!

BOYLE. Prawna; yis, the Prawna. (*Blowing gently through his lips.*) That's the Prawna!

MRS. B. Whist, whist, Jack.

BENT. The happiness of man depends upon his sympathy with this Spirit. Men who have reached a high state of excellence are called Yogi. Some men become Yogi in a short time, it may take others millions of years.

BOYLE. Yogi! I seen hundhreds of them in the streets o' San Francisco.

BENT. It is said by these Yogi that if we practise certain mental exercises that we would have powers denied to others—for instance, the faculty of seeing things that happen miles and miles away.

MRS. B. I wouldn't care to meddle with that sort o' belief; it's a very curious religion, altogether.

BOYLE. What's curious about it? Isn't all religions curious?—if they weren't, you wouldn't get any one to believe them. But religions is passin' away—they've had their day like everything else. Take the real Dublin people, f'rinstance: they know more about Charlie Chaplin an' Tommy Mix than they do about SS. Peter an' Paul!

MRS. B. You don't believe in ghosts, Mr. Bentham?

MARY. Don't you know he doesn't, mother?

BENT. I don't know that, Mary. Scientists are beginning to think that what we call ghosts are sometimes seen by persons of a certain nature. They say that sensational actions, such as the killing of a person, demand great energy, and that that energy lingers in the place where the action occurred. People may live in the place and see nothing, when someone may come along whose personality has some peculiar connection with the energy of the place, and, in a flash, the person sees the whole affair.

JOHN. (*rising swiftly, pale and affected*). What sort o' talk is this to be goin' on with? Is there nothin' betther to be talkin' about but the killin' o' people? My God, isn't it bad enough for these things to happen without talkin' about them!

(*He hurriedly goes into the room on left.*)

BENT. Oh, I'm very sorry, Mrs. Boyle; I never thought . . .

MRS. B. (*apologetically*). Never mind, Mr. Bentham, he's very touchy. (*A frightened scream is heard from* JOHNNY *inside.*)

MRS. B. Mother of God, what's that?

(*He rushes out again, his face pale, his lips twitching, his limbs trembling.*)

JOHN. Shut the door, shut the door, quick, for God's sake! Great God, have mercy on me! Blessed Mother o' God, shelter me, shelther your son!

MRS. B. (*catching him in her arms*). What's wrong with you? What ails

you? Sit down, sit down, here, on the bed . . . there now . .
there now.

MARY. Johnny, Johnny, what ails you?

JOHN. I seen him, I seen him . . . kneelin' in front o' the statue . .
merciful Jesus, have pity on me!

MRS. B. (*to* BOYLE). Get him a glass o' whisky . . . quick, man, an' don'
stand gawkin'.

(BOYLE *gets the whisky*.)

JOHN. Sit here, sit here, mother . . . between me an' the door.

MRS. B. I'll sit beside you as long as you like, only tell me what was i
came across you at all?

JOHN. (*after taking some drink*). I seen him. . . . I seen Robbie Tancred kneelin' down before the statue . . . an' the red light shinin
on him . . . an' when I went in . . . he turned an' looked at me
. . . an' I seen the wouns bleedin' in his breast. . . . Oh, why did
he look at me like that? . . . it wasn't my fault that he was done
in. . . . Mother o' God, keep him away from me!

MRS. B. There, there, child, you've imagined it all. There was nothin'
there at all—it was the red light you seen, an' the talk we had put
all the rest into your head. Here, dhrink more o' this—it'll do you
good. . . . An', now, stretch yourself down on the bed for a little.
(*To* BOYLE.) Go in, Jack, an' show him it was only in his own
head it was.

BOYLE (*making no move*). E-e-e-eh; it's all nonsense; it was only a
shadda he saw.

MARY. Mother o' God, he made me heart lep!

BENT. It was simply due to an over-wrought imagination—we all get that
way at times.

MRS. B. There, dear, lie down in the bed, an' I'll put the quilt across you
. . . e-e-e-eh, that's it . . . you'll be as right as the mail in a few
minutes.

JOHN. Mother, go into the room an' see if the light's lightin' before the
statue.

MRS. B. (*to* BOYLE). Jack, run in an' see if the light's lightin' before the
statue.

BOYLE (*to* MARY). Mary, slip in an' see if the light's lightin' before the statue. (MARY *hesitates to go in.*)

BENT. It's all right; Mary, I'll go.

(*He goes into the room; remains for a few moments, and returns.*)

BENT. Everything's just as it was—the light burning bravely before the statue.

BOYLE. Of course; I knew it was all nonsense.

(*A knock at the door.*)

BOYLE (*going to open the door*). E-e-e-e-eh. (*He opens it, and* JOXER, *followed by* MRS. MADIGAN, *enters.* MRS. MADIGAN *is a strong, dapper little woman of about forty-five; her face is almost always a widespread smile of complacency. She is a woman who, in manner at least, can mourn with them that mourn, and rejoice with them that do rejoice. When she is feeling comfortable, she is inclined to be reminiscent; when others say anything, or following a statement made by herself, she has a habit of putting her head a little to one side, and nodding it rapidly several times in succession, like a bird pecking at a hard berry. Indeed, she has a good deal of the bird in her, but the bird instinct is by no means a melodious one. She is ignorant, vulgar and forward, but her heart is generous withal. For instance, she would help a neighbour's sick child; she would probably kill the child, but her intention would be to cure it; she would be more at home helping a drayman to lift a fallen horse. She is dressed in a rather soiled grey dress and a vivid purple blouse; in her hair is a huge comb, ornamented with huge coloured beads. She enters with a gliding step, beaming smile and nodding head.* BOYLE *receives them effusively.*)

BOYLE. Come on in, Mrs. Madigan; come on in; I was afraid you weren't comin'. . . . (*Slyly.*) There's some people able to dhress, ay, Joxer?

JOX. Fair as the blossoms that bloom in the May, an' sweet as the scent of the new-mown hay. . . . Ah, well she may wear them.

MRS. MAD. (*looking at* MARY). I know some as are as sweet as the blossoms that bloom in the May—oh, no names, no pack dhrill!

BOYLE. An' now I'll inthroduce the pair o' yous to Mary's intended: Mr.

Bentham, this is Mrs. Madigan, an oul' back-parlour neighbour that, if she could help it at all, ud never see a body shuk!

BENT. (*rising, and tentatively shaking the hand of* MRS. MADIGAN). I'm sure, it's a great pleasure to know you, Mrs. Madigan.

MRS. MAD. An' I'm goin' to tell you, Mr. Bentham, you're goin' to get a nice a bit o' skirt in Mary, there, as ever you seen in your puff Not like some of the dhressed-up dolls that's knockin' abou lookin' for men when it's a skelpin' they want. I remember, a well as I remember yestherday, the day she was born—of a Tues day, the 25th o' June, in the year 1901, at thirty-three minutes pas wan in the day be Foley's clock, the pub at the corner o' the street A cowld day it was too, for the season o' the year, an' I remember sayin' to Joxer, there, who I met comin' up th' stairs, that the new arrival in Boyle's ud grow up a hardy chiselur if it lived, an' tha she'd be somethin' one o' these days that nobody suspected, an' so signs on it, here she is today, goin' to be married to a young mar lookin' as if he'd be fit to commensurate in any position in life i ud please God to call him!

BOYLE (*effusively*). Sit down, Mrs. Madigan, sit down, me oul' sport (*To* BENTHAM.) This is Joxer Daly, Past Chief Ranger of the Dea Little Shamrock Branch of the Irish National Foresters, an oul front-top neighbour, that never despaired, even in the darkes days of Ireland's sorra.

JOX. Nil desperandum, Captain, nil desperandum.

BOYLE. Sit down, Joxer, sit down. The two of us was ofen in a tigh corner.

MRS. B. Ay, in Foley's snug!

JOX. An' we kem out of it flyin', we kem out of it flyin', Captain.

BOYLE. An' now for a dhrink—I know yous won't refuse an oul' friend

MRS. MAD. (*to* JUNO). Is Johnny not well, Mrs. . . .

MRS. B. (*warningly*). S-s-s-sh.

MRS. MAD. Oh, the poor darlin'.

BOYLE. Well, Mrs. Madigan, is it tea or what?

MRS. MAD. Well, speakin' for meself, I jus' had me tea a minute ago, an I'm afraid to dhrink any more—I'm never the same when I dhrink too much tay. Thanks, all the same, Mr. Boyle.

BOYLE. Well, what about a bottle o' stout or a dhrop o' whisky?

MRS. MAD. A bottle o' stout ud be a little too heavy for me stummock afther me tay. . . . A-a-ah, I'll thry the ball o' malt.

(BOYLE *prepares the whisky*.)

MRS. MAD. There's nothin' like a ball o' malt occasional like—too much of it isn't good. (*To* BOYLE, *who is adding water*.) Ah, God, Johnny, don't put too much wather on it! (*She drinks*.) I suppose yous'll be lavin' this place.

BOYLE. I'm looking for a place near the sea; I'd like the place that you might say was me cradle, to be me grave as well. The sea is always callin' me.

JOX. She is callin', callin', callin', in the win' an' on the sea.

BOYLE. Another dhrop o' whisky, Mrs. Madigan?

MRS. MAD. Well, now, it ut be hard to refuse seein' the suspicious times that's in it.

BOYLE (*with a commanding gesture*). Song! . . . Juno . . . Mary . . . "Home to Our Mountains"!

MRS. MAD. (*enthusiastically*). Hear, hear!

JOX. Oh, tha's a darlin' song, a daarlin' song!

MARY (*bashfully*). Ah no, da; I'm not in a singin' humour.

MRS. MAD. Gawn with you, child, an' you only goin' to be marrid; I remember as well as I remember yesterday—it was on a lovely August evenin', exactly, accordin' to date, fifteen years ago, come the Tuesday folleyin' the nex' that's comin' on, when me own man—*the Lord be good to him*—an' me was sittin' shy together in a doty little nook on a counthry road, adjacent to The Stiles. "That'll scratch your lovely, little white neck," says he, ketchin' hould of a danglin' bramble branch, holdin' clusters of the love-liest flowers you ever seen, an' breakin' it off, so that his arm fell, accidental like, roun' me waist, an' as I felt it tightenin', an' tightenin', an' tightenin', I thought me buzzom was every minute goin' to burst out into a roystherin' song about

"The little green leaves that were shakin' on the threes,
    The gallivantin' butherflies, an' buzzin' o' the bees!"

BOYLE. Ordher for the song!

JUNO. Come on, Mary—we'll do our best. (JUNO *and* MARY *stand up, and*

choosing a suitable position, sing simply "Home to Our Moun-
tains." They bow to company, and return to their places.)

BOYLE (*emotionally, at the end of song*). Lull . . . me . . . to . . . rest!

JOX. (*clapping his hands*). Bravo, bravo! Darlin' girulls, darlin' girulls!

MRS. MAD. Juno, I never seen you in betther form.

BENT. Very nicely rendered indeed.

MRS. MAD. A noble call, a noble call!

MRS. B. What about yourself, Mrs. Madigan?

(*After some coaxing,* MRS. MADIGAN *rises, and in a quavering voice sings*
the following verse.)

> "If I were a blackbird I'd whistle and sing;
> I'd follow the ship that my thrue love was in;
> An' on the top riggin', I'd there build me nest,
> An' at night I would sleep on me Willie's white breast!"

(*Becoming husky, amid applause, she sits down.*)

MRS. MAD. Ah, me voice is too husky now, Juno; though I remember the
time when Maisie Madigan could sing like a nightingale at matin'
time. I remember as well as I remember yestherday, at a party
given to celebrate the comin' of the first chiselur to Annie an'
Benny Jimeson—who was the barber, yous may remember, in
Henrietta Street, that, afther Easter Week, hung out a green,
white an' orange pole, an', then, when the Tans started their Jazz
dancin', whipped it in agen, an' stuck out a red, white an' blue
wan instead, givin' as an excuse that a barber's pole was strictly
non-political—singin' "An' You'll Remember Me," with the top
notes quiverin' in a dead hush of pethrified attention, folleyed be
a clappin' o' hans that shuk the tumblers on the table, an' capped
by Jimeson, the barber, sayin' that it was the best rendherin' of
"You'll Remember Me" he ever heard in his natural!

BOYLE (*peremptorily*). Ordher for Joxer's song!

JOX. Ah no, I couldn't; don't ass me, Captain.

BOYLE. Joxer's song, Joxer's song—give us wan of your shut-eyed wans.

(JOXER *settles himself in his chair; takes a drink; clears his throat;*
solemnly closes his eyes, and begins to sing in a very querulous
voice.)

    "She is far from the lan' where her young hero sleeps,
        An' lovers around her are sighing . . . (*He hesitates.*)
        An' lovers around her are sighin' . . . sighin' . . . sighin' . . ."
(*A pause.*)

BOYLE (*imitating* JOXER).

    "And lovers around her are sighing!"
What's the use of you thryin' to sing the song if you don't know
it?

MARY. Thry another one, Mr. Daly—maybe you'd be more fortunate.

MRS. MAD. Gawn, Joxer; thry another wan.

JOX. (*starting again*).

    "I have heard the mavis singin' his love song to the morn;
    I have seen the dew-dhrop clingin' to the rose jus' newly born;
    but . . . but . . . (*frantically*)
    To the rose jus' newly born . . .
    newly born . . . born."

JOHN. Mother, put on the gramophone, for God's sake, an' stop Joxer's
bawlin'.

BOYLE (*commandingly*). Gramophone! . . . I hate to see fellas thryin'
to do what they're not able to do.

(BOYLE *arranges the gramophone, and is about to start it, when voices
are heard of persons descending the stairs.*)

MRS. B. (*warningly*). Whisht, Jack, don't put it on, don't put it on yet;
this must be poor Mrs. Tancred comin' down to go to the hospital—I forgot all about them bringin' the body to the church tonight. Open the door, Mary, an' give them a bit o' light.

(MARY *opens the door, and* MRS. TANCRED—*a very old woman, obviously
shaken by the death of her son—appears, accompanied by several
neighbours. The first few phrases are spoken before they appear.*)

1ST. NEIGHBOUR. It's a sad journey we're goin' on, but God's good, an' the
Republicans won't be always down.

MRS. TAN. Ah, what good is that to me now? Whether they're up or
down—it won't bring me darlin' boy from the grave.

MRS. B. Come in an' have a hot cup o' tay, Mrs. Tancred, before you go.

MRS. TAN. Ah, I can take nothin' now, Mrs. Boyle—I won't be long
afther him.

IST. NEIGHBOUR. Still an' all, he died a noble death, an' we'll bury him like a king.

MRS. TAN. An' I'll go on livin' like a pauper. Ah, what's the pains I suffered bringin' him into the world to carry him to his cradle, to the pains I'm sufferin' now, carryin' him out o' the world to bring him to his grave!

MARY. It would be better for you not to go at all, Mrs. Tancred, but to stay at home beside the fire with some o' the neighbours.

MRS. TAN. I seen the first of him, an' I'll see the last of him.

MRS. B. You'd want a shawl, Mrs. Tancred; it's a cowld night, an' the win's blowin' sharp.

MRS. MAD. (*rushing out*). I've a shawl above.

MRS. TAN. Me home is gone now; he was me only child, an' to think that he was lyin' for a whole night stretched out on the side of a lonely counthry lane, with his head, his darlin' head, that I often kissed an' fondled, half hidden in the wather of a runnin' brook. An' I'm told he was the leadher of the ambush where me nex' door neighbour, Mrs. Mannin', lost her Free State soldier son. An' now here's the two of us oul' women, standin' one on each side of a scales o' sorra, balanced be the bodies of our two dead darlin' sons. (MRS. MADIGAN *returns, and wraps a shawl around her.*) God bless you, Mrs. Madigan. . . . (*She moves slowly towards the door.*) Mother o' God, Mother o' God, have pity on the pair of us! . . . O Blessed Virgin, where were you when me darlin' son was riddled with bullets, when me darlin' son was riddled with bullets! . . . Sacred Heart of the Crucified Jesus, take away our hearts o' stone . . . an' give us hearts o' flesh! . . . Take away this murdherin' hate . . . an' give us Thine own eternal love!

(*They pass out of the room.*)

MRS. B. (*explanatorily to* BENTHAM). That was Mrs. Tancred of the two-pair back; her son was found, e'er yesterday, lyin' out beyant Finglas riddled with bullets. A Die-hard he was, be all accounts. He was a nice quiet boy, but lattherly he went to hell, with his Republic first, an' Republic last an' Republic over all. He ofen took tea with us here, in the oul' days, an' Johnny, there, an' him used to be always together.

JOHN. Am I always to be havin' to tell you that he was no friend o' mine? I never cared for him, an' he could never stick me. It's not because he was Commandant of the Battalion that I was Quarther-Masther of, that we were friends.

MRS. B. He's gone now—the Lord be good to him! God help his poor oul' creature of a mother, for no matther whose friend or enemy he was, he was her poor son.

BENT. The whole thing is terrible, Mrs. Boyle; but the only way to deal with a mad dog is to destroy him.

MRS. B. An' to think of me forgettin' about him bein' brought to the church tonight, an' we singin' an' all, but it was well we hadn't the gramophone goin', anyhow.

BOYLE. Even if we had aself. We've nothin' to do with these things, one way or t'other. That's the Government's business, an' let them do what we're payin' them for doin'.

MRS. B. I'd like to know how a body's not to mind these things; look at the way they're afther leavin' the people in this very house. Hasn't the whole house, nearly, been massacreed? There's young Dough-erty's husband with his leg off; Mrs. Travers that had her son blew up be a mine in Inchegeela, in County Cork; Mrs. Mannin' that lost wan of her sons in ambush a few weeks ago, an' now, poor Mrs. Tancred's only child gone west with his body made a collandher of. Sure, if it's not our business, I don't know whose business it is.

BOYLE. Here, there, that's enough about them things; they don't affect us, an' we needn't give a damn. If they want a wake, well, let them have a wake. When I was a sailor, I was always resigned to meet with a wathery grave; an' if they want to be soldiers, well, there's no use o' them squealin' when they meet a soldier's fate.

JOX. Let me like a soldier fall—me breast expandin' to th' ball!

MRS. B. In wan way, she deserves all she got; for lately, she let th' Die-hards make an open house of th' place; an' for th' last couple of months, either when th' sun was risin' or when th' sun was settin', you had C.I.D. men burstin' into your room, assin' you where were you born, where were you christened, where were you mar-ried, an' where would you be buried!

JOHN. For God's sake, let us have no more o' this talk.

MRS. MAD. What about Mr. Boyle's song before we start th' gramophone?

MARY (*getting her hat, and putting it on*). Mother, Charlie and I are goin' out for a little sthroll.

MRS. B. All right, darlin'.

BENT. (*going out with* MARY). We won't be long away, Mrs. Boyle.

MRS. MAD. Gwan, Captain, Gwan.

BOYLE. E-e-e-e-eh, I'd want to have a few more jars in me, before I'd be in fettle for singin'.

JOX. Give us that poem you writ t'other day. (*To the rest.*) Aw, it's a darlin' poem, a daarlin' poem.

MRS. B. God bless us, is he startin' to write poetry!

BOYLE (*rising to his feet*). E-e-e-e-eh.

(*He recites in an emotional, consequential manner the following verses.*)

> "Shawn an' I were friends, sir, to me he was all in all.
> His work was very heavy and his wages were very small.
> None betther on th' beach as Docker, I'll go bail,
> 'Tis now I'm feelin' lonely, for today he lies in jail.
> He was not what some call pious—seldom at church or prayer;
> For the greatest scoundrels I know, sir, goes every Sunday there.
> Fond of his pint—well, rather, but hated the Boss by creed
> But never refused a copper to comfort a pal in need."

E-e-e-e-eh. (*He sits down.*)

MRS. MAD. Grand, grand; you should folly that up, you should folly that up.

JOX. It's a daarlin' poem!

BOYLE (*delightedly*). E-e-e-e-eh.

JOHN. Are yous goin' to put on th' gramophone tonight, or are yous not?

MRS. B. Gwan, Jack, put on a record.

MRS. MAD. Gwan, Captain, gwan.

BOYLE. Well, yous'll want to keep a dead silence.

(*He sets a record, starts the machine, and it begins to play "If you're*

*Irish, come into the Parlour." As the tune is in full blare, the door is suddenly opened by a brisk, little bald-headed man, dressed circumspectly in a black suit; he glares fiercely at all in the room; he is "*NEEDLE*" NUGENT, a tailor. He carries his hat in his hand.)*

NUG. (*loudly, above the noise of the gramophone*). Are yous goin' to have that thing bawlin' an' the funeral of Mrs. Tancred's son passin' the house? Have none of yous any respect for the Irish people's National regard for the dead? (BOYLE *stops the gramophone.*)

MRS. B. Maybe, Needle Nugent, it's nearly time we had a little less respect for the dead, an' a little more regard for the livin'.

MRS. MAD. We don't want you, Mr. Nugent, to teach us what we learned at our mother's knee. You don't look yourself as if you were dyin' of grief; if y'ass Maisie Madigan anything, I'd call you a real thrue Die-hard an' live-soft Republican, attendin' Republican funerals in the day, an' stoppin' up half the night makin' suits for the Civic Guards!

(*Persons are heard running down to the street, some saying, "Here it is, here it is." NUGENT withdraws, and the rest, except JOHNNY, go to the window looking into the street, and look out. Sounds of a crowd coming nearer are heard; portion are singing.*)

> "To Jesus' Heart all burning
>   With fervent love for men,
> My heart with fondest yearning
>   Shall raise its joyful strain.
>   While ages course along,
>   Blest be with loudest song
>   The Sacred Heart of Jesus
>   By every heart and tongue."

MRS. B. Here's the hearse, here's the hearse!

BOYLE. There's t'oul' mother walkin' behin' the coffin.

MRS. MAD. You can hardly see the coffin with the wreaths.

JOX. Oh, it's a darlin' funeral, a daarlin' funeral!

MRS. MAD. W'd have a betther view from the street.

BOYLE. Yes—this place ud give you a crick in your neck.

(*They leave the room, and go down.* JOHNNY *sits moodily by the fire. ʌ* YOUNG MAN *enters; he looks at* JOHNNY *for a moment.*)

YOUNG MAN. Quarther-Masther Boyle.

JOHN. (*with a start*). The Mobilizer!

YOUNG MAN. You're not at the funeral?

JOHN. I'm not well.

YOUNG MAN. I'm glad I've found you; you were stoppin' at your aunt's I called there but you'd gone. I've to give you an ordher to attenc a Battalion Staff meetin' the night afther tomorrow.

JOHN. Where?

YOUNG MAN. I don't know; you're to meet me at the Pillar at eigh o'clock; then we're to go to a place I'll be told of tonight; there we'll meet a mothor that'll bring us to the meeting. They thin! you might be able to know somethin' about them that gave the bend where Commandant Tancred was shelterin'.

JOHN. I'm not goin', then. I know nothing about Tancred.

YOUNG MAN (*at the door*). You'd betther come for your own sake— remember your oath.

JOHN (*passionately*). I won't go! Haven't I done enough for Ireland! I've lost me arm, an' me hip's desthroyed so that I'll never be able to walk right agen! Good God, haven't I done enough for Ireland?

YOUNG MAN. Boyle, no man can do enough for Ireland!   (*He goes.*)
(*Faintly in the distance the crowd is heard saying.*)
    "Hail, Mary, full of grace, the Lord is with Thee;
    Blessed art Thou amongst women, and blessed, etc."

(CURTAIN)

ACT THREE

The same as ACT TWO. *It is about half-past six on a November evening; a bright fire burns in the grate.* MARY, *dressed to go out, is sitting on a chair by the fire, leaning forward, her hands under her chin, her elbows on her knees. A look of dejection, mingled with un-certain anxiety, is on her face. A lamp, turned low, is lighting on*

*the table. The votive light under the picture of the Virgin gleams
more redly than ever.* MRS. BOYLE *is putting on her hat and coat.
It is two months later.*

MRS. B. An' has Bentham never even written to you since—not one line
for the past month?

MARY (*tonelessly*). Not even a line, mother.

MRS. B. That's very curious. . . . What came between the two of yous
at all? To leave you so sudden, an' yous so great together. . . .
To go away t' England, an' not to even leave you his address. . . .
The way he was always bringin' you to dances, I thought he was
mad afther you. Are you sure you said nothin' to him?

MARY. No, mother—at least nothing that could possibly explain his
givin' me up.

MRS. B. You know you're a bit hasty at times, Mary, an' say things you
shouldn't say.

MARY. I never said to him what I shouldn't say, I'm sure of that.

MRS. B. How are you sure of it?

MARY. Because I love him with all my heart and soul, mother. Why, I
don't know; I often thought to myself that he wasn't the man
poor Jerry was, but I couldn't help loving him, all the same.

MRS. B. But you shouldn't be frettin' the way you are; when a woman
loses a man, she never knows what she's afther losin', to be sure,
but, then, she never knows what she's afther gainin', either. You're
not the one girl of a month ago—you look like one pinin' away.
It's long ago I had a right to bring you to the doctor, instead of
waitin' till tonight.

MARY. There's no necessity, really, mother, to go to the doctor; nothing
serious is wrong with me—I'm run down and disappointed, that's
all.

MRS. B. I'll not wait another minute; I don't like the look of you at all.
. . . I'm afraid we made a mistake in throwin' over poor Jerry.
. . . He'd have been betther for you than that Bentham.

MARY. Mother, the best man for a woman is the one for whom she has
the most love, and Charlie had it all.

MRS. B. Well, there's one thing to be said for him—he couldn't have been

thinkin' of the money, or he wouldn't ha' left you . . . it must ha'
been somethin' else.

MARY (*wearily*). I don't know . . . I don't know, mother . . . only I
think . . .

MRS. B. What d'ye think?

MARY. I imagine . . . he thought . . . we weren't . . . good enough
for him.

MRS. B. An' what was he himself, only a school teacher? Though I don't
blame him for fightin' shy of people like that Joxer fella an' that
oul' Madigan wan—nice sort o' people for your father to introduce to a man like Mr. Bentham. You might have told me all
about this before now, Mary; I don't know why you like to hide
everything from your mother; you knew Bentham, an' I'd ha'
known nothin' about it if it hadn't bin for the Will; an' it was
only today, afther long coaxin', that you let out that he's left you.

MARY. It would have been useless to tell you—you wouldn't understand.

MRS. B. (*hurt*). Maybe not. . . . Maybe I wouldn't understand. . . .
Well, we'll be off now.

(*She goes over to door left, and speaks to* BOYLE *inside.*)

MRS. B. We're goin' now to the doctor's. Are you goin' to get up this
evenin'?

BOYLE (*from inside*). The pains in me legs is terrible! It's me should be
poppin' off to the doctor instead o' Mary, the way I feel.

MRS. B. Sorra mend you! A nice way you were in last night—carried in
in a frog's march, dead to the world. If that's the way you'll go
on when you get the money it'll be the grave for you, an asylum
for me and the Poorhouse for Johnny.

BOYLE. I thought you were goin'?

MRS. B. That's what has you as you are—you can't bear to be spoken to.
Knowin' the way we are, up to our ears in debt, it's a wondher
you wouldn't ha' got up to go to th' solicitor's an' see if we could
ha' gotten a little o' the money even.

BOYLE (*shouting*). I can't be goin' up there night, noon an' mornin', can
I? He can't give the money till he gets it, can he? I can't get
blood out of a turnip, can I?

MRS. B. It's nearly two months since we heard of the Will, an' the money seems as far off as ever. . . . I suppose you know we owe twenty pouns to oul' Murphy?

BOYLE. I've a faint recollection of you tellin' me that before.

MRS. B. Well, you'll go over to the shop yourself for the things in future—I'll face him no more.

BOYLE. I thought you said you were goin'?

MRS. B. I'm goin' now; come on, Mary.

BOYLE. Ey, Juno, ey!

MRS. B. Well, what d'ye want now?

BOYLE. Is there e'er a bottle o' stout left?

MRS. B. There's two o' them here still.

BOYLE. Show us in one o' them an' leave t'other there till I get up. An' throw us in the paper that's on the table, an' the bottle o' Sloan's Liniment that's in th' drawer.

MRS. B. (*getting the liniment and the stout*). What paper is it you want—the *Messenger*? ~~The Catholic Harold~~

BOYLE. *Messenger!* The *News o' the World!*

(MRS. BOYLE *brings in the things asked for, and comes out again.*)

MRS. B. (*at door*). Mind the candle, now, an' don't burn the house over our heads. I left t'other bottle o' stout on the table.

(*She puts bottle of stout on table. She goes out with* MARY. *A cork is heard popping inside.*

(*A pause; then outside the door is heard the voice of* JOXER *lilting softly:* "Me pipe I'll smoke, as I dhrive me moke . . . are you . . . there . . . Mor . . . ee . . . ar . . . i . . . teee!" *A gentle knock is heard, and after a pause the door opens, and* JOXER, *followed by* NUGENT, *enters.*)

JOX. Be God, they must be all out; I was thinkin' there was somethin' up when he didn't answer the signal. We seen Juno an' Mary goin', but I didn't see him, an' it's very seldom he escapes me.

NUG. He's not goin' to escape me—he's not goin' to be let go to the fair altogether.

JOX. Sure, the house couldn't hould them lately; an' he goin' about like a mastherpiece of the Free State counthry; forgettin' their friends; forgettin' God—wouldn't even lift his hat passin' a chapel! Sure

they were bound to get a dhrop! An' you really think there's no
money comin' to him afther all?

NUG. Not as much as a red rex, man; I've been a bit anxious this long
time over me money, an' I went up to the solicitor's to find out
all I could—ah, man, they were goin' to throw me down the stairs.
They toul' me that the oul' cock himself had the stairs worn away
comin' up afther it, an' they black in the face tellin' him he'd get
nothin'. Some way or another that the Will is writ he won't be
entitled to get as much as a make!

JOX. Ah, I thought there was somethin' curious about the whole thing;
I've bin havin' sthrange dhreams for the last couple o' weeks. An'
I notice that that Bentham fella doesn't be comin' here now—there
must be somethin' on the mat there too. Anyhow, who, in the
name o' God, ud leave anythin' to that oul' bummer? Sure it ud
be unnatural. An' the way Juno an' him's been throwin' their
weight about for the last few months! Ah, him that goes a bor-
rowin' goes a sorrowin'!

NUG. Well, he's not goin' to throw his weight about in the suit I made
for him much longer. I'm tellin' you seven pouns aren't to be
found growin' on the bushes these days.

JOX. An' there isn't hardly a neighbour in the whole street that hasn't
lent him money on the strength of what he was goin' to get, but
they're after backing the wrong horse. Wasn't it a mercy o' God
that I'd nothin' to give him! The softy I am, you know, I'd ha'
lent him me last juice! I must have had somebody's good prayers.
Ah, afther all, an honest man's the noblest work o' God!

epigram

(BOYLE *coughs inside.*)

JOX. Whisht, damn it, he must be inside in bed.

NUG. Inside o' bed or outside of it, he's goin' to pay me for that suit, or
give it back—he'll not climb up my back as easily as he thinks.

JOX. Gwan in at wanst, man, an' get it off him, an' don't be a fool.

NUG. (*going to door left, opening it and looking in*). Ah, don't disturb
yourself, Mr. Boyle; I hope you're not sick?

BOYLE. Th' oul' legs, Mr. Nugent, the oul' legs.

NUG. I just called over to see if you could let me have anything off the
suit?

BOYLE. E-e-e-eh, how much is this it is?

NUG. It's the same as it was at the start—seven pouns.

BOYLE. I'm glad you kem, Mr. Nugent; I want a good heavy top-coat—Irish frieze, if you have it. How much would a top-coat like that be, now?

NUG. About six pouns.

BOYLE. Six pouns—six an' seven, six an' seven is thirteen—that'll be thirteen pouns I'll owe you.

(JOXER *slips the bottle of stout that is on the table into his pocket.* NUGENT *rushes into the room, and returns with suit on his arm; he pauses at the door.*)

NUG. You'll owe me no thirteen pouns. Maybe you think you're betther able to owe it than pay it!

BOYLE (*frantically*). Here, come back to hell ower that—where're you goin' with them clothes o' mine?

NUG. Where am I goin' with them clothes o' yours? Well, I like your damn cheek!

BOYLE. Here, what am I goin' to dhress meself in when I'm goin' out?

NUG. What do I care what you dhress yourself in! You can put yourself in a bolsther cover, if you like.

(*He goes towards the other door, followed by* JOXER.)

JOX. What'll he dhress himself in! Gentleman Jack an' his frieze coat!

(*They go out.*)

BOYLE (*inside*). Ey, Nugent; ey, Mr. Nugent, Mr. Nugent!

(*After a pause* BOYLE *enters hastily, buttoning the braces of his moleskin trousers; his coat and vest are on his arm; he throws these on a chair and hurries to the door on right.*)

BOYLE. Ey, Mr. Nugent, Mr. Nugent!

JOX. (*meeting him at the door*). What's up, what's wrong, Captain?

BOYLE. Nugent's been here an' took away me suit—the only things I had to go out in!

JOX. Tuk your suit—for God's sake! An' what were you doin' while he was takin' them?

BOYLE. I was in bed when he stole in like a thief in the night, an' before I knew even what he was thinkin' of, he whipped them from the chair an' was off like a redshank!

JOX. An' what, in the name o' God, did he do that for?

BOYLE. What did he do it for? How the hell do I know what he done it for?—jealousy an' spite, I suppose.

JOX. Did he not say what he done it for?

BOYLE. Amn't I afther tellin' you that he had them whipped up an' was gone before I could open me mouth?

JOX. That was a very sudden thing to do; there mus' be somethin' behin' it. Did he hear anythin', I wondher?

BOYLE. Did he hear anythin'?—you talk very queer, Joxer—what could he hear?

JOX. About you not gettin' the money, in some way or t'other?

BOYLE. An' what ud prevent me from gettin' th' money?

JOX. That's jus' what I was thinkin'—what ud prevent you from gettin' the money—nothin', as far as I can see.

BOYLE (*looking round for bottle of stout, with an exclamation*). Aw, holy God!

JOX. What's up, Jack?

BOYLE. He must have afther lifted the bottle o' stout that Juno left on the table!

JOX. (*horrified*). Ah no, ah no; he wouldn't be afther doin' that now.

BOYLE. An' who done it then? Juno left a bottle o' stout here, an' it's gone—it didn't walk, did it?

JOX. Oh, that's shockin'; ah, man's inhumanity to man makes countless thousands mourn!

MRS. MAD. (*appearing at the door*). I hope I'm not disturbin' you in any discussion on your forthcomin' legacy—if I may use the word—an' that you'll let me have a barny for a minute or two with you, Mr. Boyle.

BOYLE (*uneasily*). To be sure, Mrs. Madigan—an oul' friend's always welcome.

JOX. Come in the evenin', come in th' mornin'; come when you're assed, or come without warnin', Mrs. Madigan.

BOYLE. Sit down, Mrs. Madigan.

MRS. MAD. (*ominously*). Th' few words I have to say can be said standin'. Puttin' aside all formularies, I suppose you remember me lendin' you some time ago three pouns that I raised on blankets an' furniture in me uncle's?

BOYLE. I remember it well. I have it recorded in me book—three pouns five shillins from Maisie Madigan, raised on articles pawned; an', item: fourpence, given to make up the price of a pint, on th' principle that no bird ever flew on wan wing; all to be repaid at par, when the ship comes home.

MRS. MAD. Well, ever since I shoved in the blankets I've been perishing with th' cowld, an' I've decided, if I'll be too hot in th' nex' world aself, I'm not goin' to be too cowld in this wan; an' consequently, I want me three pouns, if you please.

BOYLE. This is a very sudden demand, Mrs. Madigan, an' can't be met; but I'm willin' to give you a receipt in full, in full.

MRS. MAD. Come on, out with th' money, an' don't be jack-actin'.

BOYLE. You can't get blood out of a turnip, can you?

MRS. MAD. (*rushing over and shaking him*). Gimme me money, y'oul' reprobate, or I'll shake the worth of it out of you!

BOYLE. Ey, houl' on, there; houl' on, there! You'll wait for your money now, me lassie!

MRS. MAD. (*looking around the room and seeing the gramophone*). I'll wait for it, will I? Well, I'll not wait long; if I can't get th' cash, I'll get th' worth of it. (*She catches up the gramophone.*)

BOYLE. Ey, ey, there, wher'r you goin' with that?

MRS. MAD. I'm goin' to th' pawn to get me three quid five shillins; I'll brin' you th' ticket, an' then you can do what you like, me bucko.

BOYLE. You can't touch that, you can't touch that! It's not my property, an' it's not ped for yet!

MRS. MAD. So much th' better. It'll be an ayse to me conscience, for I'm takin' what doesn't belong to you. You're not goin' to be swankin' it like a paycock with Maisie Madigan's money—I'll pull some o' th' gorgeous feathers out o' your tail! (*She goes off with the gramophone.*)

BOYLE. What's th' world comin' to at all? I ass you, Joxer Daly, is there any morality left anywhere?

JOX. I wouldn't ha' believed it, only I seen it with me own two eyes. I didn't think Maisie Madigan was that sort of woman; she has either a sup taken, or she's heard somethin'.

BOYLE. Heard somethin'—about what, if it's not any harm to ass you?

JOX. She must ha' heard some rumour or other that you weren't goin' to get th' money.

BOYLE. Who says I'm not goin' to get th' money?

JOX. Sure, I don't know—I was only sayin'.

BOYLE. Only sayin' what?

JOX. Nothin'.

BOYLE. You were goin' to say somethin'—don't be a twisther.

JOX. (angrily). Who's a twisther?

BOYLE. Why don't you speak your mind, then?

JOX. You never twisted yourself—no, you wouldn't know how!

BOYLE. Did you ever know me to twist; did you ever know me to twist?

JOX. (fiercely). Did you ever do anythin' else! Sure, you can't believe a word that comes out o' your mouth.

BOYLE. Here, get out, ower o' this; I always knew you were a prognosticator an' a procrastinator!

JOX. (going out as JOHNNY comes in). The anchor's weighed, farewell, ree . . . mem . . . ber . . . me. Jacky Boyle, Esquire, infernal rogue an' damned liar.

JOHN. Joxer an' you at it agen?—when are you goin' to have a little respect for yourself, an' not be always makin' a show of us all?

BOYLE. Are you goin' to lecture me now?

JOHN. Is mother back from the doctor yet, with Mary?

(MRS. BOYLE enters; it is apparent from the serious look on her face that something has happened. She takes off her hat and coat without a word and puts them by. She then sits down near the fire, and there is a few moments' pause.)

BOYLE. Well, what did the doctor say about Mary?

MRS. B. (in an earnest manner and with suppressed agitation). Sit down here, Jack; I've something to say to you . . . about Mary.

BOYLE (awed by her manner). About . . . Mary?

MRS. B. Close that door there and sit down here.

BOYLE (closing the door). More throuble in our native land, is it? (He sits down.) Well, what is it?

MRS. B. It's about Mary.

BOYLE. Well, what about Mary—there's nothin' wrong with her, is there?

MRS. B. I'm sorry to say there's a gradle wrong with her.

BOYLE. A gradle wrong with her! (*Peevishly.*) First Johnny an' now Mary; is the whole house goin' to become an hospital! It's not consumption, is it?

MRS. B. No . . . it's not consumption . . . it's worse.

JOHN. Worse! Well, we'll have to get her into some place ower this, there's no one here to mind her.

MRS. B. We'll all have to mind her now. You might as well know now, Johnny, as another time. (*To* BOYLE.) D'ye know what the doctor said to me about her, Jack?

BOYLE. How ud I know—I wasn't there, was I?

MRS. B. He told me to get her married at wanst.

BOYLE. Married at wanst! An' why did he say the like o' that?

MRS. B. Because Mary's goin' to have a baby in a short time.

BOYLE. Goin' to have a baby!—my God, what'll Bentham say when he hears that?

MRS. B. Are you blind, man, that you can't see that it was Bentham that has done this wrong to her?

BOYLE (*passionately*). Then he'll marry her, he'll have to marry her!

MRS. B. You know he's gone to England, an' God knows where he is now.

BOYLE. I'll folly him, I'll folly him, an' bring him back, an' make him do her justice. The scoundrel, I might ha' known what he was, with his yogees an' his prawna!

MRS. B. We'll have to keep it quiet till we see what we can do.

BOYLE. Oh, isn't this a nice thing to come on top o' me, an' the state I'm in! A pretty show I'll be to Joxer an' to that oul' wan, Madigan! Amn't I afther goin' through enough without havin' to go through this!

MRS. B. What you an' I'll have to go through'll be nothin' to what poor Mary'll have to go through; for you an' me is middlin' old, an' most of our years is spent; but Mary'll have maybe forty years to face an' handle, an' every wan of them'll be tainted with a bitther memory.

BOYLE. Where is she? Where is she till I tell her off? I'm tellin' you when I'm done with her she'll be a sorry girl!

MRS. B. I left her in me sister's till I came to speak to you. You'll say nothin' to her, Jack; ever since she left school she's earned her livin', an' your fatherly care never throubled the poor girl.

BOYLE. Gwan, take her part agen her father! But I'll let you see whether I'll say nothin' to her or no! Her an' her readin'! That's more o' th' blasted nonsense that has the house fallin' down on top of us! What did th' likes of her, born in a tenement house, want with readin'? Her readin's afther bringin' her to a nice pass—oh, it's madnin', madnin', madnin'!

MRS. B. When she comes back say nothin' to her, Jack, or she'll leave this place.

BOYLE. Leave this place! Ay, she'll leave this place, an' quick too!

MRS. B. If Mary goes, I'll go with her.

BOYLE. Well, go with her! Well, go, th' pair o' yous! I lived before I seen yous, an' I can live when yous are gone. Isn't this a nice thing to come rollin' in on top o' me afther all your prayin' to St. Anthony an' The Little Flower! An' she's a Child o' Mary, too— I wonder what'll the nuns think of her now? An' it'll be bellows'd all over th' disthrict before you could say Jack Robinson; an' whenever I'm seen they'll whisper, "That's th' father of Mary Boyle that had th' kid be th' swank she used to go with; d'ye know, d'ye know?" To be sure they'll know—more about it than I will meself!

JOHN. She should be dhriven out o' th' house she's brought disgrace on!

MRS. B. Hush, you, Johnny. We needn't let it be bellows'd all over the place; all we've got to do is to leave this place quietly an' go some-where where we're not known, an' nobody'll be th' wiser.

BOYLE. You're talkin' like a two-year-oul', woman. Where'll we get a a place ou' o' this?—places aren't that easily got.

MRS. B. But, Jack, when we get the money . . .

BOYLE. Money—what money?

MRS. B. Why, oul' Ellison's money, of course.

BOYLE. There's no money comin' from oul' Ellison, or any one else. Since you've heard of wan throuble, you might as well hear of another. There's no money comin' to us at all—the Will's a wash-out!

MRS. B. What are you sayin', man—no money?

JOHN. How could it be a wash-out?

BOYLE. The boyo that's afther doin' it to Mary done it to me as well. The thick made out the Will wrong; he said in th' Will, only first cousin an' second cousin, instead of mentionin' our names, an' now any one that thinks he's a first cousin or second cousin t' oul' Ellison can claim the money as well as me, an' they're springin' up in hundreds, an' comin' from America an' Australia, thinkin' to get their whack out of it, while all the time the lawyers is gobblin' it up, till there's not as much as ud buy a stockin' for your lovely daughter's baby!

MRS. B. I don't believe it, I don't believe it, I don't believe it!

JOHN. Why did you say nothin' about this before?

MRS. B. You're not serious, Jack; you're not serious!

BOYLE. I'm tellin' you the scholar, Bentham, made a banjax o' th' Will; instead o' sayin', "th' rest o' me property to be divided between me first cousin, Jack Boyle, an' me second cousin, Mick Finnegan, o' Santhry," he writ down only, "me first an' second cousins," an' the world an' his wife are afther th' property now.

MRS. B. Now I know why Bentham left poor Mary in th' lurch; I can see it all now—oh, is there not even a middlin' honest man left in th' world?

JOHN. (*to* BOYLE). An' you let us run into debt, an' you borreyed money from everybody to fill yourself with beer! An' now you tell us the whole thing's a wash-out! Oh, if it's thrue, I'm done with you, for you're worse than me sisther Mary!

BOYLE. You hole your tongue, d'ye hear? I'll not take any lip from you. Go an' get Bentham if you want satisfaction for all that's afther happenin' us.

JOHN. I won't hole me tongue, I won't hole me tongue! I'll tell you what I think of you, father an' all as you are . . . you . . .

MRS. B. Johnny, Johnny, Johnny, for God's sake, be quiet!

JOHN. I'll not be quiet, I'll not be quiet; he's a nice father, isn't he? Is it any wondher Mary went asthray, when . . .

MRS. B. Johnny, Johnny, for my sake be quiet—for your mother's sake!

BOYLE. I'm goin' out now to have a few dhrinks with th' last few makes I have, an' tell that lassie o' yours not to be here when I come back; for if I lay me eyes on her, I'll lay me hans on her, an' if I lay me hans on her, I won't be accountable for me actions!

JOHN. Take care somebody doesn't lay his hands on you—y' oul' . . .

MRS. B. Johnny, Johnny!

BOYLE (*at door, about to go out*). Oh, a nice son, an' a nicer daughter, I have. (*Calling loudly upstairs.*) Joxer, Joxer, are you there?

JOX. (*from a distance*). I'm here, More . . . ee . . . aar . . . i . . . tee!

BOYLE. I'm goin' down to Foley's—are you comin'?

JOX. Come with you? With that sweet call me heart is stirred; I'm only waiting for the word, an' I'll be with you, like a bird! (BOYLE *and* JOXER *pass the door going out.*)

JOHN. (*throwing himself on the bed*). I've a nice sisther, an' a nice father, there's no bettin' on it. I wish to God a bullet or a bomb had whipped me ou' o' this long ago! Not one o' yous, not one o' yous, have any thought for me!

MRS. B. (*with passionate remonstrance*). If you don't whisht, Johnny, you'll drive me mad. Who has kep' th' home together for the past few years—only me? An' who'll have to bear th' biggest part o' this throuble but me?—but whinin' an' whingin' isn't goin' to do any good.

JOHN. You're to blame yourself for a gradle of it—givin' him his own way in everything, an' never assin' to check him, no matther what he done. Why didn't you look afther th' money? why . . .

(*There is a knock at the door;* MRS. BOYLE *opens it;* JOHNNY *rises on his elbow to look and listen; two men enter.*)

IST. MAN. We've been sent up be th' Manager of the Hibernian Furnishing Co., Mrs. Boyle, to take back the furniture that was got a while ago.

MRS. B. Yous'll touch nothin' here—how do I know who yous are?

IST. MAN (*showing a paper*). There's the ordher, ma'am. (*Reading.*) A chest o' drawers, a table, wan easy an' two ordinary chairs;

wan mirror; wan chesterfield divan, an' a wardrobe an' two vases. (*To his comrade.*) Come on, Bill, it's afther knockin'-off time already.

JOHN. For God's sake, mother, run down to Foley's an' bring father back, or we'll be left without a stick.

(*The men carry out the table.*)

MRS. B. What good would it be?—you heard what he said before he went out.

JOHN. Can't you thry? He ought to be here, an' the like of this goin' on.

(MRS. BOYLE *puts a shawl around her, as* MARY *enters.*)

MARY. What's up, mother? I met men carryin' away the table, an' everybody's talking about us not gettin' the money after all.

MRS. B. Everythin's gone wrong, Mary, everythin'. We're not gettin' a penny out o' the Will, not a penny—I'll tell you all when I come back; I'm goin' for your father. (*She runs out.*)

JOHN. (*to* MARY, *who has sat down by the fire*). It's a wondher you're not ashamed to show your face here, afther what has happened.

(JERRY *enters slowly; there is a look of earnest hope on his face. He looks at* MARY *for a few moments.*)

JER. (*softly*). Mary!

(MARY *does not answer.*)

JER. Mary, I want to speak to you for a few moments, may I?

(MARY *remains silent;* JOHNNY *goes slowly into room on left.*)

JER. Your mother has told me everything, Mary, and I have come to you. . . . I have come to tell you, Mary, that my love for you is greater and deeper than ever. . . .

MARY (*with a sob*). Oh, Jerry, Jerry, say no more; all that is over now; anything like that is impossible now!

JER. Impossible? Why do you talk like that, Mary?

MARY. After all that has happened.

JER. What does it matter what has happened? We are young enough to be able to forget all those things. (*He catches her hand.*) Mary, Mary, I am pleading for your love. With Labour, Mary, humanity is above everything; we are the Leaders in the fight for a new life. I want to forget Bentham, I want to forget that you left me—even for a while.

MARY. Oh, Jerry, Jerry, you haven't the bitter word of scorn for me after all.

JER. (*passionately*). Scorn! I love you, love you, Mary!

MARY (*rising, and looking him in the eyes*). Even though . . .

JER. Even though you threw me over for another man; even though you gave me many a bitter word!

MARY. Yes, yes, I know; but you love me, even though . . . even though . . . I'm . . . goin' . . . goin' . . . (*He looks at her questioningly, and fear gathers in his eyes.*) Ah, I was thinkin' so. . . . You don't know everything!

JER. (*poignantly*). Surely to God, Mary, you don't mean that . . . that . . . that . . .

MARY. Now you know all, Jerry; now you know all!

JER. My God, Mary, have you fallen as low as that?

MARY. Yes, Jerry, as you say, I have fallen as low as that.

JER. I didn't mean it that way, Mary . . . it came on me so sudden, that I didn't mind what I was sayin'. . . . I never expected this—your mother never told me. . . . I'm sorry . . . God knows, I'm sorry for you, Mary.

MARY. Let us say no more, Jerry; I don't blame you for thinkin' it's terrible. . . . I suppose it is. . . . Everybody'll think the same . . . it's only as I expected—your humanity is just as narrow as the humanity of the others.

JER. I'm sorry, all the same. . . . I shouldn't have troubled you. . . . I wouldn't if I'd known. . . . If I can do anything for you . . . Mary . . . I will. (*He turns to go, and halts at the door.*)

MARY. Do you remember, Jerry, the verses you read when you gave the lecture in the Socialist Rooms some time ago, on Humanity's Strife with Nature?

JER. The verses—no; I don't remember them.

MARY. I do. They're runnin' in me head now—

> "An' we felt the power that fashion'd
> All the lovely things we saw,
> That created all the murmur
> Of an everlasting law,

Was a hand of force an' beauty,
With an eagle's tearin' claw.

Then we saw our globe of beauty
Was an ugly thing as well,
A hymn divine whose chorus
Was an agonizin' yell;
Like the story of a demon,
That an angel had to tell;

Like a glowin' picture by a
Hand unsteady, brought to ruin;
Like her craters, if their deadness
Could give life unto the moon;
Like the agonizing horror
Of a violin out of tune."

(*There is a pause, and* DEVINE *goes slowly out.*)

JOHN. (*returning*). Is he gone?

MARY. Yes.

(*The two men re-enter.*)

1ST. MAN. We can't wait any longer for t'oul' fella—sorry, Miss, but we
have to live as well as th' nex' man. (*They carry out some things.*)

JOHN. Oh, isn't this terrible! . . . I suppose you told him everything
. . . couldn't you have waited for a few days? . . . he'd have
stopped th' takin' of the things, if you'd kep' your mouth shut.
Are you burnin' to tell every one of the shame you've brought
on us?

MARY (*snatching up her hat and coat*). Oh, this is unbearable!

(*She rushes out.*)

1ST. MAN (*re-entering*). We'll take the chest o' drawers next—it's the
heaviest.

(*The votive light flickers for a moment, and goes out.*)

JOHN. (*in a cry of fear*). Mother o' God, the light's afther goin' out!

1ST. MAN. You put the win' up me the way you bawled that time. The
oil's all gone, that's all.

JOHN. (*with an agonizing cry*). Mother o' God, there's a shot I'm afther
gettin'!

1ST. MAN. What's wrong with you, man? Is it a fit you're takin'?

JOHN. I'm after feelin' a pain in me breast, like the tearin' by of a bullet!

1ST. MAN. He's goin' mad—it's a wondher they'd leave a chap like that here by himself.

(*Two* IRREGULARS *enter swiftly; they carry revolvers; one goes over to* JOHNNY; *the other covers the two furniture men.*)

1ST. IRREG. (*to the men, quietly and incisively*). Who are you?—what are yous doin' here?—quick!

1ST. MAN. Removin' furniture that's not paid for.

1ST. IRREG. Get over to the other end of the room an' turn your faces to the wall—quick!

(*The two men turn their faces to the wall, with their hands up.*)

2ND. IRREG. (*to* JOHNNY). Come on, Sean Boyle, you're wanted; some of us have a word to say to you.

JOHN. I'm sick, I can't—what do you want with me?

2ND. IRREG. Come on, come on; we've a distance to go, an' haven't much time—come on.

JOHN. I'm an oul' comrade—yous wouldn't shoot an oul' comrade.

2ND. IRREG. Poor Tancred was an oul' comrade o' yours, but you didn't think o' that when you gave him away to the gang that sent him to his grave. But we've no time to waste; come on—here, Dermot, ketch his arm. (*To* JOHNNY.) Have you your beads?

JOHN. Me beads! Why do you ass me that, why do you ass me that?

2ND. IRREG. Go on, go on, march!

JOHN. Are yous goin' to do in a comrade?—look at me arm, I lost it for Ireland.

2ND. IRREG. Commandant Tancred lost his life for Ireland.

JOHN. Sacred Heart of Jesus, have mercy on me! Mother o' God, pray for me—be with me now in the agonies o' death! . . . Hail, Mary, full o' grace . . . the Lord is . . . with Thee.

(*They drag out* JOHNNY BOYLE, *and the curtain falls. When it rises again the most of the furniture is gone.* MARY *and* MRS. BOYLE, *one on each side, are sitting in a darkened room, by the fire; it is an hour later.*)

MRS. B. I'll not wait much longer . . . what did they bring him away in the mothor for? Nugent says he thinks they had guns . . . is me throubles never goin' to be over? . . . If anything ud happen to poor Johnny, I think I'd lose me mind. . . . I'll go to the Police Station, surely they ought to be able to do somethin'.

(*Below is heard the sound of voices.*)

MRS. B. Whisht, is that something? Maybe, it's your father, though when I left him in Foley's he was hardly able to lift his head. Whisht!

(*A knock at the door, and the voice of* MRS. MADIGAN, *speaking very softly.*) Mrs. Boyle, Mrs. Boyle.

(MRS. BOYLE *opens the door.*)

MRS. MAD. Oh, Mrs. Boyle, God an' His Blessed Mother be with you this night!

MRS. B. (*calmly*). What is it, Mrs. Madigan? It's Johnny—something about Johnny.

MRS. MAD. God send it's not, God send it's not Johnny!

MRS. B. Don't keep me waitin', Mrs. Madigan; I've gone through so much lately that I feel able for anything.

MRS. MAD. Two polismen below wantin' you.

MRS. B. Wantin' me; an' why do they want me?

MRS. MAD. Some poor fella's been found, an' they think it's, it's . . .

MRS. B. Johnny, Johnny!

MARY (*with her arms round her mother*). Oh, mother, mother, me poor, darlin' mother.

MRS. B. Hush, hush, darlin'; you'll shortly have your own throuble to bear. (*To* MRS. MADIGAN.) An' why do the polis think it's Johnny, Mrs. Madigan?

MRS. MAD. Because one o' the doctors knew him when he was attendin' with his poor arm.

MRS. B. Oh, it's thrue, then; it's Johnny, it's me son, me own son!

MARY. Oh, it's thrue, it's thrue what Jerry Devine says—there isn't a God, there isn't a God; if there was He wouldn't let these things happen!

MRS. B. Mary, Mary, you mustn't say them things. We'll want all the help we can get from God an' His Blessed Mother now! These things have nothin' to do with the Will o' God. Ah, what can God do agen the stupidity o' men!

MRS. MAD. The polis want you to go with them to the hospital to see the poor body—they're waitin' below.

MRS. B. We'll go. Come, Mary, an' we'll never come back here agen. Let your father furrage for himself now; I've done all I could an' it was all no use—he'll be hopeless till the end of his days. I've got a little room in me sisther's where we'll stop till your throuble is over, an' then we'll work together for the sake of the baby.

MARY. My poor little child that'll have no father!

MRS. B. It'll have what's far betther—it'll have two mothers.

A ROUGH VOICE (*shouting from below*). Are yous goin' to keep us waitin' for yous all night?

MRS. MAD. (*going to the door, and shouting down*). Take your hour, there, take your hour! If yous are in such a hurry, skip off, then, for nobody wants you here—if they did yous wouldn't be found. For you're the same as yous were undher the British Government —never where yous are wanted! As far as I can see, the Polis as Polis, in this city, is Null an' Void!

MRS. B. We'll go, Mary, we'll go; you to see your poor dead brother, an' me to see me poor dead son!

MARY. I dhread it, mother, I dhread it!

MRS. B. I forgot, Mary, I forgot; your poor oul' selfish mother was only thinkin' of herself. No, no, you mustn't come—it wouldn't be good for you. You go on to me sisther's an' I'll face th' ordeal meself. Maybe I didn't feel sorry enough for Mrs. Tancred when her poor son was found as Johnny's been found now—because he was a Die-hard! Ah, why didn't I remember that then he wasn't a Die-hard or a Stater, but only a poor dead son! It's well I remember all that she said—an' it's my turn to say it now: What was the pain I suffered, Johnny, bringin' you into the world to carry you to your cradle, to the pains I'll suffer carryin' you out o' the world to bring you to your grave! Mother o' God, Mother o' God, have pity on us all! Blessed Virgin, where were you when me darlin' son was riddled with bullets, when me darlin' son was riddled with bullets? Sacred Heart o' Jesus, take away our hearts o' stone, and give us hearts o' flesh! Take away this murdherin hate, an' give us Thine own eternal love!

(They all go slowly out.)

(There is a pause; then a sound of shuffling steps on the stairs outside. The door opens and BOYLE *and* JOXER, *both of them very drunk, enter.)*

BOYLE. I'm able to go no farther. . . . Two polis, ey . . . what were they doin' here, I wondher? . . . Up to no good, anyhow . . . an' Juno an' that lovely daughter o' mine with them. *(Taking a sixpence from his pocket and looking at it.)* Wan single, solitary tanner left out of all I borreyed. . . . *(He lets it fall.)* The last o' the Mohicans. . . . The blinds is down, Joxer, the blinds is down!

JOX. *(walking unsteadily across the room, and anchoring at the bed).* Put all . . . your throubles . . . in your oul' kit-bag . . . an' smile . . . smile . . . smile!

BOYLE. The counthry'll have to steady itself. . . . It's goin' . . . to hell. . . . Where'r all . . . the chairs . . . gone to . . . steady itself, Joxer. . . . Chairs'll . . . have to . . . steady themselves. . . . No matther . . . what any one may . . . say. . . . Irelan' sober . . . is Irelan' . . . free.

JOX. *(stretching himself on the bed).* Chains . . . an' . . . slaveree . . . that's a darlin' motto . . . a daaarlin' . . . motto!

BOYLE. If th' worst comes . . . to th' worse . . . I can join a . . . flyin' . . . column. . . . I done . . . me bit . . . in Easther Week . . . had no business . . . to . . . be . . . there . . . but Captain Boyle's Captain Boyle!

JOX. Breathes there a man with soul . . . so . . . de . . . ad . . . this . . . me . . . o . . . wn, me nat . . . ive l . . . an'!

BOYLE *(subsiding into a sitting posture on the floor).* Commandant Kelly died . . . in them . . . arms . . . Joxer. . . . Tell me Volunteer Butties . . . says he . . . that . . . I died for . . . Irelan'!

JOX. D'jever rade Willie . . . Reilly . . . an' his own . . . Colleen . . . Bawn? It's a darlin' story, a daarlin' story!

BOYLE. I'm telling you . . . Joxer . . . th' whole worl's . . . in a terr . . . ible state o' . . . chassis!

(CURTAIN)

Eugene O'Neill

► At home and abroad, Eugene O'Neill is America's greatest dramatist. His plays have been translated into most of the important European languages and have been given almost continuous performances in the theatres of the world. No other American has matched him in the scope of his subjects, or in the power and depth of his probings into the tortuous secrets of the inner man. His dramas have produced unrivalled excitement as theatrical experiences, and this same magic intoxicant is still potent on the printed page. Though the plays are American, they are restricted by no national barriers. Wherever the human heart is disturbed and searching out the mystery of its unrest, there is the locale for O'Neill's dramas. Their universality is proclaimed by their success at the same time in America, Russia, Sweden, Germany, and England. Their native quality received the unprecedented, official recognition of three Pulitzer awards (1920, 1922, 1928); their international appeal was formally attested by the Nobel committee when it awarded O'Neill the prize in literature in 1936.

O'Neill brought to the theatre a unique experience. For one with his serious, brooding temperament and dramatic gifts, it was an experience rich in substance. It might have destroyed him, and apparently came close to doing so. But he had enough genius to take command at the right moment and shape his experience into art. A brief chart of his career reads like the outline for an O'Neill play, except that the plays generally end in frustration.

He was born October 16, 1888, quite fittingly at the Barrett House on Broadway at Forty-third Street in New York City. His father was a gifted actor who became famous for his long and successful years on the road with his own company in *The Count of Monte Cristo*. O'Neill said that his father cleared fifty thousand dollars a season with this play.

O'Neill immediately began a life that led him alternately in and out of the theatre. During his first seven years, he was carried by his itinerant parents to all the larger towns of the United States. Then until he was thirteen he was placed in various boarding schools. He graduated from Betts Academy at Stamford, Connecticut, in 1906, and entered Princeton the following autumn. Near the end of his freshman year he was suspended for irregularities of conduct—according to the best tradition, for tossing a beer-bottle through the window of the president's campus home. The president was Woodrow Wilson. By the time his suspension had expired, O'Neill was completely alienated from academic life and ready to assault the world on its hardest terms.

O'Neill's college career was ended abruptly, but his education for his future work was just beginning, though he did not know this at the time. It was divided into four episodes which roughly correspond to the freshman-to-senior sequence of the university curriculum. After a brief period as secretary for a mail-order jewelry firm, and following his first marriage, O'Neill went gold-hunting in Honduras with a mining engineer—the first of those "beyond the horizon" journeys over the sea in search of himself and the romance which eluded him at home. He found malaria instead, and returned to the United States. He then became assistant manager of the road company starring his father and Viola Allen in *The White Sister,* and stayed with it on tour from St. Louis to Boston. At the end of the season he boarded a Norwegian boat and sailed for sixty-five days to Buenos Aires on his second venture. There he tried again to become mercantile minded, successively with Westinghouse, Swift, and Singer, but without success. He went to the water-front to live; he worked occasionally, and saw and heard about life in the raw, unrefined lump. He saw enough characters and heard enough yarns to supply a writer like Jack London with material for a lifetime.

But this life soon palled, and O'Neill shipped as mule-tender on a steamer bound from Buenos Aires to Durban, Africa, where he could not even land because he was destitute. He sailed back to the Argentine, was reduced to beachcombing, and finally signed on a British tramp steamer. He got back into New York in 1911. He was turning twenty-three.

O'Neill lived in New York in a three-dollar-a-month room at a vermin-invaded, water-front dive kept by "Jimmy the Priest." He was penniless, and apparently unwilling to be aided or supervised by his family. He finally shipped again for his fourth venture, this time as an able seaman on the American liner *New York,* bound for Southampton. On his return, he joined his father's company in New Orleans, and took a minor part in the ubiquitous *Monte Cristo,* learning his part en route to Ogden, Utah, where he first became an actor. He had acquired an education somewhat different from that offered him at Princeton.

One other element was needed: the training necessary to give meaning to these experiences through the medium of words. This was supplied to order by Frederick P. Latimer of the New London *Telegraph,* who gave him a job as reporter in 1912 and printed some of his verses in a column on the editorial page from August 26 to December 9. He encouraged O'Neill; he was the first man to recognize the possibilities in the wayward boy. But the terrific beating O'Neill had given his constitution in his vagabond, drinking, carousing years now claimed its price. He developed a soft spot in his lung, and had to go to Gaylord Farm sanitarium at Wallingford, Connecticut, an account of which appears in the first part of *The Straw.*

O'Neill was now in his twenty-fifth year, and old enough to consider what this furious life of his was all about. The enforced leisure gave him time to ponder, and his resolution and understanding began to take form. He had written just enough to excite his own interest. When he left the sanitarium in the late spring, he went to live with an English family on the Connecticut coast, where he spent more than a year building up his health, and reading intensively the things he had missed that now interested him. He specialized in the great dramatists of Greece and England, in Ibsen, and particularly in Strindberg whose intense psychological plays fascinated him. He also practiced writing and turned out "eleven one-acters, two long plays, and some verse." He was ready for technical training and advice on how to transmute his experience into dramas. The best place for such instruction was the playwriting course at Harvard University.

O'Neill accordingly spent the year 1914-1915 in Professor Baker's 47 Workshop. It is not surprising that a man of O'Neill's age, type, experience, and certainty of direction found the procedure disappointing—another beyond-the-horizon quest. He was somewhat restive under the class routine. He seems to have had the scorn of a socially timid but older and more widely experienced young man for his fellow students in the course. They were trying to make plays without knowledge. When a member of the class went to the blackboard to chart the plot development of a play by Augustus Thomas, O'Neill got up and walked out. It was a characteristic gesture of impatience with the conventional, unimaginative stage techniques and their dull and partial representation of life. O'Neill didn't actually say so, but it seems obvious that he sensed the artificiality and awkwardness of the whole procedure. Everything was backwards. The students were being told how to write before they had anything to say. The exercises did not stem naturally out of a genuine creative problem. O'Neill, on the contrary, was burdened with the raw flesh of what he had seen and lived and known, and he was trying to find an effective way to give it life through the medium of drama. He had great respect for Professor Baker, but he felt that the results of the course were, for him, largely negative.

O'Neill may have carried away more than he could specify at the time; but, fortunately for him, there was at that moment a ferment in the air, and a group of play-conscious intellectuals whose interests were similar to his own. This was the Greenwich Village group who foregathered at Provincetown during the summers, beginning in 1915, and there at the improvised Wharf Theatre played several one-act pieces.

This group of young spirits included George Cram Cook, Susan Glaspell, Mary Heaton Vorse, Wilbur Daniel Steele, Harry Kemp, Hutchins Hapgood, and others. They represented in their fashion the belated arrival in America of the European currents that had produced the Théâtre Libre, the Moscow Art Theatre, and other such organizations for the advancement of the theatre.

O'Neill joined the Provincetown, as they called themselves, in the summer of 1916. Following his year at Harvard he had lived in Greenwich Village where he had learned to criticize the sorry scheme of things, where he had made acquaintance with the radical laborites, the Negroes and Italians, and had added to his collection of characters later to be used in his plays. On invitation from Susan Glaspell, he gave *Bound East for Cardiff* to a gathering of the Provincetown to read. "Then," said Miss Glaspell, "we knew what we were for." They produced this one-act play at the Wharf, and, later in the summer, a second play by O'Neill called *Thirst*. The author acted a small part in each. Both plays created a powerful and original effect on the spectators.

When the group returned to the Village, they opened the Playwright's Theatre at 139 Macdougal Street in November with

Bound East for Cardiff, in which O'Neill again played the Second Mate. They also produced O'Neill's *Before Breakfast, Fog,* and *The Sniper.* In November, 1917, they opened with his *The Long Voyage Home,* and followed on the second bill with his *Ile,* and later with *The Rope.* In the autumn of 1918 they presented his *Where the Cross Is Made,* and *The Moon of the Caribbees;* in 1919 *The Dreamy Kid;* and in 1920 *Exorcism.* Then, on February 2, 1920, at the up-town Morosco Theatre, John D. Williams produced *Beyond the Horizon,* the Pulitzer Prize play of the year, the second play to receive that award. On the evening of November 1, 1920, the Provincetown Players presented *The Emperor Jones.* Then came *Diff'rent,* on December 27; *Gold,* June 1, 1921; and a second Pulitzer Prize drama, *Anna Christie,* November 2, 1921. Thus with phenomenal timeliness the Provincetown had provided O'Neill with a perfect experimental laboratory theatre, and an assured subscription audience, the like of which no other American playwright ever enjoyed. O'Neill paid tribute to them for their aid. In a few short seasons he emerged as the foremost American dramatist.

The career and achievements of O'Neill since that time have been international news. The Provincetown Players produced *The Hairy Ape* (1922), *All God's Chillun Got Wings* (1924), and *Desire Under the Elms* (1924). The Theatre Guild began its presentations of O'Neill with *Marco Millions* and *Strange Interlude,* both in January, 1928, and has continued to be his producer. He himself has generally stayed away from New York and the theatre. He has lived at Ridgefield, Connecticut; in a chateau in France; in a gleaming white mansion on the water's edge in Bermuda; on an island off the coast of Georgia; and on his present estate, Tao House, in Contra Costa County, California, in the hills back of Berkeley.

The closest possible unity and interlinking exist between O'Neill's career as thus briefly sketched and the plays for which he is celebrated. That is a subject for special study in the psychology of creative endeavor in drama. But the effects of O'Neill's natural rebelliousness and prodigality, his dreamy passion, his knowledge of all sorts and conditions of men, and his absorption and synthesis of the discontents and the intellectual interests of Europe and America in the second and third decades of the century are visible in some form in every detail of his work. The plays themselves are so rich in interest from so many points of view that it becomes embarrassing to summarize them or to arrange them into groups.

Their themes and subject matter are extraordinarily varied. The early one-act plays, and certain scenes in the later and longer dramas, were, for the most part, concerned with sailors and the sea realistically presented. The men are rough of manner and of speech; they are violent and hard in action; they are lonely and tormented by some deep-seated malaise; and they have their moments of agitation in the presence of such beauties as life on board ship affords: "the mournful cadence of the song from the shore" that stirs Smitty's memories under the moon of the Caribbees and drives him to drink; Paddy's thoughts in *The Hairy Ape* of "clippers wid tall masts touching the sky" making sail at dawn; of the sound of a chanty song; of a glimpse of the land astern "sinking low and dying out"; or the thrill of a ship scudding south at night under the moon and the stars.

The first five long plays, all individual and searching with an energy new to American drama, were presented in quick succession. *Beyond the Horizon,* a tragedy of fate, illusion, and human frustration, was produced in February, 1920. *The Emperor Jones, Diff'rent, Gold,* and *Anna Christie* were all produced within one year—November 3, 1920, to November 2, 1921. *The Emperor Jones* was a triumph in early American expressionism.

It showed O'Neill's technical versatility in flinging on the visible stage in externalized symbols the inner, fear-stricken life, or unconscious, atavistic self of the ex-Pullman porter, the Emperor Jones. The melodramatic devices of the silver bullet and the incessant beat of the tom-tom on Jones's night of penalty and terror, together with the sequence of short, surcharged scenes, built up the entire play to a terrific climax. *Anna Christie* dealt in straightforward style with the redemption of the fallen and bedraggled Anna through the power of a sailor's love and the tradition of the sea. It was set on the fog-drenched water-front that O'Neill knew so well, and it gave a sympathetic character portrayal of Anna's father, Chris, now retired to a barge, but with a full understanding of the sinister power of "old davil sea." The character of the father, who divides the play with Anna, was a remarkable example of how O'Neill salvaged treasure out of the sunken days along the wharfs. He had known the original of Chris at Jimmy the Priest's.

These three plays, with such faults as they have, were genuine achievements. *Diff'rent,* a study of a sex-inhibited New England spinster, is interesting as a forerunner of the greater plays to come on the same subject in the same locale. *The Hairy Ape* was more ambitious in theme and technique. It contained O'Neill's nostalgic tribute to the romance of the sea, and the contrast between the age of sails and the age of steel and steam. It called upon symbols, after the fashion of expressionism, to enlarge its suggestiveness. It presented Yank's concept of "belonging," and the deterioration of the muscular stoker when he lost his conviction of the importance of his place in society. He discovered that he was only a hairy ape, hired and exploited by the idle people represented by the fretful Mildred, who called him a "filthy beast" and who fainted when she saw him at work in the stokehole of a transatlantic liner.

As a dramatist O'Neill was more concerned with personal

psychological problems in the Strindberg manner than with the social problems that aroused so many of his contemporaries. His somewhat desperate probings of the disturbed inner lives of his characters led him to call still further upon symbolistic methods to transcend the limitations of objective realism on the stage. He wrote four notable plays of this type. They are sharp and clear on certain points, baffling if not confused on others. The most subtle and elusive, as well as the most elaborately symbolic, was *The Great God Brown* (1926). This was the play in which O'Neill introduced his characters with masked faces to represent the personality with which they confront the world; when they lay bare their unspoken thoughts in static soliloquy they remove their masks. The dualism is also represented by the opposed disciplines of Dionysus (pagan acceptance of life) and St. Anthony (the Christian denial of life), in the central character whose name is Dion Anthony; and in the contrasting characters of Marguerite and Cybele, represented by Margaret and Cybel. The symbolism extends through all the details of the play, including the revelation of Brown as "the visionless demi-god of our new materialistic myth—Success," as O'Neill himself explained.

Lazarus Laughed, a literary drama written in 1927, is O'Neill's attempt to do what Browning and others had done before him: to show how a glimpse over the threshold of death affected Lazarus, and how it modified his view of life and his relations with those around him. *Dynamo* (1929) was the beginning of an ambitious, perhaps even pretentious, trilogy on man, God, and the machine age—the new and cruel god (or goddess) here being a dynamo. The play failed and O'Neill abandoned the scheme. Some of its threads of interest were combined with the dual personality theme of *The Great God Brown* to produce *Days Without End,* or John Loving's struggle with his psyche, who stands beside him at all times to represent his demon other-nature. His quest for peace and certainty after the illness of his wife leads him in the final scene to prostrate himself at the foot of the Cross and pour out his soul in faith and surrender; whereupon the corpse of his attendant other-self falls with arms outstretched "like a cripple's testimonial offering in a shrine." These exceedingly interesting and daringly experimental plays were all failures on the stage. Yet they have been among the most widely discussed of O'Neill dramas.

Of the various other plays, three represent O'Neill's supreme achievements to date. They are the dramas of sex repressions and psychological involvements so deeply studied as to become genuine tragedies: *Desire Under the Elms* (1924), *Strange Interlude* (1928), and *Mourning Becomes Electra* (1931).

The tragic dignity of *Desire Under the Elms* was somewhat tarnished by the reactions of the audiences of the 1920's which perverted the play into a *succès de scandale;* but with the passing of the years it has emerged as one of the important tragedies in American drama. Its movement is relentless. It gathers in strength from the thrice-entangled web of human emotions which it weaves and resolves.

Strange Interlude is in nine acts, which require a playing time from late afternoon through an evening. It is the study of the possessive attachment of a father for his daughter. It shows how her own life was frustrated and repressed by a denial of life when her lover went to war, and how, after an aberrant interlude of nervous disorder, she was awakened, and found fulfillment in a collective relationship with her lover, her husband, her son, and the sublimated image of her father in the person of "dear old Charlie." Instead of masks, O'Neill used the ancient device of the monologue to permit the characters to speak to the audience their secret thoughts, which in normal life would be kept in good-mannered concealment.

Mourning Becomes Electra went even further in dramatizing Freudian inner turmoil. O'Neill took an American story about the sinister New England House of Mannon at the close of the Civil War, and modeled it on the outlines of the tragic events in the Greek House of Atreus. He substituted a "modern psychological approximation of the Greek sense of fate" in the belief that this motivation might bring to life again the force that was lost when "belief in gods and supernatural retribution" was abandoned.

Following this series of searching and tragic plays, O'Neill surprised and delighted his world audience by writing a gentle comedy, *Ah, Wilderness!* (1933). He gave it a title from *The Rubaiyat* to suggest its mood and substance of wine and love and song as seen through the unfolding experiences of a boy almost seventeen with "a restless, apprehensive, defiant, shy, dreamy, self-conscious intelligence about him." It re-creates with tenderness and sympathy the almost forgotten world of 1906, when O'Neill was about the same age as Richard Miller of his play. It brings to life the day when the writings of Oscar Wilde and Swinburne were thought wicked, when the popularity of Omar was at its peak, and when the name of a new dramatist called Bernard Shaw meant to Mrs. Miller a vile play but to her young son "the greatest playwright alive today. . . ."

The crisis in the boy's life is treated with respect but not as a world-shattering tragedy. It is the kind of experience a normal family lives through and resolves with patience, understanding, and a little common sense. Though it is pitched in the comic vein, it is excellent O'Neill, and takes its place among the treasured plays of our time.

It had been written rapidly and almost without effort while O'Neill was struggling to complete the complicated, ambitious, and not very successful *Days Without End* (1934). The Theatre Guild produced it in 1933, George Cohan starred in the part of Nat Miller, and enthusiastic audiences supported it for two years, making it one of the greatest successes in the Guild's history.

In retrospect, *Ah, Wilderness!,* which seemed only a happy interlude in O'Neill's great creative career, actually marked its close. He continued to write steadily until his health failed him. The press reported from time to time during the 1930's that he was composing a series of plays about the growth and development of America, and even announced tentative plans for their production. They have not yet reached the public on stage or in print.

There was much excitement in 1946 when O'Neill again produced and published a new play called *The Iceman Cometh* (dated 1939 by the author). It was not one of the series, but a single long play set in Harry Hope's back room and bar, "a cheap ginmill of the five-cent whiskey, last-resort variety situated on the downtown West Side of New York," in the summer 1912. The characters, the mood, and the "beyond the horizon" dreams of the outcast and the defeated suggest the O'Neill of the 1920's. The play was interesting and distinguished, like all of his writings, but not overpowering. *A Moon for the Misbegotten* was given try-out production the following season. It was confusing to audiences, it was severely criticized by reviewers as unformed and unconvincing, and it was withdrawn without a New York performance. It has recently been published.

AH, WILDERNESS!

Characters

NAT MILLER, *owner of the* Evening Globe
ESSIE, *his wife*
ARTHUR, *their son*
RICHARD, *their son*
MILDRED, *their daughter*
TOMMY, *their son*
SID DAVIS, *Essie's brother, reporter on the* Waterbury Standard
LILY MILLER, *Nat's sister*
DAVID MCCOMBER, *dry-goods merchant*
MURIEL MCCOMBER, *his daughter*
WINT SELBY, *a classmate of Arthur's at Yale*
BELLE
NORA
BARTENDER
SALESMAN

Scenes

ACT ONE: *Sitting-room of the Miller home in a large small-town in Connecticut—early morning, July 4th, 1906*

ACT TWO: *Dining-room of the Miller home—evening of the same day*

ACT THREE, SCENE I: *Back room of a bar in a small hotel—10 o'clock the same night*

SCENE II: *Same as Act One—a little after 11 o'clock the same night*

ACT FOUR, SCENE I: *The Miller sitting-room—about 1 o'clock the following afternoon*

SCENE II: *A strip of beach along the harbor—about 9 o'clock that night*

SCENE III: *Same as Scene One—the sitting-room—about 10 o'clock the same night*

ACT ONE

SCENE—*Sitting-room of the* MILLER *home in a large small-town in Connecticut—about 7:30 in the morning of July 4th, 1906.*

*The room is fairly large, homely looking and cheerful in the morning
sunlight, furnished with scrupulous medium-priced tastelessness
of the period. Beneath the two windows at left, front, a sofa with
silk and satin cushions stands against the wall. At rear of sofa, a
bookcase with glass doors, filled with cheap sets, extends along
the remaining length of wall. In the rear wall, left, is a double
doorway with sliding doors and portières, leading into a dark,
windowless, back parlor. At right of this doorway, another bookcase, this time a small, open one, crammed with boys' and girls'
books and the best-selling novels of many past years—books the
family really have read. To the right of this bookcase is the mate
of the double doorway at its left, with sliding doors and portières,
this one leading to a well-lighted front parlor. In the right wall,
rear, a screen door opens on a porch. Farther forward in this wall
are two windows, with a writing desk and a chair between them.
At center is a big, round table with a green-shaded reading lamp,
the cord of the lamp running up to one of five sockets in the
chandelier above. Five chairs are grouped about the table—three
rockers at left, right, and right rear of it, two armchairs at rear
and left rear. A medium-priced, inoffensive rug covers most of the
floor. The walls are papered white with a cheerful, ugly blue
design.*

*Voices are heard in a conversational tone from the dining-room beyond
the back parlor, where the family are just finishing breakfast.
Then* MRS. MILLER's *voice, raised commandingly,* "Tommy! Come
back here and finish your milk!" *At the same moment* TOMMY
*appears in the doorway from the back parlor—a chubby, sun-
burnt boy of eleven with dark eyes, blond hair wetted and plas-
tered down in a part, and a shiny, good-natured face, a rim of
milk visible about his lips. Bursting with bottled-up energy and
a longing to get started on the Fourth, he nevertheless has hesi-
tated obediently at his mother's call.*

TOM. (*calls back pleadingly*). Aw, I'm full, Ma. And I said excuse me and you said all right. (*His* FATHER'*s voice is heard speaking to his* MOTHER. *Then she calls:* "All right, Tommy," *and* TOMMY *asks eagerly.*) Can I go out now?

MO.'S VOICE (*correctingly*). May I!

TOM. (*fidgeting, but obediently*). May I, Ma?

MO.'S VOICE. Yes. (TOMMY *jumps for the screen door to the porch at right like a sprinter released by the starting shot.*)

FA.'S VOICE (*shouts after him*). But you set off your crackers away from the house, remember! (*But* TOMMY *is already through the screen door, which he leaves open behind him.*)

(*A moment later the family appear from the back parlor, coming from the dining-room. First are* MILDRED *and* ARTHUR. MILDRED *is fifteen, tall and slender, with big, irregular features, resembling her father to the complete effacing of any pretense at prettiness. But her big, gray eyes are beautiful; she has vivacity and a fetching smile, and everyone thinks of her as an attractive girl. She is dressed in shirt-waist and skirt in the fashion of the period.*

(ARTHUR, *the eldest of the Miller children who are still living home, is nineteen. He is tall, heavy, barrel-chested and muscular, the type of football linesman of that period, with a square, stolid face, small blue eyes and thick sandy hair. His manner is solemnly collegiate. He is dressed in the latest college fashion of that day, which has receded a bit from the extreme of preceding years, but still runs to padded shoulders and pants half-pegged at the top, and so small at their wide-cuffed bottoms that they cannot be taken off with shoes on.*)

MILD. (*as they appear—inquisitively*). Where are you going today, Art?

ART. (*with superior dignity*). That's my business. (*He ostentatiously takes from his pocket a tobacco pouch with a big Y and class numerals stamped on it, and a heavy bulldog briar pipe with silver Y and numerals, and starts filling the pipe.*)

MILD. (*teasingly*). Bet I know, just the same! Want me to tell you her initials? E. R.! (*She laughs.* ARTHUR, *pleased by this insinuation at his lady-killing activities, yet finds it beneath his dignity to reply. He goes to the table, lights his pipe and picks up the local*

*morning paper, and slouches back into the armchair at left rear
of table, beginning to whistle "Oh, Waltz Me Around Again,
Willie" as he scans the headlines.* MILDRED *sits on the sofa at left,
front.*)

(*Meanwhile, their mother and their* AUNT LILY, *their father's sister, have
appeared, following them from the back parlor.* MRS. MILLER *is
around fifty, a short, stout woman with fading light-brown hair
sprinkled with gray, who must have been decidedly pretty as a
girl in a round-faced, cute, small-featured, wide-eyed fashion. She
has big brown eyes, soft and maternal—a bustling, mother-of-a-
family manner. She is dressed in shirtwaist and skirt.*

(LILY MILLER, *her sister-in-law, is forty-two, tall, dark and thin. She
conforms outwardly to the conventional type of old-maid school
teacher, even to wearing glasses. But behind the glasses her gray
eyes are gentle and tired, and her whole atmosphere is one of shy
kindliness. Her voice presents the greatest contrast to her appearance—soft and full of sweetness. She, also, is dressed in a shirt-
waist and skirt.*)

MRS. MILL. (*as they appear*). Getting milk down him is like— (*Suddenly she is aware of the screen door standing half open.*) Goodness, look at that door he's left open! The house will be alive with
flies! (*Rushing out to shut it.*) I've told him again and again—
and that's all the good it does! It's just a waste of breath! (*She
slams the door shut.*)

LILY (*smiling*). Well, you can't expect a boy to remember to shut doors
—on the Fourth of July. (*She goes diffidently to the straight-
backed chair before the desk at right, front, leaving the comfortable chairs to the others.*)

MRS. MILL. That's you all over, Lily—always making excuses for him.
You'll have him spoiled to death in spite of me. (*She sinks in
rocker at right of table.*) Phew, I'm hot, aren't you? This is going
to be a scorcher. (*She picks up a magazine from the table and
begins to rock, fanning herself.*)

(*Meanwhile, her husband and her brother have appeared from the back
parlor, both smoking cigars.* NAT MILLER *is in his late fifties, a tall,
dark, spare man, a little stoop-shouldered, more than a little bald,*

dressed with an awkward attempt at sober respectability imposed upon an innate heedlessness of clothes. His long face has large, irregular, undistinguished features, but he has fine, shrewd, humorous gray eyes.

(SID DAVIS, *his brother-in-law, is forty-five, short and fat, bald-headed, with the Puckish face of a Peck's Bad Boy who has never grown up. He is dressed in what had once been a very natty loud light suit but is now a shapeless and faded nondescript in cut and color.*)

SID (*as they appear*). Oh, I like the job first rate, Nat. Waterbury's a nifty old town with the lid off, when you get to know the ropes. I rang in a joke in one of my stories that tickled the folks there pink. Waterwagon—Waterbury—Waterloo!

MILL. (*grinning*). Darn good!

SID (*pleased*). I thought it was pretty fair myself. (*Goes on a bit ruefully, as if oppressed by a secret sorrow.*) Yes, you can see life in Waterbury, all right—that is, if you're looking for life in Waterbury!

MRS. MILL. What's that about Waterbury, Sid?

SID. I was saying it's all right in its way—but there's no place like home.

(*As if to punctuate this remark, there begins a series of bangs from just beyond the porch outside, as TOMMY inaugurates his celebration by setting off a package of firecrackers. The assembled family jump in their chairs.*)

MRS. MILL. That boy! (*She rushes to the screen door and out on the porch, calling*) Tommy! You mind what your Pa told you! You take your crackers out in the back yard, you hear me!

ART. (*frowning scornfully*). Fresh kid! He did it on purpose to scare us.

MILL. (*grinning through his annoyance*). Darned youngster! He'll have the house afire before the day's out.

SID (*grins and sings*).

> "Dunno what ter call 'im
> But he's mighty like a Rose—velt."

(*They all laugh.*)

LILY. Sid, you Crazy! (SID *beams at her.* MRS. MILLER *comes back from the porch, still fuming.*)

MRS. MILL. Well, I've made him go out back at last. Now we'll have a little peace. (*As if to contradict this, the bang of firecrackers and torpedoes begins from the rear of the house, left, and continues at intervals throughout the scene, not nearly so loud as the first explosion, but sufficiently emphatic to form a disturbing punctuation to the conversation.*)

MILL. Well, what's on the tappee for all of you today? Sid, you're coming to the Sachem Club picnic with me, of course.

SID (*a bit embarrassedly*). You bet. I mean I'd like to, Nat—that is, if—

MRS. MILL. (*regarding her brother with smiling suspicion*). Hmm! I know what that Sachem Club picnic's always meant!

LILY (*breaks in in a forced joking tone that conceals a deep earnestness*). No, not this time, Essie. Sid's a reformed character since he's been on the paper in Waterbury. At least, that's what he swore to me last night.

SID (*avoiding her eyes, humiliated—joking it off*). Pure as the driven snow, that's me. They're running me for president of the W.C.-T.U. (*They all laugh.*)

MRS. MILL. Sid, you're a caution. You turn everything into a joke. But you be careful, you hear? We're going to have dinner in the evening tonight, you know—the best shore dinner you ever tasted and I don't want you coming home—well, not able to appreciate it.

LILY. Oh, I know he'll be careful today. Won't you, Sid?

SID (*more embarrassed than ever—joking it off melodramatically*). Lily, I swear to you if any man offers me a drink, I'll kill him—that is, if he changes his mind! (*They all laugh except* LILY, *who bites her lip and stiffens.*)

MRS. MILL. No use talking to him, Lily. You ought to know better by this time. We can only hope for the best.

MILL. Now, you women stop picking on Sid. It's the Fourth of July and even a downtrodden newspaperman has a right to enjoy himself when he's on his holiday.

MRS. MILL. I wasn't thinking only of Sid.

MILL. (*with a wink at the others*). What, are you insinuating I ever—?

MRS. MILL. Well, to do you justice, no, not what you'd really call— But

I've known you to come back from this darned Sachem Club picnic— Well, I didn't need any little bird to whisper that you'd been some place besides to the well! (*She smiles good-naturedly.* MILLER *chuckles.*)

SID (*after a furtive glance at the stiff and silent* LILY—*changes the subject abruptly by turning to* ARTHUR). How are you spending the festive Fourth, Boola-Boola? (ARTHUR *stiffens dignifiedly.*)

MILD. (*teasingly*). I can tell you, if he won't.

MRS. MILL. (*smiling*). Off to the Rands', I suppose.

ART. (*with dignity*). I and Bert Turner are taking Elsie and Ethel Rand canoeing. We're going to have a picnic lunch on Strawberry Island. And this evening I'm staying at the Rands' for dinner.

MILL. You're accounted for, then. How about you, Mid?

MILD. I'm going to the beach to Anne Culver's.

ART. (*sarcastically*). Of course, there won't be any boys present! Johnny Dodd, for example?

MILD. (*giggles—then with a coquettish toss of her head*). Pooh! what do I care for him? He's not the only pebble on the beach.

MILL. Stop your everlasting teasing, you two. How about you and Lily, Essie?

MRS. MILL. I don't know. I haven't made any plans. Have you, Lily?

LILY (*quietly*). No. Anything you want to do.

MRS. MILL. Well, I thought we'd just sit around and rest and talk.

MILL. You can gossip any day. This is the Fourth. Now, I've got a better suggestion than that. What do you say to an automobile ride? I'll get out the Buick and we'll drive around town and out to the lighthouse and back. Then Sid and I will let you off here, or anywhere you say, and we'll go on to the picnic.

MRS. MILL. I'd love it. Wouldn't you, Lily?

LILY. It would be nice.

MILL. Then, that's all settled.

SID (*embarrassedly*). Lily, want to come with me to the fireworks display at the beach tonight?

MRS. MILL. That's right, Sid. You take her out. Poor Lily never has any fun, always sitting home with me.

LILY (*flustered and grateful*). I—I'd like to, Sid, thank you. (*Then an apprehensive look comes over her face.*) Only not if you come home—you know.

SID (*again embarrassed and humiliated—again joking it off, solemnly*). Evil-minded, I'm afraid, Nat. I hate to say it of your sister. (*They all laugh. Even* LILY *cannot suppress a smile.*)

ART. (*with heavy jocularity*). Listen, Uncle Sid. Don't let me catch you and Aunt Lily spooning on a bench tonight—or it'll be my duty to call a cop!

(SID *and* LILY *both look painfully embarrassed at this, and the joke falls flat, except for* MILDRED *who can't restrain a giggle at the thought of these two ancients spooning.*)

MRS. MILL. (*rebukingly*). Arthur!

MILL. (*dryly*). That'll do you. Your education in kicking a football around Yale seems to have blunted your sense of humor.

MRS. MILL. (*suddenly—startledly*). But where's Richard? We're forgetting all about him. Why, where is that boy? I thought he came in with us from breakfast.

MILD. I'll bet he's off somewhere writing a poem to Muriel McComber, the silly! Or pretending to write one. I think he just copies—

ART. (*looking back toward the dining-room*). He's still in the dining-room, reading a book. (*Turning back—scornfully.*) Gosh, he's always reading now. It's not my idea of having a good time in vacation.

MILL. (*caustically*). He read his school books, too, strange as that may seem to you. That's why he came out top of his class. I'm hoping before you leave New Haven they'll find time to teach you reading is a good habit.

MRS. MILL. (*sharply*). That reminds me, Nat. I've been meaning to speak to you about those awful books Richard is reading. You've got to give him a good talking to— (*She gets up from her chair.*) I'll go up and get them right now. I found them where he'd hid them on the shelf in his wardrobe. You just wait till you see what— (*She bustles off, rear right, through the front parlor.*)

MILL. (*plainly not relishing whatever is coming—to* SID *grumblingly*). Seems to me she might wait until the Fourth is over before bringing up— (*Then with a grin.*) I know there's nothing to it, anyway. When I think of the books I used to sneak off and read when I was a kid.

SID. Me, too. I suppose Dick is deep in Nick Carter or Old Cap Collier.

MILL. No, he passed that period long ago. Poetry's his red meat nowadays, I think—love poetry—and socialism, too, I suspect, from some dire declarations he's made. (*Then briskly.*) Well, might as well get him on the carpet. (*He calls.*) Richard. (*No answer—louder.*) Richard. (*No answer—then in a bellow.*) Richard!

ART. (*shouting*). Hey, Dick, wake up! Pa's calling you.

RICH.'s VOICE (*from the dining-room*) All right. I'm coming.

MILL. Darn him! When he gets his nose in a book, the house could fall down and he'd never—

(RICHARD *appears in the doorway from the back parlor, the book he has been reading in one hand, a finger marking his place. He looks a bit startled still, reluctantly called back to earth from another world. He is going on seventeen, just out of high school. In appearance he is a perfect blend of father and mother, so much so that each is convinced he is the image of the other. He has his mother's light-brown hair, his father's gray eyes; his features are neither large nor small; he is of medium height, neither fat nor thin. One would not call him a handsome boy; neither is he homely. But he is definitely different from both of his parents, too. There is something of extreme sensitiveness added—a restless, apprehensive, defiant, shy, dreamy, self-conscious intelligence about him. In manner he is alternately plain simple boy and a posey actor solemnly playing a role. He is dressed in prep school reflection of the college style of* ARTHUR.)

RICH. Did you want me, Pa?

MILL. I'd hoped I'd made that plain. Come and sit down a while. (*He points to the rocking chair at the right of table near his.*)

RICH. (*coming forward—seizing on the opportunity to play up his preoccupation—with apologetic superiority*). I didn't hear you, Pa. I was off in another world.

(MILDRED *slyly shoves her foot out so that he trips over it, almost falling. She laughs gleefully. So does* ARTHUR.)

ART. Good for you, Mid! That'll wake him up!

RICH. (*grins sheepishly—all boy now*). Darn you, Mid! I'll show you! (*He pushes her back on the sofa and tickles her with his free hand, still holding the book in the other. She shrieks.*)

ART. Give it to her, Dick!

MILL. That's enough, now. No more roughhouse. You sit down here, Richard. (RICHARD *obediently takes the chair at right of table, opposite his father.*) What were you planning to do with yourself today? Going out to the beach with Mildred?

RICH. (*scornfully superior*). That silly skirt party! I should say not!

MILD. He's not coming because Muriel isn't. I'll bet he's got a date with her somewheres.

RICH. (*flushing bashfully*). You shut up! (*Then to his father.*) I thought I'd just stay home, Pa—this morning, anyway.

MILL. Help Tommy set off firecrackers, eh?

RICH. (*drawing himself up—with dignity*). I should say not. (*Then frowning portentously.*) I don't believe in this silly celebrating the Fourth of July—all this lying talk about liberty—when there is no liberty!

MILL. (*a twinkle in his eye*). Hmm.

RICH. (*getting warmed up*). The land of the free and the home of the brave! Home of the slave is what they ought to call it—the wage slave ground under the heel of the capitalist class, starving, crying for bread for his children, and all he gets is a stone! The Fourth of July is a stupid farce!

MILL. (*putting a hand to his mouth to conceal a grin*). Hmm. Them are mighty strong words. You'd better not repeat such sentiments outside the bosom of the family or they'll have you in jail.

SID. And throw away the key.

RICH. (*darkly*). Let them put me in jail. But how about the freedom of speech in the Constitution, then? That must be a farce, too. (*Then he adds grimly.*) No, you can celebrate your Fourth of July. I'll celebrate the day the people bring out the guillotine again and I see Pierpont Morgan being driven by in a tumbril!

(*His father and* SID *are greatly amused;* LILY *is shocked but, taking her cue from them, smiles.* MILDRED *stares at him in puzzled wonder-*

ment, never having heard this particular line before. Only ARTHUR
betrays the outraged reaction of a patriot.)

ART. Aw say, you fresh kid, tie that bull outside! You ought to get a
punch in the nose for talking that way on the Fourth!

MILL. (*solemnly*). Son, if I didn't know it was you talking, I'd think we
had Emma Goldman with us.

ART. Never mind, Pa. Wait till we get him down to Yale. We'll take
that out of him!

RICH. (*with high scorn*). Oh, Yale! You think there's nothing in the
world besides Yale! After all, what is Yale?

ART. You'll find out what!

SID (*provocatively*). Don't let them scare you, Dick. Give 'em hell!

LILY (*shocked*). Sid! You shouldn't swear before—

RICH. What do you think I am, Aunt Lily—a baby? I've heard worse
than anything Uncle Sid says.

MILD. And said worse himself, I bet!

MILL. (*with a comic air of resignation*). Well, Richard, I've always
found I've had to listen to at least one stump speech every Fourth.
I only hope getting your extra strong one right after breakfast
will let me off for the rest of the day. (*They all laugh now, taking
this as a cue.*)

RICH. (*somberly*). That's right, laugh! After you, the deluge, you think!
But look out! Supposing it comes before? Why shouldn't the
workers of the world unite and rise? They have nothing to lose
but their chains! (*He recites threateningly.*) "The days grow hot,
O Babylon! 'Tis cool beneath thy willow trees!"

MILL. Hmm. That's good. But where's the connection, exactly? Something from that book you're reading?

RICH. (*superior*). No. That's poetry. This is prose.

MILL. I've heard there was a difference between 'em. What is the book?

RICH. (*importantly*). Carlyle's *French Revolution*.

MILL. Hmm. So that's where you drove the tumbril from and piled poor
old Pierpont in it. (*Then seriously.*) Glad you're reading it,
Richard. It's a darn fine book.

RICH. (*with unflattering astonishment*). What, have you read it?

MILL. Well, you see, even a newspaper owner can't get out of reading a book every now and again.

RICH. (*abashed*). I—I didn't mean—I know you— (*Then enthusiastically.*) Say, isn't it a great book, though—that part about Mirabeau—and about Marat and Robespierre—

MRS. MILL. (*appears from the front parlor in a great state of flushed annoyance*). Never you mind Robespierre, young man! You tell me this minute where you've hidden those books! They were on the shelf in your wardrobe and now you've gone and hid them somewheres else. You go right up and bring them to your father! (RICHARD, *for a second, looks suddenly guilty and crushed. Then he bristles defensively.*)

MILL. (*after a quick understanding glance at him*). Never mind his getting them now. We'll waste the whole morning over those darned books. And anyway, he has a right to keep his library to himself—that is, if they're not too— What books are they, Richard?

RICH. (*self-consciously*). Well—there's—

MRS. MILL. I'll tell you, if he won't—and you give him a good talking to. (*Then, after a glance at* RICHARD, *mollifiedly.*) Not that I blame Richard. There must be some boy he knows who's trying to show off as advanced and wicked, and he told him about—

RICH. No! I read about them myself, in the papers and in other books.

MRS. MILL. Well, no matter how, there they were on his shelf. Two by that awful Oscar Wilde they put in jail for heaven knows what wickedness.

ART. (*suddenly—solemnly authoritative*). He committed bigamy. (*Then as* SID *smothers a burst of ribald laughter.*) What are you laughing at? I guess I ought to know. A fellow at college told me. His father was in England when this Wilde was pinched—and he said he remembered once his mother asked his father about it and he told her he'd committed bigamy.

MILL. (*hiding a smile behind his hand*). Well then, that must be right, Arthur.

MRS. MILL. I wouldn't put it past him, nor anything else. One book was called the Picture of something or other.

RICH. *The Picture of Dorian Gray*. It's one of the greatest novels ever written!

MRS. MILL. Looked to me like cheap trash. And the second book was poetry. The Ballad of I forget what.

RICH. *The Ballad of Reading Gaol,* one of the greatest poems ever written. (*He pronounces it "Reading Goal" as in "goalpost."*)

MRS. MILL. All about someone who murdered his wife and got hung, as he richly deserved, as far as I could make out. And then there were two books by that Bernard Shaw—

RICH. The greatest playwright alive today!

MRS. MILL. To hear him tell it, maybe! You know, Nat, the one who wrote a play about—well, never mind—that was so vile they wouldn't even let it play in New York!

MILL. Hmm. I remember.

MRS. MILL. One was a book of his plays and the other had a long title I couldn't make head or tail of, only it wasn't a play.

RICH. (*proudly*). *The Quintessence of Ibsenism.*

MILD. Phew! Good gracious, what a name! What does it mean, Dick? I'll bet he doesn't know.

RICH. (*outraged*). I do, too, know! It's about Ibsen, the greatest playwright since Shakespeare!

MRS. MILL. Yes, there was a book of plays by that Ibsen there, too! And poems by Swin something—

RICH. *Poems and Ballads* by Swinburne, Ma. The greatest poet since Shelley! He tells the truth about real love!

MRS. MILL. Love! Well, all I can say is, from reading here and there, that if he wasn't flung in jail along with Wilde, he should have been. Some of the things I simply couldn't read, they were so indecent— All about—well, I can't tell you before Lily and Mildred.

SID (*with a wink at* RICHARD—*jokingly*). Remember, I'm next on that one, Dick. I feel the need of a little poetical education.

LILY (*scandalized, but laughing*). Sid! Aren't you ashamed?

MRS. MILL. This is no laughing matter. And then there was Kipling— but I suppose he's not so bad. And last there was a poem—a long one—the Rubay— What is it, Richard?

RICH. *The Rubaiyat of Omar Khayyam*. That's the best of all!

MILL. Oh, I've read that, Essie—got a copy down at the office.

SID (*enthusiastically*). So have I. It's a pippin!

LILY (*with shy excitement*). I—I've read it, too—at the library. I like—some parts of it.

MRS. MILL. (*scandalized*). Why, Lily!

MILL. Everybody's reading that now, Essie—and it don't seem to do them any harm. There's fine things in it, seems to me—true things.

MRS. MILL. (*a bit bewildered and uncertain now*). Why, Nat, I don't see how you— It looked terrible blasphemous—parts I read.

SID. Remember this one: (*he quotes rhetorically*) "Oh Thou, who didst with pitfall and gin beset the path I was to wander in—" Now, I've always noticed how beset my path was with gin—in the past, you understand! (*He casts a joking side glance at* LILY. *The others laugh. But* LILY *is in a melancholy dream and hasn't heard him.*)

MRS. MILL. (*tartly, but evidently suppressing her usual smile where he is concerned*). You would pick out the ones with liquor in them!

LILY (*suddenly—with a sad pathos, quotes awkwardly and shyly*). I like—because it's true:

> "The Moving Finger writes, and having writ,
> Moves on: nor all your Piety nor Wit
> Shall lure it back to cancel half a Line,
> Nor all your Tears wash out a Word of it."

MRS. MILL. (*astonished, as are all the others*). Why, Lily, I never knew you to recite poetry before!

LILY (*immediately guilty and apologetic*). I—it just stuck in my memory somehow.

RICH. (*looking at her as if he had never seen her before*). Good for you, Aunt Lily! (*Then enthusiastically.*) But that isn't the best. The best is:

> "A Book of Verses underneath the Bough,
> A Jug of Wine, A Loaf of Bread—and Thou
> Beside me singing in the Wilderness—"

ART. (*who, bored to death by all this poetry quoting, has wandered over to the window at rear of desk, right*). Hey! Look who's coming up the walk— Old Man McComber!

MILL. (*irritably*). Dave? Now what in thunder does that damned old— Sid, I can see where we never are going to get to that picnic.

MRS. MILL. (*vexatiously*). He'll know we're in this early, too. No use lying. (*Then appalled by another thought.*) That Norah—she's that thick, she never can answer the front door right unless I tell her each time. Nat, you've got to talk to Dave. I'll have her show him in here. Lily, you run up the back stairs and get your things on. I'll be up in a second. Nat, you get rid of him the first second you can! Whatever can the old fool want— (*She and* LILY *hurry out through the back parlor.*)

ART. I'm going to beat it—just time to catch the eight-twenty trolley.

MILD. I've got to catch that, too. Wait till I get my hat, Art! (*She rushes into the back parlor.*)

ART. (*shouts after her*). I can't wait. You can catch up with me if you hurry. (*He turns at the back-parlor door—with a grin.*) McComber may be coming to see if your intentions toward his daughter are dishonorable, Dick! You'd better beat it while your shoes are good! (*He disappears through the back-parlor door, laughing.*)

RICH. (*a bit shaken, but putting on a brave front*). Think I'm scared of him?

MILL. (*gazing at him—frowning*). Can't imagine what— But it's to complain about something, I know that. I only wish I didn't have to be pleasant with the old buzzard—but he's about the most valuable advertiser I've got.

SID (*sympathetically*). I know. But tell him to go to hell, anyway. He needs that ad more than you.

(*The sound of the bell comes from the rear of the house, off left from back parlor.*)

MILL. There he is. You clear out, Dick—but come right back as soon as he's gone, you hear? I'm not through with you, yet.

RICH. Yes, Pa.

MILL. You better clear out, too, Sid. You know Dave doesn't approve jokes.

SID. And loves me like poison! Come on, Dick, we'll go out and help Tommy celebrate. (*He takes* RICHARD's *arm and they also disappear through the back-parlor door.* MILLER *glances through the front parlor toward the front door, then calls in a tone of strained heartiness.*)

MILL. Hello, Dave. Come right in here. What good wind blows you around on this glorious Fourth?

(*A flat, brittle voice answers him:* "Good morning," *and a moment later* DAVID MC COMBER *appears in the doorway from the front parlor. He is a thin, dried-up little man with a head too large for his body perched on a scrawny neck, and a long solemn horse face with deep-set little black eyes, a blunt formless nose and a tiny slit of a mouth. He is about the same age as* MILLER *but is entirely bald, and looks ten years older. He is dressed with a prim neatness in shiny old black clothes.*)

MILL. Here, sit down and make yourself comfortable. (*Holding out the cigar box.*) Have a cigar?

MC COM. (*sitting down in the chair at the right of table—acidly.*) You're forgetting. I never smoke.

MILL. (*forcing a laugh at himself*). That's so. So I was. Well, I'll smoke alone then. (*He bites off the end of the cigar viciously, as if he wished it were* MC COMBER's *head, and sits down opposite him.*)

MC COM. You asked me what brings me here, so I'll come to the point at once. I regret to say it's something disagreeable—disgraceful would be nearer the truth—and it concerns your son, Richard!

MILL. (*beginning to bristle—but calmly*). Oh, come now, Dave, I'm sure Richard hasn't—

MC COM. (*sharply*). And I'm positive he has. You're not accusing me of being a liar, I hope.

MILL. No one said anything about liar. I only meant you're surely mistaken if you think—

MC COM. I'm not mistaken. I have proof of everything in his own handwriting!

MILL. (*sharply*). Let's get down to brass tacks. Just what is it you're charging him with?

MC COM. With being dissolute and blasphemous—with deliberately attempting to corrupt the morals of my young daughter, Muriel.

MILL. Then I'm afraid I will have to call you a liar, Dave!

MC COM. (*without taking offense—in the same flat, brittle voice*). I thought you'd get around to that, so I brought some of the proofs with me. I've a lot more of 'em at home. (*He takes a wallet from his inside coat pocket, selects five or six slips of paper, and holds them out to* MILLER.) These are good samples of the rest. My wife discovered them in one of Muriel's bureau drawers hidden under the underwear. They're all in his handwriting, you can't deny it. Anyway, Muriel's confessed to me he wrote them. You read them and then say I'm a liar. (MILLER *has taken the slips and is reading them frowningly.* MC COMBER *talks on.*) Evidently you've been too busy to take the right care about Richard's bringing up or what he's allowed to read—though I can't see why his mother failed in her duty. But that's your misfortune, and none of my business. But Muriel is my business and I can't and I won't have her innocence exposed to the contamination of a young man whose mind, judging from his choice of reading matter, is as foul—

MILL. (*making a tremendous effort to control his temper*). Why, you damned old fool! Can't you see Richard's only a fool kid who's just at the stage when he's out to rebel against all authority, and so he grabs at everything radical to read and wants to pass it on to his elders and his girl and boy friends to show off what a young hellion he is! Why, at heart you'd find Richard is just as innocent and as big a kid as Muriel is! (*He pushes the slips of paper across the table contemptuously.*) This stuff doesn't mean anything to me—that is, nothing of what you think it means. If you believe this would corrupt Muriel, then you must believe she's easily corrupted! But I'll bet you'd find she knows a lot more about life than you give her credit for—and can guess a stork didn't bring her down your chimney!

MC COM. Now you're insulting my daughter. I won't forget that.

MILL. I'm not insulting her. I think Muriel is a darn nice girl. That's why I'm giving her credit for ordinary good sense. I'd say the same about my own Mildred, who's the same age.

MC COM. I know nothing about your Mildred except that she's known all over as a flirt. (*Then more sharply.*) Well, I knew you'd prove obstinate, but I certainly never dreamed you'd have the impudence, after reading those papers, to claim your son was innocent of all wrongdoing!

MILL. And what did you dream I'd do?

MC COM. Do what it's your plain duty to do as a citizen to protect other people's children! Take and give him a hiding he'd remember to the last day of his life! You'd ought to do it for his sake, if you had any sense—unless you want him to end up in jail!

MILL. (*his fists clenched, leans across the table*). Dave, I've stood all I can stand from you! You get out! And get out quick, if you don't want a kick in the rear to help you!

MC COM. (*again in his flat, brittle voice, slowly getting to his feet*). You needn't lose your temper. I'm only demanding you do your duty by your own as I've already done by mine. I'm punishing Muriel. She's not to be allowed out of the house for a month and she's to be in bed every night by eight sharp. And yet she's blameless, compared to that—

MILL. I said I'd had enough out of you, Dave! (*He makes a threatening movement.*)

MC COM. You needn't lay hands on me. I'm going. But there's one thing more. (*He takes a letter from his wallet.*) Here's a letter from Muriel for your son. (*Puts it on the table.*) It makes clear, I think, how she's come to think about him, now that her eyes have been opened. I hope he heeds what's inside—for his own good and yours—because if I ever catch him hanging about my place again I'll have him arrested! And don't think I'm not going to make you regret the insults you've heaped on me. I'm taking the advertisement for my store out of your paper—and it won't go in again, I tell you, not unless you apologize in writing and promise to punish—

MILL. I'll see you in hell first! As for your damned old ad, take it out and go to hell!

MC COM. That's plain bluff. You know how badly you need it. So do I. (*He starts stiffly for the door.*)

MILL. Here! Listen a minute! I'm just going to call *your* bluff and tell you that, whether you want to reconsider your decision or not, I'm going to refuse to print your damned ad after tomorrow! Put that in your pipe and smoke it! Furthermore, I'll start a campaign to encourage outside capital to open a dry-goods store in opposition to you that won't be the public swindle I can prove yours is!

MC COM. (*a bit shaken by this threat—but in the same flat tone*). I'll sue you for libel.

MILL. When I get through, there won't be a person in town will buy a dishrag in your place!

MC COM. (*more shaken, his eyes shifting about furtively*). That's all bluff. You wouldn't dare— (*Then finally he says uncertainly*) well, good day (*and turns and goes out.* NAT *stands looking after him. Slowly the anger drains from his face and leaves him looking a bit sick and disgusted.* SID *appears from the back parlor. He is nursing a burn on his right hand, but his face is one broad grin of satisfaction.*)

SID. I burned my hand with one of Tommy's damned firecrackers and came in to get some vaseline. I was listening to the last of your scrap. Good for you, Nat! You sure gave him hell!

MILL. (*dully*). Much good it'll do. He knows it was all talk.

SID. That's just what he don't know, Nat. The old skinflint has a guilty conscience.

MILL. Well, anyone who knows me knows I wouldn't use my paper for a dirty, spiteful trick like that—no matter what he did to me.

SID. Yes, everyone knows you're an old sucker, Nat, too decent for your own good. But McComber never saw you like this before. I tell you you scared the pants off him. (*He chuckles.*)

MILL. (*still dejectedly*). I don't know what made me let go like that. The hell of skunks like McComber is that after being with them ten minutes you become as big skunks as they are.

SID (*notices the slips of paper on the table*). What's this? Something he brought? (*He picks them up and starts to read.*)

MILL. (*grimly*). Samples of the new freedom—from those books Essie found—that Richard's been passing on to Muriel to educate her. They're what started the rumpus. (*Then frowning.*) I've got to do something about that young anarchist or he'll be getting me, and himself, in a peck of trouble. (*Then pathetically helpless.*) But what can I do? Putting the curb bit on would make him worse. Then he'd have a harsh tyrant to defy. He'd love that, darn him!

SID (*has been reading the slips, a broad grin on his face—suddenly he whistles*). Phew! This is a warm lulu for fair! (*He recites with a joking intensity.*)

"My life is bitter with thy love; thine eyes
    Blind me, thy tresses burn me, thy sharp sighs
    Divide my flesh and spirit with soft sound—"

MILL. (*with a grim smile*). Hmm. I missed that one. That must be Mr. Swinburne's copy. I've never read him, but I've heard something like that was the matter with him.

SID. Yes, it's labelled Swinburne—"Anactoria." Whatever that is. But wait, watch and listen! The worst is yet to come! (*He recites with added comic intensity.*)

"That I could drink thy veins as wine, and eat
    Thy breasts like honey, that from face to feet
    Thy body were abolished and consumed,
    And in my flesh thy very flesh entombed!"

MILL. (*an irrepressible boyish grin coming to his face*). Hell and halle-lujah! Just picture old Dave digesting that for the first time! Gosh, I'd give a lot to have seen his face! (*Then a trace of shocked reproof showing in his voice.*) But it's no joking matter. That stuff *is* warm—too damned warm, if you ask me! I don't like this a damned bit, Sid. That's no kind of thing to be sending a decent girl. (*More worriedly.*) I thought he was really stuck on her—as one gets stuck on a decent girl at his age—all moonshine and holding hands and a kiss now and again. But this looks—I wonder if he is hanging around her to see what he can get? (*Angrily.*) By God, if that's true, he deserves that licking McComber says it's my duty to give him! I've got to draw the line somewhere!

SID. Yes, it won't do to have him getting any decent girl in trouble.

MILL. The only thing I can do is put it up to him straight. (*With pride.*) Richard'll stand up to his guns, no matter what. I've never known him to lie to me.

SID (*at a noise from the back parlor, looks that way—in a whisper*). Then now's your chance. I'll beat it and leave you alone—see if the women folks are ready upstairs. We ought to get started soon— if we're ever going to make that picnic. (*He is halfway to the entrance to the front parlor as* RICHARD *enters from the back parlor, very evidently nervous about* MC COMBER's *call.*)

RICH. (*adopting a forced, innocent tone*). How's your hand, Uncle Sid?

SID. All right, Dick, thanks—only hurts a little. (*He disappears.* MILLER *watches his son frowningly.* RICHARD *gives him a quick side glance and grows more guiltily self-conscious.*)

RICH. (*forcing a snicker*). Gee, Pa, Uncle Sid's a bigger kid than Tommy is. He was throwing firecrackers in the air and catching them on the back of his hand and throwing 'em off again just before they went off—and one came and he wasn't quick enough, and it went off almost on top of—

MILL. Never mind that. I've got something else to talk to you about besides firecrackers.

RICH. (*apprehensively*). What, Pa?

MILL. (*suddenly puts both hands on his shoulders—quietly*). Look here, Son. I'm going to ask you a question, and I want an honest answer. I warn you beforehand if the answer is "yes" I'm going to punish you and punish you hard because you'll have done something no boy of mine ought to do. But you've never lied to me before, I know, and I don't believe, even to save yourself punishment, you'd lie to me now, would you?

RICH. (*impressed—with dignity*). I won't lie, Pa.

MILL. Have you been trying to have something to do with Muriel— something you shouldn't—you know what I mean.

RICH. (*stares at him for a moment, as if he couldn't comprehend—then, as he does, a look of shocked indignation comes over his face*). No! What do you think I am, Pa? I never would! She's not that kind! Why, I—I love her! I'm going to marry her—after I get out of college! She's said she would! We're engaged!

MILL. (*with great relief*). All right. That's all I wanted to know. We won't talk any more about it. (*He gives him an approving pat on the back.*)

RICH. I don't see how you could think— Did that old idiot McComber say that about me?

MILL. (*joking now*). Shouldn't call your future father-in-law names, should you? 'Taint respectful. (*Then after a glance at* RICHARD'S *indignant face—points to the slips of paper on the table.*) Well, you can't exactly blame old Dave, can you, when you read through that literature you wished on his innocent daughter?

RICH. (*sees the slips for the first time and is overcome by embarrassment, which he immediately tries to cover up with a superior carelessness*). Oh, so that's why. He found those, did he? I told her to be careful— Well, it'll do him good to read the truth about life for once and get rid of his old-fogy ideas.

MILL. I'm afraid I've got to agree with him, though, that they're hardly fit reading for a young girl. (*Then with subtle flattery.*) They're all well enough, in their way, for you who're a man, but— Think it over, and see if you don't agree with me.

RICH. (*embarrassedly*). Aw, I only did it because I liked them—and I wanted her to face life as it is. She's so darned afraid of life— afraid of her Old Man—afraid of people saying this or that about her—afraid of being in love—afraid of everything. She's even afraid to let me kiss her. I thought, maybe, reading those things— they're beautiful, aren't they, Pa?— I thought they would give her the spunk to lead her own life, and not be—always thinking of being afraid.

MILL. I see. Well, I'm afraid she's still afraid. (*He takes the letter from the table.*) Here's a letter from her he said to give you. (RICHARD *takes the letter from him uncertainly, his expression changing to one of apprehension.* MILLER *adds with a kindly smile*) You better be prepared for a bit of a blow. But never mind. There's lots of other fish in the sea. (RICHARD *is not listening to him, but staring at the letter with a sort of fascinated dread.* MILLER *looks into his son's face a second, then turns away, troubled and embarrassed.*) Darn it! I better go upstairs and get rigged out or I never will get to that picnic. (*He moves awkwardly and self-consciously off through the front parlor.*)

(RICHARD *continues to stare at the letter for a moment—then girds up his courage and tears it open and begins to read swiftly. As he reads his face grows more and more wounded and tragic, until at the end his mouth draws down at the corners, as if he were about to break into tears. With an effort he forces them back and his face grows flushed with humiliation and wronged anger.*)

RICH. (*blurts out to himself*). The little coward! I hate her! She can't treat me like that! I'll show her! (*At the sound of voices from the front parlor, he quickly shoves the letter into the inside pocket of his coat and does his best to appear calm and indifferent, even attempting to whistle "Waiting at the Church." But the whistle peters out miserably as his* MOTHER, LILY *and* SID *enter from the front parlor. They are dressed in all the elaborate paraphernalia of motoring at that period—linen dusters, veils, goggles,* SID *in a snappy cap.*)

MRS. MILL. Well, we're about ready to start at last, thank goodness! Let's hope no more callers are on the way. What did that McComber want, Richard, do you know? Sid couldn't tell us.

RICH. You can search me. Ask Pa.

MRS. MILL. (*immediately sensing something "down" in his manner—going to him worriedly*). Why, whatever's the matter with you, Richard? You sound as if you'd lost your last friend! What is it?

RICH. (*desperately*). I—I don't feel so well—my stomach's sick.

MRS. MILL. (*immediately all sympathy—smoothing his hair back from his forehead*). You poor boy! What a shame—on the Fourth, too, of all days! (*Turning to the others.*) Maybe I better stay home with him, if he's sick.

LILY. Yes, I'll stay, too.

RICH. (*more desperately*). No! You go, Ma! I'm not really sick. I'll be all right. You go. I want to be alone! (*Then, as a louder bang comes from in back as* TOMMY *sets off a cannon cracker, he jumps to his feet.*) Darn Tommy and his darned firecrackers! You can't get any peace in this house with that darned kid around! Darn the Fourth of July, anyway! I wish we still belonged to England! (*He strides off in an indignant fury of misery through the front parlor.*)

MRS. MILL. (*stares after him worriedly—then sighs philosophically*). Well, I guess he can't be so very sick—after that. (*She shakes her head.*) He's a queer boy. Sometimes I can't make head or tail of him.

MILL. (*calls from the front door beyond the back parlor*). Come along, folks. Let's get started.

SID. We're coming, Nat. (*He and the two women move off through the front parlor.*)

(CURTAIN)

ACT TWO

SCENE—*Dining-room of the* MILLER *home—a little after 6 o'clock in the evening of the same day.*

The room is much too small for the medium-priced, formidable dining-room set, especially now when all the leaves of the table are in. At left, toward rear, is a double doorway with sliding doors and portières leading into the back parlor. In the rear wall, left, is the door to the pantry. At the right of door is the china closet with its display of the family cut glass and fancy china. In the right wall are two windows looking out on a side lawn. In front of the windows is a heavy, ugly sideboard with three pieces of old silver on its top. In the left wall, extreme front, is a screen door opening on a side porch. A dark rug covers most of the floor. The table, with a chair at each end, left and right, three chairs on the far side, facing front, and two on the near side, their backs to front, takes up most of the available space. The walls are papered in a somber brown and dark-red design.

MRS. MILLER *is supervising and helping the Second Girl,* NORAH, *in the setting of the table.* NORAH *is a clumsy, heavy-handed, heavy-footed, long-jawed, beamingly good-natured young Irish girl—a* "greenhorn."

MRS. MILL. I really think you better put on the lights, Norah. It's getting so cloudy out, and this pesky room is so dark, anyway.

NOR. Yes, Mum. (*She stretches awkwardly over the table to reach the chandelier that is suspended from the middle of the ceiling and manages to turn one light on—scornfully.*) Arrah, the contraption!

MRS. MILL. (*worriedly*). Careful!

NOR. Careful as can be, Mum. (*But in moving around to reach the next bulb she jars heavily against the table.*)

MRS. MILL. There! I knew it! I do wish you'd watch—!

NOR. (*a flustered appeal in her voice*). Arrah, what have I done wrong now?

MRS. MILL. (*draws a deep breath—then sighs helplessly*). Oh, nothing. Never mind the rest of the lights. You might as well go out in the kitchen and wait until I ring.

NOR. (*relieved and cheerful again*). Yes, Mum. (*She starts for the pantry.*)

MRS. MILL. But there's one thing— (NORAH *turns apprehensively.*) No, two things—things I've told you over and over, but you always forget. Don't pass the plates on the wrong side at dinner tonight, and do be careful not to let that pantry door slam behind you. Now you will try to remember, won't you?

NOR. Yes, Mum. (*She goes into the pantry and shuts the door behind her with exaggerated care as* MRS. MILLER *watches her apprehensively.* MRS. MILLER *sighs and reaches up with difficulty and turns on another of the four lights in the chandelier. As she is doing so,* LILY *enters from the back parlor.*)

LILY. Here, let me do that, Essie. I'm taller. You'll only strain yourself. (*She quickly lights the other two bulbs.*)

MRS. MILL. (*gratefully*). Thank you, Lily. It's a stretch for me, I'm getting so fat.

LILY. But where's Norah? Why didn't she—?

MRS. MILL. (*exasperatedly*). Oh, that girl! Don't talk about her! She'll be the death of me! She's that thick, you honestly wouldn't believe it possible.

LILY (*smiling*). Why, what did she do now?

MRS. MILL. Oh, nothing. She means all right.

LILY. Anything else I can do, Essie?

MRS. MILL. Well, she's got the table all wrong. We'll have to reset it. But you're always helping me. It isn't fair to ask you—in your vacation. You need your rest after teaching a pack of wild Indians of kids all year.

LILY (*beginning to help with the table*). You know I love to help. It makes me feel I'm some use in this house instead of just sponging—

MRS. MILL. (*indignantly*). Sponging! You pay, don't you?

LILY. Almost nothing. And you and Nat only take that little to make me feel better about living with you. (*Forcing a smile.*) I don't see how you stand me—having a cranky old maid around all the time.

MRS. MILL. What nonsense you talk! As if Nat and I weren't only too tickled to death to have you! Lily Miller, I've no patience with you when you go on like that. We've been over this a thousand times before, and still you go on! Crazy, that's what it is! (*She changes the subject abruptly.*) What time's it getting to be?

LILY (*looking at her watch*). Quarter past six.

MRS. MILL. I do hope those men folks aren't going to be late for dinner. (*She sighs.*) But I suppose with that darned Sachem Club picnic it's more likely than not. (LILY *looks worried, and sighs.* MRS. MILLER *gives her a quick side glance.*) I see you've got your new dress on.

LILY (*embarrassedly*). Yes, I thought—if Sid's taking me to the fireworks—I ought to spruce up a little.

MRS. MILL. (*looking away*). Hmm. (*A pause—then she says with an effort to be casual.*) You mustn't mind if Sid comes home feeling a bit—gay. I expect Nat to—and we'll have to listen to all those old stories of his about when he was a boy. You know what those picnics are, and Sid'd be running into all his old friends.

LILY (*agitatedly*). I don't think he will—this time—not after his promise.

MRS. MILL. (*avoiding looking at her*). I know. But men are weak. (*Then quickly.*) That was a good notion of Nat's, getting Sid the job on the Waterbury *Standard*. All he ever needed was to get away from the rut he was in here. He's the kind that's the victim of his friends. He's easily led—but there's no real harm in him, you know that. (LILY *keeps silent, her eyes downcast*. MRS. MILLER *goes on meaningly*.) He's making good money in Waterbury, too—thirty-five a week. He's in a better position to get married than he ever was.

LILY (*stiffly*). Well, I hope he finds a woman who's willing—though after he's through with his betting on horse races, and dice, and playing Kelly pool, there won't be much left for a wife—even if there was nothing else he spent his money on.

MRS. MILL. Oh, he'd give up all that—for the right woman. (*Suddenly she comes directly to the point*.) Lily, why don't you change your mind and marry Sid and reform him? You love him and always have—

LILY (*stiffly*). I can't love a man who drinks.

MRS. MILL. You can't fool me. I know darned well you love him. And he loves you and always has.

LILY. Never enough to stop drinking for. (*Cutting off* MRS. MILLER's *reply*.) No, it's no good in your talking, Essie. We've been over this a thousand times before and I'll always feel the same as long as Sid's the same. If he gave me proof he'd—but even then I don't believe I could. It's sixteen years since I broke off our engagement, but what made me break it off is as clear to me today as it was then. It was what he'd be liable to do now to anyone who married him—his taking up with bad women.

MRS. MILL. (*protests half-heartedly*). But he's always sworn he got raked into that party and never had anything to do with those harlots.

LILY. Well, I don't believe him—didn't then and don't now. I do believe he didn't deliberately plan to, but— Oh, it's no good talking, Essie. What's done is done. But you know how much I like Sid—in spite of everything. I know he was just born to be what he is—irresponsible, never meaning to harm but harming in spite of himself. But don't talk to me about marrying him—because I never could.

MRS. MILL. (*angrily*). He's a dumb fool—a stupid dumb fool, that's what he is!

LILY (*quietly*). No. He's just Sid.

MRS. MILL. It's a shame for you—a measly shame—you that would have made such a wonderful wife for any man—that ought to have your own home and children!

LILY (*winces but puts her arm around her affectionately—gently*). Now don't you go feeling sorry for me. I won't have that. Here I am, thanks to your and Nat's kindness, with the best home in the world; and as for the children, I feel the same love for yours as if they were mine, and I didn't have the pain of bearing them. And then there are all the boys and girls I teach every year. I like to feel I'm a sort of second mother to them and helping them to grow up to be good men and women. So I don't feel such a useless old maid, after all.

MRS. MILL. (*kisses her impulsively—her voice husky*). You're a good woman, Lily—too good for the rest of us. (*She turns away, wiping a tear furtively—then abruptly changing the subject.*) Good gracious, if I'm not forgetting one of the most important things! I've got to warn that Tommy against giving me away to Nat about the fish. He knows, because I had to send him to market for it, and he's liable to burst out laughing—

LILY. Laughing about what?

MRS. MILL. (*guiltily*). Well, I've never told you, because it seemed sort of a sneaking trick, but you know how Nat carries on about not being able to eat bluefish.

LILY. I know he says there's a certain oil in it that poisons him.

MRS. MILL. (*chuckling*). Poisons him, nothing! He's been eating blue-fish for years—only I tell him each time it's weakfish. We're having it tonight—and I've got to warn that young imp to keep his face straight.

LILY (*laughing*). Aren't you ashamed, Essie?

MRS. MILL. Not much, I'm not! I like bluefish! (*She laughs.*) Where is Tommy? In the sitting-room?

LILY. No, Richard's there alone. I think Tommy's out on the piazza with Mildred. (MRS. MILLER *bustles out through the back parlor.*

As soon as she is gone, the smile fades from LILY's *lips. Her face grows sad and she again glances nervously at her watch.* RICHARD *appears from the back parlor, moving in an aimless way. His face wears a set expression of bitter gloom; he exudes tragedy. For* RICHARD, *after his first outburst of grief and humiliation, has begun to take a masochistic satisfaction in his great sorrow, especially in the concern which it arouses in the family circle. On seeing his aunt, he gives her a dark look and turns and is about to stalk back toward the sitting-room when she speaks to him pityingly.*) Feel any better, Richard?

RICH. (*somberly*). I'm all right, Aunt Lily. You mustn't worry about me.

LILY (*going to him*). But I do worry about you. I hate to see you so upset.

RICH. It doesn't matter. Nothing matters.

LILY (*puts her arm around him sympathetically*). You really mustn't let yourself take it so seriously. You know, something happens and things like that come up, and we think there's no hope—

RICH. Things like what come up?

LILY. What's happened between you and Muriel.

RICH. (*with disdain*). Oh, her! I wasn't even thinking about her. I was thinking about life.

LILY. But then—if we really, *really* love—why, then something else is bound to happen soon that changes everything again, and it's all as it was before the misunderstanding, and everything works out all right in the end. That's the way it is with life.

RICH. (*with a tragic sneer*). Life! Life is a joke! And everything comes out all wrong in the end!

LILY (*a little shocked*). You mustn't talk that way. But I know you don't mean it.

RICH. I do too mean it! You can have your silly optimism, if you like, Aunt Lily. But don't ask me to be so blind. I'm a pessimist! (*Then with an air of cruel cynicism.*) As for Muriel, that's all dead and past. I was only kidding her, anyway, just to have a little fun, and she took it seriously, like a fool. (*He forces a cruel smile to his lips.*) You know what they say about women and trolley cars, Aunt Lily: there's always another one along in a minute.

ILY (*really shocked this time*). I don't like you when you say such horrible, cynical things. It isn't nice.

RICH. Nice! That's all you women think of! I'm proud to be a cynic. It's the only thing you can be when you really face life. I suppose you think I ought to be heartbroken about Muriel—a little coward that's afraid to say her soul's her own, and keeps tied to her father's apron strings! Well, not for mine! There's plenty of other fish in the sea! (*As he is finishing, his mother comes back through the back parlor.*)

MRS. MILL. Why, hello. You here, Richard? Getting hungry, I suppose?

RICH. (*indignantly*). I'm not hungry a bit! That's all you think of, Ma—food!

MRS. MILL. Well, I must say I've never noticed you to hang back at meal times. (*To* LILY.) What's that he was saying about fish in the sea?

ILY (*smiling*). He says he's through with Muriel now.

MRS. MILL. (*tartly—giving her son a rebuking look*). She's through with him, he means! The idea of your sending a nice girl like her things out of those indecent books! (*Deeply offended*, RICHARD *disdains to reply but stalks woundedly to the screen door at left, front, and puts a hand on the knob.*) Where are you going?

RICH. (*quotes from* Candida *in a hollow voice*). "Out, then, into the night with me!" (*He stalks out, slamming the door behind him.*)

MRS. MILL. (*calls*). Well, don't you go far, 'cause dinner'll be ready in a minute, and I'm not coming running after you! (*She turns to* LILY *with a chuckle.*) Goodness, that boy! He ought to be on the stage! (*She mimics.*) "Out—into the night"—and it isn't even dark yet! He got that out of one of those books, I suppose. Do you know, I'm actually grateful to old Dave McComber for putting an end to his nonsense with Muriel. I never did approve of Richard getting so interested in girls. He's not old enough for such silliness. Why, seems to me it was only yesterday he was still a baby. (*She sighs—then matter-of-factly.*) Well, nothing to do now till those men turn up. No use standing here like gawks. We might as well go in the sitting-room and be comfortable.

LILY (*the nervous, worried note in her voice again*). Yes, we might a well. (*They go out through the back parlor. They have no soon disappeared than the screen door is opened cautiously and* RICHAI *comes back in the room.*)

RICH. (*stands inside the door, looking after them—quotes bitterly* "They do not know the secret in the poet's heart." (*He com nearer the table and surveys it, especially the cut-glass dish co taining olives, with contempt and mutters disdainfully.*) Food (*But the dish of olives seems to fascinate him and presently h has approached nearer, and stealthily lifts a couple and cram them into his mouth. He is just reaching out for more when th pantry door is opened slightly and* NORAH *peers in.*)

NOR. Mister Dick, you thief, lave them olives alone, or the missus'll b swearing it was me at them!

RICH. (*draws back his hand as if he had been stung—too flustered t be anything but guilty boy for a second*). I—I wasn't eating—

NOR. Oho, no, of course not, divil fear you, you was only feeling thei pulse! (*Then warningly.*) Mind what I'm saying now, or I'll hav to tell on you to protect me good name!

(*She draws back into the pantry, closing the door.* RICHARD *stands, prey to feelings of bitterest humiliation and seething revolt agains everyone and everything. A low whistle comes from just outsid the porch door. He starts. Then a masculine voice calls:* "Hey Dick." *He goes over to the screen door grumpily—then as h recognizes the owner of the voice, his own as he answers become respectful and admiring.*)

RICH. Oh, hello, Wint. Come on in. (*He opens the door and* WINT SELB enters and stands just inside the door.* SELBY *is nineteen, a class mate of* ARTHUR'S *at Yale. He is a typical, good-looking colleg boy of the period, not the athletic but the hell-raising sport type He is tall, blond, dressed in extreme collegiate cut.*)

WINT (*as he enters—warningly, in a low tone*). Keep it quiet, Kid. don't want the folks to know I'm here. Tell Art I want to see hin a second—on the Q.T.

RICH. Can't. He's up at the Rands'—won't be home before ten, anyway

WINT (*irritably*). Damn, I thought he'd be here for dinner. (*More irritably.*) Hell, that gums the works for fair!

RICH. (*ingratiatingly*). What is it, Wint? Can't I help?

WINT (*gives him an appraising glance*). I might tell you, if you can keep your face shut.

RICH. I can.

WINT. Well, I ran into a couple of swift babies from New Haven this after, and I dated them up for tonight, thinking I could catch Art. But now it's too late to get anyone else and I'll have to pass it up. I'm nearly broke and I can't afford to blow them both to drinks.

RICH. (*with shy eagerness*). I've got eleven dollars saved up. I could loan you some.

WINT (*surveys him appreciatively*). Say, you're a good sport. (*Then shaking his head.*) Nix, Kid, I don't want to borrow your money. (*Then getting an idea.*) But say, have you got anything on for tonight?

RICH. No.

WINT. Want to come along with me? (*Then quickly.*) I'm not trying to lead you astray, understand. But it'll be a help if you would just sit around with Belle and feed her a few drinks while I'm off with Edith. (*He winks.*) See what I mean? You don't have to do anything, not even take a glass of beer—unless you want to.

RICH. (*boastfully*). Aw, what do you think I am—a rube?

WINT. You mean you're game for anything that's doing?

RICH. Sure I am!

WINT. Ever been out with any girls—I mean, real swift ones that there's something doing with, not these dead Janes around here?

RICH. (*lies boldly*). Aw, what do you think? Sure I have!

WINT. Ever drink anything besides sodas?

RICH. Sure. Lots of times. Beer and sloe-gin fizz and—Manhattans.

WINT (*impressed*). Hell, you know more than I thought. (*Then considering.*) Can you fix it so your folks won't get wise? I don't want your old man coming after me. You can get back by half-past ten or eleven, though, all right. Think you can cook up some lie

to cover that? (*As* RICHARD *hesitates—encouraging him.*) Ough
to be easy—on the Fourth.

RICH. Sure. Don't worry about that.

WINT. But you've got to keep your face closed about this, you hear?—
to Art and everybody else. I tell you straight, I wouldn't ask you
to come if I wasn't in a hole—and if I didn't know you were
coming down to Yale next year, and didn't think you're giving
me the straight goods about having been around before. I don'
want to lead you astray.

RICH. (*scornfully*). Aw, I told you that was silly.

WINT. Well, you be at the Pleasant Beach House at half-past nine then
Come in the back room. And don't forget to grab some cloves to
take the booze off your breath.

RICH. Aw, I know what to do.

WINT. See you later, then. (*He starts out and is just about to close the
door when he thinks of something.*) And say, I'll say you're a
Harvard freshman, and you back me up. They don't know a
damn thing about Harvard. I don't want them thinking I'm
travelling around with any high-school kid.

RICH. Sure. That's easy.

WINT. So long, then. You better beat it right after your dinner while
you've got a chance, and hang around until it's time. Watch your
step, Kid.

RICH. So long. (*The door closes behind* WINT. RICHARD *stands for a
moment, a look of bitter, defiant rebellion coming over his face
and mutters to himself.*) I'll show her she can't treat me the way
she's done! I'll show them all! (*Then the front door is heard
slamming, and a moment later* TOMMY *rushes in from the back
parlor.*)

TOM. Where's Ma?

RICH. (*surlily*). In the sitting-room. Where did you think, Bonehead?

TOM. Pa and Uncle Sid are coming. Mid and I saw them from the front
piazza. Gee, I'm glad. I'm awful hungry, ain't you? (*He rushes
out through the back parlor, calling.*) Ma! They're coming! Let's
have dinner quick! (*A moment later* MRS. MILLER *appears from*

the back parlor accompanied by TOMMY, *who keeps insisting urgently.*) Gee, but I'm awful hungry, Ma!

MRS. MILL. I know. You always are. You've got a tapeworm, that's what I think.

TOM. Have we got lobsters, Ma? Gee, I love lobsters.

MRS. MILL. Yes, we've got lobsters. And fish. You remember what I told you about that fish. (*He snickers.*) Now, do be quiet, Tommy! (*Then with a teasing smile at* RICHARD.) Well, I'm glad to see you've got back out of the night, Richard. (*He scowls and turns his back on her.* LILY *appears through the back parlor, nervous and apprehensive. As she does so, from the front yard* SID's *voice is heard singing "Poor John!"* MRS. MILLER *shakes her head forebodingly—but, so great is the comic spell for her even in her brother's voice, a humorous smile hovers at the corners of her lips.*) Mmm! Mmm! Lily, I'm afraid—

LILY (*bitterly*). Yes, I might have known.

(MILDRED *runs in through the back parlor. She is laughing to herself a bit shamefacedly. She rushes to her mother.*)

MILD. Ma, Uncle Sid's— (*She whispers in her ear.*)

MRS. MILL. Never mind! You shouldn't notice such things—at your age! And don't you encourage him by laughing at his foolishness, you hear!

TOM. You needn't whisper, Mid. Think I don't know? Uncle Sid's soused again.

MRS. MILL. (*shakes him by the arm indignantly*). You be quiet! Did I ever! You're getting too smart! (*Gives him a push.*) Go to your place and sit right down and not another word out of you!

TOM. (*aggrieved—rubbing his arm as he goes to his place*). Aw, Ma!

MRS. MILL. And you sit down, Richard and Mildred. You better, too, Lily. We'll get him right in here and get some food in him. He'll be all right then. (RICHARD, *preserving the pose of the bitter, disillusioned pessimist, sits down in his place in the chair at right of the two whose backs face front.* MILDRED *takes the other chair facing back, at his left.* TOMMY *has already slid into the end chair at right of those at the rear of table facing front.* LILY *sits in the one of those at left, by the head of the table, leaving the middle one* [SID's] *vacant. While they are doing this, the front screen door is heard slamming and* NAT's *and* SID's *laughing voices, raised as they come in and for a moment after, then suddenly cautiously lowered.* MRS. MILLER *goes to the entrance to the back parlor and calls peremptorily.*) You come right in here! Don't stop to wash up or anything. Dinner's coming right on the table.

MILL.'s VOICE (*jovially*). All right, Essie. Here we are! Here we are!

MRS. MILL. (*goes to pantry door, opens it and calls*). All right, Norah. You can bring in the soup. (*She comes back to the back-parlor entrance just as* MILLER *enters. He isn't drunk by any means. He is just mellow and benignly ripened. His face is one large, smiling, happy beam of utter appreciation of life. All's right with the world, so satisfyingly right that he becomes sentimentally moved even to think of it.*)

MILL. Here we are, Essie! Right on the dot! Here we are! (*He pulls her to him and gives her a smacking kiss on the ear as she jerks her head away.* MILDRED *and* TOMMY *giggle.* RICHARD *holds rigidly aloof and disdainful, his brooding gaze fixed on his plate.* LILY *forces a smile.*)

MRS. MILL. (*pulling away—embarrassedly, almost blushing*). Don't, you Crazy! (*Then recovering herself—tartly.*) So I see, you're here! And if I didn't, you've told me four times already!

MILL. (*beamingly*). Now, Essie, don't be critical. Don't be carpingly critical. Good news can stand repeating, can't it? 'Course it can! (*He slaps her jovially on her fat buttocks.* TOMMY *and* MILDRED *roar with glee. And* NORAH, *who has just entered from the pantry with a huge tureen of soup in her hands, almost drops it as she explodes in a merry guffaw.*)

MRS. MILL. (*scandalized*). Nat! Aren't you ashamed!

MILL. Couldn't resist it! Just simply couldn't resist it!

(NORAH, *still standing with the soup tureen held out stiffly in front of her, again guffaws.*)

MRS. MILL. (*turns on her with outraged indignation*). Norah! Bring that soup here this minute! (*She stalks with stiff dignity toward her place at the foot of the table, right.*)

NOR. (*guiltily*). Yes, Mum. (*She brings the soup around the head of the table, passing* MILLER.)

MILL. (*jovially*). Why, hello, Norah!

MRS. MILL. Nat! (*She sits down stiffly at the foot of the table.*)

NOR. (*rebuking him familiarly*). Arrah now, don't be making me laugh and getting me into trouble!

MRS. MILL. Norah!

NOR. (*a bit resentfully*). Yes, Mum. Here I am. (*She sets the soup tureen down with a thud in front of* MRS. MILLER *and passes around the other side, squeezing with difficulty between the china closet and the backs of chairs at the rear of the table.*)

MRS. MILL. Tommy! Stop spinning your napkin ring! How often have I got to tell you? Mildred! Sit up straight in your chair! Do you want to grow up a humpback? Richard! Take your elbows off the table!

MILL. (*coming to his place at the head of the table, rubbing his hands together genially*). Well, well, well. Well, well, well. It's good to be home again.

(NORAH *exits into the pantry and lets the door slam with a bang behind her.*)

MRS. MILL. (*jumps*). Oh! (*Then exasperatedly.*) Nat, I do wish you wouldn't encourage that stupid girl by talking to her, when I'm doing my best to train—

MILL. (*beamingly*). All right, Essie. Your word is law! (*Then laughingly.*) We did have the darndest fun today! And Sid was the life of that picnic! You ought to have heard him! Honestly, he had that crowd just rolling on the ground and splitting their sides! He ought to be on the stage.

MRS. MILL. (*as* NORAH *comes back with a dish of saltines—begins ladling soup into the stack of plates before her.*) He ought to be at this table eating something to sober him up, that's what he ought to be! (*She calls.*) Sid! You come right in here! (*Then to* NORAH, *handing her a soup plate.*) Here, Norah. (NORAH *begins passing soup.*) Sit down, Nat, for goodness' sakes. Start eating, everybody. Don't wait for me. You know I've given up soup.

MILL. (*sits down but bends forward to call to his wife in a confidential tone*). Essie—Sid's sort of embarrassed about coming—I mean I'm afraid he's a little bit—not too much, you understand—but he met such a lot of friends and—well, you know, don't be hard on him. Fourth of July is like Christmas—comes but once a year. Don't pretend to notice, eh? And don't you kids, you hear! And don't you, Lily. He's scared of you.

LILY (*with stiff meekness*). Very well, Nat.

MILL. (*beaming again—calls*). All right, Sid. The coast's clear. (*He begins to absorb his soup ravenously.*) Good soup, Essie! Good soup! (*A moment later* SID *makes his entrance from the back parlor. He is in a condition that can best be described as blurry. His movements have a hazy uncertainty about them. His shiny fat face is one broad, blurred, Puckish, naughty-boy grin; his eyes have a blurred, wondering vagueness. As he enters he makes a solemnly intense effort to appear casual and dead, cold sober. He waves his hand aimlessly and speaks with a silly gravity.*)

SID. Good evening. (*They all answer* "Good evening," *their eyes on their plates. He makes his way vaguely toward his place, continuing his grave effort at conversation.*) Beautiful evening. I never remember seeing—more beautiful sunset. (*He bumps vaguely into* LILY's *chair as he attempts to pass behind her—immediately he is all grave politeness.*) Sorry—sorry, Lily—deeply sorry.

LILY (*her eyes on her plate—stiffly*). It's all right.

SID (*manages to get into his chair at last—mutters to himself*). Wha' was I sayin'? Oh, sunsets. But why butt in? Hasn't sun—perfect right to set? Mind y'r own business. (*He pauses thoughtfully, considering this—then looks around from face to face, fixing each with a vague, blurred, wondering look, as if some deep puzzle were confronting him. Then suddenly he grins mistily and nods with satisfaction.*) And there you are! Am I right?

MILL. (*humoring him*). Right.

SID. Right! (*He is silent, studying his soup plate, as if it were some strange enigma. Finally he looks up and regards his sister and asks with wondering amazement.*) Soup?

MRS. MILL. Of course, it's soup. What did you think it was? And you hurry up and eat it.

SID (*again regards his soup with astonishment*). Well! (*Then suddenly.*) Well, all right then! Soup be it! (*He picks up his spoon and begins to eat, but after two tries in which he finds it difficult to locate his mouth, he addresses the spoon plaintively.*) Spoon, is this any way to treat a pal? (*Then suddenly comically angry, putting the spoon down with a bang.*) Down with spoons! (*He raises his soup plate and declaims.*) "We'll drink to the dead already, and hurrah for the next who dies." (*Bowing solemnly to right and left.*) Your good health, ladies *and* gents. (*He starts drinking the soup.* MILLER *guffaws and* MILDRED *and* TOMMY *giggle. Even* RICHARD *forgets his melancholy and snickers, and* MRS. MILLER *conceals a smile. Only* LILY *remains stiff and silent.*)

MRS. MILL. (*with forced severity*). Sid!

SID (*peers at her muzzily, lowering the soup plate a little from his lips*). Eh?

MRS. MILL. Oh, nothing. Never mind.

SID (*solemnly offended*). Are you—publicly rebuking me before assembled—? Isn't soup liquid? Aren't liquids drunk? (*Then considering this to himself.*) What if they are drunk? It's a good man's failing. (*He again peers mistily about at the company.*) Am I right or wrong?

MRS. MILL. Hurry up and finish your soup, and stop talking nonsense!

SID (*turning to her—again offendedly*). Oh, no, Essie, if I ever so far forget myself as to drink a leg of lamb, then you might have some—excuse for— Just think of waste effort eating soup with spoons—fifty gruelling lifts per plate—billions of soup-eaters on globe—why, it's simply staggering! (*Then darkly to himself.*) No more spoons for me! If I want to develop my biceps, I'll buy Sandow Exerciser! (*He drinks the rest of his soup in a gulp and beams around at the company, suddenly all happiness again.*) Am I right, folks?

MILL. (*who has been choking with laughter.*) Haw, haw! You're right, Sid.

SID (*peers at him blurredly and shakes his head sadly*). Poor old Nat! Always wrong—but heart of gold, heart of purest gold. And drunk again, I regret to note. Sister, my heart bleeds for you and your poor fatherless chicks!

MRS. MILL. (*restraining a giggle—severely*). Sid! Do shut up for a minute! Pass me your soup plates, everybody. If we wait for that girl to take them, we'll be here all night.

(*They all pass their plates, which* MRS. MILLER *stacks up and then puts on the sideboard. As she is doing this,* NORAH *appears from the pantry with a platter of broiled fish. She is just about to place these before* MILLER *when* SID *catches her eye mistily and rises to his feet, making her a deep, uncertain bow.*)

SID (*raptly*). Ah, Sight for Sore Eyes, my beautiful Macushla, my star-eyed Mavourneen—

MRS. MILL. Sid!

NOR. (*immensely pleased—gives him an arch, flirtatious glance*). Ah sure, Mister Sid, it's you that have kissed the Blarney Stone, when you've a drop taken!

MRS. MILL. (*outraged*). Norah! Put down that fish!

NOR. (*flusteredly*). Yes, Mum. (*She attempts to put the fish down hastily before* MILLER, *but her eyes are fixed nervously on* MRS. MILLER *and she gives* MILLER *a nasty swipe on the side of the head with the edge of the dish.*)

MILL. Ouch! (*The children, even* RICHARD, *explode into laughter.*)

NOR. (*almost lets the dish fall*). Oh, glory be to God! Is it hurted you are?

MILL. (*rubbing his head—good-naturedly*). No, no harm done. Only careful, Norah, careful.

NOR. (*gratefully*). Yes, sorr. (*She thumps down the dish in front of him with a sigh of relief.*)

SID (*who is still standing—with drunken gravity*). Careful, Mavourneen, careful! You might have hit him some place besides the head. Always aim at his head, remember—so as not to worry us.

(*Again the children explode. Also* NORAH. *Even* LILY *suddenly lets out an hysterical giggle and is furious with herself for doing so.*)

LILY. I'm so sorry, Nat. I didn't mean to laugh. (*Turning on* SID *furiously.*) Will you please sit down and stop making a fool of yourself!

(SID *gives her a hurt, mournful look and then sinks meekly down on his chair.*)

NOR. (*grinning cheerfully, gives* LILY *a reassuring pat on the back*). Ah, Miss Lily, don't mind him. He's only under the influence. Sure, there's no harm in him at all.

MRS. MILL. Norah!

(NORAH *exits hastily into the pantry, letting the door slam with a crash behind her. There is silence for a moment as* MILLER *serves the fish and it is passed around.* NORAH *comes back with the vegetables and disappears again, and these are dished out.*)

MILL. (*is about to take his first bite—stops suddenly and asks his wife*). This isn't, by any chance, bluefish, is it, my dear?

MRS. MILL. (*with a warning glance at* TOMMY). Of course not. You know we never have bluefish, on account of you.

MILL. (*addressing the table now with the gravity of a man confessing his strange peculiarities*). Yes, I regret to say, there's a certain peculiar oil in bluefish that invariably poisons me. (*At this,* TOMMY *cannot stand it any more but explodes into laughter.* MRS. MILLER, *after a helpless glance at him, follows suit; then* LILY *goes off into uncontrollable, hysterical laughter, and* RICHARD *and* MILDRED *are caught in the contagion.* MILLER *looks around at them with a weak smile, his dignity now ruffled a bit.*) Well, I must say I don't see what's so darned funny about my being poisoned.

SID (*peers around him—then with drunken cunning*). Aha! Nat, I suspect—plot! This fish looks blue to me—very blue—in fact despondent, desperate, and— (*He points his fork dramatically at* MRS. MILLER.) See how guilty she looks—a ver—veritable Lucretia Georgia! Can it be this woman has been slowly poisoning you all these years? And how well—you've stood it! What iron constitution! Even now, when you are invariably at death's door, I can't believe—

(*Everyone goes off into uncontrollable laughter.*)

MILL. (*grumpily*). Oh, give us a rest, you darned fool! A joke's a joke, but— (*He addresses his wife in a wounded tone.*) Is this true, Essie?

MRS. MILL. (*wiping the tears from her eyes—defiantly*). Yes, it is true, if you must know, and you'd never have suspected it, if it weren't for that darned Tommy, and Sid poking his nose in. You've eaten bluefish for years and thrived on it and it's all nonsense about that peculiar oil.

MILL. (*deeply offended*). Kindly allow me to know my own constitution! Now I think of it, I've felt upset afterwards every damned time we've had fish! (*He pushes his plate away from him with proud renunciation.*) I can't eat this.

MRS. MILL. (*insultingly matter-of-fact*). Well, don't then. There's lots of lobster coming and you can fill up on that.

(RICHARD *suddenly bursts out laughing again.*)

MILL. (*turns to him caustically*). You seem in a merry mood, Richard. I thought you were the original of the Heart Bowed Down today.

SID (*with mock condolence*). Never mind, Dick. Let them—scoff! What can they understand about girls whose hair sizzchels, whose lips are fireworks, whose eyes are red-hot sparks—

MILD. (*laughing*). Is that what he wrote to Muriel? (*Turning to her brother.*) You silly goat, you!

RICH. (*surlily*). Aw, shut up, Mid. What do I care about her? I'll show all of you how much I care!

MRS. MILL. Pass your plates as soon as you're through, everybody. I've rung for the lobster. And that's all. You don't get any dessert or tea after lobster, you know.

(NORAH *appears bearing a platter of cold boiled lobsters which she sets before* MILLER, *and disappears.*)

TOM. Gee, I love lobster!

(MILLER *puts one on each plate, and they are passed around and everyone starts in pulling the cracked shells apart.*)

MILL. (*feeling more cheerful after a couple of mouthfuls—determining to give the conversation another turn, says to his daughter*). Have a good time at the beach, Mildred?

MILD. Oh, fine, Pa, thanks. The water was wonderful and warm.

MILL. Swim far?

MILD. Yes, for me. But that isn't so awful far.

MILL. Well, you ought to be a good swimmer, if you take after me. I used to be a regular water rat when I was a boy. I'll have to go down to the beach with you one of these days—though I'd be rusty, not having been in in all these years. (*The reminiscent look comes into his eyes of one about to embark on an oft-told tale of childhood adventure.*) You know, speaking of swimming, I never go down to that beach but what it calls to mind the day I and Red Sisk went in swimming there and I saved his life.

(*By this time the family are beginning to exchange amused, guilty glances. They all know what is coming.*)

SID (*with a sly, blurry wink around*). Ha! Now we—have it again!

MILL. (*turning on him*). Have what?

SID. Nothing—go on with your swimming—don't mind me.

MILL. (*glares at him—but immediately is overcome by the reminiscent mood again*). Red Sisk—his father kept a blacksmith shop where the Union Market is now—we kids called him Red because he had the darnedest reddest crop of hair—

SID (*as if he were talking to his plate*). Remarkable!—the curious imagination—of little children.

MRS. MILL. (*as she sees MILLER about to explode—interposes tactfully*). Sid! Eat your lobster and shut up! Go on, Nat.

MILL. (*gives SID a withering look—then is off again*). Well, as I was saying, Red and I went swimming that day. Must have been—let me see—Red was fourteen, bigger and older than me, I was only twelve—forty-five years ago—wasn't a single house down there then—but there was a stake out where the whistling buoy is now, about a mile out. (TOMMY, *who has been having difficulty restraining himself, lets out a stifled giggle.* MILLER *bends a frowning gaze on him.*) One more sound out of you, young man, and you'll leave this table!

MRS. MILL. (*quickly interposing, trying to stave off the story*). Do eat your lobster, Nat. You didn't have any fish, you know.

MILL. (*not liking the reminder—pettishly*). Well, if I'm going to be interrupted every second anyway— (*He turns to his lobster and chews in silence for a moment.*)

MRS. MILL. (*trying to switch the subject*). How's Anne's mother's rheumatism, Mildred?

MILD. Oh, she's much better, Ma. She was in wading today. She says salt water's the only thing that really helps her bunion.

MRS. MILL. Mildred! Where are your manners? At the table's no place to speak of—

MILL. (*fallen into the reminiscent obsession again*). Well, as I was saying, there was I and Red, and he dared me to race him out to the stake and back. Well, I didn't let anyone dare me in those days. I was a spunky kid. So I said all right and we started out. We swam and swam and were pretty evenly matched; though, as I've said, he was bigger and older than me, but finally I drew ahead. I was going along easy, with lots in reserve, not a bit tired, when suddenly I heard a sort of gasp from behind me—like this —"help." (*He imitates. Everyone's eyes are firmly fixed on their plates, except* SID's.) And I turned and there was Red, his face all pinched and white, and he says weakly: "Help, Nat! I got a cramp in my leg!" Well, I don't mind telling you I got mighty scared. I didn't know what to do. Then suddenly I thought of the pile. If I could pull him to that, I could hang on to him till someone'd notice us. But the pile was still—well, I calculate it must have been two hundred feet away.

SID. Two hundred and fifty!

MILL. (*in confusion*). What's that?

SID. Two hundred *and* fifty! I've taken down the distance every time you've saved Red's life for thirty years and the mean average to that pile is two hundred and fifty feet! (*There is a burst of laughter from around the table.* SID *continues complainingly.*) Why didn't you let that Red drown, anyway, Nat? I never knew him but I know I'd never have liked him.

MILL. (*really hurt, forces a feeble smile to his lips and pretends to be a good sport about it*). Well, guess you're right, Sid. Guess I have told that one too many times and bored everyone. But it's a good true story for kids because it illustrates the danger of being foolhardy in the water—

MRS. MILL. (*sensing the hurt in his tone, comes to his rescue*). Of course it's a good story—and you tell it whenever you've a mind to. And you, Sid, if you were in any responsible state, I'd give you a good piece of my mind for teasing Nat like that.

MILL. (*with a sad, self-pitying smile at his wife*). Getting old, I guess, Mother—getting to repeat myself. Someone ought to stop me.

MRS. MILL. No such thing! You're as young as you ever were. (*She turns on SID again angrily.*) You eat your lobster and maybe it'll keep your mouth shut!

SID (*after a few chews—irrepressibly*). Lobster! Did you know, Tommy, your Uncle Sid is the man invented lobster? Fact! One day—when I was building the Pyramids—took a day off and just dashed off lobster. He was bigger'n' older than me and he had the darnedest reddest crop of hair but I dashed him off just the same. Am I right, Nat? (*Then suddenly in the tones of a side-show barker.*) Ladies *and* Gents—

MRS. MILL. Mercy sakes! Can't you shut up?

SID. In this cage you see the lobster. You will not believe me, ladies *and* gents, but it's a fact that this interesting bivalve only makes love to his mate once in every thousand years—but, dearie me, how he does enjoy it!

(*The children roar.* LILY *and* MRS. MILLER *laugh in spite of themselves—then look embarrassed.* MILLER *guffaws—then suddenly grows shocked.*)

MILL. Careful, Sid, careful. Remember you're at home.

TOM. (*suddenly in a hoarse whisper to his mother, with an awed glance of admiration at his uncle*). Ma! Look at him! He's eating that claw, shells and all!

MRS. MILL. (*horrified*). Sid, do you want to kill yourself? Take it away from him, Lily!

SID (*with great dignity*). But I prefer the shells. All famous epicures prefer the shells—to the less delicate, coarser meat. It's the same with clams. Unless I eat the shells there is a certain, peculiar oil that invariably poisons— Am I right, Nat?

MILL. (*good-naturedly*). You seem to be getting a lot of fun kidding me. Go ahead, then. I don't mind.

MRS. MILL. He better go right up to bed for a while, that's what he better do.

SID (*considering this owlishly*). Bed? Yes, maybe you're right. (*He gets to his feet.*) I am not at all well—in very delicate condition—we are praying for a boy. Am I right, Nat? Nat, I kept telling you all day I was in delicate condition and yet you kept forcing demon chowder on me, although you knew full well—even if you were full—that there is a certain peculiar oil in chowder that invariably— (*They are again all laughing—*LILY, *hysterically.*)

MRS. MILL. *Will* you get to bed, you idiot!

SID (*mutters graciously*). Immediately—if not sooner. (*He turns to pass behind* LILY, *then stops, staring down at her.*) But wait. There is still a duty I must perform. No day is complete without it. Lily, answer once and for all, will you marry me?

LILY (*with an hysterical giggle*). No, I won't—never!

SID (*nodding his head*). Right! And perhaps it's all for the best. For how could I forget the pre—precepts taught me at mother's dying knee. "Sidney," she said, "never marry a woman who drinks! Lips that touch liquor shall never touch yours!" (*Gazing at her mournfully.*) Too bad! So fine a woman once—and now such a slave to rum! (*Turning to* NAT.) What can we do to save her, Nat? (*In a hoarse, confidential whisper.*) Better put her in institution where she'll be removed from temptation! The mere smell of it seems to drive her frantic!

MRS. MILL. (*struggling with her laughter*). You leave Lily alone, and go to bed!

SID. *Right!* (*He comes around behind* LILY's *chair and moves toward the entrance to the back parlor—then suddenly turns and says with a bow.*) Good night, ladies—*and* gents. We will meet—bye and bye! (*He gives an imitation of a Salvation Army drum.*) Boom! Boom! Boom! Come and be saved, Brothers! (*He starts to sing the old Army hymn.*)

> "In the sweet
> Bye and bye
> We will meet on that beautiful shore."

(*He turns and marches solemnly out through the back parlor, singing.*)

> "Work and pray
> While you may.
> We will meet in the sky bye and bye."

(MILLER *and his wife and the children are all roaring with laughter.* LILY *giggles hysterically.*)

MILL. (*subsiding at last*). Haw, haw. He's a case, if ever there was one! Darned if you can help laughing at him—even when he's poking fun at you!

MRS. MILL. Goodness, but he's a caution! Oh, my sides ache, I declare! I was trying so hard not to—but you can't help it, he's so silly! But I suppose we really shouldn't. It only encourages him. But, my lands—!

LILY (*suddenly gets up from her chair and stands rigidly, her face working—jerkily*). That's just it—you shouldn't—even I laughed —it does encourage—that's been his downfall—everyone always laughing, everyone always saying what a card he is, what a case, what a caution, so funny—and he's gone on—and we're all responsible—making it easy for him—we're all to blame—and all we do is laugh!

MILL. (*worriedly*). Now, Lily, now, you mustn't take on so. It isn't as serious as all that.

LILY (*bitterly*). Maybe—it is—to me. Or was—once. (*Then contritely.*) I'm sorry, Nat. I'm sorry, Essie. I didn't mean to—I'm not feeling myself tonight. If you'll excuse me, I'll go in the front parlor and lie down on the sofa awhile.

MRS. MILL. Of course, Lily. You do whatever you've a mind to.

(LILY *goes out.*)

MILL. (*frowning—a little shamefaced*). Hmm. I suppose she's right. Never knew Lily to come out with things that way before. Anything special happened, Essie?

MRS. MILL. Nothing I know—except he'd promised to take her to the fireworks.

MILL. That's so. Well, supposing I take her. I don't want her to feel disappointed.

MRS. MILL. (*shaking her head*). Wild horses couldn't drag her there now.

MILL. Hmm. I thought she'd got completely over her foolishness about him long ago.

MRS. MILL. She never will.

MILL. She'd better. He's got fired out of that Waterbury job—told me at the picnic after he'd got enough Dutch courage in him.

MRS. MILL. Oh, dear! Isn't he the fool!

MILL. I knew something was wrong when he came home. Well, I'll find a place for him on my paper again, of course. He always was the best news-getter this town ever had. But I'll tell him he's got to stop his damn nonsense.

MRS. MILL. (*doubtfully*). Yes.

MILL. Well, no use sitting here mourning over spilt milk. (*He gets up, and* RICHARD, MILDRED, TOMMY *and* MRS. MILLER *follow his example, the children quiet and a bit awed.*) You kids go out in the yard and try to keep quiet for a while, so's your Uncle Sid'll get to sleep and your Aunt Lily can rest.

TOM. (*mournfully*). Ain't we going to set off the skyrockets and Roman candles, Pa?

MILL. Later, Son, later. It isn't dark enough for them yet anyway.

MILD. Come on, Tommy. I'll see he keeps quiet, Pa.

MILL. That's a good girl. (MILDRED *and* TOMMY *go out through the screen door.* RICHARD *remains standing, sunk in bitter, gloomy thoughts.* MILLER *glances at him—then irritably.*) Well, Melancholy Dane, what are you doing?

RICH. (*darkly*). I'm going out—for a while. (*Then suddenly.*) Do you know what I think? It's Aunt Lily's fault, Uncle Sid's going to ruin. It's all because he loves her, and she keeps him dangling after her, and eggs him on and ruins his life—like all women love to ruin men's lives! I don't blame him for drinking himself to death! What does he care if he dies, after the way she's treated him! I'd do the same thing myself if I were in his boots!

MRS. MILL. (*indignantly*). Richard! You stop that talk!

RICH. (*quotes bitterly*).

"Drink! for you know not whence you come nor why.
Drink! for you know not why you go nor where!"

MILL. (*losing his temper—harshly*). Listen here, young man! I've had about all I can stand of your nonsense for one day! You're growing a lot too big for your size, seems to me! You keep that damn fool talk to yourself, you hear me—or you're going to regret it! Mind now! (*He strides angrily away through the back parlor.*)

MRS. MILL. (*still indignant*). Richard, I'm ashamed of you, that's what I am. (*She follows her husband.* RICHARD *stands for a second, bitter, humiliated, wronged, even his father turned enemy, his face growing more and more rebellious. Then he forces a scornful smile to his lips.*)

RICH. Aw, what the hell do I care? I'll show them! (*He turns and goes out the screen door.*)

(CURTAIN)

ACT THREE

Scene One

SCENE—*The back room of a bar in a small hotel—a small, dingy room, dimly lighted by two fly-specked globes in a fly-specked gilt chandelier suspended from the middle of the ceiling. At left, front, is the swinging door leading to the bar. At rear of door, against the wall, is a nickel-in-the-slot player-piano. In the rear wall, right, is a door leading to the "Family Entrance" and the stairway to the upstairs rooms. In the middle of the right wall is a window with closed shutters. Three tables with stained tops, four chairs around each table, are placed at center, front, at right, toward rear, and at rear, center. A brass cuspidor is on the floor by each table. The floor is unswept, littered with cigarette and cigar butts. The hideous saffron-colored wallpaper is blotched and spotted.*

It is about 10 o'clock the same night. RICHARD *and* BELLE *are discovered sitting at the table at center,* BELLE *at left of it,* RICHARD *in the next chair at the middle of table, rear, facing front.*

BELLE *is twenty, a rather pretty peroxide blonde, a typical college "tart" of the period, and of the cheaper variety, dressed with tawdry flashiness. But she is a fairly recent recruit to the ranks, and is still a bit remorseful behind her make-up and defiantly careless manner.*

BELLE *has an empty gin-rickey glass before her,* RICHARD *a half-empty glass of beer. He looks horribly timid, embarrassed and guilty, but at the same time thrilled and proud of at last mingling with the pace that kills.*

The player-piano is grinding out "Bedelia." The BARTENDER, *a stocky young Irishman with a foxily cunning, stupid face and a cynically wise grin, stands just inside the bar entrance, watching them over the swinging door.*

BELL. *(with an impatient glance at her escort—rattling the ice in her empty glass).* Drink up your beer, why don't you? It's getting flat.

RICH. *(embarrassedly).* I let it get that way on purpose. I like it better when it's flat. *(But he hastily gulps down the rest of his glass, as if it were some nasty-tasting medicine. The* BARTENDER *chuckles audibly.* BELLE *glances at him.)*

BELL. *(nodding at the player-piano scornfully).* Say, George, is "Bedelia" the latest to hit this hick burg? Well, it's only a couple of years old! You'll catch up in time! Why don't you get a new roll for that old box?

BAR. *(with a grin).* Complain to the boss, not me. We're not used to having Candy Kiddoes like you around—or maybe we'd get up to date.

BELL. *(with a professionally arch grin at him).* Don't kid me, please. I can't bear it. *(Then she sings to the music from the piano, her eyes now on* RICHARD.) "Bedelia, I'd like to feel yer." *(The* BARTENDER *laughs. She smirks at* RICHARD.) Ever hear those words to it, Kid?

RICH. *(who has heard them but is shocked at hearing a girl say them— putting on a blasé air).* Sure, lots of times. That's old.

BELL. *(edging her chair closer and putting a hand over one of his).* Then why don't you act as if you knew what they were all about?

RICH. *(terribly flustered).* Sure, I've heard that old parody lots of times. What do you think I am?

BELL. I don't know, Kid. Honest to God, you've got me guessing.

BAR. (*with a mocking chuckle*). He's a hot sport, can't you tell it? I never seen such a spender. My head's dizzy bringing you in drinks!

BELL. (*laughs irritably—to* RICHARD) Don't let him kid you. You show him. Loosen up and buy another drink, what say?

RICH. (*humiliated—manfully*). Sure. Excuse me. I was thinking of something else. Have anything you like. (*He turns to the* BAR-TENDER *who has entered from the bar*.) See what the lady will have—and have one on me yourself.

BAR. (*coming to the table—with a wink at* BELLE). That's talking! Didn't I say you were a sport? I'll take a cigar on you. (*To* BELLE.) What's yours, Kiddo—the same?

BELL. Yes. And forget the house rules this time and remember a rickey is supposed to have gin in it.

BAR. (*grinning*). I'll try to—seeing it's you. (*Then to* RICHARD.) What's yours—another beer?

RICH. (*shyly*). A small one, please. I'm not thirsty.

BELL. (*calculatedly taunting*). Say, honest, are things that slow up at Harvard? If they had you down at New Haven, they'd put you in a kindergarten! Don't be such a dead one! Filling up on beer will only make you sleepy. Have a man's drink!

RICH. (*shamefacedly*). All right. I was going to. Bring me a sloe-gin fizz.

BELL. (*to* BARTENDER). And make it a real one.

BAR. (*with a wink*). I get you. Something that'll warm him up, eh? (*He goes into the bar, chuckling*.)

BELL. (*looks around the room—irritably*). Christ, what a dump! (RICH-ARD *is startled and shocked by this curse and looks down at the table*.) If this isn't the deadest burg I ever struck! Bet they take the sidewalks in after nine o'clock! (*Then turning on him*.) Say, honestly, Kid, does your mother know you're out?

RICH. (*defensively*). Aw, cut it out, why don't you—trying to kid me!

BELL. (*glances at him—then resolves on a new tack—patting his hand*). All right. I didn't mean to, Dearie. Please don't get sore at me.

RICH. I'm not sore.

BELL. (*seductively*). You see, it's this way with me. I think you're one of the sweetest kids I've ever met—and I could like you such a lot if you'd give me half a chance—instead of acting so cold and indifferent.

RICH. I'm not cold and indifferent. (*Then solemnly tragic.*) It's only that I've got—a weight on my mind.

BELL. (*impatiently*). Well, get it off your mind and give something else a chance to work. (*The* BARTENDER *comes in, bringing the drinks.*)

BAR. (*setting them down—with a wink at* BELLE). This'll warm him for you. Forty cents, that is—with the cigar.

RICH. (*pulls out his roll and hands a dollar bill over—with exaggerated carelessness*). Keep the change.

(BELLE *emits a gasp and seems about to protest, then thinks better of it. The* BARTENDER *cannot believe his luck for a moment—then pockets the bill hastily, as if afraid* RICHARD *will change his mind.*)

BAR. (*respect in his voice*). Thank you, sir.

RICH. (*grandly*). Don't mention it.

BAR. I hope you like the drink. I took special pains with it. (*The voice of the* SALESMAN, *who has just come in the bar, calls* "Hey! Anybody here?" *and a coin is rapped on the bar.*) I'm coming.

(*The* BARTENDER *goes out.*)

BELL. (*remonstrating gently, a new appreciation for her escort's possibilities in her voice*). You shouldn't be so generous, Dearie. Gets him in bad habits. A dime would have been plenty.

RICH. Ah, that's all right. I'm no tightwad.

BELL. That's the talk I like to hear. (*With a quick look toward the bar, she stealthily pulls up her dress—to* RICHARD's *shocked fascination —and takes a package of cheap cigarettes from her stocking.*) Keep an eye out for that bartender, Kid, and tell me if you see him coming. Girls are only allowed to smoke upstairs in the rooms, he said.

RICH. (*embarrassedly*). All right. I'll watch.

BELL. (*having lighted her cigarette and inhaled deeply, holds the package out to him*). Have a Sweet? You smoke, don't you?

RICH. (*taking one*). Sure! I've been smoking for the last two years—on the sly. But next year I'll be allowed—that is, pipes and cigars.

(*He lights his cigarette with elaborate nonchalance, puffs, but does not inhale—then, watching her, with shocked concern.*) Say, you oughtn't to inhale like that! Smoking's awful bad for girls, anyway, even if they don't—

BELL. (*cynically amused*). Afraid it will stunt my growth? Gee, Kid, you are a scream! You'll grow up to be a minister yet! (RICHARD *looks shamefaced. She scans him impatiently—then holds up her drink.*) Well, here's how! Bottoms up, now! Show me you really know how to drink. It'll take that load off your mind. (RICHARD *follows her example and they both drink the whole contents of their glasses before setting them down.*) There! That's something like! Feel better?

RICH. (*proud of himself—with a shy smile*). You bet.

BELL. Well, you'll feel still better in a minute—and then maybe you won't be so distant and unfriendly, eh?

RICH. I'm not.

BELL. Yes, you are. I think you just don't like me.

RICH. (*more manfully*). I do too like you.

BELL. How much? A lot?

RICH. Yes, a lot.

BELL. Show me how much! (*Then as he fidgets embarrassedly.*) Want me to come sit on your lap?

RICH. Yes—I— (*She comes and sits on his lap. He looks desperately uncomfortable, but the gin is rising to his head and he feels proud of himself and devilish, too.*)

BELL. Why don't you put your arm around me? (*He does so awkwardly.*) No, not that dead way. Hold me tight. You needn't be afraid of hurting me. I like to be held tight, don't you?

RICH. Sure I do.

BELL. 'Specially when it's by a nice handsome kid like you. (*Ruffling his hair.*) Gee, you've got pretty hair, do you know it? Honest, I'm awfully strong for you! Why can't you be about me? I'm not so awfully ugly, am I?

RICH. No, you're—you're pretty.

BELL. You don't say it as if you meant it.

RICH. I do mean it—honest.

BELL. Then why don't you kiss me? (*She bends down her lips toward his. He hesitates, then kisses her and at once shrinks back.*) Call that kissing? Here. (*She holds his head and fastens her lips on his and holds them there. He starts and struggles. She laughs.*) What's the matter, Honey Boy? Haven't you ever kissed like that before?

RICH. Sure. Lots of times.

BELL. Then why did you jump as if I'd bitten you? (*Squirming around on his lap.*) Gee, I'm getting just crazy about you! What shall we do about it, eh? Tell me.

RICH. I—don't know. (*Then boldly.*) I—I'm crazy about you, too.

BELL. (*kissing him again*). Just think of the wonderful time Edith and your friend, Wint, are having upstairs—while we sit down here like two dead ones. A room only costs two dollars. And, seeing I like you so much, I'd only take five dollars—from you. I'd do it for nothing—for you—only I've got to live and I owe my room rent in New Haven—and you know how it is. I get ten dollars from everyone else. Honest! (*She kisses him again, then gets up from his lap—briskly.*) Come on. Go out and tell the bartender you want a room. And hurry. Honest, I'm so strong for you I can hardly wait to get you upstairs!

RICH. (*starts automatically for the door to the bar—then hesitates, a great struggle going on in his mind—timidity, disgust at the money element, shocked modesty, and the guilty thought of* MURIEL, *fighting it out with the growing tipsiness that makes him want to be a hell of a fellow and go in for all forbidden fruit, and makes this tart a romantic, evil vampire in his eyes. Finally, he stops and mutters in confusion*). I can't.

BELL. What, are you too bashful to ask for a room? Let me do it, then. (*She starts for the door.*)

RICH. (*desperately*). No—I don't want you to—I don't want to.

BELL. (*surveying him, anger coming into her eyes*). Well, if you aren't the lousiest cheap skate!

RICH. I'm not a cheap skate!

BELL. Keep me around here all night fooling with you when I might be out with some real live ones—if there is such a thing in this burg!—and now you quit on me! Don't be such a piker! You've got five dollars! I seen it when you paid for the drinks, so don't hand me any lies!

RICH. I— Who said I hadn't? And I'm not a piker. If you need the five dollars so bad—for your room rent—you can have it without—I mean, I'll be glad to give— (*He has been fumbling in his pocket and pulls out his nine-dollar roll and holds out the five to her.*)

BELL. (*hardly able to believe her eyes, almost snatches it from his hand—then laughs and immediately becomes sentimentally grateful*). Thanks, Kid. Gee—oh, thanks— Gee, forgive me for losing my temper and bawling you out, will you? Gee, you're a regular peach! You're the nicest kid I've ever met! (*She kisses him and he grins proudly, a hero to himself now on many counts.*) Gee, you're a peach! Thanks, again!

RICH. (*grandly—and quite tipsily*). It's—nothing—only too glad. (*Then boldly.*) Here—give me another kiss, and that'll pay me back.

BELL. (*kissing him*). I'll give you a thousand, if you want 'em. Come on, let's sit down, and we'll have another drink—and this time I'll blow you just to show my appreciation. (*She calls.*) Hey, George! Bring us another round—the same!

RICH. (*a remnant of caution coming to him*). I don't know as I ought to—

BELL. Oh, another won't hurt you. And I want to blow you, see. (*They sit down in their former places.*)

RICH. (*boldly draws his chair closer and puts an arm around her—tipsily*). I like you a lot—now I'm getting to know you. You're a darned nice girl.

BELL. Nice is good! Tell me another! Well, if I'm so nice, why didn't you want to take me upstairs? That's what I don't get.

RICH. (*lying boldly*). I did want to—only I— (*Then he adds solemnly.*) I've sworn off. (*The* BARTENDER *enters with the drinks.*)

BAR. (*setting them on the table*). Here's your pleasure. (*Then regarding* RICHARD'S *arm about her waist.*) Ho-ho, we're coming on, I see. (RICHARD *grins at him muzzily.*)

BELL. (*digs into her stocking and gives him a dollar*). Here. This is mine. (*He gives her change and she tips him a dime, and he goes out. She puts the five* RICHARD *had given her in her stocking and picks up her glass.*) Here's how—and thanks again. (*She sips.*)

RICH. (*boisterously*). Bottoms up! Bottoms up! (*He drinks all of his down and sighs with exaggerated satisfaction.*) Gee, that's good stuff, all right. (*Hugging her.*) Give me another kiss, Belle.

BELL. (*kisses him*). What did you mean a minute ago when you said you'd sworn off?

RICH. (*solemnly*). I took an oath I'd be faithful.

BELL. (*cynically*). Till death do us part, eh? Who's the girl?

RICH. (*shortly*). Never mind.

BELL. (*bristling*). I'm not good enough to talk about her, I suppose?

RICH. I didn't—mean that. You're all right. (*Then with tipsy gravity.*) Only you oughtn't to lead this kind of life. It isn't right—for a nice girl like you. Why don't you reform?

BELL. (*sharply*). Nix on that line of talk! Can it, you hear! You can do a lot with me for five dollars—but you can't reform me, see. Mind your own business, Kid, and don't butt in where you're not wanted!

RICH. I—I didn't mean to hurt your feelings.

BELL. I know you didn't mean. You're only like a lot of people who mean well, to hear them tell it. (*Changing the subject.*) So you're faithful to your one love, eh? (*With an ugly sneer.*) And how about her? Bet you she's out with a guy under some bush this minute, giving him all he wants. Don't be a sucker, Kid! Even the little flies do it!

RICH. (*starting up in his chair—angrily*). Don't you say that! Don't you dare!

BELL. (*unimpressed—with a cynical shrug of her shoulders*). All right. Have it your own way and be a sucker! It cuts no ice with me.

RICH. You don't know her or—

BELL. And don't want to. Shut up about her, can't you? (*She stares before her bitterly.* RICHARD *subsides into scowling gloom. He is becoming perceptibly more intoxicated with each moment now. The* BARTENDER *and the* SALESMAN *appear just inside the swinging door.*

The BARTENDER *nods toward* BELLE, *giving the* SALESMAN *a wink. The* SALESMAN *grins and comes into the room, carrying his high-ball in his hand. He is a stout, jowly-faced man in the late thirties, dressed with cheap nattiness, with the professional breeziness and jocular, kid-'em-along manner of his kind.* BELLE *looks up as he enters and he and she exchange a glance of complete recognition. She knows his type by heart and he knows hers.*)

SALES. (*passes by her to the table at right—grinning genially*). Good evening.

BELL. Good evening.

SALES. (*sitting down*). Hope I'm not butting in on your party—but my dogs were giving out standing at that bar.

BELL. All right with me. (*Giving* RICHARD *a rather contemptuous look.*) I've got no party on.

SALES. That sounds hopeful.

RICH. (*suddenly recites sentimentally*).

"But I wouldn't do such, 'cause I loved her too much,
But I learned about women from her."

(*Turns to scowl at the* SALESMAN—*then to* BELLE.) Let's have 'nother drink!

BELL. You've had enough.

(RICHARD *subsides, muttering to himself.*)

SALES. What is it—a child poet or a child actor?

BELL. Don't know. Got me guessing.

SALES. Well, if you could shake the cradle-robbing act, maybe we could do a little business.

BELL. That's easy. I just pull my freight. (*She shakes* RICHARD *by the arm.*) Listen, Kid. Here's an old friend of mine, Mr. Smith of New Haven, just come in. I'm going over and sit at his table for a while, see. And you better go home.

RICH. (*blinking at her and scowling*). I'm never going home! I'll show them!

BELL. Have it your own way—only let me up. (*She takes his arm from around her and goes to sit by the* SALESMAN. RICHARD *stares after her offendedly.*)

RICH. Go on. What do I care what you do? (*He recites scornfully.*) "For a woman's only a woman, but a good cigar's a smoke."

SALES. (*as* BELLE *sits beside him*). Well, what kind of beer will you have, Sister?

BELL. Mine's a gin rickey.

SALES. You've got extravagant tastes, I'm sorry to see.

RICH. (*begins to recite sepulchrally*).

"Yet each man kills the thing he loves,
By each let this be heard."

SALES. (*grinning*). Say, this is rich! (*He calls encouragement.*) That's swell dope, young feller. Give us some more.

RICH. (*ignoring him—goes on more rhetorically*).

"Some do it with a bitter look,
Some with a flattering word,
The coward does it with a kiss,
The brave man with a sword!"

(*He stares at* BELLE *gloomily and mutters tragically.*) I did it with a kiss! I'm a coward.

SALES. That's the old stuff, Kid. You've got something on the ball, all right, all right! Give us another—right over the old pan, now!

BELL. (*with a laugh*). Get the hook!

RICH. (*glowering at her—tragically*).

" 'Oho,' they cried, 'the world is wide,
But fettered limbs go lame!
And once, or twice, to throw the dice
Is a gentlemanly game,
But he does not win who plays with Sin
In the secret House of Shame!' "

BELL. (*angrily*). Aw, can it! Give us a rest from that bunk!

SALES. (*mockingly*). This gal of yours don't appreciate poetry. She's a lowbrow. But I'm the kid that eats it up. My middle name is Kelly and Sheets! Give us some more of the same! Do you know "The Lobster and the Wise Guy"? (*Turns to* BELLE *seriously.*) No kidding, that's a peacherino. I heard a guy recite it at Poli's. Maybe this nut knows it. Do you, Kid? (*But* RICHARD *only glowers at him gloomily without answering.*)

BELL. (*surveying* RICHARD *contemptuously*). He's copped a fine skinful—
and gee, he's hardly had anything.

RICH. (*suddenly—with a dire emphasis*). "And then—at ten o'clock—
Eilert Lovborg will come—with vine leaves in his hair!"

BELL. And bats in his belfry, if he's you!

RICH. (*regards her bitterly—then starts to his feet bellicosely—to the*
SALESMAN). I don't believe you ever knew her in New Haven at
all! You just picked her up now! You leave her alone, you hear!
You won't do anything to her—not while I'm here to protect her!

BELL. (*laughing*). Oh, my God! Listen to it!

SALES. Ssshh! This is a scream! Wait! (*He addresses* RICHARD *in tones of
exaggerated melodrama.*) Curse you, Jack Dalton, if I won't un-
hand her, what then?

RICH. (*threateningly*). I'll give you a good punch in the snoot, that's
what! (*He moves toward their table.*)

SALES. (*with mock terror—screams in falsetto*). Help! Help! (*The* BAR-
TENDER *comes in irritably.*)

BAR. Hey. Cut out the noise. What the hell's up with you?

RICH. (*tipsily*). He's too—damn fresh!

SALES. (*with a wink*). He's going to murder me. (*Then gets a bright
idea for eliminating* RICHARD—*seriously to the* BARTENDER.) It's
none of my business, Brother, but if I were in your boots I'd give
this young souse the gate. He's under age; any fool can see that.

BAR. (*guiltily*). He told me he was over eighteen.

SALES. Yes, and I tell you I'm the Pope—but you don't have to believe
me. If you're not looking for trouble, I'd advise you to get him
started for some other gin mill and let them do the lying, if anything comes up.

BAR. Hmm. (*He turns to* RICHARD *angrily and gives him a push.*) Come
on, now. On your way! You'll start no trouble in here! Beat it
now!

RICH. I will not beat it!

BAR. Oho, won't you? (*He gives him another push that almost sends
him sprawling.*)

BELL. (*callously*). Give him the bum's rush! I'm sick of his bull!

(RICHARD *turns furiously and tries to punch the* BARTENDER.)

BAR. (*avoids the punch*). Oho, you would, would you? (*He grabs* RICH-
ARD *by the back of the neck and the seat of the pants and marches
him ignominiously toward the swinging door.*)

RICH. Leggo of me, you dirty coward!

BAR. Quiet now—or I'll pin a Mary Ann on your jaw that'll quiet you!
(*He rushes him through the screen door and a moment later the
outer doors are heard swinging back and forth.*)

SALES. (*with a chuckle*). Hand it to me, Kid. How was that for a slick
way of getting rid of him?

BELL. (*suddenly sentimental*). Poor kid. I hope he makes home all right.
I liked him—before he got soused.

SALES. Who is he?

BELL. The boy who's upstairs with my friend told me, but I didn't pay
much attention. Name's Miller. His old man runs a paper in this
one-horse burg, I think he said.

SALES. (*with a whistle*). Phew! He must be Nat Miller's kid, then.

BAR. (*coming back from the bar*). Well, he's on his way—with a good
boot in the tail to help him!

SALES. (*with a malicious chuckle*). Yes? well, maybe that boot will
cost you a job, Brother. Know Nat Miller who runs the *Globe?*
That's his kid.

BAR. (*his face falling*). The hell he is! Who said so?

SALES. This baby doll. (*Getting up.*) Say, I'll go keep cases on him—see
he gets on the trolley all right, anyway. Nat Miller's a good scout.
(*He hurries out.*)

BAR. (*viciously*). God damn the luck! If he ever finds out I served his
kid, he'll run me out of town. (*He turns on* BELLE *furiously.*) Why
didn't you put me wise, you lousy tramp, you!

BELL. Hey! I don't stand for that kind of talk—not from no hick beer-
squirter like you, see!

BAR. (*furiously*). You don't, don't you! Who was it but you told me to
hand him dynamite in that fizz? (*He gives her chair a push that
almost throws her to the floor.*) Beat it, you—and beat it quick—
or I'll call Sullivan from the corner and have you run in for street-

walking! (*He gives her a push that lands her against the family-entrance door.*) Get the hell out of here—and no long waits!

BELL. (*opens the door and goes out—turns and calls back viciously*). I'll fix you for this, you thick Mick, if I have to go to jail for it. (*She goes out and slams the door.*)

BAR. (*looks after her worriedly for a second—then shrugs his shoulders*). That's only her bull. (*Then with a sigh as he returns to the bar.*) Them lousy tramps is always getting this dump in Dutch!

(CURTAIN)

Scene Two

SCENE—*Same as Act One—Sitting-room of the* MILLER *home—about 11 o'clock the same night.*

MILLER *is sitting in his favorite rocking-chair at left of table, front. He has discarded collar and tie, coat and shoes, and wears an old, worn, brown dressing-gown and disreputable-looking carpet slippers. He has his reading specs on and is running over items in a newspaper. But his mind is plainly preoccupied and worried, and he is not paying much attention to what he reads.*

MRS. MILLER *sits by the table at right, front. She also has on her specs. A sewing basket is on her lap and she is trying hard to keep her attention fixed on the doily she is doing. But, as in the case of her husband, but much more apparently, her mind is preoccupied, and she is obviously on tenterhooks of nervous uneasiness.*

LILY *is sitting in the armchair by the table at rear, facing right. She is pretending to read a novel, but her attention wanders, too, and her expression is sad, although now it has lost all its bitterness and become submissive and resigned again.*

MILDRED *sits at the desk at right, front, writing two words over and over again, stopping each time to survey the result critically, biting her tongue, intensely concentrated on her work.*

TOMMY *sits on the sofa at left, front. He has had a hard day and is terribly sleepy but will not acknowledge it. His eyes blink shut on him, his head begins to nod, but he isn't giving up, and every time he senses any of the family glancing in his direction, he goads himself into a bright-eyed wakefulness.*

MILD. (*finally surveys the two words she has been writing and is satisfied with them*). There. (*She takes the paper over to her mother.*) Look, Ma. I've been practising a new way of writing my name. Don't look at the others, only the last one. Don't you think it's the real goods?

MRS. MILL. (*pulled out of her preoccupation*). Don't talk that horrible slang. It's bad enough for boys, but for a young girl supposed to have manners—my goodness, when I was your age, if my mother'd ever heard me—

MILD. Well, don't you think it's nice, then?

MRS. MILL. (*sinks back into preoccupation—scanning the paper—vaguely*). Yes, very nice, Mildred—very nice, indeed. (*Hands the paper back mechanically.*)

MILD. (*is a little piqued, but smiles*). Absent-minded! I don't believe you even saw it. (*She passes around the table to show her* AUNT LILY. MILLER *gives an uneasy glance at his wife and then, as if afraid of meeting her eye, looks quickly back at his paper again.*)

MRS. MILL. (*staring before her—sighs worriedly*). Oh, I do wish Richard would come home!

MILL. There now, Essie. He'll be in any minute now. Don't you worry about him.

MRS. MILL. But I do worry about him!

LILY (*surveying* MILDRED's *handiwork—smiling*). This is fine, Mildred. Your penmanship is improving wonderfully. But don't you think that maybe you've got a little too many flourishes?

MILD. (*disappointedly*). But, Aunt Lily, that's just what I was practising hardest on.

MRS. MILL. (*with another sigh*). What time is it now, Nat?

MILL. (*adopting a joking tone*). I'm going to buy a clock for in here. You have me reaching for my watch every couple of minutes. (*He has pulled his watch out of his vest pocket—with forced carelessness.*) Only a little past ten.

MRS. MILL. Why, you said it was that an hour ago! Nat Miller, you're telling me a fib, so's not to worry me. You let me see that watch!

MILL. (*guiltily*). Well, it's quarter to eleven—but that's not so late—when you remember it's Fourth of July.

MRS. MILL. If you don't stop talking Fourth of July—! To hear you go on, you'd think that was an excuse for anything from murder to picking pockets!

MILD. (*has brought her paper around to her father and now shoves it under his nose*). Look, Pa.

MILL. (*seizes on this interruption with relief*). Let's see. Hmm. Seems to me you've been inventing a new signature every week lately. What are you in training for—writing checks? You must be planning to catch a rich husband.

MILD. (*with an arch toss of her head*). No wedding bells for me! But how do you like it, Pa?

MILL. It's overpowering—no other word for it, overpowering! You could put it on the Declaration of Independence and not feel ashamed.

MRS. MILL. (*desolately, almost on the verge of tears*). It's all right for you to laugh and joke with Mildred! I'm the only one in this house seems to care— (*Her lips tremble.*)

MILD. (*a bit disgustedly*). Ah, Ma, Dick only sneaked off to the fireworks at the beach, you wait and see.

MRS. MILL. Those fireworks were over long ago. If he had, he'd be home.

LILY (*soothingly*). He probably couldn't get a seat, the trolleys are so jammed, and he had to walk home.

MILL. (*seizing on this with relief*). Yes, I never thought of that, but I'll bet that's it.

MILD. Ah, don't let him worry you, Ma. He just wants to show off he's heartbroken about that silly Muriel—and get everyone fussing over him and wondering if he hasn't drowned himself or something.

MRS. MILL. (*snappily*). You be quiet! The way you talk at times, I really believe you're that hard-hearted you haven't got a heart in you! (*With an accusing glance at her husband.*) One thing I know, you don't get that from me! (*He meets her eye and avoids it guiltily. She sniffs and looks away from him around the room. TOMMY, who is nodding and blinking, is afraid her eye is on him. He straightens alertly and speaks in a voice that, in spite of his effort, is dripping with drowsiness.*)

TOM. Let me see what you wrote, Mid.

MILD. (*cruelly mocking*). You? You're so sleepy you couldn't see it!

TOM. (*valiantly*). I am not sleepy!

MRS. MILL. (*has fixed her eye on him*). My gracious, I was forgetting you were still up! You run up to bed this minute! It's hours past your bedtime!

TOM. But it's the Fourth of July. Ain't it, Pa?

MRS. MILL. (*gives her husband an accusing stare*). There! You see what you've done? You might know he'd copy your excuses! (*Then sharply to* TOMMY.) You heard what I said, Young Man!

TOM. Aw, Ma, can't I stay up a *little* longer?

MRS. MILL. I said, no! You obey me and no more arguing about it!

TOM. (*drags himself to his feet*). Aw! I should think I could stay up till Dick—

MILL. (*kindly but firmly*). You heard your ma say no more arguing. When she says git, you better git. (TOMMY *accepts his fate resignedly and starts around kissing them all good night.*)

TOM. (*kissing her*). Good night, Aunt Lily.

LILY. Good night, dear. Sleep well.

TOM. (*pecking at* MILDRED). Good night, you.

MILD. Good night, you.

TOM. (*kissing him*). Good night, Pa.

MILL. Good night, Son. Sleep tight.

TOM. (*kissing her*). Good night, Ma.

MRS. MILL. Good night. Here! You look feverish. Let me feel of your head. No, you're all right. Hurry up, now. And don't forget your prayers.

(TOMMY *goes slowly to the doorway—then turns suddenly, the discovery of another excuse lighting up his face.*)

TOM. Here's another thing, Ma. When I was up to the water closet last—

MRS. MILL. (*sharply*). When you were *where*?

TOM. The bathroom.

MRS. MILL. That's better.

TOM. Uncle Sid was snoring like a fog horn—and he's right next to my room. How can I ever get to sleep while he's— (*He is overcome by a jaw-cracking yawn.*)

MRS. MILL. I guess you'd get to sleep all right if you were inside a fog horn. You run along now. (TOMMY *gives up, grins sleepily, and moves off to bed. As soon as he is off her mind, all her former uneasiness comes back on* MRS. MILLER *tenfold. She sighs, moves restlessly, then finally asks.*) What time is it now, Nat?

MILL. Now, Essie, I just told you a minute ago.

MRS. MILL. (*resentfully*). I don't see how you can take it so calm! Here it's midnight, you might say, and our Richard still out, and we don't even know where he is.

MILD. I hear someone on the piazza. Bet that's him now, Ma.

MRS. MILL. (*her anxiety immediately turning to relieved anger*). You give him a good piece of your mind, Nat, you hear me? You're too easy with him, that's the whole trouble! The idea of him daring to stay out like this! (*The front door is heard being opened and shut, and someone whistling "Waltz Me Around Again, Willie."*)

MILD. No, that isn't Dick. It's Art.

MRS. MILL. (*her face falling*). Oh.

(*A moment later* ARTHUR *enters through the front parlor, whistling softly, half under his breath, looking complacently pleased with himself.*)

MILL. (*surveys him over his glasses, not with enthusiasm—shortly*). So you're back, eh? We thought it was Richard.

ART. Is he still out? Where'd he go to?

MILL. That's just what we'd like to know. You didn't run into him anywhere, did you?

ART. No. I've been at the Rands' ever since dinner. (*He sits down in the armchair at left of table, rear.*) I suppose he sneaked off to the beach to watch the fireworks.

MILL. (*pretending an assurance he is far from feeling*). Of course. That's what we've been trying to tell your mother, but she insists on worrying her head off.

MRS. MILL. But if he was going to the fireworks, why wouldn't he say so? He knew we'd let him.

ART. (*with calm wisdom*). That's easy, Ma. (*He grins superiorly.*) Didn't you hear him this morning showing off bawling out the Fourth like an anarchist? He wouldn't want to renege on that to you—but he'd want to see the old fireworks just the same. (*He adds complacently.*) I know. He's at the foolish age.

MILL. (*stares at* ARTHUR *with ill-concealed astonishment, then grins*). Well, Arthur, by gosh, you make me feel as if I owed you an apology when you talk horse sense like that. (*He turns to his wife, greatly relieved.*) Arthur's hit the nail right on the head, I think, Essie. That was what I couldn't figure out—why he—but now it's clear as day.

MRS. MILL. (*with a sigh*). Well, I hope you're right. But I wish he was home.

ART. (*takes out his pipe and fills and lights it with solemn gravity*). He oughtn't to be allowed out this late at his age. I wasn't, Fourth or no Fourth—if I remember.

MILL. (*a twinkle in his eyes*). Don't tax your memory trying to recall those ancient days of your youth.

(MILDRED *laughs and* ARTHUR *looks sheepish. But he soon regains his aplomb.*)

ART. (*importantly*). We had a corking dinner at the Rands'. We had sweetbreads on toast.

MRS. MILL. (*arising momentarily from her depression*). Just like the Rands to put on airs before you! I never could see anything to sweetbreads. Always taste like soap to me. And no real nourishment to them. I wouldn't have the pesky things on my table!

(ARTHUR *again feels sat upon.*)

MILD. (*teasingly*). Did you kiss Elsie good night?

ART. Stop trying to be so darn funny all the time! You give me a pain in the ear!

MILD. And that's where she gives me a pain, the stuck-up thing!—thinks she's the whole cheese!

MILL. (*irritably*). And it's where your everlasting wrangling gives me a pain, you two! Give us a rest! (*There is silence for a moment.*)

MRS. MILL. (*sighs worriedly again*). I do wish that boy would get home!

MILL. (*glances at her uneasily, peeks surreptitiously at his watch—then has an inspiration and turns to* ARTHUR). Arthur, what's this I hear about your having such a good singing voice? Rand was telling me he liked nothing better than to hear you sing—said you did every night you were up there. Why don't you ever give us folks at home here a treat?

ART. (*pleased, but still nursing wounded dignity*). I thought you'd only sit on me.

MRS. MILL. (*perking up—proudly*). Arthur has a real nice voice. He practises when you're not at home. I didn't know you cared for singing, Nat.

MILL. Well, I do—nothing better—and when I was a boy I had a fine voice myself and folks used to say I'd ought— (*Then abruptly, mindful of his painful experience with reminiscence at dinner, looking about him guiltily.*) Hmm. But don't hide your light under a bushel, Arthur. Why not give us a song or two now? You can play for him, can't you, Mildred?

MILD. (*with a toss of her head*). I can play as well as Elsie Rand, at least!

ART. (*ignoring her—clearing his throat importantly*). I've been singing a lot tonight. I don't know if my voice—

MILD. (*forgetting her grudge, grabs her brother's hand and tugs at it*). Come on. Don't play modest. You know you're just dying to show off. (*This puts* ARTHUR *off it at once. He snatches his hand away from her angrily.*)

ART. Let go of me, you! (*Then with surly dignity*) I don't feel like singing tonight, Pa. I will some other time.

MILL. You let him alone, Mildred! (*He winks at* ARTHUR, *indicating with his eyes and a nod of his head* MRS. MILLER, *who has again sunk into worried brooding. He makes it plain by this pantomime that he wants him to sing to distract his mother's mind.*)

ART. (*puts aside his pipe and gets up promptly*). Oh—sure, I'll do the best I can. (*He follows* MILDRED *into the front parlor, where he switches on the lights.*)

MILL. (*to his wife*). It won't keep Tommy awake. Nothing could. And Sid, he'd sleep through an earthquake. (*Then suddenly, looking through the front parlor—grumpily.*) Darn it, speak of the devil, here he comes. Well, he's had a good sleep and he'd ought to be sobered up. (LILY *gets up from her chair and looks around her huntedly, as if for a place to hide.* MILLER *says soothingly.*) Lily, you just sit down and read your book and don't pay any attention to him. (*She sits down again and bends over her book tensely. From the front parlor comes the tinkling of a piano as* MILDRED *runs over the scales.*)

(*In the midst of this,* SID *enters through the front parlor. All the effervescence of his jag has worn off and he is now suffering from a bad case of hangover—nervous, sick, a prey to gloomy remorse and bitter feelings of self-loathing and self-pity. His eyes are bloodshot and puffed, his face bloated, the fringe of hair around his baldness tousled and tufty. He sidles into the room guiltily, his eyes shifting about, avoiding looking at anyone.*)

SID (*forcing a sickly, twitching smile*). Hello.

MILL. (*considerately casual*). Hello, Sid. Had a good nap? (*Then, as* SID *swallows hard and is about to break into further speech,* MILDRED'S *voice comes from the front parlor,* "I haven't played that in ever so long, but I'll try," *and she starts an accompaniment.*)

(MILLER *motions* SID *to be quiet.*) Ssshh! Arthur's going to sing for us. (SID *flattens himself against the edge of the bookcase at center, rear, miserably self-conscious and ill-at-ease there but nervously afraid to move anywhere else.* ARTHUR *begins to sing. He has a fairly decent voice but his method is untrained sentimentality to a dripping degree. He sings that old sentimental favorite,* "Then You'll Remember Me." *The effect on his audience is instant.* MILLER *gazes before him with a ruminating melancholy, his face seeming to become gently sorrowful and old.* MRS. MILLER *stares before her, her expression becoming more and more doleful.* LILY *forgets to pretend to read her book but looks over it, her face growing tragically sad. As for* SID, *he is moved to his remorseful, guilt-stricken depths. His mouth pulls down at the corners and he seems about to cry. The song comes to an end.* MILLER *starts, then claps his hands enthusiastically and calls.*) Well done, Arthur— well done! Why, you've got a splendid voice! Give us some more! You liked that, didn't you, Essie?

MRS. MILL. (*dolefully*). Yes—but it's sad—terrible sad.

SID (*after swallowing hard, suddenly blurts out*). Nat and Essie—and

Lily—I—I want to apologize—for coming home—the way I did—there's no excuse—but I didn't mean—

MILL. (*sympathetically*). Of course, Sid. It's all forgotten.

MRS. MILL. (*rousing herself—affectionately pitying*). Don't be a goose, Sid. We know how it is with picnics. You forget it.

(*His face lights up a bit but his gaze shifts to* LILY *with a mute appeal, hoping for a word from her which is not forthcoming. Her eyes are fixed on her book, her body tense and rigid.*)

SID (*finally blurts out desperately*). Lily—I'm sorry—about the fireworks. Can you—forgive me? (*But* LILY *remains implacably silent. A stricken look comes over* SID'S *face. In the front parlor* MILDRED *is heard saying,* "But I only know the chorus"—*and she starts another accompaniment.*)

MILL. (*comes to* SID'S *rescue*). Ssshh! we're going to have another song. Sit down, Sid. (SID, *hanging his head, flees to the farthest corner, left, front, and sits at the end of the sofa, facing front, hunched up, elbows on knees, face in hands, his round eyes childishly wounded and woebegone.* ARTHUR *sings the popular* "Dearie," *playing up its sentimental values for all he is worth. The effect on his audience is that of the previous song, intensified—especially upon* SID. *As he finishes,* MILLER *again starts and applauds.*) Mighty fine, Arthur! You sang that darned well! Didn't he, Essie?

MRS. MILL. (*dolefully*). Yes—but I wish he wouldn't sing such sad songs. (*Then, her lips trembling.*) Richard's always whistling that.

MILL. (*hastily—calls*). Give us something cheery, next one, Arthur. You know, just for variety's sake.

SID (*suddenly turns toward* LILY—*his voice choked with tears—in a passion of self-denunciation*). You're right, Lily!—right not to forgive me!—I'm no good and never will be!—I'm a no-good drunken bum!—you shouldn't even wipe your feet on me!—I'm a dirty, rotten drunk!—no good to myself or anybody else!—if I had any guts I'd kill myself, and good riddance!—but I haven't!—I'm yellow, too!—a yellow, drunken bum!

(*He hides his face in his hands and begins to sob like a sick little boy. This is too much for* LILY. *All her bitter hurt and steely resolve to ignore and punish him vanish in a flash, swamped by a pitying love for him. She runs and puts her arm around him—even kisses him tenderly and impulsively on his bald head, and soothes him as if he were a little boy.* MRS. MILLER, *almost equally moved, has half risen to go to her brother, too, but* MILLER *winks and shakes his head vigorously and motions her to sit down.*)

LILY. There! Don't cry, Sid! I can't bear it! Of course, I forgive you! Haven't I always forgiven you? I know you're not to blame— So don't, Sid!

SID (*lifts a tearful, humbly grateful, pathetic face to her—but a face that the dawn of a cleansed conscience is already beginning to restore to its natural Puckish expression*). Do you really forgive me— I know I don't deserve it—can you really—?

LILY (*gently*). I told you I did, Sid—and I do.

SID (*kisses her hand humbly, like a big puppy licking it*). Thanks, Lily. I can't tell you— (*In the front parlor,* ARTHUR *begins to sing rollickingly "Waiting at the Church," and after the first line or two* MILDRED *joins in.* SID's *face lights up with appreciation and, automatically, he begins to tap one foot in time, still holding fast to* LILY's *hand. When they come to "sent around a note, this is what she wrote," he can no longer resist, but joins in a shaky bawl*) "Can't get away to marry you today, My wife won't let me!" (*As the song finishes, the two in the other room laugh.* MILLER *and* SID *laugh.* LILY *smiles at* SID's *laughter. Only* MRS. MILLER *remains dolefully preoccupied, as if she hadn't heard.*)

MILL. That's fine, Arthur and Mildred. That's darned good.

SID (*turning to* LILY *enthusiastically*). You ought to hear Vesta Victoria sing that! Gosh, she's great! I heard her at Hammerstein's Victoria—you remember, that trip I made to New York.

LILY (*her face suddenly tired and sad again—for her memory of certain aspects of that trip is the opposite from what he would like her to recall at this moment—gently disengaging her hand from his— with a hopeless sigh*). Yes, I remember, Sid. (*He is overcome momentarily by guilty confusion. She goes quietly and sits down in her chair again. In the front parlor, from now on,* MILDRED *keeps starting to run over popular tunes but always gets stuck and turns to another.*)

MRS. MILL. (*suddenly*). What time is it now, Nat? (*Then without giving him a chance to answer.*) Oh, I'm getting worried something dreadful, Nat! You don't know what might have happened to Richard! You read in the papers every day about boys getting run over by automobiles.

LILY. Oh, don't say that, Essie!

MILL. (*sharply, to conceal his own reawakened apprehension*). Don't get to imagining things, now!

MRS. MILL. Well, why couldn't it happen, with everyone that owns one out tonight, and lots of those driving, drunk? Or he might have gone down to the beach dock and fallen overboard! (*On the verge of hysteria.*) Oh, I know something dreadful's happened! And you can sit there listening to songs and laughing as if— Why don't you do something? Why don't you go out and find him? (*She bursts into tears.*)

LILY (*comes to her quickly and puts her arm around her*). Essie, you mustn't worry so! You'll make yourself sick! Richard's all right. I've got a feeling in my bones he's all right.

MILD. (*comes hurrying in from the front parlor*). What's the trouble? (ARTHUR *appears in the doorway beside her. She goes to her mother and also puts an arm around her.*) Ah, don't cry, Ma! Dick'll turn up in a minute or two, wait and see!

ART. Sure, he will!

MILL. (*has gotten to his feet, frowning—soberly*). I was going out to look—if he wasn't back by twelve sharp. That'd be the time it'd take him to walk from the beach if he left after the last car. But I'll go now, if it'll ease your mind. I'll take the auto and drive out the beach road—and likely pick him up on the way. (*He has taken his collar and tie from where they hang from one corner of the bookcase at rear, center, and is starting to put them on.*) You better come with me, Arthur.

ART. Sure thing, Pa. (*Suddenly he listens and says.*) Ssshh! There's someone on the piazza now—coming around to this door, too. That must be him. No one else would—

MRS. MILL. Oh, thank God, thank God!

MILL. (*with a sheepish smile*). Darn him! I've a notion to give him hell for worrying us all like this.

(*The screen door is pushed violently open and* RICHARD *lurches in and stands swaying a little, blinking his eyes in the light. His face is a pasty pallor, shining with perspiration, and his eyes are glassy. The knees of his trousers are dirty, one of them torn from the sprawl on the sidewalk he had taken, following the* BARTENDER'S *kick. They all gape at him, too paralyzed for a moment to say anything.*)

MRS. MILL. Oh God, what's happened to him! He's gone crazy! Richard!

SID (*the first to regain presence of mind—with a grin*). Crazy, nothing. He's only soused!

ART. He's drunk, that's what! (*Then shocked and condemning.*) You've got your nerve! You fresh kid! We'll take that out of you when we get you down to Yale!

RICH. (*with a wild gesture of defiance—maudlinly dramatic*).

"Yesterday this Day's Madness did prepare
Tomorrow's Silence, Triumph, or Despair.
Drink! for—"

MILL. (*his face grown stern and angry, takes a threatening step toward him*). Richard! How dare—!

MRS. MILL. (*hysterically*). Don't you strike him, Nat! Don't you—!

SID (*grabbing his arm*). Steady, Nat! Keep your temper! No good bawling him out now! He don't know what he's doing!

MILL. (*controlling himself and looking a bit ashamed*). All right— you're right, Sid.

RICH. (*drunkenly glorying in the sensation he is creating—recites with dramatic emphasis*). "And then—I will come—with vine leaves in my hair!" (*He laughs with a double-dyed sardonicism.*)

MRS. MILL. (*staring at him as if she couldn't believe her eyes*). Richard! You're intoxicated!—you bad, wicked boy, you!

RICH. (*forces a wicked leer to his lips and quotes with ponderous mockery*). "Fancy that, Hedda!" (*Then suddenly his whole expression changes, his pallor takes on a greenish, seasick tinge, his eyes seem to be turned inward uneasily—and, all pose gone, he calls to his mother appealingly, like a sick little boy.*) Ma! I feel—rotten! (MRS. MILLER *gives a cry and starts to go to him, but* SID *steps in her way.*)

SID. You let me take care of him, Essie. I know this game backwards.

MILL. (*putting his arm around his wife*). Yes, you leave him to Sid.

SID (*his arm around* RICHARD—*leading him off through the front parlor*). Come on, Old Sport! Upstairs we go! Your old Uncle Sid'll fix you up. He's the kid that wrote the book!

MRS. MILL. (*staring after them—still aghast*). Oh, it's too terrible! Imagine our Richard! And did you hear him talking about some Hedda? Oh, I know he's been with one of those bad women, I know he has—my Richard! (*She hides her face on* MILLER's *shoulder and sobs heartbrokenly.*)

MILL. (*a tired, harassed, deeply worried look on his face—soothing her*). Now, now, you mustn't get to imagining such things! You mustn't, Essie! (LILY *and* MILDRED *and* ARTHUR *are standing about awkwardly with awed, shocked faces.*)

(CURTAIN)

ACT FOUR

Scene One

SCENE—*The same—Sitting-room of the* MILLER *house—about 1 o'clock in the afternoon of the following day.*

As the curtain rises, the family, with the exception of RICHARD, *are discovered coming in through the back parlor from dinner in the dining-room.* MILLER *and his wife come first. His face is set in an expression of frowning severity.* MRS. MILLER's *face is drawn and worried. She has evidently had no rest yet from a sleepless, tearful night.* SID *is himself again, his expression as innocent as if nothing had occurred the previous day that remotely concerned him. And, outside of eyes that are bloodshot and nerves that are shaky, he shows no aftereffects except that he is terribly sleepy.* LILY *is gently sad and depressed.* ARTHUR *is self-consciously a virtuous young*

man against whom nothing can be said. MILDRED *and* TOMMY *are
subdued, covertly watching their father.*

They file into the sitting-room in silence and then stand around uncertainly, as if each were afraid to be the first to sit down. The atmosphere is as stiltedly grave as if they were attending a funeral service. Their eyes keep fixed on the head of the house, who has gone to the window at right and is staring out frowningly, savagely chewing a toothpick.

MILL. (*finally—irritably*). Damn it, I'd ought to be back at the office putting in some good licks! I've a whole pile of things that have got to be done today!

MRS. MILL. (*accusingly*). You don't mean to tell me you're going back without seeing him? It's your duty—!

MILL. (*exasperatedly*). 'Course I'm not! I wish you'd stop jumping to conclusions! What else did I come home for, I'd like to know? Do I usually come way back here for dinner on a busy day? I was only wishing this hadn't come up—just at this particular time. (*He ends up very lamely and is irritably conscious of the fact.*)

TOM. (*who has been fidgeting restlessly—unable to bear the suspense a moment longer*). What is it Dick's done? Why is everyone scared to tell me?

MILL. (*seizes this as an escape valve—turns and fixes his youngest son with a stern forbidding eye*). Young man, I've never spanked you yet, but that don't mean I never will! Seems to me that you've been just itching for it lately! You keep your mouth shut till you're spoken to—or I warn you something's going to happen!

MRS. MILL. Yes, Tommy, you keep still and don't bother your pa. (*Then warningly to her husband.*) Careful what you say, Nat. Little pitchers have big ears.

MILL. (*peremptorily*). You kids skedaddle—all of you. Why are you always hanging around the house? Go out and play in the yard, or take a walk, and get some fresh air. (MILDRED *takes* TOMMY's *hand and leads him out through the front parlor.* ARTHUR *hangs back, as if the designation "kids" couldn't possibly apply to him.*

His father notices this—impatiently.) You, too, Arthur. (ARTHUR *goes out with a stiff, wounded dignity*.)

LILY (*tactfully*). I think I'll go for a walk, too. (*She goes out through the front parlor.* SID *makes a movement as if to follow her*.)

MILL. I'd like you to stay, Sid—for a while, anyway.

SID. Sure. (*He sits down in the rocking chair at right, rear, of table and immediately yawns*.) Gosh, I'm dead. Don't know what's the matter with me today. Can't seem to keep awake.

MILL. (*with caustic sarcasm*). Maybe that demon chowder you drank at the picnic poisoned you! (SID *looks sheepish and forces a grin. Then* MILLER *turns to his wife with the air of one who determinedly faces the unpleasant*.) Where is Richard?

MRS. MILL. (*flusteredly*). He's still in bed. I made him stay in bed to punish him—and I thought he ought to, anyway, after being so sick. But he says he feels all right.

SID (*with another yawn*). 'Course he does. When you're young you can stand anything without it feazing you. Why, I remember when I could come down on the morning after, fresh as a daisy, and eat a breakfast of pork chops and fried onions and— (*He stops guiltily*.)

MILL. (*bitingly*). I suppose that was before eating lobster shells had ruined your iron constitution.

MRS. MILL. (*regards her brother severely*). If I was in your shoes, I'd keep still! (*Then turning to her husband*.) Richard must be feeling better. He ate all the dinner I sent up, Norah says.

MILL. I thought you weren't going to give him any dinner—to punish him.

MRS. MILL. (*guiltily*). Well—in his weakened condition—I thought it best— (*Then defensively*.) But you needn't think I haven't punished him. I've given him pieces of my mind he won't forget in a hurry. And I've kept reminding him his real punishment was still to come—that you were coming home to dinner on purpose—and then he'd learn that you could be terrible stern when he did such awful things.

MILL. (*stirs uncomfortably*). Hmm!

MRS. MILL. And that's just what it's your duty to do—punish him good and hard! The idea of him daring— (*Then hastily.*) But you be careful how you go about it, Nat. Remember he's like you inside— too sensitive for his own good. And he never would have done it, I know, if it hadn't been for that darned little dunce, Muriel, and her numbskull father—and then all of us teasing him and hurting his feelings all day—and then you lost your temper and were so sharp with him right after dinner before he went out.

MILL. (*resentfully*). I see this is going to work round to where it's all my fault!

MRS. MILL. Now, I didn't say that, did I? Don't go losing your temper again. And here's another thing. You know as well as I, Richard would never have done such a thing alone. Why, he wouldn't know how! He must have been influenced and led by someone.

MILL. Yes, I believe that. Did you worm out of him who it was? (*Then angrily.*) By God, I'll make whoever it was regret it!

MRS. MILL. No, he wouldn't admit there was anyone. (*Then triumphantly.*) But there is one thing I did worm out of him—and I can tell you it relieved my mind more'n anything. You know, I was afraid he'd been with one of those bad women. Well, turns out there wasn't any Hedda. She was just out of those books he's been reading. He swears he's never known a Hedda in his life. And I believe him. Why, he seemed disgusted with me for having such a notion. (*Then lamely.*) So somehow—I can't kind of feel it's all as bad as I thought it was. (*Then quickly and indignantly.*) But it's bad enough, goodness knows—and you punish him good just the same. The idea of a boy of his age—! Shall I go up now and tell him to get dressed, you want to see him?

MILL. (*helplessly—and irritably*). Yes! I can't waste all day listening to you!

MRS. MILL. (*worriedly*). Now you keep your temper, Nat, remember! (*She goes out through the front parlor.*)

MILL. Darn women, anyway! They always get you mixed up. Their minds simply don't know what logic is! (*Then he notices that* SID *is dozing—sharply.*) Sid!

SID (*blinking—mechanically*). I'll take the same. (*Then hurriedly.*) What'd you say, Nat?

MILL. (*caustically*). What I didn't say was what'll you have. (*Irritably.*) Do you want to be of some help, or don't you? Then keep awake and try and use your brains! This is a damned sight more serious than Essie has any idea! She thinks there weren't any girls mixed up with Richard's spree last night—but I happen to know there were! (*He takes a letter from his pocket.*) Here's a note a woman left with one of the boys downstairs at the office this morning— didn't ask to see me, just said give me this. He'd never seen her before—said she looked like a tart. (*He has opened the letter and reads.*) "Your son got the booze he drank last night at the Pleasant Beach House. The bartender there knew he was under age but served him just the same. He thought it was a good joke to get him soused. If you have any guts you will run that bastard out of town." Well, what do you think of that? It's a woman's handwriting—not signed, of course.

SID. She's one of the babies, all right—judging from her elegant language.

MILL. See if you recognize the handwriting.

SID (*with a reproachful look*). Nat, I resent the implication that I correspond with all the tramps around this town. (*Looking at the letter.*) No, I don't know who this one could be. (*Handing the letter back.*) But I deduce that the lady had a run-in with the barkeep and wants revenge.

MILL. (*grimly*). And I deduce that before that she must have picked up Richard—or how would she know who he was?—and took him to this dive.

SID. Maybe. The Pleasant Beach House is nothing but a bed house— (*Quickly.*) At least, so I've been told.

MILL. That's just the sort of damned fool thing he might do to spite Muriel, in the state of mind he was in—pick up some tart. And she'd try to get him drunk so—

SID. Yes, it might have happened like that—and it might not. How're we ever going to prove it? Everyone at the Pleasant Beach will lie their heads off.

MILL. (*simply and proudly*). Richard won't lie.

SID. Well, don't blame him if he don't remember everything that hap-

pened last night. (*Then sincerely concerned.*) I hope you're
wrong, Nat. That kind of baby is dangerous for a kid like Dick—
in more ways than one. You know what I mean.

MILL. (*frowningly*). Yep—and that's just what's got me worried. Damn
it, I've got to have a straight talk with him—about women and all
those things. I ought to have long ago.

SID. Yes. You ought.

MILL. I've tried to a couple of times. I did it all right with Wilbur and
Lawrence and Arthur, when it came time—but, hell, with Richard
I always get sort of ashamed of myself and can't get started right.
You feel, in spite of all his bold talk out of books, that he's so
darned innocent inside.

SID. I know. I wouldn't like the job. (*Then after a pause—curiously.*)
How were you figuring to punish him for his sins?

MILL. (*frowning*). To be honest with you, Sid, I'm damned if I know.
All depends on what I feel about what he feels when I first size
him up—and then it'll be like shooting in the dark.

SID. If I didn't know you so well, I'd say don't be too hard on him. (*He
smiles a little bitterly.*) If you remember, I was always getting
punished—and see what a lot of good it did me!

MILL. (*kindly*). Oh, there's lots worse than you around, so don't take
to boasting. (*Then, at a sound from the front parlor—with a
sigh.*) Well, here comes the Bad Man, I guess.

SID (*getting up*). I'll beat it. (*But it is* MRS. MILLER *who appears in the
doorway, looking guilty and defensive.* SID *sits down again.*)

MRS. MILL. I'm sorry, Nat—but he was sound asleep and I didn't have
the heart to wake him. I waited for him to wake up but he didn't.

MILL. (*concealing a relief of which he is ashamed—exasperatedly*). Well,
I'll be double damned! If you're not the—

MRS. MILL. (*defensively aggressive*). Now don't lose your temper at me,
Nat Miller! You know as well as I do he needs all the sleep he
can get today—after last night's ructions! Do you want him to be
taken down sick? And what difference does it make to you, anyway? You can see him when you come home for supper, can't
you? My goodness, I never saw you so savage-tempered! You'd
think you couldn't bear waiting to punish him!

MILL. (*outraged*). Well, I'll be eternally— (*Then suddenly he laughs.*) No use talking, you certainly take the cake! But you know darned well I told you I'm not coming home to supper tonight. I've got a date with Jack Lawson that may mean a lot of new advertising and it's important.

MRS. MILL. Then you can see him when you do come home.

MILL. (*covering his evident relief at this respite with a fuming manner*). All right! All right! I give up! I'm going back to the office. (*He starts for the front parlor.*) Bring a man all the way back here on a busy day and then you— No consideration— (*He disappears, and a moment later the front door is heard shutting behind him.*)

MRS. MILL. Well! I never saw Nat so bad-tempered.

SID (*with a chuckle*). Bad temper, nothing. He's so tickled to get out of it for a while he can't see straight!

MRS. MILL. (*with a sniff*). I hope I know him better than you. (*Then fussing about the room, setting this and that in place, while* SID *yawns drowsily and blinks his eyes.*) Sleeping like a baby—so innocent-looking. You'd think butter wouldn't melt in his mouth. It all goes to show you never can tell by appearances—not even when it's your own child. The idea!

SID (*drowsily*). Oh, Dick's all right, Essie. Stop worrying.

MRS. MILL. (*with a sniff*). Of course, you'd say that. I suppose you'll have him out with you painting the town red the next thing! (*As she is talking,* RICHARD *appears in the doorway from the sitting-room. He shows no ill effects from his experience the night before. In fact, he looks surprisingly healthy. He is dressed in old clothes that look as if they had been hurriedly flung on. His expression is one of hang-dog guilt mingled with a defensive defiance.*)

RICH. (*with self-conscious unconcern, ignoring his mother*). Hello, Sid.

MRS. MILL. (*whirls on him*). What are you doing here, Young Man? I thought you were asleep! Seems to me you woke up pretty quick—just after your pa left the house!

RICH. (*sulkily*). I wasn't asleep. I heard you in the room.

MRS. MILL. (*outraged*). Do you mean to say you were deliberately deceiving—

RICH. I wasn't deceiving. You didn't ask if I was asleep.

MRS. MILL. It amounts to the same thing and you know it! It isn't enough your wickedness last night, but now you have to take to lying!

RICH. I wasn't lying, Ma. If you'd asked if I was asleep I'd have said no.

MRS. MILL. I've a good mind to send you straight back to bed and make you stay there!

RICH. Ah, what for, Ma? It was only giving me a headache, lying there.

MRS. MILL. If you've got a headache, I guess you know it doesn't come from that! And imagine me standing there, and feeling sorry for you, like a fool—even having a run-in with your pa because— But you wait till he comes back tonight! If you don't catch it!

RICH. (*sulkily*). I don't care.

MRS. MILL. You don't care? You talk as if you weren't sorry for what you did last night!

RICH. (*defiantly*). I'm not sorry.

MRS. MILL. Richard! You ought to be ashamed! I'm begining to think you're hardened in wickedness, that's what!

RICH. (*with bitter despondency*). I'm not sorry because I don't care a darn what I did, or what's done to me, or anything about anything! I won't do it again—

MRS. MILL. (*seizing on this to relent a bit*). Well, I'm glad to hear you say that, anyway!

RICH. But that's not because I think it was wicked or any such old-fogy moral notion, but because it wasn't any fun. It didn't make me happy and funny like it does Uncle Sid—

SID (*drowsily*). What's that? Who's funny?

RICH. (*ignoring him*). It only made me sadder—and sick—so I don't see any sense in it.

MRS. MILL. Now you're talking sense! That's a good boy.

RICH. But I'm not sorry I tried it once—curing the soul by means of the senses, as Oscar Wilde says. (*Then with despairing pessimism.*) But what does it matter what I do or don't do? Life is all a stupid farce! I'm through with it! (*With a sinister smile.*) It's lucky there aren't any of General Gabler's pistols around—or you'd see if I'd stand it much longer!

MRS. MILL. (*worriedly impressed by this threat—but pretending scorn*).

I don't know anything about General Gabler—I suppose that's more of those darned books—but you're a silly gabbler yourself when you talk that way!

RICH. (*darkly*). That's how little you know about me.

MRS. MILL. (*giving in to her worry*). I wish you wouldn't say those terrible things—about life and pistols! You don't want to worry me to death, do you?

RICH. (*reassuringly stoical now*). You needn't worry, Ma. It was only my despair talking. But I'm not a coward. I'll face—my fate.

MRS. MILL. (*stands looking at him puzzledly—then gives it up with a sigh*). Well, all I can say is you're the queerest boy I ever did hear of! (*Then solicitously, putting her hand on his forehead.*) How's your headache? Do you want me to get you some Bromo Seltzer?

RICH. (*taken down—disgustedly*). No, I don't! Aw, Ma, you don't understand anything!

MRS. MILL. Well, I understand this much: It's your liver, that's what! You'll take a good dose of salts tomorrow morning, and no nonsense about it! (*Then suddenly.*) My goodness, I wonder what time it's getting to be. I've got to go upstreet. (*She goes to the front-parlor doorway—then turns.*) You stay here, Richard, you hear? Remember you're not allowed out today—for a punishment. (*She hurries away.* RICHARD *sits in tragic gloom.* SID, *without opening his eyes, speaks to him drowsily.*)

SID. Well, how's my fellow Rum Pot, as good old Dowie calls us? Got a head?

RICH. (*startled—sheepishly*). Aw, don't go dragging that up, Uncle Sid. I'm never going to be such a fool again, I tell you.

SID (*with drowsy cynicism—not unmixed with bitterness at the end*). Seems to me I've heard someone say that before. Who could it have been, I wonder? Why, if it wasn't Sid Davis! Yes, sir, I've heard him say that very thing a thousand times, must be. But then he's always fooling; you can't take a word he says seriously; he's a card, that Sid is!

RICH. (*darkly*). I was desperate, Uncle—even if she wasn't worth it. I was wounded to the heart.

SID. I like to the quick better myself—more stylish. (*Then sadly.*) But you're right. Love is hell on a poor sucker. Don't I know it? (RICHARD *is disgusted and disdains to reply.* SID's *chin sinks on his chest and he begins to breathe noisily, fast asleep.* RICHARD *glances at him with aversion. There is a sound of someone on the porch and the screen door is opened and* MILDRED *enters. She smiles on seeing her uncle, then gives a start on seeing* RICHARD.)

MILD. Hello! Are you allowed up?

RICH. Of course, I'm allowed up.

MILD. (*comes and sits in her father's chair at right, front, of table*). How did Pa punish you?

RICH. He didn't. He went back to the office without seeing me.

MILD. Well, you'll catch it later. (*Then rebukingly.*) And you ought to. If you'd ever seen how awful you looked last night!

RICH. Ah, forget it, can't you?

MILD. Well, are you ever going to do it again, that's what I want to know.

RICH. What's that to you?

MILD. (*with suppressed excitement*). Well, if you don't solemnly swear you won't—then I won't give you something I've got for you.

RICH. Don't try to kid me. You haven't got anything.

MILD. I have, too.

RICH. What?

MILD. Wouldn't you like to know! I'll give you three guesses.

RICH. (*with disdainful dignity*). Don't bother me. I'm in no mood to play riddles with kids!

MILD. Oh, well, if you're going to get snippy! Anyway, you haven't promised yet.

RICH. (*a prey to keen curiosity now*). I promise. What is it?

MILD. What would you like best in the world?

RICH. I don't know. What?

MILD. And you pretend to be in love! If I told Muriel that!

RICH. (*breathlessly*). Is it—from her?

MILD. (*laughing*). Well, I guess it's a shame to keep you guessing. Yes. It is from her. I was walking past her place just now when I saw her waving from their parlor window, and I went up and she said give this to Dick, and she didn't have a chance to say anything else because her mother called her and said she wasn't allowed to have company. So I took it—and here it is. (*She gives him a letter folded many times into a tiny square.* RICHARD *opens it with a trembling eagerness and reads.* MILDRED *watches him curiously—then sighs affectedly.*) Gee, it must be nice to be in love like you are—all with one person.

RICH. (*his eyes shining*). Gee, Mid, do you know what she says—that she didn't mean a word in that other letter. Her old man made her write it. And she loves me and only me and always will, no matter how they punish her!

MILD. My! I'd never think she had that much spunk.

RICH. Huh! You don't know her! Think I could fall in love with a girl that was afraid to say her soul's her own? I should say not! (*Then more gleefully still.*) And she's going to try and sneak out and meet me tonight. She says she thinks she can do it. (*Then suddenly feeling this enthusiasm before* MILDRED *is entirely the wrong note for a cynical pessimist—with an affected bitter laugh.*) Ha! I knew darned well she couldn't hold out—that she'd ask to see me again. (*He misquotes cynically.*) "Women never know when the curtain has fallen. They always want another act."

MILD. Is that so, Smarty?

RICH. (*as if he were weighing the matter*). I don't know whether I'll consent to keep this date or not.

MILD. Well, I know! You're not allowed out, you silly! So you can't!

RICH. (*dropping all pretense—defiantly*). Can't I, though! You wait and see if I can't! I'll see her tonight if it's the last thing I ever do! I don't care how I'm punished after!

MILD. (*admiringly*). Goodness! I never thought you had such nerve!

RICH. You promise to keep your face shut, Mid—until after I've left—then you can tell Pa and Ma where I've gone—I mean, if they're worrying I'm off like last night.

MILD. All right. Only you've got to do something for me when I ask.

RICH. 'Course I will. (*Then excitedly.*) And say, Mid! Right now's the best chance for me to get away—while everyone's out! Ma'll be coming back soon and she'll keep watching me like a cat— (*He starts for the back parlor.*) I'm going. I'll sneak out the back.

MILD. (*excitedly*). But what'll you do till nighttime? It's ages to wait.

RICH. What do I care how long I wait! (*Intensely sincere now.*) I'll think of her—and dream! I'd wait a million years and never mind it—for her! (*He gives his sister a superior scornful glance.*) The trouble with you is, you don't understand what love means! (*He disappears through the back parlor.* MILDRED *looks after him admiringly.* SID *puffs and begins to snore peacefully.*)

(CURTAIN)

Scene Two

SCENE—*A strip of beach along the harbor. At left, a bank of dark earth, running half-diagonally back along the beach, marking the line where the sand of the beach ends and fertile land begins. The top of the bank is grassy and the trailing boughs of willow trees extend out over it and over a part of the beach. At left, front, is a path leading up the bank, between the willows. On the beach, at center, front, a white, flat-bottomed rowboat is drawn up, its bow about touching the bank, the painter trailing up the bank, evidently made fast to the trunk of a willow. Halfway down the sky, at rear, left, the crescent of the new moon casts a soft, mysterious, caressing light over everything. The sand of the beach shimmers palely. The forward half (left of center) of the rowboat is in the deep shadow cast by the willow, the stern section is in moonlight. In the distance, the orchestra of a summer hotel can be heard very faintly at intervals.*

RICHARD *is discovered sitting sideways on the gunwale of the rowboat near the stern. He is facing left, watching the path. He is in a great state of anxious expectancy, squirming about uncomfortably on the narrow gunwale, kicking at the sand restlessly, twirling his straw hat, with a bright-colored band in stripes, around on his finger.*

RICH. (*thinking aloud*). Must be nearly nine. . . . I can hear the Town Hall clock strike, it's so still tonight . . . Gee, I'll bet Ma had a fit when she found out I'd sneaked out . . . I'll catch hell when I get back, but it'll be worth it . . . if only Muriel turns up . . . she didn't say for certain she could . . . gosh, I wish she'd come! . . . am I sure she wrote nine? . . . (*He puts the straw hat on the seat amidships and pulls the folded letter out of his pocket and peers at it in the moonlight.*) Yes, it's nine, all right. (*He starts to put the note back in his pocket, then stops and kisses it—then shoves it away hastily, sheepish, looking around him shamefacedly, as if afraid he were being observed.*) Aw, that's silly . . . no, it isn't either . . . not when you're really in love. . . . (*He jumps to his feet restlessly.*) Darn it, I wish she'd show up! . . . think of something else . . . that'll make the time pass quicker . . . where was I this time last night? . . . waiting outside the Pleasant Beach House . . . Belle . . . ah, forget her! . . . now, when Muriel's coming . . . that's a fine time to think of—! . . . but you hugged and kissed her . . . not until I was drunk, I didn't . . . and then it was all showing off . . . darned fool! . . . and I didn't go upstairs with her . . . even if she was pretty . . . aw, she wasn't pretty . . . she was all painted up . . . she was just a whore . . . she was everything dirty . . . Muriel's a million times prettier anyway . . . Muriel and I will go upstairs . . . when we're married . . . but that will be beautiful . . . but I oughtn't even to think of that yet . . . it's not right . . . I'd never—now . . . and she'd never . . . she's a decent girl . . . I couldn't love her if she wasn't . . . but after we're married. . . . (*He gives a little shiver of passionate longing—then resolutely turns his mind away from these improper, almost desecrating thoughts.*) That damned barkeep kicking me . . . I'll bet you if I hadn't been drunk I'd have given him one good punch in the nose, even if he could have licked me after! . . . (*Then with a shiver of shamefaced revulsion and self-disgust.*) Aw, you deserved a kick in the pants . . . making such a darned slob of yourself . . . reciting the *Ballad of Reading Gaol* to those lowbrows! . . . you must have been a fine sight when you got home! . . . having to be put to bed and getting sick! . . . Phaw! . . .

(*He squirms disgustedly.*) Think of something else, can't you?
. . . recite something . . . see if you remember . . .

"Nay, let us walk from fire unto fire

From passionate pain to deadlier delight—

I am too young to live without desire,

Too young art thou to waste this summernight—"

. . . gee, that's a peach! . . . I'll have to memorize the rest and
recite it to Muriel the next time. . . . I wish I could write poetry
. . . about her and me. . . . (*He sighs and stares around him at
the night.*) Gee, it's beautiful tonight . . . as if it was a special
night . . . for me and Muriel. . . . Gee, I love tonight. . . . I
love the sand, and the trees, and the grass, and the water and the
sky, and the moon . . . it's all in me and I'm in it . . . God, it's
so beautiful! (*He stands staring at the moon with a rapt face.
From the distance the Town Hall clock begins to strike. This
brings him back to earth with a start.*) There's nine now. . . .
(*He peers at the path apprehensively.*) I don't see her . . . she
must have got caught. . . . (*Almost tearfully.*) Gee, I hate to go
home and catch hell . . . without having seen her! . . . (*Then
calling a manly cynicism to his aid.*) Aw, who ever heard of a
woman ever being on time. . . . I ought to know enough about
life by this time not to expect . . . (*Then with sudden excitement.*) There she comes now. . . . Gosh! (*He heaves a huge sigh
of relief—then recites dramatically to himself, his eyes on the
approaching figure.*)

"And lo my love, mine own soul's heart, more dear

Than mine own soul, more beautiful than God,

Who hath my being between the hands of her—"

(*Then hastily.*) Mustn't let her know I'm so tickled. . . . I ought to be
mad about that first letter, anyway . . . if women are too sure of
you, they treat you like slaves . . . let her suffer, for a change.
. . . (*He starts to stroll around with exaggerated carelessness,
turning his back on the path, hands in pockets, whistling with
insouciance "Waiting at the Church."*)

(MURIEL MCCOMBER *enters from down the path, left front. She is fifteen,
going on sixteen. She is a pretty girl with a plump, graceful little*

figure, fluffy, light-brown hair, big naïve wondering dark eyes, a round, dimpled face, a melting drawly voice. Just now she is in a great thrilled state of timid adventurousness. She hesitates in the shadow at the foot of the path, waiting for RICHARD *to see her; but he resolutely goes on whistling with back turned, and she has to call him.*)

MUR. Oh, Dick.

RICH. (*turns around with an elaborate simulation of being disturbed in the midst of profound meditation*). Oh, hello. Is it nine already? Gosh, time passes—when you're thinking.

MUR. (*coming toward him as far as the edge of the shadow—disappointedly*). I thought you'd be waiting right here at the end of the path. I'll bet you'd forgotten I was even coming.

RICH. (*strolling a little toward her but not too far—carelessly*). No, I hadn't forgotten, honest. But I got to thinking about life.

MUR. You might think of me for a change, after all the risk I've run to see you! (*Hesitating timidly on the edge of the shadow.*) Dick! You come here to me. I'm afraid to go out in that bright moonlight where anyone might see me.

RICH. (*coming toward her—scornfully*). Aw, there you go again—always scared of life!

MUR. (*indignantly*). Dick Miller, I do think you've got an awful nerve to say that after all the risks I've run making this date and then sneaking out! You didn't take the trouble to sneak any letter to me, I notice!

RICH. No, because after your first letter, I thought everything was dead and past between us.

MUR. And I'll bet you didn't care one little bit! (*On the verge of humiliated tears.*) Oh, I was a fool ever to come here! I've got a good notion to go right home and never speak to you again! (*She half turns back toward the path.*)

RICH. (*frightened—immediately becomes terribly sincere—grabbing her hand*). Aw, don't go, Muriel! Please! I didn't mean anything like that, honest I didn't! Gee, if you knew how broken-hearted I was by that first letter, and how darned happy your second letter made me—!

MUR. (*happily relieved—but appreciates she has the upper hand now and doesn't relent at once*). I don't believe you.

RICH. You ask Mid how happy I was. She can prove it.

MUR. She'd say anything you told her to. I don't care anything about what she'd say. It's you. You've got to swear to me—

RICH. I swear!

MUR. (*demurely*). Well then, all right, I'll believe you.

RICH. (*his eyes on her face lovingly—genuine adoration in his voice*). Gosh, you're pretty tonight, Muriel! It seems ages since we've been together! If you knew how I've suffered—!

MUR. I did, too.

RICH. (*unable to resist falling into his tragic literary pose for a moment*). The despair in my soul— (*He recites dramatically.*) "Something was dead in each of us, And what was dead was Hope!" That was me! My hope of happiness was dead! (*Then with sincere boyish fervor.*) Gosh, Muriel, it sure is wonderful to be with you again! (*He puts a timid arm around her awkwardly.*)

MUR. (*shyly*). I'm glad—it makes you happy. I'm happy, too.

RICH. Can't I—won't you let me kiss you—now? Please! (*He bends his face toward hers.*)

MUR. (*ducking her head away—timidly*). No. You mustn't. Don't—

RICH. Aw, why can't I?

MUR. Because—I'm afraid.

RICH. (*discomfited—taking his arm from around her—a bit sulky and impatient with her*). Aw, that's what you always say! You're always so afraid! Aren't you ever going to let me?

MUR. I will—sometime.

RICH. When?

MUR. Soon, maybe.

RICH. Tonight, will you?

MUR. (*coyly*). I'll see.

RICH. Promise?

MUR. I promise—maybe.

RICH. All right. You remember you've promised. (*Then coaxingly.*) Aw, don't let's stand here. Come on out and we can sit down in the boat.

MUR. (*hesitantly*). It's so bright out there.

RICH. No one'll see. You know there's never anyone around here at night.

MUR. (*illogically*). I know there isn't. That's why I thought it would be the best place. But there might be someone.

RICH. (*taking her hand and tugging at it gently*). There isn't a soul. (MURIEL *steps out a little and looks up and down fearfully.* RICHARD *goes on insistently.*) Aw, what's the use of a moon if you can't see it!

MUR. But it's only a new moon. That's not much to look at.

RICH. But I want to see you. I can't here in the shadow. I want to— drink in—all your beauty.

MUR. (*can't resist this*). Well, all right—only I can't stay only a few minutes. (*She lets him lead her toward the stern of the boat.*)

RICH. (*pleadingly*). Aw, you can stay a little while, can't you? Please! (*He helps her in and she settles herself in the stern seat of the boat, facing diagonally left front.*)

MUR. A little while. (*He sits beside her.*) But I've got to be home in bed again pretending to be asleep by ten o'clock. That's the time Pa and Ma come up to bed, as regular as clock work, and Ma always looks into my room.

RICH. But you'll have oodles of time to do that.

MUR. (*excitedly*). Dick, you have no idea what I went through to get here tonight! My, but it was exciting! You know Pa's punishing me by sending me to bed at eight sharp, and I had to get all undressed and into bed 'cause at half-past he sends Ma up to make sure I've obeyed, and she came up, and I pretended to be asleep, and she went down again, and I got up and dressed in such a hurry—I must look a sight, don't I?

RICH. You do not! You look wonderful!

MUR. And then I sneaked down the back stairs. And the pesky old stairs squeaked, and my heart was in my mouth, I was so scared, and then I sneaked out through the back yard, keeping in the dark under the trees, and— My, but it was exciting! Dick, you don't realize how I've been punished for your sake. Pa's been so mean and nasty, I've almost hated him!

RICH. And you don't realize what I've been through for you—and what I'm in for—for sneaking out— (*Then darkly.*) And for what I did last night—what your letter made me do!

MUR. (*made terribly curious by his ominous tone*). What did my letter make you do?

RICH. (*beginning to glory in this*). It's too long a story—and let the dead past bury its dead. (*Then with real feeling.*) Only it isn't past, I can tell you! What I'll catch when Pa gets hold of me!

MUR. Tell me, Dick! Begin at the beginning and tell me!

RICH. (*tragically*). Well, after your old—your father left our place I caught holy hell from Pa.

MUR. You mustn't swear!

RICH. (*somberly*). Hell is the only word that can describe it. And on top of that, to torture me more, he gave me your letter. After I'd read that I didn't want to live any more. Life seemed like a tragic farce.

MUR. I'm so awful sorry, Dick—honest I am! But you might have known I'd never write that unless—

RICH. I thought your love for me was dead. I thought you'd never loved me, that you'd only been cruelly mocking me—to torture me!

MUR. Dick! I'd never! You know I'd never!

RICH. I wanted to die. I sat and brooded about death. Finally I made up my mind I'd kill myself.

MUR. (*excitedly*). Dick! You didn't!

RICH. I did, too! If there'd been one of Hedda Gabler's pistols around, you'd have seen if I wouldn't have done it beautifully! I thought, when I'm dead, she'll be sorry she ruined my life!

MUR. (*cuddling up a little to him*). If you ever had! I'd have died, too! Honest, I would!

RICH. But suicide is the act of a coward. That's what stopped me. (*Then with a bitter change of tone.*) And anyway, I thought to myself, she isn't worth it.

MUR. (*huffily*). That's a nice thing to say!

RICH. Well, if you meant what was in that letter, you wouldn't have been worth it, would you?

MUR. But I've told you Pa—

RICH. So I said to myself, I'm through with women; they're all alike!

MUR. I'm not.

RICH. And I thought, what difference does it make what I do now? I might as well forget her and lead the pace that kills, and drown my sorrows! You know I had eleven dollars saved up to buy you something for your birthday, but I thought, she's dead to me now and why shouldn't I throw it away? (*Then hastily.*) I've still got almost five left, Muriel, and I can get you something nice with that.

MUR. (*excitedly*). What do I care about your old presents? You tell me what you did!

RICH. (*darkly again*). After it was dark, I sneaked out and went to a low dive I know about.

MUR. Dick Miller, I don't believe you ever!

RICH. You ask them at the Pleasant Beach House if I didn't! They won't forget me in a hurry!

MUR. (*impressed and horrified*). You went there? Why, that's a terrible place! Pa says it ought to be closed by the police!

RICH. (*darkly*). I said it was a dive, didn't I? It's a "secret house of shame." And they let me into a secret room behind the barroom. There wasn't anyone there but a Princeton Senior I know—he belongs to Tiger Inn and he's fullback on the football team—and he had two chorus girls from New York with him, and they were all drinking champagne.

MUR. (*disturbed by the entrance of the chorus girls*). Dick Miller! I hope you didn't notice—

RICH. (*carelessly*). I had a highball by myself and then I noticed one of the girls—the one that wasn't with the fullback—looking at me. She had strange-looking eyes. And then she asked me if I wouldn't drink champagne with them and come and sit with her.

MUR. She must have been a nice thing! (*Then a bit falteringly.*) And did—you?

RICH. (*with tragic bitterness*). Why shouldn't I, when you'd told me in that letter you'd never see me again?

MUR. (*almost tearfully*). But you ought to have known Pa made me—

RICH. I didn't know that then. (*Then rubbing it in.*) Her name was

Belle. She had yellow hair—the kind that burns and stings you!

MUR. I'll bet it was dyed!

RICH. She kept smoking one cigarette after another—but that's nothing for a chorus girl.

MUR. (*indignantly*). She was low and bad, that's what she was or she couldn't be a chorus girl, and her smoking cigarettes proves it! (*Then falteringly again.*) And then what happened?

RICH. (*carelessly*). Oh, we just kept drinking champagne—I bought a round—and then I had a fight with the barkeep and knocked him down because he'd insulted her. He was a great big thug but—

MUR. (*huffily*). I don't see how he could—insult that kind! And why did you fight for her? Why didn't the Princeton fullback who'd brought them there? He must have been bigger than you.

RICH. (*stopped for a moment—then quickly*). He was too drunk by that time.

MUR. And were you drunk?

RICH. Only a little then. I was worse later. (*Proudly.*) You ought to have seen me when I got home! I was on the verge of delirium tremens!

MUR. I'm glad I didn't see you. You must have been awful. I hate people who get drunk. I'd have hated you!

RICH. Well, it was all your fault, wasn't it? If you hadn't written that letter—

MUR. But I've told you I didn't mean— (*Then faltering but fascinated.*) But what happened with that Belle—after—before you went home?

RICH. Oh, we kept drinking champagne and she said she'd fallen in love with me at first sight and she came and sat on my lap and kissed me.

MUR. (*stiffening*). Oh!

RICH. (*quickly, afraid he has gone too far*). But it was only all in fun, and then we just kept on drinking champagne, and finally I said good night and came home.

MUR. And did you kiss her?

RICH. No, I didn't.

MUR. (*distractedly*). You did, too! You're lying and you know it. You did, too! (*Then tearfully.*) And there I was right at that time lying in bed not able to sleep, wondering how I was ever going to see you again and crying my eyes out, while you—! (*She suddenly jumps to her feet in a tearful fury.*) I hate you! I wish you were dead! I'm going home this minute! I never want to lay eyes on you again! And this time I mean it! (*She tries to jump out of the boat but he holds her back. All the pose has dropped from him now and he is in a frightened state of contrition.*)

RICH. (*imploringly*). Muriel! Wait! Listen!

MUR. I don't want to listen! Let me go! If you don't I'll bite your hand!

RICH. I won't let you go! You've got to let me explain! I never—! Ouch! (*For* MURIEL *has bitten his hand and it hurts, and, stung by the pain, he lets go instinctively, and she jumps quickly out of the boat and starts running toward the path.* RICHARD *calls after her with bitter despair and hurt.*) All right! Go if you want to—if you haven't the decency to let me explain! I hate you, too! I'll go and see Belle!

MUR. (*seeing he isn't following her, stops at the foot of the path—defiantly*). Well, go and see her—if that's the kind of girl you like! What do I care? (*Then as he only stares before him broodingly, sitting dejectedly in the stern of the boat, a pathetic figure of injured grief.*) You can't explain! What can you explain? You owned up you kissed her!

RICH. I did not. I said she kissed me.

MUR. (*scornfully, but drifting back a step in his direction*). And I suppose you just sat and let yourself be kissed! Tell that to the Marines!

RICH. (*injuredly*). All right! If you're going to call me a liar every word I say—

MUR. (*drifting back another step*). I didn't call you a liar. I only meant —it sounds fishy. Don't you know it does?

RICH. I don't know anything. I only know I wish I was dead!

MUR. (*gently reproving*). You oughtn't to say that. It's wicked. (*Then after a pause.*) And I suppose you'll tell me you didn't fall in love with her?

RICH. (*scornfully*). I should say not! Fall in love with that kind of girl! What do you take me for?

MUR. (*practically*). How do you know what you did if you drank so much champagne?

RICH. I kept my head—with her. I'm not a sucker, no matter what you think!

MUR. (*drifting nearer*). Then you didn't—love her?

RICH. I hated her! She wasn't even pretty! And I had a fight with her before I left, she got so fresh. I told her I loved you and never could love anyone else, and for her to leave me alone.

MUR. But you said just now you were going to see her—

RICH. That was only bluff. I wouldn't—unless you left me. Then I wouldn't care what I did—any more than I did last night. (*Then suddenly defiant.*) And what if I did kiss her once or twice? I only did it to get back at you!

MUR. Dick!

RICH. You're a fine one to blame me—when it was all your fault! Why can't you be fair? Didn't I think you were out of my life forever? Hadn't you written me you were? Answer me that!

MUR. But I've told you a million times that Pa—

RICH. Why didn't you have more sense than to let him make you write it? Was it my fault you didn't?

MUR. It was your fault for being so stupid! You ought to have known he stood right over me and told me each word to write. If I'd refused, it would only have made everything worse. I had to pretend, so I'd get a chance to see you. Don't you see, Silly? And I had sand enough to sneak out to meet you tonight, didn't I? (*He doesn't answer. She moves nearer.*) Still I can see how you felt the way you did—and maybe I am to blame for that. So I'll forgive and forget, Dick—if you'll swear to me you didn't even think of loving that—

RICH. (*eagerly*). I didn't! I swear, Muriel. I couldn't. I love you!

MUR. Well, then—I still love you.

RICH. Then come back here, why don't you?

MUR. (*coyly*). It's getting late.

RICH. It's not near half-past yet.

MUR. (*comes back and sits down by him shyly*). All right—only I'll have to go soon, Dick. (*He puts his arm around her. She cuddles up close to him.*) I'm sorry—I hurt your hand.

RICH. That was nothing. It felt wonderful—even to have you bite!

MUR. (*impulsively takes his hand and kisses it*). There! That'll cure it. (*She is overcome by confusion at her boldness.*)

RICH. You shouldn't—waste that—on my hand. (*Then tremblingly.*) You said—you'd let me—

MUR. I said, maybe.

RICH. Please, Muriel. You know—I want it so!

MUR. Will it wash off—her kisses—make you forget you ever—for always?

RICH. I should say so! I'd never remember—anything but it—never want anything but it—ever again.

MUR. (*shyly lifting her lips*). Then—all right—Dick. (*He kisses her tremblingly and for a moment their lips remain together. Then she lets her head sink on his shoulder and sighs softly.*) The moon *is* beautiful, isn't it?

RICH. (*kissing her hair*). Not as beautiful as you! Nothing is! (*Then after a pause.*) Won't it be wonderful when we're married?

MUR. Yes—but it's so long to wait.

RICH. Perhaps I needn't go to Yale. Perhaps Pa will give me a job. Then I'd soon be making enough to—

MUR. You better do what your pa thinks best—and I'd like you to be at Yale. (*Then patting his face.*) Poor you! Do you think he'll punish you awful?

RICH. (*intensely*). I don't know and I don't care! Nothing would have kept me from seeing you tonight—not if I'd had to crawl over red-hot coals! (*Then falling back on Swinburne—but with passionate sincerity.*) You have my being between the hands of you! You are "my love, mine own soul's heart, more dear than mine own soul, more beautiful than God!"

MUR. (*shocked and delighted*). Ssshh! It's wrong to say that.

RICH. (*adoringly*). Gosh, but I love you! Gosh, I love you—Darling!

MUR. I love you, too—Sweetheart! (*They kiss. Then she lets her head sink on his shoulder again and they both sit in a rapt trance, star-*

ing at the moon. After a pause—dreamily.) Where'll we go on our honeymoon, Dick? To Niagara Falls?

RICH. (*scornfully*). That dump where all the silly fools go? I should say not! (*With passionate romanticism.*) No, we'll go to some far-off wonderful place! (*He calls on Kipling to help him.*) Somewhere out on the Long Trail—the trail that is always new—on the road to Mandalay! We'll watch the dawn come up like thunder out of China!

MUR. (*hazily but happily*). That'll be wonderful, won't it?

(CURTAIN)

Scene Three

SCENE—*The sitting-room of the* MILLER *house again—about 10 o'clock the same night.* MILLER *is sitting in his rocker at left, front, of table, his wife in the rocker at right, front, of table. Moonlight shines through the screen door at right, rear. Only the green-shaded reading lamp is lit and by its light* MILLER, *his specs on, is reading a book while his wife, sewing basket in lap, is working industriously on a doily.* MRS. MILLER's *face wears an expression of unworried content.* MILLER's *face has also lost its look of harassed preoccupation, although he still is a prey to certain misgivings, when he allows himself to think of them. Several books are piled on the table by his elbow, the books that have been confiscated from* RICHARD.

MILL. (*chuckles at something he reads—then closes the book and puts it on the table.* MRS. MILLER *looks up from her sewing*). This Shaw's a comical cuss—even if his ideas are so crazy they oughtn't to allow them to be printed. And that Swinburne's got a fine swing to his poetry—if he'd only choose some other subjects besides loose women.

MRS. MILL. (*smiling teasingly*). I can see where you're becoming corrupted by those books, too—pretending to read them out of duty to Richard, when your nose has been glued to the page!

MILL. No, no—but I've got to be honest. There's something to them. That *Rubaiyat of Omar Khayyam,* now. I read that over again and liked it even better than I had before—parts of it, that is, where it isn't all about boozing.

MRS. MILL. (*has been busy with her own thoughts during this last—with a deep sigh of relief*). My, but I'm glad Mildred told me where Richard went off to. I'd have worried my heart out if she hadn't. But now, it's all right.

MILL. (*frowning a little*). I'd hardly go so far as to say that. Just because we know he's all right tonight doesn't mean last night is wiped out. He's still got to be punished for that.

MRS. MILL. (*defensively*). Well, if you ask me, I think after the way I punished him all day, and the way I know he's punished himself, he's had about all he deserves. I've told you how sorry he was, and how he said he'd never touch liquor again. It didn't make him feel happy like Sid, but only sad and sick, so he didn't see anything in it for him.

MILL. Well, if he's really got that view of it driven into his skull, I don't know but I'm glad it all happened. That'll protect him more than a thousand lectures—just horse sense about himself. (*Then frowning again.*) Still, I can't let him do such things and go scot-free. And then, besides, there's another side to it— (*He stops abruptly.*)

MRS. MILL. (*uneasily*). What do you mean, another side?

MILL. (*hastily*). I mean, discipline. There's got to be some discipline in a family. I don't want him to get the idea he's got a stuffed shirt at the head of the table. No, he's got to be punished, if only to make the lesson stick in his mind, and I'm going to tell him he can't go to Yale, seeing he's so undependable.

MRS. MILL. (*up in arms at once*). Not go to Yale! I guess he can go to Yale! Every man of your means in town is sending his boys to college! What would folks think of you? You let Wilbur go, and you'd have let Lawrence, only he didn't want to, and you're letting Arthur! If our other children can get the benefit of a college education, you're not going to pick on Richard—

MILL. Hush up, for God's sake! If you'd let me finish what I started to say! I said I'd *tell* him that now—bluff—then later on I'll change my mind, if he behaves himself.

MRS. MILL. Oh well, if that's all— (*Then defensively again.*) But it's your duty to give him every benefit. He's got an exceptional brain, that boy has! He's proved it by the way he likes to read all those deep plays and books and poetry.

MILL. But I thought you— (*He stops, grinning helplessly.*)

MRS. MILL. You thought I what?

MILL. Never mind.

MRS. MILL. (*sniffs, but thinks it better to let this pass*). You mark my words, that boy's going to turn out to be a great lawyer, or a great doctor, or a great writer, or—

MILL. (*grinning*). You agree he's going to be great, anyway.

MRS. MILL. Yes, I most certainly have a lot of faith in Richard.

MILL. Well, so have I, as far as that goes.

MRS. MILL. (*after a pause—judicially*). And as for his being in love with Muriel, I don't see but what it might work out real well. Richard could do worse.

MILL. But I thought you had no use for her, thought she was stupid.

MRS. MILL. Well, so I did, but if she's good for Richard and he wants her— (*Then inconsequentially.*) Ma used to say you weren't over-bright, but she changed her mind when she saw I didn't care if you were or not.

MILL. (*not exactly pleased by this*). Well, I've been bright enough to—

MRS. MILL. (*going on as if he had not spoken*). And Muriel's real cute-looking, I have to admit that. Takes after her mother. Alice Briggs was the prettiest girl before she married.

MILL. Yes, and Muriel will get big as a house after she's married, the same as her mother did. That's the trouble. A man never can tell what he's letting himself in for— (*He stops, feeling his wife's eyes fixed on him with indignant suspicion.*)

MRS. MILL. (*sharply*). I'm not too fat and don't you say it!

MILL. Who was talking about you?

MRS. MILL. And I'd rather have some flesh on my bones than be built like a string bean and bore a hole in a chair every time I sat down —like some people!

MILL. (*ignoring the insult—flatteringly*). Why, no one'd ever call you fat, Essie. You're only plump, like a good figure ought to be.

MRS. MILL. (*childishly pleased—gratefully giving tit for tat*). Well, you're not skinny, either—only slender—and I think you've been putting on weight lately, too. (*Having thus squared matters she takes up her sewing again. A pause. Then* MILLER *asks incredulously.*)

MILL. You don't mean to tell me you're actually taking this Muriel crush of Richard's seriously, do you? I know it's a good thing to encourage right now but—pshaw, why, Richard'll probably forget all about her before he's away six months, and she'll have forgotten him.

MRS. MILL. Don't be so cynical. (*Then, after a pause, thoughtfully.*) Well, anyway, he'll always have it to remember—no matter what happens after—and that's something.

MILL. You bet that's something. (*Then with a grin.*) You surprise me at times with your deep wisdom.

MRS. MILL. You don't give me credit for ever having common sense, that's why. (*She goes back to her sewing.*)

MILL. (*after a pause*). Where'd you say Sid and Lily had gone off to?

MRS. MILL. To the beach to listen to the band. (*She sighs sympathetically.*) Poor Lily! Sid'll never change, and she'll never marry him. But she seems to get some queer satisfaction out of fussing over him like a hen that's hatched a duck—though Lord knows I wouldn't in her shoes!

MILL. Arthur's up with Elsie Rand, I suppose?

MRS. MILL. Of course.

MILL. Where's Mildred?

MRS. MILL. Out walking with her latest. I've forgot who it is. I can't keep track of them. (*She smiles.*)

MILL. (*smiling*). Then, from all reports, we seem to be completely surrounded by love!

MRS. MILL. Well, we've had our share, haven't we? We don't have to begrudge it to our children. (*Then has a sudden thought.*) But I've done all this talking about Muriel and Richard and clean forgot how wild old McComber was against it. But he'll get over that, I suppose.

MILL. (*with a chuckle*). He has already. I ran into him upstreet this afternoon and he was meek as pie. He backed water and said he guessed I was right. Richard had just copied stuff out of books, and kids would be kids, and so on. So I came off my high horse a bit—but not too far—and I guess all that won't bother anyone any more. (*Then rubbing his hands together—with a boyish grin of pleasure.*) And I told you about getting that business from Lawson, didn't I? It's been a good day, Essie—a darned good day!

(*From the hall beyond the front parlor the sound of the front door being opened and shut is heard.* MRS. MILLER *leans forward to look, pushing her specs up.*)

MRS. MILL. (*in a whisper*). It's Richard.

MILL. (*immediately assuming an expression of becoming gravity*). Hmm. (*He takes off his spectacles and puts them back in their case and straightens himself in his chair.*)

(RICHARD *comes slowly in from the front parlor. He walks like one in a trance, his eyes shining with a dreamy happiness, his spirit still too exalted to be conscious of his surroundings, or to remember the threatened punishment. He carries his straw hat dangling in his hand, quite unaware of its existence.*)

RICH. (*dreamily, like a ghost addressing fellow shades*). Hello.

MRS. MILL. (*staring at him worriedly*). Hello, Richard.

MILL. (*sizing him up shrewdly*). Hello, Son.

(RICHARD *moves past his mother and comes to the far corner, left front, where the light is dimmest, and sits down on the sofa, and stares before him, his hat dangling in his hand.*)

MRS. MILL. (*with frightened suspicion now*). Goodness, he acts queer! Nat, you don't suppose he's been—?

MILL. (*with a reassuring smile*). No. It's love, not liquor, this time.

MRS. MILL. (*only partly reassured—sharply*). Richard! What's the matter with you? (*He comes to himself with a start. She goes on scoldingly.*) How many times have I told you to hang up your hat in the hall when you come in! (*He looks at his hat as if he were surprised at its existence. She gets up fussily and goes to him.*) Here. Give it to me. I'll hang it up for you this once. And what are you sitting over here in the dark for? Don't forget your father's been waiting to talk to you! (*She comes back to the table and he follows her, still half in a dream, and stands by his father's chair.* MRS. MILLER *starts for the hall with his hat.*)

MILL. (*quietly but firmly now*). You better leave Richard and me alone for a while, Essie.

MRS. MILL. (*turns to stare at him apprehensively*). Well—all right. I'll go sit on the piazza. Call me if you want me. (*Then a bit pleadingly.*) But you'll remember all I've said, Nat, won't you? (MILLER *nods reassuringly. She disappears through the front parlor.* RICHARD, *keenly conscious of himself as the about-to-be-sentenced criminal by this time, looks guilty and a bit defiant, searches his father's expressionless face with uneasy side glances, and steels himself for what is coming.*)

MILL. (*casually, indicating* MRS. MILLER's *rocker*). Sit down, Richard. (RICHARD *slumps awkwardly into the chair and sits in a self-conscious, unnatural position.* MILLER *sizes him up keenly—then suddenly smiles and asks with quiet mockery.*) Well, how are the vine leaves in your hair this evening?

RICH. (*totally unprepared for this approach—shamefacedly mutters*). I don't know, Pa.

MILL. Turned out to be poison ivy, didn't they? (*Then kindly.*) But you needn't look so alarmed. I'm not going to read you any temperance lecture. That'd bore me more than it would you. And, in spite of your damn foolishness last night, I'm still giving you credit for having brains. So I'm pretty sure anything I could say to you you've already said to yourself.

RICH. (*his head down—humbly*). I know I was a darned fool.

MILL. (*thinking it well to rub in this aspect—disgustedly*). You sure were—not only a fool but a downright, stupid, disgusting fool! (RICHARD *squirms, his head still lower.*) It was bad enough for you to let me and Arthur see you, but to appear like that before your mother and Mildred—! And I wonder if Muriel would think you were so fine if she ever saw you as you looked and acted then. I think she'd give you your walking papers for keeps. And you couldn't blame her. No nice girl wants to give her love to a stupid drunk!

RICH. (*writhing*). I know, Pa.

MILL. (*after a pause—quietly*). All right. Then that settles—the booze end of it. (*He sizes* RICHARD *up searchingly—then suddenly speaks sharply.*) But there is another thing that's more serious. How about that tart you went to bed with at the Pleasant Beach House?

RICH. (*flabbergasted—stammers*). You know—? But I didn't! If they've told you about her down there, they must have told you I didn't! She wanted me to—but I wouldn't. I gave her the five dollars just so she'd let me out of it. Honest, Pa, I didn't! She made everything seem rotten and dirty—and—I didn't want to do a thing like that to Muriel—no matter how bad I thought she'd treated me—even after I felt drunk, I didn't. Honest!

MILL. How'd you happen to meet this lady, anyway?

RICH. I can't tell that, Pa. I'd have to snitch on someone—and you wouldn't want me to do that.

MILL. (*a bit taken aback*). No. I suppose I wouldn't. Hmm. Well, I believe you—and I guess that settles that. (*Then, after a quick, furtive glance at* RICHARD, *he nerves himself for the ordeal and begins with a shamefaced, self-conscious solemnity.*) But listen here, Richard, it's about time you and I had a serious talk about—hmm—certain matters pertaining to—and now that the subject's come up of its own accord, it's a good time—I mean, there's no use in procrastinating further—so, here goes. (*But it doesn't go smoothly and as he goes on he becomes more and more guiltily embarrassed and self-conscious and his expressions more stilted.* RICHARD *sedulously avoids even glancing at him, his own embarrassment made tenfold more painful by his father's.*) Richard, you have now come to the age when— Well, you're a fully developed man, in a way, and it's only natural for you to have certain desires of the flesh, to put it that way— I mean, pertaining to the opposite sex—certain natural feelings and temptations—that'll want to be gratified—and you'll want to gratify them. Hmm—well, human society being organized as it is, there's only one outlet for—unless you're a scoundrel and go around ruining decent girls—which you're not, of course. Well, there are a certain class of women—always have been and always will be as long as human nature is what it is— It's wrong, maybe, but what can you do about it? I mean, girls like that one you—girls there's something doing with —and lots of 'em are pretty, and it's human nature if you— But that doesn't mean to ever get mixed up with them seriously! You just have what you want and pay 'em and forget it. I know that sounds hard and unfeeling, but we're talking facts and— But don't think I'm encouraging you to— If you can stay away from 'em, all the better—but if—why—hmm— Here's what I'm driving at, Richard. They're apt to be whited sepulchres—I mean, your whole life might be ruined if—so, darn it, you've got to know how to— I mean, there are ways and means— (*Suddenly he can go no farther and winds up helplessly.*) But, hell, I suppose you boys talk all this over among yourselves and you know more about it than I do. I'll admit I'm no authority. I never had anything to do with such women, and it'll be a hell of a lot better for you if you never do!

RICH. (*without looking at him*). I'm never going to, Pa. (*Then shocked indignation coming into his voice.*) I don't see how you could think I could—now—when you know I love Muriel and am going to marry her. I'd die before I'd—!

MILL. (*immensely relieved—enthusiastically*). That's the talk! By God, I'm proud of you when you talk like that! (*Then hastily.*) And now that's all of that. There's nothing more to say and we'll forget it, eh?

RICH. (*after a pause*). How are you going to punish me, Pa?

MILL. I *was* sort of forgetting that, wasn't I? Well, I'd thought of telling you you couldn't go to Yale—

RICH. (*eagerly*). Don't I have to go? Gee, that's great! Muriel thought you'd want me to. I was telling her I'd rather you gave me a job on the paper because then she and I could get married sooner. (*Then with a boyish grin.*) Gee, Pa, you picked a lemon. That isn't any punishment. You'll have to do something besides that.

MILL. (*grimly—but only half concealing an answering grin*). Then you'll go to Yale and you'll stay there till you graduate, that's the answer to that! Muriel's got good sense and you haven't! (RICHARD *accepts this philosophically.*) And now we're finished, you better call your mother.

(RICHARD *opens the screen door and calls* "Ma," *and a moment later she comes in. She glances quickly from son to husband and immediately knows that all is well and tactfully refrains from all questions.*)

MRS. MILL. My, it's a beautiful night. The moon's way down low—almost setting. (*She sits in her chair and sighs contentedly.* RICHARD *remains standing by the door, staring out at the moon, his face pale in the moonlight.*)

MILL. (*with a nod at* RICHARD, *winking at his wife*). Yes, I don't believe I've hardly ever seen such a beautiful night—with such a wonderful moon. Have you, Richard?

RICH. (*turning to them—enthusiastically*). No! It was wonderful—down at the beach— (*He stops abruptly, smiling shyly.*)

MILL. (*watching his son—after a pause—quietly*). I can only remember a few nights that were as beautiful as this—and they were long ago, when your mother and I were young and planning to get married.

RICH. (*stares at him wonderingly for a moment, then quickly from his father to his mother and back again, strangely, as if he'd never seen them before—then he looks almost disgusted and swallows as if an acrid taste had come into his mouth—but then suddenly his face is transfigured by a smile of shy understanding and sympathy. He speaks shyly*). Yes, I'll bet those must have been wonderful nights, too. You sort of forget the moon was the same way back then—and everything.

MILL. (*huskily*). You're all right, Richard. (*He gets up and blows his nose.*)

MRS. MILL. (*fondly*). You're a good boy, Richard. (RICHARD *looks dreadfully shy and embarrassed at this. His father comes to his rescue.*)

MILL. Better get to bed early tonight, Son, hadn't you?

RICH. I couldn't sleep. Can't I go out on the piazza and sit for a while—until the moon sets?

MILL. All right. Then you better say good night now. I don't know about your mother, but I'm going to bed right away. I'm dead tired.

MRS. MILL. So am I.

RICH. (*goes to her and kisses her*). Good night, Ma.

MRS. MILL. Good night. Don't you stay up till all hours now.

RICH. (*comes to his father and stands awkwardly before him*). Good night, Pa.

MILL. (*puts his arm around him and gives him a hug*). Good night, Richard. (RICHARD *turns impulsively and kisses him—then hurries out the screen door.* MILLER *stares after him—then says huskily.*) First time he's done that in years. I don't believe in kissing between fathers and sons after a certain age—seems mushy and silly—but that meant something! And I don't think we'll ever have to worry about his being safe—from himself—again. And I guess no matter what life will do to him, he can take care of it now. (*He sighs with satisfaction and, sitting down in his chair, begins to unlace his shoes.*) My darned feet are giving me fits!

MRS. MILL. (*laughing*). Why do you bother unlacing your shoes now, you big goose—when we're going right up to bed?

MILL. (*as if he hadn't thought of that before, stops*). Guess you're right. (*Then getting to his feet—with a grin.*) Mind if I don't say my prayers tonight, Essie? I'm certain God knows I'm too darned tired.

MRS. MILL. Don't talk that way. It's real sinful. (*She gets up—then laughing fondly.*) If that isn't you all over! Always looking for an excuse to— You're worse than Tommy! But all right. I suppose tonight you needn't. You've had a hard day. (*She puts her hand on the reading-lamp switch.*) I'm going to turn out the light. All ready?

MILL. Yep. Let her go, Gallagher. (*She turns out the lamp. In the ensuing darkness the faint moonlight shines full in through the screen door. Walking together toward the front parlor they stand full in it for a moment, looking out.* MILLER *puts his arm around her. He says in a low voice.*) There he is—like a statue of Love's Young Dream. (*Then he sighs and speaks with a gentle nostalgic melancholy.*) What's it that *Rubaiyat* says:

"Yet Ah, that Spring should vanish with the Rose!
That Youth's sweet-scented manuscript should close!"

(*Then throwing off his melancholy, with a loving smile at her.*)

Well, Spring isn't everything, is it, Essie? There's a lot to be said for Autumn. That's got beauty, too. And Winter—if you're together.

MRS. MILL. (*simply*). Yes, Nat. (*She kisses him and they move quietly out of the moonlight, back into the darkness of the front parlor.*)

(CURTAIN)

Thomas Stearns Eliot

► Thomas Stearns Eliot, whose family was connected with the New England family of Eliots, was born in St. Louis in 1888. He went to Harvard (A.B., 1909; A.M., 1910), where he began writing during his undergraduate days. After receiving his A.M., Eliot spent a year at the Sorbonne, and then returned to Harvard for three more years of graduate study and teaching. Thence he went, in 1914, to Merton College, Oxford, for still another year of study. In 1915, he went down from Oxford to London, which was to become his permanent home. He married an Englishwoman, and in 1927 became a British subject. In an oft-quoted passage from *For Lancelot Andrewes* (1928) he announced that he was "an Anglo-Catholic in religion, a classicist in literature, and a royalist in politics." He has belied the conventional concept of the limitations of the poetic temperament by his success in the business world. At various times he has worked in a bank, edited a magazine, and served as a director of a publishing house.

Eliot is perhaps the most influential poet of his generation, and a distinguished critic as well. Among his contemporaries his influence in both realms has been enormous; he has been looked upon with awe and imitated with reverence by younger poets and critics. This vast reputation, even greater in France and England than in America, rests upon a relatively small output of verses, whose roots lie in French Symbolism, and on two or three volumes of critical essays. The loftiness and obscurity of his poems, their urbane and esoteric allusions, and their classic precision and compression of style (*The Waste Land,* which Eliot himself has annotated heavily, is the epic example) have, however, prevented their author from becoming a popular favorite. In his earlier poetry Eliot portrayed the hollowness and futility of an age without faith; in his more recent work he has been concerned with the rebuilding of faith and with the spiritual regeneration of the individual.

Eliot's interest in drama as a literary form became evident during the 1930's. The fragments of *Sweeney Agonistes* (1933) and the pageant *The Rock* (1934), for example, are cast in a dramatic mold. But it was not until *Murder in the Cathedral* (1935) that Eliot achieved a poetic composition suitable for stage presentation, and capable of being enhanced by performance. This play was specially written for production at the Chapter House adjoining the cloisters of Canterbury to help raise funds for the restoration of the Cathedral. It captured the attention of the English theatre public and was moved to the Mercury Theatre in London. There, and on a later tour of the provinces, it was performed six hundred times. In 1936 it was presented by the Federal Theatre of WPA at the cathedral-like Manhattan Theatre in New York, where it was enthusiastically received for thirty-eight performances. In February 1938 the original English company, with the English sets, brought it to the Ritz Theatre in New York for a brief run of twenty-one performances. And in 1952 New York saw the première of the screen version, for which Mr. Eliot himself had adapted the play.

In 1939 Eliot's second verse play, *The Family Reunion,* appeared, and in 1949 a third poetic drama, *The Cocktail Party.* Despite its rare intellectual quality and the demands it made upon the audience, *The Cocktail Party* proved to be the most popular of Eliot's plays thus far. It was first produced at the Edinburgh Festival in the summer of 1949, before it was brought to New York, where it had a phenomenal (for a poetic drama) run of 153 performances. Toward the end of 1952 Mr. Eliot was completing work on a fourth verse play, which, like the last two, is on a modern theme.

Although Eliot has continued to write poetry and criticism—indeed, one of his major poems, *Four Quartets,* was not completed until 1943—he has declared that his chief interest now lies in poetic drama. In a lecture at Harvard in 1951 he gave the following analysis of that dramatic form and of his special interest in it:

"It seems to me that if we are to have a poetic drama, it is more likely to come from poets learning how to write plays, than from skilful prose dramatists learning to write poetry. That some poets can learn how to write plays, and write good ones, may be only a hope, but I believe a not unreasonable hope; but that a man who has started by writing successful prose plays should then learn how to write good poetry, seems to me extremely unlikely. And, under present-day conditions, and until the verse play is recognised by the larger public as a possible source of entertainment, the poet is likely to get his first opportunity to work for the stage only after making some sort of reputation for himself as the author of other kinds of verse. . . .

"I should . . . like . . . to set before myself, and, if I can, before you, though only in dim outline, the ideal towards which it seems to me that poetic drama should strive. It is an unattainable ideal: and that is why it interests me, for it provides an incentive towards further experiment and exploration, beyond any goal which there is prospect of attaining. It is a function of all art to give us some perception of an order in life, by imposing an order upon it. The painter works by selection, combination, and emphasis among the elements of the visible world; the musician, in the world of sound. It seems to

me that beyond the nameable, classifiable emotions and motives of our conscious life when directed towards action—the
part of life which prose drama is wholly adequate to express—
there is a fringe of indefinite extent, of feeling which we can
only detect, so to speak, out of the corner of the eye and can
never completely focus; of feeling of which we are only aware
in a kind of temporary detachment from action. There are
great prose dramatists—such as Ibsen and Chekhov—who have
at times done things of which I would not otherwise have supposed prose to be capable, but who seem to me, in spite of their
success, to have been hampered in expression by writing in
prose. This peculiar range of sensibility can be expressed by
dramatic poetry, at its moments of greatest intensity. At such
moments, we touch the border of those feelings which only
music can express. We can never emulate music, because to
arrive at the condition of music would be the annihilation of
poetry, and especially of dramatic poetry. Nevertheless, I have
before my eyes a kind of mirage of the perfection of verse
drama, which would be a design of human action and of
words, such as to present at once the two aspects of dramatic
and of musical order. It seems to me that Shakespeare achieved
this at least in certain scenes—even rather early, for there is the
balcony scene of *Romeo and Juliet*—and that this was what he
was striving towards in his late plays. To go as far in this direction as it is possible to go, without losing that contact with
the ordinary everyday world with which drama must come to
terms, seems to me the proper aim of dramatic poetry." [1]

Murder in the Cathedral is a richly construed play of classic
dimensions, religious in spirit and universal in theme. Its action,

[1] Reprinted by permission of the publishers from T. S. Eliot, *Poetry and Drama*,
Cambridge, Mass.: Harvard University Press, Copyright, 1951, by The President
and Fellows of Harvard College.

concentrated within the month of December 1170, deals with the final days and the martyrdom of Archbishop Thomas Becket. Though the central occurrence is historical, the play is not documentary and makes no attempt to re-create realistically the original events. Instead, it is cast in the mold of Greek drama, and uses the classic device of the chorus to create the mood and carry much of the narrative.

The mood is one of gloom, of impending disaster, and of deep foreboding. It is voiced in the first few sentences by the Women of Canterbury in the Archbishop's Hall:

"Here let us stand, close by the cathedral. Here let us wait. . . .
Some presage of an act
Which our eyes are compelled to witness, has forced our feet
Toward the cathedral. We are forced to bear witness."

This dolorous lament is immediately heightened by the appearance of Becket, returning from an exile of seven years only to be murdered. The substance of the play, including much of its dramatic development, is the probing of the Archbishop's faith and the motives—both his own and his murderers'—for his martyrdom.

The probing is achieved through the device of the four Tempters, after the fashion of the temptation of Jesus. The first three Tempters represent worldly and selfish motives which Becket has already surmounted; but the fourth Tempter represents spiritual pride and forces Becket to face the possibility that he may be unworthily seeking personal glory through his martyrdom. Becket rejects this temptation also, and his purer faith triumphs.

Murder in the Cathedral has achieved the unique distinction of being a great religious drama in a period when previous efforts in this field have failed in their purpose. However, though it acts well on the stage, its studied diction and highly compressed lines are too charged with meaning and with connotation to be easily communicated across the footlights. The play therefore is especially rewarding in thoughtful reading, where the lines may be said again and again until their richness of sound and sense has been fully savored.

MURDER

IN THE

CATHEDRAL

PART ONE

Characters

A CHORUS OF WOMEN OF CANTERBURY

THREE PRIESTS OF THE CATHEDRAL

A HERALD

ARCHBISHOP THOMAS BECKET

FOUR TEMPTERS

ATTENDANTS

The Scene is the Archbishop's Hall,
on December 2nd, 1170.

CHOR. Here let us stand, close by the cathedral. Here let us wait.
Are we drawn by danger? Is it the knowledge of safety, that draws our feet
Towards the cathedral? What danger can be
For us, the poor, the poor women of Canterbury? what tribulation
With which we are not already familiar? There is no danger
For us, and there is no safety in the cathedral. Some presage of an act
Which our eyes are compelled to witness, has forced our feet
Towards the cathedral. We are forced to bear witness.
Since golden October declined into sombre November
And the apples were gathered and stored, and the land became brown sharp points of death in a waste of water and mud.
The New Year waits, breathes, waits, whispers in darkness.
While the labourer kicks off a muddy boot and stretches his hand to the fire,
The New Year waits, destiny waits for the coming.
Who has stretched out his hand to the fire and remembered the Saints at All Hallows,
Remembered the martyrs and saints who wait? and who shall
Stretch out his hand to the fire, and deny his master? who shall be warm
By the fire, and deny his master?

Seven years and the summer is over
Seven years since the Archbishop left us,
He who was always kind to his people.
But it would not be well if he should return.
King rules or barons rule;
We have suffered various oppression,
But mostly we are left to our own devices,
And we are content if we are left alone.
We try to keep our households in order;
The merchant, shy and cautious, tries to compile a little fortune,
And the labourer bends to his piece of earth, earth-colour, his own colour,

Preferring to pass unobserved.
Now I fear disturbance of the quiet seasons:
Winter shall come bringing death from the sea,
Ruinous spring shall beat at our doors,
Root and shoot shall eat our eyes and our ears,
Disastrous summer burn up the beds of our streams
And the poor shall wait for another decaying October.
Why should the summer bring consolation
For autumn fires and winter fogs?
What shall we do in the heat of summer
But wait in barren orchards for another October?
Some malady is coming upon us. We wait, we wait,
And the saints and martyrs wait, for those who shall be martyrs
    and saints.
Destiny waits in the hand of God, shaping the still unshapen:
I have seen these things in a shaft of sunlight.
Destiny waits in the hand of God, not in the hands of statesmen
Who do, some well, some ill, planning and guessing,
Having their aims which turn in their hands in the pattern of
    time.
Come, happy December, who shall observe you, who shall pre-
    serve you?
Shall the Son of Man be born again in the litter of scorn?
For us, the poor, there is no action,
But only to wait and to witness.

(*Enter* PRIESTS.)

1ST. PR. Seven years and the summer is over.
    Seven years since the Archbishop left us.

2ND PR. What does the Archbishop do, and our Sovereign Lord the Pope
    With the stubborn King and the French King
    In ceaseless intrigue, combinations,
    In conference, meetings accepted, meetings refused,
    Meetings unended or endless
    At one place or another in France?

3RD PR. I see nothing quite conclusive in the art of temporal government,
    But violence, duplicity and frequent malversation.

King rules or barons rule:
The strong man strongly and the weak man by caprice.
They have but one law, to seize the power and keep it,
And the steadfast can manipulate the greed and lust of others,
The feeble is devoured by his own.

1ST PR. Shall these things not end
    Until the poor at the gate
    Have forgotten their friend, their Father in God, have forgotten
    That they had a friend?

(*Enter* HERALD.)

HER. Servants of God, and watchers of the temple,
    I am here to inform you, without circumlocution:
    The Archbishop is in England, and is close outside the city.
    I was sent before in haste
    To give you notice of his coming, as much as was possible,
    That you may prepare to meet him.

1ST PR. What, is the exile ended, is our Lord Archbishop
    Reunited with the King? what reconciliation
    Of two proud men? what peace can be found
    To grow between the hammer and the anvil? Tell us,
    Are the old disputes at an end, is the wall of pride cast down
    That divided them? Is it peace or war? Does he come
    In full assurance, or only secure
    In the power of Rome, the spiritual rule,
    The assurance of right, and the love of the people,
    Contemning the hatred and envy of barons?

HER. You are right to express a certain incredulity.
    He comes in pride and sorrow, affirming all his claims,
    Assured, beyond doubt, of the devotion of the people,
    Who receive him with scenes of frenzied enthusiasm,
    Lining the road and throwing down their capes,
    Strewing the way with leaves and late flowers of the season.
    The streets of the city will be packed to suffocation,
    And I think that his horse will be deprived of its tail,
    A single hair of which becomes a precious relic.

He is at one with the Pope, and with the King of France,
Who indeed would have liked to detain him in his kingdom:
But as for our King, that is another matter.

1ST PR. But again, is it war or peace?

HER.   Peace, but not the kiss of peace.
A patched up affair, if you ask my opinion.
And if you ask me, I think the Lord Archbishop
Is not the man to cherish any illusions,
Or yet to diminish the least of his pretensions.
If you ask my opinion, I think that this peace
Is nothing like an end, or like a beginning.
It is common knowledge that when the Archbishop
Parted from the King, he said to the King,
My Lord, he said, I leave you as a man
Whom in this life I shall not see again.
I have this, I assure you, on the highest authority;
There are several opinions as to what he meant
But no one considers it a happy prognostic.   (*Exit.*)

1ST PR. I fear for the Archbishop, I fear for the Church,
I know that the pride bred of sudden prosperity
Was but confirmed by bitter adversity.
I saw him as Chancellor, flattered by the King,
Liked or feared by courtiers, in their overbearing fashion,
Despised and despising, always isolated,
Never one among them, always insecure;
His pride always feeding upon his own virtues,
Pride drawing sustenance from impartiality,
Pride drawing sustenance from generosity,
Loathing power given by temporal devolution,
Wishing subjection to God alone.
Had the King been greater, or had he been weaker
Things had perhaps been different for Thomas.

2ND PR. Yet our Lord is returned. Our Lord has come back to his own
again.
We have had enough of waiting, from December to dismal December.

The Archbishop shall be at our head, dispelling dismay and doubt.

He will tell us what we are to do, he will give us our orders, instruct us.

Our Lord is at one with the Pope, and also the King of France.

We can lean on a rock, we can feel a firm foothold

Against the perpetual wash of tides of balance of forces of barons and landholders.

The rock of God is beneath our feet. Let us meet the Archbishop with cordial thanksgiving:

Our Lord, our Archbishop returns. And when the Archbishop returns

Our doubts are dispelled. Let us therefore rejoice,

I say rejoice, and show a glad face for his welcome.

I am the Archbishop's man. Let us give the Archbishop welcome!

3RD PR. For good or ill, let the wheel turn.

The wheel has been still, these seven years, and no good.

For ill or good, let the wheel turn.

For who knows the end of good or evil?

Until the grinders cease

And the door shall be shut in the street,

And all the daughters of music shall be brought low.

CHOR. Here is no continuing city, here is no abiding stay.

Ill the wind, ill the time, uncertain the profit, certain the danger.

O late late late, late is the time, late too late, and rotten the year;

Evil the wind, and bitter the sea, and grey the sky, grey grey grey.

O Thomas, return, Archbishop; return, return to France.

Return. Quickly. Quietly. Leave us to perish in quiet.

You come with applause, you come with rejoicing, but you come bringing death into Canterbury:

A doom on the house, a doom on yourself, a doom on the world.

We do not wish anything to happen.

Seven years we have lived quietly,

Succeeded in avoiding notice,

Living and partly living.

There have been oppression and luxury,
There have been poverty and licence,
There has been minor injustice.
Yet we have gone on living,
Living and partly living.
Sometimes the corn has failed us,
Sometimes the harvest is good,
One year is a year of rain,
Another a year of dryness,
One year the apples are abundant,
Another year the plums are lacking.
Yet we have gone on living,
Living and partly living.
We have kept the feasts, heard the masses,
We have brewed beer and cyder,
Gathered wood against the winter,
Talked at the corner of the fire,
Talked at the corners of streets,
Talked not always in whispers,
Living and partly living.
We have seen births, deaths and marriages,
We have had various scandals,
We have been afflicted with taxes,
We have had laughter and gossip,
Several girls have disappeared
Unaccountably, and some not able to.
We have all had our private terrors,
Our particular shadows, our secret fears.

But now a great fear is upon us, a fear not of one but of many,
A fear like birth and death, when we see birth and death alone
In a void apart. We
Are afraid in a fear which we cannot know, which we cannot
    face, which none understands,
And our hearts are torn from us, our brains unskinned like the
    layers of an onion, our selves are lost lost

In a final fear which none understands. O Thomas Archbishop,
O Thomas our Lord, leave us and leave us be, in our humble and
tarnished frame of existence, leave us; do not ask us
To stand to the doom on the house, the doom on the Archbishop,
the doom on the world.
Archbishop, secure and assured of your fate, unaffrayed among
the shades, do you realise what you ask, do you realise what
it means
To the small folk drawn into the pattern of fate, the small folk
who live among small things,
The strain on the brain of the small folk who stand to the doom
of the house, the doom of their Lord, the doom of the world?
O Thomas, Archbishop, leave us, leave us, leave sullen Dover, and
set sail for France. Thomas our Archbishop still our Archbishop even in France. Thomas Archbishop, set the white sail
between the grey sky and the bitter sea, leave us, leave us for
France.

2ND PR. What a way to talk at such a juncture!
You are foolish, immodest and babbling women.
Do you not know that the good Archbishop
Is likely to arrive at any moment?
The crowds in the streets will be cheering and cheering,
You go on croaking like frogs in the treetops:
But frogs at least can be cooked and eaten.
Whatever you are afraid of, in your craven apprehension,
Let me ask you at the least to put on pleasant faces,
And give a hearty welcome to our good Archbishop.

(*Enter* THOMAS.)

THOM. Peace. And let them be, in their exaltation.
They speak better than they know, and beyond your under-
standing.
They know and do not know, what it is to act or suffer.
They know and do not know, that acting is suffering
And suffering is action. Neither does the actor suffer
Nor the patient act. But both are fixed
In an eternal action, an eternal patience

To which all must consent that it may be willed
And which all must suffer that they may will it,
That the pattern may subsist, for the pattern is the action
And the suffering, that the wheel may turn and still
Be forever still.

2ND PR. O my Lord, forgive me, I did not see you coming,
Engrossed by the chatter of these foolish women.
Forgive us, my Lord, you would have had a better welcome
If we had been sooner prepared for the event.
But your Lordship knows that seven years of waiting,
Seven years of prayer, seven years of emptiness,
Have better prepared our hearts for your coming,
Than seven days could make ready Canterbury.
However, I will have fires laid in all your rooms
To take the chill off our English December,
Your Lordship now being used to a better climate.
Your Lordship will find your rooms in order as you left them.

THOM. And will try to leave them in order as I find them.
I am more than grateful for all your kind attentions.
These are small matters. Little rest in Canterbury
With eager enemies restless about us.
Rebellious bishops, York, London, Salisbury,
Would have intercepted our letters,
Filled the coast with spies and sent to meet me
Some who hold me in bitterest hate.
By God's grace aware of their prevision
I sent my letters on another day,
Had fair crossing, found at Sandwich
Broc, Warenne, and the Sheriff of Kent,
Those who had sworn to have my head from me.
Only John, the Dean of Salisbury,
Fearing for the King's name, warning against treason,
Made them hold their hands. So for the time
We are unmolested.

IST PR.   But do they follow after?

THOM. For a little time the hungry hawk
        Will only soar and hover, circling lower,
        Waiting excuse, pretence, opportunity.
        End will be simple, sudden, God-given.
        Meanwhile the substance of our first act
        Will be shadows, and the strife with shadows.
        Heavier the interval than the consummation.
        All things prepare the event. Watch.

(*Enter* FIRST TEMPTER.)

1ST TEM. You see, my Lord, I do not wait upon ceremony:
        Here I have come, forgetting all acrimony,
        Hoping that your present gravity
        Will find excuse for my humble levity
        Remembering all the good time past.
        Your Lordship won't despise an old friend out of favour?
        Old Tom, gay Tom, Becket of London,
        Your Lordship won't forget that evening on the river
        When the King, and you and I were all friends together?
        Friendship should be more than biting Time can sever.
        What, my Lord, now that you recover
        Favour with the King, shall we say that summer's over
        Or that the good time cannot last?
        Fluting in the meadows, viols in the hall,
        Laughter and apple-blossom floating on the water,
        Singing at nightfall, whispering in chambers,
        Fires devouring the winter season,
        Eating up the darkness, with wit and wine and wisdom!
        Now that the King and you are in amity,
        Clergy and laity may return to gaiety,
        Mirth and sportfulness need not walk warily.

THOM. You talk of seasons that are past. I remember
        Not worth forgetting.

TEM.   And of the new season.
        Spring has come in winter. Snow in the branches
        Shall float as sweet as blossoms. Ice along the ditches

Mirror the sunlight. Love in the orchard
Send the sap shooting. Mirth matches melancholy.

THOM. We do not know very much of the future
Except that from generation to generation
The same things happen again and again.
Men learn little from others' experience.
But in the life of one man, never
The same time returns. Sever
The cord, shed the scale. Only
The fool, fixed in his folly, may think
He can turn the wheel on which he turns.

TEM. My Lord, a nod is as good as a wink.
A man will often love what he spurns.
For the good times past, that are come again
I am your man.

THOM.   Not in this train.
Look to your behaviour. You were safer
Think of penitence and follow your master.

TEM. Not at this gait!
If you go so fast, others may go faster.
Your Lordship is too proud!
The safest beast is not the one that roars most loud.
This was not the way of the King our master!
You were not used to be so hard upon sinners
When they were your friends. Be easy, man!
The easy man lives to eat the best dinners.
Take a friend's advice. Leave well alone,
Or your goose may be cooked and eaten to the bone.

THOM. You come twenty years too late.

TEM. Then I leave you to your fate.
I leave you to the pleasures of your higher vices,
Which will have to be paid for at higher prices.
Farewell, my Lord, I do not wait upon ceremony,
I leave as I came, forgetting all acrimony,
Hoping that your present gravity
Will find excuse for my humble levity.

If you will remember me, my Lord, at your prayers,
I'll remember you at kissing-time below the stairs.

THOM. Leave-well-alone, the springtime fancy,
So one thought goes whistling down the wind.
The impossible is still temptation.
The impossible, the undesirable,
Voices under sleep, waking a dead world,
So that the mind may not be whole in the present.

(*Enter* SECOND TEMPTER.)

2ND TEM. Your Lordship has forgotten me, perhaps. I will remind you.
We met at Clarendon, at Northampton,
And last at Montmirail, in Maine. Now that I have recalled them,
Let us but set these not too pleasant memories
In balance against other, earlier
And weightier ones: those of the Chancellorship.
See how the late ones rise! The master of policy
Whom all acknowledged, should guide the state again.

THOM. Your meaning?

TEM.   The Chancellorship that you resigned
When you were made Archbishop—that was a mistake
On your part—still may be regained. Think, my Lord,
Power obtained grows to glory,
Life lasting, a permanent possession,
A templed tomb, monument of marble.
Rule over men reckon no madness.

THOM. To the man of God what gladness?

TEM.   Sadness
Only to those giving love to God alone.
Fare forward, shun two files of shadows:
Mirth merrymaking, melting strength in sweetness,
Fiddling to feebleness, doomed to disdain;
And godlovers' longings, lost in God.
Shall he who held the solid substance
Wander waking with deceitful shadows?
Power is present. Holiness hereafter.

THOM. Who then?

TEM.   The Chancellor. King and Chancellor.
King commands. Chancellor richly rules.
This is a sentence not taught in the schools.
To set down the great, protect the poor,
Beneath the throne of God can man do more?
Disarm the ruffian, strengthen the laws,
Rule for the good of the better cause,
Dispensing justice make all even,
Is thrive on earth, and perhaps in heaven.

THOM. What means?

TEM.   Real power
Is purchased at price of a certain submission.
Your spiritual power is earthly perdition.
Power is present, for him who will wield.

THOM. Whose was it?

TEM.   His who is gone.

THOM. Who shall have it?

TEM.   He who will come.

THOM. What shall be the month?

TEM.   The last from the first.

THOM. What shall we give for it?

TEM.   Pretence of priestly power.

THOM. Why should we give it?

TEM.   For the power and the glory.

THOM. No!

TEM.   Yes! Or bravery will be broken,
Cabined in Canterbury, realmless ruler,
Self-bound servant of a powerless Pope,
The old stag, circled with hounds.

THOM. No!

TEM.   Yes! men must manoeuvre. Monarchs also,
Waging war abroad, need fast friends at home.
Private policy is public profit;
Dignity still shall be dressed with decorum.

THOM. You forget the bishops
Whom I have laid under excommunication.

TEM. Hungry hatred
Will not strive against intelligent self-interest.
THOM. You forget the barons. Who will not forget
Constant curbing of petty privilege.
TEM. Against the barons
Is King's cause, churl's cause, Chancellor's cause.
THOM. No! shall I, who keep the keys
Of heaven and hell, supreme alone in England,
Who bind and loose, with power from the Pope,
Descend to desire a punier power?
Delegate to deal the doom of damnation,
To condemn kings, not serve among their servants,
Is my open office. No! Go.
TEM. Then I leave you to your fate.
Your sin soars sunward, covering kings' falcons.
THOM. Temporal power, to build a good world,
To keep order, as the world knows order.
Those who put their faith in worldly order
Not controlled by the order of God,
In confident ignorance, but arrest disorder,
Make it fast, breed fatal disease,
Degrade what they exalt. Power with the King—
I *was* the King, his arm, his better reason.
But what was once exaltation
Would now be only mean descent.

(*Enter* THIRD TEMPTER.)

3RD TEM. I am an unexpected visitor.
THOM.   I expected you.
TEM. But not in this guise, or for my present purpose.
THOM. No purpose brings surprise.
TEM.   Well, my Lord,
I am no trifler, and no politician.
To idle or intrigue at court
I have no skill. I am no courtier.
I know a horse, a dog, a wench;

I know how to hold my estates in order,
A country-keeping lord who minds his own business.
It is we country lords who know the country
And we who know what the country needs.
It is our country. We care for the country.
We are the backbone of the nation.
We, not the plotting parasites
About the King. Excuse my bluntness:
I am a rough straightforward Englishman.

THOM. Proceed straight forward.

TEM.   Purpose is plain.
Endurance of friendship does not depend
Upon ourselves, but upon circumstance.
But circumstance is not undetermined.
Unreal friendship may turn to real
But real friendship, once ended, cannot be mended.
Sooner shall enmity turn to alliance.
The enmity that never knew friendship
Can sooner know accord.

THOM.   For a countryman
You wrap your meaning in as dark generality
As any courtier.

TEM.   This is the simple fact!
You have no hope of reconciliation
With Henry the King. You look only
To blind assertion in isolation.
That is a mistake.

THOM.   O Henry, O my King!

TEM.   Other friends
May be found in the present situation.
King in England is not all-powerful;
King is in France, squabbling in Anjou;
Round him waiting hungry sons.
We are for England. We are in England.
You and I, my Lord, are Normans.

England is a land for Norman
Sovereignty. Let the Angevin
Destroy himself, fighting in Anjou.
He does not understand us, the English barons.
We are the people.

THOM. To what does this lead?

TEM.   To a happy coalition
Of intelligent interests.

THOM.   But what have you—
If you do speak for barons—

TEM.   For a powerful party
Which has turned its eyes in your direction—
To gain from you, your Lordship asks.
For us, Church favour would be an advantage,
Blessing of Pope powerful protection
In the fight for liberty. You, my Lord,
In being with us, would fight a good stroke
At once, for England and for Rome,
Ending the tyrannous jurisdiction
Of king's court over bishop's court,
Of king's court over baron's court.

THOM. Which I helped to found.

TEM.   Which you helped to found.
But time past is time forgotten.
We expect the rise of a new constellation.

THOM. And if the Archbishop cannot trust the King,
How can he trust those who work for King's undoing?

TEM. Kings will allow no power but their own;
Church and people have good cause against the throne.

THOM. If the Archbishop cannot trust the Throne,
He has good cause to trust none but God alone.
It is not better to be thrown
To a thousand hungry appetites than to one.
At a future time this may be shown.
I ruled once as Chancellor
And men like you were glad to wait at my door.

Not only in the court, but in the field
And in the tilt-yard I made many yield.
Shall I who ruled like an eagle over doves
Now take the shape of a wolf among wolves?
Pursue your treacheries as you have done before:
No one shall say that I betrayed a king.

TEM. Then, my Lord, I shall not wait at your door;
And I well hope, before another spring
The King will show his regard for your loyalty.

THOM. To make, then break, this thought has come before,
The desperate exercise of failing power.
Samson in Gaza did no more.
But if I break, I must break myself alone.

(*Enter* FOURTH TEMPTER.)

4TH TEM. Well done, Thomas, your will is hard to bend.
And with me beside you, you shall not lack a friend.

THOM. Who are you? I expected
Three visitors, not four.

TEM. Do not be surprised to receive one more.
Had I been expected, I had been here before.
I always precede expectation.

THOM.   Who are you?

TEM. As you do not know me, I do not need a name,
And, as you know me, that is why I come.
You know me, but have never seen my face.
To meet before was never time or place.

THOM. Say what you come to say.

TEM.   It shall be said at last.
Hooks have been baited with morsels of the past.
Wantonness is weakness. As for the King,
His hardened hatred shall have no end.
You know truly, the King will never trust
Twice, the man who has been his friend.
Borrow use cautiously, employ
Your services as long as you have to lend.

You would wait for trap to snap
Having served your turn, broken and crushed.
As for barons, envy of lesser men
Is still more stubborn than king's anger.
Kings have public policy, barons private profit,
Jealousy raging possession of the fiend.
Barons are employable against each other;
Greater enemies must kings destroy.

THOM. What is your counsel?

TEM.   Fare forward to the end.
All other ways are closed to you
Except the way already chosen.
But what is pleasure, kingly rule,
Or rule of men beneath a king,
With craft in corners, stealthy stratagem,
To general grasp of spiritual power?
Man oppressed by sin, since Adam fell—
You hold the keys of heaven and hell.
Power to bind and loose: bind, Thomas, bind,
King and bishop under your heel.
King, emperor, bishop, baron, king:
Uncertain mastery of melting armies,
War, plague, and revolution,
New conspiracies, broken pacts;
To be master or servant within an hour,
This is the course of temporal power.
The Old King shall know it, when at last breath,
No sons, no empire, he bites broken teeth.
You hold the skein: wind, Thomas, wind
The thread of eternal life and death.
You hold this power, hold it.

THOM.   Supreme, in this land?

TEM. Supreme, but for one.

THOM.   That I do not understand.

TEM. It is not for me to tell you how this may be so;
I am only here, Thomas, to tell you what you know.

тном. How long shall this be?

тем. Save what you know already, ask nothing of me.
     But think, Thomas, think of glory after death.
     When king is dead, there's another king,
     And one more king is another reign.
     King is forgotten, when another shall come:
     Saint and Martyr rule from the tomb.
     Think, Thomas, think of enemies dismayed,
     Creeping in penance, frightened of a shade;
     Think of pilgrims, standing in line
     Before the glittering jewelled shrine,
     From generation to generation
     Bending the knee in supplication.
     Think of the miracles, by God's grace,
     And think of your enemies, in another place.

тном. I have thought of these things.

тем.   That is why I tell you.
     Your thoughts have more power than kings to compel you.
     You have also thought, sometimes at your prayers,
     Sometimes hesitating at the angles of stairs,
     And between sleep and waking, early in the morning,
     When the bird cries, have thought of further scorning.
     That nothing lasts, but the wheel turns,
     The nest is rifled, and the bird mourns;
     That the shrine shall be pillaged, and the gold spent,
     The jewels gone for light ladies' ornament,
     The sanctuary broken, and its stores
     Swept into the laps of parasites and whores.
     When miracles cease, and the faithful desert you,
     And men shall only do their best to forget you.
     And later is worse, when men will not hate you
     Enough to defame or to execrate you,
     But pondering the qualities that you lacked
     Will only try to find the historical fact.
     When men shall declare that there was no mystery
     About this man who played a certain part in history.

THOM. But what is there to do? what is left to be done?
    Is there no enduring crown to be won?
TEM. Yes, Thomas, yes; you have thought of that too.
    What can compare with glory of Saints
    Dwelling forever in presence of God?
    What earthly glory, of king or emperor,
    What earthly pride, that is not poverty
    Compared with richness of heavenly grandeur?
    Seek the way of martyrdom, make yourself the lowest
    On earth, to be high in heaven.
    And see far off below you, where the gulf is fixed,
    Your persecutors, in timeless torment,
    Parched passion, beyond expiation.
THOM.   No!
    Who are you, tempting with my own desires?
    Others have come, temporal tempters,
    With pleasure and power at palpable price.
    What do you offer? what do you ask?
TEM. I offer what you desire. I ask
    What you have to give. Is it too much
    For such a vision of eternal grandeur?
THOM. Others offered real goods, worthless
    But real. You only offer
    Dreams to damnation.
TEM.   You have often dreamt them.
THOM. Is there no way, in my soul's sickness,
    Does not lead to damnation in pride?
    I well know that these temptations
    Mean present vanity and future torment.
    Can sinful pride be driven out
    Only by more sinful? Can I neither act nor suffer
    Without perdition?
TEM. You know and do not know, what it is to act or suffer.
    You know and do not know, that acting is suffering,
    And suffering action. Neither does the actor suffer
    Nor the patient act. But both are fixed

In an eternal action, an eternal patience
To which all must consent that it may be willed
And which all must suffer that they may will it,
That the pattern may subsist, that the wheel may turn and still
Be forever still.

CHOR. There is no rest in the house. There is no rest in the street.

I hear restless movement of feet. And the air is heavy and thick.

Thick and heavy the sky. And the earth presses up beneath my
feet.

What is the sickly smell, the vapour? the dark green light from
a cloud on a withered tree? The earth is heaving to parturition
of issue of hell. What is the sticky dew that forms on the back
of my hand?

THE FOUR TEMPTERS.

Man's life is a cheat and a disappointment;
All things are unreal,
Unreal or disappointing:
The Catherine wheel, the pantomime cat,
The prizes given at the children's party,
The prize awarded for the English Essay,
The scholar's degree, the statesman's decoration.
All things become less real, man passes
From unreality to unreality.
This man is obstinate, blind, intent
On self-destruction,
Passing from deception to deception,
From grandeur to grandeur to final illusion,
Lost in the wonder of his own greatness,
The enemy of society, enemy of himself.

THE THREE PRIESTS.

O Thomas my Lord do not fight the intractable tide,
Do not sail the irresistible wind; in the storm,
Should we not wait for the sea to subside, in the night
Abide the coming of day, when the traveller may find his way,
The sailor lay course by the sun?

(CHORUS, PRIESTS *and* TEMPTERS *alternately*.)

c. Is it the owl that calls, or a signal between the trees?

p. Is the window-bar made fast, is the door under lock and bolt?

t. Is it rain that taps at the window, is it wind that pokes at the door?

c. Does the torch flame in the hall, the candle in the room?

p. Does the watchman walk by the wall?

t. Does the mastiff prowl by the gate?

c. Death has a hundred hands and walks by a thousand ways.

p. He may come in the sight of all, he may pass unseen unheard.

t. Come whispering through the ear, or a sudden shock on the skull.

c. A man may walk with a lamp at night, and yet be drowned in a ditch.

p. A man may climb the stair in the day, and slip on a broken step.

t. A man may sit at meat, and feel the cold in his groin.

CHOR. We have not been happy, my Lord, we have not been too happy.

We are not ignorant women, we know what we must expect and not expect.

We know of oppression and torture,

We know of extortion and violence,

Destitution, disease,

The old without fire in winter,

The child without milk in summer,

Our labour taken away from us,

Our sins made heavier upon us.

We have seen the young man mutilated,

The torn girl trembling by the mill-stream.

And meanwhile we have gone on living,

Living and partly living,

Picking together the pieces,

Gathering faggots at nightfall,

Building a partial shelter,

For sleeping, and eating and drinking and laughter.

God gave us always some reason, some hope; but now a new terror has soiled us, which none can avert, none can avoid, flowing under our feet and over the sky;

Under doors and down chimneys, flowing in at the ear and the
  mouth and the eye.
God is leaving us, God is leaving us, more pang, more pain, than
  birth or death.
Sweet and cloying through the dark air
Falls the stifling scent of despair;
The forms take shape in the dark air:
Puss-purr of leopard, football of padding bear,
Palm-pat of nodding ape, square hyaena waiting
For laughter, laughter, laughter. The Lords of Hell are here.
They curl round you, lie at your feet, swing and wing through
  the dark air.
O Thomas Archbishop, save us, save us, save yourself that we
  may be saved;
Destroy yourself and we are destroyed.

THOM. Now is my way clear, now is the meaning plain:
  Temptation shall not come in this kind again.
  The last temptation is the greatest treason:
  To do the right deed for the wrong reason.
  The natural vigour in the venial sin
  Is the way in which our lives begin.
  Thirty years ago, I searched all the ways
  That lead to pleasure, advancement and praise.
  Delight in sense, in learning and in thought,
  Music and philosophy, curiosity,
  The purple bullfinch in the lilac tree,
  The tiltyard skill, the strategy of chess,
  Love in the garden, singing to the instrument,
  Were all things equally desirable.
  Ambition comes when early force is spent
  And when we find no longer all things possible.
  Ambition comes behind and unobservable.
  Sin grows with doing good. When I imposed the King's **law**
  In England, and waged war with him against Toulouse,
  I beat the barons at their own game. I
  Could then despise the men who thought me most contemptible,

The raw nobility, whose manners matched their fingernails.
While I ate out of the King's dish
To become servant of God was never my wish.
Servant of God has chance of greater sin
And sorrow, than the man who serves a king.
For those who serve the greater cause may make the cause serve
    them,
Still doing right: and striving with political men
May make that cause political, not by what they do
But by what they are. I know
What yet remains to show you of my history
Will seem to most of you at best futility,
Senseless self-slaughter of a lunatic,
Arrogant passion of a fanatic.
I know that history at all times draws
The strangest consequence from remotest cause.
But for every evil, every sacrilege,
Crime, wrong, oppression and the axe's edge,
Indifference, exploitation, you, and you,
And you, must all be punished. So must you.
I shall no longer act or suffer, to the sword's end.
Now my good Angel, whom God appoints
To be my guardian, hover over the swords' points.

INTERLUDE

THE ARCHBISHOP (*preaches in the Cathedral on Christmas Morning,
    1170*). "Glory to God in the highest, and on earth peace, good
    will toward men." *The fourteenth verse of the second chapter of
    the Gospel according to Saint Luke.* In the Name of the Father,
    and of the Son, and of the Holy Ghost. Amen.

Dear children of God, my sermon this morning will be a very short
    one. I wish only that you should ponder and meditate the deep
    meaning and mystery of our masses of Christmas Day. For when-

ever Mass is said, we re-enact the Passion and Death of Our Lord; and on this Christmas Day we do this in celebration of His Birth. So that at the same moment we rejoice in His coming for the salvation of men, and offer again to God His Body and Blood in sacrifice, oblation and satisfaction for the sins of the whole world. It was in this same night that has just passed, that a multitude of the heavenly host appeared before the shepherds at Bethlehem, saying, "Glory to God in the highest, and on earth peace, good will toward men"; at this same time of all the year that we cele- brate at once the Birth of Our Lord and His Passion and Death upon the Cross. Beloved, as the World sees, this is to behave in a strange fashion. For who in the World will both mourn and re- joice at once and for the same reason? For either joy will be over- borne by mourning, or mourning will be cast out by joy; so it is only in these our Christian mysteries that we can rejoice and mourn at once for the same reason. But think for a while on the meaning of this word "peace." Does it seem strange to you that the angels should have announced Peace, when ceaselessly the world has been stricken with War and the fear of War? Does it seem to you that the angelic voices were mistaken, and that the promise was a disappointment and a cheat?

Reflect now, how Our Lord Himself spoke of Peace. He said to His disciples, "My peace I leave with you, my peace I give unto you." Did He mean peace as we think of it: the kingdom of England at peace with its neighbours, the barons at peace with the King, the householder counting over his peaceful gains, the swept hearth, his best wine for a friend at the table, his wife singing to the children? Those men His disciples knew no such things: they went forth to journey afar, to suffer by land and sea, to know torture, imprisonment, disappointment, to suffer death by martyr- dom. What then did He mean? If you ask that, remember then that He said also, "Not as the world gives, give I unto you." So then, He gave to His disciples peace, but not peace as the world gives.

Consider also one thing of which you have probably never thought. Not only do we at the feast of Christmas celebrate at once Our

Lord's Birth and His Death: but on the next day we celebrate the martyrdom of His first martyr, the blessed Stephen. Is it an accident, do you think, that the day of the first martyr follows immediately the day of the Birth of Christ? By no means. Just as we rejoice and mourn at once, in the Birth and in the Passion of Our Lord; so also, in a smaller figure, we both rejoice and mourn in the death of martyrs. We mourn, for the sins of the world that has martyred them; we rejoice, that another soul is numbered among the Saints in Heaven, for the glory of God and for the salvation of men.

Beloved, we do not think of a martyr simply as a good Christian who has been killed because he is a Christian: for that would be solely to mourn. We do not think of him simply as a good Christian who has been elevated to the company of the Saints: for that would be simply to rejoice: and neither our mourning nor our rejoicing is as the world's is. A Christian martyrdom is no accident. Saints are not made by accident. Still less is a Christian martyrdom the effect of a man's will to become a Saint, as a man by willing and contriving may become a ruler of men. Ambition fortifies the will of man to become ruler over other men: it operates with deception, cajolery, and violence, it is the action of impurity upon impurity. Not so in Heaven. A martyr, a saint, is always made by the design of God, for His love of men, to warn them and to lead them, to bring them back to His ways. A martyrdom is never the design of man; for the true martyr is he who has become the instrument of God, who has lost his will in the will of God, not lost it but found it, for he has found freedom in submission to God. The martyr no longer desires anything for himself, not even the glory of martyrdom. So thus as on earth the Church mourns and rejoices at once, in a fashion that the world cannot understand; so in Heaven the Saints are most high, having made themselves most low, seeing themselves not as we see them, but in the light of the Godhead from which they draw their being.

I have spoken to you today, dear children of God, of the martyrs of the past, asking you to remember especially our martyr of Canterbury, the blessed Archbishop Elphege; because it is fitting, on Christ's birthday, to remember what is that Peace which He brought; and because, dear children, I do not think I shall ever preach to you again; and because it is possible that in a short time you may have yet another martyr, and that one perhaps not the last. I would have you keep in your hearts these words that I say, and think of them at another time. In the Name of the Father, and of the Son, and of the Holy Ghost. Amen.

PART TWO

Characters	THREE PRIESTS
	FOUR KNIGHTS
	ARCHBISHOP THOMAS BECKET
	CHORUS OF WOMEN OF CANTERBURY
	ATTENDANTS

The first scene is in the Archbishop's Hall,
the second scene is in the Cathedral,
on December 29th, 1170.

CHOR. Does the bird sing in the South?
Only the sea-bird cries, driven inland by the storm.
What sign of the spring of the year?
Only the death of the old: not a stir, not a shoot, not a breath.
Do the days begin to lengthen?
Longer and darker the day, shorter and colder the night.
Still and stifling the air: but a wind is stored up in the East.
The starved crow sits in the field, attentive; and in the wood
The owl rehearses the hollow note of death.

What signs of a bitter spring?
The wind stored up in the East.
What, at the time of the birth of Our Lord, at Christmastide,
Is there not peace upon earth, goodwill among men?
The peace of this world is always uncertain, unless men keep the
    peace of God.
And war among men defiles this world, but death in the Lord
    renews it,
And the world must be cleaned in the winter, or we shall have
    only
A sour spring, a parched summer, an empty harvest.
Between Christmas and Easter what work shall be done?
The ploughman shall go out in March and turn the same earth
He has turned before, the bird shall sing the same song.
When the leaf is out on the tree, when the elder and may
Burst over the stream, and the air is clear and high,
And voices trill at windows, and children tumble in front of the
    door,
What work shall have been done, what wrong
Shall the bird's song cover, the green tree cover, what wrong
Shall the fresh earth cover? We wait, and the time is short
But waiting is long.

(*Enter the* FOUR KNIGHTS.)

1ST KNI. Servants of the King.

1ST PR.   And known to us.
    You are welcome. Have you ridden far?

1ST KNI. Not far today, but matters urgent
    Have brought us from France. We rode hard,
    Took ship yesterday, landed last night,
    Having business with the Archbishop.

2ND KNI. Urgent business.

3RD KNI.   From the King.

4TH KNI. By the King's order.

1ST KNI.   Our men are outside.

1ST PR. You know the Archbishop's hospitality.
    We are about to go to dinner.

The good Archbishop would be vexed
If we did not offer you entertainment
Before your business. Please dine with us.
Your men shall be looked after also.
Dinner before business. Do you like roast pork?

1ST KNI. Business before dinner. We will roast your pork
First, and dine upon it after.

2ND KNI. We must see the Archbishop.

3RD KNI.   Go, tell the Archbishop
We have no need of his hospitality.
We will find our own dinner.

1ST PR. (*to* ATTENDANT). Go, tell His Lordship.

4TH KNI.   How much longer will you keep us waiting?

(*Enter* THOMAS.)

THOM. (*to* PRIESTS). However certain our expectation
The moment foreseen may be unexpected
When it arrives. It comes when we are
Engrossed with matters of other urgency.
On my table you will find
The papers in order, and the documents signed.
(*To* KNIGHTS).
You are welcome, whatever your business may be.
You say, from the King?

1ST KNI.   Most surely from the King.
We must speak with you alone.

THOM. (*to* PRIESTS).   Leave us then alone.
Now what is the matter?

1ST KNI.   This is the matter.

THE FOUR KNIGHTS.

You are the Archbishop in revolt against the King; in rebellion to
    the King and the law of the land;
You are the Archbishop who was made by the King; whom he
    set in your place to carry out his command.
You are his servant, his tool, and his jack,
You wore his favours on your back,

You had your honours all from his hand; from him you had the
power, the seal and the ring.

This is the man who was the tradesman's son: the backstairs brat
who was born in Cheapside;

This is the creature that crawled upon the King; swollen with
blood and swollen with pride.

Creeping out of the London dirt,

Crawling up like a louse on your shirt,

The man who cheated, swindled, lied; broke his oath and betrayed his King.

THOM. This is not true.

Both before and after I received the ring

I have been a loyal vassal to the King.

Saving my order, I am at his command,

As his most faithful vassal in the land.

1ST KNI. Saving your order! let your order save you—

As I do not think it is like to do.

Saving your ambition is what you mean,

Saving your pride, envy and spleen.

2ND KNI. Saving your insolence and greed.

Won't you ask us to pray to God for you, in your need?

3RD KNI. Yes, we'll pray for you!

4TH KNI.   Yes, we'll pray for you!

THE FOUR KNIGHTS.

Yes, we'll pray that God may help you!

THOM. But, gentlemen, your business

Which you said so urgent, is it only

Scolding and blaspheming?

1ST KNI.   That was only

Our indignation, as loyal subjects.

THOM. Loyal? to whom?

1ST KNI.   To the King!

2ND KNI.   The King!

3RD KNI. The King!

4TH KNI.   God bless him!

THOM. Then let your new coat of loyalty be worn
  Carefully, so it get not soiled or torn.
  Have you something to say?
IST KNI.   By the King's command.
  Shall we say it now?
2ND KNI.   Without delay,
  Before the old fox is off and away.
THOM.   What you have to say
  By the King's command—if it be the King's command—
  Should be said in public. If you make charges,
  Then in public I will refute them.
IST KNI.   No! here and now!
(*They make to attack him, but the* PRIESTS *and* ATTENDANTS *return and
  quietly interpose themselves.*)
THOM. Now and here!
IST KNI. Of your earlier misdeeds I shall make no mention.
  They are too well known. But after dissension
  Had ended, in France, and you were endued
  With your former privilege, how did you show your gratitude?
  You had fled from England, not exiled
  Or threatened, mind you; but in the hope
  Of stirring up trouble in the French dominions.
  You sowed strife abroad, you reviled
  The King to the King of France, to the Pope,
  Raising up against him false opinions.
2ND KNI. Yet the King, out of his charity,
  And urged by your friends, offered clemency,
  Made a pact of peace, and all dispute ended
  Sent you back to your See as you demanded.
3RD KNI. And burying the memory of your transgressions
  Restored your honours and your possessions.
  All was granted for which you sued:
  Yet how, I repeat, did you show your gratitude?
4TH KNI. Suspending those who had crowned the young prince,
  Denying the legality of his coronation;

Binding with the chains of anathema,
Using every means in your power to evince
The King's faithful servants, everyone who transacts
His business in his absence, the business of the nation.
1ST KNI. These are the facts.
Say therefore if you will be content
To answer in the King's presence. Therefore were we sent.
THOM. Never was it my wish
To uncrown the King's son, or to diminish
His honour and power. Why should he wish
To deprive my people of me and keep me from my own
And bid me sit in Canterbury, alone?
I would wish him three crowns rather than one,
And as for the bishops, it is not my yoke
That is laid upon them, or mine to revoke.
Let them go to the Pope. It was he who condemned them.
1ST KNI. Through you they were suspended.
2ND KNI.   By you be this amended.
3RD KNI. Absolve them.
4TH KNI.   Absolve them.
THOM.   I do not deny
That this was done through me. But it is not I
Who can loose whom the Pope has bound.
Let them go to him, upon whom redounds
Their contempt towards me, their contempt towards the Church
    shown.
1ST KNI. Be that as it may, here is the King's command:
That you and your servants depart from this land.
THOM. If that *is* the King's command, I will be bold
To say: seven years were my people without
My presence; seven years of misery and pain.
Seven years a mendicant on foreign charity
I lingered abroad: seven years is no brevity.
I shall not get those seven years back again.
Never again, you must make no doubt,
Shall the sea run between the shepherd and his fold.

1ST KNI. The King's justice, the King's majesty,
   You insult with gross indignity;
   Insolent madman, whom nothing deters
   From attainting his servants and ministers.

THOM. It is not I who insult the King,
   And there is higher than I or the King.
   It is not I, Becket from Cheapside,
   It is not against me, Becket, that you strive.
   It is not Becket who pronounces doom,
   But the Law of Christ's Church, the judgement of Rome.
   Go then to Rome, or let Rome come
   Here, to you, in the person of her most unworthy son.
   Petty politicians in your endless adventure!
   Rome alone can absolve those who break Christ's indenture.

1ST KNI. Priest, you have spoken in peril of your life.

2ND KNI. Priest, you have spoken in danger of the knife.

3RD KNI. Priest, you have spoken treachery and treason.

4TH KNI. Priest! traitor confirmed in malfeasance.

THOM. I submit my cause to the judgement of Rome.
   But if you kill me, I shall rise from my tomb
   To submit my cause before God's throne.

KNIGHTS. Priest! monk! and servant! take, hold, detain,
   Restrain this man, in the King's name;
   Or answer with your bodies, if he escape before we come,
   We come for the King's justice, we come again.   (*Exeunt.*)

THOM. Pursue those who flee, track down those who evade;
   Come for arrest, come with the sword,
   Here, here, you shall find me ready, in the battle of the Lord.
   At whatsoever time you are ready to come,
   You will find me still more ready for martyrdom.

CHOR. I have smelt them, the death-bringers, senses are quickened
   By subtile forebodings; I have heard
   Fluting in the nighttime, fluting and owls, have seen at noon
   Scaly wings slanting over, huge and ridiculous. I have tasted
   The savour of putrid flesh in the spoon. I have felt
   The heaving of earth at nightfall, restless, absurd. I have heard

Laughter in the noises of beasts that make strange noises: jackal, jackass, jackdaw; the scurrying noise of mouse and jerboa; the laugh of the loon, the lunatic bird. I have seen

Grey necks twisting, rat tails twining, in the thick light of dawn. I have eaten

Smooth creatures still living, with the strong salt taste of living things under sea; I have tasted

The living lobster, the crab, the oyster, the whelk and the prawn; and they live and spawn in my bowels, and my bowels dissolve in the light of dawn. I have smelt

Death in the rose, death in the hollyhock, sweet pea, hyacinth, primrose and cowslip. I have seen

Trunk and horn, tusk and hoof, in odd places;

I have lain on the floor of the sea and breathed with the breathing of the sea-anemone, swallowed with ingurgitation of the sponge. I have lain in the soil and criticised the worm. In the air

Flirted with the passage of the kite, I have plunged with the kite and cowered with the wren. I have felt

The horn of the beetle, the scale of the viper, the mobile hard insensitive skin of the elephant, the evasive flank of the fish. I have smelt

Corruption in the dish, incense in the latrine, the sewer in the incense, the smell of sweet soap in the woodpath, a hellish sweet scent in the woodpath, while the ground heaved. I have seen

Rings of light coiling downwards, leading

To the horror of the ape. Have I not known, not known

What was coming to be? It was here, in the kitchen, in the passage,

In the mews in the barn in the byre in the market place

In our veins our bowels our skulls as well

As well as in the plottings of potentates

As well as in the consultations of powers.

What is woven on the loom of fate

What is woven in the councils of princes

Is woven also in our veins, our brains,
Is woven like a pattern of living worms
In the guts of the women of Canterbury.

I have smelt them, the death-bringers; now is too late
For action, too soon for contrition.
Nothing is possible but the shamed swoon
Of those consenting to the last humiliation.
I have consented, Lord Archbishop, have consented.
Am torn away, subdued, violated,
United to the spiritual flesh of nature,
Mastered by the animal powers of spirit,
Dominated by the lust of self-demolition,
By the final utter uttermost death of spirit,
By the final ecstasy of waste and shame,
O Lord Archbishop, O Thomas Archbishop, forgive us, forgive
  us, pray for us that we may pray for you, out of our shame.

THOM. Peace, and be at peace with your thoughts and visions.
These things had to come to you and you to accept them.
This is your share of the eternal burden,
The perpetual glory. This is one moment,
But know that another
Shall pierce you with a sudden painful joy
When the figure of God's purpose is made complete.
You shall forget these things, toiling in the household,
You shall remember them, droning by the fire,
When age and forgetfulness sweeten memory
Only like a dream that has often been told
And often been changed in the telling. They will seem unreal.
Human kind cannot bear very much reality.

PRIESTS (*severally*). My Lord, you must not stop here. To the minster.
Through the cloister. No time to waste. They are coming back,
armed. To the altar, to the altar. They are here already. To the
sanctuary. They are breaking in. We can barricade the minster
doors. You cannot stay here. Force him to come. Seize him.

THOM. All my life they have been coming, these feet. All my life
   I have waited. Death will come only when I am worthy,
   And if I am worthy, there is no danger.
   I have therefore only to make perfect my will.

PRIESTS. My Lord, they are coming. They will break through presently.
   You will be killed. Come to the altar.

THOM. Peace! be quiet! remember where you are, and what is hap-
        pening;
   No life here is sought for but mine,
   And I am not in danger: only near to death.

PRIESTS. Make haste, my Lord. Don't stop here talking. It is not right.
   What shall become of us, my Lord, if you are killed; what shall
        become of us?

THOM. That again is another theme
   To be developed and resolved in the pattern of time.
   It is not for me to run from city to city;
   To meet death gladly is only
   The only way in which I can defend
   The Law of God, the holy canons.

PRIESTS. My Lord, to vespers! You must not be absent from vespers.
   You must not be absent from the divine office. To vespers. Into
   the cathedral!

THOM. Go to vespers, remember me at your prayers.
   They shall find the shepherd here; the flock shall be spared.
   I have had a tremor of bliss, a wink of heaven, a whisper,
   And I would no longer be denied; all things
   Proceed to a joyful consummation.

PRIESTS. Seize him! force him! drag him!

THOM. Keep your hands off!

PRIESTS. To vespers! Take his feet! Up with him! Hurry.

(*They drag him off. While the* CHORUS *speak, the scene is changed to
   the cathedral.*)

CHOR. (*while a* Dies Irae *is sung in Latin by a choir in the distance*).
   Numb the hand and dry the eyelid,
   Still the horror, but more horror
   Than when tearing in the belly.

Still the horror, but more horror
Than when twisting in the fingers,
Than when splitting in the skull.

More than footfall in the passage,
More than shadow in the doorway,
More than fury in the hall.

The agents of hell disappear, the human, they shrink and dissolve
Into dust on the wind, forgotten, unmemorable; only is here
The white flat face of Death, God's silent servant,
And behind the face of Death the Judgement
And behind the Judgement the Void, more horrid than active
    shapes of hell;
Emptiness, absence, separation from God;
The horror of the effortless journey, to the empty land
Which is no land, only emptiness, absence, the Void,
Where those who were men can no longer turn the mind
To distraction, delusion, escape into dream, pretence,
Where the soul is no longer deceived, for there are no objects, no
    tones,
No colours, no forms to distract, to divert the soul
From seeing itself, foully united forever, nothing with nothing,
Not what we call death, but what beyond death is not death,
We fear, we fear. Who shall then plead for me,
Who intercede for me, in my most need?

Dead upon the tree, my Saviour,
Let not be in vain Thy labour;
Help me, Lord, in my last fear.

Dust I am, to dust am bending,
From the final doom impending
Help me, Lord, for death is near.

(*In the cathedral.* THOMAS *and* PRIESTS.)

PRIESTS. Bar the door. Bar the door.

The door is barred.
We are safe. We are safe.
The enemy may rage outside, he will tire
In vain. They cannot break in.
They dare not break in.
They cannot break in. They have not the force.
We are safe. We are safe.

THOM. Unbar the doors! throw open the doors!
I will not have the house of prayer, the church of Christ,
The sanctuary, turned into a fortress.
The Church shall protect her own, in her own way, not
As oak and stone; stone and oak decay,
Give no stay, but the Church shall endure.
The church shall be open, even to our enemies. Open the door!

PRIESTS. My Lord! these are not men, these come not as men come, but
Like maddened beasts. They come not like men, who
Respect the sanctuary, who kneel to the Body of Christ,
But like beasts. You would bar the door
Against the lion, the leopard, the wolf or the boar,
Why not more
Against beasts with the souls of damned men, against men
Who would damn themselves to beasts. My Lord! My Lord!

THOM. Unbar the door!
You think me reckless, desperate and mad.
You argue by results, as this world does,
To settle if an act be good or bad.
You defer to the fact. For every life and every act
Consequence of good and evil can be shown.
And as in time results of many deeds are blended
So good and evil in the end become confounded.
It is not in time that my death shall be known;
It is out of time that my decision is taken
If you call that decision
To which my whole being gives entire consent.
I give my life
To the Law of God above the Law of Man.

Those who do not the same
How should they know what I do?
How should you know what I do? Yet how much more
Should you know than these madmen beating on the door.
Unbar the door! unbar the door!
We are not here to triumph by fighting, by stratagem, or by
resistance,
Not to fight with beasts as men. We have fought the beast
And have conquered. We have only to conquer
Now, by suffering. This is the easier victory.
Now is the triumph of the Cross, now
Open the door! I command it. OPEN THE DOOR!

(*The door is opened. The* KNIGHTS *enter, slightly tipsy.*)

PRIESTS. This way, my Lord! Quick. Up the stair. To the roof. To the
crypt. Quick. Come. Force him.

KNIGHTS (*one line each*).
Where is Becket, the traitor to the King?
Where is Becket, the meddling priest?
Come down Daniel to the lions' den,
Come down Daniel for the mark of the beast.

Are you washed in the blood of the Lamb?
Are you marked with the mark of the beast?
Come down Daniel to the lions' den,
Come down Daniel and join in the feast.

Where is Becket the Cheapside brat?
Where is Becket the faithless priest?
Come down Daniel to the lions' den,
Come down Daniel and join the feast.

THOM. It is the just man who
Like a bold lion, should be without fear.
I am here.
No traitor to the King. I am a priest,
A Christian, saved by the blood of Christ,
Ready to suffer with my blood.

This is the sign of the Church always,
The sign of blood. Blood for blood.
His blood given to buy my life,
My blood given to pay for His death,
My death for His death.

KNIGHTS. Absolve all those you have excommunicated.
Resign the powers you have arrogated.
Restore to the King the money you appropriated.
Renew the obedience you have violated.

THOM. For my Lord I am now ready to die,
That His Church may have peace and liberty.
Do with me as you will, to your hurt and shame;
But none of my people, in God's name,
Whether layman or clerk, shall you touch.
This I forbid.

KNIGHTS. Traitor! traitor! traitor! traitor!

THOM. You, Reginald, three times traitor you:
Traitor to me as my temporal vassal,
Traitor to me as your spiritual lord,
Traitor to God in desecrating His Church.

1ST KNI. No faith do I owe to a renegade,
And what I owe shall now be paid.

THOM. Now to Almighty God, to the Blessed Mary ever Virgin, to the
blessed John the Baptist, the holy apostles Peter and Paul, to the
blessed martyr Denys, and to all the Saints, I commend my cause
and that of the Church.

(*While the* KNIGHTS *kill him, we hear the* CHORUS.)

CHOR. Clear the air! clean the sky! wash the wind! take stone from stone
and wash them.
The land is foul, the water is foul, our beasts and ourselves de-
filed with blood.
A rain of blood has blinded my eyes. Where is England? where
is Kent? where is Canterbury?
O far far far far in the past; and I wander in a land of barren
boughs: if I break them, they bleed; I wander in a land of dry
stones: if I touch them they bleed.

How how can I ever return, to the soft quiet seasons?
Night stay with us, stop sun, hold season, let the day not come,
    let the spring not come.
Can I look again at the day and its common things, and see them
    all smeared with blood, through a curtain of falling blood?
We did not wish anything to happen.
We understood the private catastrophe,
The personal loss, the general misery,
Living and partly living;
The terror by night that ends in daily action,
The terror by day that ends in sleep;
But the talk in the market-place, the hand on the broom,
The nighttime heaping of the ashes,
The fuel laid on the fire at daybreak,
These acts marked a limit to our suffering.
Every horror had its definition,
Every sorrow had a kind of end:
In life there is not time to grieve long.
But this, this is out of life, this is out of time,
An instant eternity of evil and wrong.
We are soiled by a filth that we cannot clean, united to super-
    natural vermin,
It is not we alone, it is not the house, it is not the city that is
    defiled,
But the world that is wholly foul.
Clear the air! clean the sky! wash the wind! take the stone from
    the stone, take the skin from the arm, take the muscle from
    the bone, and wash them. Wash the stone, wash the bone,
    wash the brain, wash the soul, wash them wash them!

(*The* KNIGHTS, *having completed the murder, advance to the front of
    the stage and address the audience.*)

IST KNI. We beg you to give us your attention for a few moments. We
    know that you may be disposed to judge unfavourably of our
    action. You are Englishmen, and therefore you believe in fair
    play: and when you see one man being set upon by four, then
    your sympathies are all with the under dog. I respect such feelings,

I share them. Nevertheless, I appeal to your sense of honour. You are Englishmen, and therefore will not judge anybody without hearing both sides of the case. That is in accordance with our long established principle of Trial by Jury. I am not myself qualified to put our case to you. I am a man of action and not of words. For that reason I shall do no more than introduce the other speakers, who, with their various abilities, and different points of view, will be able to lay before you the merits of this extremely complex problem. I shall call upon our youngest member to speak first. William de Traci.

2ND KNI. I am afraid I am not anything like such an experienced speaker as Reginald Fitz Urse would lead you to believe. But there is one thing I should like to say, and I might as well say it at once. It is this: in what we have done, and whatever you may think of it, we have been perfectly disinterested. (*The other* KNIGHTS: "Hear! hear!") *We* are not getting anything out of this. We have much more to lose than to gain. We are four plain Englishmen who put our country first. I dare say that we didn't make a very good impression when we came in. The fact is that we knew we had taken on a pretty stiff job; I'll only speak for myself, but I had drunk a good deal—I am not a drinking man ordinarily—to brace myself up for it. When you come to the point, it does go against the grain to kill an Archbishop, especially when you have been brought up in good Church traditions. So if we seemed a bit rowdy, you will understand why it was; and for my part I am awfully sorry about it. We realised that this was our duty, but all the same we had to work ourselves up to it. And, as I said, *we* are not getting a penny out of this. We know perfectly well how things will turn out. King Henry—God bless him—will have to say, for reasons of state, that he never meant this to happen; and there is going to be an awful row; and at the best we shall have to spend the rest of our lives abroad. And even when reasonable people come to see that the Archbishop *had* to be put out of the way —and personally I had a tremendous admiration for him—you must have noticed what a good show he put up at the end—they won't give *us* any glory. No, we have done for ourselves, there's no mistake about that. So, as I said at the beginning, please give us at least the credit for being completely disinterested in this business. I think that is about all I have to say.

1st KNI. I think we will all agree that William de Traci has spoken well and has made a very important point. The gist of his argument is this: that we have been completely disinterested. But our act itself needs more justification than that; and you must hear our other speakers. I shall next call upon Hugh de Morville.

3rd KNI. I should like first to recur to a point that was very well put by our leader, Reginald Fitz Urse: that you are Englishmen, and therefore your sympathies are always with the under dog. It is the English spirit of fair play. Now the worthy Archbishop, whose good qualities I very much admired, has throughout been presented as the under dog. But is this really the case? I am going to appeal not to your emotions but to your reason. You are hard-headed sensible people, as I can see, and not to be taken in by emotional clap-trap. I therefore ask you to consider soberly: what were the Archbishop's aims? and what are King Henry's aims? In the answer to these questions lies the key to the problem.

The King's aim has been perfectly consistent. During the reign of the late Queen Matilda and the irruption of the unhappy usurper Stephen, the kingdom was very much divided. Our King saw that the one thing needful was to restore order: to curb the excessive powers of local government, which were usually exercised for selfish and often for seditious ends, and to systematise the judiciary. There was utter chaos: there were three kinds of justice and three kinds of court: that of the King, that of the Bishops, and that of the baronage. I must repeat one point that the last speaker has made. While the late Archbishop was Chancellor, he whole-heartedly supported the King's designs: this is an important point, which, if necessary, I can substantiate. Now the King intended that Becket, who had proved himself an extremely able administrator—no one denies that—should unite the offices of Chancellor and Archbishop. No one would have grudged him that; no one than he was better qualified to fill at once these two most important posts. Had Becket concurred with the King's wishes, we should have had an almost ideal State: a union of spiritual and temporal administration, under the central government. I knew Becket well, in various official relations; and I may say that I have never known a man so well qualified for the highest rank of the Civil Service. And what happened? The moment that Becket, at the King's instance, had been made Archbishop, he resigned the office of Chancellor, he became more priestly than the priests, he ostentatiously and offensively adopted an ascetic manner of life, he openly abandoned every policy that he had heretofore supported; he affirmed immediately that there was a higher order than that which our King, and he as the King's servant, had for so many years striven to establish; and that—God knows why— the two orders were incompatible.

You will agree with me that such interference by an Archbishop offends the instincts of a people like ours. So far, I know that I have your approval: I read it in your faces. It is only with the measures we have had to adopt, in order to set matters to rights, that you take issue. No one regrets the necessity for violence more than we do. Unhappily, there are times when violence is the only way in which social justice can be secured. At another time, you would condemn an Archbishop by vote of Parliament and execute him formally as a traitor, and no one would have to bear the burden of being called murderer. And at a later time still, even such temperate measures as these would become unnecessary. But, if you have now arrived at a just subordination of the pretensions of the Church to the welfare of the State, remember that it is we who took the first step. We have been instrumental in bringing about the state of affairs that you approve. We have served your interests; we merit your applause; and if there is any guilt whatever in the matter, you must share it with us.

IST KNI. Morville has given us a great deal to think about. It seems to me that he has said almost the last word, for those who have been able to follow his very subtle reasoning. We have, however, one more speaker, who has I think another point of view to express. If there are any who are still unconvinced, I think that Richard Brito will be able to convince them. Richard Brito.

4TH KNI. The speakers who have preceded me, to say nothing of our leader, Reginald Fitz Urse, have all spoken very much to the point. I have nothing to add along their particular lines of argument. What I have to say may be put in the form of a question: *Who killed the Archbishop?* As you have been eye-witnesses of this lamentable scene, you may feel some surprise at my putting it in this way. But consider the course of events. I am obliged, very briefly, to go over the ground traversed by the last speaker. While the late Archbishop was Chancellor, no one, under the King, did more to weld the country together, to give it the unity, the stability, order, tranquillity, and justice that it so badly needed. From the moment he became Archbishop, he completely reversed his policy; he showed himself to be utterly indifferent to the fate of the country, to be, in fact, a monster of egotism, a menace to society. This egotism grew upon him, until it became at last an undoubted mania. Every means that had been tried to conciliate him, to restore him to reason, had failed. Now I have unimpeachable evidence to the effect that before he left France he clearly prophesied, in the presence of numerous witnesses, that he had not long to live, and that he would be killed in England. He used every means of provocation; from his conduct, step by step, there can be no inference except that he had determined upon a death by martyrdom. This man, formerly a great public servant, had become a wrecker. Even at the last, he could have given us reason: you have seen how he evaded our questions. And when he had deliberately exasperated us beyond human endurance, he could still have easily escaped; he could have kept himself from us long enough to allow our righteous anger to cool. That was just what he did not wish to happen; he insisted, while we were still inflamed with wrath, that the doors should be opened. Need I say more? I think, with these facts before you, you will unhesitatingly render a verdict of Suicide while of Unsound Mind. It is the only charitable verdict you can give, upon one who was, after all, a great man.

IST KNI. Thank you, Brito. I think that there is no more to be said; and I suggest that you now disperse quietly to your homes. Please be

careful not to loiter in groups at street corners, and do nothing
that might provoke any public outbreak.   (*Exeunt* KNIGHTS.)

1ST PR. O father, father, gone from us, lost to us,
How shall we find you, from what far place
Do you look down on us? You now in Heaven,
Who shall now guide us, protect us, direct us?
After what journey through what further dread
Shall we recover your presence? when inherit
Your strength? The Church lies bereft,
Alone, desecrated, desolated, and the heathen shall build on the
ruins,
Their world without God. I see it. I see it.

3RD PR. No. For the Church is stronger for this action,
Triumphant in adversity. It is fortified
By persecution: supreme, so long as men will die for it.
Go, weak sad men, lost erring souls, homeless in earth or heaven.
Go where the sunset reddens the last grey rock
Of Brittany, or the Gates of Hercules.
Go venture shipwreck on the sullen coasts
Where blackamoors make captive Christian men;
Go to the northern seas confined with ice
Where the dead breath makes numb the hand, makes dull the
brain;
Find an oasis in the desert sun,
Go seek alliance with the heathen Saracen,
To share his filthy rites, and try to snatch
Forgetfulness in his libidinous courts,
Oblivion in the fountain by the date-tree;
Or sit and bite your nails in Aquitaine.
In the small circle of pain within the skull
You still shall tramp and tread one endless round
Of thought, to justify your action to yourselves,
Weaving a fiction which unravels as you weave,
Pacing forever in the hell of make-believe
Which never is belief: this is your fate on earth
And we must think no further of you. O my Lord

The glory of whose new state is hidden from us,
Pray for us of your charity; now in the sight of God
Conjoined with all the saints and martyrs gone before you,
Remember us. Let our thanks ascend
To God, who has given us another Saint in Canterbury.

CHOR. (*while a* Te Deum *is sung in Latin by a choir in the distance*).

We praise Thee, O God, for Thy glory displayed in all the creatures of the earth,

In the snow, in the rain, in the wind, in the storm; in all of Thy creatures, both the hunters and the hunted.

For all things exist only as seen by Thee, only as known by Thee, all things exist

Only in Thy light, and Thy glory is declared even in that which denies Thee; the darkness declares the glory of light.

Those who deny Thee could not deny, if Thou didst not exist; and their denial is never complete, for if it were so, they would not exist.

They affirm Thee in living; all things affirm Thee in living; the bird in the air, both the hawk and the finch; the beast on the earth, both the wolf and the lamb; the worm in the soil and the worm in the belly.

Therefore man, whom Thou hast made to be conscious of Thee, must consciously praise Thee, in thought and in word and in deed.

Even with the hand to the broom, the back bent in laying the fire, the knee bent in cleaning the hearth, we, the scrubbers and sweepers of Canterbury,

The back bent under toil, the knee bent under sin, the hands to the face under fear, the head bent under grief,

Even in us the voices of seasons, the snuffle of winter, the song of spring, the drone of summer, the voices of beasts and of birds, praise Thee.

We thank Thee for Thy mercies of blood, for Thy redemption by blood. For the blood of Thy martyrs and saints

Shall enrich the earth, shall create the holy places.

For wherever a saint has dwelt, wherever a martyr has given his
  blood for the blood of Christ,
There is holy ground, and the sanctity shall not depart from it
Though armies trample over it, though sightseers come with
  guide-books looking over it;
From where the western seas gnaw at the coast of Iona,
To the death in the desert, the prayer in forgotten places by the
  broken imperial column,
From such ground springs that which forever renews the earth
Though it is forever denied. Therefore, O God, we thank Thee
Who hast given such blessing to Canterbury.

Forgive us, O Lord, we acknowledge ourselves as type of the
  common man,
Of the men and women who shut the door and sit by the fire;
Who fear the blessing of God, the loneliness of the night of God,
  the surrender required, the deprivation inflicted;
Who fear the injustice of men less than the justice of God;
Who fear the hand at the window, the fire in the thatch, the fist
  in the tavern, the push into the canal,
Less than we fear the love of God.
We acknowledge our trespass, our weakness, our fault; we ac-
  knowledge
That the sin of the world is upon our heads; that the blood of
  the martyrs and the agony of the saints
Is upon our heads.
Lord, have mercy upon us.
Christ, have mercy upon us.
Lord, have mercy upon us.
Blessed Thomas, pray for us.

Tennessee Williams

► A new and distinctive talent was introduced to the American theatre in *The Glass Menagerie*. It opened in Chicago on the night after Christmas, 1944, to critical acclaim but a sparse audience. The critics refused to let the play die. Their insistence soon had Chicago people flocking to see it, and it played for three months before capacity crowds. It moved on to the Playhouse in New York, March 31, 1945, and ran for a year and a half. It was selected for the Drama Critics' Circle award as the best play written by an American and produced in New York in the season 1944-45. In Williams' own words, "I was snatched out of virtual oblivion and thrust into sudden prominence." He has sustained that prominence by the unique quality of his art and his perception of some of the more illusive values in the national life.

Williams came up the rough road and hammered out his art from his own unremitting struggles. His career fits the legendary pattern of an artist's development through obstacles, disappointment, frustration, and perseverance. He was born Thomas Lanier Williams at Columbus, Mississippi, March 26, 1914. He was reared in St. Louis, where his father held a position with a shoe company. He began writing poetry and short stories at the University of Missouri, which he attended from 1931 to 1933. When the depression forced him to give up college, he went to work with the shoe company. He was temperamentally unfit for this kind of employment. He solaced himself after work-hours by writing. His health broke down, and he took time off to recuperate. Then he proceeded with his college work at Washington University in 1936-37, went on to the University of Iowa, and received his A.B., with a major in drama, in 1938.

No enchanted doors into the theatre opened to him. He waited on tables in a New Orleans French Quarter restaurant, and worked on a pigeon ranch in California. He kept on writing. His one act plays, distilled from this hard-won but valuable experience, caught the notice of a New York agent. He was given a scholarship to the playwrights' seminar directed by Theresa Helburn and John Gassner at the New School for Social Research. He won a Rockefeller Foundation Fellowship in 1940, and a thousand dollar grant for work in drama. These subsidies provided him with food and shelter while he worked at perfecting his art. His first play, *Battle of Angels,* produced by the Theatre Guild, was abandoned after its opening in Boston on December 30, 1940. The next few years were a well-nigh desperate contest with drama and destitution. He resorted to odd jobs to keep going. Finally, while on a Hollywood contract, he wrote *The Glass Menagerie.* This was it. He adopted his pen name, Tennessee Williams, to symbolize his metamorphosis into a new period of professional life.

The hard, astringent facts of living which he had seen and experienced might well have induced him to compose plays of the genre of Gorki's *The Lower Depths.* But instead, like Anton Chekhov, whose work he admires, his compassion and his perception have allowed him to see behind the repellent facts to the dreams and illusions by which men live and sustain their spirits while they endure the assault of these facts. The mother, Amanda, in *The Glass Menagerie,* one of his best creations, lives in a world of sentimental illusion of her own creation; if she accepted the alley in St. Louis at its real value with all its devastating drabness and absence of hope, she would perish. She lives where she dreams, and tomorrow will be better. Her daughter Laura, crippled in body and withdrawn from the world in spirit, lives in a world of make-believe more delicate and tenuous than her mother could ever perceive. She becomes another fragile piece in the collection of the glass menagerie. And the son Tom, narrator of the play, works in a warehouse but escapes intermittently and desperately into a poet's dream world. "I give you truth," he says, "in the pleasant disguise of illusion."

Williams' problem is to catch this gossamer world in the setting of the alley apartment and to make the audience share the illusion by suspending their disbelief. The technique is designed to facilitate this adventure. It calls upon the narrator to speak directions to his listeners, and to help them philosophize about the significance of memory and reality; it uses music, recurring themes, gauze curtains, special lighting effects, and symbolic lantern slides to help create the mood. Opinion is divided as to whether these devices are merely superficial "literary" tricks external to the play, or whether they are an inherent part of the total structure. To this spectator and reader they are so skillfully handled that they are absorbed into the living tissue of the play.

A Streetcar Named Desire, which began its sensational run at the Barrymore Theater on December 3, 1947, dispensed with the devices and the external symbols of make-believe to root itself in a gross and turbulent segment of New Orleans life. It is written "straight," and the make-believe world of Blanche DuBois is conveyed from within the play itself through the power of its character creation. It relies on no external stage tricks to achieve its ultimately tender and tragic effect. It was awarded the Pulitzer Prize in 1948.

The most distinctive values in Tennessee Williams' work have been their absorbing human warmth and compassion. Our contemporary stage has not always been notable for these fine qualities. Their presence in *A Streetcar Named Desire* makes acceptable a heaping measure of what would otherwise be a devastating and seamy realism. Seen through this magic casement the tragedies of Laura and Blanche and the others are invested with the softening aura of poetry.

These same values gave quality to another play closely related to the previous ones. *Summer and Smoke* (1948) appealed to Margo Jones, and she produced it with splendid effect at Dallas in her experimental Theatre-in-the-Round. She brought it to the Music Box in the autumn of 1948. The imaginative sets made for it by Jo Mielziner caught the mood and the temper of the play perfectly and won much acclaim. The play closed after 100 performances.

Summer and Smoke did not have the wistful symbolism of *The Glass Menagerie,* nor the fierce melodrama of *A Streetcar Named Desire;* instead it had a greater simplicity and naturalness, and a sensitive understanding of the frustrations which kept Alma forever separated, physically and spiritually, from the young doctor whom she had loved from childhood. Its period, from the turn of the century through 1916, is the same as that of *Ah, Wilderness!,* but the provincial Mississippi town of Glorious Hill and the Rev. Winemiller's family have little in common with the small town in Connecticut and the Miller family. The circumscribed parish environment of Alma, and the prim code by which she was taught conformity, successfully walled her off from the gay freedom and extroversion of the wayward young medical student, whom she could not win, and of her voice pupil Nellie, who married him. The whole composition is fragile but firmly wrought, and it adds another to the haunting feminine misfits which Williams has portrayed so successfully.

In his fourth major play, *The Rose Tattoo* (1951), Williams for the first time tried his hand at folk-comedy. While this play has the same human warmth and compassion found in the playwright's other important work, it is marked less with poignancy than with gusto, thus demonstrating a still further range of this young dramatist's art.

SUMMER AND SMOKE

Characters

ALMA, *as a child*	ROSA GONZALES
JOHN, *as a child*	NELLIE EWELL
REV. WINEMILLER	ROGER DOREMUS
MRS. WINEMILLER	MRS. BASSETT
JOHN BUCHANAN, JR.	VERNON
A GIRL	ROSEMARY
DUSTY	PAPA GONZALES
DR. BUCHANAN	MR. KRAMER
ALMA WINEMILLER	

Part One—a summer

Prologue: The Fountain.
Scene One: The Same.
Scene Two: The Rectory Interior and Doctor's Office.
Scene Three: The Rectory Interior.
Scene Four: The Doctor's Office.
Scene Five: The Rectory Interior.
Scene Six: The Arbor.

Part Two—a winter

Scene Seven: The Rectory and Doctor's Office.
Scene Eight: The Doctor's Office.
Scene Nine: The Rectory and Doctor's Office.
Scene Ten: The Fountain.
Scene Eleven: The Doctor's Office.
Scene Twelve: The Fountain.

The entire action of the play takes place in Glorious Hill, Mississippi.
The time is the turn of the century through 1916.

Author's Production Notes

As the concept of a design grows out of reading a play I will not do more than indicate what I think are the most essential points.

First of all—The Sky.

There must be a great expanse of sky so that the entire action of the play takes place against it. This is true of interior as well as exterior scenes. But in fact there are no really interior scenes, for the walls are omitted or just barely suggested by certain necessary fragments such as might be needed to hang a picture or to contain a door-frame.

During the day scenes the sky should be a pure and intense blue (like the sky of Italy as it is so faithfully represented in the religious paintings of the Renaissance) and costumes should be selected to form dramatic color contrasts to this intense blue which the figures stand against. (Color harmonies and other visual effects are tremendously important.)

In the night scenes, the more familiar constellations, such as Orion and the Great Bear and the Pleiades, are clearly projected on the night sky, and above them, splashed across the top of the cyclorama, is the nebulous radiance of the Milky Way. Fleecy cloud forms may also be projected on this cyclorama and made to drift across it.

So much for The Sky.

Now we descend to the so-called interior sets of the play. There are two of these "interior" sets, one being the parlor of an Episcopal Rectory and the other the home of a doctor next door to the Rectory. The architecture of these houses is barely suggested but is of an American Gothic design of the Victorian era. There are no actual doors or windows or walls. Doors and windows are represented by delicate frameworks of Gothic design. These frames have strings of ivy clinging to them, the leaves of emerald and amber. Sections of wall are used only where they are functionally required. There should be a fragment of wall in back of the Rectory sofa, supporting a romantic landscape in a gilt frame. In the doctor's house there should be a section of wall to support the chart of anatomy. Chirico has used fragmentary walls and interiors in a very evocative way in his painting called "Conversation among the Ruins."

We will deal more specifically with these interiors as we come to them in the course of the play.

Now we come to the main exterior set which is a promontory in a park or public square in the town of Glorious Hill. Situated on this promontory is a fountain in the form of a stone angel, in a gracefully crouching position with wings lifted and her hands held together to form a cup from which water flows, a public drinking fountain. The stone angel of the fountain should probably be elevated so that it appears in the background of the interior scenes as a symbolic figure (Eternity) brooding over the course of the play. This entire exterior set may be on an upper level, above that of the two fragmentary interiors. *I would like all three units to form an harmonious whole like one complete picture rather than three separate ones. An imaginative designer may solve these plastic problems in a variety of ways and should not feel bound by any of my specific suggestions.*

There is one more set, a very small exterior representing an arbor, which we will describe when we reach it.

Everything possible should be done to give an unbroken fluid quality to the sequence of scenes.

There should be no curtain except for the intermission. The other divisions of the play should be accomplished by changes of lighting.

Finally, the matter of music. One basic theme should recur and the points of recurrence have been indicated here and there in the stage directions.

Rome, March, 1948.

PART ONE—A SUMMER

Prologue

In the park near the angel of the fountain. At dusk of an evening in May, in the first few years of this Century.

ALMA, *as a child of ten, comes into the scene. She wears a middy blouse and has ribboned braids. She already has the dignity of an adult;*

there is a quality of extraordinary delicacy and tenderness or spirituality in her, which must set her distinctly apart from other children. She has a habit of holding her hands, one cupped under the other in a way similar to that of receiving the wafer at Holy Communion. This is a habit that will remain with her as an adult. She stands like that in front of the stone angel for a few moments; then bends to drink at the fountain.

While she is bent at the fountain, JOHN, *as a child, enters. He shoots a pea-shooter at* ALMA's *bent-over back. She utters a startled cry and whirls about. He laughs.*

JOHN. Hi, Preacher's daughter. (*He advances toward her.*) I been looking for you.

ALMA (*hopefully*). You have?

JOHN. Was it you that put them handkerchiefs on my desk? (ALMA *smiles uncertainly.*) Answer up!

ALMA. I put a box of handkerchiefs on your desk.

JOHN. I figured it was you. What was the idea, Miss Priss?

ALMA. You needed them.

JOHN. Trying to make a fool of me?

ALMA. Oh, no!

JOHN. Then what was the idea?

ALMA. You have a bad cold and your nose has been running all week. It spoils your appearance.

JOHN. You don't have to look at me if you don't like my appearance.

ALMA. I like your appearance.

JOHN (*coming closer*). Is that why you look at me all the time?

ALMA. I—don't!

JOHN. Oh, yeh, you do. You been keeping your eyes on me all the time. Every time I look around I see them cat eyes of yours looking at me. That was the trouble today when Miss Blanchard asked you where the river Amazon was. She asked you twice and you still didn't answer because you w' lookin' at me. What's the idea? What've'y' got on y' mind anyhow?

ALMA. I was only thinking how handsome you'd be if your face wasn't dirty. You know why your face is dirty? Because you don't use a handkerchief and you wipe your nose on the sleeve of that dirty old sweater.

JOHN (*indignantly*). Hah!

ALMA. That's why I put the handkerchiefs on your desk and I wrapped them up so nobody would know what they were. It isn't my fault that you opened the box in front of everybody!

JOHN. What did you think I'd do with a strange box on my desk? Just leave it there till it exploded or something? Sure I opened it up. I didn't expect to find no—*handkerchief!*—in it . . .

ALMA (*in a shy trembling voice*). I'm sorry that you were embarrassed. I honestly am awfully sorry that you were embarrassed. Because I wouldn't embarrass you for the world!

JOHN. Don't flatter yourself that I was embarrassed. I don't embarrass that easy.

ALMA. It was stupid and cruel of those girls to laugh.

JOHN. Hah!

ALMA. They should all realize that you don't have a mother to take care of such things for you. It was a pleasure to me to be able to do something for you, only I didn't want you to know it was me who did it.

JOHN. Hee-haw! Ho-hum! Take 'em back! (*He snatches out the box and thrusts it toward her.*)

ALMA. *Please* keep them.

JOHN. What do I want with them?

(*She stares at him helplessly. He tosses the box to the ground and goes up to the fountain and drinks. Something in her face mollifies him and he sits down at the base of the fountain with a manner that does not preclude a more friendly relation. The dusk gathers deeper.*)

ALMA. Do you know the name of the angel?

JOHN. Does she have a name?

ALMA. Yes, I found out she does. It's carved in the base, but it's all worn away so you can't make it out with your eyes.

JOHN. Then how do you know it?

ALMA. You have to read it with your fingers. I did and it gave me cold shivers! *You* read it and see if it doesn't give *you* cold shivers! Go on! Read it with your fingers!

JOHN. Why don't you tell me and save me the trouble?

ALMA. I'm not going to tell you.

(JOHN *grins indulgently and turns to the pediment, crouching before it and running his fingers along the worn inscription.*)

JOHN. E?

ALMA. Yes, E is the first letter!

JOHN. T?

ALMA. Yes!

JOHN. E?

ALMA. E!

JOHN. K?

ALMA. No, no, not K!—R! (*He slowly straightens up.*)

JOHN. Eternity?

ALMA. *Eternity!*—Didn't it give you the cold shivers?

JOHN. Nahh.

ALMA. Well, it did me!

JOHN. Because you're a preacher's daughter. Eternity. What is eternity?

ALMA (*in a hushed wondering voice*). It's something that goes on and on when life and death and time and everything else is all through with.

JOHN. There's no such thing.

ALMA. There is. It's what people's souls live in when they have left their bodies. My name is Alma and Alma is Spanish for soul. Did you know that?

JOHN. Hee-haw! Ho-hum! Have you ever seen a dead person?

ALMA. No.

JOHN. I have. They made me go in the room when my mother was dying and she caught hold of my hand and wouldn't let me go— and so I screamed and hit her.

ALMA. Oh, you didn't do that.

JOHN (*somberly*). Uh-huh. She didn't look like my mother. Her face was all ugly and yellow and—terrible—bad-smelling! And so I hit her to make her let go of my hand. They told me that I was a devil!

ALMA. You didn't know what you were doing.

JOHN. My dad is a doctor.

ALMA. I know.

JOHN. He wants to send me to college to study to be a doctor but I wouldn't be a doctor for the world. And have to go in a room and watch people dying! . . . Jesus!

ALMA. You'll change your mind about that.

JOHN. Oh, no, I won't. I'd rather *be* a devil, like they called me and go to South America on a boat! . . . Give me one of them handkerchiefs. (*She brings them eagerly and humbly to the fountain. He takes one out and wets it at the fountain and scrubs his face with it.*) Is my face clean enough to suit you now?

ALMA. Yes!—Beautiful!

JOHN. *What!*

ALMA. I said "Beautiful"!

JOHN. Well—let's—kiss each other.

(ALMA *turns away.*)

JOHN. Come on, let's just try it!

(*He seizes her shoulders and gives her a quick rough kiss. She stands amazed with one hand cupping the other.*

(*The voice of a child in the distance calls "Johnny! Johnny!"*

(*He suddenly snatches at her hair-ribbon, jerks it loose and then runs off with a mocking laugh. Hurt and bewildered,* ALMA *turns back to the stone angel, for comfort. She crouches at the pediment and touches the inscription with her fingers. The scene dims out with music.*)

Scene One

Before the curtain rises a band is heard playing a patriotic anthem, punctuated with the crackle of fireworks.

The scene is the same as for the Prologue. It is the evening of July 4th in a year shortly before the first World War. There is a band concert and a display of fireworks in the park. During the scene the light changes from faded sunlight to dusk. Sections of roof, steeples, weathervanes, should have a metallic surface that catches

*the mellow light on the backdrop; when dusk has fallen the stars
should be visible.*

As the curtain rises, the REV. *and* MRS. WINEMILLER *come in and sit on
the bench near the fountain.* MRS. WINEMILLER *was a spoiled and
selfish girl who evaded the responsibilities of later life by slipping
into a state of perverse childishness. She is known as* MR. WINE-
MILLER'S *"Cross."*

MR. WINE. (*suddenly rising*). There is Alma, getting on the bandstand!
(MRS. WINEMILLER *is dreamily munching popcorn.*)

AN ANNOUNCER'S VOICE (*at a distance*). The Glorious Hill Orchestra
brings you Miss Alma Winemiller, The Nightingale of the Delta,
singing . . . "La Golondrina."

MR. WINE. (*sitting back down again*). This is going to provoke a lot of
criticism.

(*The song commences. The voice is not particularly strong, but it has
great purity and emotion.* JOHN BUCHANAN *comes along. He is
now a Promethean figure, brilliantly and restlessly alive in a stag-
nant society. The excess of his power has not yet found a channel.
If it remains without one, it will burn him up. At present he is
unmarked by the dissipations in which he relieves his demoniac
unrest; he has the fresh and shining look of an epic hero. He
walks leisurely before the* WINEMILLER'S *bench, negligently touching the crown of his hat but not glancing at them; climbs the
steps to the base of the fountain, then turns and looks in the direction of the singer. A look of interest touched with irony appears
on his face. A couple, strolling in the park, pass behind the fountain.*)

GIRL. Look who's by the fountain!

MAN. Bright as a new silver dollar!

JOHN. Hi, Dusty! Hi, Pearl!

MAN. How'd you make out in that floating crap game?

JOHN. I floated with it as far as Vicksburg, then sank.

GIRL. Everybody's been calling: "Johnny, Johnny—where's Johnny?"

(JOHN'S *father,* DR. BUCHANAN, *comes on from the right, as* REV. *and* MRS.
WINEMILLER *move off the scene to the left, toward the band music.*

DR. BUCHANAN *is an elderly man whose age shows in his slow and stiff movements. He walks with a cane.* JOHN *sees him coming, but pretends not to and starts to walk off.*)

DR. BUCH. John!

JOHN (*slowly turning around, as the couple move off*). Oh! Hi, Dad. . . . (*They exchange a long look.*) I—uh—meant to wire you but I must've forgot. I got tied up in Vicksburg Friday night and just now got back to town. Haven't been to the house yet. Is everything . . . going okay? (*He takes a drink of water at the fountain.*)

DR. BUCH. (*slowly, in a voice hoarse with emotion*). There isn't any room in the medical profession for wasters, drunkards and lechers. And there isn't any room in my house for wasters—drunkards—lechers! (*A child is heard calling* "I sp-yyyyyy!" *in the distance.*) I married late in life. I brought over five hundred children into this world before I had one of my own. And by God it looks like I've given myself the rottenest one of the lot. . . . (JOHN *laughs uncertainly.*) You will find your things at the Alhambra Hotel.

JOHN. Okay. If that's how you want it.

(*There is a pause. The singing comes through on the music.* JOHN *tips his hat diffidently and starts away from the fountain. He goes a few feet and his father suddenly calls after him.*)

DR. BUCH. John! (JOHN *pauses and looks back.*) Come here.

JOHN. Yes, Sir? (*He walks back to his father and stands before him.*)

DR. BUCH. (*hoarsely*). Go to the Alhambra Hotel and pick up your things and—bring them back to the house.

JOHN (*gently*). Yes, Sir. If that's how you want it. (*He diffidently extends a hand to touch his father's shoulder.*)

DR. BUCH. (*brushing the hand roughly off*). You! . . . You infernal *whelp,* you!"

(DR. BUCHANAN *turns and goes hurriedly away.* JOHN *looks after him with a faint, affectionate smile, then sits down on the steps with an air of relief, handkerchief to forehead, and a whistle of relief. Just then the singing at the bandstand ends and there is the sound of applause.* MRS. WINEMILLER *comes in from the left, followed by her husband.*)

MRS. WINE. Where is the ice cream man?

MR. WINE. Mother, hush! (*He sees his daughter approaching.*) Here we are, Alma!

(*The song ends. There is applause. Then the band strikes up the "Santiago Waltz."*)

(ALMA WINEMILLER *enters.* ALMA *had an adult quality as a child and now, in her middle twenties, there is something prematurely spinsterish about her. An excessive propriety and self-consciousness is apparent in her nervous laugher; her voice and gestures belong to years of church entertainment, to the position of hostess in a rectory. People her own age regard her as rather quaintly and humorously affected. She has grown up mostly in the company of her elders. Her true nature is still hidden even from herself. She is dressed in pale yellow and carries a yellow silk parasol. As* ALMA *passes in front of the fountain,* JOHN *slaps his hands resoundingly together a few times. She catches her breath in a slight laughing sound, makes as if to retreat, with a startled "Oh!", but then goes quickly to her parents. The applause from the crowd continues.*)

MR. WINE. They seem to want to hear you sing again, Alma.

(*She turns nervously about, touching her throat and her chest.* JOHN *grins, applauding by the fountain. When the applause dies out,* ALMA *sinks faintly on the bench.*)

ALMA. Open my bag, Father. My fingers have frozen stiff! (*She draws a deep labored breath.*) I don't know what came over me—absolute panic! Never, never again, it isn't worth it—the tortures that I go through!

MR. WINE. (*anxiously*). You're having one of your nervous attacks?

ALMA. My heart's beating so! It seemed to be in my *throat* the whole time I was singing! (JOHN *laughs audibly from the fountain.*) Was it noticeable, Father?

MR. WINE. You sang extremely well, Alma. But you know how I feel about this, it was contrary to my wishes and I cannot imagine why you wanted to do it, especially since it seemed to upset you so.

ALMA. I don't see how anyone could object to my singing at a patriotic occasion. If I had just sung well! But I barely got through it. At one point I thought that I wouldn't. The words flew out of my mind. Did you notice the pause? Blind panic! They really never came back, but I went on singing—I think I must have been improvising the lyric! Whew! Is there a handkerchief in it?

MRS. WINE. (*suddenly*). Where is the ice cream man?

ALMA (*rubbing her fingers together*). Circulation is slowly coming back . . .

MR. WINE. Sit back quietly and take a deep breath, Alma.

ALMA. Yes, my handkerchief—now . . .

MRS. WINE. Where is the ice cream man?

MR. WINE. Mother, there isn't any ice cream man.

ALMA. No, there isn't any ice cream man, Mother. But on the way home Mr. Doremus and I will stop by the drug store and pick up a pint of ice cream.

MR. WINE. Are you intending to stay here?

ALMA. Until the concert is over. I promised Roger I'd wait for him.

MR. WINE. I suppose you have noticed who is by the fountain?

ALMA. *Shhh!*

MR. WINE. Hadn't you better wait on a different bench?

ALMA. This is where Roger will meet me.

MR. WINE. Well, Mother, we'll run along now. (MRS. WINEMILLER *has started vaguely toward the fountain,* MR. WINEMILLER *firmly restraining her.*) This way, this way, Mother! (*He takes her arm and leads her off.*)

MRS. WINE. (*calling back, in a high, childish voice*). Strawberry, Alma. Chocolate, chocolate and strawberry mixed! Not vanilla!

ALMA (*faintly*). Yes, yes, Mother—vanilla . . .

MRS. WINE. (*furiously*). I said *not* vanilla. (*Shouting.*) Strawberry!

MR. WINE. (*fiercely*). Mother! We're attracting attention. (*He propels her forcibly away.*)

(JOHN *laughs by the fountain.* ALMA *moves her parasol so that it shields her face from him. She leans back closing her eyes.* JOHN *notices a firecracker by the fountain. He leans over negligently to pick it up. He grins and lights it and tosses it toward* ALMA's *bench.*

When it goes off she springs up with a shocked cry, letting the parasol drop.)

JOHN *(jumping up as if outraged)*. Hey! Hey, you! *(He looks off to the right.* ALMA *sinks back weakly on the bench.* JOHN *solicitously advances.)* Are you all right?

ALMA. I can't seem to—catch my breath! Who threw it?

JOHN. Some little rascal.

ALMA. Where?

JOHN. He ran away quick when I hollered!

ALMA. There ought to be an ordinance passed in this town forbidding firecrackers.

JOHN. Dad and I treated fifteen kids for burns the last couple of days. I think you need a little restorative, don't you? *(He takes out a flask.)* Here!

ALMA. What is it?

JOHN. Applejack brandy.

ALMA. No thank you.

JOHN. Liquid dynamite.

ALMA. I'm sure.

*(*JOHN *laughs and returns it to his pocket. He remains looking down at her with one foot on the end of her bench. His steady, smiling look into her face is disconcerting her. In* ALMA'S *voice and manner there is a delicacy and elegance, a kind of "airiness," which is really natural to her as it is, in a less marked degree, to many Southern girls. Her gestures and mannerisms are a bit exaggerated but in a graceful way. It is understandable that she might be accused of "putting on airs" and of being "affected" by the other young people of the town. She seems to belong to a more elegant age, such as the Eighteenth Century in France. Out of nervousness and self-consciousness she has a habit of prefacing and concluding her remarks with a little breathless laugh. This will be indicated at points, but should be used more freely than indicated; however, the characterization must never be stressed to the point of making her at all ludicrous in a less than sympathetic way.)*

ALMA. You're—home for the summer? *(*JOHN *gives an affirmative grunt.)* Summer is not the pleasantest time of year to renew an acquaintance with Glorious Hill—is it? (JOHN *gives an indefinite grunt.* ALMA *laughs airily.*) The Gulf wind has failed us this year, disappointed us dreadfully this summer. We used to be able to rely on the Gulf wind to cool the nights off for us, but this summer has been an exceptional season. (*He continues to grin disconcertingly down at her; she shows her discomfiture in flurried gestures.*)

JOHN (*slowly*). Are you—disturbed about something?

ALMA. That firecracker was a shock.

JOHN. You should be over that shock by now.

ALMA. I don't get over shocks quickly.

JOHN. I see you don't.

ALMA. You're planning to stay here and take over some of your father's medical practice?

JOHN. I haven't made up my mind about anything yet.

ALMA. I hope so, we all hope so. Your father was telling me that you have succeeded in isolating the germ of that fever epidemic that's broken out at Lyon.

JOHN. Finding something to kill it is more of a trick.

ALMA. You'll do that! He's so positive that you will. He says that you made a special study of bacter—bacter . . .

JOHN. Bacteriology!

ALMA. Yes! At Johns Hopkins! That's in Boston, isn't it?

JOHN. No. Baltimore.

ALMA. Oh, Baltimore. Baltimore, Maryland. Such a beautiful combination of names. And bacteriology—isn't that something you do with a microscope?

JOHN. Well—partly. . . .

ALMA. I've looked through a telescope, but never a microscope. What . . . what do you—see?

JOHN. A—universe, Miss Alma.

ALMA. What kind of a universe?

JOHN. Pretty much the same kind that you saw through the lens of a telescope—a mysterious one. . . .

ALMA. Oh, yes. . . .

JOHN. Part anarchy—and part order!

ALMA. The footprints of God!

JOHN. But not God.

ALMA (*ecstatically*). To be a doctor! And deal with these mysteries under the microscope lens . . . I think it is more religious than being a priest! There is so much suffering in the world it actually makes one sick to think about it, and most of us are so helpless to relieve it. . . . But a physician! Oh, my! With his magnificent gifts and training what a joy it must be to know that he is equipped and appointed to bring relief to all of this fearful suffering—and fear! And it's an expanding profession, it's a profession that is continually widening its horizons. So many diseases have already come under scientific control but the commencement is just—beginning! I mean there is so much more that is yet to be done, such as mental afflictions to be brought under control. . . . And with your father's example to inspire you! Oh, my!

JOHN. I didn't know you had so many ideas about the medical profession.

ALMA. Well, I am a great admirer of your father, as well as a patient. It's such a comfort knowing that he's right next door, within arm's reach as it were!

JOHN. Why? Do you have fits? . . .

ALMA. Fits? (*She throws back her head with a peal of gay laughter.*) Why no, but I do have attacks!—of nervous heart trouble. Which can be so alarming that I run straight to your father!

JOHN. At two or three in the morning?

ALMA. Yes, as late as that, even . . . occasionally. He's very patient with me.

JOHN. But does you no good?

ALMA. He always reassures me.

JOHN. Temporarily?

ALMA. Yes . . .

JOHN. Don't you want more than that?

ALMA. What?

JOHN. It's none of my business.

ALMA. What were you going to say?

JOHN. You're Dad's patient. But I have an idea . . .

ALMA. Please go on! (JOHN *laughs a little.*) Now you have to go on! You can't leave me up in the air! What were you going to tell me?

JOHN. Only that I suspect you need something more than a little temporary reassurance.

ALMA. *Why?* Why? You think it's more serious than . . . ?

JOHN. You're swallowing air.

ALMA. I'm what?

JOHN. You're swallowing air, Miss Alma.

ALMA. I'm swallowing air?

JOHN. Yes, you swallow air when you laugh or talk. It's a little trick that hysterical women get into.

ALMA (*uncertainly*). Ha-ha . . . !

JOHN. You swallow air and it presses on your heart and gives you palpitations. That isn't serious in itself but it's a symptom of something that is. Shall I tell you frankly?

ALMA. Yes!

JOHN. Well, what I think you have is a *doppelganger!* You have a *doppelganger* and the *doppelganger* is badly irritated.

ALMA. Oh, my goodness! I have an irritated *doppelganger!* (*She tries to laugh, but is definitely uneasy.*) How awful that sounds! What exactly *is* it?

JOHN. It's none of *my* business. You are not *my* patient.

ALMA. But that's downright wicked of you! To tell me I have something awful-sounding as that, and then refuse to let me know what it is! (*She tries to laugh again, unsuccessfully.*)

JOHN. I shouldn't have said anything! I'm not your doctor. . . .

ALMA. Just how did you arrive at this—diagnosis of my case? (*She laughs.*) But of course you're teasing me. Aren't you? . . . There, the Gulf wind is stirring! He's actually moving the leaves of the palmetto! And listen to them complaining. . . .

(*As if brought in by this courier from the tropics,* ROSA GONZALES *enters and crosses to the fountain. Her indolent walk produces a sound and an atmosphere like the Gulf wind on the palmettos, a whispering of silk and a slight rattle of metallic ornaments. She is dressed in an almost outrageous finery, with lustrous feathers on her hat, greenish blue, a cascade of them, also diamond and emerald earrings.*)

JOHN (*sharply*). *Who is that?*

ALMA. I'm surprised that you don't know.

JOHN. I've been away quite a while.

ALMA. That's the Gonzales girl. . . . Her father's the owner of the gambling casino on Moon Lake. (ROSA *drinks at the fountain and wanders leisurely off.*) She smiled at you, didn't she?

JOHN. I thought she did.

ALMA. I hope that you have a strong character. (*He places a foot on the end of the bench.*)

JOHN. Solid rock.

ALMA (*nervously*). The pyrotechnical display is going to be brilliant.

JOHN. The what?

ALMA. The fireworks.

JOHN. Aw!

ALMA. I suppose you've lost touch with most of your *old* friends here.

JOHN (*laconically*). Yeah.

ALMA. You must make some *new* ones! I belong to a little group that meets every ten days. I think you'd enjoy them, too. They're young people with—intellectual and artistic interests. . . .

JOHN (*sadly*). Aw, I see . . . intellectual. . . .

ALMA. You must come!—sometime—I'm going to remind you of it. . . .

JOHN. Thanks. Do you mind if I sit down?

ALMA. Why, certainly not, there's room enough for two! Neither of us are—terribly large in diameter! (*She laughs shrilly.*)

(*A girl's voice is heard calling: "Goodbye, Nellie!" and another answers: "Goodbye!"* NELLIE EWELL *enters—a girl of sixteen with a radiantly fresh healthy quality.*)

ALMA. Here comes someone much nicer! One of my adorable little vocal pupils, the youngest and prettiest one with the least gift for music.

JOHN. I know that one.

ALMA. Hello, there, Nellie dear!

NELL. Oh, Miss Alma, your singing was so beautiful it made me cry.

ALMA. It's sweet of you to fib so. I sang terribly.

NELL. You're just being modest, Miss Alma. Hello, Dr. John! Dr. John?

JOHN. Yeah?

NELL. That book you gave me is too full of long words.

JOHN. Look 'em up in the dictionary, Nellie.

NELL. I did, but you know how dictionaries are. You look up one long word and it gives you another and you look up that one and it gives you the long word you looked up in the first place. (JOHN *laughs.*) I'm coming over tomorrow for you to explain it all to me. (*She laughs and goes off.*)

ALMA. What book is she talking about?

JOHN. A book I gave her about the facts of nature. She came over to the office and told me her mother wouldn't tell her anything and she had to know because she'd fallen in love.

ALMA. Why the precocious little—imp! (*She laughs.*)

JOHN. What sort of a mother has she?

ALMA. Mrs. Ewell's the merry widow of Glorious Hill. They say that she goes to the depot to meet every train in order to make the acquaintance of traveling salesmen. Of course she is ostracized by all but a few of her own type of women in town, which is terribly hard for Nellie. It isn't fair to the child. Father didn't want me to take her as a pupil because of her mother's reputation, but I feel that one has a duty to perform toward children in such—circumstances. . . . And I always say that life is such a mysteriously complicated thing that no one should really presume to judge and condemn the behavior of anyone else! (*There is a faraway "puff" and a burst of golden light over their heads. Both look up. There is a long-drawn "Ahhh . . ." from the invisible crowd. This is an effect that will be repeated at intervals during the scene.*) There goes the first sky-rocket! Oh, look at it burst into a million stars!

(JOHN *leans way back to look up and allows his knees to spread wide apart so that one of them is in contact with* ALMA'S. *The effect upon her is curiously disturbing.*)

JOHN (*after a moment*). Do you have a chill?

ALMA. Why, no!—no. Why?

JOHN. You're shaking.

ALMA. Am I?

JOHN. Don't you feel it?

ALMA. I have a touch of malaria lingering on.

JOHN. You have malaria?

ALMA. Never severely, never really severely. I just have touches of it that come and go. (*She laughs airily.*)

JOHN (*with a gentle grin*). Why do you laugh that way?

ALMA. What way?

(JOHN *imitates her laugh.* ALMA *laughs again in embarrassment.*)

JOHN. Yeah. That way.

ALMA. I do declare, you haven't changed in the slightest. It used to delight you to embarrass me and it still does!

JOHN. I guess I shouldn't tell you this, but I heard an imitation of you at a party.

ALMA. Imitation? Of what?

JOHN. You.

ALMA. I?—I? Why, *what* did they imitate?

JOHN. You singing at a wedding.

ALMA. My voice?

JOHN. Your gestures and facial expression!

ALMA. How mystifying!

JOHN. No, I shouldn't have told you. You're upset about it.

ALMA. I'm not in the least upset, I am just mystified.

JOHN. Don't you know that you have a reputation for putting on airs a a little—for gilding the lily a bit?

ALMA. I have no idea what you are talking about.

JOHN. Well, some people seem to have gotten the idea that you are just a little bit—affected!

ALMA. Well, well, well, well. (*She tries to conceal her hurt.*) That may be so, it may seem so to some people. But since I am innocent of any attempt at affectation, I really don't know what I can do about it.

JOHN. You have a rather fancy way of talking.

ALMA. Have I?

JOHN. Pyrotechnical display instead of fireworks, and that sort of thing.

ALMA. So?

JOHN. And how about that accent?

ALMA. Accent? This leaves me quite speechless! I have sometimes been accused of having a put-on accent by people who disapprove of good diction. My father was a Rhodes scholar at Oxford, and while over there he fell into the natural habit of using the long A where it is correct to use it. I suppose I must have picked it up from him, but it's entirely unconscious. Who gave this imitation at this party you spoke of?

JOHN (*grinning*). I don't think she'd want that told.

ALMA. Oh, it was a *she* then?

JOHN. You don't think a man could do it?

ALMA. No, and I don't think a lady would do it either!

JOHN. I didn't think it would have made you so mad, or I wouldn't have brought it up.

ALMA. Oh, I'm not mad. I'm just mystified and amazed as I always am by unprovoked malice in people. I don't understand it when it's directed at me and I don't understand it when it is directed at anybody else. I just don't understand it, and perhaps it is better not to understand it. These people who call me affected and give these unkind imitations of me—I wonder if they stop to think that I have had certain difficulties and disadvantages to cope with—which may be partly the cause of these peculiarities of mine—which they find so offensive!

JOHN. Now, Miss Alma, you're making a mountain out of a molehill!

ALMA. I wonder if they stop to think that my circumstances are somewhat different from theirs? My father and I have a certain—cross —to bear!

JOHN. What cross?

ALMA. Living next door to us, you should know what cross.

JOHN. Mrs. Winemiller?

ALMA. She had her breakdown while I was still in high school. And from that time on I have had to manage the Rectory and take over the social and household duties that would ordinarily belong to a minister's wife, not his daughter. And that may have made me seem strange to some of my more critical contemporaries. In a way it may have—deprived me of—my youth. . . . (*Another rocket goes up. Another "Ahhh . . ." from the crowd.*)

JOHN. You ought to go out with young people.

ALMA. I am not a recluse. I don't fly around here and there giving imitations of other people at parties. But I am not a recluse by any manner of means. Being a minister's daughter I have to be more selective than most girls about the—society I keep. But I do go out now and then. . . .

JOHN. I have seen you in the public library and the park, but only two or three times have I seen you out with a boy and it was always someone like this Roger Doremus.

ALMA. I'm afraid that you and I move in different circles. If I wished to be as outspoken as you are, which is sometimes just an excuse for being rude—I might say that I've yet to see you in the company of a—well, a—reputable young woman. You've heard unfavorable talk about me in your circle of acquaintances and I've heard equally unpleasant things about you in mine. And the pity of it is that you are preparing to be a doctor. You're intending to practice your father's profession here in Glorious Hill. (*She catches her breath in a sob.*) Most of us have no choice but to lead useless lives! But you have a gift for scientific research! You have a chance to serve humanity. Not just to go on enduring for the sake of endurance, but to serve a noble, humanitarian cause, to relieve human suffering. And what do you do about it? Everything that you can to alienate the confidence of nice people who love and respect your father. While he is devoting himself to the fever at Lyon you drive your automobile at a reckless pace from one disorderly roadhouse to another! You say you have seen two things through the microscope, anarchy and order? Well, obviously *order* is not the thing that impressed you . . . conducting yourself like some overgrown schoolboy who wants to be known as the wildest fellow in town! And you—a gifted young doctor— *Magna cum Laude!* (*She turns aside, touching her eyelids with a handkerchief.*) You know what I call it? I call it a *desecration!* (*She sobs uncontrollably. Then she springs up from the bench.* JOHN *catches her hand.*)

JOHN. You're not going to run off, are you?

ALMA. Singing in public always—always upsets me!—Let go of my hand. (*He holds on to it, grinning up at her in the deepening dusk. The stars are coming out in the cyclorama with its leisurely floating cloud-forms. In the distance the band is playing "La Golondrina."*) Please let go of my hand.

JOHN. Don't run off mad.

ALMA. Let's not make a spectacle of ourselves.

JOHN. Then sit back down.

(*A skyrocket goes up. The crowd "Ahhh . . .s."*)

ALMA. You threw that firecracker and started a conversation just in order to tease me as you did as a child. You came to this bench in order to embarrass me and to hurt my feelings with the report of that vicious—imitation! No, let go of my hand so I can leave, now. You've succeeded in your purpose. I *was* hurt, I *did* make a fool of myself as you intended! So let me go now!

JOHN. You're attracting attention! Don't you know that I really *like* you, Miss Alma?

ALMA. No, you don't.

(*Another skyrocket.*)

JOHN. Sure I do. A lot. Sometimes when I come home late at night I look over at the Rectory. I see something white at the window. Could that be you, Miss Alma? Or, is it your *doppelganger,* looking out of the window that faces my way?

ALMA. Enough about *doppelganger*—whatever that is!

JOHN. There goes a nice one, Roman candle they call it!

(*This time the explosion is in back of them. A Roman candle shoots up puffs of rainbow-colored light in back of the stone angel of the fountain. They turn in profile to watch it.*)

JOHN (*counting the puffs of light*). Four—five—six—that's all? No— seven! (*There is a pause.* ALMA *sits down slowly.*)

ALMA (*vaguely*). Dear me . . . (*She fans herself.*)

JOHN. How about going riding?

ALMA (*too eagerly*). When . . . now?

(ROSA GONZALES *has wandered up to the fountain again.* JOHN's *attention drifts steadily toward her and away from* ALMA.)

JOHN (*too carelessly*). Oh . . . some afternoon.

ALMA. Would you observe the speed limit?

JOHN. Strictly with you, Miss Alma.

ALMA. Why then, I'd be glad to—John.

(JOHN *has risen from the bench and crosses to the fountain.*)

JOHN. And wear a hat with a plume!

ALMA. I don't have a hat with a plume!

JOHN. Get one!

(*Another skyrocket goes up, and there is another long "Ahhh . . ."
from the crowd.* JOHN *saunters up to the fountain.* ROSA *has lingered beside it. As he passes her he whispers something. She
laughs and moves leisurely off.* JOHN *takes a quick drink at the
fountain, then follows* ROSA, *calling back "Good night" to* ALMA.
There is a sound of laughter in the distance. ALMA *sits motionless
for a moment, then touches a small white handkerchief to her
lips and nostrils.* MR. DOREMUS *comes in, carrying a French horn
case. He is a small man, somewhat like a sparrow.*)

ROG. *Whew!* Golly! Moses!—Well, how did it go, Miss Alma?

ALMA. How did—what—go?

ROG. (*annoyed*). My solo on the French horn.

ALMA (*slowly, without thinking*). I paid no attention to it. (*She rises
slowly and takes his arm.*) I'll have to hang on your arm—I'm
feeling so dizzy!

(*The scene dims out. There is a final skyrocket and a last "Ahhh . . ."
from the crowd in the distance. Music is heard, and there is light
on the angel.*)

Scene Two

Inside the Rectory, which is lighted. MRS. WINEMILLER *comes in and
makes her way stealthily to the love seat, where she seats herself.
Opening her parasol, she takes out a fancy white-plumed hat
which she had concealed there. Rising, she turns to the mirror on
the wall over the love seat and tries on the hat. She draws a long,
ecstatic breath as she places it squarely on her head. At that mo-*

ment the telephone rings. Startled, she snatches off the hat, hides it behind the center table and quickly resumes her seat. The telephone goes on ringing. ALMA *comes in to answer it.*

ALMA. Hello. . . . Yes, Mr. Gillam. . . . She did? . . . Are you sure? . . . How shocking! . . . (MRS. WINEMILLER *now retrieves the hat, seats herself in front of* ALMA *and puts the hat on.*) Thank you, Mr. Gillam . . . the hat is here.

(MR. WINEMILLER *comes in. He is distracted.*)

MR. WINE. Alma! Alma, your mother . . . !

ALMA (*coming in*). I know, Father, Mr. Gillam just phoned. He told me she picked up a white plumed hat and he pretended not to notice in order to save you the embarrassment, so I—told him to just charge it to us.

MR. WINE. That hat looks much too expensive.

ALMA. It's fourteen dollars. You pay six of it, Father, and I'll pay eight. (*She gives him the parasol.*)

MR. WINE. What an insufferable cross we have to bear. (*He retires despairingly from the room.*)

(ALMA *goes over to her mother and seats her in a chair at the table.*)

ALMA. I have a thousand and one things to do before my club meeting tonight, so you work quietly on your picture puzzle or I shall take the hat back, plume and all.

MRS. WINE. (*throwing a piece of the puzzle on the floor*). The pieces don't fit! (ALMA *picks up the piece and puts it on the table.*) The pieces don't fit!

(ALMA *stands for a moment in indecision. She reaches for the phone, then puts it down. Then she takes it up again, and gives a number. The telephone across the way in the doctor's office rings and that part of the scene lights up.* JOHN *comes in.*)

JOHN (*answering the phone*). Hello?

ALMA. John! (*She fans herself rapidly with a palm leaf clutched in her free hand and puts on a brilliant, strained smile as if she were actually in his presence.*)

JOHN. Miss Alma?

ALMA. You recognized my voice?

JOHN. I recognized your laugh.

ALMA. Ha-ha! How are you, you stranger you?

JOHN. I'm pretty well, Miss Alma. How're you doing?

ALMA. Surviving, just surviving! Isn't it fearful?

JOHN. Uh-huh.

ALMA. You seem unusually laconic. Or perhaps I should say more than usually laconic.

JOHN. I had a big night and I'm just recovering from it.

ALMA. Well, sir, I have a bone to pick with you!

JOHN. What's that, Miss Alma? (*He drains a glass of bromo.*)

ALMA. The time of our last conversation on the Fourth of July, you said you were going to take me riding in your automobile.

JOHN. Aw. Did I say that?

ALMA. Yes indeed you did, sir! And all these hot afternoons I've been breathlessly waiting and hoping that you would remember that promise. But now I know how insincere you are. Ha-ha! Time and again the four-wheeled phenomenon flashes by the Rectory and I have yet to put my—my quaking foot in it!

(MRS. WINEMILLER *begins to mock* ALMA's *speech and laughter.*)

JOHN. What was that, Miss Alma? I didn't understand you.

ALMA. I was just reprimanding you, sir! Castigating you verbally! Ha-ha!

MRS. WINE. (*grimacing*). Ha-ha.

JOHN. What about, Miss Alma? (*He leans back and puts his feet on table.*)

ALMA. Never mind. I know how busy you are! (*She whispers.*) Mother, hush!

JOHN. I'm afraid we have a bad connection.

ALMA. I hate telephones. I don't know why but they always make me laugh as if someone were poking me in the ribs! I swear to goodness they do!

JOHN. Why don't you just go to your window and I'll go to mine and we can holler across?

ALMA. The yard's so wide I'm afraid it would crack my voice! And I've got to sing at somebody's wedding tomorrow.

JOHN. You're going to sing at a wedding?

ALMA. Yes. "The Voice That Breathed O'er Eden!" And I'm as hoarse as a frog! (*Another gale of laughter almost shakes her off her feet.*)

JOHN. Better come over and let me give you a gargle.

ALMA. Nasty gargles—I hate them!

MRS. WINE. (*mockingly*). Nasty gargles—I hate them!

ALMA. Mother, shhh!—please! As you no doubt have gathered, there is some interference at this end of the line! What I wanted to say is—you remember my mentioning that little club I belong to?

JOHN. Aw! Aw, yes! Those intellectual meetings!

ALMA. Oh, now, don't call it that. It's just a little informal gathering every Wednesday and we talk about the new books and read things out loud to each other!

JOHN. Serve any refreshments?

ALMA. Yes, we serve refreshments!

JOHN. Any liquid refreshments?

ALMA. Both liquid and solid refreshments.

JOHN. Is this an invitation?

ALMA. Didn't I promise I'd ask you? It's going to be tonight!—at eight at my house, at the Rectory, so all you'll have to do is cross the yard!

JOHN. I'll try to make it, Miss Alma.

ALMA. Don't say try as if it required some Herculean effort! All you have to do is . . .

JOHN. Cross the yard! Uh-huh—reserve me a seat by the punch bowl.

ALMA. That gives me an idea! We *will* have punch, fruit punch, with claret in it. Do you like claret?

JOHN. I just dote on claret.

ALMA. Now you're being sarcastic! Ha-ha-ha!

JOHN. Excuse me, Miss Alma, but Dad's got to use this phone.

ALMA. I won't hang up till you've said you'll come without fail!

JOHN. I'll be there, Miss Alma. You can count on it.

ALMA. Au revoir, then! Until eight.

JOHN. G'bye, Miss Alma. (JOHN *hangs up with an incredulous grin.* ALMA *remains holding the phone with a dazed smile until the office interior has dimmed slowly out.*)

MRS. WINE. Alma's in love—in love. (*She waltzes mockingly.*)

ALMA (*sharply*). Mother, you are wearing out my patience! Now I am expecting another music pupil and I have to make preparations for the club meeting so I suggest that you . . . (NELLIE *rings the bell.*) Will you go up to your room? (*Then she calls sweetly.*) Yes, Nellie, coming, Nellie. All right, stay down here then. But keep your attention on your picture puzzle or there will be no ice cream for you after supper!

(*She admits* NELLIE, *who is wildly excited over something. This scene should be played lightly and quickly.*)

NELL. Oh, Miss Alma! (*She rushes past* ALMA *in a distracted manner, throws herself on the sofa and hugs herself with excited glee.*)

ALMA. What is it, Nellie? Has something happened at home? (NELLIE *continues her exhilaration.*) Oh, now, Nellie, stop that! Whatever it is, it can't be *that* important!

NELL. (*blurting out suddenly*). Miss Alma, haven't you ever had—*crushes?*

ALMA. What?

NELL. Crushes?

ALMA. Yes—I suppose I have. (*She sits down.*)

NELL. Did you know that I used to have a crush on *you,* Miss Alma?

ALMA. No, Nellie.

NELL. Why do you think that I took singing lessons?

ALMA. I supposed it was because you wished to develop your voice.

NELL. (*cutting in*). Oh, you know, and I know, I never had any voice. I had a crush on you though. Those were the days when I had crushes on girls. Those days are all over, and now I have crushes on boys. Oh, Miss Alma, you know about Mother, how I was brought up so nobody nice except you would have anything to do with us—Mother meeting the trains to pick up the traveling salesmen and bringing them home to drink and play poker—all of them acting like pigs, pigs, pigs!

MRS. WINE. (*mimicking*). Pigs, pigs, pigs!

NELL. Well, I thought I'd always hate men. Loathe and despise them. But last night— Oh!

ALMA. Hadn't we better run over some scales until you are feeling calmer?

NELL. (*cutting in*). I'd heard them downstairs for hours but didn't know who it was—I'd fallen asleep—when all of a sudden my door banged open. He'd thought it was the bathroom!

ALMA (*nervously*). Nellie, I'm not sure I want to hear any more of this story.

NELL. (*interrupting*). Guess who it was?

ALMA. I couldn't possibly guess.

NELL. Someone you know. Someone I've seen you with.

ALMA. Who?

NELL. The wonderfullest person in all the big wide world! When he saw it was me he came and sat down on the bed and held my hand and we talked and talked until Mother came up to see what had happened to him. You should have heard him bawl her out. Oh, he laid the law down! He said she ought to send me off to a girl's school because she wasn't fit to bring up a daughter! Then she started to bawl him out. You're a fine one to talk, she said, you're not fit to call yourself a doctor. (ALMA *rises abruptly.*)

ALMA. John Buchanan?

NELL. Yes, of course, Dr. Johnny.

ALMA. Was—with—your—mother?

NELL. Oh, he wasn't her beau! He had a girl with him, and Mother had somebody else!

ALMA. Who—did—he—have?

NELL. Oh, some loud tacky thing with a Z in her name!

ALMA. Gonzales? Rosa Gonzales?

NELL. Yes, that was it! (ALMA *sits slowly back down.*) But him! Oh, Miss Alma! He's the *wonderfullest* person that I . . .

ALMA (*interrupting*). Your mother was right! He isn't fit to call himself a doctor! I hate to disillusion you, but this wonderfullest person is pitiably weak.

(*Someone calls "Johnny" outside.*)

NELL. (*in hushed excitement*). Someone is calling him now!

ALMA. Yes, these people who shout his name in front of his house are of such a character that the old doctor cannot permit them to come inside the door. And when they have brought him home at night, left him sprawling on the front steps, sometimes at day-break—it takes two people, his father and the old cook, one push-ing and one pulling, to get him upstairs. (*She sits down.*) All the gifts of the gods were showered on him. . . . (*The call of "Johnny" is repeated.*) But all he cares about is indulging his senses! (*Another call of "Johnny."*)

NELL. Here he comes down the steps! (ALMA *crosses toward the window.*) Look at him jump!

ALMA. Oh.

NELL. Over the banisters. Ha-ha!

ALMA. Nellie, don't lean out the window and have us caught spying.

MRS. WINE. (*suddenly*). Show Nellie how *you* spy on him! Oh, she's a good one at spying. She stands behind the curtain and *peeks* around it, and . . .

ALMA (*frantically*). *Mother!*

MRS. WINE. She spies on him. Whenever he comes in at night she rushes down stairs to watch him out of this window!

ALMA (*interrupting her*). Be still!

MRS. WINE. (*going right on*). She called him just now and had a fit on the telephone! (*The old lady cackles derisively.* ALMA *snatches her cigarette from her and crushes it under her foot.*) Alma's in love! Alma's in love!

ALMA (*interrupting*). Nellie, Nellie, please go.

NELL. (*with a startled giggle*). All right, Miss Alma, I'm going. (*She crosses quickly to the door, looking back once with a grin.*) Good night, Mrs. Winemiller!

(NELLIE *goes out gaily, leaving the door slightly open.* ALMA *rushes to it and slams it shut. She returns swiftly to* MRS. WINEMILLER, *her hands clenched with anger.*)

ALMA. If ever I hear you say such a thing again, if ever you dare to repeat such a thing in my presence or anybody else's—then it will be the last straw! You understand me? Yes, you understand me. You act like a child, but you have the devil in you. And God will punish you—yes! I'll punish you too. I'll take your cigarettes from you and give you no more. I'll give you no ice cream either. Be cause I'm tired of your malice. Yes, I'm tired of your malice and your self-indulgence. People wonder why I'm tied down here! They pity me—think of me as an old maid already! In spite of I'm young. Still young! It's you—it's you, you've taken my youth away from me! I wouldn't say that—I'd try not even to think it— if you were just kind, just simple! But I could spread my life out like a rug for you to step on and you'd step on it, and not even say "Thank you, Alma!" Which is what you've done always—and now you dare to tell a disgusting lie about me—in front of that girl!

MRS. WINE. Don't you think I hear you go to the window at night to watch him come in and . . .

ALMA. Give me that plumed hat, Mother! It goes back now, it goes back!

MRS. WINE. *Fight! Fight!*

(ALMA *snatches at the plumed hat.* MRS. WINEMILLER *snatches too. The hat is torn between them.* MRS. WINEMILLER *retains the hat. The plume comes loose in* ALMA's *hand. She stares at it a moment with a shocked expression.*)

ALMA (*sincerely*). Heaven have mercy upon us!

Scene Three

Inside the Rectory.

The meeting is in progress, having just opened with the reading of the minutes by ALMA. *She stands before the green plush sofa and the others. This group includes* MR. DOREMUS, VERNON, *a willowy younger man with an open collar and Byronic locks, the widow* BASSETT, *and a wistful older girl with a long neck and thick-lensed glasses.*

ALMA (*reading*). Our last meeting which fell on July fourteenth . . .

MRS. BASS. Bastille Day!

ALMA. Pardon me?

MRS. BASS. It fell on Bastille Day! But, honey, that was the meeting before last.

ALMA. You're perfectly right. I seem to be on the wrong page. . . . (*She drops the papers.*)

MRS. BASS. Butterfingers!

ALMA. Here we are! July twenty-fifth! Correct?

MRS. BASS. Correct! (*A little ripple of laughter goes about the circle.*)

ALMA (*continuing*). It was debated whether or not we ought to suspend operations for the remainder of the summer as the departure of several members engaged in the teaching profession for their summer vacations . . .

MRS. BASS. Lucky people!

ALMA. . . . had substantially contracted our little circle.

MRS. BASS. Decimated our ranks! (*There is another ripple of laughter.*) (JOHN *appears outside the door-frame and rings the bell.*)

ALMA (*with agitation*). Is that—is that—the doorbell?

MRS. BASS. It sure did sound like it to me.

ALMA. Excuse me a moment. I think it may be . . .

(*She crosses to the door-frame and makes the gesture of opening the door.* JOHN *steps in, immaculately groomed and shining, his white linen coat over his arm and a white Panama hat in his hand. He is a startling contrast to the other male company, who seem to be outcasts of a state in which he is a prominent citizen.*)

ALMA (*shrilly*). Yes, it is—our guest of honor! Everybody, this is Dr. John Buchanan, Jr.

JOHN (*easily glancing about the assemblage*). Hello, everybody.

MRS. BASS. I never thought he'd show up. Congratulations, Miss Alma.

JOHN. Did I miss much?

ALMA. Not a thing! Just the minutes— I'll put you on the sofa. Next to me. (*She laughs breathlessly and makes an uncertain gesture. He settles gingerly on the sofa. They all stare at him with a curious sort of greediness.*) Well, now! we are completely assembled!

MRS. BASS. (*eagerly*). Vernon has his verse play with him tonight!

ALMA (*uneasily*). Is that right, Vernon?

(*Obviously, it is.* VERNON *has a pile of papers eight inches thick on his knees. He raises them timidly with downcast eyes.*)

ROG. (*quickly*). We decided to put that off till cooler weather. Miss

Rosemary is supposed to read us a paper tonight on William Blake.

MRS. BASS. Those dead poets can keep!

(JOHN *laughs*.)

ALMA (*excitedly jumping up*). Mrs. Bassett, everybody! This is the way I feel about the verse play. It's too important a thing to read under any but ideal circumstances. Not only atmospheric—on some cool evening with music planned to go with it!—but everyone present so that nobody will miss it! Why don't we . . .

ROG. Why don't we take a standing vote on the matter?

ALMA. Good, good, perfect!

ROG. All in favor of putting the verse play off till cooler weather, stand up!

(*Everybody rises but* ROSEMARY *and* MRS. BASSETT. ROSEMARY *starts vaguely to rise, but* MRS. BASSETT *jerks her arm.*)

ROSE. Was this a vote?

ROG. Now, Mrs. Bassett, no rough tactics, please!

ALMA. Has everybody got fans? John, you haven't got one! (*She looks about for a fan for him. Not seeing one, she takes* ROGER'S *out of his hand and gives it to* JOHN. ROGER *is nonplussed.* ROSEMARY *gets up with her paper.*)

ROSE. The poet—William Blake.

MRS. BASS. Insane, insane, that man was a mad fanatic! (*She squints her eyes tight shut and thrusts her thumbs into her ears. The reactions range from indignant to conciliatory.*)

ROG. Now, Mrs. Bassett!

MRS. BASS. This is a free country. I can speak my opinion. And I have *read up* on him. Go on, Rosemary. I wasn't criticizing your paper. (*But* ROSEMARY *sits down, hurt.*)

ALMA. Mrs. Bassett is only joking, Rosemary.

ROSE. No, I don't want to read it if she feels that strongly about it.

MRS. BASS. Not a bit, don't be silly! I just don't see why we should encourage the writings of people like that who have already gone into a drunkard's grave!

VARIOUS VOICES (*exclaiming*). Did he? I never heard that about him. Is that true?

ALMA. Mrs. Bassett is mistaken about that. Mrs. Bassett, you have confused Blake with someone else.

MRS. BASS. (*positively*). Oh, no, don't tell me. I've read up on him and know what I'm talking about. He traveled around with that Frenchman who took a shot at him and landed them both in jail! Brussels, Brussels!

ROG. (*gaily*). Brussels sprouts!

MRS. BASS. That's where it happened, fired a gun at him in a drunken stupor, and later one of them died of T.B. in the gutter! All right. I'm finished. I won't say anything more. Go on with your paper, Rosemary. There's nothing like contact with culture!

(ALMA *gets up.*)

ALMA. Before Rosemary reads her paper on Blake, I think it would be a good idea, since some of us aren't acquainted with his work, to preface the critical and biographical comments with a reading of one of his loveliest lyric poems.

ROSE. I'm not going to read anything at all! Not I!

ALMA. Then let me read it then. (*She takes a paper from* ROSEMARY.) . . . This is called "Love's Secret." (*She clears her throat and waits for a hush to settle.* ROSEMARY *looks stonily at the carpet.* MRS. BASSETT *looks at the ceiling.* JOHN *coughs.*)

> "Never seek to tell thy love,
>   Love that never told can be,
>   For the gentle wind doth move
>   Silently, invisibly.
>   I told my love, I told my love,
>   I told him all my heart.
>   Trembling, cold in ghastly fear
>   Did my love depart.
>
>   No sooner had he gone from me
>   Than a stranger passing by,
>   Silently, invisibly,
>   Took him with a sigh!"

(*There are various effusions and enthusiastic applause.*)

MRS. BASS. Honey, you're right. That isn't the man I meant. I was thinking about the one who wrote about "the bought red lips." Who
was it that wrote about the "bought red lips"?

(JOHN *has risen abruptly. He signals to* ALMA *and points to his watch.
He starts to leave.*)

ALMA (*springing up*). John!

JOHN (*calling back*). I have to call on a patient!

ALMA. Oh, John! (*She calls after him so sharply that the group is
startled into silence.*)

ROSE. (*interpreting this as a cue to read her paper*). "The poet, William
Blake, was born in 1757 . . ."

(ALMA *suddenly rushes to the door and goes out after* JOHN.)

ROG. Of poor but honest parents.

MRS. BASS. No supercilious comments out of you, sir. Go on, Rosemary.
(*She speaks loudly.*) She has such a beautiful *voice!*

(ALMA *returns inside, looking stunned.*)

ALMA. Please excuse the interruption, Rosemary. Dr. Buchanan had to
call on a patient.

MRS. BASS. (*archly*). I bet I know who the patient was. Ha-ha! That
Gonzales girl whose father owns Moon Lake Casino and
goes everywhere with two pistols strapped on his belt. Johnny
Buchanan will get himself shot in that crowd!

ALMA. Why, Mrs. Bassett, what gave you such an idea? I don't think
that John even knows that Gonzales girl!

MRS. BASS. He knows her, all right. In the Biblical sense of the word, if
you'll excuse me!

ALMA. No, I will not excuse you! A thing like that is inexcusable!

MRS. BASS. Have you fallen for him, Miss Alma? Miss Alma has fallen
for the young doctor! They tell me he has lots of new lady
patients!

ALMA. Stop it! (*She stamps her foot furiously and crushes the palm leaf
fan between her clenched hands.*) I won't have malicious talk
here! You drove him away from the meeting after I'd bragged so
much about how bright and interesting you all were! You put
your worst foot forward and simpered and chattered and carried

on like idiots, idiots! What am I saying? I—I—please excuse me! (*She rushes out the inner door.*)

ROG. I move that the meeting adjourn.

MRS. BASS. I second the motion.

ROSE. I don't understand. What happened?

MRS. BASS. Poor Miss Alma!

ROG. She hasn't been herself lately. . . .

(*They all go out. After a moment* ALMA *reenters with a tray of refreshments, looks about the deserted interior and bursts into hysterical laughter. The light dims out.*)

Scene Four

In the doctor's office.

JOHN *has a wound on his arm which he is bandaging with* ROSA's *assistance.*

JOHN. Hold that end. Wrap it around. Pull it tight. (*There is a knock at the door. They look up silently. The knock is repeated.*) I better answer before they wake up the old man. (*He goes out. A few moments later he returns followed by* ALMA. *He is rolling down his sleeve to conceal the bandage.* ALMA *stops short at the sight of* ROSA.) Wait outside, Rosa. In the hall. But be quiet! (ROSA *gives* ALMA *a challenging look as she withdraws from the lighted area.* JOHN *explains about* ROSA.) A little emergency case.

ALMA. The patient you had to call on. (JOHN *grins*) I want to see your father.

JOHN. He's asleep. Anything I can do?

ALMA. No, I think not. I have to see your father.

JOHN. It's two A.M., Miss Alma.

ALMA. I know, I'm afraid I'll have to see him.

JOHN. What's the trouble?

(*The voice of* JOHN's *father is heard, calling from above.*)

DR. BUCH. John! What's going on down there?

JOHN (*at the door*). Nothing much, Dad. Somebody got cut in a fight.

DR. BUCH. I'm coming down.

JOHN. No. Don't! Stay in bed! (*He rolls up his sleeve to show* ALMA *the bandaged wound. She gasps and touches her lips.*) I've patched him up, Dad. You sleep! (JOHN *executes the gesture of closing a door quietly on the hall.*)

ALMA. You've been in a brawl with that—woman! (JOHN *nods and rolls the sleeve back down.* ALMA *sinks faintly into a chair.*)

JOHN. Is your *doppelganger* cutting up again?

ALMA. It's your father I want to talk to.

JOHN. Be reasonable, Miss Alma. You're not that sick.

ALMA. Do you suppose I would come here at two o'clock in the morning if I were not seriously ill?

JOHN. It's no telling what you would do in a state of hysteria. (*He puts some powders in a glass of water.*) Toss that down, Miss Alma.

ALMA. What is it?

JOHN. A couple of little white tablets dissolved in water.

ALMA. What kind of tablets?

JOHN. You don't trust me?

ALMA. You are not in any condition to inspire much confidence. (JOHN *laughs softly. She looks at him helplessly for a moment, then bursts into tears. He draws up a chair beside hers and puts his arm gently about her shoulders.*) I seem to be all to pieces.

JOHN. The intellectual meeting wore you out.

ALMA. You made a quick escape from it.

JOHN. I don't like meetings. The only meetings I like are between two people.

ALMA. Such as between yourself and the lady outside?

JOHN. Or between you and me.

ALMA (*nervously*). Where is the . . . ?

JOHN. Oh. You've decided to take it?

ALMA. Yes, if you . . . (*She sips and chokes. He gives her his handkerchief. She touches her lips with it.*)

JOHN. Bitter?

ALMA. Awfully bitter.

JOHN. It'll make you sleepy.

ALMA. I do hope so. I wasn't able to sleep.

JOHN. And you felt panicky?

ALMA. Yes. I felt walled in.

JOHN. You started hearing your heart?

ALMA. Yes, like a drum!

JOHN. It scared you?

ALMA. It always does.

JOHN. Sure. I know.

ALMA. I don't think I will be able to get through the summer.

JOHN. You'll get through it, Miss Alma.

ALMA. How?

JOHN. One day will come after another and one night will come after another till sooner or later the summer will be all through with and then it will be fall, and you will be saying, I don't see how I'm going to get through the fall.

ALMA. Oh . . .

JOHN. That's right. Draw a deep breath!

ALMA. Ah . . .

JOHN. Good. Now draw another!

ALMA. Ah . . .

JOHN. Better? Better?

ALMA. A little.

JOHN. Soon you'll be much better. (*He takes out a big silver watch and holds her wrist.*) Did y' know that time is one side of the four-dimensional continuum we're caught in?

ALMA. What?

JOHN. Did you know space is curved, that it turns back onto itself like a soap-bubble, adrift in something that's even less than space. (*He laughs a little as he replaces the watch.*)

ROSA (*faintly from outside.*) Johnny!

JOHN (*looking up as if the cry came from there*). Did you know that the Magellanic clouds are a hundred thousand light years away from the earth? No? (ALMA *shakes her head slightly.*) That's something to think about when you worry over your heart, that little red fist that's got to keep knocking, knocking against the big black door.

ROSA (*more distinctly*). Johnny! (*She opens the door a crack.*)

JOHN. *Calla de la boca!* (*The door closes and he speaks to* ALMA.)

There's nothing wrong with your heart but a little functional disturbance, like I told you before. You want me to check it? (ALMA *nods mutely.* JOHN *picks up his stethoscope.*)

ALMA. The lady outside, I hate to keep her waiting.

JOHN. Rosa doesn't mind waiting. Unbutton your blouse.

ALMA. Unbutton . . . ?

JOHN. The blouse.

ALMA. Hadn't I better—better come back in the morning, when your father will be able to . . . ?

JOHN. Just as you please, Miss Alma. (*She hesitates. Then begins to un-button her blouse. Her fingers fumble.*) Fingers won't work?

ALMA (*breathlessly*). They are just as if frozen!

JOHN (*smiling*). Let me. (*He leans over her.*) Little pearl buttons . . .

ALMA. If your father discovered that woman in the house . . .

JOHN. He won't discover it.

ALMA. It would distress him terribly.

JOHN. Are you going to tell him?

ALMA. Certainly not! (*He laughs and applies the stethoscope to her chest.*)

JOHN. Breathe! . . . Out! . . . Breathe! . . . Out!

ALMA. Ah . . .

JOHN. Um-hmmm . . .

ALMA. What do you hear?

JOHN. Just a little voice saying—"Miss Alma is lonesome!" (*She rises and turns her back to him.*)

ALMA. If your idea of helping a patient is to ridicule and insult . . .

JOHN. My idea of helping you is to tell you the truth. (ALMA *looks up at him. He lifts her hand from the chair arm.*) What is this stone?

ALMA. A topaz.

JOHN. Beautiful stone. . . . Fingers still frozen?

ALMA. A little. (*He lifts her hand to his mouth and blows his breath on her fingers.*)

JOHN. I'm a poor excuse for a doctor, I'm much too selfish. But let's try to think about you.

ALMA. Why should you bother about me? (*She sits down.*)

JOHN. You know I like you and I think you're worth a lot of consideration.

ALMA. Why?

JOHN. Because you have a lot of feeling in your heart, and that's a rare thing. It makes you too easily hurt. Did I hurt you tonight?

ALMA. You hurt me when you sprang up from the sofa and rushed from the Rectory in such—in such mad haste that you left your coat behind you!

JOHN. I'll pick up the coat sometime.

ALMA. The time of our last conversation you said you would take me riding in your automobile sometime, but you forgot to.

JOHN. I didn't forget. Many's the time I've looked across at the Rectory and wondered if it would be worth trying, you and me. . . .

ALMA. You decided it wasn't?

JOHN. I went there tonight, but it wasn't you and me. . . . Fingers warm now?

ALMA. Those tablets work quickly. I'm already feeling drowsy. (*She leans back with her eyes nearly shut.*) I'm beginning to feel almost like a water lily. A water lily on a Chinese lagoon.

(*A heavy iron bell strikes three.*)

ROSA. *Johnny?*

(ALMA *starts to rise.*)

ALMA. I *must* go.

JOHN. I will call for you Saturday night at eight o'clock.

ALMA. What?

JOHN. I'll give you this box of tablets but watch how you take them. Never more than one or two at a time.

ALMA. Didn't you say something else a moment ago?

JOHN. I said I would call for you at the Rectory Saturday night.

ALMA. Oh . . .

JOHN. Is that all right?

(ALMA *nods speechlessly. She remains with the box resting in the palm of her hand as if not knowing it was there.* JOHN *gently closes her fingers on the box.*)

ALMA. Oh! (*She laughs faintly.*)

ROSA (*outside*). *Johnny!*

JOHN. Do you think you can find your way home, Miss Alma?

(ROSA *steps back into the office with a challenging look.* ALMA *catches her breath sharply and goes out the side door.*)

(JOHN *reaches above him and turns out the light. He crosses to* ROSA *by the anatomy chart and takes her roughly in his arms. The light lingers on the chart as the interior dims out.*)

Scene Five

In the Rectory.

Before the light comes up a soprano voice is heard singing "From the Land of the Sky Blue Waters."

As the curtain rises, ALMA *gets up from the piano.* MR. *and* MRS. WINE-MILLER, *also, are in the lighted room.*

ALMA. What time is it, Father? (*He goes on writing. She raises her voice.*) What time is it, Father?

MR. WINE. Five of eight. I'm working on my sermon.

ALMA. Why don't you work in the study?

MR. WINE. The study is suffocating. So don't disturb me.

ALMA. Would there be any chance of getting Mother upstairs if someone should call?

MR. WINE. Are you expecting a caller?

ALMA. Not expecting. There is just a chance of it.

MR. WINE. Whom are you expecting?

ALMA. I said I wasn't expecting anyone, that there was just a possibility . . .

MR. WINE. Mr. Doremus? I thought that this was his evening with his mother?

ALMA. Yes, it is his evening with his mother.

MR. WINE. Then who is coming here, Alma?

ALMA. Probably no one. Probably no one at all.

MR. WINE. This is all very mysterious.

MRS. WINE. That tall boy next door is coming to see her, that's who's coming to see her.

ALMA. If you will go upstairs, Mother, I'll call the drug store and ask them to deliver a pint of fresh peach ice cream.

MRS. WINE. I'll go upstairs when I'm ready—good and ready, and you can put that in your pipe and smoke it, Miss Winemiller! (*She lights a cigarette.* MR. WINEMILLER *turns slowly away with a profound sigh.*)

ALMA. I may as well tell you who might call, so that if he calls there will not be any unpleasantness about it. Young Dr. John Buchanan said he might call.

MRS. WINE. See!

MR. WINE. You can't be serious.

MRS. WINE. Didn't I tell you?

ALMA. Well, I am.

MR. WINE. That young man might come here?

ALMA. He asked me if he might and I said, yes, if he wished to. But it is now after eight so it doesn't look like he's coming.

MR. WINE. If he does come you will go upstairs to your room and I will receive him.

ALMA. If he does come I'll do no such thing, Father.

MR. WINE. You must be out of your mind.

ALMA. I'll receive him myself. You may retire to your study and Mother upstairs. But if he does come I'll receive him. I don't judge people by the tongues of gossips. I happen to know that he has been grossly misjudged and misrepresented by old busybodies who're envious of his youth and brilliance and charm.

MR. WINE. If you're not out of your senses, then I'm out of mine.

ALMA. I daresay we're all a bit peculiar, Father. . . .

MR. WINE. Well, I have had one almost insufferable cross to bear and perhaps I can bear another. But if you think I'm retiring into my study when this young man comes, probably with a whiskey bottle in one hand and a pair of dice in the other, you have another think coming. I'll sit right here and look at him until he leaves. (*He turns back to his sermon.*)

(*A whistle is heard outside the open door.*)

ALMA (*speaking quickly*). As a matter of fact I think I'll walk down to the drug store and call for the ice cream myself. (*She crosses to the door, snatching up her hat, gloves and veil.*)

MRS. WINE. There she goes to him! Ha-ha! (ALMA *rushes out.*)

MR. WINE. (*looking up*). Alma! Alma!

MRS. WINE. Ha-ha-haaaaa!

MR. WINE. Where is Alma?—Alma! (*He rushes through the door.*) Alma!

MRS. WINE. Ha-ha! Who got fooled? Who got fooled! Ha-haaaa! Insufferable cross yourself, you old—windbag. . . .

(*The curtain comes down.*)

Scene Six

A delicately suggested arbor, enclosing a table and two chairs. Over the table is suspended a torn paper lantern. This tiny set may be placed way downstage in front of the two interiors, which should be darkened out, as in the fountain scenes. In the background, as it is throughout the play, the angel of the fountain is dimly visible.

Music from the nearby pavilion of the Casino can be used when suitable for background.

JOHN's *voice is audible before he and* ALMA *enter.*

JOHN (*from the darkness*). I don't understand why we can't go in the Casino.

ALMA. You do understand. You're just pretending not to.

JOHN. Give me one reason.

ALMA (*coming into the arbor*). I am a minister's daughter.

JOHN. That's no reason. (*He follows her in. He wears a white linen suit, carrying the coat over his arm.*)

ALMA. You're a doctor. That's a better reason. You can't any more afford to be seen in such places than I can—less!

JOHN (*bellowing*). Dusty!

DUSTY (*from the darkness.*) Coming!

JOHN. What are you fishing in that pocketbook for?

ALMA. Nothing.

JOHN. What have you got there?

ALMA. Let go!

JOHN. Those sleeping tablets I gave you?

ALMA. Yes.

JOHN. What for?

ALMA. I need one.

JOHN. *Now?*

ALMA. Yes.

JOHN. Why?

ALMA. Why? Because I nearly died of heart failure in your automobile. What possessed you to drive like that? A demon?

(DUSTY *enters.*)

JOHN. A bottle of vino rosso.

DUST. Sure. (*He withdraws.*)

JOHN. Hey! Tell Shorty I want to hear the "Yellow Dog Blues."

ALMA. Please give me back my tablets.

JOHN. You want to turn into a dope-fiend taking this stuff? I said take one when you need one.

ALMA. I need one now.

JOHN. Sit down and stop swallowing air. (DUSTY *returns with a tall wine bottle and two thin-stemmed glasses.*) When does the cock-fight start?

DUST. 'Bout ten o'clock, Dr. Johnny.

ALMA. When does *what start?*

JOHN. They have a cock-fight here every Saturday night. Ever seen one?

ALMA. Perhaps in some earlier incarnation of mine.

JOHN. When you wore a brass ring in your nose?

ALMA. Then maybe I went to exhibitions like that.

JOHN. You're going to see one tonight.

ALMA. Oh, no, I'm not.

JOHN. That's what we came here for.

ALMA. I didn't think such exhibitions were legal.

JOHN. This is Moon Lake Casino where anything goes.

ALMA. And you're a frequent patron?

JOHN. I'd say constant.

ALMA. Then I'm afraid you must be serious about giving up your medical career.

JOHN. You bet I am! A doctor's life is walled in by sickness and misery and death.

ALMA. May I be so presumptuous as to inquire what you'll do when you quit?

JOHN. You may be so presumptuous as to inquire.

ALMA. But you won't tell me?

JOHN. I haven't made up my mind, but I've been thinking of South America lately.

ALMA (*sadly*). Oh . . .

JOHN. I've heard that cantinas are lots more fun than saloons, and senoritas are caviar among females.

ALMA. Dorothy Sykes' brother went to South America and was never heard of again. It takes a strong character to survive in the tropics. Otherwise it's a quagmire.

JOHN. You think my character's weak?

ALMA. I think you're confused, just awfully, awfully confused, as confused as I am—but in a different way. . . .

JOHN (*stretching out his legs*). Hee-haw, ho-hum.

ALMA. You used to say that as a child—to signify your disgust!

JOHN (*grinning*). Did I?

ALMA (*sharply*). Don't sit like that!

JOHN. Why not?

ALMA. You look so indolent and worthless.

JOHN. Maybe I am.

ALMA. If you must go somewhere, why don't you choose a place with a bracing climate?

JOHN. Parts of South America are as cool as a cucumber.

ALMA. I never knew that.

JOHN. Well, now you do.

ALMA. Those Latins all dream in the sun—and indulge their senses.

JOHN. Well, it's yet to be proven that anyone on this earth is crowned with so much glory as the one that uses his senses to get all he can in the way of—satisfaction.

ALMA. Self-satisfaction?

JOHN. What other kind is there?

ALMA. I will answer that question by asking you one. Have you ever seen, or looked at, a picture of a Gothic cathedral?

JOHN. Gothic cathedrals? What about them?

ALMA. How everything reaches up, how everything seems to be straining for something out of the reach of stone—or human—fingers? . . . The immense stained windows, the great arched doors that are five or six times the height of the tallest man—the vaulted ceiling and all the delicate spires—all reaching up to something beyond attainment! To me—well, that is the secret, the principle back of existence—the everlasting struggle and aspiration for more than our human limits have placed in our reach. . . . Who was that said that—oh, so beautiful thing!—"All of us are in the gutter, but some of us are looking at the stars!"

JOHN. Mr. Oscar Wilde.

ALMA (*somewhat taken aback*). Well, regardless of who said it, it's still true. Some of us are looking at the stars! (*She looks up raptly and places her hand over his.*)

JOHN. It's no fun holding hands with gloves on, Miss Alma.

ALMA. That's easily remedied. I'll just take the gloves off. (*Music is heard.*)

JOHN. Christ! (*He rises abruptly and lights a cigarette.*) Rosa Gonzales is dancing in the Casino.

ALMA. You *are* unhappy. You hate me for depriving you of the company inside. Well, you'll escape by and by. You'll drive me home and come back out by yourself. . . . I've only gone out with three young men at all seriously, and with each one there was a desert between us.

JOHN. What do you mean by a desert?

ALMA. Oh—wide, wide stretches of uninhabitable ground.

JOHN. Maybe you made it that way by being stand-offish.

ALMA. I made quite an effort with one or two of them.

JOHN. What kind of an effort?

ALMA. Oh, I—tried to entertain them the first few times. I would play and sing for them in the Rectory parlor.

JOHN. With your father in the next room and the door half open.

ALMA. I don't think that was the trouble.

JOHN. What was the trouble?

ALMA. I—I didn't have my heart in it. (*She laughs uncertainly.*) A silence would fall between us. You know, a silence?

JOHN. Yes, I know a silence.

ALMA. I'd try to talk and he'd try to talk and neither would make a go of it.

JOHN. Then silence would fall?

ALMA. Yes, the enormous silence.

JOHN. Then you'd go back to the piano?

ALMA. I'd twist my ring. Sometimes I twisted it so hard that the band cut my finger! He'd glance at his watch and we'd both know that the useless undertaking had come to a close. . . .

JOHN. You'd call it quits?

ALMA. Quits is—what we'd call it. . . . One or two times I was rather sorry about it.

JOHN. But you didn't have your heart in it?

ALMA. None of them really engaged my serious feelings.

JOHN. You do have serious feelings—of that kind?

ALMA. Doesn't everyone—sometimes?

JOHN. Some women are cold. Some women are what is called frigid.

ALMA. Do I give that impression?

JOHN. Under the surface you have a lot of excitement, a great deal more than any other woman I have met. So much that you have to carry these sleeping pills with you. The question is why? (*He leans over and lifts her veil.*)

ALMA. What are you doing that for?

JOHN. So that I won't get your veil in my mouth when I kiss you.

ALMA (*faintly*). Do you want to do that?

JOHN (*gently*). Miss Alma. (*He takes her arms and draws her to her feet.*) Oh, Miss Alma, Miss Alma! (*He kisses her.*)

ALMA (*in a low, shaken voice*). Not "Miss" any more. Just Alma.

JOHN (*grinning gently*). "Miss" suits you better, Miss Alma. (*He kisses her again. She hesitantly touches his shoulders, but not quite to push him away.* JOHN *speaks softly to her.*) Is it so hard to forget you're a preacher's daughter?

ALMA. There is no reason for me to forget that I am a minister's daughter. A minister's daughter's no different from any other young lady who tries to remember that she *is* a lady.

JOHN. This lady stuff, is that so important?

ALMA. Not to the sort of girls that you may be used to bringing to Moon Lake Casino. But suppose that some day . . . (*she crosses out of the arbor and faces away from him*) suppose that some day you—*married.* . . . The woman that you selected to be your wife, and not only your wife but—the mother of your children! (*She catches her breath at the thought.*) Wouldn't you want that woman to be a lady? Wouldn't you want her to be somebody that you, as her husband, and they as her precious children—could look up to with very deep respect? (*There is a pause.*)

JOHN. There's other things between a man and a woman besides respect. Did you know that, Miss Alma?

ALMA. Yes. . . .

JOHN. There's such a thing as intimate relations.

ALMA. Thank you for telling me that. So plainly.

JOHN. It may strike you as unpleasant. But it does have a good deal to do with—connubial felicity, as you'd call it. There are some women that just give in to a man as a sort of obligation imposed on them by the—cruelty of nature! (*He finishes his glass and pours another.*) And there you are.

ALMA. There *I* am?

JOHN. I'm speaking generally.

ALMA. Oh.

(*Hoarse shouts go up from the Casino.*)

JOHN. The cock-fight has started!

ALMA. Since you have spoken so plainly, I'll speak plainly, too. There are some women who turn a possibly beautiful thing into something no better than the coupling of beasts!—but love is what you bring to it.

JOHN. You're right about that.

ALMA. Some people bring just their bodies. But there are some people, there are some women, John—who can bring their hearts to it, also—who can bring their souls to it!

JOHN (*derisively*). Souls again, huh?—those Gothic cathedrals you dream of! (*There is another hoarse prolonged shout from the Casino.*) Your name is Alma and Alma is Spanish for soul. Some time I'd like to show you a chart of the human anatomy that I have in the office. It shows what our insides are like, and maybe you can show me where the beautiful soul is located on the chart. (*He drains the wine bottle.*) Let's go watch the cock-fight.

ALMA. No! (*There is a pause.*)

JOHN. I know something else we could do. There are rooms above the Casino. . . .

ALMA (*her back stiffening.*) I'd heard that you made suggestions like that to girls that you go out with, but I refused to believe such stories were true. What made you think I might be amenable to such a suggestion?

JOHN. I counted your pulse in the office the night you ran out because you weren't able to sleep.

ALMA. The night I was ill and went to your father for help.

JOHN. It was me you went to.

ALMA. It was your father, and you wouldn't call your father.

JOHN. Fingers frozen stiff when I . . .

ALMA (*rising*). Oh! I want to go home. But I won't go with you. I will go in a taxi! (*She wheels about hysterically.*) Boy! Boy! Call a taxi!

JOHN. I'll call one for you, Miss Alma.—Taxi! (*He goes out of the arbor.*)

ALMA (*wildly*). You're not a gentleman!

JOHN (*from the darkness*). Taxi!

ALMA. You're not a gentleman!

(*As he disappears she makes a sound in her throat like a hurt animal. The light fades out of the arbor and comes up more distinctly on the stone angel of the fountain.*)

PART TWO—A WINTER

Scene Seven

The sky and the southern constellations, almost imperceptibly moving with the earth's motion, appear on the great cyclorama.

The Rectory interior is lighted first, disclosing ALMA *and* ROGER DOREMUS *seated on the green plush sofa under the romantic landscape in its heavy gilt frame. On a tiny table beside them is a cut glass pitcher of lemonade with cherries and orange slices in it, like a little aquarium of tropical fish.* ROGER *is entertaining* ALMA *with a collection of photographs and postcards, mementoes of his mother's trip to the Orient. He is enthusiastic about them and describes them in phrases his mother must have assimilated from a sedulous study of literature provided by Cook's Tours.* ALMA *is less enthusiastic; she is preoccupied with the sounds of a wild party going on next door at the doctor's home. At present there is Mexican music with shouts and stamping.*

Only the immediate area of the sofa is clearly lighted; the fountain is faintly etched in light and the night sky walls the interior.

ROG. And this is Ceylon, The Pearl of the Orient!

ALMA. And who is this fat young lady?

ROG. That is Mother in a hunting costume.

ALMA. The hunting costume makes her figure seem bulky. What was your mother hunting?

ROG. (*gaily*). Heaven knows what she was hunting! But she found Papa.

ALMA. Oh, she met your father on this Oriental tour?

ROG. Ha-ha!—yes. . . . He was returning from India with dysentery and they met on the boat.

ALMA (*distastefully*). Oh . . .

ROG. And here she is on top of a ruined temple!

ALMA. How did she get up there?

ROG. Climbed up, I suppose.

ALMA. What an active woman.

ROG. Oh, yes, active—is no word for it! Here she is on an elephant's back in Burma.

ALMA. Ah!

ROG. You're looking at it upside down, Miss Alma!

ALMA. Deliberately—to tease you. (*The doorbell rings.*) Perhaps that's your mother coming to fetch you home.

ROG. It's only ten-fifteen. I never leave till ten-thirty.

(MRS. BASSETT *comes in.*)

ALMA. Mrs. Bassett!

MRS. BASS. I was just wondering who I could turn to when I saw the Rectory light and I thought to myself, Grace Bassett, you trot yourself right over there and talk to Mr. Winemiller!

ALMA. Father has retired.

MRS. BASS. Oh, what a pity. (*She sees* ROGER.) Hello, Roger! . . . I saw that fall your mother took this morning. I saw her come skipping out of the Delta Planters' Bank and I thought to myself, now isn't that remarkable, a woman of her age and weight so light on her feet? And just at that very moment—*down she went!* I swear to goodness I thought she had broken her hip! Was she bruised much?

ROG. Just shaken up, Mrs. Bassett.

MRS. BASS. Oh, how lucky! She certainly must be made out of India rubber! (*She turns to* ALMA.) Alma—Alma, if it is not too late for human intervention, your father's the one right person to call up old Dr. Buchanan at the fever clinic at Lyon and let him know!

ALMA. About—what?

MRS. BASS. You must be stone-deaf if you haven't noticed what's been going on next door since the old doctor left to fight the epidemic. One continual orgy! Well, not five minutes ago a friend of mine who works at the County Courthouse called to inform me that young Dr. John and Rosa Gonzales have taken a license out and are going to be married tomorrow!

ALMA. Are you—quite certain?

MRS. BASS. Certain? I'm always certain before I speak!

ALMA. Why would he—do such a thing?

MRS. BASS. August madness! They say it has something to do with the falling stars. Of course it might also have something to do with the fact that he lost two or three thousand dollars at the Casino which he can't pay except by giving himself to Gonzales' daughter. (*She turns to* ALMA.) Alma, what are you doing with that picture puzzle?

ALMA (*with a faint, hysterical laugh*). The pieces don't fit!

MRS. BASS. (*to* ROGER). I shouldn't have opened my mouth.

ALMA. Will both of you please go!

(ROGER *goes out.*)

MRS. BASS. I knew this was going to upset you. Good night, Alma. (*She leaves.* ALMA *suddenly springs up and seizes the telephone.*)

ALMA. Long distance. . . . Please get me the fever clinic at Lyon. . . . I want to speak to Dr. Buchanan.

(*The light in the Rectory dims out and light comes on in the doctor's office.* ROSA's *voice is heard calling.*)

ROSA. *Johnny!*

(*The offstage calling of* JOHN's *name is used throughout the play as a cue for theme music.* JOHN *enters the office interior. He is dressed, as always, in a white linen suit. His face has a look of satiety and confusion. He throws himself down in a swivel chair at the desk.*

(ROSA GONZALES *comes in. She is dressed in a flamenco costume and has been dancing. She crosses and stands before the anatomy chart and clicks her castanets to catch his attention, but he remains looking up at the roofless dark. She approaches him.*)

ROSA. You have blood on your face!

JOHN. You bit my ear.

ROSA. Ohhh . . . (*She approaches him with exaggerated concern.*)

JOHN. You never make love without scratching or biting or something. Whenever I leave you I have a little blood on me. Why is that?

ROSA. Because I know I can't hold you.

JOHN. I think you're doing a pretty good job of it. Better than anyone else. Tomorrow we leave here together and Father or somebody else can tell old Mrs. Arbuckle her eighty-five years are enough and she's got to go now on the wings of carcinoma. Dance, Rosa! (*Accordion music is heard. She performs a slow and joyless dance*

around his chair. John continues while she dances.) Tomorrow
we leave here together. We sail out of Galveston, don't we?

ROSA. You say it but I don't believe it.

JOHN. I have the tickets.

ROSA. Two pieces of paper that you can tear in two.

JOHN. We'll go all right, and live on fat remittances from your Papa!
Ha-ha!

ROSA. Ha-ha-ha!

JOHN. Not long ago the idea would have disgusted me, but not now.
(*He catches her by the wrist.*) Rosa! Rosa Gonzales! Did anyone
ever slide downhill as fast as I have this summer? Ha-ha! Like a
greased pig. And yet every evening I put on a clean white suit.
I have a dozen. Six in the closet and six in the wash. And there
isn't a sign of depravity in my face. And yet all summer I've sat
around here like *this,* remembering last night, anticipating the
next one! The trouble with me is, I should have been *castrated!*
(*He flings his wine glass at the anatomy chart. She stops dancing.*) Dance, Rosa! Why don't you dance? (ROSA *shakes her head
dumbly.*) What is the matter, Rosa? Why don't you go on dancing? (*The accordion continues; he thrusts her arm savagely over
her head in the flamenco position.*)

ROSA (*suddenly weeping*). *I can't dance any more!* (*She throws herself
to the floor, pressing her weeping face to his knees. The voice of
her father is heard, bellowing, in the next room.*)

GONZ. *The sky is the limit!*

(JOHN *is sobered.*)

JOHN. Why does your father want me for a son-in-law?

ROSA (*sobbing*). *I want you—I, I want you!*

JOHN (*raising her from the floor*). Why do you?

ROSA (*clinging to him*). Maybe because—I was born in Piedras Negras,
and grew up in a one room house with a dirt floor, and all of us
had to sleep in that one room, five Mexicans and three geese and
a little game-cock named Pepe! Ha-ha! (*She laughs hysterically.*)
Pepe was a good fighter! That's how Papa began to make money,
winning bets on Pepe! Ha-ha! We all slept in the one room. And
in the night, I would hear the love-making. Papa would grunt

like a pig to show his passion. I thought to myself, how dirty it was, love-making, and how dirty it was to be Mexicans and all have to sleep in one room with a dirt floor and not smell good because there was not any bathtub! (*The accordion continues.*)

JOHN. What has that got to do with . . . ?

ROSA. Me wanting you? You're tall! You smell good! And, oh, I'm so glad that you never grunt like a pig to show your passion! (*She embraces him convulsively.*) Ah, but *quien sabe!* Something might happen tonight, and I'll wind up with some dark little friend of Papa's.

GONZ. (*imperiously*). Rosa! Rosa!

ROSA. *Si, si,* Papa, *aqui estoy!*

GONZ. (*entering unsteadily*). The gold beads . . . (*He fingers a necklace of gold beads that* ROSA *is wearing.*) Johnny . . . (*He staggers up to* JOHN *and catches him in a drunken embrace.*) Listen! When my girl Rosa was little she see a string a gold bead and she want those gold bead so bad that she cry all night for it. I don' have money to buy a string of gold bead so next day I go for a ride up to Eagle Pass and I walk in a dry good store and I say to the man: "Please give me a string a gold bead." He say: "Show me the money!" And I reach down to my belt and I pull out— not the money—but this! (*He pulls out a revolver.*) Now—now I have money, but I still have this! (*Laughing.*) She got the gold bead. Anything that she want I get for her with this (*he pulls out a roll of bills*) or this! (*He waves the revolver.*)

JOHN (*pushing* GONZALES *away*). Keep your stinking breath out of my face, Gonzales!

ROSA. *Dejalo, dejalo,* Papa!

GONZ. (*moving unsteadily to the couch, with* ROSA *supporting him*). *Le doy la tierra y si la tierra no basta—le doy el cielo!* (*He collapses onto the couch.*) The sky is the limit!

ROSA (*to* JOHN). Let him stay there. Come on back to the party.

(ROSA *leaves the room.* JOHN *goes over to the window facing the Rectory and looks across. The light comes up in the Rectory living room as* ALMA *enters, dressed in a robe. She goes to the window and looks across at the doctor's house. As* ALMA *and* JOHN *stand at the*

*windows looking toward each other through the darkness music
is heard. Slowly, as if drawn by the music,* JOHN *walks out of his
house and crosses over to the Rectory.* ALMA *remains motionless at
the window until* JOHN *enters the room, behind her. The music
dies away and there is a murmur of wind. She slowly turns to face*
JOHN.)

JOHN. I took the open door for an invitation. The Gulf wind is blowing
tonight . . . cools things off a little. But my head's on fire. . . .
(ALMA *says nothing.* JOHN *moves a few steps toward her.*) The
silence? (ALMA *sinks onto the love seat, closing her eyes.*) Yes, the
enormous silence. (*He goes over to her.*) I will go in a minute,
but first I want you to put your hands on my face. . . . (*He
crouches beside her.*) Eternity and Miss Alma have such cool
hands. (*He buries his face in her lap. The attitude suggests a
stone* Pieta. ALMA's *eyes remain closed.*)

(*On the other side of the stage* DR. BUCHANAN *enters his house and the
light builds a little as he looks around in the door of his office.
The love theme music fades out and the Mexican music comes up
strongly, with a definitely ominous quality, as* ROSA *enters the office from the other side.*)

ROSA. Johnny! (*She catches sight of* DR. BUCHANAN *and checks herself in
surprise.*) Oh! I thought you were Johnny! . . . But you are
Johnny's father. . . . I'm Rosa Gonzales!

DR. BUCH. I know who you are. What's going on in my house?

ROSA (*nervously*). John's giving a party because we're leaving tomorrow.
(*Defiantly.*) Yes! Together! I hope you like the idea, but if you
don't, it don't matter, because *we* like the idea and my father likes
the idea.

GONZ. (*drunkenly, sitting up on the couch*). The sky is the limit!

(DR. BUCHANAN *slowly raises his silver-headed cane in a threatening gesture.*)

DR. BUCH. Get your—swine out of—my house! (*He strikes* GONZALES
with his cane.)

GONZ. (*staggering up from the couch in pain and surprise*). Aieeee!

ROSA (*breathlessly, backing against the chart of anatomy*). No! No,
Papa!

DR. BUCH. (*striking at the chest of the bull-like man with his cane*). Get your swine out, I said! Get them out of my house!

(*He repeats the blow. The drunken Mexican roars with pain and surprise. He backs up and reaches under his coat.*)

ROSA (*wildly and despairingly*). No, no, no, no, no, no!

(*She covers her face against the chart of anatomy. A revolver is fired. There is a burst of light. The cane drops. The music stops short. Everything dims out but a spot of light on* ROSA *standing against the chart of anatomy with closed eyes and her face twisted like that of a tragic mask.*)

ROSA (*senselessly*). Aaaaaahhhhhh . . . Aaaaaahhhhhh . . .

(*The theme music is started faintly and light disappears from everything but the wings of the stone angel.*)

Scene Eight

The doctor's office.

The stone angel is dimly visible above.

JOHN *is seated in a hunched position at the table.* ALMA *enters with a coffee tray. The sounds of a prayer come through the inner door.*

JOHN. What is that mumbo-jumbo your father is spouting in there?

ALMA. A prayer.

JOHN. Tell him to quit. We don't want that wornout magic.

ALMA. You may not want it, but it's not a question of what you want any more. I've made you some coffee.

JOHN. I don't want any.

ALMA. Lean back and let me wash your face off, John. (*She presses a towel to the red marks on his face.*) It's such a fine face, a fine and sensitive face, a face that has power in it that shouldn't be wasted.

JOHN. Never mind that. (*He pushes her hand away.*)

ALMA. You have to go in to see him.

JOHN. I couldn't. He wouldn't want me.

ALMA. This happened because of his devotion to you.

JOHN. It happened because some meddlesome Mattie called him back here tonight. Who was it did that?

ALMA. I did.

JOHN. It *was* you then!

ALMA. I phoned him at the fever clinic in Lyon as soon as I learned what you were planning to do. I wired him to come here and stop it.

JOHN. You brought him here to be shot.

ALMA. You can't put the blame on anything but your weakness.

JOHN. *You* call me weak?

ALMA. Sometimes it takes a tragedy like this to make a weak person strong.

JOHN. You—white-blooded spinster! You so right people, pious pompous mumblers, preachers and preacher's daughter, all muffled up in a lot of wornout magic! And I was supposed to minister to your neurosis, give you tablets for sleeping and tonics to give you the strength to go on mumbling your wornout mumbo-jumbo!

ALMA. Call me whatever you want, but don't let your father hear your drunken shouting. (*She tries to break away from him.*)

JOHN. Stay here! I want you to look at something. (*He turns her about.*) This chart of anatomy, look!

ALMA. I've seen it before. (*She turns away.*)

JOHN. You've never dared to look at it.

ALMA. Why should I?

JOHN. You're scared to.

ALMA. You must be out of your senses.

JOHN. You talk about weakness but can't even look at a picture of human insides.

ALMA. They're not important.

JOHN. That's your mistake. You think you're stuffed with rose-leaves. Turn around and look at it, it may do you good!

ALMA. How can you behave like this with your father dying and you so . . .

JOHN. Hold still!

ALMA. . . . so much to blame for it!

JOHN. No more than you are!

ALMA. At least for this little while . . .

JOHN. Look here!

ALMA. . . . you could feel some shame!

JOHN (*with crazy, grinning intensity*). Now listen here to the anatomy lecture! This upper story's the brain which is hungry for something called truth and doesn't get much but keeps on feeling hungry! This middle's the belly which is hungry for food. This part down here is the sex which is hungry for love because it is sometimes lonesome. I've fed all three, as much of all three as I could or as much as I wanted— You've fed none—nothing. Well—maybe your belly a little—watery subsistence— But love or truth, nothing but—nothing but hand-me-down notions!—attitudes!—poses. (*He releases her.*) Now you can go. The anatomy lecture is over.

ALMA. So that is your high conception of human desires. What you have here is not the anatomy of a beast, but a man. And I—I reject your opinion of where love is, and the kind of truth you believe the brain to be seeking!—There is something not shown on the chart.

JOHN. You mean the part that Alma is Spanish for, do you?

ALMA. Yes, that's not shown on the anatomy chart! But it's there, just the same, yes, there! Somewhere, not seen, but there. And it's *that* that I loved you with—that! Not what you mention!—Yes, did love you with, John, did nearly *die* of when you hurt me! (*He turns slowly to her and speaks gently.*)

JOHN. I wouldn't have made love to you.

ALMA (*uncomprehendingly*). What?

JOHN. The night at the Casino—I wouldn't have made love to you. Even if you had consented to go upstairs. I couldn't have made love to you. (*She stares at him as if anticipating some unbearable hurt.*) Yes, yes! Isn't that funny? I'm more afraid of your soul than you're afraid of my body. You'd have been as safe as the angel of the fountain—because I wouldn't feel *decent* enough to touch you. . . .

(MR. WINEMILLER *comes in.*)

MR. WINE. He's resting more easily now.

ALMA. Oh . . . (*She nods her head.* JOHN *reaches for his coffee cup.*) It's cold. I'll heat it.

JOHN. It's all right.

MR. WINE. Alma, Dr. John wants you.

ALMA. I . . .

MR. WINE. He asked if you would sing for him.

ALMA. I—couldn't—now!

JOHN. Go in and sing to him, Miss Alma!

(MR. WINEMILLER *withdraws through the outer door.* ALMA *looks back at* JOHN *hunched over the coffee cup. He doesn't return her look. She passes into the blurred orange space beyond the inner door, leaving it slightly open. After a few minutes her voice rises softly within, singing.* JOHN *suddenly rises. He crosses to the door, shoves it slowly open and enters.*)

JOHN (*softly and with deep tenderness*). Father?

(*The light dims out in the house, but lingers on the stone angel.*)

Scene Nine

The cyclorama is the faint blue of a late afternoon in autumn. There is band-music—a Sousa march, in the distance. As it grows somewhat louder, ALMA *enters the Rectory interior in a dressing gown and with her hair hanging loose. She looks as if she had been through a long illness, the intensity drained, her pale face listless. She crosses to the window frame but the parade is not in sight so she returns weakly to the sofa and sits down closing her eyes with exhaustion.*

The REV. *and* MRS. WINEMILLER *enter the outer door frame of the Rectory, a grotesque-looking couple.* MRS. WINEMILLER *has on her plumed hat, at a rakish angle, and a brilliant scarf about her throat. Her face wears a roguish smile that suggests a musical comedy pirate. One hand holds the minister's arm and with the other she is holding an ice cream cone.*

MR. WINE. Now you may let go of my arm, if you please! She was on her worst behavior. Stopped in front of the White Star Pharmacy on Front Street and stood there like a mule; wouldn't budge till I bought her an ice cream cone. I had it wrapped in tissue paper because she had promised me that she wouldn't eat it till we got home. The moment I gave it to her she tore off the paper and walked home licking it every step of the way!—just—just to humiliate me! (MRS. WINEMILLER *offers him the half-eaten cone, saying "Lick?"*) No, thank you!

ALMA. Now, now, children.

(MR. WINEMILLER'S *irritation shifts to* ALMA.)

MR. WINE. Alma! Why don't you get dressed? It hurts me to see you sitting around like this, day in, day out, like an invalid when there is nothing particularly wrong with you. I can't read your mind. You may have had some kind of disappointment, but you must not make it an excuse for acting as if the world had come to an end.

ALMA. I have made the beds and washed the breakfast dishes and phoned the market and sent the laundry out and peeled the potatoes and shelled the peas and set the table for lunch. What more do you want?

MR. WINE. (*sharply*). I want you to either get dressed or stay in your room. (ALMA *rises indifferently, then her father speaks suddenly.*) At night you get dressed. Don't you? Yes, I heard you slipping out of the house at two in the morning. And that was not the first time.

ALMA. I don't sleep well. Sometimes I have to get up and walk for a while before I am able to sleep.

MR. WINE. What am I going to tell people who ask about you?

ALMA. Tell them I've changed and you're waiting to see in what way.

(*The band music becomes a little louder.*)

MR. WINE. Are you going to stay like this indefinitely?

ALMA. Not indefinitely, but you may wish that I had.

MR. WINE. Stop twisting that ring! Whenever I look at you you're twisting that ring. Give me that ring! I'm going to take that ring off your finger! (*He catches her wrist. She breaks roughly away from him.*)

MRS. WINE. (*joyfully*). Fight! Fight!

MR. WINE. Oh, I give up!

ALMA. That's better. (*She suddenly crosses to the window as the band music gets louder.*) Is there a parade in town?

MRS. WINE. Ha-ha—yes! They met him at the station with a great big silver loving-cup!

ALMA. Who? Who did they . . . ?

MRS. WINE. That boy next door, the one you watched all the time!

ALMA. Is that true, Father?

MR. WINE. (*unfolding his newspaper*). Haven't you looked at the papers?

ALMA. No, not lately.

MR. WINE. (*wiping his eyeglasses*). These people are grasshoppers, just as likely to jump one way as another. He's finished the work his father started, stamped out the fever and gotten all of the glory. Well, that's how it is in this world. Years of devotion and sacrifice are overlooked an' forgotten while someone young an' lucky walks off with the honors!

(ALMA *has crossed slowly to the window. The sun brightens and falls in a shaft through the frame.*)

ALMA (*suddenly crying out*). There he is! (*She staggers away from the window. There is a roll of drums and then silence.* ALMA *now speaks faintly.*) What . . . happened? Something . . . struck me! (MR. WINEMILLER *catches her arm to support her.*)

MR. WINE. Alma . . . I'll call a doctor.

ALMA. No, no, don't. Don't call anybody to help me. I want to die! (*She collapses on the sofa.*)

The band strikes up again and recedes down the street. The Rectory interior dims out. Then the light is brought up in the doctor's office. JOHN *enters, with his loving-cup. He is sprucely dressed and his whole manner suggests a new-found responsibility. While he is setting the award on the table, removing his coat and starched collar,* NELLIE EWELL *appears in the door behind him. She stands by the anatomy chart and watches him until he discovers her presence.* NELLIE *has abruptly grown up, and wears very adult clothes, but has lost none of her childish impudence and brightness.* JOHN *gives a startled whistle as he sees her.* NELLIE *giggles.*)

JOHN. High heels, feathers . . . and paint!

NELL. Not paint!

JOHN. Natural color?

NELL. Excitement.

JOHN. Over what?

NELL. Everything! You! You here! Didn't you see me at the depot? I shouted and waved my arm off! I'm home for Thanksgiving.

JOHN. From where?

NELL. Sophie Newcombe's. (*He remains staring at her, unbelieving. At last she draws a book from under her arm.*) Here is that nasty book you gave me last summer when I was pretending such ignorance of things!

JOHN. Only pretending?

NELL. Yes. (*He ignores the book. She tosses it on the table.*) . . . Well? (JOHN *laughs uneasily and sits on the table.*) Shall I go now, or will you look at my tongue? (*She crosses to him, sticking out her tongue.*)

JOHN. Red as a berry!

NELL. Peppermint drops! Will you have one? (*She holds out a sack.*)

JOHN. Thanks. (NELLIE *giggles as he takes one.*) What's the joke, Nellie?

NELL. They make your mouth so sweet!

JOHN. So?

NELL. I always take one when I hope to be kissed.

JOHN (*after a pause*). Suppose I took you up on that?

NELL. I'm not scared. Are you?

(*He gives her a quick kiss. She clings to him, raising her hand to press his head against her own. He breaks free after a moment and turns the light back on.*)

JOHN (*considerably impressed*). Where did you learn such tricks?

NELL. I've been away to school. But they didn't teach me to love.

JOHN. Who are you to be using that long word?

NELL. That isn't a long word!

JOHN. No? (*He turns away from her.*) Run along Nellie before we get into trouble.

NELL. Who's afraid of trouble, you or me?

JOHN. I am. Run along! Hear me?

NELL. Oh, I'll go. But I'll be back for Christmas! (*She laughs and runs out. He whistles and wipes his forehead with a handkerchief.*)

Scene Ten

An afternoon in December. At the fountain in the park. It is very windy.

ALMA *enters. She seems to move with an effort against the wind. She sinks down on the bench.*

A widow with a flowing black veil passes across the stage and pauses by ALMA's *bench. It is* MRS. BASSETT.

MRS. BASS. Hello, Alma.

ALMA. Good afternoon, Mrs. Bassett.

MRS. BASS. Such wind, such wind!

ALMA. Yes, it nearly swept me off my feet. I had to sit down to catch my breath for a moment.

MRS. BASS. I wouldn't sit too long if I were you.

ALMA. No, not long.

MRS. BASS. It's good to see you out again after your illness.

ALMA. Thank you.

MRS. BASS. Our poor little group broke up after you dropped out.

ALMA (*insincerely*). What a pity.

MRS. BASS. You should have come to the last meeting.

ALMA. Why, what happened?

MRS. BASS. Vernon read his verse play!

ALMA. Ah, how was it received?

MRS. BASS. Maliciously, spitefully and vindictively torn to pieces, the way children tear the wings of butterflies. I think next spring we might reorganize. (*She throws up her black-gloved hands in a deploring gesture.*)

(NELLIE EWELL *appears. She is dressed very fashionably and carrying a fancy basket of Christmas packages.*)

NELL. Miss Alma!

MRS. BASS. (*rushing off*). Goodbye!

NELL. Oh, there you are!

ALMA. Why Nellie . . . Nellie Ewell!

NELL. I was by the Rectory. Just popped in for a second; the holidays are so short that every minute is precious. They told me you'd gone to the park.

ALMA. This is the first walk I've taken in quite a while.

NELL. You've been ill!

ALMA. Not ill, just not very well. How you've grown up, Nellie.

NELL. It's just my clothes. Since I went off to Sophie Newcombe I've picked out my own clothes, Miss Alma. When Mother had jurisdiction over my wardrobe, she tried to keep me looking like a child!

ALMA. Your voice is grown-up, too.

NELL. They're teaching me diction, Miss Alma. I'm learning to talk like you, long A's and everything, such as "cahn't" and "bahth" and "lahf" instead of "laugh." Yesterday I slipped. I said I "lahfed and lahfed till I nearly died laughing." Johnny was so amused at me!

ALMA. Johnny?

NELL. Your nextdoor neighbor!

ALMA. Oh! I'm sure it must be a very fashionable school.

NELL. Oh yes, they're preparing us to be young ladies in society. What a pity there's no society here to be a young lady in . . . at least not for me, with Mother's reputation!

ALMA. You'll find other fields to conquer.

NELL. What's this I hear about *you*?

ALMA. I have no idea, Nellie.

NELL. That you've quit teaching singing and gone into retirement.

ALMA. Naturally I had to stop teaching while I was ill and as for retiring from the world . . . it's more a case of the world retiring from me.

NELL. I know somebody whose feelings you've hurt badly.

ALMA. Why, who could that be, Nellie?

NELL. Somebody who regards you as an angel!

ALMA. I can't think who might hold me in such esteem.

NELL. Somebody who says that you refused to see him.

ALMA. I saw nobody. For several months. The long summer wore me out so.

NELL. Well, anyhow, I'm going to give you your present. (*She hands her a small package from the basket.*)

ALMA. Nellie, you shouldn't have given me anything.

NELL. I'd like to know why not!

ALMA. I didn't expect it.

NELL. After the trouble you took with my horrible voice?

ALMA. It's very sweet of you, Nellie.

NELL. Open it!

ALMA. Now?

NELL. Why, sure.

ALMA. It's so prettily wrapped I hate to undo it.

NELL. I love to wrap presents and since it was for you, I did a specially dainty job of it.

ALMA (*winding the ribbon about her fingers*). I'm going to save this ribbon. I'm going to keep this lovely paper too, with the silver stars on it. And the sprig of holly . . .

NELL. Let me pin it on your jacket, Alma.

ALMA. Yes, do. I hardly realized that Christmas was coming. . . . (*She unfolds the paper, revealing a lace handkerchief and a card.*) What an exquisite handkerchief.

NELL. I hate to give people handkerchiefs, it's so unimaginative.

ALMA. I love to get them.

NELL. It comes from Maison Blanche!

ALMA. Oh, does it really?

NELL. Smell it!

ALMA. Sachet *Roses!* Well, I'm just more touched and pleased than I can possibly tell you!

NELL. The card!

ALMA. Card?

NELL. You dropped it. (*She snatches up the card and hands it to* ALMA.)

ALMA. Oh, how clumsy of me! Thank you, Nellie. "Joyeux Noel . . . to Alma . . . from Nellie and . . . (*she looks up slowly*) *John?*"

NELL. He helped me wrap presents last night and when we came to

yours we started talking about you. Your ears must have burned!
(*The wind blows loudly.* ALMA *bends stiffly forward.*)

ALMA. You mean you—spoke well of me?

NELL. "Well of"! We raved, simply raved! Oh, he told me the influence
you'd had on him!

ALMA. Influence?

NELL. He told me about the wonderful talks he'd had with you last summer when he was so mixed up and how you inspired him and you
more than anyone else was responsible for his pulling himself together, after his father was killed, and he told me about . . .
(ALMA *rises stiffly from the bench.*) Where are you going, Miss
Alma?

ALMA. To drink at the fountain.

NELL. He told me about how you came in the house that night like an
angel of mercy!

ALMA (*laughing harshly by the fountain*). This is the only angel in
Glorious Hill. (*She bends to drink.*) Her body is stone and her
blood is mineral water.

(*The wind is louder.*)

NELL. How penetrating the wind is!

ALMA. I'm going home, Nellie. You run along and deliver your presents
now. . . .

(*She starts away.*)

NELL. But wait till I've told you the wonderfullest thing I . . .

ALMA. I'm going home now. Goodbye.

NELL. Oh— Goodbye, Miss Alma.

(*She snatches up her festive basket and rushes in the other direction
with a shrill giggle as the wind pulls at her skirts. The lights dim
out.*)

Scene Eleven

An hour later. In JOHN's *office.*

*The interior is framed by the traceries of Victorian architecture and
there is one irregular section of wall supporting the anatomy
chart. Otherwise the stage is open to the cyclorama.*

*In the background mellow golden light touches the vane of a steeple
(a gilded weathercock). Also the wings of the stone angel. A singing wind rises and falls throughout scene.*

JOHN *is seated at a white enameled table examining a slide through a
microscope.*

A bell tolls the hour of five as ALMA *comes hesitantly in. She wears a
russet suit and a matching hat with a plume. The light changes,
the sun disappearing behind a cloud, fading from the steeple and
the stone angel till the bell stops tolling. Then it brightens again.*

ALMA. No greetings? No greetings at all?

JOHN. Hello, Miss Alma.

ALMA (*speaking with animation to control her panic*). How white it is
here, such glacial brilliance! (*She covers her eyes, laughing.*)

JOHN. New equipment.

ALMA. Everything new but the chart.

JOHN. The human anatomy's always the same old thing.

ALMA. And such a tiresome one! I've been plagued with sore throats.

JOHN. Everyone has here lately. These Southern homes are all improp-
erly heated. Open grates aren't enough.

ALMA. They burn the front of you while your back is freezing!

JOHN. Then you go into another room and get chilled off.

ALMA. Yes, yes, chilled to the bone.

JOHN. But it never gets quite cold enough to convince the damn fools
that a furnace is necessary so they go on building without them.
(*There is the sound of wind.*)

ALMA. Such a strange afternoon.

JOHN. Is it? I haven't been out.

ALMA. The Gulf wind is blowing big, white—what do they call them?
cumulus?—clouds over! Ha-ha! It seemed determined to take the
plume off my hat, like that fox terrier we had once, named Jacob,
snatched the plume off a hat and dashed around and around the
back yard with it like a trophy!

JOHN. I remember Jacob. What happened to him?

ALMA. Oh, Jacob. Jacob was such a mischievous thief. We had to send

him out to some friends in the country. Yes, he ended his days as
—a country squire! The tales of his exploits . . .

JOHN. Sit down, Miss Alma.

ALMA. If I'm disturbing you . . . ?

JOHN. No—I called the Rectory when I heard you were sick. Your
father told me you wouldn't see a doctor.

ALMA. I needed a rest, that was all. . . . You were out of town
mostly. . . .

JOHN. I was mostly in Lyon, finishing up Dad's work in the fever clinic.

ALMA. Covering yourself with sudden glory!

JOHN. Redeeming myself with good works.

ALMA. It's rather late to tell you how happy I am, and also how proud.
I almost feel as your father might have felt—if . . . And—are
you—happy now, John?

JOHN (*uncomfortably, not looking at her*). I've settled with life on fairly
acceptable terms. Isn't that all a reasonable person can ask for?

ALMA. He can ask for much more than that. He can ask for the coming
true of his most improbable dreams.

JOHN. It's best not to ask for too much.

ALMA. I disagree with you. I say, ask for all, but be prepared to get nothing! (*She springs up and crosses to the window. She continues.*)
No, I haven't been well. I've thought many times of something
you told me last summer, that I have a *doppelganger*. I looked
that up and I found that it means another person inside me, another self, and I don't know whether to thank you or not for making me conscious of it!—I haven't been well. . . . For a while I
thought I was dying, that that was the change that was coming.

JOHN. When did you have that feeling?

ALMA. August. September. But now the Gulf wind has blown that feeling away like a cloud of smoke, and I know now I'm not dying,
that it isn't going to turn out to be that simple. . . .

JOHN. Have you been anxious about your heart again? (*He retreats to
a professional manner and takes out a silver watch, putting his
fingers on her wrist.*)

ALMA. And now the stethoscope? (*He removes the stethoscope from the
table and starts to loosen her jacket. She looks down at his ben*

*head. Slowly, involuntarily, her gloved hands lift and descend on
the crown of his head. He gets up awkwardly. She suddenly leans
toward him and presses her mouth to his.)* Why don't you say
something? Has the cat got your tongue?

JOHN. Miss Alma, what can I say?

ALMA. You've gone back to calling me "Miss Alma" again.

JOHN. We never really got past that point with each other.

ALMA. Oh, yes we did. We were so close that we almost breathed together!

JOHN (*with embarrassment*). I didn't know that.

ALMA. No? Well, I did, I knew it. (*Her hand touches his face tenderly.*)
You shave more carefully now? You don't have those little razor
cuts on your chin that you dusted with gardenia talcum. . . .

JOHN. I shave more carefully now.

ALMA. So that explains it! (*Her fingers remain on his face, moving
gently up and down it like a blind person reading Braille. He is
intensely embarrassed and gently removes her hands from him.*)
Is it—impossible now?

JOHN. I don't think I know what you mean.

ALMA. You know what I mean, all right! So be honest with me. One
time I said "no" to something. You may remember the time, and
all that demented howling from the cock-fight? But now I have
changed my mind, or the girl who said "no," she doesn't exist any
more, she died last summer—suffocated in smoke from something
on fire inside her. No, she doesn't live now, but she left me her
ring— You see? This one you admired, the topaz ring set in
pearls. . . . And she said to me when she slipped this ring on my
finger—"Remember I died empty-handed, and so make sure that
your hands have *something in them!*" (*She drops her gloves. She
clasps his head again in her hands.*) I said, "But what about
pride?"—She said, "Forget about pride whenever it stands between you and what you must have!" (*He takes hold of her
wrists.*) And then I said, "But what if he doesn't want me?" I
don't know what she said then. I'm not sure whether she said
anything or not—her lips stopped moving—yes, I think she
stopped breathing! (*He gently removes her craving hands from*

his face.) No? (*He shakes his head in dumb suffering.*) Then the answer is "no"!

JOHN (*forcing himself to speak*). I have a respect for the truth, and I have a respect for you—so I'd better speak honestly if you want me to speak. (ALMA *nods slightly.*) You've won the argument that we had between us.

ALMA. What—argument?

JOHN. The one about the chart.

ALMA. Oh—the chart! (*She turns from him and wanders across to the chart. She gazes up at it with closed eyes, and her hands clasped in front of her.*)

JOHN. It shows that we're not a package of rose leaves, that every interior inch of us is taken up with something ugly and functional and no room seems to be left for anything else in there.

ALMA. No . . .

JOHN. But I've come around to your way of thinking, that something else is in there, an immaterial something—as thin as smoke—which all of those ugly machines combine to produce and that's their whole reason for being. It can't be seen so it can't be shown on the chart. But it's there, just the same, and knowing it's there—why, then the whole thing—this—this unfathomable experience of ours—takes on a new value, like some—some wildly romantic work in a laboratory! Don't you see?

(*The wind comes up very loud, almost like a choir of voices. Both of them turn slightly,* ALMA *raising a hand to her plumed head as if she were outdoors.*)

ALMA. Yes, I see! Now that you no longer want it to be otherwise you're willing to believe that a spiritual bond can exist between us two!

JOHN. Can't you believe that I am sincere about it?

ALMA. Maybe you are. But I don't want to be talked to like some incurably sick patient you have to comfort. (*A harsh and strong note comes into her voice.*) Oh, I suppose I am sick, one of those weak and divided people who slip like shadows among you solid strong ones. But sometimes, out of necessity, we shadowy people take on a strength of our own. I have that now. You needn't try to deceive me.

JOHN. I wasn't.

ALMA. You needn't try to comfort me. I haven't come here on any but equal terms. You said, let's talk truthfully. Well, let's do! Unsparingly, truthfully, even shamelessly, then! It's no longer a secret that I love you. It never was. I loved you as long ago as the time I asked you to read the stone angel's name with your fingers. Yes, I remember the long afternoons of our childhood, when I had to stay indoors to practice my music—and heard your playmates calling you, "Johnny, Johnny!" How it went through me, just to hear your name called! And how I—rushed to the window to watch you jump the porch railing! I stood at a distance, halfway down the block, only to keep in sight of your torn red sweater, racing about the vacant lot you played in. Yes, it had begun that early, this affliction of love, and has never let go of me since, but kept on growing. I've lived next door to you all the days of my life, a weak and divided person who stood in adoring awe of your singleness, of your strength. And that is my story! Now I wish *you* would tell *me*—why didn't it happen between us? Why did I fail? Why did you come almost close enough—and no closer?

JOHN. Whenever we've gotten together, the three or four times that we have . . .

ALMA. As few as that?

JOHN. It's only been three or four times that we've come face to face. And each of those times—we seemed to be trying to find something in each other without knowing what it was that we wanted to find. It wasn't a body hunger although—I acted as if I thought it might be the night I wasn't a gentleman—at the Casino—it wasn't the physical you that I really wanted!

ALMA. I know, you've already . . .

JOHN. You didn't have that to give me.

ALMA. Not at that time.

JOHN. You had something else to give.

ALMA. What did I have?

(JOHN *strikes a match. Unconsciously he holds his curved palm over the flame of the match to warm it. It is a long kitchen match and it makes a good flame. They both stare at it with a sorrowful un-*

derstanding that is still perplexed. It is about to burn his fingers.
She leans forward and blows it out, then she puts on her gloves.)

JOHN. You couldn't name it and I couldn't recognize it. I thought it was just a Puritanical ice that glittered like flame. But now I believe it *was* flame, mistaken for ice. I still don't understand it, but I know it was there, just as I know that your eyes and your voice are the two most beautiful things I've ever known—and also the warmest, although they don't seem to be set in your body at all. . . .

ALMA. You talk as if my body had ceased to exist for you, John, in spite of the fact that you've just counted my pulse. Yes, that's it! You tried to avoid it, but you've told me plainly. The tables have turned, yes, the tables have turned with a vengeance! You've come around to my old way of thinking and I to yours like two people exchanging a call on each other at the same time, and each one finding the other one gone out, the door locked against him and no one to answer the bell! (*She laughs.*) I came here to tell you that being a gentleman doesn't seem so important to me any more, but you're telling me I've got to remain a lady. (*She laughs rather violently.*) The tables have turned with a vengeance!—The air in here smells of ether— It's making me dizzy . . .

JOHN. I'll open a window.

ALMA. Please.

JOHN. There now.

ALMA. Thank you, that's better. Do you remember those little white tablets you gave me? I've used them all up and I'd like to have some more.

JOHN. I'll write the prescription for you. (*He bends to write.*)

(NELLIE *is in the waiting room. They hear her voice.*)

ALMA. Someone is waiting in the waiting room, John. One of my vocal pupils. The youngest and prettiest one with the least gift for music. The one that you helped wrap up this handkerchief for me. (*She takes it out and touches her eyes with it.*)

(*The door opens, first a crack.* NELLIE *peers in and giggles. Then she throws the door wide open with a peal of merry laughter. She has holly pinned on her jacket. She rushes up to* JOHN *and hugs him with childish squeals.*)

NELL. I've been all over town just shouting, shouting!

JOHN. Shouting what?

NELL. Glad tidings!

(JOHN *looks at* ALMA *over* NELLIE's *shoulder.*)

JOHN. I thought we weren't going to tell anyone for a while.

NELL. I couldn't stop myself. (*She wheels about.*) Oh, Alma, has he told you?

ALMA (*quietly*). He didn't need to, Nellie. I guessed . . . from the Christmas card with your two names written on it!

(NELLIE *rushes over to* ALMA *and hugs her. Over* NELLIE's *shoulder* ALMA *looks at* JOHN. *He makes a thwarted gesture as if he wanted to speak. She smiles desperately and shakes her head. She closes her eyes and bites her lips for a moment. Then she releases* NELLIE *with a laugh of exaggerated gaiety.*)

NELL. So, Alma, you were really the first to know!

ALMA. I'm proud of that, Nellie.

NELL. See on my finger! This was the present I couldn't tell you about!

ALMA. Oh, what a lovely, lovely solitaire! But solitaire is such a wrong name for it. Solitaire means single and this means *two!* It's blinding, Nellie! Why it . . . hurts my eyes!

(JOHN *catches* NELLIE's *arm and pulls her to him. Almost violently* ALMA *lifts her face; it is bathed in tears. She nods gratefully to* JOHN *for releasing her from* NELLIE's *attention. She picks up her gloves and purse.*)

JOHN. Excuse her, Miss Alma. Nellie's still such a child.

ALMA (*with a breathless laugh*). I've got to run along now.

JOHN. Don't leave your prescription.

ALMA. Oh, yes, where's my prescription?

JOHN. On the table.

ALMA. I'll take it to the drug store right away!

(NELLIE *struggles to free herself from* JOHN's *embrace which keeps her from turning to* ALMA.)

NELL. Alma, don't go! Johnny, let go of me, Johnny! You're hugging me so tight I can't breathe!

ALMA. Goodbye.

NELL. Alma! Alma, you know you're going to sing at the wedding!

The very first Sunday in spring!—which will be Palm Sunday! "The Voice That Breathed O'er Eden."

(ALMA *has closed the door.* JOHN *shuts his eyes tight with a look of torment. He rains kisses on* NELLIE's *forehead and throat and lips. The scene dims out with music.*)

Scene Twelve

In the park near the angel of the fountain. About dusk.

ALMA *enters the lighted area and goes slowly up to the fountain and bends to drink. Then she removes a small white package from her pocketbook and starts to unwrap it. While she is doing this, a* YOUNG MAN *comes along. He is dressed in a checked suit and a derby. He pauses by the bench. They glance at each other.*

A train whistles in the distance. The YOUNG MAN *clears his throat. The train whistle is repeated. The* YOUNG MAN *crosses toward the fountain, his eyes on* ALMA. *She hesitates, with the unwrapped package in her hand. Then she crosses toward the bench and stands hesitantly in front of it. He stuffs his hands in his pockets and whistles. He glances with an effect of unconcern back over his shoulder.*

ALMA *pushes her veil back with an uncertain gesture. His whistle dies out. He sways back and forth on his heels as the train whistles again. He suddenly turns to the fountain and bends to drink.* ALMA *slips the package back into her purse. As the young man straightens up, she speaks in a barely audible voice.*

ALMA. The water—is—cool.

YNG. MAN (*eagerly*). Did you say something?

ALMA. I said, the water is cool.

YNG. MAN. Yes, it sure is, it's nice and cool!

ALMA. It's always cool.

YNG. MAN. Is it?

ALMA. Yes. Yes, even in summer. It comes from deep underground.

YNG. MAN. That's what keeps it cool.

ALMA. Glorious Hill is famous for its artesian springs.

YNG. MAN. I didn't know that.

(*The* YOUNG MAN *jerkily removes his hands from his pockets. She gathers confidence before the awkwardness of his youth.*)

ALMA. Are you a stranger in town?

YNG. MAN. I'm a traveling salesman.

ALMA. Ah, you're a salesman who travels! (*She laughs gently.*) But you're younger than most of them are, and not so fat!

YNG. MAN. I'm just starting out. I travel for Red Goose shoes.

ALMA. Ah! The Delt's your territory?

YNG. MAN. From the Peabody Lobby to Cat-Fish Row in Vicksburg.

(ALMA *leans back and looks at him under half-closed lids, perhaps a little suggestively.*)

ALMA. The life of a traveling salesman is interesting . . . but lonely.

YNG. MAN. You're right about that. Hotel bedrooms are lonely.

(*There is a pause. Far away the train whistles again.*)

ALMA. All rooms are lonely where there is only one person. (*Her eyes fall shut.*)

YNG. MAN (*gently*). You're tired, aren't you?

ALMA. I? Tired? (*She starts to deny it; then laughs faintly and confesses the truth.*) Yes . . . a little. . . . But I shall rest now. I've just now taken one of my sleeping tablets.

YNG. MAN. So early?

ALMA. Oh, it won't put me to sleep. It will just quiet my nerves.

YNG. MAN. What are you nervous about?

ALMA. I won an argument this afternoon.

YNG. MAN. That's nothing to be nervous over. You ought to be nervous if you *lost* one.

ALMA. It wasn't the argument that I wanted to win. . . .

YNG. MAN. Well, I'm nervous too.

ALMA. What over?

YNG. MAN. It's my first job and I'm scared of not making good.

(*The mysteriously sudden intimacy that sometimes occurs between strangers more completely than old friends or lovers moves them both.* ALMA *hands the package of tablets to him.*)

ALMA. Then you must take one of my tablets.

YNG. MAN. Shall I?

ALMA. Please take one!

YNG. MAN. Yes, I shall.

ALMA. You'll be surprised how infinitely merciful they are. The prescription number is 96814. I think of it as the telephone number of God! (*They both laugh. He places one of the tablets on his tongue and crosses to the fountain to wash it down.*)

YNG. MAN (*to the stone figure*). Thanks, angel. (*He gives her a little salute, and crosses back to* ALMA.)

ALMA. Life is full of little mercies like that, not *big* mercies but comfortable *little* mercies. And so we are able to keep on going. . . . (*She has leaned back with half-closed eyes.*)

YNG. MAN (*returning*). You're falling asleep.

ALMA. Oh no, I'm not. I'm just closing my eyes. You know what I feel like now? I feel like a water-lily.

YNG. MAN. A water-lily?

ALMA. Yes, I feel like a water-lily on a Chinese lagoon. Won't you sit down? (*The* YOUNG MAN *does.*) My name is Alma. Spanish for soul! What's yours?

YNG. MAN. Ha-ha! Mine's Archie Kramer. *Mucho gusto,* as they say in Spain.

ALMA. *Usted habla Español, señor?*

YNG. MAN. *Un poquito! Usted habla Español, señorita?*

ALMA. *Me tambien. Un poquito!*

YNG. MAN (*delightedly*). Ha . . . ha . . . ha! Sometimes *un poquito* is plenty! (ALMA *laughs . . . in a different way than she has ever laughed before, a little wearily, but quite naturally. The* YOUNG MAN *leans toward her confidentially.*) What's there to do in this town after dark?

ALMA. There's not much to do in this town after dark, but there are resorts on the lake that offer all kinds of after-dark entertainment. There's one called Moon Lake Casino. It's under new management, now, but I don't suppose its character has changed.

YNG. MAN. What was its character?

ALMA. Gay, very gay, Mr. Kramer. . . .

YNG. MAN. Then what in hell are we sitting here for? *Vamonos!*

ALMA. *Como no, señor!*

YNG. MAN. Ha-ha-ha! (*He jumps up.*) I'll call a taxi. (*He goes off shouting "Taxi."*)

(ALMA *rises from the bench. As she crosses to the fountain the grave mood of the play is reinstated with a phrase of music. She faces the stone angel and raises her gloved hand in a sort of valedictory salute. Then she turns slowly about toward the audience with her hand still raised in a gesture of wonder and finality as . . . the curtain falls.*)

Jean Giraudoux

▶ Jean Giraudoux was born in the small French provincial town of Bellac in 1882. He was gifted, sensitive, and poetic. He loved books and learning and, even more than was normal for French boys of his generation, he responded to the Greek and Roman classics. "Latin is the language to which I owe most," he said. Because he found the title "professor" annoying, he gave up his youthful ambition of becoming a teacher, and devoted his energy to writing. But the rewards for writing, he soon found, would not support him, and he turned to public service for a living. After attending the Consular School he received a post in the Ministry of Foreign Affairs. As a diplomat he was able to satisfy an eagerness for travel to foreign countries: he visited Canada, Mexico, Russia, the Orient, and spent a great deal of time in Germany. He was an officer-instructor in the United States during World War I, and out of his experiences he wrote in 1918 an appreciative book about America, which he called *Amica America*. At the beginning of World War II, he was appointed Commissioner General for Information, a post which made him at once chief of the press bureau in the French Foreign Office and chief of French propaganda abroad. Giraudoux remained in Paris after the German occupation, "tacitly" accepting collaboration, and died there in 1944.

Throughout his life, Giraudoux combined the professions of literature and diplomacy, although he was always better known as a writer than as a diplomat. During the first two decades of his work as a writer he concentrated on short stories and novels. They were published in the literary magazines of small circulation, and were read chiefly by the select coterie which gathered around him. He published five books of fiction in rapid succession between 1918 and 1922, with growing critical acclaim for his wit, style, fantasy, and artistry. This rising reputation was officially recognized and publicized by the award of the Grand Prix Balzac for his *Siegfried et le Limousin* (1922).

Giraudoux turned toward the theatre after his long apprenticeship in the field of the impressionistic novel. The impact of his imaginative creation in an era largely preoccupied with astringent realism was first felt with the production in Paris in 1928 of his first play *Siegfried,* based upon his prize-winning novel. The Siegfried of the play is an amnesic French soldier, wounded in the war, who for a time becomes a German personality and minister in the post-war German state. His French fiancée restores his memory and poses the question whether he shall remain a German or return to France. He returns. The play was enormously successful in France, and was well-received in New York in Eva Le Gallienne's production.

Amphitryon 38, which followed immediately in 1929, was an even greater success and has continued to delight audiences and readers with its gay wit, its audacious humor, and dramatic fantasy centering around the loves of Jupiter and Alcmène. It was brilliantly enacted in New York in 1937, in S. N. Behrman's adaptation, by Alfred Lunt and Lynn Fontanne. It gave point to Giraudoux's remark about himself following the publication of his *Elpenor,* "I became the Charlie Chaplin of the Odyssey."

These successes led to a series of plays in which all of Giraudoux's qualities seemed to reach their full maturity. Among these qualities were a style of remarkable precision, verve, and elegance; a gift for scintillating verbal passages and dramatic manipulation of ideas; an effervescence of spirit at Olympian play among the tragic and comic concerns of earth-bound mankind.

One of these concerns was the ominous drift toward another war that in the 1930's was becoming as obvious as doom in a Greek tragedy. Giraudoux wrote one of his best plays on this theme, using for his cast of characters the personages of Homer's *Iliad* as they supposedly existed just prior to the Trojan War, and, without being too obvious about it, implying the deadly parallel between their day and his own with respect to the folly of mankind and the laughter of the gods. He gave his play the arresting title of *La Guerre de Troie n'aura pas lieu*. It was produced by Louis Jouvet, who also played the part of Hector, at the Théâtre de l'Athénée in November 1935. It has had no publication or production in English.

Electre, Intermezzo, Fin de Siegfried, Judith, L'Impromptu de Paris, and the fairy tale *Ondine*, which came out as Hitler invaded the Rhineland, were also limited largely to French audiences. But during the German occupation of Paris in World War II, and while Giraudoux was in Switzerland, he wrote for Jouvet a new play which was to achieve an international success. Its English title was *The Madwoman of Chaillot*. Giraudoux, who died in 1944, did not live to see it performed. It was produced at the Théâtre de l'Athénée in December 1945, and at the Belasco Theatre in New York in December 1948, with the same charming sets which Christian Berard had designed for the original Paris production.

After a slow and doubtful opening which, momentarily at least, confused the New York critics, the play caught the fancy of the American audience, and became one of the most talked-about plays of the season. The Critics' Circle voted it the best foreign play of 1948-49. To an audience which had been valiantly struggling with the gloom, the surrender, and general hopelessness of Sartre's postwar existentialism, Giraudoux's fantasy seemed clean and cool. It left overtones and symbolic implications spiraling about in the mind, as though one were trying to peer around the corner or lean over the rim of the world to glimpse more than had been shown. It was expressionism grown mature. It used a symbolism that remained on the visible perimeter of reality. It was even more intriguing to have realistic sets, in contrast to Strindberg's distorted Dream World, with characters having all the external appearance of realistic Parisians, and at the same time up-ending the real world and creating mental havoc by their straight-faced madness.

The tone is set by the time of the play, "a little before noon in the Spring of next year." It is sprinkled with bright, satirical lines, like those of the President who has sold stock in a bogus company and is now troubled because "we have a tremendous capital, and not the slightest idea what to do with it," and like the passage at the end of the brilliant scene between the Madwoman and her mad companions just before the President and his colleagues are sent down to their doom. The Madwoman says solemnly, "And so you see why I have asked you to come here today. The world has gone out of its mind. Unless we do something, humanity is doomed! Constance, have you any suggestions?" And the whole zany business is resolved on a note of high irony when the Madwoman says, "Well, there we are. The world is saved. And you see how simple it all was? Nothing is ever so wrong in this world that a sensible woman can't set it right in the course of an afternoon. . . . Well, let's get on to more important things. Four o'clock. My poor cats must be starved. What a bore for them if humanity had to be saved every afternoon."

The play was adapted for the American stage by Maurice Valency of Columbia University. His discerning comment on it is worth pondering: "There is a marked tendency in contemporary French dramatic literature to explore the penumbral regions of thought and feeling far beyond anything in our current practice. It is this technique that gives extraordinary richness of overtone to such a play, for example, as *The Madwoman of Chaillot*."

The Madwoman of Chaillot is reprinted here in Maurice Valency's English adaptation.

THE MADWOMAN
OF CHAILLOT

Characters

THE WAITER	DR. JADIN
THE LITTLE MAN	COUNTESS AURELIA, *Madwoman of Chaillot*
THE PROSPECTOR	THE DOORMAN
THE PRESIDENT	THE POLICEMAN
THE BARON	PIERRE
THERESE	THE SERGEANT
THE STREET SINGER	THE SEWER-MAN
THE FLOWER GIRL	MME. CONSTANCE, *Madwoman of Passy*
THE RAGPICKER	MLLE. GABRIELLE, *Madwoman of St. Sulpice*
PAULETTE	MME. JOSEPHINE, *Madwoman of La Concorde*
THE DEAF-MUTE	THE PRESIDENTS
IRMA	THE PROSPECTORS
THE SHOE-LACE PEDDLER	THE PRESS AGENTS
THE BROKER	THE LADIES
THE STREET JUGGLER	THE ADOLPHE BERTAUTS

Scenes

ACT ONE: *The Café Terrace of* Chez Francis.

ACT TWO: *The Countess' Cellar—21 Rue de Chaillot.*

ACT ONE

SCENE: *The café terrace at* Chez Francis, *on the Place de l'Alma in Paris. The Alma is in the stately quarter of Paris known as Chaillot, between the Champs Élysées and the Seine, across the river from the Eiffel Tower.*

Chez Francis *has several rows of tables set out under its awning, and, as it is lunch time, a good many of them are occupied. At a table, downstage, a somewhat obvious* BLONDE *with ravishing legs is sipping a vermouth-cassis and trying hard to engage the attention of the* PROSPECTOR, *who sits at an adjacent table taking little sips of water and rolling them over his tongue with the air of a connoisseur. Downstage right, in front of the tables on the sidewalk, is the usual Paris bench, a stout and uncomfortable affair provided by the municipality for the benefit of those who prefer to sit without drinking. A* POLICEMAN *lounges about, keeping the peace without unnecessary exertion.*

TIME: *It is a little before noon in the Spring of next year.*

AT RISE: *The* PRESIDENT *and the* BARON *enter with importance, and are ushered to a front table by the* WAITER.

PRES. Baron, sit down. This is a historic occasion. It must be properly celebrated. The waiter is going to bring out my special port.

BAR. Splendid.

PRES. (*offers his cigar case*). Cigar? My private brand.

BAR. Thank you. You know, this all gives me the feeling of one of those enchanted mornings in the *Arabian Nights* when thieves foregather in the market place. Thieves—pashas . . .

(*He sniffs the cigar judiciously, and begins lighting it.*)

PRES. (*chuckles*). Tell me about yourself.

BAR. Well, where shall I begin?

(*The* STREET SINGER *enters. He takes off a battered black felt with a flourish and begins singing an ancient mazurka.*)

ST. SING. (*sings*).

> "Do you hear, Mademoiselle,
> Those musicians of hell?"

PRES. Waiter! Get rid of that man.

WAIT. He is singing *La Belle Polonaise*.

PRES. I didn't ask for the program. I asked you to get rid of him. (*The* WAITER *doesn't budge. The* SINGER *goes by himself.*) As you were saying, Baron . . . ?

BAR. Well, until I was fifty . . . (*the* FLOWER GIRL *enters through the café door, center*) my life was relatively uncomplicated. It consisted of selling off one by one the various estates left me by my father. Three years ago, I parted with my last farm. Two years ago, I lost my last mistress. And now—all that is left me is . . .

FLOW. GIRL (*to the* BARON). Violets, sir?

PRES. Run along.

(*The* FLOWER GIRL *moves on.*)

BAR. (*staring after her*). So that, in short, all I have left now is my name.

PRES. Your name is precisely the name we need on our board of directors.

BAR. (*with an inclination of his head*). Very flattering.

PRES. You will understand when I tell you that mine has been a very different experience. I came up from the bottom. My mother spent most of her life bent over a washtub in order to send me to school. I'm eternally grateful to her, of course, but I must confess that I no longer remember her face. It was no doubt beautiful—but when I try to recall it, I see only the part she invariably showed me—her rear.

BAR. Very touching.

PRES. When I was thrown out of school for the fifth and last time, I decided to find out for myself what makes the world go round. I ran errands for an editor, a movie star, a financier. . . . I began to understand a little what life is. Then, one day, in the subway, I saw a face. . . . My rise in life dates from that day.

BAR. Really?

PRES. One look at that face, and I knew. One look at mine, and he knew. And so I made my first thousand—passing a boxful of counterfeit notes. A year later, I saw another such face. It got me a nice berth in the narcotics business. Since then, all I do is to look out for such faces. And now here I am—president of eleven corporations, director of fifty-two companies, and, beginning today, chairman of the board of the international combine in which you have been so good as to accept a post. (*The* RAGPICKER *passes, sees something under the* PRESIDENT's *table, and stoops to pick it up.*) Looking for something?

RAG. Did you drop this?

PRES. I never drop anything.

RAG. Then this hundred-franc note isn't yours?

PRES. Give it here. (*The* RAGPICKER *gives him the note, and goes out.*)

BAR. Are you sure it's yours?

PRES. All hundred-franc notes, Baron, are mine.

BAR. Mr. President, there's something I've been wanting to ask you. What exactly is the purpose of our new company? Or is that an indiscreet question . . . ?

PRES. Indiscreet? Not a bit. Merely unusual. As far as I know, you're the first member of a board of directors ever to ask such a question.

BAR. Do we plan to exploit a commodity? A utility?

PRES. My dear sir, I haven't the faintest idea.

BAR. But if you don't know—who does?

PRES. Nobody. And at the moment, it's becoming just a trifle embarrassing. Yes, my dear Baron, since we are now close business associates, I must confess that for the time being we're in a little trouble.

BAR. I was afraid of that. The stock issue isn't going well?

PRES. No, no—on the contrary. The stock issue is going beautifully. Yesterday morning at ten o'clock we offered 500,000 shares to the general public. By 10:05 they were all snapped up at par. By 10:20, when the police finally arrived, our offices were a shambles. . . . Windows smashed—doors torn off their hinges—you never saw anything so beautiful in your life! And this morning our stock is being quoted over the counter at 124 with no sellers, and the orders are still pouring in.

BAR. But in that case—what is the trouble?

PRES. The trouble is we have a tremendous capital, and not the slightest idea of what to do with it.

BAR. You mean all those people are fighting to buy stock in a company that has no object?

PRES. My dear Baron, do you imagine that when a subscriber buys a share of stock, he has any idea of getting behind a counter or digging a ditch? A stock certificate is not a tool, like a shovel, or a commodity, like a pound of cheese. What we sell a customer is not a share in a business, but a view of the Elysian Fields. A financier is a creative artist. Our function is to stimulate the imagination. We are poets!

BAR. But in order to stimulate the imagination, don't you need some field of activity?

PRES. Not at all. What you need for that is a name. A name that will stir the pulse like a trumpet call, set the brain awhirl like a movie star, inspire reverence like a cathedral. *United General International Consolidated!* Of course that's been used. That's what a corporation needs.

BAR. And do we have such a name?

PRES. So far we have only a blank space. In that blank space a name must be printed. This name must be a masterpiece. And if I seem a little nervous today, it's because—somehow—I've racked my brains, but it hasn't come to me. Oho! Look at that! Just like the answer to a prayer . . . ! (*The* BARON *turns and stares in the direction of the* PROSPECTOR.) You see? There's one. And what a beauty!

BAR. You mean that girl?

PRES. No, no, not the girl. That face. You see . . . ? The one that's drinking water.

BAR. You call that a face? That's a tombstone.

PRES. It's a milestone. It's a signpost. But is it pointing the way to steel, or wheat, or phosphates? That's what we have to find out. Ah! He sees me. He understands. He will be over.

BAR. And when he comes . . . ?

PRES. He will tell me what to do.

BAR. You mean business is done this way? You mean, you would trust a stranger with a matter of this importance?

PRES. Baron, I trust neither my wife, nor my daughter, nor my closest friend. My confidential secretary has no idea where I live. But a face like that I would trust with my inmost secrets. Though we have never laid eyes on each other before, that man and I know each other to the depths of our souls. He's no stranger—he's my brother, he's myself. You'll see. He'll be over in minute. (*The* DEAF MUTE *enters and passes slowly among the tables, placing a small envelope before each customer. He comes to the* PRESIDENT's *table.*) What is this anyway? A conspiracy? We don't want your envelopes. Take them away. (*The* DEAF MUTE *makes a short but pointed speech in sign language.*) Waiter, what the devil's he saying?

WAIT. Only Irma understands him.

PRES. Irma? Who's Irma?

WAIT. (*calls*). Irma! It's the waitress inside, sir. Irma!

(IRMA *comes out. She is twenty. She has the face and figure of an angel.*)

IRMA. Yes?

WAIT. These gentlemen would . . .

PRES. Tell this fellow to get out of here, for God's sake! (*The* DEAF MUTE *makes another manual oration.*) What's he trying to say, anyway?

IRMA. He says it's an exceptionally beautiful morning, sir. . . .

PRES. Who asked him?

IRMA. But, he says, it was nicer before the gentleman stuck his face in it.

PRES. Call the manager!

(IRMA *shrugs. She goes back into the restaurant. The* DEAF MUTE *walks off, Left. Meanwhile a* SHOELACE PEDDLER *has arrived.*)

PED. Shoelaces? Postcards?

BAR. I think I could use a shoelace.

PRES. No, no . . .

PED. Black? Tan?

BAR. (*showing his shoes*). What would you recommend?

PED. Anybody's guess.

BAR. Well, give me one of each.

PRES. (*putting a hand on the* BARON's *arm*). Baron, although I am your chairman, I have no authority over your personal life—none, that is, except to fix the amount of your director's fees, and eventually to assign a motor car for your use. Therefore, I am asking you, as a personal favor to me, not to purchase anything from this fellow.

BAR. How can I resist so gracious a request? (*The* PEDDLER *shrugs, and passes on.*) But I really don't understand. . . . What difference would it make?

PRES. Look here, Baron. Now that you're with us, you must understand that between this irresponsible riff-raff and us there is an impenetrable barrier. *We* have no dealings whatever with *them*.

BAR. But without us, the poor devil will starve.

PRES. No, he won't. He expects nothing from us. He has a clientele of his own. He sells <u>shoelaces</u> exclusively to those who have no shoes. Just as the necktie peddler sells only to those who wear no shirts. And that's why these street hawkers can afford to be insolent, disrespectful and independent. They don't need us. They have a world of their own. Ah! My broker. Splendid. He's beaming.

(*The* BROKER *walks up and grasps the* PRESIDENT's *hand with enthusiasm.*)

BRO. Mr. President! My heartiest congratulations! What a day! What a day!

(*The* STREET JUGGLER *appears, Right. He removes his coat, folds it carefully, and puts it on the bench. Then he opens a suitcase, from which he extracts a number of colored clubs.*)

PRES. (*presenting the* BROKER). Baron Tommard, of our Board of Directors. My broker. (*The* BROKER *bows. So does the* JUGGLER. *The* BROKER *sits down and signals for a drink. The* JUGGLER *prepares to juggle.*) What's happened?

BRO. Listen to this. Ten o'clock this morning. The market opens. (*As he speaks, the* JUGGLER *provides a visual counterpart to the* BROKER's *lines, his clubs rising and falling in rhythm to the* BROKER's *words.*) Half million shares issued at par, par value a hundred, quoted on the curb at 124 and we start buying at 126, 127, 129—and it's going up—up—up—(*the* JUGGLER's *clubs rise higher and higher*)—132—133—138—141—141—141—141 . . .

BAR. May I ask . . . ?

PRES. No, no—any explanation would only confuse you.

BRO. Ten forty-five we start selling short on rumors of a Communist

plot, market bearish. . . . 141—138—133—132—and it's down—
down—down—102—and we start buying back at 93. Eleven
o'clock, rumors denied—95—98—101—106—124—141—and by
11:30 we've got it all back—net profit three and a half million
francs.

PRES. Classical. Pure. (*The* JUGGLER *bows again. A* LITTLE MAN *leans over
from a near-by table, listening intently, and trembling with excitement.*) And how many shares do we reserve to each member of
the board?

BRO. Fifty, as agreed.

PRES. Bit stingy, don't you think?

BRO. All right—three thousand.

PRES. That's a little better. (*To the* BARON.) You get the idea?

BAR. I'm beginning to get it.

BRO. And now we come to the exciting part . . . (*The* JUGGLER *prepares to juggle with balls of fire.*) Listen carefully: With 35 percent of our funded capital under Section 32 I buy 50,000 United
at 36 which I immediately reconvert into 32,000 National Amalga-
mated two's preferred which I set up as collateral on 150,000
General Consols which I deposit against a credit of fifteen billion
to buy Eastern Hennequin which I immediately turn into Argentine wheat realizing 136 percent of the original investment which
naturally accrues as capital gain and not as corporate income thus
saving twelve millions in taxes, and at once convert the 25 percent
cotton reserve into lignite, and as our people swing into action in
London and New York, I beat up the price on greige goods from
26 to 92—114—203—306—(*the* JUGGLER *by now is juggling his fireballs in the sky. The balls no longer return to his hands*) 404 . . .
(*The* LITTLE MAN *can stand no more. He rushes over and dumps
a sackful of money on the table.*)

L. MAN. Here—take it—please, take it!

BRO. (*frigidly*). Who is this man? What is this money?

L. MAN. It's my life's savings. Every cent. I put it all in your hands.

BRO. Can't you see we're busy?

L. MAN. But I beg you . . . It's my only chance . . . Please don't turn
me away.

BRO. Oh, all right. (*He sweeps the money into his pocket.*) Well?

L. MAN. I thought—perhaps you'd give me a little receipt. . . .

PRES. My dear man, people like us don't give receipts for money. We take them.

L. MAN. Oh, pardon. Of course. I was confused. Here it is. (*Scribbles a receipt.*) Thank you—thank you—thank you. (*He rushes off joyfully. The* STREET SINGER *reappears.*)

ST. SING. (*sings*).
>   "Do you hear, Mademoiselle,
>   Those musicians of hell?"

PRES. What, again? Why does he keep repeating those two lines like a parrot?

WAIT. What else can he do? He doesn't know any more and the song's been out of print for years.

BAR. Couldn't he sing a song he knows?

WAIT. He likes this one. He hopes if he keeps singing the beginning someone will turn up to teach him the end.

PRES. Tell him to move on. We don't know the song.

(*The* PROFESSOR *strolls by, swinging his cane. He overhears.*)

PROF. (*stops and addresses the* PRESIDENT *politely*). Nor do I, my dear sir. Nor do I. And yet, I'm in exactly the same predicament. I remember just two lines of my favorite song, as a child. A mazurka also, in case you're interested. . . .

PRES. I'm not.

PROF. Why is it, I wonder, that one always forgets the words of a mazurka? I suppose they just get lost in that damnable rhythm. All I remember is: (*He sings.*)
>   "From England to Spain
>   I have drunk, it was bliss . . ."

ST. SING. (*walks over, and picks up the tune*).
>   "Red wine and champagne
>   And many a kiss."

PROF. Oh, God! It all comes back to me . . . ! (*He sings.*)
>   "Red lips and white hands I have known
>   Where the nightingales dwell. . . ."

PRES. (*holding his hands to his ears*). Please—please . . .

ST. SING.

      "And to each one I've whispered, 'My own,'
        And to each one, I've murmured: 'Farewell.' "

PRES. Farewell. Farewell.

ST. SING. }
PROF.   } (*duo*).

      "But there's one I shall never forget. . . ."

PRES. This isn't a café. It's a circus!

(*The two go off, still singing:* "There is one that's engraved in my heart." *The* PROSPECTOR *gets up slowly and walks toward the* PRESI-DENT's *table. He looks down without a word. There is a tense silence.*)

PROS. Well?

PRES. I need a name.

PROS. (*nods, with complete comprehension*). I need fifty thousand.

PRES. For a corporation.

PROS. For a woman.

PRES. Immediately.

PROS. Before evening.

PRES. Something . . .

PROS. Unusual?

PRES. Something . . .

PROS. Provocative?

PRES. Something . . .

PROS. Practical.

PRES. Yes.

PROS. Fifty thousand. Cash.

PRES. I'm listening.

PROS. *International Substrate of Paris, Inc.*

PRES. (*snaps his fingers*). That's it! (*To the* BROKER.) Pay him off. (*The* BROKER *pays with the* LITTLE MAN's *money.*) Now—what does it mean?

PROS. It means what it says. I'm a prospector.

PRES. (*rises*). A prospector! Allow me to shake your hand. Baron. You are in the presence of one of nature's noblemen. Shake his hand.

This is Baron Tommard. (*They shake hands.*) It is this man, my
dear Baron, who smells out in the bowels of the earth those deposits of metal or liquid on which can be founded the only social
unit of which our age is capable—the corporation. Sit down,
please. (*They all sit.*) And now that we have a name . . .

PROS. You need a property.

PRES. Precisely.

PROS. I have one.

PRES. A claim?

PROS. Terrific.

PRES. Foreign?

PROS. French.

BAR. In Indo-China?

BRO. Morocco?

PRES. In France?

PROS. (*matter of fact*). In Paris.

PRES. In Paris? You've been prospecting in Paris?

BAR. For women, no doubt.

PRES. For art?

BRO. For gold?

PROS. Oil.

BRO. He's crazy.

PRES. Sh! He's inspired.

PROS. You think I'm crazy. Well, they thought Columbus was crazy.

BAR. Oil in Paris?

BRO. But how is it possible?

PROS. It's not only possible. It's certain.

PRES. Tell us.

PROS. You don't know, my dear sir, what treasures Paris conceals. Paris
is the least prospected place in the world. We've gone over the rest
of the planet with a fine-tooth comb. But has anyone ever thought
of looking for oil in Paris? Nobody. Before me, that is.

PRES. Genius!

PROS. No. Just a practical man. I use my head.

BAR. But why has nobody ever thought of this before?

PROS. The treasures of the earth, my dear sir, are not easy to find nor to get at. They are invariably guarded by dragons. Doubtless there is some reason for this. For once we've dug out and consumed the internal ballast of the planet, the chances are it will shoot off on some irresponsible tangent and smash itself up in the sky. Well, that's the risk we take. Anyway, that's not my business. A prospector has enough to worry about.

BAR. I know—snakes—tarantulas—fleas . . .

PROS. Worse than that, sir. Civilization.

PRES. Does that annoy you?

PROS. Civilization gets in our way all the time. In the first place, it covers the earth with cities and towns which are damned awkward to dig up when you want to see what's underneath. It's not only the real-estate people—you can always do business with them —it's human sentimentality. How do you do business with that?

PRES. I see what you mean.

PROS. They say that where we pass, nothing ever grows again. What of it? Is a park any better than a coal mine? What's a mountain got that a slag pile hasn't? What would you rather have in your garden—an almond tree or an oil well?

PRES. Well . . .

PROS. Exactly. But what's the use of arguing with these fools? Imagine the choicest place you ever saw for an excavation, and what do they put there? A playground for children! Civilization!

PRES. Just show us the point where you want to start digging. We'll do the rest. Even if it's in the middle of the Louvre. Where's the oil?

PROS. Perhaps you think it's easy to make an accurate fix in an area like Paris where everything conspires to put you off the scent? Women—perfume—flowers—history. You can talk all you like about geology, but an oil deposit, gentlemen, has to be smelled out. I have a good nose. I go further. I have a phenomenal nose. But the minute I get the right whiff—the minute I'm on the scent—a fragrance rises from what I take to be the spiritual deposits of the past—and I'm completely at sea. Now take this very point, for example, this very spot.

BAR. You mean—right here in Chaillot?

PROS. Right under here.

PRES. Good heavens! (*He looks under his chair.*)

PROS. It's taken me months to locate this spot.

BAR. But what in the world makes you think . . . ?

PROS. Do you know this place, Baron?

BAR. Well, I've been sitting here for thirty years.

PROS. Did you ever taste the water?

BAR. The water? Good God, no!

PROS. It's plain to see that you are no prospector! A prospector, Baron, is addicted to water as a drunkard to wine. Water, gentlemen, is the one substance from which the earth can conceal nothing. It sucks out its innermost secrets and brings them to our very lips. Well—beginning at Notre Dame, where I first caught the scent of oil three months ago, I worked my way across Paris, glassful by glassful, sampling the water, until at last I came to this café. And here—just two days ago—I took a sip. My heart began to thump. Was it possible that I was deceived? I took another, a third, a fourth, a fifth. I was trembling like a leaf. But there was no mistake. Each time that I drank, my taste-buds thrilled to the most exquisite flavor known to a prospector—the flavor of— (*with utmost lyricism*) petroleum!

PRES. Waiter! Some water and four glasses. Hurry. This round, gentlemen, is on me. And as a toast—I shall propose International Substrate of Paris, Incorporated. (*The* WAITER *brings a decanter and the glasses. The* PRESIDENT *pours out the water amid profound silence. They taste it with the air of connoisseurs savoring something that has never before passed human lips. Then they look at each other doubtfully. The* PROSPECTOR *pours himself a second glass and drinks it off.*) Well . . .

BRO. Ye-es . . .

BAR. Mm . . .

PROS. Get it?

BAR. Tastes queer.

PROS. That's it. To the unpracticed palate it tastes queer. But to the taste-buds of the expert—ah!

BAR. Still, there's one thing I don't quite understand . . .

PROS. Yes?

BAR. This café doesn't have its own well, does it?

PROS. Of course not. This is Paris water.

BRO. Then why should it taste different here than anywhere else?

PROS. Because, my dear sir, the pipes that carry this water pass deep through the earth, and the earth just here is soaked with oil, and this oil permeates the pores of the iron and flavors the water it carries. Ever so little, yes—but quite enough to betray its presence to the sensitive tongue of the specialist.

BAR. I see.

PROS. I don't say everyone is capable of tasting it. No. But I—I can detect the presence of oil in water that has passed within fifteen miles of a deposit. Under special circumstances, twenty.

PRES. Phenomenal!

PROS. And so here I am with the greatest discovery of the age on my hands—but the blasted authorities won't let me drill a single well unless I show them the oil! Now how can I show them the oil unless they let me dig? Completely stymied! Eh?

PRES. What? A man like you?

PROS. That's what they think. That's what they want. Have you noticed the strange glamor of the women this morning? And the quality of the sunshine? And this extraordinary convocation of vagabonds buzzing about protectively like bees around a hive? Do you know why it is? Because they know. It's a plot to distract us, to turn us from our purpose. Well, let them try. I know there's oil here. And I'm going to dig it up, even if I . . . (*He smiles.*) Shall I tell you my little plan?

PRES. By all means.

PROS. Well . . . For heaven's sake, what's that?

(*At this point, the* MADWOMAN *enters. She is dressed in the grand fashion of 1885, a taffeta skirt with an immense train—which she has gathered up by means of a clothespin—ancient button shoes, and a hat in the style of Marie Antoinette. She wears a lorgnette on a chain, and an enormous cameo pin at her throat. In her hand she carries a small basket. She walks in with great dignity, extracts*

a dinner bell from the bosom of her dress, and rings it sharply.
IRMA *appears.*)

COUNT. Are my bones ready, Irma?

IRMA. There won't be much today, Countess. We had broilers. Can you wait? While the gentleman inside finishes eating?

COUNT. And my gizzard?

IRMA. I'll try to get it away from him.

COUNT. If he eats my gizzard, save me the giblets. They will do for the tomcat that lives under the bridge. He likes a few giblets now and again.

IRMA. Yes, Countess. (IRMA *goes back into the café. The* COUNTESS *takes a few steps and stops in front of the* PRESIDENT's *table. She examines him with undisguised disapproval.*)

PRES. Waiter. Ask that woman to move on.

WAIT. Sorry, sir. This is her café.

PRES. Is she the manager of the café?

WAIT. She's the Madwoman of Chaillot.

PRES. A Madwoman? She's mad?

WAIT. Who says she's mad?

PRES. You just said so yourself.

WAIT. Look, sir. You asked me who she was. And I told you. What's mad about her? She's the Madwoman of Chaillot.

PRES. Call a policeman.

(*The* COUNTESS *whistles through her fingers. At once, the* DOORMAN *runs out of the café. He has three scarves in his hands.*)

COUNT. Have you found it? My feather boa?

DOOR. Not yet, Countess. Three scarves. But no boa.

COUNT. It's five years since I lost it. Surely you've had time to find it.

DOOR. Take one of these, Countess. Nobody's claimed them.

COUNT. A boa like that doesn't vanish, you know. A feather boa nine feet long!

DOOR. How about this blue one?

COUNT. With my pink ruffle and my green veil? You're joking! Let me see the yellow. (*She tries it on.*) How does it look?

DOOR. Terrific.

(*With a magnificent gesture, she flings the scarf about her, upsetting*

the PRESIDENT's *glass and drenching his trousers with water. She
stalks off without a glance at him.*)

PRES. Waiter! I'm making a complaint.

WAIT. Against whom?

PRES. Against her! Against you! The whole gang of you! That singer!
That shoelace peddler! That female lunatic! Or whatever you
call her!

BAR. Calm yourself, Mr. President. . . .

PRES. I'll do nothing of the sort! Baron, the first thing we have to do
is to get rid of these people! Good heavens, look at them! Every
size, shape, color and period of history imaginable. It's utter
anarchy! I tell you, sir, the only safeguard of order and discipline
in the modern world is a standardized worker with interchange-
able parts. That would solve the entire problem of management.
Here, the manager . . . And there—one composite drudge grunt-
ing and sweating all over the world. Just we two. Ah, how beautiful! How easy on the eyes! How restful for the conscience!

BAR. Yes, yes—of course.

PRES. Order. Symmetry. Balance. But instead of that, what? Here in
Chaillot, the very citadel of management, these insolent phantoms
of the past come to beard us with their raffish individualism—with
the right of the voiceless to sing, of the dumb to make speeches,
of trousers to have no seats and bosoms to have dinner bells!

BAR. But, after all, do these people matter?

PRES. My dear sir, wherever the poor are happy, and the servants are
proud, and the mad are respected, our power is at an end. Look
at that! That waiter! That madwoman! That flower girl! Do I
get that sort of service? And suppose that I—president of twelve
corporations and ten times a millionaire—were to stick a gladiolus
in my buttonhole and start yelling— (*He tinkles his spoon in a
glass violently, yelling.*) Are my bones ready, Irma?

BAR. (*reprovingly*). Mr. President . . .

(*People at the adjoining tables turn and stare with raised eyebrows. The
WAITER starts to come over.*)

PRES. You see? Now.

PROS. We were discussing my plan.

PRES. Ah yes, your plan. (*He glances in the direction of the* MAD-WOMAN's *table.*) Careful—she's looking at us.

PROS. Do you know what a bomb is?

PRES. I'm told they explode.

PROS. Exactly. You see that white building across the river. Do you happen to know what that is?

PRES. I do not.

PROS. That's the office of the City Architect. That man has stubbornly refused to give me a permit to drill for oil anywhere within the limits of the city of Paris. I've tried everything with him—influence, bribes, threats. He says I'm crazy. And now . . .

PRES. Oh, my God! What is this one trying to sell us?

(*A little* OLD MAN *enters Left, and doffs his hat politely. He is somewhat ostentatiously respectable—gloved, pomaded, and carefully dressed, with a white handkerchief peeping out of his breast pocket.*)

DR. JAD. Nothing but health, sir. Or rather the health of the feet. But remember—as the foot goes, so goes the man. May I present myself . . . ? Dr. Gaspard Jadin, French Navy, retired. Former specialist in the extraction of ticks and chiggers. At present specializing in the extraction of bunions and corns. In case of sudden emergency, Martial the waiter will furnish my home address. My office is here, second row, third table, week days, twelve to five. Thank you very much. (*He sits at his table.*)

WAIT. Your vermouth, Doctor?

DR. JAD. My vermouth. My vermouths. How are your gallstones today, Martial?

WAIT. Fine. Fine. They rattle like anything.

DR. JAD. Splendid. (*He spies the* COUNTESS.) Good morning, Countess. How's the floating kidney? Still afloat? (*She nods graciously.*) Splendid. Splendid. So long as it floats, it can't sink.

PRES. This is impossible! Let's go somewhere else.

PROS. No. It's nearly noon.

PRES. Yes. It is. Five to twelve.

PROS. In five minutes' time you're going to see that City Architect blown up, building and all—boom!

BRO. Are you serious?

PROS. That imbecile has no one to blame but himself. Yesterday noon, he got my ultimatum—he's had twenty-four hours to think it over. No permit? All right. Within two minutes my agent is going to drop a little package in his coal bin. And three minutes after that, precisely at noon . . .

BAR. You prospectors certainly use modern methods.

PROS. The method may be modern. But the idea is old. To get at the treasure, it has always been necessary to slay the dragon. I guarantee that after this, the City Architect will be more reasonable. The new one, I mean.

PRES. Don't you think we're sitting a little close for comfort?

PROS. Oh no, no. Don't worry. And, above all, don't stare. We may be watched. (*A clock strikes.*) Why, that's noon. Something's wrong! Good God! What's this? (*A* POLICEMAN *staggers in bearing a lifeless body on his shoulders in the manner prescribed as "The Fireman's Lift."*) It's Pierre! My agent! (*He walks over with affected nonchalance.*) I say, Officer, what's that you've got?

POLICE. Drowned man. (*He puts him down on the bench.*)

WAIT. He's not drowned. His clothes are dry. He's been slugged.

POLICE. Slugged is also correct. He was just jumping off the bridge when I came along and pulled him back. I slugged him, naturally, so he wouldn't drag me under. Life Saving Manual, Rule 5: "In cases where there is danger of being dragged under, it is necessary to render the subject unconscious by means of a sharp blow." He's had that. (*He loosens the clothes and begins applying artificial respiration.*)

PROS. The stupid idiot! What the devil did he do with the bomb? That's what comes of employing amateurs!

PRES. You don't think he'll give you away?

PROS. Don't worry. (*He walks over to the* POLICEMAN.) Say, what do you think you're doing?

POLICE. Lifesaving. Artificial respiration. First aid to the drowning.

PROS. But he's not drowning.

POLICE. But he thinks he is.

PROS. You'll never bring him round that way, my friend. That's meant for people who drown in water. It's no good at all for those who drown without water.

POLICE. What am I supposed to do? I've just been sworn in. It's my first day on the beat. I can't afford to get in trouble. I've got to go by the book.

PROS. Perfectly simple. Take him back to the bridge where you found him and throw him in. Then you can save his life and you'll get a medal. This way, you'll only get fined for slugging an innocent man.

POLICE. What do you mean, innocent? He was just going to jump when I grabbed him.

PROS. Have you any proof of that?

POLICE. Well, I saw him.

PROS. Written proof? Witnesses?

POLICE. No, but . . .

PROS. Then don't waste time arguing. You're in trouble. Quick—before anybody notices—throw him in and dive after him. It's the only way out.

POLICE. But I don't swim.

PRES. You'll learn how on the way down. Before you were born, did you know how to breathe?

POLICE. (*convinced*). All right. Here we go. (*He starts lifting the body.*)

DR. JAD. One moment, please. I don't like to interfere, but it's my professional duty to point out that medical science has definitely established the fact of intra-uterine respiration. Consequently, this policeman, even before he was born, knew not only how to breathe but also how to cough, hiccup and belch.

PRES. Suppose he did—how does it concern you?

DR. JAD. On the other hand, medical science has never established the fact of intra-uterine swimming or diving. Under the circumstances, we are forced to the opinion, Officer, that if you dive in you will probably drown.

POLICE. You think so?

PROS. Who asked you for an opinion?

PRES. Pay no attention to that quack, Officer.

DR. JAD. Quack, sir?

PROS. This is not a medical matter. It's a legal problem. The officer has made a grave error. He's new. We're trying to help him.

BRO. He's probably afraid of the water.

POLICE. Nothing of the sort. Officially, I'm afraid of nothing. But I always follow doctor's orders.

DR. JAD. You see, Officer, when a child is born . . .

PROS. Now, what does he care about when a child is born? He's got a dying man on his hands. . . . Officer, if you want my advice . . .

POLICE. It so happens, I care a lot about when a child is born. It's part of my duty to aid and assist any woman in childbirth or labor.

PRES. Can you imagine!

POLICE. Is it true, Doctor, what they say, that when you have twins, the first born is considered to be the youngest?

DR. JAD. Quite correct. And what's more, if the twins happen to be born at midnight on December 31st, the older is a whole year younger. He does his military service a year later. That's why you have to keep your eyes open. And that's the reason why a queen always gives birth before witnesses. . . .

POLICE. God! The things a policeman is supposed to know! Doctor, what does it mean if, when I get up in the morning sometimes . . .

PROS. (*nudging the* PRESIDENT *meaningfully*). The old woman . . .

BRO. Come on, Baron.

PRES. I think we'd better all run along.

PROS. Leave him to me.

PRES. I'll see you later. (*The* PRESIDENT *steals off with the* BROKER *and the* BARON.)

POLICE. (*still in conference with* DR. JADIN). But what's really worrying me, Doctor, is this—don't you think it's a bit risky for a man to marry after forty-five?

(*The* BROKER *runs in breathlessly.*)

BRO. Officer! Officer!

POLICE. What's the trouble?

BRO. Quick! Two women are calling for help—on the sidewalk—Avenue Wilson!

POLICE. Two women at once? Standing up or lying down?

BRO. You'd better go and see. Quick!

PROS. You'd better take the Doctor with you.

POLICE. Come along, Doctor, come along. . . . (*Pointing to* PIERRE.) Tell him to wait till I get back. Come along, Doctor. (*He runs out, the* DOCTOR *following. The* PROSPECTOR *moves over toward* PIERRE, *but* IRMA *crosses in front of him and takes the boy's hand.*)

IRMA. How beautiful he is! Is he dead, Martial?

WAIT. (*handing her a pocket mirror*). Hold this mirror to his mouth. If it clouds over . . .

IRMA. It clouds over.

WAIT. He's alive. (*He holds out his hand for the mirror.*)

IRMA. Just a sec— (*She rubs it clean and looks at herself intently. Before handing it back, she fixes her hair and applies her lipstick. Meanwhile the* PROSPECTOR *tries to get around the other side, but the* COUNTESS' *eagle eye drives him off. He shrugs his shoulders and exits with the* BARON.) Oh, look—he's opened his eyes!

(PIERRE *opens his eyes, stares intently at* IRMA *and closes them again with the expression of a man who is among the angels.*)

PIERRE (*murmurs*). Oh! How beautiful!

VOICE (*from within the café*). Irma!

IRMA. Coming. Coming. (*She goes in, not without a certain reluctance. The* COUNTESS *at once takes her place on the bench, and also the* YOUNG MAN'S *hand.* PIERRE *sits up suddenly, and finds himself staring, not at* IRMA, *but into the very peculiar face of the* COUNTESS. *His expression changes.*)

COUNT. You're looking at my iris? Isn't it beautiful?

PIERRE. Very. (*He drops back, exhausted.*)

COUNT. The Sergeant was good enough to say it becomes me. But I no longer trust his taste. Yesterday, the flower girl gave me a lily, and he said it didn't suit me.

PIERRE (*weakly*). It's beautiful.

COUNT. He'll be very happy to know that you agree with him. He's really quite sensitive. (*She calls.*) Sergeant!

PIERRE. No, please—don't call the police.

COUNT. But I must. I think I hurt his feelings.

PIERRE. Let me go, Madame.

COUNT. No, no. Stay where you are. Sergeant! (PIERRE *struggles weakly to get up.*)

PIERRE. Please let me go.

COUNT. I'll do nothing of the sort. When you let someone go, you never see him again. I let Charlotte Mazumet go. I never saw her again

PIERRE. Oh, my head.

COUNT. I let Adolphe Bertaut go. And I was holding him. And I never saw him again.

PIERRE. Oh, God!

COUNT. Except once. Thirty years later. In the market. He had changed a great deal—he didn't know me. He sneaked a melon from right under my nose, the only good one of the year. Ah, here we are. Sergeant! (*The* POLICE SERGEANT *comes in with importance.*)

SERG. I'm in a hurry, Countess.

COUNT. With regard to the iris. This young man agrees with you. He says it suits me.

SERG. (*going*). There's a man drowning in the Seine.

COUNT. He's not drowning in the Seine. He's drowning here. Because I'm holding him tight—as I should have held Adolphe Bertaut. But if I let him go, I'm sure he will go and drown in the Seine. He's a lot better looking than Adolphe Bertaut, wouldn't you say? (PIERRE *sighs deeply.*)

SERG. How would I know?

COUNT. I've shown you his photograph. The one with the bicycle.

SERG. Oh, yes. The one with the harelip.

COUNT. I've told you a hundred times! Adolphe Bertaut had no harelip. That was a scratch in the negative. (*The* SERGEANT *takes out his notebook and pencil.*) What are you doing?

SERG. I am taking down the drowned man's name, given name and date of birth.

COUNT. You think that's going to stop him from jumping in the river? Don't be silly, Sergeant. Put that book away and try to console him.

SERG. I should try and console him?

COUNT. When people want to die, it is your job as a guardian of the state to speak out in praise of life. Not mine.

SERG. I should speak out in praise of life?

COUNT. I assume you have some motive for interfering with people's attempts to kill each other, and rob each other, and run each other over? If you believe that life has some value, tell him what it is Go on.

SERG. Well, all right. Now look, young man . . .

COUNT. His name is Roderick.

PIERRE. My name is not Roderick.

COUNT. Yes, it is. It's noon. At noon all men become Roderick.

SERG. Except Adolphe Bertaut.

COUNT. In the days of Adolphe Bertaut, we were forced to change the men when we got tired of their names. Nowadays, we're more practical—each hour on the hour all names are automatically changed. The men remain the same. But you're not here to discuss Adolphe Bertaut, Sergeant. You're here to convince the young man that life is worth living.

PIERRE. It isn't.

SERG. Quiet. Now then—what was the idea of jumping off the bridge, anyway?

COUNT. The idea was to land in the river. Roderick doesn't seem to be at all confused about that.

SERG. Now how can I convince anybody that life is worth living if you keep interrupting all the time?

COUNT. I'll be quiet.

SERG. First of all, Mr. Roderick, you have to realize that suicide is a crime against the state. And why is it a crime against the state? Because every time anybody commits suicide, that means one soldier less for the army, one taxpayer less for the . . .

COUNT. Sergeant, isn't there something about life that you really enjoy?

SERG. That I enjoy?

COUNT. Well, surely, in all these years, you must have found something worth living for. Some secret pleasure, or passion. Don't blush. Tell him about it.

SERG. Who's blushing? Well, naturally, yes—I have my passions—like everybody else. The fact is, since you ask me—I love—to play— casino. And if the gentleman would like to join me, by and by

when I go off duty, we can sit down to a nice little game in the
back room with a nice cold glass of beer. If he wants to kill an
hour, that is.

COUNT. He doesn't want to kill an hour. He wants to kill himself. Well?
Is that all the police force has to offer by way of earthly bliss?

SERG. Huh? You mean— (*He jerks a thumb in the direction of the
pretty* BLONDE, *who has just been joined by a* BRUNETTE *of the same
stamp.*) Paulette? (*The young man groans.*)

COUNT. You're not earning your salary, Sergeant. I defy anybody to stop
dying on your account.

SERG. Go ahead, if you can do any better. But you won't find it easy.

COUNT. Oh, this is not a desperate case at all. A young man who has just
fallen in love with someone who has fallen in love with him!

PIERRE. She hasn't. How could she?

COUNT. Oh, yes, she has. She was holding your hand, just as I'm holding
it, when all of a sudden . . . Did you ever know Marshal Canrobert's niece?

SERG. How could he know Marshal Canrobert's niece?

COUNT. Lots of people knew her—when she was alive. (PIERRE *begins to
struggle energetically.*) No, no, Roderick—stop—stop!

SERG. You see? You won't do any better than I did.

COUNT. No? Let's bet. I'll bet my iris against one of your gold buttons.
Right?—Roderick, I know very well why you tried to drown
yourself in the river.

PIERRE. You don't at all.

COUNT. It's because that Prospector wanted you to commit a horrible
crime.

PIERRE. How did you know that?

COUNT. He stole my boa, and now he wants you to kill me.

PIERRE. Not exactly.

COUNT. It wouldn't be the first time they've tried it. But I'm not so easy
to get rid of, my boy, oh, no . . . Because . . .

(*The* DOORMAN *rides in on his bicycle. He winks at the* SERGEANT, *who
has now seated himself while the* WAITER *serves him a beer.*)

DOOR. Take it easy, Sergeant.

SERG. I'm busy saving a drowning man.

COUNT. They can't kill me because—I have no desire to die.

PIERRE. You're fortunate.

COUNT. To be alive is to be fortunate, Roderick. Of course, in the morning, when you first awake, it does not always seem so very gay. When you take your hair out of the drawer, and your teeth out of the glass, you are apt to feel a little out of place in this world. Especially if you've just been dreaming that you're a little girl on a pony looking for strawberries in the woods. But all you need to feel the call of life once more is a letter in your mail giving you your schedule for the day—your mending, your shopping, that letter to your grandmother that you never seem to get around to. And so, when you've washed your face in rosewater, and powdered it—not with this awful rice-powder they sell nowadays, which does nothing for the skin, but with a cake of pure white starch—and put on your pins, your rings, your brooches, bracelets, earrings and pearls—in short, when you are dressed for your morning coffee—and have had a good look at yourself—not in the glass, naturally—it lies—but in the side of the brass gong that once belonged to Admiral Courbet—then, Roderick, then you're armed, you're strong, you're ready—you can begin again. (PIERRE *is listening now intently. There are tears in his eyes.*)

PIERRE. Oh, Madame . . . ! Oh, Madame . . . !

COUNT. After that, everything is pure delight. First the morning paper. Not, of course, these current sheets full of lies and vulgarity. I always read the *Gaulois,* the issue of March 22, 1903. It's by far the best. It has some delightful scandal, some excellent fashion notes, and, of course, the last-minute bulletin on the death of Leonide Leblanc. She used to live next door, poor woman, and when I learn of her death every morning, it gives me quite a shock. I'd gladly lend you my copy, but it's in tatters.

SERG. Couldn't we find him a copy in some library?

COUNT. I doubt it. And so, when you've taken your fruit salts—not in water, naturally—no matter what they say, it's water that gives you gas—but with a bit of spiced cake—then in sunlight or rain, Chaillot calls. It is time to dress for your morning walk. This takes much longer, of course—without a maid, impossible to do it under an hour, what with your corset, corset-cover and drawers all of which lace or button in the back. I asked Madame Lanvin, a while ago, to fit the drawers with zippers. She was quite charming, but she declined. She thought it would spoil the style.

(*The* DEAF-MUTE *comes in.*)

WAIT. I know a place where they put zippers on anything.

(*The* RAGPICKER *enters.*)

COUNT. I think Lanvin knows best. But I really manage very well, Martial. What I do now is, I lace them up in front, then twist them around to the back. It's quite simple, really. Then you choose a lorgnette, and then the usual fruitless search for the feather boa that the prospector stole—I know it was he: he didn't dare look me in the eye—and then all you need is a rubber band to slip around your parasol—I lost the catch the day I struck the cat that was stalking the pigeon—it was worth it—ah, that day I earned my wages!

RAG. Countess, if you can use it, I found a nice umbrella catch the other day with a cat's eye in it.

COUNT. Thank you, Ragpicker. They say these eyes sometimes come to life and fill with tears. I'd be afraid . . .

PIERRE. Go on, Madame, go on . . .

COUNT. Ah! So life is beginning to interest you, is it? You see how beautiful it is?

PIERRE. What a fool I've been!

COUNT. Then, Roderick, I begin my rounds. I have my cats to feed, my dogs to pet, my plants to water. I have to see what the evil ones are up to in the district—those who hate people, those who hate plants, those who hate animals. I watch them sneaking off in the morning to put on their disguises—to the baths, to the beauty parlors, to the barbers. But they can't deceive me. And when they come out again with blonde hair and false whiskers, to pull up my flowers and poison my dogs, I'm there, and I'm ready. All you have to do to break their power is to cut across their path from the left. That isn't always easy. Vice moves swiftly. But I have a good long stride and I generally manage. . . . Right, my friends?

(*The* WAITER *and the* RAGPICKER *nod their heads with evident ap-*

proval.) Yes, the flowers have been marvelous this year. And the butcher's dog on the Rue Bizet, in spite of that wretch that tried to poison him, is friskier than ever. . . .

SERG. That dog had better look out. He has no license.

COUNT. He doesn't seem to feel the need for one.

RAG. The Duchess de la Rochefoucauld's whippet is getting awfully thin. . . .

COUNT. What can I do? She bought that dog full grown from a kennel where they didn't know his right name. A dog without his right name is bound to get thin.

RAG. I've got a friend who knows a lot about dogs—an Arab . . .

COUNT. Ask him to call on the Duchess. She receives Thursdays, five to seven. You see, then, Roderick. That's life. Does it appeal to you now?

PIERRE. It seems marvelous.

COUNT. Ah! Sergeant. My button. (*The* SERGEANT *gives her his button and goes off. At this point the* PROSPECTOR *enters.*) That's only the morning. Wait till I tell you about the afternoon!

PROS. All right, Pierre. Come along now.

PIERRE. I'm perfectly all right here.

PROS. I said, come along now.

PIERRE (*to the* COUNTESS). I'd better go, Madame.

COUNT. No.

PIERRE. It's no use. Please let go my hand.

PROS. Madame, will you oblige me by letting my friend go?

COUNT. I will not oblige you in any way.

PROS. All right. Then I'll oblige you . . . ! (*He tries to push her away. She catches up a soda water siphon and squirts it in his face.*)

PIERRE. Countess . . .

COUNT. Stay where you are. This man isn't going to take you away. In the first place, I shall need you in a few minutes to take me home. I'm all alone here and I'm very easily frightened.

(*The* PROSPECTOR *makes a second attempt to drag* PIERRE *away. The* COUNTESS *cracks him over the skull with the siphon. They join battle. The* COUNTESS *whistles. The* DOORMAN *comes, then the other* VAGABONDS, *and lastly the* POLICE SERGEANT.)

PROS. Officer! Arrest this woman!

SERG. What's the trouble here?

PROS. She refuses to let this man go.

SERG. Why should she?

PROS. It's against the law for a woman to detain a man on the street.

IRMA. Suppose it's her son whom she's found again after twenty years?

RAG. (*gallantly*). Or her long-lost brother? The Countess is not so old.

PROS. Officer, this is a clear case of disorderly conduct.

(*The* DEAF-MUTE *interrupts with frantic signals.*)

COUNT. Irma, what is the Deaf-Mute saying?

IRMA (*interpreting*). The young man is in danger of his life. He mustn't go with him.

PROS. What does he know?

IRMA. He knows everything.

PROS. Officer, I'll have to take your number.

COUNT. Take his number. It's 2133. It adds up to nine. It will bring you luck.

SERG. Countess, between ourselves, what are you holding him for, anyway?

COUNT. I'm holding him because it's very pleasant to hold him. I've never really held anybody before, and I'm making the most of it. And because so long as *I* hold him, he's free.

PROS. Pierre, I'm giving you fair warning. . . .

COUNT. And I'm holding him because Irma wants me to hold him. Because if I let him go, it will break her heart.

IRMA. Oh, Countess!

SERG. (*to the* PROSPECTOR). All right, you—move on. Nobody's holding you. You're blocking traffic. Move on.

PROS. (*menacingly*). I have your number. (*And murderously, to* PIERRE.) You'll regret this, Pierre. (*Exit* PROSPECTOR.)

PIERRE. Thank you, Countess.

COUNT. They're blackmailing you, are they? (PIERRE *nods.*) What have you done? Murdered somebody?

PIERRE. No.

COUNT. Stolen something?

PIERRE. No.

COUNT. What then?

PIERRE. I forged a signature.

COUNT. Whose signature?

PIERRE. My father's. To a note.

COUNT. And this man has the paper, I suppose?

PIERRE. He promised to tear it up, if I did what he wanted. But I couldn't do it.

COUNT. But the man is mad! Does he really want to destroy the whole neighborhood?

PIERRE. He wants to destroy the whole city.

COUNT. (*laughs*). Fantastic.

PIERRE. It's not funny, Countess. He can do it. He's mad, but he's powerful, and he has friends. Their machines are already drawn up and waiting. In three months' time you may see the city covered by a forest of derricks and drills.

COUNT. But what are they looking for? Have they lost something?

PIERRE. They're looking for oil. They're convinced that Paris is sitting on a lake of oil.

COUNT. Suppose it is. What harm does it do?

PIERRE. They want to bring the oil to the surface, Countess.

COUNT. (*laughs*). How silly! Is that a reason to destroy a city? What do they want with this oil?

PIERRE. They want to make war, Countess.

COUNT. Oh, dear, let's forget about these horrible men. The world is beautiful. It's happy. That's how God made it. No man can change it.

WAIT. Ah, Countess, if you only knew . . .

COUNT. If I only knew what?

WAIT. Shall we tell her now? Shall we tell her?

COUNT. What is it you are hiding from me?

RAG. Nothing, Countess. It's you who are hiding.

WAIT. You tell her. You've been a pitchman. You can talk.

ALL. Tell her. Tell her. Tell her.

COUNT. You're frightening me, my friends. Go on. I'm listening.

RAG. Countess, there was a time when old clothes were as good as new—in fact, they were better. Because when people wore clothes, they gave something to them. You may not believe it, but right this minute, the highest-priced shops in Paris are selling clothes that were thrown away thirty years ago. They're selling them for new. That's how good they were.

COUNT. Well?

RAG. Countess, there was a time when garbage was a pleasure. A garbage can was not what it is now. If it smelled a little strange, it was because it was a little confused—there was everything there—sardines, cologne, iodine, roses. An amateur might jump to a wrong conclusion. But to a professional—it was the smell of God's plenty.

COUNT. Well?

RAG. Countess, the world has changed.

COUNT. Nonsense. How could it change? People are the same, I hope.

RAG. No, Countess. The people are not the same. The people are different. There's been an invasion. An infiltration. From another planet. The world is not beautiful any more. It's not happy.

COUNT. Not happy? Is that true? Why didn't you tell me this before?

RAG. Because you live in a dream, Countess. And we don't like to disturb you.

COUNT. But how could it have happened?

RAG. Countess, there was a time when you could walk around Paris, and all the people you met were just like yourself. A little cleaner, maybe, or dirtier, perhaps, or angry, or smiling—but you knew them. They were you. Well, Countess, twenty years ago, one day, on the street, I saw a face in the crowd. A face, you might say, without a face. The eyes—empty. The expression—not human. Not a human face. It saw me staring, and when it looked back at me with its gelatine eyes, I shuddered. Because I knew that to make room for this one, one of us must have left the earth. A while after, I saw another. And another. And since then, I've seen hundreds come in—yes—thousands.

COUNT. Describe them to me.

RAG. You've seen them yourself, Countess. Their clothes don't wrinkle. Their hats don't come off. When they talk, they don't look at you. They don't perspire.

COUNT. Have they wives? Have they children?

RAG. They buy the models out of shop windows, furs and all. They ani-
mate them by a secret process. Then they marry them. Naturally,
they don't have children.

COUNT. What work do they do?

RAG. They don't do any work. Whenever they meet, they whisper, and
then they pass each other thousand-franc notes. You see them
standing on the corner by the Stock Exchange. You see them at
auctions—in the back. They never raise a finger—they just stand
there. In theater lobbies, by the box office—they never go inside.
They don't do anything, but wherever you see them, things are
not the same. I remember well the time when a cabbage could sell
itself just by being a cabbage. Nowadays it's no good being a cabbage—unless you have an agent and pay him a commission. Nothing is free any more to sell itself or give itself away. These days,
Countess, every cabbage has its pimp.

COUNT. I can't believe that.

RAG. Countess, little by little, the pimps have taken over the world. They
don't do anything, they don't make anything—they just stand
there and take their cut. It makes a difference. Look at the shop-
keepers. Do you ever see one smiling at a customer any more?
Certainly not. Their smiles are strictly for the pimps. The butcher
has to smile at the meat-pimp, the florist at the rose-pimp, the
grocer at the fresh-fruit-and-vegetable pimp. It's all organized
down to the slightest detail. A pimp for bird-seed. A pimp for
fishfood. That's why the cost of living keeps going up all the time.
You buy a glass of beer—it costs twice as much as it used to.
Why? 10 per cent for the glass-pimp, 10 per cent for the beer-pimp,
20 per cent for the glass-of-beer-pimp—that's where our money
goes. Personally, I prefer the old-fashioned type. Some of those
men at least were loved by the women they sold. But what feelings can a pimp arouse in a leg of lamb? Pardon my language,
Irma.

COUNT. It's all right. She doesn't understand it.

RAG. So now you know, Countess, why the world is no longer happy.
We are the last of the free people of the earth. You saw them

looking us over today. Tomorrow, the street-singer will start paying the song-pimp, and the garbage-pimp will be after me. I tell you, Countess, we're finished. It's the end of free enterprise in this world!

COUNT. Is this true, Roderick?

PIERRE. I'm afraid it's true.

COUNT. Did you know about this, Irma?

IRMA. All I know is the doorman says that faith is dead.

DOOR. I've stopped taking bets over the phone.

JUG. The very air is different, Countess. You can't trust it any more. If I throw my torches up too high, they go out.

RAG. The sky-pimp puts them out.

FLOW. GIRL. My flowers don't last over night now. They wilt.

JUG. Have you noticed, the pigeons don't fly any more?

RAG. They can't afford to. They walk.

COUNT. They're a lot of fools and so are you! You should have told me at once! How can you bear to live in a world where there is unhappiness? Where a man is not his own master? Are you cowards? All we have to do is to get rid of these men.

PIERRE. How can we get rid of them? They're too strong.

(*The* SERGEANT *walks up again.*)

COUNT. (*smiling*). The Sergeant will help us.

SERG. Who? Me?

IRMA. There are a great many of them, Countess. The Deaf-Mute knows them all. They employed him once, years ago, because he was deaf. (*The* DEAF-MUTE *wigwags a short speech.*) They fired him because he wasn't blind. (*Another flash of sign language.*) They're all connected like the parts of a machine.

COUNT. So much the better. We shall drive the whole machine into a ditch.

SERG. It's not that easy, Countess. You never catch these birds napping. They change before your very eyes. I remember when I was in the detectives. . . . You catch a president, pfft! He turns into a trustee. You catch him as trustee, and pfft! he's not a trustee—he's an honorary vice-chairman. You catch a Senator dead to rights: he becomes Minister of Justice. You get after the Minister of

Justice—he is Chief of Police. And there you are—no longer in
the detectives.

PIERRE. He's right, Countess. They have all the power. And all the
money. And they're greedy for more.

COUNT. They're greedy? Ah, then, my friends, they're lost. If they're
greedy, they're stupid. If they're greedy—don't worry, I know exactly what to do. Roderick, by tonight you will be an honest man.
And, Juggler, your torches will stay lit. And your beer will flow
freely again, Martial. And the world will be saved. Let's get to
work.

RAG. What are you going to do?

COUNT. Have you any kerosene in the house, Irma?

IRMA. Yes. Would you like some?

COUNT. I want just a little. In a dirty bottle. With a little mud. And
some mange-cure, if you have it. (*To the* DEAF-MUTE.) Deaf-Mute!
Take a letter. (IRMA *interprets in sign language. To the* SINGER.)
Singer, go and find Madame Constance. (IRMA *and the* WAITER *go
into the café.*)

SING. Yes, Countess.

COUNT. Ask her to be at my house by two o'clock. I'll be waiting for her
in the cellar. You may tell her we have to discuss the future of
humanity. That's sure to bring her.

SING. Yes, Countess.

COUNT. And ask her to bring Mademoiselle Gabrielle and Madame
Josephine with her. Do you know how to get in to speak to Madame Constance? You ring twice, and then meow three times like
a cat. Do you know how to meow?

SING. I'm better at barking.

COUNT. Better practise meowing on the way. Incidentally, I think Madame Constance knows all the verses of your mazurka. Remind
me to ask her.

SING. Yes, Countess.   (*Exit.*)

(IRMA *comes in. She is shaking the oily concoction in a little perfume
vial, which she now hands the* COUNTESS.)

IRMA. Here you are, Countess.

COUNT. Thanks, Irma. (*She assumes a presidential manner.*) Deaf-Mute! Ready?

(IRMA *interprets in sign language. The* WAITER *has brought out a portfolio of letter paper and placed it on a table. The* DEAF-MUTE *sits down before it, and prepares to write.*)

IRMA (*speaking for the* DEAF-MUTE). I'm ready.

COUNT. My dear Mr.— What's his name?

(IRMA *wigwags the question to the* DEAF-MUTE, *who answers in the same manner. It is all done so deftly that it is as if the* DEAF-MUTE *were actually speaking.*)

IRMA. They are all called Mr. President.

COUNT. My dear Mr. President: I have personally verified the existence of a spontaneous outcrop of oil in the cellar of Number 21 Rue de Chaillot, which is at present occupied by a dignified person of unstable mentality. (*The* COUNTESS *grins knowingly.*) This explains why, fortunately for us, the discovery has so long been kept secret. If you should wish to verify the existence of this outcrop for yourself, you may call at the above address at three P.M. today. I am herewith enclosing a sample so that you may judge the quality and consistency of the crude. Yours very truly. Roderick, can you sign the prospector's name?

PIERRE. You wish me to?

COUNT. One forgery wipes out the other. (PIERRE *signs the letter. The* DEAF-MUTE *types the address on an envelope.*)

IRMA. Who is to deliver this?

COUNT. The Doorman, of course. On his bicycle. And as soon as you have delivered it, run over to the prospector's office. Leave word that the President expects to see him at my house at three.

DOOR. Yes, Countess.

COUNT. I shall leave you now. I have many pressing things to do. Among others, I must press my red gown.

RAG. But this only takes care of two of them, Countess.

COUNT. Didn't the Deaf-Mute say they are all connected like the works of a machine?

IRMA. Yes.

COUNT. Then, if one comes, the rest will follow. And we shall have them all. My boa, please.

DOOR. The one that's stolen, Countess?

COUNT. Naturally. The one the prospector stole.

DOOR. It hasn't turned up yet, Countess. But someone has left an ermine collar.

COUNT. Real ermine?

DOOR. Looks like it.

COUNT. Ermine and iris were made for each other. Let me see it.

DOOR. Yes, Countess. *(Exit DOORMAN.)*

COUNT. Roderick, you shall escort me. You still look pale. I have some old Chartreuse at home. I always take a glass each year. Last year I forgot. You shall have it.

PIERRE. If there is anything I can do, Countess . . . ?

COUNT. There is a great deal you can do. There are all the things that need to be done in a room that no man has been in for twenty years. You can untwist the cord on the blind and let in a little sunshine for a change. You can take the mirror off the wardrobe door, and deliver me once and for all from the old harpy that lives in the mirror. You can let the mouse out of the trap. I'm tired of feeding it. *(To her friends.)* Each man to his post. See you later, my friends. *(The DOORMAN puts the ermine collar around her shoulders.)* Thank you, my boy. It's rabbit. *(One o'clock strikes.)* Your arm, Valentine.

PIERRE. Valentine?

COUNT. It's just struck one. At one, all men become Valentine.

PIERRE *(he offers his arm)*. Permit me.

COUNT. Or Valentino. It's obviously far from the same, isn't it, Irma? But they have that much choice. *(She sweeps out majestically with PIERRE. The others disperse. All but IRMA.)*

IRMA *(clearing off the table)*. I hate ugliness. I love beauty. I hate meanness. I adore kindness. It may not seem so grand to some to be a waitress in Paris. I love it. A waitress meets all sorts of people. She observes life. I hate to be alone. I love people. But I have never said I love you to a man. Men try to make me say it. They put their arms around me—I pretend I don't see it. They pinch me—I pretend I don't feel it. They kiss me—I pretend I don't know it. They take me out in the evening and make me drink— but I'm careful, I never say it. If they don't like it, they can leave me alone. Because when I say I love you to Him, He will know just by looking in my eyes that many have held me and pinched me and kissed me, but I have never said I love you to anyone in the world before. Never. No. (*Looking off in the direction in* which PIERRE *has gone, she whispers softly:*) I love you.

VOICE (*from within the café*). Irma!

IRMA. Coming. (*Exits.*)

(CURTAIN)

ACT TWO

SCENE: *The cellar of the* COUNTESS' *house. An ancient vault set deep in the ground, with walls of solid masonry, part brick and part great ashlars, mossy and sweating. A staircase of medieval pattern is built into the thickness of the wall, and leads up to the street level from a landing halfway down. In the corners of the cellar are piled casks, packing cases, bird cages, and other odds and ends—the accumulation of centuries—the whole effect utterly fantastic.*

In the center of the vast underground room, some furniture has been arranged to give an impression of a sitting-room of the 1890's. There is a venerable chaise-longue piled with cushions that once were gay, three armchairs, a table with an oil lamp and a bowl of flowers, a shaggy rug. It is two P.M., the same day.

AT RISE: *The* COUNTESS *is sitting over a bit of mending, in one of the armchairs.* IRMA *appears on the landing and calls down.*

IRMA. Countess! The Sewer Man is here.

COUNT. Thank goodness, Irma. Send him down. (*The* SEWER MAN *enters. He carries his hip-boots in his hand.*) How do you do, Mr. Sewer Man? (*The* SEWER MAN *bows.*) But why do you have your boots in your hand instead of on your feet?

SEWER MAN. Etiquette, Countess. Etiquette.

COUNT. How very American! I'm told that Americans nowadays apolo-

gize for their gloves if they happen to take one's hand. As if the
skin of a human were nicer to touch than the skin of a sheep!
And particularly if they have sweaty hands . . . !

SEWER MAN. My feet never sweat, Countess.

COUNT. How very nice! But please don't stand on ceremony here. Put
your boots on. Put them on.

SEWER MAN (*complying*). Thanks very much, Countess.

COUNT. (*while he draws on his boots*). I'm sure you must have a very
poor opinion of the upper world, from what you see of it. The
way people throw their filth into your territory is absolutely
scandalous! I burn all my refuse, and I scatter the ashes. All I
ever throw in the drain is flowers. Did you happen to see a lily
float by this morning? Mine. But perhaps you didn't notice?

SEWER MAN. We notice a lot more down there, Countess, than you might
think. You'd be surprised the things we notice. There's lots of
things come along that were obviously intended for us—little
gifts, you might call them—sometimes a brand-new shaving brush
—sometimes, *The Brothers Karamazov*. . . . Thanks for the lily,
Countess. A very sweet thought.

COUNT. Tomorrow you shall have this iris. But now, let's come to the
point. I have two questions to ask you.

SEWER MAN. Yes, Countess?

COUNT. First—and this has nothing to do with our problem—it's just
something that has been troubling me. . . . Tell me, is it true
that the sewer men of Paris have a king?

SEWER MAN. Oh, now, Countess, that's another of those fairy tales out
of the Sunday supplements. It just seems those writers can't keep
their minds off the sewers! It fascinates them. They keep thinking
of us moving around in our underground canals like gondoliers
in Venice, and it sends them into a fever of romance! The things
they say about us! They say we have a race of girls down there
who never see the light of day! It's completely fantastic! The girls
naturally come out—every Christmas and Easter. And orgies by
torchlight with gondolas and guitars! With troops of rats that
dance as they follow the piper! What nonsense! The rats are not

allowed to dance. No, no, no. Of course we have no king. Down in the sewers, you'll find nothing but good Republicans.

COUNT. And no queen?

SEWER MAN. No. We may run a beauty contest down there once in a while. Or crown a mermaid Queen of the May. But no queen what you'd call a queen. And, as for these swimming races they talk so much about . . . possibly once in a while—in the summer—in the dog days . . .

COUNT. I believe you. I believe you. And now tell me. Do you remember that night I found you here in my cellar—looking very pale and strange—you were half-dead as a matter of fact—and I gave you some brandy. . . .

SEWER MAN. Yes, Countess.

COUNT. That night you promised if ever I should need it—you would tell me the secret of this room.

SEWER MAN. The secret of the moving stone?

COUNT. I need it now.

SEWER MAN. Only the King of the Sewer Men knows this secret.

COUNT. I'm sure of it. I know most secrets, of course. As a matter of fact, I have three magic words that will open any door that words can open. I have tried them all—in various tones of voice. They don't seem to work. And this is a matter of life and death.

SEWER MAN. Look, Countess. (*He locates a brick in the masonry, and pushes it. A huge block of stone slowly pivots and uncovers a trap from which a circular staircase winds into the bowels of the earth.*)

COUNT. Good heavens! Where do those stairs lead?

SEWER MAN. Nowhere.

COUNT. But they must go somewhere.

SEWER MAN. They just go down.

COUNT. Let's go and see.

SEWER MAN. No, Countess. Never again. That time you found me, I had a pretty close shave. I kept going down and around, and down and around for an hour, a year—I don't know. There's no end to it, Countess. Once you start you can't stop. . . . Your head begins to turn—you're lost. No—once you start down, there's no coming up.

COUNT. You came up.

SEWER MAN. I—I am a special case. Besides, I had my tools, my ropes. And I stopped in time.

COUNT. You could have screamed—shouted.

SEWER MAN. You could fire off a cannon.

COUNT. Who could have built a thing like this?

SEWER MAN. Paris is old, you know. Paris is very old.

COUNT. You don't suppose, by any chance, there is oil down there?

SEWER MAN. There's only death down there.

COUNT. I should have preferred a little oil too—or a vein of gold—or emeralds. You're quite sure there is nothing?

SEWER MAN. Not even rats.

COUNT. How does one lower this stone?

SEWER MAN. Simple. To open, you press here. And to close it, you push there. (*He presses the brick. The stone descends.*) Now there's two of us in the world that know it.

COUNT. I won't remember long. Is it all right if I repeat my magic words while I press it?

SEWER MAN. It's bound to help.

(IRMA *enters.*)

IRMA. Countess, Madame Constance and Mademoiselle Gabrielle are here.

COUNT. Show them down, Irma. Thank you very much, Mr. Sewer Man.

SEWER MAN. Like that story about the steam laundry that's supposed to be running day and night in my sewer . . . I can assure you. . . .

COUNT. (*edging him toward the door*). Thank you very much.

SEWER MAN. Pure imagination! They never work nights. (*He goes off, bowing graciously.*)

(CONSTANCE, *the Madwoman of Passy, and* GABRIELLE, *the Madwoman of St. Sulpice, come down daintily.* CONSTANCE *is all in white. She wears an enormous hat graced with ostrich plumes, and a lavender veil.* GABRIELLE *is costumed with the affected simplicity of the 1880's. She is atrociously made up in a remorseless parody of blushing innocence, and she minces down the stairs with macabre coyness.*)

CON. Aurelia! Don't tell us they've found your feather boa?

GAB. You don't mean Adolphe Bertaut has proposed at last! I knew he would.

COUNT. How are you, Constance? (*She shouts.*) How are you, Gabrielle?

GAB. You needn't shout today, my dear. It's Wednesday. Wednesdays, I hear perfectly.

CON. It's Thursday.

GAB. Oh, dear. Well, never mind. I'm going to make an exception just this once.

CON. (*to an imaginary dog who has stopped on the landing*). Come along, Dickie. Come along. And stop barking. What a racket you're making! Come on, darling—we've come to see the longest boa and the handsomest man in Paris. Come on.

COUNT. Constance, it's not a question of my boa today. Nor of poor Adolphe. It's a question of the future of the human race.

CON. You think it has a future?

COUNT. Please don't make silly jokes. Sit down and listen to me. Today we must make a decision which may alter the fate of the world.

CON. Couldn't we do it tomorrow? I want to wash my slippers. Now, Dickie—please!

COUNT. We haven't a moment to waste. Where is Josephine? Well, we'd best have our tea, and the moment Josephine comes . . .

GAB. Josephine is sitting on her bench in front of the palace waiting for President Wilson to come out. She says she's sorry, but she positively must see him today.

CON. Dickie!

COUNT. What a pity! (*She gets the tea things from the side table, pours tea and serves cake and honey.*) I wish she were here to help us. She has a first-class brain.

CON. Go ahead, dear. We're listening. (*To* DICKIE.) What is it, Dickie? You want to sit in Aunt Aurelia's lap. All right, darling. Go on. Jump, Dickie.

COUNT. Constance, we love you, as you know. And we love Dickie. But this is a serious matter. So let's stop being childish for once.

CON. And what does that mean, if you please?

COUNT. It means Dickie. You know perfectly well that we love him and fuss over him just as if he were still alive. He's a sacred memory and we wouldn't hurt his feelings for the world. But please don't plump him in my lap when I'm settling the future of mankind. His basket is in the corner—he knows where it is, and he can just go and sit in it.

CON. So you're against Dickie too! You too!

COUNT. Constance! I'm not in the least against Dickie! I adore Dickie. But you know as well as I that Dickie is only a convention with us. It's a beautiful convention—but it doesn't have to bark all the time. Besides, it's you that spoil him. The time you went to visit your niece and left him with me, we got on marvelously together. He didn't bark, he didn't tear things, he didn't even eat. But when you're with him, one can pay attention to nothing else. I'm not going to take Dickie in my lap at a solemn moment like this, no, not for anything in the world. And that's that!

GAB. (*very sweetly*). Constance, dear, I don't mind taking him in my lap. He loves to sit in my lap, don't you, darling?

CON. Kindly stop putting on angelic airs, Gabrielle. I know you very well. You're much too sweet to be sincere. There's plenty of times that I make believe that Dickie is here, when really I've left him home, and you cuddle and pet him just the same.

GAB. I adore animals.

CON. If you adore animals, you shouldn't pet them when they're not there. It's a form of hypocrisy.

COUNT. Now, Constance, Gabrielle has as much right as you . . .

CON. Gabrielle has no right to do what she does. Do you know what she does? She invites *people* to come to tea with us. *People* whom we know nothing about. *People* who exist only in her imagination.

COUNT. You think that's not an existence?

GAB. I don't invite them at all. They come by themselves. What can I do?

CON. You might introduce us.

COUNT. If you think they're only imaginary, there's no point in your meeting them, is there?

CON. Of course they're imaginary. But who likes to have imaginary people staring at one? Especially strangers.

GAB. Oh, they're really very nice. . . .

CON. Tell me just one thing, Gabrielle—are they here now?

COUNT. Am I to be allowed to speak? Or is this going to be the same as the argument about inoculating Josephine's cat, when we didn't get to the subject at all?

CON. Never! Never! Never! I'll never give my consent to that. (*To* DICKIE.) I'd never do a thing like that to you, Dickie sweet. . . . Oh, no! Oh, no! (*She begins to weep softly.*)

COUNT. Good heavens! Now we have her in tears. What an impossible creature! With the fate of humanity hanging in the balance! All right, all right, stop crying. I'll take him in my lap. Come, Dickie, Dickie.

CON. No. He won't go now. Oh, how can you be so cruel? Don't you suppose I know about Dickie? Don't you think I'd rather have him here alive and woolly and frisking around the way he used to? You have your Adolphe. Gabrielle has her birds. But I have only Dickie. Do you think I'd be so silly about him if it wasn't that it's only by pretending that he's here all the time that I get him to come sometimes, really? Next time I won't bring him!

COUNT. Now let's not get ourselves worked up over nothing. Come here, Dickie. . . . Irma is going to take you for a nice walk. (*She rings her bell.*) Irma!

(IRMA *appears on the landing.*)

CON. No. He doesn't want to go. Besides, I didn't bring him today. So there!

COUNT. Very well, then. Irma, make sure the door is locked.

IRMA. Yes, Countess. (IRMA *exits.*)

CON. What do you mean? Why locked? Who's coming?

COUNT. If you'd let me get a word in, you'd know by now. A terrible thing has happened. This morning, this very morning, exactly at noon . . .

CON. (*thrilled*). Oh, how exciting!

COUNT. Be quiet. This morning, exactly at noon, thanks to a young man who drowned himself in the Seine . . . Oh, yes, while I think of it—do you know a mazurka called *La Belle Polonaise?*

CON. Yes, Aurelia.

COUNT. Could you sing it now? This very minute?

CON. Yes, Aurelia.

COUNT. All of it?

CON. Yes, Aurelia. But who's interrupting now, Aurelia?

COUNT. You're right. Well, this morning, exactly at noon, I discovered a horrible plot. There is a group of men who intend to tear down the whole city!

CON. Is that all?

GAB. But I don't understand, Aurelia. Why should men want to tear down the city? It was they themselves who put it up.

COUNT. You are so innocent, my poor Gabrielle. There are people in the world who want to destroy everything. They have the fever of destruction. Even when they pretend that they're building, it is only in order to destroy. When they put up a new building, they quietly knock down two old ones. They build cities so that they can destroy the countryside. They destroy space with telephones and time with airplanes. Humanity is now dedicated to the task of universal destruction. I am speaking, of course, primarily of the male sex.

GAB. (*shocked*). Oh . . . !

CON. Aurelia! Must you talk sex in front of Gabrielle?

COUNT. There *are* two sexes.

CON. Gabrielle is a virgin, Aurelia!

COUNT. Oh, she can't be as innocent as all that. She keeps canaries.

GAB. I think you're being very cruel about men, Aurelia. Men are big and beautiful, and as loyal as dogs. I preferred not to marry, it's true. But I hear excellent reports from friends who have had an opportunity to observe them closely.

COUNT. My poor darling! You are still living in a dream. But one day, you will wake up as I have, and then you will see what is happening in the world. The tide has turned, my dear. Men are changing back into beasts. They know it. They no longer try to hide it. There was once such a thing as manners. I remember a time when the hungriest was the one who took the longest to pick up his fork. The one with the broadest grin was the one who needed most to go to the . . . It was such fun to keep them grinning like that for hours. But now they no longer pretend. Just look at them—snuffling their soup like pigs, tearing their meat like tigers, crunching their lettuce like crocodiles! A man doesn't take your hand nowadays. He gives you his paw.

CON. Would that trouble you so much if they turned into animals? Personally, I think it's a good idea.

GAB. Oh, I'd love to see them like that. They'd be sweet.

CON. It might be the salvation of the human race.

COUNT. (*to* CONSTANCE). You'd make a fine rabbit, wouldn't you?

CON. I?

COUNT. Naturally. You don't think it's only the men who are changing? You change along with them. Husbands and wives together. We're all one race, you know.

CON. You think so? And why would my poor husband have to be a rabbit if he were alive?

COUNT. Remember his front teeth? When he nibbled his celery?

CON. I'm happy to say, I remember absolutely nothing about him. All I remember on that subject is the time that Father Lacordaire tried to kiss me in the park.

COUNT. Yes, yes, of course.

CON. And what does that mean, if you please, "Yes, yes, of course"?

COUNT. Constance, just this once, look us in the eye and tell us truly— did that really happen or did you read about it in a book?

CON. Now I'm being insulted!

COUNT. We promise you faithfully that we'll believe it all over again afterwards, won't we, Gabrielle? But tell us the truth this once.

CON. How dare you question my memories? Suppose I said your pearls were false!

COUNT. They were.

CON. I'm not asking what they were. I'm asking what they are. Are they false or are they real?

COUNT. Everyone knows that little by little, as one wears pearls, they become real.

CON. And isn't it exactly the same with memories?

COUNT. Now do not let us waste time. I must go on.

CON. I think Gabrielle is perfectly right about men. There are still plenty who haven't changed a bit. There's an old Senator who bows to Gabrielle every day when he passes her in front of the palace. And he takes off his hat each time.

GAB. That's perfectly true, Aurelia. He's always pushing an empty baby carriage, and he always stops and bows.

COUNT. Don't be taken in, Gabrielle. It's all make-believe. And all we can expect from these make-believe men is itself make-believe. They give us face powder made of stones, sausages made of saw-dust, shirts made of glass, stockings made of milk. It's all a vulgar pretense. And if that is the case, imagine what passes, these days, for virtue, sincerity, generosity and love! I warn you, Gabrielle, don't let this Senator with the empty baby carriage pull the wool over your eyes.

GAB. He's really the soul of courtesy. He seems very correct.

COUNT. Those are the worst. Gabrielle, beware! He'll make you put on black riding boots, while he dances the can-can around you, sing-ing God knows what filth at the top of his voice. The very thought makes one's blood run cold!

GAB. You think that's what he has in mind?

COUNT. Of course. Men have lost all sense of decency. They are all equally disgusting. Just look at them in the evening, sitting at their tables in the café, working away in unison with their tooth-picks, hour after hour, digging up roast beef, veal, onion . . .

CON. They don't harm anyone that way.

COUNT. Then why do you barricade your door, and make your friends meow before you let them come up? Incidentally, we must make an interesting sight, Gabrielle and I, yowling together on your doorstep like a couple of tomcats!

CON. There's no need at all for you to yowl together. One would be quite enough. And you know perfectly well why I have to do it. It's because there are murderers.

COUNT. I don't quite see what prevents murderers from meowing like anybody else. But why are there murderers?

CON. Why? Because there are thieves.

COUNT. And why are there thieves? Why is there almost nothing but thieves?

CON. Because they worship money. Because money is king.

COUNT. Ah—now we've come to it. Because we live in the reign of the Golden Calf. Did you realize that, Gabrielle? Men now publicly worship the Golden Calf!

GAB. How awful! Have the authorities been notified?

COUNT. The authorities do it themselves, Gabrielle.

GAB. Oh! Has anyone talked to the bishop?

COUNT. Nowadays only money talks to the bishop. And so you see why I asked you to come here today. The world has gone out of its mind. Unless we do something, humanity is doomed! Constance, have you any suggestions?

CON. I know what I always do in a case like this. . . .

COUNT. You write to the Prime Minister.

CON. He always does what I tell him.

COUNT. Does he ever answer your letters?

CON. He knows I prefer him not to. It might excite gossip. Besides, I don't always write. Sometimes I wire. The time I told him about the Archbishop's frigidaire, it was by wire. And they sent a new one the very next day.

COUNT. There was probably a commission in it for someone. And what do you suggest, Gabrielle?

CON. Now, how can she tell you until she's consulted her voices?

GAB. I could go right home and consult them, and we could meet again after dinner.

COUNT. There's no time for that. Besides, your voices are not real voices.

GAB. (*furious*). How dare you say a thing like that?

COUNT. Where do your voices come from? Still from your sewing-machine?

GAB. Not at all. They've passed into my hot-water bottle. And it's much nicer that way. They don't chatter any more. They gurgle. But they haven't been a bit nice to me lately. Last night they kept telling me to let my canaries out. "Let them out. Let them out. Let them out."

CON. Did you?

GAB. I opened the cage. They wouldn't go.

COUNT. I don't call that *voices*. Objects talk—everyone knows that. It's the principle of the phonograph. But to ask a hot-water bottle for advice is silly. What does a hot-water bottle know? No, all we have to consult here is our own judgment.

CON. Very well then, tell us what you have decided. Since you're asking our opinion, you've doubtless made up your mind.

COUNT. Yes, I've thought the whole thing out. All I really needed to discover was the source of the infection. Today I found it.

CON. Where?

COUNT. You'll see soon enough. I've baited a trap. In just a few minutes, the rats will be here.

GAB. (*in alarm*). Rats!

COUNT. Don't be alarmed. They're still in human form.

GAB. Heavens! What are you going to do with them?

COUNT. That's just the question. Suppose I get these wicked men all here at once—in my cellar—have I the right to exterminate them?

GAB. To kill them?

(COUNTESS *nods.*)

CON. That's not a question for us. You'll have to ask Father Bridet.

COUNT. I have asked him. Yes. One day, in confession, I told him frankly that I had a secret desire to destroy all wicked people. He said: "By all means, my child. And when you're ready to go into action, I'll lend you the jawbone of an ass."

CON. That's just talk. You get him to put that in writing.

GAB. What's your scheme, Aurelia?

COUNT. That's a secret.

CON. It's not so easy to kill them. Let's say you had a tank full of vitriol all ready for them. You could never get them to walk into it. There's nothing so stubborn as a man when you want him to do something.

COUNT. Leave that to me.

CON. But if they're killed, they're bound to be missed, and then we'll be fined. They fine you for every little thing these days.

COUNT. They won't be missed.

GAB. I wish Josephine were here. Her sister's husband was a lawyer. She knows all about these things.

COUNT. Do you miss a cold when it's gone? Or the germs that caused it? When the world feels well again, do you think it will regret its illness? No, it will stretch itself joyfully, and it will smile— that's all.

CON. Just a moment! Gabrielle, are they here now? Yes or no?

COUNT. What's the matter with you now?

CON. I'm simply asking Gabrielle if her friends are in the room or not. I have a right to know.

GAB. I'm not allowed to say.

CON. I know very well they are. I'm sure of it. Otherwise you wouldn't be making faces.

COUNT. May I ask what difference it makes to you if her friends are in the room?

CON. Just this: If they're here, I'm not going to say another word! I'm certainly not going to commit myself in a matter involving the death sentence in the presence of third parties, whether they exist or not.

GAB. That's not being very nice to my guests, is it?

COUNT. Constance, you must be mad! Or are you so stupid as to think that just because we're alone, there's nobody with us? Do you consider us so boring or repulsive that of all the millions of beings, imaginary or otherwise, who are prowling about in space, there's not one who might possibly enjoy spending a little time with us? On the contrary, my dear—my house is full of guests always. They know that here they have a place in the universe where they can come when they're lonely and be sure of a welcome. For my part, I'm delighted to have them.

GAB. Thank you, Aurelia.

CON. You know perfectly well, Aurelia . . .

COUNT. I know perfectly well that at this moment the whole universe is listening to us—and that every word we say echoes to the remotest star. To pretend otherwise is the sheerest hypocrisy.

CON. Then why do you insult me in front of everybody? I'm not mean. I'm shy. I feel timid about giving an opinion in front of such a crowd. Furthermore, if you think I'm so bad and so stupid, why did you invite me, in the first place?

COUNT. I'll tell you. And I'll tell you why, disagreeable as you are, I always give you the biggest piece of cake and my best honey. It's because when you come there's always, someone with you—and I don't mean Dickie—I mean someone who resembles you like a sister, only she's young and lovely, and she sits modestly to one side and smiles at me tenderly all the time you're bickering and quarreling, and never says a word. That's the Constance to whom I give the cake that you gobble, and it's because of her that you're here today, and it's her vote that I'm asking you to cast in this crucial moment. And not yours, which is of no importance whatever.

CON. I'm leaving.

COUNT. Be so good as to sit down. I can't let her go yet.

CON. (*crossing toward the stairs*). No. This is too much. I'm taking her with me.

(IRMA *enters*.)

IRMA. Madame Josephine.

COUNT. Thank heaven!

GAB. We're saved.

(JOSEPHINE, *the Madwoman of La Concorde, sweeps in majestically in a get-up somewhere between the regal and the priestly*.)

JOS. My dear friends, today once again, I waited for President Wilson—but he didn't come out.

COUNT. You'll have to wait quite a while longer before he does. He's been dead since 1924.

JOS. I have plenty of time.

COUNT. In anyone else, Josephine, these extravagances might seem a little childish. But a person of your judgment doubtless has her reasons for wanting to talk to a man to whom no one would listen when he was alive. We have a legal problem for you. Suppose you had all the world's criminals here in this room. And suppose you had a way of getting rid of them forever. Would you have the right to do it?

JOS. Why not?

COUNT. Exactly my point.

GAB. But, Josephine, so many people!

JOS. *De minimis non curat lex!* The more there are, the more legal it is.

It's impersonal. It's even military. It's the cardinal principle of battle—you get all your enemies in one place, and you kill them all together at one time. Because if you had to track them down one by one in their houses and offices, you'd get tired, and sooner or later you'd stop. I believe your idea is very practical, Aurelia. I can't imagine why we never thought of it before.

GAB. Well, if you think it's all right to do it. . . .

JOS. By all means. Your criminals have had a fair trial, I suppose?

COUNT. Trial?

JOS. Certainly. You can't kill anybody without a trial. That's elementary. "No man shall be deprived of his life, liberty and property without due process of law."

COUNT. They deprive us of ours.

JOS. That's not the point. You're not accused of anything. Every accused—man, woman or child—has the right to defend himself at the bar of justice. Even animals. Before the Deluge, you will recall, the Lord permitted Noah to speak in defense of his fellow mortals. He evidently stuttered. You know the result. On the other hand, Captain Dreyfus was not only innocent—he was defended by a marvelous orator. The result was precisely the same. So you see, in having a trial, you run no risk whatever.

COUNT. But if I give them the slightest cause for suspicion—I'll lose them.

JOS. There's a simple procedure prescribed in such cases. You can summon the defendants by calling them three times—mentally, if you like. If they don't appear, the court may designate an attorney who will represent them. This attorney can then argue their case to the court, *in absentia,* and a judgment can then be rendered, *in contumacio.*

COUNT. But I don't know any attorneys. And we have only ten minutes.

GAB. Hurry, Josephine, hurry!

JOS. In case of emergency, it is permissible for the court to order the first passer-by to act as attorney for the defense. A defense is like a baptism. Absolutely indispensable, but you don't have to know anything to do it. Ask Irma to get you somebody. Anybody.

COUNT. The Deaf-Mute?

JOS. Well—that's getting it down a bit fine. That might be questionable on appeal.

COUNT. (*calls*). Irma! What about the Police Sergeant?

JOS. He won't do. He's under oath to the state.

(IRMA *appears*.)

IRMA. Yes, Countess?

COUNT. Who's out there, Irma?

IRMA. All our friends, Countess. There's the Ragpicker and . . .

COUNT. Send down the Ragpicker.

CON. Do you think it's wise to have all those millionaires represented by a ragpicker?

JOS. It's a first-rate choice. Criminals are always represented by their opposites. Murderers, by someone who obviously wouldn't hurt a fly. Rapists, by a member of the League for Decency. Experience shows it's the only way to get an acquittal.

COUNT. But we must not have an acquittal. That would mean the end of the world!

JOS. Justice is justice, my dear.

(*The* RAGPICKER *comes down, with a stately air. Behind him, on the landing, appear the other* VAGABONDS.)

RAG. Greetings, Countess. Greetings, ladies. My most sincere compliments.

COUNT. Has Irma told you . . . ?

RAG. She said something about a trial.

COUNT. You have been appointed attorney for the defense.

RAG. Terribly flattered, I'm sure.

COUNT. You realize, don't you, how much depends on the outcome of this trial?

JOS. Do you know the defendants well enough to undertake the case?

RAG. I know them to the bottom of their souls. I go through their garbage every day.

CON. And what do you find there?

RAG. Mostly flowers.

GAB. It's true, you know, the rich are always surrounded with flowers.

CON. How beautiful!

COUNT. Are you trying to prejudice the court?

RAG. Oh no, Countess, no.

COUNT. We want a completely impartial defense.

RAG. Of course, Countess, of course. Permit me to make a suggestion.

COUNT. Will you preside, Josephine?

RAG. Instead of speaking as attorney, suppose you let me speak directly as defendant. It will be more convincing, and I can get into it more.

JOS. Excellent idea. Motion granted.

COUNT. We don't want you to be too convincing, remember.

RAG. Impartial, Countess, impartial.

JOS. Well? Have you prepared your case?

RAG. How rich am I?

JOS. Millions. Billions.

RAG. How did I get them? Theft? Murder? Embezzlement?

COUNT. Most likely.

RAG. Do I have a wife? A mistress?

COUNT. Everything.

RAG. All right. I'm ready.

GAB. Will you have some tea?

RAG. Is that good?

CON. Very good for the voice. The Russians drink nothing but tea. And they talk like anything.

RAG. All right. Tea.

JOS. (*to the* VAGABONDS). Come in. Come in. All of you. You may take places. The trial is public. (*The* VAGABONDS *dispose themselves on the steps and elsewhere.*) Your bell, if you please, Aurelia.

COUNT. But what if I should need to ring for Irma?

JOS. Irma will sit here, next to me. If you need her, she can ring for herself. (*To the* POLICE SERGEANT *and the* FOLICEMAN.) Conduct the accused to the bar. (*The officers conduct the* RAGPICKER *to a bar improvised with a rocking chair and a packing case marked* "Fragile." *The* RAGPICKER *mounts the box. She rings the bell.*) The court is now in session. (*All sit.*) Counsel for the defense, you may take the oath.

RAG. I swear to tell the truth, the whole truth, and nothing but the truth, so help me God.

JOS. Nonsense! You're not a witness. You're an attorney. It's your duty to lie, conceal and distort everything, and slander everybody.

RAG. All right. I swear to lie, conceal and distort everything, and slander everybody.

(JOSEPHINE *rings stridently*.)

JOS. Quiet! Begin.

RAG. May it please the honorable, august and elegant Court . . .

JOS. Flattery will get you nowhere. That will do. The defense has been heard. Cross-examination.

COUNT. Mr. President . . .

RAG. (*bowing with dignity*). Madame.

COUNT. Do you know what you are charged with?

RAG. I can't for the life of me imagine. My life is an open book. My ways are known to all. I am a pillar of the church and the sole support of the Opera. My hands are spotless.

COUNT. What an atrocious lie! Just look at them!

CON. You don't have to insult the man. He's only lying to please you.

COUNT. Be quiet, Constance! You don't get the idea at all. (*To the* RAG-PICKER.) You are charged with the crime of worshipping money.

RAG. Worshipping money? Me?

JOS. Do you plead guilty or not guilty? Which is it?

RAG. Why, Your Honor . . .

JOS. Yes or no?

RAG. Yes or no? No! I don't worship money, Countess. Heavens, no! Money worships me. It adores me. It won't let me alone. It's damned embarrassing, I can tell you.

JOS. Kindly watch your language.

COUNT. Defendant, tell the Court how you came by your money.

RAG. The first time money came to me, I was a mere boy, a little golden-haired child in the bosom of my dear family. It came to me suddenly in the guise of a gold brick which, in my innocence, I picked out of a garbage can one day while playing. I was horrified, as you can imagine. I immediately tried to get rid of it by swapping it for a little rundown one-track railroad which, to my consternation, at once sold itself for a hundred times its value. In a desperate effort to get rid of this money, I began to buy things. I bought the Northern Refineries, the Galeries Lafayette, and the Schneider-Creusot Munition Works. And now I'm stuck with them. It's a horrible fate—but I'm resigned to it. I don't ask for your sympathy, I don't ask for your pity—all I ask for is a little common human understanding. . . . (*He begins to cry.*)

COUNT. I object. This wretch is trying to play on the emotions of the Court.

JOS. The Court has no emotions.

RAG. Everyone knows that the poor have no one but themselves to blame for their poverty. It's only just that they should suffer the consequences. But how is it the fault of the rich if they're rich?

COUNT. Dry your tears. You're deceiving nobody. If, as you say, you're ashamed of your money, why is it you hold onto it with such a death-grip?

RAG. Me?

ST. PED. You never part with a franc!

JUG. You wouldn't even give the poor Deaf-Mute a sou!

RAG. Me, hold onto money? What slander! What injustice! What a thing to say to me in the presence of this honorable, august and elegant Court! I spend all my time trying to spend my money. If I have tan shoes, I buy black ones. If I have a bicycle, I buy a motor car. If I have a wife, I buy . . .

JOS. (*rings*). Order!

RAG. I dispatch a plane to Java for a bouquet of flowers. I send a steamer to Egypt for a basket of figs. I send a special representative to New York to fetch me an ice-cream cone. And if it's not just exactly right, back it goes. But no matter what I do, I can't get rid of my money! If I play a hundred to one shot, the horse comes in by twenty lengths. If I throw a diamond in the Seine, it turns up in the trout they serve me for lunch. Ten diamonds—ten trout. Well, now, do you suppose I can get rid of forty millions by giving a sou to a deaf-mute? Is it even worth the effort?

CON. He's right.

RAG. Ah! You see, my dear? At last, there is somebody who understands me! Somebody who is not only beautiful, but extraordinarily sensitive and intelligent.

COUNT. I object!

JOS. Overruled!

RAG. I should be delighted to send you some flowers, Miss—directly I'm acquitted. What flowers do you prefer?

CON. Roses.

RAG. You shall have a bale every morning for the next five years. Money means nothing to me.

CON. And amaryllis.

RAG. I'll make a note of the name. (*In his best lyrical style.*) The lady understands, ladies and gentlemen. The lady is no fool. She's been around and she knows what's what. If I gave the Deaf-Mute a franc, twenty francs, twenty million francs—I still wouldn't make a dent in the forty times a thousand million francs that I'm afflicted with! Right, little lady?

CON. Right.

JOS. Proceed.

RAG. Like on the Stock Exchange. If *you* buy a stock, it sinks at once like a plummet. But if *I* buy a stock, it turns around and soars like an eagle. If I buy it at 33 . . .

PED. It goes up to a thousand.

RAG. It goes to twenty thousand! That's how I bought my twelve chateaux, my twenty villas, my 234 farms. That's how I endow the Opera and keep my twelve ballerinas.

FLOW. GIRL. I hope every one of them deceives you every moment of the day!

RAG. How can they deceive me? Suppose they try to deceive me with the male chorus, the general director, the assistant electrician or the English horn—I own them all, body and soul. It would be like deceiving me with my big toe.

CON. Don't listen, Gabrielle.

GAB. Listen to what?

RAG. No. I am incapable of jealousy. I have all the women—or I can have them, which is the same thing. I get the thin ones with caviar—the fat ones with pearls . . .

COUNT. So you think there are no women with morals?

RAG. I mix morals with mink—delicious combination. I drip pearls into protests. I adorn resistance with rubies. My touch is jeweled; my smile, a motor car. What woman can withstand me? I lift my little finger—and do they fall?—Like leaves in autumn—like tin cans from a second-story window.

CON. That's going a little too far!

COUNT. You see where money leads.

RAG. Of course. When you have no money, nobody trusts you, nobody believes you, nobody likes you. Because to have money is to be virtuous, honest, beautiful and witty. And to be without is to be ugly and boring and stupid and useless.

COUNT. One last question. Suppose you find this oil you're looking for. What do you propose to do with it?

RAG. I propose to make war! I propose to conquer the world!

COUNT. You have heard the defense, such as it is. I demand a verdict of guilty.

RAG. What are you talking about? Guilty? I? I am never guilty!

JOS. I order you to keep quiet!

RAG. I am never quiet!

JOS. Quiet, in the name of the law!

RAG. I am the law. When I speak, that is the law. When I present my backside, it is etiquette to smile and to apply the lips respectfully. It is more than etiquette—it is a cherished national privilege, guaranteed by the Constitution.

JOS. That's contempt of court. The trial is over.

COUNT. And the verdict?

ALL. Guilty!

JOS. Guilty as charged.

COUNT. Then I have full authority to carry out the sentence?

ALL. Yes!

COUNT. I can do what I like with them?

ALL. Yes!

COUNT. I have the right to exterminate them?

ALL. Yes!

JOS. Court adjourned!

COUNT. (*to the* RAGPICKER). Congratulations, Ragpicker. A marvelous defense. Absolutely impartial.

RAG. Had I known a little before, I could have done better. I could have prepared a little speech, like the time I used to sell the Miracle Spot Remover. . . .

JOS. No need for that. You did very well, extempore. The likeness was striking and the style reminiscent of Clemenceau. I predict a brilliant future for you. Good-bye, Aurelia. I'll take our little Gabrielle home.

CON. I'm going to walk along the river. (*To* DICKIE.) Oh! So here you are. And your ear all bloody! Dickie! Have you been fighting again? Oh, dear . . . !

COUNT. (*to the* RAGPICKER). See that she gets home all right, won't you? She loses everything on the way. And in the queerest places. Her prayer book in the butcher shop. And her corset in church.

RAG. (*bowing and offering his arm*). Permit me, Madame.

ST. SING. Oh, Countess—my mazurka. Remember?

COUNT. Oh, yes. Constance, wait a moment. (*To the* SINGER.) Well? Begin.

SING. (*sings*).
     "Do your hear, Mademoiselle,
     Those musicians of hell?"

CON. Why, of course, it's *La Belle Polonaise*. . . . (*She sings.*)
     "From Poland to France
     Comes this marvelous dance,
         So gracious,
         Audacious,
     Will you foot it, perchance?"

SING. I'm saved!

JOS. (*reappearing at the head of the stairs.*)
     "Now my arm I entwine
     Round these contours divine,
     So pure, so impassioned,
     Which Cupid has fashioned. . . ."

GAB. (*reappearing also, she sings a quartet with the others*).
> "Come, let's dance the mazurka, that devilish measure,
>> 'Tis a joy that's reserved to the gods for their pleasure—
>>> Let's gallop, let's hop,
>>> With never a stop,
>>> My blonde Polish miss,
>> Let our heads spin and turn
>> As the dance-floor we spurn—
>> There was never such pleasure as this!"

(*They all exit, dancing.*)

IRMA. It's time for your afternoon nap.

COUNT. But suppose they come, Irma!

IRMA. I'll watch out for them.

COUNT. Thank you, Irma. I *am* tired. (*She smiles.*) Did you ever see a trial end more happily in your life?

IRMA. Lie down and close your eyes a moment.

(*The* COUNTESS *stretches out on the chaise-longue and shuts her eyes.* IRMA *tiptoes out. In a moment,* PIERRE *comes down softly, the feather boa in his hands. He stands over the chaise-longue, looking tenderly down at the sleeping woman, then kneels beside her and takes her hand.*)

COUNT. (*without opening her eyes*). Is it you, Adolphe Bertaut?

PIERRE. It's only Pierre.

COUNT. Don't lie to me, Adolphe Bertaut. These are your hands. Why do you complicate things always? Say that it's you.

PIERRE. Yes. It is I.

COUNT. Would it cost you so much to call me Aurelia?

PIERRE. It's I, Aurelia.

COUNT. Why did you leave me, Adolphe Bertaut? Was she so very lovely, this Georgette of yours?

PIERRE. No. You are a thousand times lovelier.

COUNT. But she was clever.

PIERRE. She was stupid.

COUNT. It was her soul, then, that drew you? When you looked into her eyes, you saw a vision of heaven, perhaps?

PIERRE. I saw nothing.

COUNT. That's how it is with men. They love you because you are beautiful and clever and soulful—and at the first opportunity they leave you for someone who is plain and dull and soulless. But why does it have to be like that, Adolphe Bertaut? Why?

PIERRE. Why, Aurelia?

COUNT. I know very well she wasn't rich. Because when I saw you that time at the grocer's, and you snatched the only good melon from right under my nose, your cuffs, my poor friend, were badly frayed. . . .

PIERRE. Yes. She was poor.

COUNT. "Was" poor? Is she dead then? If it's because she's dead that you've come back to me—then no. Go away. I will not take their leavings from the dead. I refuse to inherit you. . . .

PIERRE. She's quite well.

COUNT. Your hands are still the same, Adolphe Bertaut. Your touch is young and firm. Because it's the only part of you that has stayed with me. The rest of you is pretty far gone, I'm afraid. I can see why you'd rather not come near me when my eyes are open. It's thoughtful of you.

PIERRE. Yes. I've aged.

COUNT. Not I. I am young because I haven't had to live down my youth, like you. I have it with me still, as fresh and beautiful as ever. But when you walk now in the park at Colombes with Georgette, I'm sure . . .

PIERRE. There is no longer a park at Colombes.

COUNT. Is there a park still at St. Cloud? Is there a park at Versailles? I've never gone back to see. But I think, if they could move, those trees would have walked away in disgust the day you went there with Georgette. . . .

PIERRE. They did. Not many are left.

COUNT. You take her also, I suppose, to hear *Denise?*

PIERRE. No one hears *Denise* any more.

COUNT. It was on the way home from *Denise,* Adolphe Bertaut, that I first took your arm. Because it was windy and it was late. I have never set foot in that street again. I go the other way round. It's not easy, in the winter, when there's ice. One is quite apt to fall. I often do.

PIERRE. Oh, my darling—forgive me.

COUNT. No, never. I will never forgive you. It was very bad taste to take her to the very places where we'd been together.

PIERRE. All the same, I swear, Aurelia . . .

COUNT. Don't swear. I know what you did. You gave her the same flowers. You bought her the same chocolates. But has she any left? No. I have all your flowers still. I have twelve chocolates. No, I will never forgive you as long as I live.

PIERRE. I always loved you, Aurelia.

COUNT. You "loved" me? Then you too are dead, Adolphe Bertaut?

PIERRE. No. I love you. I shall always love you, Aurelia.

COUNT. Yes. I know. That much I've always known. I knew it the moment you went away, Adolphe, and I knew that nothing could ever change it. Georgette is in his arms now—yes. But he loves me. Tonight he's taken Georgette to hear *Denise*—yes. But he loves me. . . . I know it. You never loved her. Do you think I believed for one moment that absurd story about her running off with the osteopath? Of course not. Since you didn't love her, obviously she stayed with you. And, after that, when she came back, and I heard about her going off with the surveyor—I knew that couldn't be true, either. You'll never get rid of her, Adolphe Bertaut—never. Because you don't love her.

PIERRE. I need your pity, Aurelia. I need your love. Don't forget me. . . .

COUNT. Farewell, Adolphe Bertaut. Farewell. Let go my hand, and give it to little Pierre. (PIERRE *lets go her hand, and after a moment takes it again. The* COUNTESS *opens her eyes.*) Pierre? Ah, it's you. Has he gone?

PIERRE. Yes, Countess.

COUNT. I didn't hear him go. Oh, he knows how to make a quick exit, that one. (*She sees the boa.*) Good heavens! Wherever did you find it?

PIERRE. In the wardrobe, Countess. When I took off the mirror.

COUNT. Was there a purple felt shopping bag with it?

PIERRE. Yes, Countess.

COUNT. And a little child's sewing box?

PIERRE. No, Countess.

COUNT. Oh, they're frightened now. They're trembling for their lives. You see what they're up to? They're quietly putting back all the things they have stolen. I never open that wardrobe, of course, on account of the old woman in the mirror. But I have sharp eyes. I don't need to open it to see what's in it. Up to this morning, that wardrobe was empty. And now—you see? But, dear me, how stupid they are! The one thing I really miss is my little sewing box. It's something they stole from me when I was a child. They haven't put it back? You're quite sure?

PIERRE. What was it like?

COUNT. Green cardboard with paper lace and gold stamping. I got it for Christmas when I was seven. They stole it the very next day. I cried my eyes out every time I thought of it—until I was eight.

PIERRE. It's not there, Countess.

COUNT. The thimble was gilt. I swore I'd never use any other. Look at my poor fingers. . . .

PIERRE. They've kept the thimble too.

COUNT. Splendid! Then I'm under no obligation to be merciful. Put the boa around my neck, Pierre. I want them to see me wearing it. They'll think it's a real boa. (IRMA *runs in excitedly.*)

IRMA. Here they come, Countess! You were right—it's a procession. The street is full of limousines and taxis!

COUNT. I will receive them. (*As* PIERRE *hesitates to leave her.*) Don't worry. There's nothing to be frightened of. (PIERRE *goes out.*) Irma, did you remember to stir the kerosene into the water?

IRMA. Yes, Countess. Here it is.

COUNT. (*looking critically at the bottle*). You might as well pour in what's left of the tea. (IRMA *shakes up the liquid.*) Don't forget, I'm supposed to be deaf. I want to hear what they're thinking.

IRMA. Yes, Countess.

COUNT. (*putting the finishing touches to her make-up*). I don't have to be merciful—but, after all, I do want to be just. . . .

(IRMA *goes up to the landing and exits. As soon as she is alone, the* COUNTESS *presses the brick, and the trap door opens. There is a* confused sound of auto horns in the street above, and the noise of an approaching crowd.)

IRMA (offstage). Yes, Mr. President. Come in, Mr. President. You're expected, Mr. President. This way, Mr. President. (The PRESIDENTS come down, led by the PRESIDENT. They all look alike, are dressed alike, and all have long cigars.) The Countess is quite deaf, gentlemen. You'll have to shout. (She announces.) The presidents of the boards of directors!

PRES. I had a premonition, Madame, when I saw you this morning, that we should meet again. (The COUNTESS smiles vaguely. He continues, a tone louder.) I want to thank you for your trust. You may place yourself in our hands with complete confidence.

2ND. PRES. Louder. The old trot can't hear you.

PRES. I have a letter here, Madame, in which . . .

2ND. PRES. Louder. Louder.

3RD. PRES. (shouting). Is it true that you've located . . . ? (the COUNTESS stares at him blankly. He shouts at the top of his voice) Oil? (The COUNTESS nods with a smile, and points down. The PRESIDENT produces a legal paper and a fountain pen.) Sign here.

COUNT. What is it? I haven't my glasses.

PRES. Your contract. (He offers the pen.)

COUNT. Thank you.

2ND. PRES. (normal voice). What is it?

3RD. PRES. Waiver of all rights. (He takes it back signed.) Thank you. (He hands it to the SECOND PRESIDENT.) Witness. (The SECOND PRESIDENT witnesses it. The PRESIDENT passes it on to the THIRD PRESIDENT.) Notarize. (The paper is notarized. The PRESIDENT turns to the COUNTESS and shouts.) My congratulations. And now, Madame— (He produces a gold brick wrapped in tissue paper.) If you'll show us the well, this package is yours.

COUNT. What is it?

PRES. Pure gold. Twenty-four karat. For you.

COUNT. Thank you very much. (She takes it.) It's heavy.

2ND. PRES. Are you going to give her that?

PRES. Don't worry. We'll pick it up again on the way out. (He shouts at the COUNTESS, pointing at the trap door.) Is this the way?

COUNT. That's the way.

(*The* SECOND PRESIDENT *tries to slip in first. The* PRESIDENT *pulls him back.*)

PRES. Just a minute, Mr. President. After me, if you don't mind. And watch those cigars. It's oil, you know. (*But as he is about to descend, the* COUNTESS *steps forward.*)

COUNT. Just one moment . . .

PRES. Yes?

COUNT. Did any of you happen to bring along a little sewing box?

PRES. Sewing box? (*He pulls back another impatient* PRESIDENT.) Take it easy.

COUNT. Or a little gold thimble?

PRES. Not me.

PRESIDENTS. Not us.

COUNT. What a pity!

PRES. Can we go down now?

COUNT. Yes. You may go down now. Watch your step!

(*They hurry down eagerly. When they have quite disappeared,* IRMA *appears on the landing and announces the next echelon.*)

IRMA. Countess, the Prospectors.

COUNT. Heavens! Are there more than one?

IRMA. There's a whole delegation.

COUNT. Send them down.

(*The* PROSPECTOR *comes in, following his nose.*)

IRMA. Come in, please.

PROS. (*sniffing the air like a bloodhound*). I smell something. . . . Who's that?

IRMA. The Countess. She is very deaf.

PROS. Good.

(*The* PROSPECTORS *also look alike. Sharp clothes, Western hats and long noses. They crowd down the stairs after the* PROSPECTOR, *sniffing in unison. The* PROSPECTOR *is especially talented. He casts about on the scent until it leads him to the decanter on the table. He pours himself a glass, drinks it off, and belches with much satisfaction. The others join him at once, and follow his example. They all belch in unison.*)

PROSPECTORS. Oil?

PROS. Oil!

COUNT. Oil.

PROS. Traces? Puddles?

COUNT. Pools. Gushers.

2ND. PROS. Characteristic odor? (*He sniffs.*)

PROS. Chanel Number 5. Nectar! Undoubtably—the finest—rarest! (*He drinks.*) Sixty gravity crude: straight gasoline! (*To the* COUNTESS.) How found? By blast? Drill?

COUNT. By finger.

PROS. (*whipping out a document*). Sign here, please.

COUNT. What is it?

PROS. Agreement for dividing the profits. . . . (*The* COUNTESS *signs.*)

2ND. PROS. (*to* IST. PROSPECTOR). What is it?

PROS. (*pocketing the paper*). Application to enter a lunatic asylum. Down there?

COUNT. Down there. (*The* PROSPECTORS *go down, sniffing.*)

(IRMA *enters.*)

IRMA. The gentlemen of the press are here.

COUNT. The rest of the machine! Show them in.

IRMA. The Public Relations Counsellors! (*They enter, all shapes and sizes, all in blue pin-striped suits and black homburg hats.*) The Countess is very deaf, gentlemen. You'll have to shout!

IST. PR. AGENT. You don't say— Delighted to make the acquaintance of so charming and beautiful a lady. . . .

2ND. PR. AGENT. Louder. She can't hear you.

IST. PR. AGENT. What a face! (*Shouts.*) Madame, we are the press. You know our power. We fix all values. We set all standards. Your entire future depends on us.

COUNT. How do you do?

IST. PR. AGENT. What will we charge the old trull? The usual thirty?

2ND. PR. AGENT. Forty.

3RD. PR. AGENT. Sixty.

IST. PR. AGENT. All right—seventy-five. (*He fills in a form and offers it to the* COUNTESS.) Sign here, Countess. This contract really gives you a break.

COUNT. That is the entrance.

1ST. PR. AGENT. Entrance to what?

COUNT. The oil well.

1ST. PR. AGENT. Oh, we don't need to see that, Madame.

COUNT. Don't need to see it?

1ST. PR. AGENT. No, no—we don't have to see it to write about it. We can imagine it. An oil well is an oil well. "That's oil we know on earth, and oil we need to know." (*He bows.*)

COUNT. But if you don't see it, how can you be sure the oil is there?

1ST. PR. AGENT. If it's there, well and good. If it's not, by the time we get through, it will be. You underestimate the creative aspect of our profession, Madame. (*The* COUNTESS *shakes her head, handing back the papers.*) I warn you, if you insist on rubbing our noses in this oil, it will cost you 10 per cent extra.

COUNT. It's worth it. (*She signs. They cross toward the trap door.*)

2ND. PR. AGENT (*descending*). You see, Madame, we of the press can refuse a lady nothing.

3RD. PR. AGENT. Especially, such a lady. (THIRD PRESS AGENT *starts going down.*)

2ND. PR. AGENT (*going down. Gallantly*). It's plain to see, Madame, that even fountains of oil have their nymphs. . . . I can use that somewhere. That's copy!

(*The* PRESS AGENTS *go down. As he disappears, the* FIRST PRESS AGENT *steals the gold brick and blows a kiss gallantly to the* COUNTESS, *who blows one back.*)

(*There is a high-pitched chatter offstage, and* IRMA *comes in, trying hard to hold back* THREE WOMEN *who pay no attention to her whatever. These* WOMEN *are tall, slender, and as soulless as if they were molded of wax. They march down the steps, erect and abstracted like animated window models, but chattering incessantly.*)

IRMA. But, ladies, please—you have no business here—you are not expected. (*To the* COUNTESS.) There are some strange ladies coming. . . .

COUNT. Show them in, Irma. (*The* WOMEN *come down, without taking the slightest interest in their surroundings.*) Who are you?

1ST. WOM. Madame, we are the most powerful pressure group in the world.

2ND. WOM. We are the ultimate dynamic.

3RD. WOM. The mainspring of all combinations.

1ST. WOM. Nothing succeeds without our assistance. Is that the well, Madame?

COUNT. That is the well.

1ST. WOM. Put out your cigarettes, girls. We don't want any explosions. Not with my brand-new eyelashes. (*They go down, still chattering. The* COUNTESS *crosses to the wall to close the trap. As she does so, there is a commotion on the landing.*)

IRMA. Countess . . .

(*A* MAN *rushes in breathlessly.*)

MAN. Just a minute! Just a minute! (*He rushes for the trap door.*)

COUNT. Wait! Who are you?

MAN. I'm in a hurry. Excuse me. It's my only chance! (*He rushes down.*)

COUNT. But . . . (*But he is gone. She shrugs her shoulders, and presses the brick. The trap closes. She rings the bell for* IRMA.) My gold brick! Why, they've stolen my gold brick! (*She moves toward the trap. It is now closed.*) Well, let them take their god with them.

(IRMA *enters and sees with astonishment that the stage is empty of all but the* COUNTESS. *Little by little, the scene is suffused with light, faint at first, but increasing as if the very walls were glowing with the quiet radiance of universal joy. Only around the closed trap a shadow lingers.*)

IRMA. But what's happened? They've gone! They've vanished!

COUNT. They've evaporated, Irma. They were wicked. Wickedness evaporates.

(PIERRE *enters. He is followed by the* VAGABONDS, *all of them. The new radiance of the world is now very perceptible. It glows from their faces.*)

PIERRE. Oh, Countess . . . !

WAIT. Countess, everything's changed. Now you can breathe again. Now you can see.

PIERRE. The air is pure! The sky is clear!

IRMA. Life is beautiful again.

RAG. (*rushes in*). Countess—the pigeons! The pigeons are flying!

FLOW. GIRL. They don't have to walk any more.

RAG. They're flying. . . . The air is like crystal. And young grass is sprouting on the pavements.

COUNT. Is it possible?

IRMA (*interpreting for the* DEAF-MUTE). Now, Juggler, you can throw your fireballs up as high as you please—they won't go out.

SERG. On the street, utter strangers are shaking hands, they don't know why, and offering each other almond bars!

COUNT. Oh, my friends . . .

WAIT. Countess, we thank you. . . .

(*They go on talking with happy and animated gestures, but we no longer hear them, for their words blend into a strain of unearthly music which seems to thrill from the uttermost confines of the universe. And out of this music comes a voice.*)

1ST. VOICE. Countess . . . (*Only the* COUNTESS *hears it. She turns from the group of* VAGABONDS *in wonder.*)

2ND. VOICE. Countess . . .

3RD. VOICE. Countess . . . (*As she looks up in rapture, the* FIRST VOICE *speaks again.*)

1ST. VOICE. Countess, we thank you. We are the friends of animals.

2ND. VOICE. We are the friends of people.

3RD. VOICE. We are the friends of friendship.

1ST. VOICE. You have freed us!

2ND. VOICE. From now on, there will be no hungry cats. . . .

3RD. VOICE. And we shall tell the Duchess her dog's right name!

(*The* VOICES *fade off. And now another group of voices is heard.*)

1ST. VOICE. Countess, we thank you. We are the friends of flowers.

2ND. VOICE. From now on, every plant in Paris will be watered. . . .

3RD. VOICE. And the sewers will be fragrant with jasmine!

(*These voices, too, are silent. For an instant, the stage is vibrant with music. Then the* DEAF-MUTE *speaks, and his voice is the most beautiful of all.*)

DEAF-MUTE. Sadness flies on the wings of the morning, and out of the heart of darkness comes the light.

(*Suddenly a group of figures detaches itself from the shadows. These are exactly similar in face and figure and in dress. They are shabby in the fashion of 1900 and their cuffs are badly frayed. Each bears in his hand a ripe melon.*)

1ST. ADOLPHE BERTAUT. Countess, we thank you. We, too, are freed at last. We are the Adolphe Bertauts of the world.

2ND. ADOLPHE BERTAUT. We are no longer timid.

3RD. ADOLPHE BERTAUT. We are no longer weak.

1ST. ADOLPHE BERTAUT. From this day on, we shall hold fast to what we love. For your sake, henceforth, we shall be handsome, and our cuffs forever immaculate and new. Countess, we bring you this melon and with it our hearts . . . ! (*They all kneel.*) Will you do us the honor to be our wife?

COUNT. (*sadly*). Too late! Too late! (*She waves them aside. They take up their melons sadly and vanish. The voices of the* VAGABONDS *are heard again, and the music dies.*) Too late! Too late!

PIERRE. Too late, Countess?

IRMA. Too late for what?

COUNT. I say that it's too late for them. On the twenty-fourth of May, 1881, the most beautiful Easter in the memory of man, it was not too late. And on the fifth of September, 1887, the day they caught the trout and broiled it on the open fire by the brook at Ville-neuve, it was not too late. And it was even not too late for them on the twenty-first of August, 1897, the day the Czar visited Paris with his guard. But they did nothing and they said nothing, and now—kiss each other, you two, this very instant!

IRMA. You mean . . . ?

PIERRE. You mean . . . ?

IRMA. But, Countess . . .

COUNT. It's three hours since you've met and known and loved each other. Kiss each other quickly. (PIERRE *hesitates.*) Look at him. He hesitates. He trembles. Happiness frightens him. . . . How like a man! Oh, Irma, kiss him, kiss him! If two people who love each other let a single instant wedge itself between them, it grows —it becomes a month, a year, a century; it becomes too late. Kiss him, Irma, kiss him while there is time, or in a moment his hair will be white and there will be another madwoman in Paris! Oh, make her kiss him, all of you! (*They kiss.*) Bravo! Oh, if only you'd had the courage to do that thirty years ago, how different I would be today! Dear Deaf-Mute, be still—your words dazzle our eyes! And Irma is too busy to translate for you. (*They kiss once more.*) Well, there we are. The world is saved. And you see how simple it all was? Nothing is ever so wrong in this world that a sensible woman can't set it right in the course of an afternoon. Only, the next time, don't wait until things begin to look black. The minute you notice anything, tell me at once.

RAG. We will, Countess. We will.

COUNT. (*puts on her hat. Her tone becomes businesslike*). Irma. My bones. My gizzard.

IRMA. I have them ready, Countess.

COUNT. Good. (*She puts the bones into her basket and starts for the stairs.*) Well, let's get on to more important things. Four o'clock. My poor cats must be starved. What a bore for them if humanity had to be saved every afternoon. They don't think much of it, as it is.

(CURTAIN)

Sidney Kingsley

▶ At the age of twenty-seven Sidney Kingsley won the Pulitzer award with his first play, *Men in White* (1933). In the depths of the great depression, which closed so many theatres, and made it difficult to find producers and backers, the Group Theatre and James Ullman courageously staged the play and were rewarded by brilliant success. It played for three hundred and fifty-one New York performances, toured the country, and introduced a vigorous new dramatist to America and the world.

Kingsley was born in New York City in 1906. At Cornell University, where he spent the four years from 1924 to 1928 on a state scholarship, he was absorbed in the drama and was an active member of the Dramatic Club. In this encouraging environment he began to write plays, and after graduation and his return to New York he played with a stock company at the Tremont Theatre, and later had a part in *Subway Express*. In the meantime he was at work on a play of his own, *Crisis*, which dealt with a moment of decision in the life of a young intern who had to choose between a sensible marriage along with a routine medical practice and further rigorous training in Vienna in the field of surgery.

This was the play, renamed *Men in White* and produced with serious and understanding realism, with suggestive sets on a sparse, semi-barren stage, that became an overnight sensation.

Two years later, in October 1935, Norman Bel Geddes

staged Kingsley's second play. It was called *Dead End,* and it was even more of a smash hit than *Men in White.* Attuned to the temper of the mid-thirties, with the suggestive symbolism of its title and the diseased lives of its poverty- and vice-ridden characters, *Dead End* proved to be a piece of photographic realism, as though the author had used a camera and a sound track to record the lives of the kids of this dead-end street in the Fifties on the East River.

The set itself, one of Bel Geddes' best, stabbed the audience with its photographically powerful representation of luxury and squalor rubbing shoulders. The audience sat as though out on the East River looking at the wharf and river front, which had been constructed in the orchestra pit and the footlight trough. The dreary squalidness of the wharf abutments suggested the filth and scum and floating refuse of this polluted river. To the left of the stage was "a high terrace and a white iron gate leading to the back of the exclusive East River Terrace Apartments" with "a glimpse of the tops of gaily colored sun umbrellas" on the shrubbed terrace. "Hugging the terrace and filing up the street are a series of squalid tenement houses . . . close, dark and crumbling." The street itself is filthy, littered with old newspapers and garbage, with wash lines and a police call box in prominent view. And here, with unflagging tension and realism, the Dead End Kids enacted their deadly education in the school of crime and juvenile delinquency.

It was an interesting coincidence that Maxwell Anderson's *Winterset,* with a somewhat similar setting and theme, should have been presented at the same time. The two plays offered the sharpest possible contrast in language: the meticulous reproduction of the speech of the Dead End boys and the poetic idealization of what Mio and Miriamne might have said if they had possessed the winged words to phrase their own halting thoughts and emotions. Both plays were fine examples of their respective types.

With these two public and critical successes behind him, Kingsley wrote and personally financed and produced a play entitled *Ten Million Ghosts* (1936). It dealt with the theme of the role of munitions makers in international discord and war, a subject earnestly explored and debated during the 1930's when the war clouds of a second world conflict were gathering. However important the concept and timely the topic, the play failed in the terms and within the setting of the theatre. Neither *The World We Make* (1939), a dramatization of Millen Brand's novel, nor the historical study of a decade in the life of Thomas Jefferson called *The Patriots* (1943) equaled the appeal of his first two plays.

In *Detective Story,* produced in March 1949, Kingsley returned to the method and the milieu of *Dead End*. Once again he had done careful research, in the manner of a good reporter or a trained social case worker. He visited the station houses to witness the nightly drama of crime and maladjustment as the police bring in their routine catch of human flotsam. Each victim is a drama in himself; massed together in the common meeting place of the same precinct station, they form a tragic pattern of misfortune and vice. With an ear trained to catch the vocabulary and rhythm of their speech with all of its vulgarity, roughness, and vigor; with a sharp eye for distinguishing marks of character, and with an experienced technician's sure touch for dramatic values and form, he succeeded in weaving the web of police bookings into a moving play. Its commentary is no less significant because he called it a melodrama. And one of the less apparent merits of the play is its skillful delineation of individualized characters who come vividly to life before us, each with his own bitter personal tragedy.

This play, aside from its intrinsic quality, is a choice example of the rich tradition of meticulous realism by a master of the art, as it has been developing in the America of the present century. It contrasts sharply with the intellectualized fantasy of *The Madwoman of Chaillot,* the philosophical poetry of *Murder in the Cathedral,* and the symbolic study of the principle of Evil in *Billy Budd.*

DETECTIVE

STORY

Characters

DETECTIVE DAKIS	SUSAN CARMICHAEL
SHOPLIFTER	PATROLMAN KEOGH
DETECTIVE GALLAGHER	PATROLMAN BAKER
MRS. FARRAGUT	WILLY
JOE FEINSON	MISS HATCH
DETECTIVE CALLAHAN	MRS. FEENEY
DETECTIVE O'BRIEN	MR. FEENEY
DETECTIVE BRODY	CRUMB-BUM
MR. SIMS	MR. GALLANTZ
DETECTIVE MC LEOD	MR. PRITCHETT
ARTHUR KINDRED	MARY MC LEOD
PATROLMAN BARNES	TAMI GIACOPPETTI
1ST BURGLAR (CHARLEY)	PHOTOGRAPHER
2ND BURGLAR (LEWIS)	LADY
MRS. BAGATELLE	GENTLEMAN
DR. SCHNEIDER	MR. BAGATELLE
LT. MONOGHAN	INDIGNANT CITIZEN

ACT ONE: A day in August. 5:30 P.M.

ACT TWO: 7:30 P.M.

ACT THREE: 8:30 P.M.

TIME: *The present. The entire action of the play takes place in the detective squad-room of a New York precinct police station.*

ACT ONE

SCENE: *The 21st Detective Squad, second floor of the 21st Precinct Police Station, New York City. The major area of the stage is occupied by the squad-room; to the right separated by a door and an invisible wall we glimpse a fragment of the* LIEUTENANT's *office. Severe, nakedly institutional, ghost-ridden, these rooms are shabby, three-quarters of a century old, with an effluvium of their own compounded of seventy-five years of the tears and blood of human anguish, despair, passion, rage, terror and violent death. The walls are olive green to the waist and light green above. In the wall upstage, two ceiling-high windows guarded by iron-grill work. The entrance, stage left, is surrounded by an iron railing with a swinging gate. Tacked to the wall, a height chart; next to it a folding fingerprint shelf; above that a green-shaded light. Adjoining, a bulletin board upon which are tacked several notices and photographs of criminals, etc. In the center of the room is the phone desk, on which are two phones. Downstage left is another desk, on it a typewriter. High on the main wall a large electric clock, beneath it a duty board with replaceable celluloid letters, reading "On Duty—*DET. GALLAGHER, DET. DAKIS, LT. MONOGHAN.*" *In the segment of the* LIEUTENANT's *office, a desk, a swivel chair, several small chairs, some files, a water-cooler, a coat-rack, etc. A small window in the* LIEUTENANT's *office looks out upon an air shaft. Through it we catch a glimpse of the window of the wash-room, the door to which is upstage right.*

The light is fading. It is late afternoon, five-twenty by the clock on the wall. Through the main windows a magnificent view of the city and its towering skyscrapers; dominating the panorama are a General Motors sign, a church spire and a cross.

At the curtain's rise, NICHOLAS DAKIS *is seated at the typewriter desk making out a form and interrogating a young woman who has been picked up for shoplifting. At the phone desk his partner,* GALLAGHER, *is writing up some "squeals," and sipping Coca-Cola from the bottle. A traffic policeman in uniform pauses momentarily in the doorway to murmur a greeting to another uniformed policeman; then they vanish. Detective* GALLAGHER *is a young man, third-grade, a novice about 27 years of age, and good-looking in spite of a broken nose. The heat has him a little down: he is sweating profusely and every once in a while he plucks at his moist shirt which clings to his body. He and his partner, Detective* DAKIS, *are in their shirt sleeves, their collars open.*

DAKIS *is a bull of a man as wide as he is high. He has a voice like the roll of a kettle-drum. He is a middle-aged Greek American. He tackles his job efficiently and unemotionally, in an apparently off-hand, casual manner—as indeed do most of the detectives.*

The SHOPLIFTER *is a shapeless, moronic little creature with a Bronx accent. Her voice is the blat of a moose-calf, and, in spite of her avowed guilt, she has all the innocence of ignorance.*

DAK. Hair? (*Squints at her frazzled hair.*)

SHOP. Brown.

DAK. (*typing, hunt and peck system*). Brown. (*He squints at her eyes.*) Eyes?

SHOP. Blue.

DAK. (*types*). Blue.

(*The phone rings.* GALLAGHER *picks up the receiver.*)

GALLA. 21st Squad Detectives, Gallagher. Yes, Madame, what is your name, please? (*He reaches for a pencil and pad, glances at the clock, writes.*) Address? Phone number? Plaza 9-1855 . . .

DAK. Weight?

GALLA. (*as the other desk phone rings*). One second, please. (*He picks up the other receiver, balancing the first on his shoulder.*) 21st Squad Detectives, Gallagher.

SHOP. 109, I think.

DAK. (*types*). 109 will do. . . . (*He squints at her potato sack of a figure.*) Height?

SHOP. I don't know. About . . .

DAK. Stand up against the wall! (*He waves her to the height chart.*) Over there.

GALLA. (*on phone*). Hello, Loot. No, nothing. A shoplifter. Best's. A pocketbook. (*He calls to* DAKIS.) Hey, Nick, what was the price on that purse she lifted?

SHOP. (*mournfully*). Six dollars.

DAK. (*to the* SHOPLIFTER). Five foot one. All right, come back. (*The* SHOPLIFTER *returns to the desk.*)

GALLA. (*on the phone*). Six bucks.

DAK. Age?

SHOP. Twenty-seven. (*Corrects herself, quickly.*) Twenty-two.

DAK. (*squints at her, types*). Twenty—seven.

GALLA. (*on the phone*). Right, Loot. It come in too late. Night court. Right, chief. (*He hangs up, applies the other receiver.*) Sorry, Mrs. . . . (*Glances at his pad.*) Andrews. Yes. Have you a list of just what's missing? It would help. Any cash? You do? One of the servants? All right. I'll be there. Yes, Madame. (*Hangs up, makes some notes on the scratch pad, sips at the Coca-Cola bottle.*)

SHOP. My God, the times I spent twice as much for a pocketbook.

DAK. (*matter of fact, no animus*). Well, you took it.

SHOP. I don't know why. It was crazy.

DAK. (*shrugs it off*). It's your first offense. You'll get off on probation.

SHOP. I didn't need it. I didn't even like it. Crazy!

(*A burst of song offstage: an overmellow baritone pouring out Canio's heartbreak from* I Pagliacci, *making up in vigor all that it lacks in sweetness: "Ma il vizio alberga sol ne l' alma tua negletta." The* SHOPLIFTER, *puzzled, glances about, hunches her shoulders at* DAKIS *inquisitively, but he is absorbed in his work and he does not even glance up. The singing comes closer. More heartbreak! "Tu viscere non hai . . . sol legge." Enter* GUS KEOGH, *a uniformed policeman with a normally smiling, smooth, white Irish face, twisted for the moment with the agony of the tragic song he is pouring forth.*)

KEO. "*è 'l senso a te . . .*" (*Breaks off, beaming.*) Got any 61's?

GALLA. A couple. You're off key today, Gus. (*Hands him several slips.* KEOGH *studies them; his face contorts again with the emotion of the song as he goes off.*)

KEO. "*vo' ne lo sprezzo mio schiacciarti . . .* (*and fades off down the hall with a sob*) *sotto piè.*"

DAK. (*rises, crosses to fingerprint board, rolls ink on pad, beckons to the* SHOPLIFTER). Come here! (*The* SHOPLIFTER *crosses to* DAKIS. *He takes her hand. She stiffens. He reassures her gently—in the interests of efficiency.*) Take it easy, girlie. Let me do the work. You just supply the finger.

SHOP. Ooh!!

DAK. This finger. Relax, now, I'm not going to hurt you. Just r-r-r-roll it. . . . (*He presses her finger down on the sheet.*)

GALLA. (*glances up, toward door into hallway at someone approaching*). Uh, uh! Here comes trouble. (*To* DAKIS.) Look at the calendar!

DAK. (*glances at the calendar on the wall*). A full moon tonight.

GALLA. (*groans*). It never fails. (*Enter an elderly, aristocratic-looking woman, dressed in the style of a by-gone era.* GALLAGHER *rises gallantly.*) Come in, Mrs. Farragut! Are those people still bothering you?

MRS. FARR. Worse than ever, Officer. If I hadn't awakened last night and smelled that gas coming through the walls, I'd be gone—we'd all be gone.

GALLA. (*solicitously*). Have a chair.

MRS. FARR. Why haven't you given me protection? I demand protection.

GALLA. (*"conning" her*). I got twelve men on duty guarding you.

MRS. FARR. But whose side are they really on? Are you sure you can trust them?

GALLA. (*wounded*). Mrs. Farragut! One of them is my own *brother*.

MRS. FARR. Oh, I'm sorry! I didn't mean to offend you. (*She sits, leans toward him, confidentially.*) Only it's so important. You see, they know I know all about it— Atom bombs! (GALLAGHER *nods sagely.*) They're making them—these foreigners next door and they blow this atomic vapor through the wall at me. And they have a man watching me from the top of the Empire State Building . . . with radar . . .

GALLA. That man we got covered.

MRS. FARR. You have?

GALLA. Day and night.

MRS. FARR. Does the President know about this?

GALLA. I talked to him only an hour ago.

MRS. FARR. That's important, very important. These foreigners know I have electronic vision. I can see everything around us vibrating with electricity. . . . Billions of atoms like stars in a universe, turning, vibrating, vibrating. Out there in the streets ten million living dynamos—coming and going . . . They create cross-currents; and those great tall skyscrapers draw all this human electricity to the top of the Empire State Building, where that man sits, and he turns it back and shoots it down on us. It's a terrifying situation . . . terrifying!! Do something!—Or it's the end of the world!! (*She rises, having worked herself into a frenzy of terror.*)

(JOE FEINSON, *police-reporter, enters, leans his head on the rail watching; a tiny man, few inches more than five feet, exaggerated nose, crooked features,* JOE's *superficially wise-cracking police-reporter attitude is only the persona with which he cloaks a genuine philosophic, humanistic outlook. Nothing escapes his humorous, beady, bird-like eyes.*)

GALLA. (*rises, crosses around to her, takes her arm reassuringly*). Now, Mrs. Farragut, I'm watching it, every second; and I got it all under control. Tell you what—I'm going to *double* the men I got guarding you. Twenty-five picked men day and night. How's that?

MRS. FARR. (*calms down*). Oh, that's better. Much better. Thank you.

(*Exit* MRS. FARRAGUT.)

GALLA. (*plucking at his damp shirt*). Get out the butterfly net.

JOE. You give the customers a good massage.

GALLA. Hell, this job is ninety percent salesmanship!

DAK. (*finishes the fingerprints*). O.K., girlie, wash your hands. In there! (*He points to the wash-room door. The* SHOPLIFTER *crosses to the wash-room, dangling her lamp-blacked fingers before her so as not to soil her dress.*)

JOE. What's new?

GALLA. It's quiet. (*Knocks wood.*)

JOE. The town's dead as Kelcey's. (*He saunters over to* GALLAGHER's *desk.*)

SHOP. (*opens the door, frowning, calls out*). There isn't any lock on the door.

DAK. Just wash your hands, girlie.

SHOP. (*indignantly*). A fine howdoyoudo! (*She slams the door.*)

JOE. Story for me?

GALLA. No. Shoplifter.

JOE. She anybody?

GALLA. Nobody at all.

JOE. Any angles?

GALLA. Nah! Just a slob.

(*Two detectives enter. One of them,* CALLAHAN, *is very exuberant and high-spirited, Tenth Avenue in his speech, dressed in a yellow polo shirt and baggy trousers, which do not match his wrinkled jacket. The other, Detective* O'BRIEN, *is an older man, spectacled, neatly dressed, soft-spoken.*)

CALL. (*tears off his jacket, revealing the full splendor of his polo shirt— Hawaiian in motif, with brilliant foliage woven into the pattern*). Hi, Tom, Nick, Joe! Phew, it's hot out! Sweat your kolonjas off!

JOE. What the hell are you dressed up for? Must be Halloween?

CALL. I wonder what he means?

O'BRI. Saks-Fifth Avenue pays Mike to advertise their clothes.

CALL. Gese, were we given a run around! We tailed a guy for two hours, from Fifty-thoid to Ninety-foist and back. I thought for sure, "This one belongs to us."

O'BRI. Looked like a good man.

CALL. Then the jerko took a bus. (*Glances at the schedule hanging on the wall.*) Moider! Sunday again! What the hell am I?—A Sunday detective? My kids'll grow up, they won't even know me. (*To* JOE.) Say, Joe, there's a big story on Third Avenue. You get it? The brewery truck?

JOE. No, what about it?

CALL. A brewery truck backed up into the sidewalk and a barrel of beer fell right out inna baby carriage.

JOE (*rising*). Was the baby in it?

CALL. Yeah.

JOE. Was it killed?

CALL. No, it was light beer! Boyeeng! (*He doubles over, holding his sides with laughter.*) Ha, ha, ha!

JOE (*groans and sinks back into his chair*). You're a cute kid. What's your name, Berle?

(*The* SHOPLIFTER *returns from the wash-room. As she crosses* CALLAHAN *studies her face, squinting his eyes professionally.*)

O'BRI. Busy day?

GALLA. Quiet.

O'BRI. Good. (*He knocks wood.*)

GALLA. Too quiet.

O'BRI. We're due. We're ripe for a homicide.

GALLA. Ssh. Wait till I get out of here. (*The desk phone rings,* GALLAGHER *groans.*) Can't you keep your big mouth shut? (*He picks up the receiver.*) 21st Squad Detectives, Gallagher. Yes, Madame. That's right. Where? Now what is it you lost?

JOE. Her virginity.

GALLA. In a taxicab?

JOE. Hell of a place!

GALLA. Did you get his number? Can you describe it?

JOE. This is going to be educational.

GALLA. What's your name? Address? Yes, Madame. I'll check that for you. Not at all.

JOE (*simultaneously with* GALLAGHER's *last speech*). I got a squeal for you. I lost something. My manhood.

CALL. We don't take cases *that* old, Joe.

GALLA. (*hanging up*). Outlawed by the statute of limitations.

(*Detective* LOU BRODY *enters with several containers of coffee, Coca-Colas, and a bag of sandwiches.* BRODY *is a huge man, deceptively obese and clumsy in appearance; bald-head, ugly, carbuncled face, lit up, however, by sad, soft, gentle eyes. He hands one bag to* DAKIS.)

BRO. Here you are, Nick!

DAK. I appreciate that.

BRO. My pleasure. Here you are, Miss.

SHOP. With Russian Dressing? (*Standing up, searching in her purse.*)

BRO. They ran out. (*He crosses, places the remaining sandwiches and coffee on the long table, then goes into the* LIEUTENANT's *office, hangs his hat and packet on the coat-tree.*)

SHOP. How much do I owe you?

DAK. It's on the house.

SHOP. You're all awful decent, really, awful decent.

DAK. Well, you didn't kill anyone.

(*A man carrying a briefcase enters, stands at the gate a moment, taps on it impatiently. He is about thirty-five, erect in bearing, sharply chiseled features, self-possessed, apparently immune to the heat; he is crisp and cool even to the starched collar. When he speaks his voice is equally crisp and starched, and carries considerable authority.*)

GALLA. Yes, sir?

(*The man fishes a card out of his wallet and presents it.*)

MAN. My name is Sims, Endicott Sims. I'm an attorney.

GALLA. What can we do for you, Counselor?

SIMS. I represent Mr. Kurt Schneider. Your office has a warrant out for him?

DAK. Hey, Lou! This is Jim's squeal, ain't it? Kurt Schneider?

BRO. Yeah, I'll take it. (*Crosses to* SIMS.) This is my partner's case. What about Schneider, Counselor? Where is he?

SIMS. He's ready to surrender himself into your custody.

BRO. Fine, bring him in.

SIMS. First, however, I have here some photographs. . . . (*He takes some pictures from his briefcase, and hands them to* BRODY.) He had these taken half an hour ago.

BRO. (*examines them*). Nudes? Ugly, ain't he?

SIMS (*smiles wryly*). He's no Mr. America.

BRO. No, that he ain't.

SIMS. The purpose is not aesthetic. I don't want any rubber hoses used on him.

BRO. Counselor, how long have you been practicing law? We don't assault our prisoners.

SIMS. Who's handling this case here?

BRO. My partner.

SIMS. A man named James McLeod?

BRO. Yeah.

SIMS. I've heard a good deal about him. A law unto himself. You will please tell him for me . . .

BRO. Wait a minute. Tell him for yourself. Here he is.

(JAMES MC LEOD *enters, his big hand gripping the arm of a stunned, sensitive-looking young man whom he guides into the room.* JAMES MC LEOD *is tall, lean, handsome, has powerful shoulders, uncompromising mouth, a studied, immobile, mask-like face betrayed by the deep-set, impatient, mocking eyes which reveal the quick flickers of mood, the deep passions of the man possessed by his own demon.*)

BRO. Oh, Jim, this is your squeal. (*To* SIMS.) This is Detective McLeod, Mr. Sims.

MC. How do you do, sir? (*Takes out a handkerchief, mops his brow, wipes the sweat-band of his hat.*)

SIMS. How do you do?

BRO. Mr. Sims is an attorney.

MC. And very clever. I've seen him in court.

SIMS. Thank you.

BRO. He's here for Kurt Schneider.

MC. (*the quick flicker of mockery in his eyes*). Oh, yes. (*To* SIMS.) I had the pleasure of arresting your client a year ago.

SIMS. So I am informed.

MC. He's changed his lawyer since, if not his business.

SIMS. Kurt Schneider is a successful truck farmer from New Jersey.

MC. With a little abortion mill in New York for a sideline. Nothing fancy, just a quick ice-tong job. I've a considerable yen for your client.

SIMS. I'm aware of that. (*To* BRODY.) Show him those pictures! (BRODY *hands the photographs to* MC LEOD.)

MC. (*looks at the pictures, grimaces*). There's no doubt the process of evolution is beginning to reverse itself.

SIMS. You understand, Officer, that my client has certain rights. I am here to see that those rights are respected.

MC. (*urbanely*). One second, Counselor. I'll be right with you. Have a chair. (*He guides the young man into the squad-room.*)

GALLA. Jim, call your wife!

MC. Thanks, Tom. (*He searches the young man for weapons; the quick "frisk," ankles, legs, thighs, front and rear.*) All right, Buster. Sit down over there. (*To* GALLAGHER.) When'd she phone?

GALLA. Twenty minutes ago. (*The phone rings.*) 21st Squad Detectives, Gallagher. Yes, sir. (*He hands the phone to* MC LEOD.) The Lieutenant.

MC. (*takes the phone and it is evident from his grimace at the phone that he has no great love for his lieutenant. He sits on the desk*). Yes, Lieutenant? I just got back.

JOE (*crosses down, drapes himself on the chair next to* MC LEOD). Hiya, Seamus!

MC. (*smothers the mouthpiece of the phone, murmurs quickly*). Oh, Yussel, Yussel! You're supposed to be an intelligent reporter.

JOE. What's the matter, Seamus?

MC. That Langdon story!

JOE. Didn't I spell your name right?

MC. It's the only thing you did get right. (*On the phone.*) Yes, Lieutenant. I just brought him in. (*To* ARTHUR.) Arthur, were you arrested before?

ART. I told you.

MC. Tell me again.

ART. No.

MC. (*back to phone*). Says no. We'll check his prints. Yes, sir. Yes, sir. (*He covers the mouthpiece.*) You're degenerating into a real sob-sister, Yussel. Grrrim grray prrrison walls! Wish you'd have seen Langdon in the bull-pen. "Hiya, Jack! Hiya, Charley!" Smiling. He was happy! He was home again! (*On phone.*) Yes, Lieutenant. Yes, sir.

JOE. The mortal God—McLeod! Captain Ahab pursuing the great gray Leviathan! A fox with rabies bit him in the ass when he was two years old, and neither of them recovered. Don't throw water on him. He goes rabid!

MC. (*hangs up, pulls* JOE's *bow-tie*). You apple-headed member of the fourth estate, to look natural you should have a knife and fork sticking out of the top of your head. City College is going to be proud of you yet! (*Rises, talks Yiddish.*) Mir daft ihr dihagginun!

JOE (*laughs, ties his tie*). It this story worth a picture?

MC. Mm . . . Possibly. (*To* ARTHUR.) Don't try running for it, Buster.

You'd just about reach that door and suddenly you'd put on weight. Bullets are supersonic.

ART. Don't worry.

MC. I won't. Either way.

(BRODY, *at the sound of the young man's voice, stops and turns quickly. He comes over, scrutinizes the young man's face.*)

MC. Know him?

BRO. No . . . No . . . I . . . (*Shakes his head.*)

MC. (*calls across the room to* MR. SIMS). One second, Counselor. (*He crosses to the* LIEUTENANT'S *office, comes face to face with* CALLAHAN. *He pauses to survey* CALLAHAN'S *sartorial splendor. Shakes his head.*) Strictly Pier 6!

CALL. I ain't no friggin barber-college detective with pleats in my pants.

MC. (*sardonically*). No, you *ain't.* . . . (*Goes into* LIEUTENANT'S *office, closes the door, dials a number.*)

CALL. (*miffed*). Remind me to get that college graduate a bicycle pump for Christmas to blow up that big head of his.

(O'BRIEN *and* GALLAGHER *laugh.*)

O'BRI. He needling you again?

CALL. Mm! Big needle-man from sew-and-sew.

MC. (*on the phone*). Hello, darling. (*His voice at once takes on warmth and tenderness; his eyes, his smile, his whole being seem to undergo a metamorphosis.*) What did the doctor say? . . . Thank God! Nothing organic? Sure, now, Mary? . . . How does he explain those palpitations? . . . Psychosomatic? Mm! And how does he explain that? . . . What tensions? (*Laughs.*) What'd he prescribe, short of a new world? Phenobarbital and Vitamin B-one? The history of our time. (*He laughs.*) Oh, Mary! You're wonderful! I love you! Of course, I was worried *sick.* Mm. Yes . . . Thank you, my angel. I'll call you later. Good-bye.

(*In the squad-room,* ARTHUR'S *face turns gray, he clutches his stomach and bites his lip.* BRODY, *who has been studying him, crosses to him.*)

BRO. What's the matter, sonny?

ART. Nothing.

(BRODY *points to the wash-room.* ARTHUR *crosses to it, quickly. Once inside, alone, his bravado falls away. He is a sick and desperate boy. He dry-retches over the sink for a moment. Breathing heavily, he looks about in sudden panic.*)

BRO. (*glances toward the wash-room, goes to his files, takes out a bottle, goes to the wash-room, props open the door, stands there, watching.* ARTHUR *controls himself, turns on the water in the sink, buries his face in it.* BRODY *takes a paper cup, pours out a drink, offers it to him*). Have a bomb?

ART. No, thanks. (*Dries his face.*)

(BRODY *tosses off the drink, himself. They return to the squad-room. The desk phone rings.* GALLAGHER *reaches for it.*)

BRO. (*glances at the clock*). O.K., Tom. I'll take over now. Go on home. (*Picks up the phone.*)

GALLA. Home? I got a squeal. (*Goes off into the next room.*)

BRO. (*on the phone*). 21st Squad, Detective Brody. Yeah? Get his license number? . . . (*He glances at the clock, scribbles data on a pad.*)

MC. (*enters the squad-room, crosses to* MR. SIMS). Now, Counselor?

SIMS (*presents him with the photographs again*). You will observe there are no scars or lacerations of any kind! (*Points to photos.*) This is the way I'm delivering my client to you, and this is the way I want him back.

MC. (*studies them gravely*). I should think that any change whatsoever would be an improvement, Counselor.

SIMS. I want you to know I'm not going to allow you to violate his Constitutional rights. You're not to abuse him physically or degrade his dignity as a human being, do you understand?

MC. (*bites this off sharply*). Counselor, I never met a criminal yet who didn't wrap himself in the Constitution from head to toe, or a hoodlum who wasn't filled to the nostrils with habeas corpus and the rights of human dignity. Did you ever see the girl your client operated on last year—in the morgue—on a marble slab? Wasn't much human left of her, Counselor—and very little dignity!

SIMS. My client was innocent of that charge. The court acquitted him.

MC. He was guilty.

SIMS. Are you setting yourself above the courts of the land?

MC. There's a higher court, Counselor.

SIMS. I'm sure there is, Officer. Are you qualified to speak for it? I'm not. God doesn't come down and whisper in my ear. But when it comes to the man-made law on terra firma, I know it, I obey it, and I respect it.

MC. What do you want to do?—Try the case here? This isn't a court. Save it for the Judge. Now, Counselor, I'm busy. Your client will be treated with as much delicacy as he is entitled to. So bring him in—or get off the pot.

SIMS. I've heard about you. You're quite an anomaly, McLeod, quite an anomaly. It's going to be a real pleasure to examine you on the witness stand.

MC. Anything to give you a thrill, Counselor.

SIMS. We may have a thrill or two in store for you.

MC. Meaning?

SIMS. For over a year you personally have been making my client's life a living hell. Why?

MC. I beg your pardon?

SIMS. Why?

MC. (*sardonically*). Because I'm annoyed by criminals that get away with murder. They upset me.

SIMS. You're easily upset.

MC. Oh, I'm *very* sensitive. (*Dismissing him.*) To me your client is just another criminal. (*Turns away.*) O.K., Arthur! In there! (*He indicates the* LIEUTENANT's *office.* ARTHUR *rises, enters the office.*)

SIMS. That's your story. At considerable expense we have investigated and discovered *otherwise*.

(MC LEOD *turns to stare at him.* SIMS *smiles knowingly and goes.*)

BRO. What the hell's he driving at?

MC. A fishing expedition. That's a shrewd mouthpiece. I've seen him operate. (*He enters the* LIEUTENANT's *office. To* ARTHUR.) Empty your pockets! Take everything out. Put it on the desk! (ARTHUR *empties the contents of his pockets on the desk.*) That all?

ART. Yes.

MC. Turn your pockets inside out. (ARTHUR *obeys.*) Sit down! Over there! What'd you do with the money?

ART. I spent it.

MC. (*examines the articles one by one, very carefully*). All of it?

ART. Yes.

MC. (*picks up a book of matches*). When were you at the Stork Club?

ART. Wednesday night.

MC. Been doing the hot spots?

ART. Some.

MC. Any of the money left?

ART. How far can you go with four hundred dollars?

MC. Four hundred and eighty.

ART. Was it four eighty?

MC. So your employer claims.

ART. He ought to know.

MC. Arthur, why'd you take the money?

ART. What's the difference? I took it, I admit it, I took it!

MC. Where'd you spend last night?

ART. In my room.

MC. I was there. Where were you? Under the bed?

ART. I sat in the Park.

MC. All night?

ART. Yes.

MC. It rained.

ART. Drizzled.

MC. You sat in the drizzle?

ART. Yes.

MC. What were you doing?

ART. Just dreaming.

MC. In the park at night?—Dreaming?

ART. Night is the time for dreams.

MC. And *thieves*! (*He examines the articles in* ARTHUR'S *pockets.* . . .
    The phone in the squad-room rings. BRODY *answers.*)

BRO. 21st Squad, Detective Brody . . . Callahan, for you!

CALL. (*crosses to phone, throwing a parking ticket on the desk*). A kiss
    from Judge Bromfield. (*Into phone.*) Callahan, 21st.

JOE (*examines the ticket*). You got a parking ticket?

DAK. (*morosely*). I got one, too. In front of the Criminal Court Building. You're such a big shot, Joe, why don't you throw a little weight around?

JOE. Mind if I use the phone?

BRO. (*nods*). The outside one.

(JOE *dials a number.*)

O'BRI. Some of these judges haven't the brains God gave them. They refrigerate them in law-school.

DAK. It ain't enough we use our own cars to take prisoners to court, and our own gas—we can't even deduct it from our income tax. Where's your justice?

JOE (*into phone*). Hello, Jerry—this is Joe Feinson. (*Suddenly yelling at the top of his lungs.*) Who the hell does that Judge Bromfield think he is? . . . He's persecutin' cops, that's what! Parkin' tickets on duty. I'm going to stir up the goddamnedest hornet's nest! . . . All right! All right! . . . (*Calmly.*) Yeah. Fine. Sure. I got one here. Yeah. (*He hangs up, takes the ticket.*) O.K. Forget it. It's fixed. (*Crosses to get* DAKIS' *ticket.*)

O'BRI. You frighten him?

JOE. I frightened myself. (*Holds up his trembling hand.*) Look at my hand! Shaking!

(DAKIS *laughs—a bellow that makes the room vibrate.*)

CALL. A cop's got to get a reporter to fix a ticket for him. I seen everything now.

JOE. That's the way it should be. A free press is the tocsin of a free people. The law keeps you in line, we keep the law in line, the people keep us in line, you keep the people in line. Everybody kicks everybody else in the ass! That way nobody gets too big for his britches. That's democracy! (*Crosses to the gate.*)

DAK. You have the gall to call that yellow, monopolistic sheet—a free press? Ha! Ha! (*Bellows again.*) You kill me!

(*Exit* JOE, *waving the ticket triumphantly.*)

SHOP. So.

DAK. So what?

SHOP. So what happens to me now?

DAK. We wait here till night court opens. Nine o'clock. Then the magistrate will probably set bail for you.

O'BRI. Have you got a lawyer? You might save the bail bond.

SHOP. My brother-in-law's a lawyer.

DAK. (*belches*). Excuse me. Call him up . . .

SHOP. Gee, I hate to. He's kind of a new brother-in-law. If my sister finds out, oh, God! she'll die! And she's in the fourth month, too.

O'BRI. It's up to you.

DAK. Suit yourself. The court'll appoint you one.

SHOP. Gee, I don't know what to do!

MC. (*completes his examination of the articles in* ARTHUR's *pockets*). Ever been arrested before, Arthur?

ART. I told you no.

MC. You sure?

ART. Yes.

MC. It would help your case if you returned the money.

ART. I know. But I can't. I told you it's gone.

(BRODY *enters the* LIEUTENANT's *office and listens to the interrogation.*)

MC. What's this pawn ticket for?

ART. Textbooks.

MC. Where did you get them?

ART. College.

MC. Graduate?

ART. No.

MC. What stopped you?

ART. World War Two, the first time.

MC. And the second time?

ART. World War Three.

MC. Foolish question, foolish answer. (*Examining contents of* ARTHUR's *pockets.*) Have you any identifying marks on you, Arthur? Any scars? . . . Roll up your sleeves. . . . (ARTHUR *obeys. On his left wrist is a tattoo mark.*) A tattoo mark. A heart. And what's the name? J—O—Y! Who's Joy?

ART. A girl.

MC. Your girl?

ART. No.

MC. Whose girl?

ART. What's the difference?

MC. What branch of the service were you in?

ART. Navy.

MC. How long?

ART. Five years.

MC. What rank?

ART. Chief Petty Officer.

MC. You married?

ART. No.

MC. How old are you?

ART. Twenty-seven.

MC. How long you been in New York?

ART. A year.

MC. Where you from?

ART. Ann Arbor, Michigan.

MC. What's your father's business?

ART. My father's dead.

MC. What *was* his business?

ART. He was a teacher. Music. History of music.

MC. History of music? He must've been proud of you. Where's your mother?

ART. She's dead.

MC. (*looking through* ARTHUR's *address book*). Ah! Here's Joy again—Joy Carmichael. Maybe I better give her a ring.

ART. What for? Why drag her into this? She doesn't know anything about it.

MC. (*mockingly*). You wouldn't lie to me, would you, Arthur?

ART. Why should I lie?

MC. I don't know. Why should you steal? Maybe it's because you're just no damn good, hm, Arthur? The judge asks me and I'm going to throw the book at you.—Tattoo *that* on your arm! (MC LEOD *rises.*)

BRO. Admission?

MC. Yes.

BRO. Get the money?

MC. No. He doesn't milk easily. A superman. I've got an angle. (*Crosses into the squad-room, dials phone.*)

BRO. (*to* ARTHUR). Sonny, you look like a nice boy. How'd you get into this mess?

ART. (*rises*). What is this? Are you going to give me a sermon?

BRO. Don't get funny with me, son. I'll knock you right through the floor! Sit down! (ARTHUR *sits*.) How'd you get into this mess, son?

ART. I don't know. You get trapped.

BRO. Where's the money?

ART. (*shakes his head*). Gone! It's gone.

BRO. What did you do with it?

ART. Spent it.

BRO. (*pauses, takes out a cigarette, offers* ARTHUR *one, lights them*). You went to college? What did you study?

ART. Majored in History.

BRO. History? What for?

ART. To teach. I wanted to be a teacher.

BRO. Much of a career in that?

ART. I used to think so.

BRO. You're a long way from home?

ART. Yes.

BRO. Why didn't you finish?

ART. No time. The war washed that up. There's no time. You can't start from scratch at 25.

(BRODY *studies him, shakes his head. The sudden babble of voices is heard, off.*)

MC. (*looks up from phone*). Uh-uh! Here comes trouble! A couple of customers.

(*A uniformed* POLICEMAN, *Negro, enters herding in front of him* TWO BURGLARS *handcuffed to each other. They are followed by other policemen, a hysterical woman, and at the tail of the parade,* WILLY, *the janitor, with broom, pail and inquisitive look.*

(*The Negro* POLICEMAN *is a big man of erect carriage, with a fine, intelligent face. The* TWO BURGLARS *are a study in contrasting personalities. The* FIRST *is nervous, thin, short, wiry, with long expressive hands that are never still, forever weaving in and out. He has jet-black hair which keeps falling over his forehead in bangs, tiny black eyes, an olive complexion and a slight Italian accent. He is protesting his innocence with percussive indignation. He is wearing an expensive suit and a pink shirt with no tie. The* SECOND BURGLAR *is a chunky, sandy-haired young fellow, slow-moving, slower-thinking, who is inclined to take this arrest as a minor nuisance at worst. He is wearing a "zoot suit" with extremely narrow cuffs on the trousers. He moves slouching slowly, swaying from side to side. There is something "off-beat," something disturbing about both these men.* WILLY, *the janitor, is a thin, sour, grizzled man with a pockmarked face and a moth-eaten tooth-brush moustache. He wears a worn black shirt and old, torn trousers. The hysterical woman is a short, dumpy, elderly Frenchwoman whose hair is in disarray and whose slip is showing. She is wringing her hands, crying and gabbling half in French, half in English. As they enter, they are all talking at once. The first burglar's percussive cries and the Frenchwoman's wails dominate the hub-bub.)*

(BRODY, *hearing the noise, crosses back into squad-room.)*

MC. What have you got there?

BARN. (NEGRO PATROLMAN). Burglars. Caught 'em red-handed. Forcible entry.

WOM. (*in a French accent*). I come up to my apartment. The door was open. The lock was burst wide open. The jamb was broken down. They were inside. I started to run. This one grabbed me and choked me.

IST. BURG. It's a lie! It's a pack of lies! I don't know what she's talking about. . . .

BARN. I was right across the street when I heard her scream. They come running down the stairs. I collared them. . . . This one put up a struggle.

IST. BURG. (*screaming*). I was walkin' down the stairs mindin' my own business—the cop jumps on me and starts beatin' the crap outa me. . . .

MC. (*roars*). All right! (*The* FIRST BURGLAR *stops screaming, pantomimes his innocence.)* We'll come to you. (*He takes his revolver out of his holster, puts it in his pocket.* BRODY *takes out his revolver, places it in the desk drawer.* DAKIS *does likewise. This is official routine which* CALLAHAN *alone neglects to observe.)*

1ST. BURG. (*softly*). Think I'm crazy to do a thing like this?

BRO. Sh! You'll get your turn to talk. Sit down.

BARN. On this one I found this jimmy, and this . . . (*Takes out a jimmy and a revolver, hands them to* MC LEOD.)

BRO. Twenty-two?

MC. (*nods*). Loaded. (*He unloads the cylinder, places the cartridges on the desk.*)

BRO. (*to the first burglar*). What's your name? Stand up! (*Searches him more thoroughly.*)

1ST. BURG. Gennini. Charles Gennini. And I don't know nothin'. I don't even know this guy. Ask him! (*To the other burglar.*) Do I know you? (*To* BRODY.) No!

BRO. Take it easy, Charley. Sit down! (*To the other burglar.*) What's your name?

2ND. BURG. Lewis Abbott.

BRO. (*brandishes revolver and jimmy*). Were you carrying these, Lewis?

LEW. (*thinks for a moment, nods, unemotionally*). Ya.

WOM. (*begins to cry*). By the throat he grabbed me! How can this happen in New York?

MC. (*gently*). Take it easy, Madame. You're all right, now. Sit down, Madame. I'll get you a glass of water.

WOM. Oh, please, please!

(MC LEOD *crosses to the water-cooler.*)

BRO. (*searches* LEWIS). You're a bad boy, Lewis, and what's more, you're a bad thief. Don't you know a good thief never carries a loaded pistol? It means five years added to your sentence, Lewis.

LEW. I'd never use it.

BRO. That's what you think, Lewis. But it'd happen. You're lucky you were picked up. Probably saved you from a murder rap. Just once you'd walk in, a woman, she'd scream, resist, you'd get scared . . .

CALL. Boom! Boom! (*Sings a funeral dirge.*) Ta da de da da de da de da de dum . . .

BRO. You like the smell a burning flesh? Your own?

LEW. (*thinks, shakes his head*). Na.

(MC LEOD *returns with the glass of water, hands it to the hysterical woman.*)

BRO. Getting dropped today was the luckiest thing ever happened to you, Lewis. (*Turns to* CHARLEY.) Now, *you!*

(CHARLEY *rises.* BRODY *searches him more carefully.*)

CHAR. (*his hands weaving*). I got nothing to do with this, I swear. You think I got rocks in my head?

BRO. (*producing a large wad of bills from* CHARLEY's *pockets*). Look at this!

MC. Quite a bundle! How much is here, Charley?

CHAR. Fourteen hundred bucks.

MC. (*digs into his own pocket, takes out a slim roll of bills*). Eleven! Why is it every time one of you bums comes in, you've got fourteen hundred dollars in your kick and I've got eleven in mine?

BRO. You don't live right.

MC. No, evidently not. (*To* CHARLEY.) Where'd you get this?

CHAR. I saved it. I worked.

MC. Where?

CHAR. I was a bricklayer.

MC. (*hands the money to the patrolman*). Count it! This goes to the custodian. We don't want Charley suing us. (*To* CHARLEY.) Let's see your hands! (*He feels them.*) The only thing you ever "laid," Charley, was a two-dollar floozy.

CALL. Do you always carry so much money around?

CHAR. Yeah.

MC. What's the matter, Charley, don't you trust the banks?

BRO. When were you in stir last, Charley?

CHAR. Me? In jail? Never! I swear to God on a stack of Bibles!

MC. What's your B number?

CHAR. I ain't got none.

MC. You sure?

CHAR. On my mother's grave, I ain't got no B card.

CALL. You're stupid.

MC. (*looks at the others, shakes his head and laughs softly*). You just gave yourself away, Charley. How do you know what a B card is if you never had one?

CHAR. I . . . heard. I been around.

MC. I'll bet you have. You've been working this precinct since October.

CHAR. No. I swear . . .

MC. (*laughs in his face*). Who the hell do you think you're kidding? (CHARLEY *glares at him*.) I know that face. This is a good man. He's been in jail before.

CHAR. Never, so help me God! What are you tryin' to do, hang me? I wanta call my lawyer.

MC. Shut up! Print him. You'll find he's got a sheet as long as your arm.

CHAR. I don't know what you're talkin' about. I swear to God! I get down on my knees . . . (*He falls to his knees, crying.*) What do you want me to . . .

MC. Get up! Get up! I can smell you. He's a cat burglar. A real murderer!

CALL. How many women you raped? (CALLAHAN *stands near by, his back to the prisoner, his revolver sticking out of the holster.* CHARLEY *looks at it, licks his lips.*)

MC. (*to* CALLAHAN). Watch the roscoe! What's the matter with you? (CALLAHAN *takes his revolver out of his holster, puts it in his pocket. To* CHARLEY.) Sit down! Over there.

WOM. Isn't anybody going to take care of me?

MC. Look, Madame! You're very upset. We don't need you here. Why don't you go home and rest up?

WOM. No, no, no! I am afraid to go back there now. I'm afraid even to go out in the street.

MC. (*laughs*). Now, come on! You've got nothing to be afraid of.

WOM. No, no! I am! I am afraid!

MC. Suppose I send a policeman with you? . . . What time do you expect your husband back?

WOM. Seven o'clock.

MC. I'll send a policeman home with you to keep you company. A nice handsome Irish cop. How's that?

WOM. (*thinks it over, giggles at him, nods*). That would be fine. Thank you, very much.

MC. (*turns her over to* KEOGH). Gus, see that this lady gets home safely. (GUS, *grinning, takes her in tow. Exit* GUS *and the woman, giggling.*)

SHOP. I think I better call my brother-in-law.

DAK. What's the number?

SHOP. Jerome 7-2577.

(DAKIS *crosses to phone, dials the number.*)

BRO. (*moves a chair center, turns to* LEWIS). Now, Lewis, sit down! (LEWIS *sits.*) You're in trouble.

MC. (*steps close to* LEWIS). You help us, we'll help you. We'll ask the D.A. to give you a break.

BRO. Tell us the truth. How many burglaries you committed here? (LEWIS *is silent.* BRODY *hands him a cigarette.*)

CALL. (*comes in from behind, lights his cigarette*). Be a man. You got dropped! Face it!

O'BRI. (*closes the circle around* LEWIS). Why not get the agony over with?

CALL. If you don't, we're gonna get the D.A. to throw away the key.

DAK. (*to* SHOPLIFTER, *holding out the phone*). Here you are, girlie! Come and get it.

SHOP. (*crossing rapidly*). Oh, God, what'll I tell her? What should I say? (*She takes the phone and assumes her most casual singsong.*) Hello, Milly! . . . Yeah! . . . Nothin'! I just didn't have any change. How are you? Yeah? Fine! How was the party? You went to Brooklyn? In your delicate condition? Milly! (*She laughs feebly.*) Say, Milly, is Jack there by any chance? Could I talk to him? Oh, nothin'! Some friend of mine wants some advice on somethin'. I don't know what. (*She puts phone down.*) He's there. What should I tell him? I don't know what to tell him.

DAK. Tell him to meet you at night court, 100 Center Street.

SHOP. Shall I tell him to bring hard cash?

DAK. He'll know better than we.

SHOP. (*whispers hoarsely into phone*). Hello, Jack? Listen—can Milly hear me? I don't want her to know, but I'm in a jam. I need your help. So don't let on. Make out like it's nothing. I can't give you all the details. I'm at the police station. Yeah. I took a bag. Best's. (*Blatting.*) I had to admit it, Jack, it was on my arm. Thanks, Jack! 100 Center Street. If Milly asks, tell her . . . Gee, Jack, you're a . . . (*She hangs up slowly, sighs with relief to Detective* DAKIS.) Boy! Am I relieved!

(ENDICOTT SIMS *appears with* KURT SCHNEIDER, *and they stand within the gate, talking softly.* SCHNEIDER *is gaunt, neatly attired, dark, sullen, narrow, ferret-like face, bulging eyes, well-trimmed, waxed moustache.*)

MC. (*coming out of the* LIEUTENANT'S *office, crosses to them*). Hello, Kurt! Come on in.

SIMS (*to* MC LEOD). I have advised my client of his legal rights. He will answer no questions other than his name and address. Remember, Kurt! Name and address, that's all. Is that understood?

MC. As you say, Counselor.

SIMS. When are you going to book him?

MC. In a couple of hours, when we get around to it.

SIMS. I want to arrange his bail bond.

MC. You'll have to get Judge Crater to stand bail for him.

SIMS. Suppose you tend to your business and I'll tend to mine.

MC. I'll be glad to, if you'll get the hell out of here and let me.

SIMS. Remember, Kurt! Name and address, that's all.   (*Exit.*)

MC. Sit down, Kurt. Over here! How've you been?

KURT. So, so.

MC. You look fit. That farm life agrees with you. Some coffee, Kurt?

KURT. You got enough?

MC. There's plenty. (*Pours some.*) Here you are! Sandwich?

KURT. I just ate.

MC. Cruller?

KURT. I'm full—

MC. Be right with you. (*Hands him a newspaper, crosses to the phone, looks up a number in his notebook, dials it.*)

BRO. (*to Patrolman* BARNES, *pointing at* CHARLEY *and indicating the wash-room*). Steve!

PATROL. BARN. (*nods*). Come on, Charley, in here! (*Takes* CHARLEY *off into the wash-room.*)

BRO. (*to* LEWIS). Charley let *you* carry the gun and the jimmy. . . . You're the one that's going to burn. Don't you see how he's crossed you?

CALL. You ever hear of the guy who sold his buddy up the river for thirty pieces of silver?

LEW. Ya. (*The ring of men closes around* LEWIS.)

O'BRI. Well? Think!

BRO. When were you in jail last?

(*Silence.*)

MC. Look, Lewis, we're gonna finger-print you. In half an hour we'll know your whole record, anyway.

BRO. Make it easy for yourself. How many burglaries you committed in New York, Lewis?

LEW. What'll I get?

CALL. Were you in jail before?

LEW. Ya. Elmira. I got out in March.

BRO. How long were you in?

LEW. Three and a half years.

BRO. What for?

LEW. Burglary.

BRO. Well, I'd say, seven and a half, to ten; maybe less, if you co-operate, if not—fifteen to twenty!

LEW. What do you want to know?

BRO. How many burglaries you committed in New York?

LEW. Nine or ten.

CALL. That's better.

BRO. What'd you do with the stuff?

LEW. Gave it to Charley.

CALL. He was in on it then?

LEW. Ya.

BRO. You sell it?

LEW. Ya.

BRO. Where?

LEW. In Boston . . . I think.

BRO. You *think?* Didn't he tell you?

LEW. Na.

CALL. You're a bit of a shmuck, ain't you, Lewis?

BRO. No, Lewis is regular. He's co-operating. (*To* LEWIS.) How much did he give you altogether?

LEW. Half. Four hundred dollars.

CALL. Wha . . . a . . . t?

BRO. This stuff was worth thirty to forty thousand dollars.

LEW. Charley said it was mostly fake.

BRO. Look! Here's the list! See for yourself!

(LEWIS *looks at it, his face drops.*)

MC. Lewis, you've been robbed!

LEW. Ya.

BRO. Where does Charley live?

LEW. 129th Street, West. I know the house. I don't know the number. I can show it to you.

BRO. Fine.

(DAKIS *crosses to the toilet, opens the door, nods to Patrolman* BARNES *who brings* CHARLEY *back into the room.*)

CALL. That's using your . . . (*taps* LEWIS' *head*) . . . tokas, Lewis.

(LIEUTENANT MONOGHAN *enters. He is an old-time police officer, ruddy, moon-faced, a cigar always thrust in the jaw, gray hair, muscle gone a bit to fat, his speech, crude New Yorkese interlarded with the vivid thieves' vernacular, crackles with authority.*)

O'BRI. Hello, Chief!

BRO. Hi, Lieutenant!

LIEUT. (*looking around*). Busy house!

O'BRI. Yes, sir, we're bouncin', all of a sudden.

CALL. John! Got your car here? (O'BRIEN *nods.*) Run us over? We're gonna hit this bum's flat, Chief.

LIEUT. (*squints at* LEWIS). What's your name?

LEW. Lewis. Abbott.

CALL. (*shows* LIEUTENANT *the jimmy*). Look at this . . . (*Shows him the gun*) . . . and this.

LIEUT. Loaded?

CALL. Yeah.

BRO. (*indicating* CHARLEY). The other burglar.

LIEUT. What's your name?

CHAR. Gennini. I don't know nothing about this, Lieutenant. I was . . .

LIEUT. (*snorts, turns his back on* CHARLEY). Print him!

CALL. Yes, sir.

LIEUT. Who made the collar?

BRO. Uniform arrest. Patrolman Barnes.

LIEUT. (*to* BARNES). Nice goin'!

MC. (*indicating* KURT *to* LIEUTENANT). Kurt Schneider. Turned himself in.

LIEUT. That mouthpiece of his got hold of me downstairs, chewed my ear off. I wanna have a talk with you. (*Beckons him inside.*)

DAK. Charley, on your feet! Let's go. (*Leads* CHARLEY *over to the finger-print board and "prints" him.*)

MC. (*in the* LIEUTENANT's *office, indicates* ARTHUR). Kindred. The Pritchett complaint.

LIEUT. Admission?

MC. Yes.

LIEUT. Step inside, lad.—In there. (*He indicates an ante-room off right.* ARTHUR *exits off right. To* MC LEOD.) Shut the door. (MC LEOD *shuts door to the squad-room. The* LIEUTENANT *takes off his hat and jacket, tosses them onto the coat-rack.*) On Schneider—what's your poisonal angle?

MC. (*subtly mimics the* LIEUTENANT's *speech*). Poisonal angle! None. Why?

LIEUT. (*looks up sharply*). His mouthpiece hinted at something or other.

MC. Fishing expedition.

LIEUT. You sure?

MC. Sure, I'm sure. What did Mr. Sims imply?

LIEUT. (*takes off his shoulder holster, hangs it on the rack, transferring the revolver to his hip-pocket*). Just vague hints.

MC. You can write those on the air!

LIEUT. What've you got? (*Takes off his shirt, hangs it up.*)

MC. Girl—Miss Harris in the hospital. Critical. I called the D.A.'s office. I'm taking Schneider over to the hospital for a positive identification. I've got a corroborating witness. I phoned her. She's on her way over here. And I want to get a signed statement from Schneider.

LIEUT. How?

MC. "Persuasion."

(JOE *saunters into the outer office.*)

LIEUT. Keep your big mitts off. That's an order.

MC. Were you ever in those railroad flats of his? Did you ever see that kitchen table covered by a filthy, blood-stained oilcloth on which Kurt Schneider performs his delicate operations?

LIEUT. (*crosses to desk, opens drawer, takes out shaving articles and towel*). This is an impoisonal business! Your moral indignation is beginning to give me a quick pain in the butt. You got a Messianic complex. You want to be the judge and the jury, too. Well, you can't do it. It says so in the book. I don't like lawyers coming in here with photos. It marks my squad lousy. I don't like it—and I won't have it. You understand?

MC. Yes, sir.

LIEUT. Can't you say, "yes, sir," without making it sound like an insult? (*Pause.*)

MC. (*the sting still in his voice*). Yes, sir.

LIEUT. (*furious*). You're too damn superior, that's your trouble. For the record, I don't like you any more'n you like me; but you got a value here and I need you on my squad. That's the only reason you're not wearing a white badge again.

MC. (*reaches in his pocket for his shield*). You wouldn't want it back now, would you?

LIEUT. When I do, I'll ask for it.

MC. Because you can have it—with instructions.

LIEUT. (*controls himself*). Get what you can out of Schneider, but no roughhouse! You know the policy of this administration.

MC. I don't hold with it.

LIEUT. What the hell ice does that cut?

MC. I don't believe in coddling criminals.

LIEUT. Who tells you to?

MC. You do. The whole damn system does.

LIEUT. Sometimes, McLeod, you talk like a maniac.

MC. (*starts to speak*). May I . . .

LIEUT. No! You got your orders. That's all.

MC. May I have the keys to the files, *sir*?

LIEUT. You got to have the last word, don't you? (*Tosses the keys on the desk, stalks off right.*)

DAK. (*finishes finger-printing* CHARLEY, *waves him to the wash-room*). Charley, wash up! In there!

JOE (*to* BRODY). How many burglaries?

BRO. Nine or ten.

(*A tall, slender girl enters and stands at the gate. Her face is handsome with a bony, freckled, intelligent, scrubbed handsomeness; wide, soft, generous lips, huge clear eyes, at the moment very troubled, indeed.*)

JOE. Any important names? Any good addresses?

BRO. (*moans*). We don't know yet. You'll get it. Don't rush us, will you, Joey?

YNG. GIRL. Is Detective McLeod here?

CALL. (*crosses up to gate*). Yes, Miss?

YNG. GIRL. May I see Detective McLeod?

CALL. He's busy. Anything I can do for you? (*He scrutinizes her, grins, a little "on the make."*) I seen your face before?

YNG. GIRL. No.

CALL. I never forget a face.

(JOE *looks at her, then wanders into the* LIEUTENANT's *office.*)

YNG. GIRL. You probably saw my sister.

CALL. Who's your sister?

YNG. GIRL. Please tell him Miss Susan Carmichael is here.

CALL. Yes, Miss. Just a minute. (*Replaces the cards in the files.*)

MC. (*in the* LIEUTENANT's *office, examining burglary sheets, still fuming at his* LIEUTENANT). Ignorant, gross ward-heeler! Why don't you print the truth for once, Yussel?

JOE. Which truth?—Yours, his, theirs, mine?

MC. *The* truth.

JOE. Oh, that one? Who would know it? If it came up and blew in your ear, who would know it?

CALL. (*pokes his head into the doorway, addresses* MC LEOD). Kid outside for you! (*Returns to his files.*)

JOE. A nice, tall, long-stemmed kid. (*He sits down, picks his teeth, rambles on, almost to himself.* MC LEOD, *who is going through the files and grinding his teeth in anger, pays no heed to* JOE's *reflections.*) I love these tall kids today. I got a nephew, 17, six-foot-three, blond hair, blue eyes. (*Sucks his teeth.*) Science tells us at the turn of the century the average man and woman's going to be seven-foot tall. Seven foot! That's for me. We know the next fifty years are gonna be lousy: war, atom-bombs, whole friggin' civilization's caving in. But I don't wake up at four A.M. to bury myself, any more. I got the whole thing licked—I'm skipping the next fifty years. I'm concentrating on the twenty-first century and all those seven-foot beauties. . . .

MC. (*impatiently*). I've no time for a philosophic discussion today, Yussel. (*Starts for outer office.*)

JOE (*following, murmurs*). Don't throw water on McLeod. He goes rabid.

BARN. (*to* CHARLEY *as he comes out of wash-room*). O.K., Charley. Come with me. (*They exit through gate.*)

MC. (*calls to* O'BRIEN *who is about to exit with* LEWIS *in tow*). Hey, John, I need eight or ten fellows up here for a line-up. Ask a couple of the men downstairs to get into civvies!

O'BRI. Line-up? Sure.   (*Exit.*)

MC. (*coming down to the desk, addresses the young lady at the gate*). Miss Carmichael?

SUS. Yes. I'm Susan Carmichael.

MC. Come in, please!

SUS. (*enters through the gate, crosses down to the desk facing* MC LEOD). Are you the officer who phoned?

MC. Yes. I'm Detective McLeod.

SUS. Where's Arthur? What happened to him? What's this about?

MC. Did you contact your sister?

SUS. (*hesitating*). N . . . no!

MC. Why not?

SUS. I couldn't reach her.

MC. Where is she?

SUS. Visiting some friends in Connecticut. I don't know the address. Where's Arthur? Is he all right?

MC. Yes. He's inside. How well do you know Arthur Kindred?

SUS. Very. All my life. We lived next door to each other in Ann Arbor.

MC. Kind of a wild boy, wasn't he?

SUS. Arthur?? Not at all. He was always very serious. Why?

MC. Did he give your sister any money?

SUS. My sister earns $25 an hour. She's a very successful model. She averages $300 to $400 a week for herself. Will you please tell me what this is about?

MC. Let me ask the questions? Do you mind?

SUS. Sorry!

MC. Arthur was in the Navy?

SUS. Five years.

MC. He got a dishonorable discharge.

SUS. What are you talking about?

(BRODY *becomes interested, edges over, listening.*)

MC. That's a question.

SUS. You didn't punctuate it.

MC. Correction. (*He smiles.*) Did he?

SUS. Arthur was cited four times. He got the silver star. He carried a sailor up three decks of a burning ship. He had two ships sunk under him. He floated around once in the Pacific Ocean for seventeen hours with sharks all around him. When they picked him up, he was out of his head, trying to climb onto a concrete platform that wasn't there. He was in the hospital for ten weeks after that. Any more questions?

MC. What is his relationship to your sister?

SUS. I told you, we all grew up together.

MC. Is he in love with her?

SUS. My sister is one of the most beautiful girls in New York. A lot of men are in love with her. May I talk to Arthur, now, please?

MC. He didn't give her any money, then?

SUS. (*impatiently*). No.

MC. Did he give it to you?

SUS. Are you kidding?

MC. I'm afraid not. Your sister's boy-friend is in trouble.

SUS. What trouble?

MC. He's a thief.

SUS. Who says so?

MC. He does.

SUS. I don't believe you.

MC. Sit down. (*He calls through door of the* LIEUTENANT'S *office, off right.*) Arthur! In here!

(ARTHUR *enters, sees* SUSAN, *stops in his tracks.*)

SUS. Jiggs! What happened?

ART. Suzy! (*He glares indignantly at* MC LEOD.) Did you have to drag children into this?

MC. (*ironically*). Now, Jiggs!

ART. Susan, you shouldn't have come here.

SUS. What happened?

ART. I took some money.

SUS. Who from?

ART. The man I worked for.

SUS. But why, Jiggs, why?

ART. None of your business.

BRO. (*scanning a list*). Say, Jim!

MC. Yes?

(BRODY *beckons to him.* MC LEOD *turns up, talks to* BRODY *sotto voce.* ARTHUR *whispers to* SUSAN, *urgently.*)

ART. Suzy, go home—quick—go home—get out of here.

SUS. (*whispers*). Jiggs, what happened? Have you got a lawyer?

ART. No!

SUS. I'll phone Joy and tell her.

ART. Do you want to get her involved? There are newspapermen here. You want to ruin her career?

SUS. (*whispering*). But, Jiggs—

ART. (*whispering*). Get out of here, will you?

(MC LEOD *returns.*)

MC. Well, young lady—satisfied?

SUS. How much did he take?

MC. $480.

ART. What's the difference? Will you please tell her to go home, Officer? She's only a kid.

SUS. (*indignantly*). I'm not. I wish you'd . . .

ART. She shouldn't be here. She's got nothing to do with this.

MC. All right, young lady. I'm sorry to have bothered you. Have your sister get in touch with me as soon as you hear from her.

ART. What for? Don't you do it, Suzy—you don't have to. (*To* MC-LEOD.) You're not going to get her involved in this.

MC. You shut up! (*To* SUSAN.) O.K. (*Motions* SUSAN *to go. She bites her lip to keep from crying, and goes.*)

BRO. (*comes down to* ARTHUR). Is it true that you carried a wounded sailor on your shoulders up three decks of a burning ship?

ART. Yes.

BRO. Pretty good.

ART. Could I have that drink now? Please!

BRO. Sure. (*Crosses up to his files, takes out a bottle of whiskey, cleans a glass, pours a drink.* MC LEOD *ambles down to* KURT, *sipping coffee from a container.*)

MC. You're looking pretty well, Kurt.

KURT. Could be better.

MC. (*sits at typewriter, inserts a sheet of paper*). How's the farm?

KURT. All right!

MC. Wasn't there a drought in Jersey this year? (*Starts to type statement.*)

KURT. I irrigate my crops. I've got plenty of water.

MC. What do you raise?

KURT. Cabbage . . . Lettuce . . . Kale! Truck stuff!

MC. (*typing*). That's the life. Picturesque country, North Jersey. Nice hills, unexpected!

KURT. Yes. How're things with you?

MC. This is one business never has a depression. (*Drinks—surveys his container.*) They make a pretty good cup of coffee across the street.

KURT. Mm. So, so.

BRO. (*comes down, hands drink to* ARTHUR.) Here you are, son! (*Crosses up again to replace bottle in his file.* ARTHUR *tosses down the drink.*)

MC. (*types*). When I retire I'm going to buy myself a little farm like yours, settle down. Does it really pay for itself?

KURT. If you work it.

MC. How much can a man average a year? (*Types.*)

KURT. Varies. Two thousand a good year.

MC. Clear? That's pretty good. (*Types.*)

KURT. Sometimes you lose a crop.

MC. (*types*). How long you had that farm?

KURT. Eleven years.

MC. And you average two thousand a year? (*Stops typing, fixes him with a sharp, searching glance.*)

KURT. What's . . . ?

MC. Then how'd you manage to accumulate $56,000 in the bank, Kurt? Hm? (*Silence.*) Hm, Kurt? How?

KURT. Who says I have?

MC. I do. I checked. $56,000. That's a lot of kale. (*Takes out a note-book from his pocket.*) You got it in four banks. Passaic—Oakdale—two in Newark. Here are the figures. How'd you get that money, Kurt?

KURT. I got it honestly.

MC. How? How?

KURT. I don't have to tell you that.

MC. Oh, come on, Kurt. How? (KURT *shakes his head.*) Make it easy for yourself. You're still running that abortion mill, aren't you?

KURT. My name is Kurt Schneider—I live in Oakdale, New Jersey. That's all I have to answer.

MC. You operated on Miss Harris, didn't you?

KURT. No, I did not!

MC. She identified your picture. (*He rips the sheet of paper out of the typewriter and sets it down before* KURT.) Sign that, Kurt!

KURT. What is it?

MC. An admission.

KURT. You think I'm crazy.

MC. We've got you dead to rights. Make it easy for yourself.

KURT. I'm not saying anything more on advice of counsel!

MC. I'm getting impatient! You better talk, Kurt.

KURT. I'm standing on my Constitutional rights!

MC. (*rising nervously, moving above the desk and down to* KURT). Hold your hats, boys, here we go again. (*Looking down on* KURT *from behind him, murmurs softly.*) You're lucky, Kurt. You got away with it once. But the postman rings twice. And this time we've

got you, Kurt. Why don't you cop a plea? Miss Harris is waiting
for you. We're going to visit her in the hospital. She's anxious to
see you. And what you don't know is . . . There was a corroborating witness, and she's downstairs ready to identify you, right
now. . . . You're getting pale, Kurt. (KURT *laughs softly to himself.*) What are you laughing at?

KURT. Nothing.

MC. That's right! That's just what you've got to laugh about—nothing.
You're on the bottom of this joke.

KURT. Maybe I am. Maybe I'm not. Maybe somebody else is.

MC. What's that mean?

KURT. I know why you're out to get me.

MC. Why? . . . (KURT *shakes his head.*) Why, Kurt? This is your last
chance. Do you want to talk?

KURT. My name is Kurt Schneider. I live in Oakdale, New Jersey. That's
all I'm obliged to say by law.

MC. You should have been a lawyer, Kurt. A Philadelphia lawyer.
(*Crosses to the rail, shouts downstairs.*) Line-up, Gus!

GUS (*off-stage, shouts up*). Coming. (*He can be heard approaching
singing the melody of* The Rose of Tralee.)

MC. (*to* DAKIS). Nick, put on your hat and coat for a line-up.

(BRODY *crosses down to* ARTHUR *again.* ARTHUR *hands him the glass.*)

ART. Thanks.

(*A pause. As* BRODY *looks at the boy, something of agony creeps into
his face.*)

BRO. My boy was in the Navy, too. The *Juneau.* Know her?

ART. She was a cruiser.

BRO. Yeah.

ART. Didn't she go down with all hands? In the Pacific?

BRO. There were ten survivors. He wasn't one of them.

ART. Too bad.

BRO. Yeah! He was my only boy. It's something you never get over. You
never believe it. You keep waiting for a bell to ring . . . phone
. . . door. Sometimes I hear a voice on the street, or see a young
fellow from the back, the set of his shoulders—like you—for a

minute it's him. Your whole life becomes like a dream . . . a walking dream.

ART. Maybe he was one of the lucky ones.

BRO. Don't say that!

ART. Why not?

BRO. Because it wouldn't make sense then.

ART. Does it?

BRO. (*fiercely*). Yes, damn it! Yes.

MC. Say, Lou! Will you put on your hat and coat for a line-up?

(*Enter policemen in civilian clothes, and detectives putting on hats and coats, joking and laughing.*)

BRO. Yeah.

MC. John, Nick, hat and coat!

(*The men line up.*)

DAK. (*to* CHARLEY). Sit over there, Charley. (*Indicates the bench.*)

MC. (*coming down to* KURT). Kurt. Put on your hat and coat. Pick your spot. End, middle, any place. No alibis later. (KURT *finds a place in the line and stands there stiffly.* MC LEOD *calls off.*) Come in, Miss Hatch. (*Enter* MISS HATCH, *a hard-looking young woman with hair bleached a lemon yellow. She wears an elaborate fur stole.*) How do you do, Miss Hatch?

MISS H. I'm fine, thank you. (*Crosses down to* MC LEOD. MC LEOD *scrutinizes her, frowns.*) What's the matter?

MC. (*indicating the fur piece*). Rushing the season, aren't you?

MISS H. (*laughs nervously*). Oh!

MC. New?

MISS H. Yes.

MC. Mink?

MISS H. Uh, uh! Dyed squirrel! Looks real though, doesn't it?

MC. Mmm. It was nice of you to come down and help us. We appreciate that.

MISS H. Don't mention it. Let's just get it over with, huh? I got an engagement. What do I— (*She looks about for an ash tray in which to deposit her cigarette.*)

MC. Throw it on the floor. (*She obeys. He steps on it.*) You have your instructions?

MISS H. Yeah. I look at them all, then touch the one on the shoulder. (*He nods. She walks slowly down the line, nervously scrutinizing the faces, a little too quickly to be convincing. She turns to* MC LEOD.) He isn't here.

MC. You haven't looked.

MISS H. I looked. Of course I did.

CALL. It's the new look.

MC. Just look, will you. Not at me. Over there.

MISS H. I don't recognize anyone. I never saw any of them in my life before.

MC. You identified a picture of one of these men.

MISS H. What are you trying to do . . . make me give you a wrong identification? Well, I ain't gonna do it.

MC. (*rubs his thumb and forefinger together, suggestively*). Do you know what this means?

MISS H. (*sharply*). Yeah. That's your cut on the side.

MC. You're fresh! (*Phone rings,* BRODY *answers it.*)

BRO. 2-1 Squad. Brody. (*Conversation sotto voce.*)

MC. I've a good mind to prefer charges against you.

MISS H. (*screams at him*). That's what I get for coming all the way downtown to help you. You cops are all the same. Give you a badge and you think you can push the world around.

MC. You identified one of these men. Now point him out or I'm going to throw you in the clink.

MISS H. You'll do *what?*

BRO. (*hangs up the phone, calls him to one side*). Jim!

MC. Yes?

BRO. (*in subdued tones*). That was the D.A.'s office. The Harris girl died.

MC. When?

BRO. A couple of hours ago.

MC. Why weren't we informed?

BRO. I don't know.

MC. There goes the case.

BRO. The D.A. says just go through the motions. He can't get an indictment now. Just book him and forget it, he says.

MC. Sure, forget it. Let him fill the morgues! (*Crosses over to* KURT.) Congratulations, Kurt! The girl died. Sit down over there, Kurt. All right, Miss Hatch. You've earned your fur piece. I hope you'll enjoy it.

MISS H. (*flaring*). You can't talk to me that way. I'm no tramp that you can talk to me that way. Who the hell do you think you are anyway?

MC. Get out! Take a couple of drop-dead pills! Get lost!

MISS H. (*exit, murmuring*). Big cheese! See my lawyer about him.

MC. All right, men, thank you.

(*As they go, we hear snatches of the following conversation from the men.*)

GUS. I was waiting for her to put the finger on you, boy.

DAK. Me? Do I look like an ice-tong man?

O'BRI. Regular Sarah Heartburn.

CALL. One minute more we'd have gotten the witches' scene from *Macbeth*.   (*Exit.*)

(WILLIE, *the janitor, has entered during the above.*)

WILL. (*sweeping vigorously, muttering all the while*). Now look at this joint, will you? You filthy slobs. You live in a stable. (*To* SHOPLIFTER.) Come on, get up. (*She rises. He sweeps right through her.*) Wouldn't think I swept it out an hour ago. Boy, I'd like to see the homes you bums live in. Pig pens, I bet.   (*Exit.*)

MC. (*crosses up to the duty chart, takes it off the wall, crosses down to the desk with it, murmuring for* JOE's *benefit*). Why am I wasting my life here? I could make more driving a hack. I like books, I like music, I've got a wonderful, wonderful wife—I could get a dozen jobs would give me more time to enjoy the good things of life. I should have my head examined. All this work, these hours! What for? It's a phony. (*He removes the letters spelling out* GALLAGHER *and* DAKIS, *places them in the drawer, takes out other letters, inserts his name and* BRODY's.)

JOE (*comes down*). Was she *reached*, you think?

MC. What do *you* think?

JOE. I don't know.

MC. (*groans*). Oh, Yussel.

JOE. I don't know.

MC. This is a phony. The thieves and murderers could have written the penal code themselves. Your democracy, Yussel, is a Rube Goldberg contraption. An elaborate machine a block long—you set it all in motion, 3,000 wheels turn, it goes *ping.* (*He crosses up again, replaces the chart on the wall.*)

JOE. That's what's great about it. That's what I love. It's so confused, it's wonderful. (*Crosses to* MC LEOD.) After all, Seamus, guilt and innocence!—The epistomological question! Just the knowing . . . the mere knowing . . . the ability to ken. Maybe he didn't do it. Maybe she can't identify him. How do you know?

(BRODY *enters, sits at desk.*)

MC. How do you know anything? You've got a nose, you can smell; you've got taste buds, you can taste; you've got nerve endings, you can feel; and, theoretically, you've got intelligence . . . you can judge.

JOE. Ah, ha! That's where it breaks down!

MC. (*to* BRODY). Got an aspirin?

(BRODY *hands him a box of aspirin,* MC LEOD *takes the box and crosses over into the* LIEUTENANT's *office.* JOE *follows him.*)

JOE. I was talking to Judge Mendez today. He just got on the bench last year, Seamus. Twenty-nine years a successful lawyer. He thought this would be a cinch. He's lost forty pounds. He's nervous as a cat. His wife thinks he has a mistress. He has:—The Law. He said to me, "Joe! I've got to sentence a man to death tomorrow. How can I do it? Who am I to judge? It takes a God to know!—To really know!"

MC. (*in* LIEUTENANT's *office, draws a glass of water, tosses the aspirin into his mouth*). Bunk!

JOE. I'm quoting Judge Mendez.

MC. Then he's a corrupt man, himself. All lawyers are, anyway. I say hang all the lawyers, and let justice triumph. (*Washes down the aspirin with a drink, sits, takes off his tie, rolls up his sleeve, then slowly, with mounting bitterness.*) Evil has a stench of its own. A child can spot it. I know . . . I know, Yussel. My own father was one of them. No good he was . . . possessed. Every day and every night of my childhood I saw and heard him abuse and maliciously torment my mother. I saw that sadistic son-of-a-bitch of a father of mine with that criminal mind of his drive my mother straight into a lunatic asylum. She died in a lunatic asylum. (*He controls himself.*) Yes, I know it when I smell it. I learned it early and deep. I was fourteen and alone in the world. I made war on it. Every time I look at one of these babies, I see my father's face!

(*Phone rings in the outer office.* BRODY *answers.*)

BRO. 2-1 Squad. Brody. (*Pause.*) Lock the door. Don't let him out! I'll be right over. (*Hangs up, rushes into the inner office, grabs his hat and coat.*) Say, Jim, there's a guy at O'Donovan's bar with a badge and gun, arresting a woman. Claims he's a cop. Might be, might be a shakedown. I'll be right back. Catch the phone for me! (*Takes his gun out of the drawer and runs off.*)

JOE (*runs after him*). Could be some shooting. Wait for me, baby!

(*Exit.*)

(MC LEOD *comes out of* LIEUTENANT'S *office, his face grim, black, the veins in his temple standing out.*)

MC. (*to* KURT). You're a lucky man, Kurt. Kissed in your cradle by a vulture. So the girl died, Kurt.

KURT. That's too bad.

MC. What have you got, Kurt, in place of a conscience? (KURT *starts to speak.*) Don't answer!—I know—a lawyer. I ought to fall on you like the sword of God.

KURT. That sword's got two edges. You could cut your own throat.

MC. (*takes out a cigarette, turns away to light it, his face twitching neurotically*). *Look!* The gate's open! While I'm lighting my cigarette—why don't you run for it? One second, you'll be out in the street.

KURT. I'll go free anyway. Why should I run?

MC. Give me the little pleasure— (*Touching his gun.*) of putting a hole in the back of your head.

KURT. You wouldn't do that. Talk!

MC. Is it?

KURT. You're an intelligent man. You're not foolish.

MC. Try me, Kurt. Why don't you? Go ahead, dance down that hall!

KURT (*smiles and shakes his head*). Soon as you book me, I'm out on bail. When I go to trial, they couldn't convict me in a million years. You know that. Even if I were guilty, which I'm not . . . The girl is dead. There are not witnesses. That's the law.

MC. You've been well briefed. You know your catechism.

KURT. I know more than my catechism!

MC. What, for example? (KURT *smiles and nods*.) What, Kurt? What goes on under that monkey-skull of yours, I wonder! (KURT *is silent*.) On your feet! (KURT *looks up at* MC LEOD's *face, is frightened by its almost insane intensity*. MC LEOD *roars at him*.) Get up!! (KURT *rises*.) Go in there! (*Points to the* LIEUTENANT's *office*. KURT *goes into the* LIEUTENANT's *office*. MC LEOD *follows him, shuts the door*.) Sit down, Kurt. (KURT *sits*.) I'm going to give you a piece of advice. When the courts and the juries and the judges let you free this time, get out of New York. Go to Georgia. They won't extradite criminals to us. So, you see, Kurt, take my advice, go to Georgia, or go to hell, but you butcher one more girl in this city, and law or no law, I'll find you and I'll put a bullet in the back of your head, and I'll drop your body in the East River, and I'll go home and I'll sleep sweetly.

KURT. You have to answer to the law the same as I. You don't frighten me. Now, I'll give you some advice. I've got plenty on you, too. I know why you're so vindictive. And you watch your step! Because I happen to have friends, too, downtown . . . with pull, lots of pull!

MC. Have you? What do you know? Aren't you the big shot! *Pull!* Have you got any friends with *push!* Like *that!* (*Kicks him;* KURT *goes over, chair and all*.)

KURT. Cut that out! You let me alone now. . . . (MC LEOD *grabs him by the lapels, pulls him to his feet*.) You let me go! Let me go!

MC. No. Kurt! Everybody else is going to let you go. You got it all figured . . . exactly. The courts, the juries, the judges—(*He slaps him*.) Everybody except me. (*He slaps him again*. KURT *starts to resist, growls and tries to push* MC LEOD *away*. MC LEOD *hits him in the belly*. KURT *crumples to the floor*. MC LEOD's *rage subsides. He sighs, disgusted with himself for losing his temper*.) Why didn't you obey your lawyer and keep your mouth shut? All right! Get up, Kurt! Come on! Get up!

KURT (*moaning and writhing*). I can't . . . I can't . . . Something inside . . . broke! (*He calls feebly.*) Help! (*He screams.*) Help!

MC. Get up! You're all right. Get up!

(KURT's *eyes roll up exposing the whites.* LIEUTENANT MONOGHAN *enters quickly, wiping shaving-lather off his face with a towel.*)

LIEUT. What's going on? (*He sees* KURT, *goes to him, bends down.*)

KURT. Inside! It broke. He hurt me . . .

(DAKIS *rushes in.*)

LIEUT. Take it easy, son, you'll be all right.

KURT. I feel terrible.

LIEUT. Nick! Quick! Get an ambulance.

DAK. Yes, sir. (*Goes to the phone, puts in a call.*)

LIEUT. Did he resist you?

(GALLAGHER *enters on the double.*)

MC. No.

LIEUT. No? You lunatic! Didn't I just get through warning you. (*To* KURT *who is on the floor, moaning in agony.*) What happened?

KURT (*gasping for breath*). He tried to kill me!

LIEUT. Why should he do that?

KURT. Tami Giacoppetti . . . Same thing! . . . She got him after me too. . . . Tami Giacoppetti . . . (KURT's *mouth opens and closes with scarcely any further sound emerging.*)

LIEUT. What? Tami Giacoppetti? Who's he? What about him? (*Puts his ear to* KURT's *mouth.*) A little louder! Just try and talk a little louder, lad. (KURT's *eyes close, his head falls back. To* GALLAGHER.) Wet some towels! (GALLAGHER *rushes to the wash-room.* DAKIS *loosens* KURT's *collar, tries to restore him to consciousness. The* LIEUTENANT *rises, confronts* MC LEOD, *glaring at him.*) Who's Tami Giacoppetti?

MC. I've no idea.

LIEUT. What's the pitch here, McLeod?

MC. He needled me. He got fresh. He begged for it, and I let him have it. That's all.

(GALLAGHER *returns with several wet towels.* DAKIS *takes them from him, applies them to* KURT's *head.*)

LIEUT. Don't con me! That ain't all. Come on! Let's have it! What about this Tami Giacoppetti?

MC. I never heard of him.

GALLA. Giacoppetti? I know him. A black-market guy. Runs a creep joint in the village.

(KURT *groans.*)

MC. He's putting on an act, Lieutenant. Can't you see . . .

(KURT *groans.*)

LIEUT. This could be a very hot potato. If this man's hurt, the big brass'll be down here throwin' questions at me. And I'm going to have the answers. What plays between you two guys? What's he got on you? What's the clout?

MC. Nothing.

LIEUT. Then what was his mouthpiece yellin' and screamin' about?

MC. Red herring. Red, red herring!

LIEUT. That I'm gonna god-damn well find out for myself. There's something kinky about this. McLeod, if you're concealing something from me, I'll have your head on a plate. (*To* GALLAGHER.) This Giacoppetti! Find him and bring him in!

GALLA. Yes, sir. (*Goes.*)

LIEUT. (*calls after him*). My car's downstairs. Use it.

GALLA. Yes, sir. (*Goes.*)

(*The* LIEUTENANT *bends down to* KURT. MC LEOD, *grim-faced, lights another cigarette.*)

(CURTAIN)

ACT TWO

SCENE: *The scene is the same, fifty-four minutes later by the clock on the wall.*

At rise, the lawyer, ENDICOTT SIMS, *is closeted in the* LIEUTENANT's *office, scolding the* LIEUTENANT *and* MC LEOD. *In the squad-room the* SHOP-LIFTER *is reading the comics.* ARTHUR *is seated quietly, his head bowed in thought.* DAKIS, *the janitor and* GUS *are in a huddle, whispering, glancing over toward the* LIEUTENANT'S *door.* BRODY *is talking sotto voce to an excited man and woman, who are glaring at a tough-looking specimen. The setting sun is throwing long and ominous shadows into the darkening room.*

SIMS (*fulminating at* MC LEOD *who pointedly ignores him by focusing attention on a hangnail*). How dare you take the law in your own hands? Who are you to constitute yourself a court of last appeal?

LIEUT. (*oil on the surging waters*). Nah, Counselor . . .

(*The phone rings in the squad-room.* BRODY *crosses to answer.*)

BRO. 21st Squad, Detective Brody . . . Yeah! . . . The hospital! Yeah. How is he? (*Jotting notation.*)

SIMS. No, Lieutenant! This is a felony. (*Wheels back to* MC LEOD.) I'm going to press a felonious assault here. So help me, I'm going to see you in jail!

MC. (*calmly, biting the hangnail*). On which side of the bars, Counselor?

SIMS. Be careful. I'm an attorney and an officer of the court, and I don't like that talk.

MC. I'm an officer of the peace and I don't like collusion.

SIMS. What do you mean by that?

MC. (*looks up, sharply*). By that I mean *collusion*. Subornation of witnesses, Counselor.

SIMS. What the devil are you talking about?

MC. I'm charging you with subornation.

SIMS. Your lips are blistering with lies.

MC. (*sardonically*). Praise from an expert. I had a witness here today you bought off, Counselor.

SIMS. That's so absurd, I'm not even going to answer it.

MC. I'll prove it!

LIEUT. All right! Cut it! Cut it out. Enough's enough.

SIMS (*to* LIEUTENANT). I intend to carry this to the Commissioner.

LIEUT. (*pushes the phone across the desk toward* SIMS). Call him now. That's your privilege.

SIMS. And don't think *you're* entirely free of blame in this, Lieutenant.

LIEUT. Me? What have I . . .

SIMS. I warned you personal motives are involved in this case. I was afraid this was going to happen. You should have taken the necessary steps to prevent it. Luckily, I came armed with photos and affidavits.

LIEUT. Mystery! Mystery! *What* motives?

MC. (*rises*). Yes. Why don't you tell us? Let's get it out in the open! What are these motives?

SIMS. It is not to my client's interests to reveal them at this moment.

MC. Legal bull.

LIEUT. I'm beginning to think so, myself.

SIMS. Sure. One hand washes the other. (BRODY *knocks at the door.*)

LIEUT. Come in!

BRO. Phone, Lieutenant.

LIEUT. (*picks up the phone*). 21st Squad, Lieutenant Monoghan . . . Yeah . . . Yeah . . .

(BRODY *returns to the squad-room, hangs up the phone.*)

SIMS (*softly, to* MC LEOD). On what evidence do you make these serious charges?

MC. (*taunting him*). The evidence of my intelligent observation.

SIMS. Insufficient, incompetent and irrelevant.

LIEUT. (*looks up, annoyed*). Sh! Sh! (*Turns back to the phone.*)

SIMS. You're pretty cagey, McLeod, but your tactics don't fool me for a second. You're not going to duck out of this so easily. You're in a position of responsibility here and you have to answer for your actions. You can't use your badge for personal vengeance. That doesn't go. The public isn't your servant; you're theirs. You're going to be broken for this.

MC. (*roaring back at him*). Go ahead! Break me! You're worse than the criminals you represent, Counselor. You're so damn respectable. Yet, look at you! The clothes you wear, your car downstairs, your house in Westchester, all bought with stolen money, tainted with blood.

LIEUT. Shut up! I got the hospital.

SIMS. How is he? (*They listen attentively.*)

LIEUT. (*on phone*). Yes. Yes. I see. Keep in touch with me. Let me know right away. (*Hangs up.*) See, Counselor, it always pays to await the event. There are no external lacerations on your client that would warrant a felony assault. They're now making X-rays and tests to see if there are any internal injuries. So far you haven't got a leg to stand on.

MC. Let him, let him! (*To* SIMS.) Bring your felony charge. It'll give me a chance to get your client on the stand and really tear his clothes off. And yours, too, Counselor.

LIEUT. McLeod! Step outside!

(MC LEOD *crosses out of the* LIEUTENANT'S *office, shuts the door.*)

BRO. (*murmurs to* MC LEOD). What's the score?

MC. Tempest in a teapot. (*Turns to his personal file.*)

SIMS. What kind of an officer is that?

LIEUT. Detectives are like fingerprints. No two alike. He has his quoiks.

SIMS. The understatement of the year.

LIEUT. We've all got 'em. He has a value here. He's honest. He ain't on the take. I stand up for him on that. Got no tin boxes.

SIMS. I wasn't saying he had.

LIEUT. I thought you was, maybe.

SIMS. No . . .

LIEUT. Then what was you saying? I guess I fumbled it.

SIMS. I can't discuss it with you.

LIEUT. (*sarcastically*). I'd love to discuss it with someone. Who do you suggest?

SIMS. McLeod.

LIEUT. Nah, Counselor!

SIMS. Or his wife!

LIEUT. (*looks up sharply*). His wife? What do you mean by that?

SIMS. Never mind! Skip it!

LIEUT. You mentioned his wife. What do you mean by that? Look! I got to get a clear-up here. A little co-operation would go a long way.

SIMS. When it serves my client's interests . . . not before.

LIEUT. Four years ago I threw my radio set the hell outa the window. You know why? Because, goddamn it, I hate mysteries.

SIMS (*smiles, shakes his head*). Lieutenant, I'm not free to discuss this, yet. (*Looks at his watch.*) Gouverneur Hospital?

LIEUT. Yeah.

SIMS. I want to see my client. Will I be allowed in?

LIEUT. Yeah, yeah.

SIMS. I'll be back. (*He leaves the* LIEUTENANT'S *office. In the squad-room, he pauses to confront* MC LEOD.) I'll be back. I'm not through with you.

MC. I can't wait.

(*Exit* SIMS.)

BRO. (*to* MC LEOD, *indicating the tough, surly-looking character*). This creep was impersonating an officer.

WOM. I didn't know. I thought he might be a policeman. His badge looked real.

BRO. A shake-down. After he got you outside he'd a taken all your money and let you go. You see, Mrs. Feeney, that's how we get a bad reputation. Now you will appear in court in the morning, won't you?

MRS. F. Oh, yes.

MR. F. Tomorrow morning? Hey! . . . I've got a job.

MRS. F. You'll explain to your boss. You'll just take off, that's all.

MR. F. But, Isabel . . .

MRS. F. He'll be there. Don't you worry. Thank you. Thank you. (*They go off, arguing.*)

BRO. (*to* MC LEOD). I'm going down to book this crumb-bum.

CR.-B. (*aggressively*). What did you call me?

BRO. A crumb-bum. Come on! (*Exit* BRODY *and the glowering* CRUMB-BUM.)

(*Inside, the* LIEUTENANT *squints at his cigar a moment, rises, bellows.*)

LIEUT. McLeod!

MC. (*crosses to the* LIEUTENANT'S *door, opens it*). Yes, sir?

LIEUT. What the hell is this about? What's he driving at? I want the truth.

MC. Lieutenant, I give you my solemn word of honor . . .

LIEUT. (*pauses, studies him, sighs, waves him out*). Shut the door!

(MC LEOD *shuts the door and crosses to the desk. A sad-looking man appears at the gate.*)

MC. Yes, sir? What can I do for you?

MAN. I want to report someone picked my pocket.

MC. (*sitting at the desk*). Come in!

MAN (*exposes his back-side, revealing a patch cut out of his trousers*). Look! They cut it right out.

MC. They work that way, with a razor blade. Sit down! Did you see the man?

MAN. No. First I knew I was in a restaurant. (*Sits down.*) I ate a big meal, reached in my pocket to pay the check. Boy, I almost dropped dead. I'm lucky I'm not here under arrest myself.

MC. (*smiles*). Yes. What's your name?

MAN. Gallantz. D. David.

MC. Address?

WILL. (*pail in one hand, broom in the other, taps* GALLANTZ *on the shoulder with the broom*). Git up!

GALL. (*rises, staring at* WILLY). 419 West 80th Street.

WILL. (*bends down to the basket under the desk, empties the contents into his pail, muttering under his breath, rises heavily, paying no attention to anyone as he crosses off*). Look at this room, will you? Wouldn't think I cleaned up an hour ago! Detectives! The brains of the department?! Ha! Couldn't find a Chinaman on Mott Street. (*Exit.*)

MC. What did you lose?

GALL. My wallet.

MC. Can you describe it?

GALL. Black leather.

MC. (*picks up the phone*). Lost property. McLeod.

SHOP. (*lays down the newspaper, addresses* DAKIS). Have you got one of them two-way radio wrist-watches like Dick Tracy?

DAK. No.

SHOP. Behind the times, ain't you?

DAK. Yeah, behind the behind.

SHOP. (*feels her pulse*). Gee, I think I'm getting a reaction. Emotions are bad for me. I got diabetes. I'm not supposed to get emotions.

DAK. (*belches, then, indignantly*). I got ulcers—I'm not supposed to eat sandwiches. A hot meal was waiting for me at home. Do me a favor!—Next time get yourself arrested before four o'clock. Let a fellow eat a home-cooked meal.

SHOP. (*genuinely contrite*). I'm sorry.

DAK. Do you realize this is on my own time? (*With mounting anger.*) Look at all these forms I had to type up. And when we get to court, what'll happen? The judge'll probably let you off. I won't even get a conviction. You cause me all this work for nothin'.

SHOP. I'm sorry.

DAK. That's a big help.

(*In his office the* LIEUTENANT *fishes an address book out of his desk-drawer, thumbs through it for a number, reaches for the phone, dials.*)

MC. (*hangs up. To* GALLANTZ). Sorry. Nothing yet. We'll follow it up. If we hear anything, we'll let you know.

GALL. Thanks! (*As he goes, he looks mournfully at his exposed derrière.*) My best pants, too.　　　　　　　　　　　　　　　　　　　　　　(*Exit.*)

LIEUT. (*on the phone*). Hello, Mrs. McLeod? This is Lieutenant Monoghan of the 21st. No, no! He's all right. Nothing like that!

(*The rest of his conversation is drowned out by the entrance of* CALLAHAN, *Policeman* BARNES, BRODY *and* CHARLEY, *the burglar, all talking at once.* CALLAHAN *and* BARNES *are carrying two suitcases and several pillowcases filled with "loot" from* CHARLEY'S *apartment.* BRODY *completes the parade, carrying more loot.* CALLAHAN *knocks at the* LIEUTENANT'S *door.*)

LIEUT. Come in!

CALL. (*opens the* LIEUTENANT'S *door, holds up the "loot"*). Look what we found, boss. And by a strange coincidence—in Charley's apartment.

(*The* LIEUTENANT *covers the phone, nods approval.*)

BARN. (*unlocks* CHARLEY'S *handcuffs*). Sit down! There! (CHARLEY *sits in the designated chair.*)

CALL. O'Brien is taking Lewis around to identify the houses.

LIEUT. Good! (*Waves him out.*) Shut the door!

(CALLAHAN *slams the door with his knee; then aided by* MC LEOD *and* BRODY *and* DAKIS, *he begins unloading the stolen goods.*)

CALL. (*holding up some "loot"*). Look at this! These jockeys sure get around! . . . (*The* LIEUTENANT *picks up his phone and continues his conversation, which is drowned out by the racket in the squad-room as the men proceed to lay out and examine the stolen goods.* CALLAHAN *holds up an expensive clock, shakes it.*) This worth anything?

MC. (*examines it*). Very good piece—Tiffany. Where'd you get this, Charley.

CHAR. I bought it.

MC. Where?

CHAR. Outside the jewelry exchange. On the street.

MC. Who from?

CHAR. Some guy.

MC. What's his name?

CHAR. I don't know. I never saw him again.

MC. Or before?

CHAR. (*nods*). Yeah.

MC. Or at all. The little man that wasn't there.

SHOP. (*feeling her pulse*). I am getting a reaction. Emotions are bad for me.

DAK. (*checking a stolen article against a list*). Girls with diabetes shouldn't steal pink panties.

SHOP. It wasn't pink pants.

DAK. (*sighs*). I know.

SHOP. It was a bag. . . .

DAK. (*closes his eyes, sighs*). I know.

SHOP. Alligator.

DAK. I know.

SHOP. Imitation alligator.

DAK. (*sorry he started it all*). I know.

BRO. (*holds up a piece of jewelry*). This any good?

MC. (*examines it*). Junk! Wait! Here's something! Monogrammed: J. G. (*Checks with list.*) Sure. This is some of the Gordon stuff. Where'd you get this, Charley?

CHAR. (*hangs his head, disgusted*). I ain't talking.

BRO. Where?

(CHARLEY *shakes his head.*)

CALL. Where'd you get it, Charley? (*Takes out a "billy."*) Know what this is? A "persuader." (*Bangs it on the desk.*)

CHAR. Go ahead! Beat me! Beat me unconscious. Go ahead!

(*The* JANITOR *enters.*)

CALL. (*laughs, puts the "persuader" away*). You're too eager, Charley. Some-a them creeps like it, you know. Gives 'em a thrill. Look at that kisser! I'm a son-of-a-bitch, I'm right.

BRO. (*holding up a piece of silver*). Where'd you get this, Charley? (CHARLEY *hangs his head.*)

DAK. (*annoyed, walks over to him*). Why don't you be professional, Charley. He's talking to you. . . . What's the matter? What are you hanging your head for? What are you ashamed of? Nobody made you be a burglar. You wanted to be a burglar—you're a burglar. So be a good one! Be proud of your chosen profession! Hold your head up. (DAKIS *lifts* CHARLEY's *head up by the chin.*) That's better. You're a good thief, Charley. You're no bum. They wear sweaters. Not you!—You got a hundred-dollar suit on you. You . . . Wait a minute! (*Opens* CHARLEY's *coat, looks at label.*) Take it off, you bum. Stolen! The name's still in it. Where'd you get it?

CHAR. (*takes off the coat, talking fast*). You mean it's stolen? O.K. O.K. I'll tell you the whole story . . . may I drop dead on this spot.

CALL. On this one? Be careful, Charley.

CHAR. (*faster and faster, the nervous hands weaving in the air*). Honest! The truth! But don't tell Lewis!—He'll kill me. He makes out like he's a dummy, don't he? He ain't. He's smart. Ooh, he's as smart as they come. Look . . . I just been in New York two weeks. I came here from Pittsburgh two weeks ago. So help me, I lose my valise in the station. I meet this guy, Lewis, in a pool-room. . . .

CALL. Where? What poolroom?

CHAR. 14th Street, corner of 7th Avenue . . . Look it up! Check it! I'm telling you the truth, so help me. I shoot a game of pool with him. He says to me, "You got a place to stay?" I says, "No." He says, "Share my flat." I say, "O.K." My suit's all dirty. He lends me this one. Says it belongs to his brother who's in Florida. (*Pause.*

He looks up at the unbelieving faces circling him, smiles feebly.)
So help me.

CALL. Charley, my boy—I could tell you a story would bring tears to
your eyes. Get in there and take off your pants! (*He pushes*
CHARLEY *into the wash-room.*)

BRO. Willy! Got an old pair of pants?

WILL. Yeah, I got some downstairs! (*Exit.*)

BRO. Not even smart enough to take out the label. The name's still in it.
Jerome Armstrong . . .

CALL. (*examining his list*). Wait! I got that squeal right here. I think
there was a rape connected with this one.

BRO. I wouldn't be surprised. (*Leaves the door of the toilet for a second.
Goes to the desk, picks up the lists.*)

LIEUT. (*calls*). Dakis!

(DAKIS *hurries to the* LIEUTENANT'S *door, opens it.*)

DAK. Yes, sir?

LIEUT. (*beckons him in; then, softly*). Wait downstairs for Mrs.
McLeod. When she gets here let me know foist.

DAK. (*startled, murmurs*). Right, Chief.

LIEUT. And . . . a . . . Nick . . . (*Touches his lips*) Button 'em up.

DAK. Yes, sir.

(*As he crosses to the gate, he glances at* MC LEOD, *his forehead furrows.
Exit. The* LIEUTENANT *studies his cigar, frowns, goes off. Through
the little window we see* CHARLEY *throw up the bathroom shade
and tug at the iron grill-work.* MC LEOD *crosses to the wash-room
door, calls in.*)

MC. The only way you can get out of there, Charley, is to jump down
the toilet and pull the chain.

(JOE FEINSON *comes in, tense and disturbed. He glances at* MC LEOD *curiously, comes over to* BRODY.)

JOE. Lots of loot. They do the Zaza robbery?

BRO. (*calls in to* CHARLEY). You robbed that Zaza dame's flat, Charley?

CHAR. (*calls out*). I don't know nuttin'!

BRO. He don't know from nuttin'!

CALL. He's ignorant and he's proud of it.

JOE. Any good names?

BRO. Don't know yet—

JOE. Any good addresses?

BRO. They're taking the other bum around. He's identifying the houses. We'll crack it in an hour.

JOE (*saunters over to* MC LEOD). What's with Kurt Schneider?

MC. No story.

JOE. He left here twenty-five minutes ago in an ambulance. What happened? He trip?

MC. Yes.

JOE. Over his schnozzola?

MC. Could have. It's long enough.

JOE. No story?

MC. No.

JOE. His lawyer's sore as a boil. What happened?

MC. You tell me. You always have the story in your pocket.

JOE. Look, Seamus! There are angles here I don't feel happy about.

MC. What angles?

JOE. I don't know . . . yet. Come! Give! Off the record.

MC. You can print it if you want to. Kurt Schneider was a butcher who murdered two girls and got away with it. High time somebody put the fear of God in him. The law wouldn't, so I did. Print it, Yussel. Go ahead. You don't like cops. Here's your chance?

JOE. I don't like cops? For a smart guy, Seamus, you can be an awful schmoe. If I got fired tomorrow, you'd still find me here, hanging around, running errands for you guys, happy as a bird dog! I'm a buff from way back. I found a home. You know that.

MC. Sentimental slop, Yussel.

(*A short, stout, timid man enters and looks about apprehensively.*)

JOE. My sixth sense is still bothering me, Seamus.

MC. Have a doctor examine it. (*To the newcomer.*) Yes, sir? (*The nervous man looks about, moistens his lips with his tongue, mops his brow, starts to speak.* MC LEOD *recognizes him.*) Oh! Come in, Mr. Pritchett. We've been waiting for you.

MR. PRIT. Did you get my money back?

MC. I'm afraid not.

MR. PRIT. What'd he do with it?

MC. Women and plush saloons.

MR. PRIT. Cabarets? I wouldn't have thought it. He seemed such an honest boy. I don't make many mistakes. I'm a pretty good student of human nature . . . usually.

MC. You'll be in court tomorrow morning?

MR. PRIT. Oh, yes.

MC. We can count on you?

MR. PRIT. When I make my mind up, I'm like iron.

MC. Fine! Thank you, Mr. Pritchett.

MR. PRIT. Like iron.

MC. Arthur, on your feet! (ARTHUR *rises*.) Is this the boy?

MR. PRIT. (*with a huge sigh*). I'm afraid it is.

MC. Arthur, over here. (ARTHUR *crosses to them. The phone rings.* MC LEOD *goes to the desk, picks up the receiver*.) 21st Squad! McLeod!

BARN. (*at the wash-room door*). All right, Charley. (*He leads* CHARLEY *back into the squad-room*. CHARLEY *is now wearing an ill-fitting, torn and filthy pair of trousers at which the eloquent hands pantomime disgust*.)

MR. PRIT. Well, Arthur, is this your journey's end?

ART. I guess so.

MR. PRIT. Did I treat you badly?

ART. No, Mr. Pritchett.

MR. PRIT. Did I pay you a decent salary?

ART. Yes.

MR. PRIT. Then why did you do this to me?

(SUSAN *appears at the gate*.)

SUS. (*catches* MC LEOD's *eyes*). May I? (*He nods. She enters, fumbling in her purse*.)

MR. PRIT. (*to* ARTHUR). You spent my money on fast women?

ART. Just a second . . .

MR. PRIT. No! I didn't grow my money on trees. I built up my business from a hole in the wall where I sold neckties two for a quarter. Thirty years I built it. By the sweat of my brow. I worked darn hard for it. I want my money back.

SUS. And you'll get it. I promise you. (*She takes some money out of her purse.*) The bank was closed. All I could scrape together, tonight, was $120. (*She hands the money to* MR. PRITCHETT.) I'll have the rest for you tomorrow.

ART. Susan! Take that back!

SUS. Let me alone! Don't interfere, Jiggs!

MR. PRIT. Who is this? Who are you, Miss?

SUS. I'm an old friend of Mr. Kindred's family. And I'd like to straighten this out with you, Mister . . . What is your name?

MR. PRIT. Pritchett, Albert J. Pritchett.

SUS. Mr. Pritchett. How do you do? I'm Susan Carmichael.

MR. PRIT. How do you do? You say you're prepared to return the rest of my money, young lady?

SUS. Yes. I'll sign a promissory note, or whatever you suggest.

MC. (*into the phone*). One second! (*To* SUSAN.) Where'd you get that cash, Miss Carmichael?

SUS. I had some and I pawned some jewelry. Here are the tickets. Do you want to see them?

MC. If you don't mind. (*Takes them, examines them.*) Anything of your sister's here?

SUS. Nothing. Not a bobby pin.

MR. PRIT. Is this the young lady who . . .

ART. No. She doesn't know anything about it.

SUS. I know all there is to know. (*To* MR. PRITCHETT.) Mr. Pritchett, this whole mess you can blame on *my sister*.

ART. What's the matter with you, Suzy? What are you dragging Joy into this for? She's got nothing to do with it.

SUS. Hasn't she?

ART. No.

SUS. I've got news for you. I just spoke to her on the phone. (*Pause.*)

ART. You didn't tell her?

SUS. Of course I did.

ART. What'd she say?

SUS. She was upset.

ART. Naturally, she would be. You shouldn't have . . .

SUS. Naturally! My blue-eyed sister was in a tizzy because she didn't want to get involved in your troubles. You know where I called her? At Walter Forbes' in Connecticut. She's afraid this might crimp her chance to be the next Mrs. Forbes. . . . Big deal!

ART. I know, Suzy. That's not news to me. I know.

SUS. Till ten minutes ago, I thought my sister was the cherub of the world. There wasn't anything I wouldn't have done for her. But if she can do this to you—to you, Jiggs—then I don't want any part of her. And I mean that. I'm through with her. I loathe her.

ART. Suzy! Take it easy.

SUS. All my life everything I wanted Joy got. All right! I didn't mind. I felt she was so special. She was entitled to be Queen. But now I'm through.

ART. Suzy, maybe you don't understand. Like everybody else, Joy is frightened. She wants to grab a little security. Don't blame her for it. I don't.

SUS. Security? You've seen Walter Forbes. He's had four wives. He gets falling-down drunk every single night of his life. Some security!

ART. He's very rich. You can't have everything.

SUS. Jiggs! Don't! Don't you be disgusting too. (*To* MR. PRITCHETT.) Should I make out a note for the rest?

MC. Wait a minute. (*He hangs up the phone, crosses to* MR. PRITCHETT, *takes the money from him and hands it back to* SUSAN.) We don't run a collection agency here! This man is a thief. We're here to prosecute criminals, not collect money.

(*Detective* DAKIS *enters, crosses into the* LIEUTENANT's *office.*)

SUS. He's not a criminal.

MC. Miss Carmichael, you seem like a very nice young lady. I'm going to give you some advice. I've seen a thousand like him. *He's no good!* Take your money and run.

DAK. (*to the* LIEUTENANT). She's downstairs.

LIEUT. (*grunts, rises, goes to the door, calls*). McLeod!

MC. Yes, sir?

LIEUT. Get me the old files on that Cottsworth squeal!

MC. (*thinks*). 1938?

LIEUT. Yeah.

MC. March 12th . . . (LIEUTENANT *nods.*) That'll be buried under a pile inside, I'll have to dig them up.

LIEUT. Dig 'em up! Do it now!

MC. Yes, sir. (*As he crosses off left, he throws his judgment at* ARTHUR *and* SUSAN.) He spells one thing for you—*misery* the rest of your life. He's no good. Believe me, I know!   (*Exit.*)

SUS. (*indignantly*). That isn't true! (*To* MR. PRITCHETT.) That isn't true. I've known Arthur all my life. He never did anything before that was dishonorable. He was the most respected boy in Ann Arbor.

(*The* LIEUTENANT *nods to* DAKIS, *who goes off to bring up* MRS. MC LEOD. BRODY *crosses down, listening to* SUSAN *and* MR. PRITCHETT.)

MR. PRIT. Little lady, once I saw a picture, *Less Miserables.*—A dandy! That was before your time. This Gene Valjeane—his sister's nine children are starving. He steals a loaf of bread. He goes to jail for—I don't know—twenty years. I'm on Gene Valjeane's side there. Impressed me very much. I gave a little talk on it at my lodge. . . . But this? I don't go along with. He wasn't starving. He had a good job. He went cabareting . . . with my money. Heck, I don't go to them myself!

BRO. Mr. Pritchett, maybe once a year we get someone in here steals because he's actually hungry. And we're all on his side. I'd do the same, wouldn't you?

MR. PRIT. Absolutely. I always say self-preservation is the first law of nature.

BRO. But that's one in a thousand cases.

MR. PRIT. Exactly my point! And what did *he* do it for?

ART. (*softly*). I did it because I was hungry.

MR. PRIT. What?

ART. Hungry. You can be hungry for other things besides bread. You've been decent to me, Mr. Pritchett. You trusted me, and I let you down. I'm sorry . . . It's hard to explain, even to myself. I'd been separated from my girl for five years—five long, bloody years! The one human being in the world I loved. She's very beautiful, Mr. Pritchett. Tall, a silvery blonde girl, warm, understanding.

SUS. Jiggs, don't!

ART. At least she was right. She was, Susan. We all change. When I came back from the war, I tried going back to school, but I couldn't get settled. I came to New York just to be near her.

She'd moved on into a new world. She was out of my reach. I should have accepted that. I couldn't. To take her out to dinner and hold her hand cost a month's salary. I hung on anyway. Last Wednesday I had to face it. I was going to lose my girl. She told me she wanted to marry someone else. I made a final grandstand play for her. Late collections had come in. Your money was in my pocket. I blew the works on her. I didn't give a damn about anything except holding on to her. It was my last chance. I lost anyway. . . .

BRO. You admit you did wrong?

ART. Yes, God, yes!

BRO. You're willing to make restitution?

ART. If I get the chance.

SUS. Tomorrow morning. I promise you!

BRO. That's in his favor. How do you feel, Mr. Pritchett?

MR. PRIT. Well . . .

BRO. This kid has a fine war record, too, remember.

MR. PRIT. I know.

BRO. He took a lot of chances for us. Maybe we ought to take one for him. You see, these kids today got problems nobody ever had. We don't even understand them. New blood. We're varicosed. If a new world is gonna be made outa this mess looks like they're the ones gotta do it.

MR. PRIT. It's funny you should say that. I was talking to my brother-in-law only the other night about my nephew and I made exactly that point. I was saying to him . . .

BRO. Mr. Pritchett, do you mind stepping over here a minute?

MR. PRIT. Not at all! (*Rises, follows him.*)

BRO. You, too, Miss!

(SUSAN *follows* BRODY *off left.*)

CHAR. (*stamps his foot*). Give me another cigarette.

BARN. What do you do? Eat these things?

CHAR. Give me a cigarette!

(BARNES *gives him another cigarette.* DAKIS *enters, leading* MRS. MC LEOD *to the* LIEUTENANT'S *office.* MARY MC LEOD *is a pretty young woman, with blonde hair, big gray, troubled eyes, a sweet mouth and deli-*

cate nose. She is inexpensively but attractively dressed. There is something immediately appealing about her. She is very feminine and very soft, and at the moment her evident terror augments these qualities.)

JOE (*sees her, is startled, rises, stops her*). How do you do, Mrs. McLeod! Remember me? I'm Joe Feinson, the reporter.

MARY (*disturbed and overwrought, studies him for a split second, then recalls him*). Oh, yes, of course. I met you with my husband. (*Her mouth trembles.* JOE *smiles, nods.*) What's happened to Jim?

JOE (*grins, reassuringly*). Nothing. He's all right. He's in there.

MARY. Mr. Feinson, please tell me!

JOE. I am.

DAK. This way, please . . . (*She follows him into the* LIEUTENANT'S *office.*)

LIEUT. How do you do, Mrs. McLeod?

MARY. Lieutenant Monoghan?

LIEUT. Yes, mam.

MARY. What is this about, Lieutenant?

LIEUT. Have a seat?

MARY. Where's my husband?

LIEUT. He'll be back in a few minutes.

MARY. He hasn't been *shot?*

LIEUT. (*reassuringly*). No!

MARY. I had a terrible feeling that he . . .

LIEUT. Nothing like that. He's all right.

MARY. You're sure? You're not trying to break it easy?

LIEUT. Nothing like that! I give you my word. You'll see him in a few minutes.

MARY. Then what is it? What's wrong?

LIEUT. A certain situation has come up, and you might be able to help us out.

MARY. Me? . . . I'm all at sea, Lieutenant!

LIEUT. Mrs. McLeod, your husband and I never got along too well, but I want you to know that right now I'm sticking my neck out a mile to save him. I'm not doing it because I like him—I don't. I'm doing it because he has a value here and I need him on the squad. So, like I say, I'm going to help him, if you help me.

MARY. What kind of trouble is Jim in?

LIEUT. A prisoner here was assaulted, maybe injured, by your husband.

MARY. Jim wouldn't do that.

LIEUT. He did. You'll have to take my word for it.

MARY. Then there must have been a reason. A very good reason.

LIEUT. That's what I have to find out.

MARY. Jim is kind and gentle.

LIEUT. That's one side of him.

MARY. It's the only side I know. I've never seen any other. (*Pause.*)

LIEUT. Please sit down!

MARY. Is this man badly hurt?

LIEUT. I don't know yet. This could become serious, Mrs. McLeod. This might cost your husband his job. He could even wind up in jail.

MARY (*sinks into the chair*). How can I help?

LIEUT. By answering some questions. By telling me the truth. Are you willing to go along?

MARY. Yes, of course.

LIEUT. Did you ever run into a man named Kurt Schneider?

MARY (*hoarsely*). No. (*Coughs.*)

LIEUT. My cigar bothering you?

MARY. No. I love the smell of a cigar. My father always smoked them.

LIEUT. Did you ever hear your husband mention that name?

MARY. What name?

LIEUT. This prisoner's name. Kurt Schneider.

MARY (*shakes her head*). Jim made it a rule never to discuss his work with me.

LIEUT. It's a good rule. We don't like to bring this sordid stuff into our homes.

MARY. I'm well trained now. I don't ask.

LIEUT. How long you been married?

MARY. Three years.

LIEUT. It took me ten years to train my wife. It's a tough life—being married to a cop.

MARY. I don't think so. I'm happy.

LIEUT. You love your husband?

MARY. Very much.

LIEUT. Where did you live before you were married?

(*The phone in the squad-room rings.*)

DAK. (*picks up the receiver*). 21st Squad—Detective Dakis.

MARY. New York.

LIEUT. You don't sound like a native. Where you from? Upstate?

MARY. Highland Falls. You've got a good ear.

LIEUT. It's my business.

DAK. (*knocks at the* LIEUTENANT'S *door, opens it*). Captain on the phone, Lieutenant.

LIEUT. (*nods to* MRS. MC LEOD). Excuse me! . . . (*He picks up the phone, turns away from her, and talks into the mouthpiece sotto voce. In the squad-room, the* SHOPLIFTER *rises and stretches.*)

SHOP. (*coyly to* CALLAHAN, *who is at the desk, typing*). You don't look like a detective.

CALL. No? What does a detective look like?

SHOP. They wear derbies. (*She giggles archly.*) You're a nice-looking fellow.

CALL. Thanks.

SHOP. Are you married?

CALL. Yes.

SHOP. (*disgusted—this is the story of her life*). Ya-a-a! (*She slaps the paper on the chair, sits down again.*)

LIEUT. Thanks, Captain! (*Hangs up, turns to* MRS. MC LEOD, *resumes his interrogation.*) When'd you leave Highland Falls?

MARY. The spring of 1941. I got a job in a defense plant.

LIEUT. Where?

MARY. In Newark.

LIEUT. This doctor was practicing in Newark at about that time.

MARY. Doctor?

LIEUT. Schneider.

MARY. Oh, he's a doctor?

LIEUT. Yes. You never met him? Around Newark, maybe?

MARY. No. I don't know him.

LIEUT. He knows you.

MARY. What makes you think that?

LIEUT. He said so.

MARY (*avoids his probing stare*). I'm afraid he's mistaken.

LIEUT. He was positive . . . Kurt Schneider! Ring any bells?

MARY. No. I'm afraid not.

LIEUT. You averted my gaze then. Why?

MARY. Did I? I wasn't conscious of it.

LIEUT. Are you sure a Dr. Schneider never treated you?

MARY (*indignantly*). Certainly not. I just told you, "No."

LIEUT. Why are you so indignant? I didn't say what he treated you for.

MARY. Did this man tell my husband he treated me?

LIEUT. If you'll tell the truth, Mrs. McLeod, you'll help your husband. You'll save me time and trouble. But that's all. In the end I'll get the correct answers. We got a hundred ways of finding out the truth.

MARY. I don't know what you're talking about, Lieutenant. I'm not lying.

(*Detective* GALLAGHER *enters with* TAMI GIACOPPETTI, *handsome, swarthy, on the sharp, loud side, very sure of himself, very sure.*)

GIAC. Can I use the phone, Champ?

GALLA. Not yet, Tami. (*Knocks at the* LIEUTENANT'S *door.*)

GIAC. O.K., Champ.

LIEUT. Yeah! (GALLAGHER *enters and hands a note to the* LIEUTENANT. *The* LIEUTENANT *glances at it, pockets it and dismisses* GALLAGHER *with a gesture.*) Mrs. McLeod, I'm going to ask you a very personal question. Now, don't get angry. I would never dream of asking any woman this type of question unless I had to. You must regard me as the impersonal voice of the law. Mrs. McLeod, did Dr. Schneider ever perform an abortion on you?

MARY. You've no right to ask me that.

LIEUT. I have to do my job—and my job is to find out the truth. Let's not waste any more time! Please answer that question!

MARY. It seems to me I have some rights to privacy. My past life concerns nobody but me.

LIEUT. You have the right to tell the truth. Did he?

MARY. No, Lieutenant Monoghan, he did not.

LIEUT. Does this name mean anything to you: Tami Giacoppetti?

MARY. No.

(*The* LIEUTENANT *goes to the door, beckons.* GALLAGHER *nudges* TAMI, *who walks inside, sees* MARY, *stops in his tracks. The smile on his face fades.*)

GIAC. (*very softly*). Hello, Mary.

(*She withers, all evasion gone, her head droops as she avoids their glances.*)

LIEUT. (*to* MRS. MC LEOD, *indicating the ante-room*). Would you mind stepping in here a minute! (*To* GIACOPPETTI.) Be right with you. (*He leads her into the ante-room.*)

(*Whistling a gay tune, Detective* O'BRIEN *enters the squad-room, followed by the burglar,* LEWIS, *and a cop.*)

BARN. Here's your boy friend, Charley!

DAK. How'd you do?

O'BRI. We got the addresses and most of the names.

DAK. How many?

O'BRI. Nine. (*To* LEWIS.) Sit down! Over here! Lewis has been very co-operative.

(CALLAHAN *has taken off his coat and puts his gun in his holster again. As he bends down over the desk,* CHARLEY *eyes the gun, tries to edge over, stands up.*)

CALL. Whither to, Charley?

CHAR. I got to go.

CALL. Again? This makes the sixth time.

CHAR. Well, I'm noivous.

BARN. Sit down, Charley!

CALL. He's noivous, poor kid.

O'BRI. He needs a vacation.

DAK. He's gonna get one. A long one. At state expense.

CALL. (*dialing a number*). Nuttin's too good for Charley. (*On phone.*) Hello, Mrs. Lundstrom? This is Detective Callahan of the Twenty-foist Precinct. We got that property was burglarized from your apartment. Will you please come down and identify it? Yeah! Yeah! We got 'em. Right. Yes, Ma'am. (*Hangs up, looks at the squeal card, dials another number.*)

O'BRI. (*on phone, simultaneously*). Hello, Mr. Donatello, please . . . Mr. Donatello? This is Detective O'Brien of the 21st Squad. Yes, sir. I think we've caught them. Yes. I have some articles here. Not all. Would you mind coming down to the station house and identifying them? Right. (*He hangs up.*)

CALL. (*on phone*). Hello! Mrs. Demetrios? This is Detective Callahan. Remember me? Twenty-foist Squad. Yeah. I'm still roarin'! How are you, Toots? (*Laughs.*) Retoin match? Where's your husband tonight? O.K. (MC LEOD *enters with an ancient bundle of records wrapped in a sheet of dusty paper and tied with twine. He is blowing off clouds of dust.*) I'll be off duty after midnight. (*Starts to hang up, suddenly remembers the purpose of the phone call.*) Oh, by the way, we got that stuff was boiglarized from your apartment. Come down and identify it. O.K., yuh barracuda! (*Hangs up.*) A man-eater.

O'BRI. You watch it!

CALL. What I don't do for the good of the soivice. I should be getting foist-grade money.

MC. (*undoing the package*). You'll be getting a "foist"-grade knock on the head.

CALL. (*disdainfully*). Brain trust. (*He walks away.*)

BRO. (*approaches* MC LEOD). Say, Jim. I had a long talk with Mr. Pritchett and he's willing to drop the charges.

MC. He is? (*Turns to* MR. PRITCHETT.) What's this about, Mr. Pritchett?

MR. PRIT. I decided not to bring charges against . . . (*Nods toward* ARTHUR.)

MC. I thought you were going to go through with this.

MR. PRIT. I'd like to give the boy another chance.

MC. To steal from someone else?

MR. PRIT. I wouldn't want this on my conscience.

MC. Supposing he commits a worse crime. What about your conscience then, Mr. Pritchett?

MR. PRIT. I'll gamble. I'm a gambler. I bet on horses—this once I'll bet on a human being.

MC. Stick to horses—the percentage is better.

BRO. Wait a minute, Jim. I advised Mr. Pritchett to do this. I thought . . .

MC. (*harshly*). You had no right to do that, Lou. This is my case. You know better.

BRO. I didn't think you'd mind.

MC. Well, I do.

BRO. (*angrily*). Well, I'm sorry!!

SUS. But I'm going to return the money. And if he's satisfied, what difference does it make to you?

MC. It isn't as easy as that. This isn't a civil action: this is a *criminal* action.

GUS (*enters with sheet in his hand*). Jim! Look at this sheet on Charley! (MC LEOD *takes it, studies it.*) As long as your arm. (*To* BARNES.) Keep your eye on that son-of-a-bitch!

MC. (*studying the sheet grimly*). Hm! (*He crosses with* GUS *to the gate, exits into the hallway.*)

MR. PRIT. (*to* BRODY). But you said . . .

BRO. I'm sorry. I made a mistake. It's his case. The disposition of it is up to him.

SUS. But if everybody concerned is . . .

BRO. I'm sorry, girlie. You gotta leave me outa this. I got no right to interfere. Take it up with him. (*Walks off left leaving* SUSAN *and* PRITCHETT *suspended in mid-air.* SUSAN *sinks into a chair awaiting* MC LEOD's *return, glancing off despairingly in his direction.* PRITCHETT *walks up to the gate, leans on it, looking off into the hallway. The* LIEUTENANT *returns to his office from the anteroom.*)

GIAC. (*rises*). What's this about, Champ?

LIEUT. Sit down, Tami! (*Picks up* TAMI's *hat from the desk, looks at the label in it.*) Dobbs Beaver? (*Impressed.*) A twenty-buck hat. You must be rolling. (*Hands* TAMI *his hat.*)

GIAC. (*taking it*). Forty bucks. I'm comfortable. No complaints. What's on your mind, Champ?

LIEUT. The woman you just said hello to.

GIAC. Mary! What kind of trouble could she be in?

LIEUT. I'd just like a little information.

GIAC. (*frowns*). That girl's a hundred percent. I wouldn't say a word against her.

LIEUT. You don't have to. She ain't in no trouble.

GIAC. No. That's good. What do you want from me, Champ?

LIEUT. Mr. Giacoppetti, all this is off the record.

GIAC. When I talk, it's always for the record, Champ. I only say something when I got something to say, Champ.

LIEUT. Look, Giacoppetti, I'm Lieutenant Monoghan. I'm in charge here. Keep your tongue in your mouth, and we'll get along.

GIAC. Mind if I phone my lawyer?

LIEUT. It ain't necessary.

GIAC. My lawyer gets mad.

LIEUT. Nothing you say here will be held against you, understand? I give you my woid.

GIAC. I won't hurt that girl.

LIEUT. I don't want you to. She's only a witness. It's someone else.

GIAC. O.K. Shoot!

LIEUT. Married?

GIAC. Yeah.

LIEUT. How long?

GIAC. Fifteen years. What a racket that is!

LIEUT. You're an expert, ain't you?

GIAC. On what? Marriage?

LIEUT. Rackets.

GIAC. I'm a legitimate business man. Take it up with my attorney.

LIEUT. Look, Mr. Giacoppetti. We've got a sheet on you. We know you're in black market up to your neck. But we don't operate in the State of New Jersey. And what went on there ain't none of our business. Unless you make it so. Kapish?

GIAC. Yeah, I kapish.

LIEUT. Got any kids?

GIAC. No.

LIEUT. I got five. You don't know what you're missing, Tami.

GIAC. (*rises, furious*). Don't rub salt in! I know. I got a wife as big as the Sahara Desert—and twice as sterile. I got nine brothers, four sisters . . . all on my payroll. None of 'em worth anything. They got kids—like rabbits they got 'em—nephews, nieces, all over the lot. But a guy like me, I should become a nation, and I got no kids. Not one. So don't rub salt in, eh?

LIEUT. (*laughs*). O.K. I guess I know how you feel.

GIAC. (*controls himself, smiles sheepishly*). You're a sharpshooter, Champ. You hit me right on my spot.

LIEUT. When did you know this girl?

GIAC. Seven years ago.

LIEUT. You like her?

GIAC. I was crazy about her. She was my girl. I'd a married her, if I could a gotten a divorce.

LIEUT. What broke it up?

GIAC. I don't know.

LIEUT. What do you think?

GIAC. I think maybe I better call my lawyer.

LIEUT. Come on, Giacoppetti. What the hell—You've gone this far. It's off the record.

GIAC. Aah, she give me the air! She got "caught" . . . and that soured her on me. Dames! Who can understand them?

LIEUT. Send her to a doctor?

GIAC. To a doctor? Me? I wanted that kid. I told her: "Give me a son—anything goes." Anything she wants. The moon out of the sky . . . I'd get it for her. Dames! Who can understand them? She goes off. That's the last I see of her. Next thing I know I hear she went to some doctor. I went looking for her. If I'd'a' found her, I'd'a' broken her neck. I found him though. I personally beat the hell out of him. Sent him to a hospital.

LIEUT. What was his name?

GIAC. A Dutchman. Schneider . . . something.

LIEUT. Kurt Schneider.

GIAC. That's it.

LIEUT. (*rises*). Thank you, Tami!

GIAC. That all?

(LIEUTENANT *opens the door of the anteroom, beckons to* MARY.)

LIEUT. Almost.

GIAC. Now will you tell me what this is about?

LIEUT. Just a minute. (MARY *enters.*) Mrs. McLeod, Mr. Giacoppetti has told me everything.

MARY. He has?

GIAC. In a case like this, they find out anyway. It's better to . . .

(MARY *begins to weep.*)

LIEUT. Now, now! . . . (*Pause.*) I'm sorry, Mrs. McLeod. Would you like a glass of water?

MARY (*nods*). Please! (*He fetches her a glass of water.*)

LIEUT. Mr. Giacoppetti! (*Nods toward the anteroom. They both exit.*)

(*Outside, night perceptibly lowers over the city. The squad-room grows ominously dark.* MC LEOD *enters,* CHARLEY'S *sheet in his hand.*)

MC. So you didn't done it, Charley? (*He switches on the lights.*)

CHAR. (*weeping and wringing his hands*). No! No! On my mother's grave!

MC. And you never been in jail?

CHAR. (*wailing*). May I drop dead on this spot! What do you guys want from me?

MC. (*to* MR. PRITCHETT). Heartbreaking, isn't it? (*Crosses to* CHARLEY.) These are your fingerprints, Charley. They never lie. (*He reads the sheet.*) Burglary, eight arrests. Five assaults. Seven muggings. Three rapes. Two arrests for murder. Six extortions. Three jail sentences. One prison break! Nice little sheet, Charley? (*To* BARNES.) He's a four-time loser. You have a club. If he makes one false move—you know what to do with it—hit him over the head.

BARN. Don't worry, I will.

MC. Book him! (*Nods in* LEWIS' *direction.*) This bum, too.

(LEWIS *rises.*)

CHAR. (*abandons his weeping act abruptly, looks at* MC LEOD, *and begins to grin*). Got a cigarette?

MC. (*furiously*). What do you want—room service?

CHAR. (*laughing*). It's the green-light hotel, ain't it?

MC. Take him away!

BARN. O.K., Charley. (*To* LEWIS.) Come on.

(*Exit* BARNES, LEWIS *and* CHARLEY, *the latter laughing raucously at* MC-LEOD.)

MC. (*turns to* PRITCHETT). Don't invest these criminals with your nervous system, Mr. Pritchett. Sure! They laugh, they cry; but don't think it's your laughter or your tears. It isn't. They're a different species, a different breed. Believe me, I know.

(JOE FEINSON *enters.*)

SUS. (*shrilly*). My God—didn't you ever make a mistake?

MC. Yes. When I was new on this job we brought in two boys who were caught stealing from a car. They looked like babies. They cried. I let them go. Two nights later—two nights later—one of them held up a butcher in Harlem. Shot him through the head and killed him. Yes, I made a mistake, and I'm not going to make it again.

SUS. But, Officer, you . . .

MC. (*harshly*). Young lady, I don't want to discuss this with you. Now don't interrupt me!

ART. (*rises*). Don't talk to her like that. She has a right to speak.

MC. (*his face goes black with anger. He roars at* ARTHUR). Shut up! Sit down! (ARTHUR *sits.* MC LEOD *controls himself, lights a cigarette, his hand trembling.*) When you're dealing with the criminal mind, softness is dangerous, Mr. Pritchett.

MR. PRIT. But if it's a first offense.

MC. It's never a first offense: it's just the first time they get caught.

SUS. Why are you so vicious?

MC. I'm not vicious, young lady. I didn't steal this man's money. (*Extinguishes the match violently and hurls it in* ARTHUR's *direction.*) He did. (*To* MR. PRITCHETT.) This is a war, Mr. Pritchett. We know it, they know it, but you don't. We're your army. We're here to protect you. But you've got to co-operate. I'm sick and tired of massaging the complainant into doing his simple duty! You civilians are too lazy or too selfish or too scared or just too indifferent to even want to appear in court and see the charges through that you, yourselves, bring. That makes us—street-cleaners. They have a stick, sweep out the streets, we have a stick, sweep out the human garbage; they pile it in wagons, dump it in the East River, we pile it in wagons, dump it in the Tombs. And what happens? —The next day . . . all back again.

MR. PRIT. But if I get paid . . .

MC. (*impatiently*). I don't care about that. This is a criminal action. Are you or aren't you going through with it? Because I'm not going to let him go.

MR. PRIT. If I don't bring charges?

MC. Then I'm going to book him, anyway, and *subpoena you* into court.

MR. PRIT. Well . . . I . . . I . . .

MC. It's my duty to protect you, in spite of yourself.

MR. PRIT. I guess I've got to leave it up to you, Officer. Whatever you say.

MC. I say, "Prosecute!"

MR. PRIT. All right! You know best. (*To* SUSAN.) I'm sorry. But he had no right to rob me in the first place. That was a terrible thing to do.

MC. (*takes him by the arm, leads him to the gate*). We won't take up any more of your time. I'll see you in court tomorrow morning at ten.

(MR. PRITCHETT *goes.*)

SUS. Mister Pritchett . . . (*She rises and runs after him.*)

MC. (*witheringly*). There goes John Q. Public, "a man of iron."

JOE. Humble yourself, sweetheart, humble yourself!

MC. What?

JOE. Seamus, Seamus, why must you always make everything so black and white? Remember, we're all of us falling down all the time. Don't be so intolerant.

MC. You're out of line.

JOE. Listen to me, Seamus. Listen! I love you, and I'm trying to warn you.

MC. What about? What's on your mind?

JOE. You're digging your own grave. A bottomless pit, baby. It's right there in front of you. One more step and you're in. Humble yourself, sweetheart, humble yourself!

MC. You're very Delphia today, Yussel. What's the oracle of CCNY trying to tell me?

(*There's a long pause.* JOE *examines his face. All friendship is gone out of it. It's hard as granite, now, the jaw muscles bulging.* JOE *smiles sadly to himself, shakes his head.*)

JOE. Nothing. Forget it. (*He goes.*)

LIEUT. (*returns to his office, followed by* GIACOPPETTI. MARY *rises*). Feel better now?

MARY. Yes. Thank you.

LIEUT. Are you ready to tell me the truth?

MARY. Yes.

LIEUT. Your husband's been persecutin' Schneider for over a year because of this?

MARY. No.

LIEUT. Schneider's attorney says so.

MARY. I don't care what he says. Jim never knew. He never knew. I'm sure of that.

LIEUT. Careful now! Weigh your words. This is very important. Any minute that phone'll ring. If Schneider is critically hurt, it's out of my hands. The next second this case'll be with the homicide squad. The Commissioner'll be here, the District Attorney. If that happens I gotta have all the facts.

MARY. Jim didn't know.

LIEUT. That's the question I gotta be sure of . . . now. (*Thinks a moment, goes to the door, calls.*) McLeod!

MC. Yes, sir? (*The* LIEUTENANT *motions him in.* MC LEOD *enters, sees* MARY, *stops short.*) Mary! What are you doing here? What's this, Lieutenant? What's my wife . . .

LIEUT. I sent for her.

MC. Why?

LIEUT. This is Mr. Giacoppetti.

GIAC. Hi, Champ!

MC. What's this about, Lieutenant?

LIEUT. Schneider! Why'd you lie to me?

MC. I didn't lie to you.

MARY. May I . . . may I . . . please.

LIEUT. Yes. Go ahead. (*Watching* MC LEOD.)

MARY. Jim, the Lieutenant won't believe me that you knew nothing about this . . .

MC. About what, Mary?

MARY. Dr. Schneider.

MC. What's he got to do with you?

MARY. This man you struck, this Dr. Schneider . . .

MC. Don't keep saying that, Mary. He's no doctor.

MARY. He isn't? I thought he was. I . . . had occasion to see him once. I went to him once when I needed help.

MC. You *what?* (*After a long pause, studies her, murmurs to himself.*)

MARY. A long time ago, Jim. (*To the* LIEUTENANT.) I told you he didn't . . .

MC. Wait a minute! (*Turns to* GIACOPPETTI.) What's he got to do with this?

MARY. We were going together.

MC. I see.

MARY. I . . .

MC. O.K. Diagrams aren't necessary. I get the picture.

GIAC. I beat the hell out of this Schneider myself. (*He touches* MC LEOD *on the arm.* MC LEOD, *with a growl, slaps his hand.*) Geeze! (*Holds his hand in agony.*)

LIEUT. Cut that out!

GIAC. I don't have to take that from you, Champ!

MC. Touch me again and I'll tear your arm out of the socket.

LIEUT. (*to* MC LEOD). You cut that out! In one second I'm going to flatten you, myself. (*There is a long pause.*)

MC. Do you mind if I talk to my wife . . . alone?

(*The* LIEUTENANT *looks at* MARY.)

MARY. Please!

LIEUT. All right, Tami. You can go.

(GIACOPPETTI *goes. The* LIEUTENANT *walks into his anteroom, slams the door.*)

MARY. I'm terribly sorry, Jim. Please forgive me. (*She touches him; he moves away to avoid her touch.*) Is this man badly hurt?

MC. No.

MARY. Then you're not in serious trouble, Jim?

MC. He's only acting. Nothing will come of it.

MARY. You're sure?

MC. Yes.

MARY. Thank God for that.

MC. My immaculate wife!

MARY. I never said I was.

MC. You never said you weren't! Why didn't you tell me?

MARY. I loved you and I was afraid of losing you.

MC. How long did you go with him?

MARY. A few months.

MC. How many?

MARY. About four.

MC. Four isn't a few.

MARY. No, I suppose not.

MC. Did he give you money?

MARY. No.

MC. But he did give you presents?

MARY. Yes. He gave me some presents, of course.

MC. Expensive ones?

MARY. I don't know.

MC. What do you mean you don't know?

MARY. I don't know. What difference does it make?

MC. This difference. I'd just as soon Schneider died. I'd sooner go to
jail for twenty years—than find out this way that my wife was a
whore.

MARY. Don't say that, Jim.

MC. That's the word, I didn't invent it. That's what they call it.

MARY. I don't care about "they." I only care about you, Jim, and it isn't
true. You know it isn't true.

MC. Why didn't you tell me?

MARY. I wanted to, but I didn't dare. I would have lost you.

MC. I thought I knew you. I thought you were everything good and
pure . . . And with a pig like that! Live dirt!

MARY. Jim, don't judge me. Try and understand. Right and wrong
aren't always as simple as they seem to you. I was on my own for
the first time in a large city. The war was on. Everything was
feverish! I'd only been out with kids my own age until I met this
man. He paid me a lot of attention. I was flattered. I'd never met

anyone like him before in my whole life. I thought he was romantic and glamorous. I thought I was in love with him.

MC. Are you trying to justify yourself in those terms?

MARY. Not justify! Just explain. It was wrong. I know it. I discovered that for myself.

MC. When? Just now?

(*The phone rings.* DAKIS *answers it.*)

MARY. I'm trying to make my life everything you want it to be. If I could make my past life over I'd do that, too, gladly. But I can't. No one can. I made a mistake. I admit it. I've paid for it . . . plenty. Isn't that enough?

DAK. (*crosses to the* LIEUTENANT's *office, enters*). Where's the Lieutenant?

MC. Inside.

DAK. (*shouting off*). Lieutenant!—Hospital's on the phone.

LIEUT. (*enters and picks up the phone*). Yeah! . . . Put him on! . . . Yeah? You're sure? O.K., Doc. Thank you. (*He hangs up.*) The devil takes care of his own! . . . It looks like Schneider's all right. They can't find anything wrong with him.

(*There is a long pause.*)

MARY. May I go now?

LIEUT. Yes, Mrs. McLeod.

(*Exit* LIEUTENANT.)

MARY. Jim, I beg you. Please understand.

MC. What's there to understand? . . . You got undressed before him . . .

MARY. Jim!

MC. You went to bed with him.

MARY. Jim! I can't take much more of this.

MC. You carried his child awhile inside you . . . and then you killed it.

MARY. Yes. That's true.

MC. Everything I hate . . . even murder . . . What the hell's left to understand!

(MARY, *completely stunned, looks at his face, swollen with anger, the face of a madman. She backs up to the door, suddenly opens it, turns, flees.*)

(CURTAIN)

ACT THREE

SCENE: *The scene is the same, eight-thirty by the clock on the wall. Night has fallen. The black, looming masses and the million twinkling eyes of "the city that never sleeps," the flashing General Motors sign, the church spire and cross seem to enter into and become a part of this strange room.*

At rise, the LIEUTENANT's *office is dark and empty. The squad-room, however, is crowded and humming like a dynamo. Half a dozen civilians under the guidance of* DAKIS *and* CALLAHAN *are identifying the stolen property piled high on the table.* BRODY *is fingerprinting* LEWIS. CHARLEY *is sitting, pantomiming to himself, the colored officer watching him closely.* MC LEOD *is seated at the typewriter tapping off* ARTHUR's *"squeal";* ARTHUR *is seated to the right of the typewriter desk, his eyes registering the nightmare.* SUSAN, *behind* ARTHUR's *chair, hovers over him, staring down at him like some impotent guardian angel. Near the same desk the* SHOPLIFTER's *big innocent calf eyes are busy watching, darting in all directions at once, enjoying the Roman holiday. A very chic* LADY *and* GENTLEMAN *in formal evening attire, who are here to claim stolen property, are being photographed by a newspaper photographer.* JOE *weaves in and out of the throng gleaning his information and jotting it down in a notebook.*

PHOT. (*to the chic lady in the evening gown, who is posing for him, holding a stolen silver soup tureen*). Hold up the loot! Little higher, please! (*She holds it higher. Flash!*) Just one more, please!

MC. (*at the desk, to* ARTHUR). Hair?

ART. Brown.

MC. Eyes?

ART. Eyes? I don't know . . . greenish?

MC. (*peering at* ARTHUR). Look brown.

SUS. Hazel. Brown and green flecked with gold.

(*Photographer flash!*)

MC. Hazel. (*Types.*)

PHOT. Ankyou! (*Reloads his camera.*)

DAK. (*to the* GENTLEMAN). Sign here. (*He signs.*) That's all. We'll notify you when to come down to pick up the rest of your property.

GENT. (*plucks out some tickets from his wallet, hands them to* DAKIS). Excellent work, Officer, excellent! My compliments.

(*Exit* GENTLEMAN *and* LADY.)

PHOT. (*to* JOE). Did you get the name?

JOE (*writing story in notebook*). I got it, I got it.

PHOT. Park Avenue?

JOE. Spell it backwards.

PHOT. K-R-A-P.

JOE. You got it.

(*The* PHOTOGRAPHER *chortles.*)

DAK. (*examines the tickets with a slow, mounting burn. To* CALLAHAN). How do you like that jerk? Two tickets for the *flower* show yet! There are two kinds of people in this precinct—the crumbs and the eelite; and the eelite are crumbs.

(CALLAHAN *laughs through his nose.* DAKIS *sits down and checks through his "squeals."*)

MC. (*typing*). You might as well go home now, young lady; as soon as we finish this we're through.

SUS. A few minutes more . . . Please!

MC. (*sighs. To* ARTHUR). Weight?

ART. A hundred and fifty-two.

MC. Height?

ART. Five eleven.

MC. Identifying marks? Scars? Come here! (*Pulls* ARTHUR's *face around.*) Scar on the left cheek. (*Types.*) And a tattoo. Which arm was that on? (ARTHUR *raises his left hand.*) Left? A heart and the name "Joy."

(*The phone rings.* CALLAHAN *answers it.*)

CALL. 21st Squad Detectives, Callahan. Yeah? A jumper? Fifty-thoid Street? (MC LEOD *stops typing, listens.*) Her name? Mc . . . what . . . ? Geeze!

MC. (*calls across the room, sharply*). What was that name?

CALL. (*on the phone*). Wait a minute . . . ! (*To* MC LEOD.) What's 'at, Jim?

MC. (*tense with sudden apprehension*). You got a jumper?

CALL. Yeah.

MC. Woman?

CALL. Yeah.

MC. She killed?

CALL. Sixteenth floor.

MC. Who is it?

CALL. What's with you?

MC. Who is it?

CALL. Name is McFadden. Old lady. Her son just identified her. Why?

MC. (*mops his brow with his handkerchief, mumbles*). Nothing. That's my street. 53rd.

(CALLAHAN *looks at* MC LEOD *with puzzlement, concludes his phone conversation sotto voce.*)

SUS. (*smiling sadly at* ARTHUR). A tattoo?

ART. (*sheepishly*). The others all had them. It made me feel like a real sailor. I was *such* a kid. Seven years ago.

SUS. Seven? It was yesterday, Jiggs.

ART. Seven years. Another world.

BRO. (*finishes fingerprinting* LEWIS). All done, Lewis! Go in there and wash your hands. Next . . .

(LEWIS, *dumb bravo, walks to the wash-room, slowly, nonchalantly, his head lolling from side to side as if it were attached to his spine by a rubber band.*)

MC. Arthur!

(ARTHUR *rises, walks slowly to* BRODY *at the fingerprint board. They exchange glances.*)

BRO. (*softly*). This hand, son. Just relax it. Aaat's it. This finger. Roll it toward me.

DAK. (*rises*). Well, three old squeals polished off. I'm clean! (*He crosses, replaces the cards in the file.*)

CALL. There's one here I'm sure they did. . . . (*Propels himself in the swivel chair over to* CHARLEY.) Charley, did you burglarize this apartment? (CHARLEY *sniffs a contemptuous silence!*) Why don't you give us a break? You do us a favor we might help you.

CHAR. How the hell you gonna help me? I'm a four-time loser. I'm gone to jail for life. How the hell you gonna help me?

CALL. You lived a louse, you wanta die a louse?

CHAR. Yaa!

CALL. You quif!

CHAR. Careful! De sign says courtesy.

CALL. Coitesy? For you? You want coitesy? Here! (*Tears off the sign, hits him on the head with it.* CHARLEY *laughs.* LEWIS *comes swaggering out of the wash-room.*)

BRO. (*finishes fingerprinting* ARTHUR). That's all, son. Go inside and wash your hands.

(ARTHUR *goes in to the wash-room.* SUSAN *holds on to herself tightly.*)

SHOP. (*rises—to* SUSAN, *comforting her*). It don't hurt. You roll it. (*Demonstrates.*) Like that. It just gets your hands a little dirty. It washes right off. It's nothing. (SUSAN *crumples into a chair.*) What's a matter? Did I say something? (SUSAN *shakes her head.*) Are you married? (SUSAN *shakes her head.*) Me neither. Everybody tells you why don't you get married. You should get married. My mother, my father, my sisters, my brother—"Get married!" As if I didn't *want* to get married. Where do you find a man? Get me a man, I'll marry him. *Anything!* As long as it's got pants. Big, little, fat, thin . . . I'll marry him. You think I'd be *here?* For a lousy crocodile bag? I'd be home, cooking him such a meal. Get married!! It's easy to talk! (*She sits again, wrapped up in the tragedy of her spinsterhood.*)

MC. (*at the main desk—to* LEWIS). Sign your name here, Lewis! (LEWIS *signs. The* PHOTOGRAPHER *signals* JOE.)

JOE (*to* BARNES). O.K., Steve! Get 'em over here.

BARN. (*elbowing* LEWIS *over, nudges* CHARLEY *with his stick*). Rise and shine, Charley. (*They line up in front of the desk.*)

PHOT. (*to* BARNES). Stand on the end! (*Patrolman* BARNES *obeys.*)

BARN. Stand here, Lewis.

LEW. (*comes close to* CHARLEY, *murmurs in his ear*). You louse! I ought to kill you.

CHAR. (*mutters*). *Me?* The thanks I get.

JOE (*to* PHOTOGRAPHER). Wait a minute! I want to line up those bullets.

I want 'em in the shot. (*He stands the bullets on end.*) Can you get 'em in?

(MC LEOD *picks up* ARTHUR'S *"sheet," and crosses to the desk.*)

PHOT. Yeah! Ready?

LEW. Thirty grand.

CHAR. Thirty bull!

LEW. I saw the list.

PHOT. (*to* BARNES, *posing them for the shot*). Grab that one by the arm!

CHAR. (*mutters*). Lists? It's a racket! People get big insurance on fake stuff. They collect on it.

BARN. (*smiling for the photo, mutters through his gleaming teeth*). Sh! You spoil the picture. (*Flash. The picture is taken.* BARNES *drops the smile.*) Over there! (*He waves them to a seat with his club, turns to the* PHOTOGRAPHER *to make sure his name is spelled correctly.*)

LEW. What about that fourteen hundred dollars?

CHAR. (*indignantly*). I had it on me for your protection. If this flatfoot had any sense, he was supposed to take it and let us go. . . . Dumb cop! Can I help it?

LEW. (*pushes his face into* CHARLEY'S, *threateningly*). I want my share.

CHAR. All right, Lewis. I'm not gonna argue with you. If it'll make you happy, I'll give you the whole fourteen hundred. Satisfied?

LEW. (*thinks it over*). Ya.

CHAR. Good.

BARN. (*crosses over to them*). No talking—you!

MC. (*to* ARTHUR). Your signature. Here! (ARTHUR *glances at the card, hesitates.*)

SUS. Shouldn't he see a lawyer first?

MC. It's routine.

SUS. Anyway a lawyer should . . .

(MC LEOD *presses his temples, annoyed.*)

ART. Susan! (*Shakes his head.*)

SUS. Excuse me. (*She forces a wan smile, nods, puts her fingers to her lips.* MC LEOD *hands* ARTHUR *the pen.* ARTHUR *looks about seeking a depository for his cigarette butt.*)

MC. On the floor. (ARTHUR *throws it on the floor.*) Step on it! (ARTHUR *steps on butt.*)

ART. Where do I sign?

MC. Here. (*Indicates the line on the card.* ARTHUR *signs.* SUSAN *rises.*)

SUS. I believe in you, Arthur. I want you to know. Deep inside—deep down, no matter what happens—I have faith in you.

JOE (*to* PHOTOGRAPHER). Now, this one. (*To* MC LEOD.) You want to be in this?

MC. (*pressing his temples*). No! Got an aspirin, Yussel?

JOE (*curtly*). No. (*Walks away.*)

PHOT. (*to* ARTHUR). You mind standing up?

(*The flash, as he snaps the picture, galvanizes* SUSAN.)

SUS. (*hysterically*). No! No! They don't have to do that to him! They don't have to. . . . (*To* BRODY.) Officer Brody. They're not going to print that in the papers, are they?

ART. (*goes to her*). It's all right, Suzy! Stop trembling. Please. I don't care. . . .

BRO. (*beckons* JOE *and* PHOTOGRAPHER *out through the gate*). Joe! Teeney! (*They follow him off.*)

SUS. I'm not . . . really. . . . It was the sudden flash! (*She buries her head in her hands, turns away to control herself.* CHARLEY *laughs softly.*)

DAK. (*putting on his hat and jacket, glances at the clock*). Well, quarter to nine. Night Court'll be open by the time we get there.

SHOP. (*rising, picking up her bag and scarf*). What do I do?

DAK. They'll tell you. Your brother-in-law's gonna be there, ain't he?

SHOP. Yeah. All I can do is thank goodness my sister's sexy. Well . . . (*She looks about.*) So long everybody! You been very nice to me. Really very nice. And I'm sorry I caused you all this trouble! Good-bye! (*She and* DAKIS *go.*)

MC. (*to* SUSAN). You better go home now, young lady. It's all over.

SUS. May I talk to Arthur? For two minutes, alone? Then I'll go. I won't make any more trouble, I promise.

MC. All right. (*He handcuffs* ARTHUR *to the chair.*) Two minutes. (*He goes into the* LIEUTENANT'S *office, sits in the darkened room.*)

SUS. (*to* ARTHUR, *her lips trembling*). Jiggs . . .

ART. (*quickly*). Don't!

SUS. (*dragging a chair over to him*). I'm not going to cry. This is no time for emotionalism. I mean we must be calm and wise. We must be realists. (*She sits down, takes his hand.*) The minute I walk out of here I'm going to call Father.

ART. No, Susan, don't do that!

SUS. But he likes you so much, Arthur. He'll be glad to help.

ART. I don't want him to know. I'm ashamed. I'm so ashamed of myself.

SUS. Jiggs, it's understandable.

ART. Is it? God Almighty, I don't understand it! I stole, Suzy. I stole money from a man who trusted me! Where am I? Am I still floating around in the middle of the Pacific, looking for concrete platforms that aren't there? How mixed up can you get?

SUS. But, Jiggs, everybody gets mixed up, some time or other.

ART. They don't steal. (*Pause.*) Delirium, isn't it?

SUS. O.K. So it is delirium, Jiggs. So what? You're coming out of it fine.

ART. (*shakes his head*). Look around, Susan. Look at this. (*Studies the handcuffs.*) The dreams I had—the plans I made . . . to end like this.

SUS. This isn't the end of the world, Jiggs.

ART. It is for me. (*He rattles the handcuffs.*) All I ever wanted was to live quietly in a small college town . . . to study and teach. No! (*Bitterly.*) This isn't a time for study and teachers . . . this is a time for generals.

SUS. (*passionately*). I hate that kind of talk, Jiggs. Everywhere I hear it. . . . I don't believe it. Whatever happens to you, you can still pick up and go on. If ever there was a time for students and teachers, this is it. I know you can still make whatever you choose of your life. (*She pauses, aware of his black anguish.*) Arthur! Do you want Joy? Would that help? Would you like to see her and talk to her?

ART. No.

SUS. I'll go to Connecticut and bring her back?

ART. I don't want her.

SUS. I'll get her here. Say the word. I'll bring her here, Arthur. She'll come. You know she will.

ART. I don't want her, Suzy. I don't want Joy.

SUS. You're sure?

ART. Yes. (*Pause.*) For five years I've been in love with a girl that doesn't exist. I wouldn't know what to say to her now. (*The noises of the city outside rise and fall.*) That's finished. Washed up.

SUS. Oh, Arthur! Why couldn't you have fallen in love with me?

ART. (*looks at her, for a long time, then, tenderly*). I've always loved you, Suzy. You were always . . . my baby.

SUS. I've news for you. I voted for the President in the last election. I'm years past the age of consent.

ART. Just an old bag?

SUS. Arthur, why didn't you fall in love with me? I'd have been so much better for you. I know I'm not as beautiful as Joy, but . . .

ART. But you are. Joy's prettier than you, Susan, but you're more beautiful.

SUS. Oh, Jiggs, you fracture me! Let us not . . . (*She almost cries.*)

ART. Let us not be emotional. We were going to be "realists." Remember?

SUS. Yes.

ART. Suzy, when I go to jail . . . (*Her lip quivers again.*) Now . . . "Realists"??

SUS. I'm not going to cry.

ART. Be my sensible Susan!

SUS. Jiggs, I can't be sensible about you. I love you.

ART. Suzy, darling . . .

SUS. Jiggs, whatever happens, when it's over—let's go back home again.

ART. That would be wonderful, Suzy. That would be everything I ever wanted.

CHAR. (*pretends to play a violin, humming "Hearts and Flowers." Then he laughs raucously, nudging* LEWIS). Hear that, Lewis? He's facin' five to ten? Wait'll the boys go to work on him. (ARTHUR *and* SUSAN *look at him. To* SUSAN.) What makes you think *he'll* want *you* then?

SUS. What?

CHAR. A kid like this in jail. They toss for him.

sus. What do you mean?

CHAR. To see whose chicken he's gonna be!

sus. What does that mean? What's he talking about?

ART. Don't listen to him. (*To* CHARLEY.) Shut up! Who asked you
to . . .

CHAR. After a while you get to like it. Lots a guys come out, they got no
use for dames after that.

ART. Shut up!

CHAR. Look at Lewis, there. He's more woman than man, ain't you,
ain't you, Lewis? (LEWIS *grins.*)

ART. (*rises in a white fury, goes for* CHARLEY, *dragging the chair to
which he's handcuffed*). Shut up! I'll crack your goddamn skull!
(BARNES *runs over to* CHARLEY.)

sus. Stop it! Stop! (BRODY *enters quickly.*) Officer Brody, make him
stop! Make him stop!

BRO. (*to* ARTHUR). Take it easy! Sit down! (*Kicks* CHARLEY *in the shins.*)
Why don't you shut up?

sus. Oh, Officer Brody, help us! Help us!

BRO. Take it easy. He ain't convicted yet. The Judge might put him on
probation. He might get off altogether. A lot of things might
happen.

CHAR. (*bending over, feeling his bruised shin*). Yak! Yak!

BRO. One more peep outa you! One! (*He slaps* CHARLEY, *turns to* BARNES,
irritated.) Take them inside!

(BARNES *waves* CHARLEY *and* LEWIS *into the next room. As they pass* AR-
THUR, LEWIS *eyes* ARTHUR *up and down, grinning and nodding.*
CHARLEY *hums his mockery,* "Hearts and Flowers." BARNES *prods*
CHARLEY *with his night-stick, muttering,* "We heard the voice be-
fore." *They exit.*)

BRO. (*to* SUSAN). If the complainant still wants to give him a break,
that'll help. You got a good lawyer? (*She shakes her head.*) I'll
give you the name of a crackerjack! I'm not supposed to, but I'll
call him myself. There are a lot of tricks to this business.

sus. Don't let it happen!

BRO. Here's your picture. (*Crumples up the photographic plate, tosses it into the waste-basket; goes to his locker, fishes out his bottle of liquor.* SUSAN *begins to weep.*)

ART. Susan! Susan! The rest of my life I'm going to find ways to make this up to you. I swear. Whatever happens . . . (*He puts his arms around her, pulls her down into the chair alongside him, holds her tight.*)

SUS. (*clinging to him*). Arthur, I . . .

ART. Sh! Don't say anything more, Suzy. We've a minute left. Let's just sit here like this . . . quietly. (SUSAN *starts to speak.*) Sh! Quiet! (*She buries her head in his shoulder and they sit there in a gentle embrace. After a second's silence, she relaxes.*) Better?

SUS. (*nods*). Mm!

BRO. (*goes into the* LIEUTENANT'S *office, looking for* MC LEOD). What are you sitting here in the dark for? (*He switches on the light.*) Want a drink, Jim?

MC. No.

BRO. (*pours himself a stiff one*). Jim, I've been your partner for thirteen years. I ever ask you for a favor?

MC. (*pressing his hand to his temples*). What is it, Lou?

BRO. That kid outside. (MC LEOD *groans.*) I want you to give him a break.

MC. You know better. I can't adjudicate this case.

BRO. And what the hell do you think you're doing?

MC. What makes him so special?

BRO. A lot. I think he's a good kid. He's got stuff on the ball. Given another chance . . . (*Pause.*) Jim, he reminds me of my boy.

MC. Mike?—was a hero.

BRO. Why? Because he was killed? If Mike'd be alive today, he'd have the same problems this kid has.

MC. Lou, Lou—how can you compare?

BRO. Thousands like 'em, I guess. New generation, a screwed-up world. We don't even understand them, Jim. I didn't Mike, till he was killed. (*Pause.*) Too late then. (*He swallows his drink.*) How about it?

MC. Don't ask me, will you?

BRO. But, I am.

мс. I can't. I can't do it, Lou. I can't drop the charges.

вко. Louder, please! I don't seem to hear so good outa this ear.

мс. This fellow and Mike—day and night— There's no comparison.

вко. Jim, this is me, Lou Brody. Remember me? What do you mean you can't drop it? You coulda let him go two hours ago. You still can. The complainant left it up to you. I heard him.

мс. Be logical, Lou.

вко. To hell with logic. I seen you logic the life out of a thing. Heart! Heart! The world's crying for a little heart. (*Pause.*) What do you say?

мс. No, Lou. No dice!

вко. My partner! Arrest his own mother.

мс. I'm too old to start compromising now.

вко. There's a full moon out tonight. It shows in your puss.

мс. You shouldn't drink so much, Lou. It melts the lining of your brain.

вко. (*pushes the bottle to him*). Here! You take it. Maybe that's what you need. Maybe it'll melt that rock you got in there for a heart.

мс. (*a moan of anguish*). For Christ's sake, stop it, Lou, will you? My nerves are like banjo strings.

вко. Well, play something on them. Play "Love's Old Sweet Song."

мс. Shut up! Lay off! God damn it! I'm warning you. Lay off! (*Silence.*)

вко. (*studies him, then . . . softer*). What's the matter?

мс. I'm drowning, Lou. I'm drowning. That's all. I'm drowning in my own juices.

вко. I wish I could understand what makes you tick.

мс. I don't expect you to understand me, Lou. I know I'm different than the others. I think differently. I'm not a little boy who won't grow up, playing cops and robbers all his life, like Callahan; and I'm not an insurance salesman, like you, Lou. I'm here out of principle!! Principle, Lou. All my life I've lived according to principle! And, God damn it, I couldn't deviate even if I wanted to.

вко. Sometimes you gotta bend with the wind . . . or break. Be a little human, Jim! Don't be such a friggin' monument!

мс. How, how? How do you compromise? How do you compromise,

Christ!—convictions that go back to the roots of your childhood?
I hate softness. I don't believe in it. My mother was soft; it killed
her. I'm no Christian. I don't believe in the other cheek. I hate
mushiness. You ask me to compromise for this kid? Who the hell
is he? Now, right now, Lou, I'm faced with a problem of my own
that's ripping me up like a .22 bullet bouncing around inside, and
I can't compromise on that. So what do I do? What do I do?

(*A long pause.* JOE *has entered quietly and has been standing in the
doorway, listening.*)

JOE. Try picking up that phone and calling her.

MC. Who?

JOE. Mary. (*Tosses an aspirin box onto the desk.*) Here's your aspirin.

MC. What are you talking about?

JOE. This ".22 bullet" of yours.

MC. You don't know anything about it.

JOE. It's one story I had in my pocket years before it happened.

MC. Listening at keyholes, Yussel?

JOE. No, I'm prescient. (*Pause.*) I met Mary years before you did. The
spring of '41—I was on the Newark *Star.* She didn't remember
me. I never forgot her, though. It's one of those faces you don't
forget. She's one in a million, your Mary. I know. She's a fine girl,
Seamus. She could have had anything she wanted—materially—
anything. She chose you instead. Why? What'd you have to offer
her? Buttons!—These crazy hours, this crazy life? She loves you.
You don't know how lucky you are. I know. I'm little and ugly—
and because I'm a lover of beauty I'm going to live and die alone.
But you? . . . The jewel was placed in your hands. Don't throw
it away. You'll never get it back, again!

(CALLAHAN *re-enters the squad-room, crossing to the files. He pauses to
light a cigarette.*)

BRO. (*softly*). You know what you were like before you met Mary? You
remember?

MC. Yes.

BRO. Like a stick!—Thin.

MC. (*his voice hoarse with emotion*). Yes.

BRO. Dried up, lonely, cold.

MC. Yes.

BRO. And you know what tenderness and warmth she brought to your life?

MC. I know. I know better than you.

BRO. So what the hell you asking me what to do? Pick up the phone! Get on your knees. Crawl!

(MARY *enters the squad-room, stands within the gate, pale, worn.* CAL-LAHAN *clears his throat, approaches her, adjusting his tie, a little "makey.")*

CALL. Yesss, Miss?

MARY. Is Detective McLeod here?

CALL. He's busy, Miss.

MARY (*wearily*). It's *Mrs.*, Mrs. McLeod.

CALL. Oh! Yes, Ma'am. I'll tell him you're here. (*Crosses. Pokes his head into the* LIEUTENANT'S *office to* MC LEOD.) Your wife is out here. (MC LEOD *rises at once, comes out to* MARY. JOE *and* BRODY *follow him out, and discreetly vanish into the wash-room.*)

MARY (*digs into her purse to avoid his eyes. Her voice is low and brittle*). I'm leaving now, Jim. I thought I'd come up and tell you. Here are the keys.

MC. (*softly*). Come inside.

MARY. My taxi's waiting.

MC. Send it away.

MARY. No. My things are in it.

MC. What things?

MARY. My valises and my trunk.

MC. Oh, Mary, be sensible.

MARY. I intend to. Let's not drag it out, Jim! Please! I don't want any more arguments. I can't stand them. (*Her voice becomes shrill.* CALLAHAN *passes by. She clamps the controls on, becoming almost inaudible.*) It's only going to make things worse.

MC. Come inside! I can't talk to you here.

MARY. The meter's ticking.

MC. (*firmly*). Let it tick! Come! (*She obeys, follows him into the* LIEU-TENANT'S *office. He shuts the door, turns to her.*) Mary, this isn't the time or place to discuss our lives, past, present or future. I want you to take your things and go home. I'll be back at eight A.M. and we'll work this out then.

MARY. You think we can?

MC. We'll have to.

MARY. I don't. I don't think it's possible.

MC. Wait a minute! Wait one minute! I don't get this. What are *you* so bitter about? Who's to blame for tonight? You put me in a cement-mixer. And now you're acting as if I were the . . .

MARY. The whore?

MC. Don't say that!

MARY. I didn't invent the word, either, Jim.

MC. I wasn't myself.

MARY. You were never more yourself, Jim. (*Pause.*)

MC. I'm sorry, Mary.

MARY. It's all right. I'm beyond feeling. I'm nice and numb.

MC. You're certainly in no condition to discuss this, tonight.

MARY. I've thought everything over and over and over again and I don't see any other way out. Our life is finished. We couldn't go on from here.

MC. You're married to me. You can't just walk out. Marriage is a sacrament, Mary. You don't dissolve it like that.

MARY. You once told me when you bring a married prostitute in here, if she's convicted, her marriage can be dissolved just like that! Well, I've been brought in and I've been convicted.

MC. I don't like that. Stop that talk, will you, Mary? I'm trying, I'm trying . . .

MARY. To what?

MC. To put all this behind me.

MARY. But you can't do it?

MC. If you'll let me.

MARY. Me? What have I got to say about it? I know the way your mind works. It never lets go. The rest of our days, we'll be living with this. If you won't be saying it you'll be thinking it. (*Pause.*) It's no good. It won't work. I don't want to live a cat-and-dog existence. I couldn't take it. I'd dry up. I'd dry up and die.

MC. Why didn't you ever tell me? If you'd come to me once, just once . . .

MARY. How could I? What good would it have done? Would you have understood? Would you have been able to forgive me?

MC. Wasn't I entitled to know?

MARY. Yes, yes!

MC. Why didn't you tell me?

MARY. Jim, I can't go over this again and again and again. I refuse to.

MC. If I didn't love you and need you so, it'd be simple, you understand?

MARY. I understand.

MC. Simple. You go home now and wait till morning.

MARY. That won't help us. Please, I'm so tired. Let me go now, Jim.

MC. To what? What'll you go to? You, who turn on every light in the house when I'm not there!

MARY. Let me go, Jim.

MC. You, who can't fall asleep unless my arms are around you! Where will you go?

MARY. Jim, I beg you . . .

MC. No, Mary, I'm not going to. (*He grasps her by the arm.*)

MARY. You're hurting my arm. Jim!

MC. I'm sorry . . . I'm sorry. (*He lets her go.*)

MARY. You ripped my sleeve.

MC. You'll sew it up.

MARY. The taxi's waiting. Please, Jim, let me go, without any more razor-slashing. I hate it.

MC. You'd go without a tear?

MARY. I wouldn't say that. One or two, perhaps. I haven't many left.

MC. Mary, I . . . (CALLAHAN *enters the* LIEUTENANT'S *office, leaves paper on his desk, and goes.*) Mary, you just don't stop loving someone.

MARY. I wouldn't have thought so. I wouldn't have believed it could happen. But, there it is. I suppose in this life we all die many times before they finally bury us. This was one of those deaths. Sudden, unexpected, like being run over by a bus. It happens.

MC. Who do you think you're kidding?

MARY. No one! (*Begins to cry.*) Least of all, myself.

MC. (*takes her in his arms*). Mary, I love you.

MARY (*clinging to him, sobbing*). Then help me! I'm trying to be a human being. I'm trying to bundle myself together. It took every bit of strength to go this far. Help me, Jim!

MC. (*caressing her*). It's no use, sweetheart, it's no use. I couldn't go home if you weren't waiting for me with the radio going and the smell of coffee on the stove. I'd blow out my brains. I would, Mary, if I went home to an empty flat—I wouldn't dare take my gun with me. (*He gives her his handkerchief. She dries her eyes.*) Now powder your nose! Put on some lipstick. (*She kisses him.* SIMS *appears at the gate, outside.*)

CALL. (*crosses to* SIMS). Yes, Counselor?

SIMS. I want to see Detective McLeod.

CALL. All right, Counselor. Come in. (*Knocks on the door.*)

MC. Come in!

CALL. Someone outside to see you.

MARY. I'll go home, now.

MC. No. Wait a minute.

MARY (*smiling now*). That taxi bill is going to break us.

MC. (*grins back at her*). Let it break us. What do we care? (*He goes out, sees* SIMS, *his face goes grim again. He crosses to* SIMS.) You see, Counselor? I told you your client was acting.

SIMS. He's still in shock.

MC. He'll be okay in the morning.

SIMS. No thanks to you. When he's brought back here tomorrow, though, he'd better remain okay. This is not to happen again! You're not to lay a finger on him. If you do . . .

MC. Then advise him again to keep his mouth shut. And see that he does.

SIMS. You're lucky you're not facing a murder charge yourself right now.

MC. I could always get you to defend me.

SIMS. And I probably would. That's my job, no matter how I feel personally.

MC. As long as you get your fee?

SIMS. I've defended many men at my own expense.

MC. That was very noble of you.

SIMS. Nobility doesn't enter into it. Every man has a right to counsel, no matter how guilty he might seem to you, or to me, for that matter. Every man has a right not to be arbitrarily judged, particularly by men in authority; not by you, not by the Congress, not even by the President of the United States. The theory being these human rights are derived from God himself.

MC. I know the theory, Counselor.

SIMS. But you don't go along with it? Well, you're not alone. There are others. You've a lot of friends all over the world. Read the headlines. But don't take it on yourself to settle it. Let history do that.

MC. Save it for the Fourth of July, Counselor.

SIMS. I'll save it for the Commissioner. I intend to see him about you. I'm not going to let you get away with this.

MC. As long as Schneider gets away with it, Counselor, all's well. Why do you take cases like this, if you're so high-minded? Schneider killed the Harris girl—he's guilty. You know it as well as I do.

SIMS. I don't know it. I don't even permit myself to speculate on his guilt or innocence. The moment I do that, I'm judging . . . and it is not my job to judge. My job is to defend my client, not to judge him. That remains with the courts. (*He turns to go.*)

MC. And you've got that taken care of, Counselor. Between bought witnesses and perjured testimony . . . (SIMS *stops in his tracks, suddenly white with fury.*)

SIMS. If you're so set on hanging Schneider, why don't you ask Mrs. McLeod if she can supply a corroborating witness?

(MC LEOD *is stopped in turn, as if he'd been hit by a meat-axe.* SIMS *goes.* CHARLEY, LEWIS *and* BARNES *enter.*)

BARN. Charley, sit over there. Over there for you, Lewis.

(MC LEOD *looks a little sick. He lights a cigarette slowly. He returns to the* LIEUTENANT's *office, his face twitching.* MARY *is just finishing powdering her face and removing the traces of the tears.*)

MARY. What's the matter, dear?

MC. Nothing.

MARY. This has been our black day.

MC. Yes.

MARY (*puts her vanity case back into her bag*). I'm sorry, darling. And yet, in a way I'm glad it's out in the open. This has been hanging over my head so long. I've had such a terrible feeling of guilt all the time.

MC. (*mutters*). All right! All right!

MARY (*ignores the storm warnings*). I needed help and there was no one. I couldn't even go to my parents.

MC. They didn't know?

MARY. No.

MC. You didn't tell them?

MARY. I didn't dare. I didn't want to hurt them. You know how sweet and simple they are.

MC. You didn't go home then? After?

MARY. No.

MC. (*acidly*). Where'd you go?

MARY. That's when I came to New York.

MC. And how long was that before I met you, Mary?

MARY. Two years.

MC. Who'd you go with, then?

MARY. No one.

MC. How many others were there, Mary?

MARY. Others?

MC. (*all control gone*). How many other *men*?

MARY. None. (*Alarmed now.*) What's the matter with you, Jim?

MC. Wait a minute! Wait a minute! (*He turns away, trying to control the insane turbulence inside.*)

MARY. No! What's the matter with you?

MC. At an autopsy yesterday I watched the medical examiner saw off the top of a man's skull, take out the brain, and hold it in his hand—(*he holds out his hand*) like that.

MARY (*horrified*). Why are you telling me this?

MC. Because I'd give everything I own to be able to take out my brain and hold it under the faucet and wash away the dirty pictures you put there tonight.

MARY. Dirty pictures?

MC. Yes!

MARY. Oh! I see. (*A long pause. The brakes of a truck outside the win-*

dow suddenly screech like a horribly wounded living thing.) I see. (*To herself.*) Yes. That would be fine, if we could. (*She straightens, turns to him, wearily.*) But when you wash away what I may have put there, you'll find you've a rotten spot in your brain, Jim, and it's growing. I know, I've watched it. . . .

MC. (*hoarsely*). Mary! That's enough.

MARY (*stronger than he, at last*). No, let's have the truth! I could never find it in my heart to acknowledge one tiny flaw in you because I loved you so—and God help me, I still do—but let's have the truth, for once, wherever it leads. You think you're on the side of the angels? You're not! You haven't even a drop of ordinary human forgiveness in your whole nature. You're a cruel and vengeful man. You're everything you've always said you hated in your own father.

MC. (*starts to throw on his jacket*). I'm not going to let you wander off in the streets this way. I'm going to take you home, myself.

MARY. What for? To kill me the way your father killed your mother!! (*His hands drop to his side. He stares at her dumbly, stricken. She puts the keys down on the desk, turns to go.*)

MC. Where are you going? (*Pause. She looks at him sadly.*)

MARY. Far away . . . you won't find me. I'm scorching my earth . . . burning my cities.

MC. When will I see you?

MARY. Never. . . . Good-bye. (*She goes.* MC LEOD, *dazed, walks slowly back to the squad-room.* BRODY *sees him from the wash-room and enters with* JOE.)

BRO. How'd it go?

MC. (*almost inaudibly*). Fine.

BRO. I mean Mary.

MC. Fine. Dandy. (*To* SUSAN.) All right, young lady, your two minutes are up.

(*The* LIEUTENANT *enters.*)

LIEUT. (*to* MC LEOD). What the hell's the matter with you?

MC. Nothing. . . .

LIEUT. Don't you feel well?

MC. Yes, sir. Feel all right.

LIEUT. (*to* BRODY). Am I crazy? Look at him.

BRO. You've gone all green, Jim.

MC. I've got a headache.

LIEUT. You better go home. Buzz your doctor.

MC. I've got a squeal to finish off, Lieutenant.

LIEUT. Brody! You finish it off.

BRO. (*reluctantly*). Yes, sir.

MC. I'd rather do it, myself.

LIEUT. You go home. That's an order.

MC. Yes, sir.

LIEUT. Callahan! You catch for Jim tonight.

CALL. Yes, sir. (*He crosses up to the duty chart, takes it off the wall.*)

BRO. (*to* MC LEOD). What happened, Jim? What's wrong?

MC. (*sits heavily*). Mary left me. Walked out. We're finished.

BRO. Too bad. She'll come back.

MC. No. This was for keeps.

(*The* LIEUTENANT *crosses.*)

LIEUT. What are you sitting there for? Why don't you go home?

(*Exit* LIEUTENANT.)

MC. Because I haven't got any.

JOE (*comes down to him*). You drove her away, didn't you? Why? (MC LEOD *doesn't answer.*) I tried to warn you, you damn fool. Why?

MC. I don't know. Why? Why do we do these things, Yussel? Who knows? . . . I built my whole life on hating my father—and all the time he was inside me, laughing—or maybe he was crying, the poor bastard, maybe he couldn't help himself, either.

(*An excited woman enters, rattles the gate.*)

CALL. Yes, Miss? (*He is at the desk now, reaching into the bottom drawer for the celluloid letters to replace the name on the duty chart.*)

WOM. Someone snatched my purse. . . .

CALL. Come in, Miss. We'll take care of you. (*He bends over to pick up a letter.*)

WOM. This happened to me once before . . . on 72nd Street. . . .

(CHARLEY *lunges for* CALLAHAN's *exposed gun, grabs it, hits* CALLAHAN *on the head with the butt, knocking him to the floor.* BARNES *raises his club.*)

CHAR. Drop that club! (*He aims at* BARNES.)

BRO. Drop it! He's a four-time loser. He'll kill you. (BARNES *drops his club.*)

CHAR. Goddamn right! Rot in jail the rest of my life? I take five or six a you bastards with me first. (BARNES *makes a movement.*)

BRO. Take it easy! He can't get by the desk.

CHAR. Shut up! One word! One move! Anybody! (MC LEOD, *seated center, laughs softly.*)

MC. I was wondering when you'd get around to it, Charley.

CHAR. None of your guff, you!

MC. (*rises*). Give me that gun!

CHAR. In the gut you'll get it. One step! I'm warnin' you. One!

BRO. Easy, Jim. He can't get by the desk.

MC. (*lunges for the gun*). You evil son-of-a-bitch!

(CHARLEY *fires point-blank at* MC LEOD. *One, two, three quick shots.* MC-LEOD *is hurled back and whirled around by the impact.* BARNES *goes into action, knocks the gun out of* CHARLEY'S *hand and starts beating him over the head with his billy. Several of the others rush in and swarm all over* CHARLEY. *He screams twice and is silent.* MC LEOD *staggers, clutching his stomach.*)

BRO. (*rushes to him, puts his arms around him, supporting him*). Jim! Did he get you? Are you hurt?

MC. Slightly. . . . (*He unbuttons his coat. His shirt is a bloody rag. The sight stuns and sickens him.*) God! (*A little boy for one second.*) Oh, Mary, Mary, Mary . . . (*He wraps the coat tightly about him as if to shut in the escaping stream of life. He looks up, smiles crookedly.*) Slightly killed, I should say. . . .

(*The* LIEUTENANT *comes running in, a number of policemen crowd in through the gate.*)

LIEUT. What's happened?

BARN. That son-of-a-bitch shot Jim!

LIEUT. Take him inside! Get him into bed, quick.

BRO. (*to* MC LEOD). Easy, baby. Come, I'll carry you to bed. . . .

MC. Wait a minute.

BRO. Now, Jim.

MC. No, don't! Don't pull at me. . . . (*He sinks back into a chair.*)

JOE. You got to lie down, Seamus.

MC. No. Once I lie down I'm not going to get up again. No.

LIEUT. Notify the Communication Bureau! Get an ambulance. Quick!

MC. Never mind the doctor. Get a priest.

BRO. Feel that bad, Jim?

GALLA. (*on the phone*). Communication Bureau.

LIEUT. Why don't you lie down, Jim?

MC. Get me a drink. (*He gasps, unable to speak.* BRODY *starts for the water-cooler.*)

LIEUT. (*whispers to* BRODY). With a belly wound . . . ?

BRO. (*whispers*). What difference does it make . . . ? Look at him!

MC. Don't whisper, Lou. I can hear you.

(*The* LIEUTENANT *goes for glass of water.*)

BRO. Sure you can. You're all right, baby. They can't hurt you. You're one of the indestructibles, you're immortal, baby.

MC. Almost, Lou, almost. Don't rush me. Give me your hand, Lou. Squeeze! Harder!

(SUSAN *begins to sob.*)

ART. Don't cry, Suzy. Don't cry!

MC. (*glances up at* ARTHUR, *studies him, turns to* BRODY). Give me Buster's prints! I don't know. I hope you're right, Lou. Maybe he'll come in tomorrow with a murder rap. I don't know any more. Get me his prints. (BRODY *goes for them.* CHARLEY *is dragged off, half unconscious, moaning.*)

JOE. How're you feeling, Seamus?

MC. Yussel! Find her! Ask her to forgive me. And help her. She needs help . . . will you?

JOE. Sure. Now take it easy.

(BRODY *hands* ARTHUR's *fingerprint sheet to* MC LEOD.)

MC. Tear it up! (BRODY *tears it.*) Unchain him, Lou. The keys are in my pocket. We have no case here, Lieutenant. The complainant withdrew. (*He crosses himself.*) In the name of the Father and of the Son and of the Holy Ghost. Oh, my God, I am heartily sorry for having offended Thee and I detest all my sins because I dread the loss of Heaven. . . . (*He falls.* BRODY *catches him, eases him to the ground, feels for his pulse.* JOE *kneels to help him. After an interminable pause.*)

BRO. He's gone!

JOE. He's dead.

LIEUT. (*completes the Act of Contrition*). I firmly resolve with the help of Thy Grace to confess my sins, to do penance and to amend my life. Amen. (*Crosses himself.*)

BRO. (*murmurs*). Amen. (BARNES *uncovers, crosses himself.* BRODY *crosses himself, rises clumsily, goes to* ARTHUR, *unlocks his handcuffs.*) All right, son. Go on home! Don't make a monkey outa me! If I see you . . . (BRODY *is crying now*) up here again, I'll kick the guts outa you. Don't make a monkey outa me!

ART. Don't wory! I won't.

SUS. He won't.

BRO. Now get the hell outa here!

(SUSAN *takes* ARTHUR's *hand. They go. At the door* ARTHUR *pauses to look back.* BRODY *has turned to watch him go. They exchange glances.*)

GALLA. (*on the phone*). St. Vincent's? Will you please send a priest over to the 21st Precinct Police Station to administer last rites?

LIEUT. (*on the phone*). Communication Bureau? Notify the Commissioner, the D.A., the homicide squad . . . 21st Precinct . . . Detective shot . . . killed.

(BRODY, *his face twisted, glances down at* MC LEOD. JOE *rises, slowly, taking off his hat.*)

(CURTAIN.)

Louis O. Coxe and Robert Chapman

▶ *Billy Budd* is a dramatization of Herman Melville's last novel of the same title. Melville began writing this novel in November 1888 and finished it in the spring of 1891, a few months before his death. The fact that he dedicated it to Jack Chase is a significant clue to its origin. During his early sailing days, Melville had encountered all types of sea captains and sailors, and the narrow confines of a ship on a long and monotonous voyage concentrated all their virtues and vices into a single burning point. He had seen the ruthless and cynical brutality of a Claggart with all his inexplicable evil; and he had known, in the person of Jack Chase, captain of the maintop, the generous understanding and honesty of Captain Vere. Chase had been a kind of father to the young sailor in the harsh loneliness of the sea voyage, and Melville drew heavily upon the experience for the material and the theme of *Billy Budd*.

Like Melville's greatest novel, *Moby Dick*, *Billy Budd* is a study of evil and of the inexorable workings of justice toward paradoxical ends through machinery devised by man's odd codes of behavior. In this play the poetic justice which overtakes Claggart must, under the code of human law, be paid for by the execution of its morally innocent agent, Billy.

The characters of the play are living, individual men, and at the same time the symbols and personifications, in a Platonic sense, of the conflict between the good and evil principles in life itself. As with Job, Billy Budd is by definition, and therefore by his words and deeds, a *naturally* good man. There is no evil in him. By the simple and natural process of acting according to his nature, he is distinguished and set apart from the rest of the seamen. They recognize his qualities and respond to them. They pay him the tribute of making him their favorite, seeing in him a testimony to the force of righteousness in an environment which normally denies its existence.

By the same token, Claggart is the personification of unprovoked and unmotivated evil. He is poisonous by nature, like an adder, and Billy Budd, by the mere fact of being what he is, incites his venom. Since Billy is an able and willing hand and a stabilizing influence on the ship, Claggart should value him and encourage him; instead he sets about systematically, with diabolic cunning, to destroy him.

Captain Vere is the agent through whom this conflict must reach its climax and be resolved, and by whom the considerations in this perplexing dilemma must be voiced. He understands the guilt of Claggart and the justice of his punishment. He also understands that Budd, by striking a superior officer in a fit of desperation, has brought an equal punishment upon himself. He argues well the conflicting claims of a higher and a lower justice, of a kindly disposed and merciful man moved by understanding and pity and the master of a British naval vessel in a tense and mutinous period who must preserve order, discipline, and stern obedience to the letter of the law even at the sacrifice of Billy Budd. And it is a part of the principle of good, as portrayed by Budd, that Billy should see the justice of this apparent miscarriage of justice and should go willingly to his death, blessing the Captain who had ordered his execution.

This keen and searching study has always been overshadowed by the power and the majesty of *Moby Dick*. By comparison with the demonic intensity of Captain Ahab's pursuit of the white whale to his own destruction, Billy Budd's innocent conflict with the devilish machinations of Claggart seems on the surface to be of a less searching order of significance. But the very simplicity of the drama, its intense concentration, on board ship but not involving the sea, and its inexorable movement toward its climax and readjusted equilibrium, give it a delayed, explosive force that continues to haunt the mind long after the curtain has fallen. For in this world, evil is an active force, not merely the absence of good. It acts for its own purposes and for its own ends. And the triumph of good over evil is, from the human viewpoint, metaphysical.

Louis O. Coxe and Robert Chapman were classmates at Princeton in the late thirties and early forties, and both joined the navy after the outbreak of World War II. Their collaboration started in 1947. Today Mr. Coxe is in the English department at the University of Minnesota and Mr. Chapman in the English department at Harvard.

These two playwrights have given the story of *Billy Budd* a masterly dramatization, stripping it to a rare concentration of dialogue and action, and extracting its full dramatic value. The play, after a try-out at the Experimental Theatre early in 1949, had a critical success in its regular New York performances, in the 1950-51 season. This success was not duplicated at the box office, however. Like many other great compositions in dramatic form, *Billy Budd* can be most fully savored through the imaginative production of the thoughtful reader.

BILLY

BUDD

The entire action takes places aboard H.M.S. Indomitable
*at sea, August, 1798, the year following
the Naval mutinies at Spithead and the Nore.*

ACT ONE

Scene One

Although outside it is a fine morning in early August, the between-decks compartment of the crew's quarters assigned to the main-topmen is dark and shadowy except for the light spilling down the companionway from above and, through the open gun-ports, the flicker of sunlight reflected on the water. The smoking-lamp burns feebly over a wooden mess table and two benches lowered for use.

JENKINS *sits at the table mending a piece of clothing. In the shadow the* DANSKER *sits motionless on a low sea chest, smoking a pipe. Neither man speaks for a long minute.*

Then JACKSON *appears on deck at the top of the companionway and lurches down into the compartment. He is doubled up in pain.*

CLAG. (*off*). You there! Jackson!

JACK. Oh Christ, he's followed me!

JEN. Who?

JACK. Master-at-Arms. He'll send me aloft again sure, and I can't hang on . . .

JEN. What the devil's wrong with you, jack? Here, sit down.

CLAG. (*entering down the companionway*). Why have you come down off the mainmast, Jackson? Your watch over?

JACK. Sick, Mister Claggart, I'm bloody sick, so I'm shaking up there on the yard till I near fell off.

JEN. Grab an arm, mate, I'll take you along to sick-bay.

CLAG. Stand away from him, Jenkins. (*To* JACKSON.) Just where does this sickness strike you, in the guts, or limbs? Or in the head? Does it exist at all?

JEN. You can see he's sick as a puking cat, plain as your stick.

CLAG. The role of Good Samaritan hardly fits you, Jenkins. (*To* JACKSON.) Now up, man. Turn topside.

JACK. I can't, I can't, I'm deathly sick, God help me, sir!

CLAG. That's hard. But this ship needs all hands. We're undermanned. The aches and pains of landsmen have their cures, but ours have none. You'll have to get aloft. Now move!

JACK. I ain't bluffing, sir, swear I'm not! Please, Mister Claggart . . . I got Cooper's leave, he says all right, I can come down.

CLAG. You have not got my leave. Cooper is captain of the maintop and ought to know better. Four men to every spar, and no replacements. Now up. Back where you belong.

JACK. (*starts up the ladder*). God, sir, I can't, I can't stand it! It'll be my death, sure!

CLAG. No more talk, man! Up you get! Start! (JACKSON *goes painfully up the ladder and out of sight on deck.* CLAGGART *starts out after him.*)

JEN. (*mutters*). God damn your bloody heart!

CLAG. Did you say something, Jenkins? (JENKINS *does not answer.* CLAGGART *goes out, calling after* JACKSON.) Now Jackson, get along. Up! Up!

JEN. I'll stick him one day before long! I will, if I hang for it.

(*Laughter and talk in the next compartment followed by entrance of* BUTLER, TALBOT *and* KINCAID.)

BUT. Messboy!

TAL. Haul in the slops!

KIN. Suppose we'll get the new man? The jack they 'pressed this morning off that merchantman? I see 'em come alongside just now.

TAL. I pity that poor bastard, so I do. I hear they get good pay on merchant ships. Eat good, too, and them treated like the God-damn Prince of Wales. (MESSBOY *enters with an iron pot of food and spits on the deck.*) Spit in it, damn you. Can't taste no worse.

MESS. Ain't nobody making you eat it, mate. You can wash your feet in it if you like. (O'DANIEL *and* PAYNE *enter.*)

TAL. What's eating you, Jenkins? Ain't you going to join the banquet?

JEN. By God, I seen a thing just now I won't stand for! I'm sitting here off watch, and I seen it all. That blacksnake Claggart kicked Jackson back aloft, and him sick as a pinkass baby in a cradle, as any fool could see.

PAY. He's the Master-at-Arms, ain't he?

JEN. Cooper sent him down. Who's captain of the starboard watch, him or Claggart? Cooper could have found him a relief. Plain murder, by God!

TAL. You think Claggart can get away with what he does without Captain Starry Vere knows what's going on? Him and that red snapper Seymour, and them other bloody officers!

JEN. Jackson'll fall. By God, no man can hang to a spar sick like that. He'll fall sure.

O'DAN. Tush, man, nobody falls in His Majesty's Navy. We lose our footing. 'Tis flying we do, to be sure.

TAL. I tell you it's Vere that's the cause of it! Our glorious fine Captain Vere, with a league of braid around his arm and a ramrod up his bum.

O'DAN. Vere, is it. As captains go, mate, let me tell you, he's an angel with a harp alongside of the skipper on the *Royal George*. Every day that one flogged a dozen men. Picked 'em by lottery, by God. Never took the gratings down till they was rusty with blood. Ho! This Vere's a saint in heaven after him.

JEN. Ram the *Royal George* and everybody in her! Claggart's the man we want, and the sooner the better, say I!

O'DAN. Ah, we'd had him puking his blood at Spithead, the devil rot his wick.

BUT. You was there, O'Daniel? At Spithead?

O'DAN. Aye. I was. Wherever you do find Englishmen doing a smart thing, you'll find an Irishman is at the bottom of it. Oho, fine it was, every day of it, with the officers quaking in their cabins, spitting green, and the whole English government wetting their breeches from the fear of us! Ah, lovely it was, lovely!

TAL. Belay your Irish noise, you fat-mouthed mackerel-snatcher. I'll tell you this, we need men on here is not afraid to use their knives if it come to that. And you can be bloody sure it will come to that, mind my word, Mickey Cork.

JEN. What did you ever use your knife for, Talbot, but to scratch your lice? Ah, you're a dancing daredevil, you are for sure.

TAL. I'll be happy to show you, if you like.

JEN. Trouble will be hunting you out, mate, if you're not careful.

TAL. Trouble! You whoreson cockney cullion! There's not a man aboard don't know you for a coward, you whining bitch-boy!

JEN. Get out.

TAL. Damn your seed, I'm not afraid of you, or your sniveling hangbys, either!

JEN. Move! Get out of it, or by God I'll run my knife to the hilts in you!

TAL. You son of a whore! Pigsticker!

(*They attack one another with drawn knives,* JENKINS *reaching suddenly across the table to seize* TALBOT. *Silently they thrash around the compartment upsetting benches and food while the others look on unmoved.*)

O'DAN. Ah, I do love to see two Englishmen fighting each other. It's fonder they are of killing themselves than fighting their proper enemies. (*Laughs hoarsely.*)

PAY. Tomorrow's rum on Jenkins. Any bets?

KIN. He's never lost one yet.

(JENKINS *throws* TALBOT *on the deck and holds the knife at his throat for a moment before letting him up, first taking his knife. He holds out his hand.*)

JEN. I'm leading seaman in this compartment, mind that. (TALBOT *hits* JENKINS' *hand and goes off angrily.*)

KIN. You're captain, that's all right by me.

O'DAN. Eyes in the boat, lads. Here comes *pfft*-face.

(SQUEAK, BILLY *and* GARDINER *appear on deck and start down the companionway.*)

GARD. Hang it, step lively, boy! Your ship is . . . Doff your hat to officers when they speak to you! By God, I'll teach you to touch your hat to a midshipman's coat, if it's only stuck on a broomstick to dry!

BILL. Aye, sir. (*The men react to* GARDINER *with yawns and gestures behind his back.*)

GARD. Very well. Your ship is *H.M.S. Indomitable* now, and we sail her tautly, and we tolerate no nonsense. Is that clear?

BILL. Aye, sir.

GARD. (*to* SQUEAK). See this new man is assigned to a watch, and get him squared away. (*To* BILLY.) You're green, of course, I can see that. But I expect we'll ripen you. (*He trips going up the ladder and* SQUEAK *tries to help him.*) Carry on.　　　　　(GARDINER *exits.*)

sq. My name's Squeak. I'm the Master-at-Arms' man. Have you met the Master-at-Arms yet, Mister Claggart? (BILLY *shakes his head.*) Oh, you'll like him. He's a nice fellow. (O'DANIEL *chokes on his pipe smoke and the other men react similarly.*) Stow your gear along in there. This here's the larboard section of the maintop. Captain of the watch is Jenkins. Him, there. Report to him. (*He pats* BILLY *on the chest and grins before starting up the ladder.*)

JEN. What's a green hand dumped in here for?

sq. Complaining, Jenkins?

JEN. I'm asking. What's wrong with that?

sq. Mister Claggart wants him here, that's why. Maybe he wants for Billy Boy to set you pigs an example. Refer any more complaints to the Master-at-Arms!

(*Exits.* BILLY *grins at the men, who return his look.*)

BILL. My name is Budd. Billy, if you like.

KIN. I'm Kincaid. This is where you swing your hammock. That's O'Daniel, this here's Payne, and Butler. This is Jenkins, captain of the watch, and that old jack's called the Dansker. Don't know why, unless maybe he's Danish. You ever had a real name, Dansker?

DANS. Not for many years.

BUT. You'd be the new impressed man?

BILL. Aye, so I am. I just came off the *Rights of Man* this morning.

DANS. Forget about the *Rights of Man* now, lad.

JEN. How long you been going to sea, baby?

BILL. About ten years, but in the merchant service.

O'DAN. Merchant service! Whissht! (*Laughs hoarsely.*)

BILL. I know I'm new at Navy work, and probably there'll be some things I'll need help with.

JEN. No doubt, little boy.

BILL. I'll learn fast, never fear. But she's a big old girl, this ship. I never was in a ship-of-the-line before. I'd have got lost trying to find the mess by myself. Maybe fallen in the magazine!

O'DAN. Ah, you get used to it. She's big, is this tub, but she's not so big you can get lost in her.

PAY. Sometimes I wish to God you could. Maybe we could lose O'Daniel.

(BILLY *laughs and the others join.*)

BILL. You're Irish, aren't you? I like the Irish. There was an Irishman on the *Rights of Man,* with big red whiskers . . . when I came away, he gave me a silver knife. This is it.

O'DAN. It's a beauty. Mind you keep an eye on it.

BUT. What's the matter, boy?

BILL. I was just thinking, maybe I won't ever see my friends again.

O'DAN. If they was Irish, don't you worry at all. The Irish is liable to turn up almost anywheres, excepting England and the fires of hell, which is much the same.

PAY. Danny, if it wasn't for the harps, the devil wouldn't have nothing to do. What was potato-eaters doing on a merchant ship?

BILL. Just sailors, like me. Most of us had no other home, even the skipper. He was a kind old bloke. Looked fierce, but he always had a kind word. Used to keep a bird in a cage in his cabin. The skipper let me feed the bird sometimes. Worms right out of the ship's biscuit. That was mostly all the meat we got.

O'DAN. The bargemen is in Navy biscuit would eat the bird.

KIN. Sit down here, Bill. Maggots or not, this is what we get. You hungry?

BILL. I'm always hungry.

KIN. Try your first sample of His Majesty's bounty. We don't know what it is, but we been eating it for a long time.

BUT. Here, eat mine. Tastes like it's been eat before, anyhow.

JEN. Give him more lobscouse, Butler. We got to keep the roses in his cheeks, ain't we, boy?

BILL. (*laughing*). I could eat anything right now. Even this.

O'DAN. Help you to forget about home and mother, lad.

JEN. Tell us about home and mother, Baby Budd.

BILL. There's not much to tell. I've got no home, and never had a family to remember.

JEN. Ain't that too bad.

BILL. Oh, I'd feel a lot worse if I'd been 'pressed with a wife and children.

KIN. That's the truth.

O'DAN. We're all patriotic volunteers.

KIN. Guano! Wait till my hitch is up, you won't see no more of me.

BUT. Three weeks drunk in Portsmouth, then back in the ruddy fleet.

DANS. Men like us got no other home.

O'DAN. No other home, is it? Ah 'tis so thick the sweet thoughts is in here, I can scarce breathe.

PAY. Then you can strangle or get out.

JEN. Aye, get along, you lousy harp, give us some fresh air.

O'DAN. If you begged me to stay itself, I'd be off to where there's smarter lads. Boy, let you pay no heed to these white mice, mind what I say. And be hanged, the lot of yous! (*He starts up the ladder.*)

KIN. You'll catch it, Danny, if Captain holds an inspection.

O'DAN. (*returning*). Ah whissht, I was forgetting that. And I do think that me figure shows up better here below than it does in the broad daylight.

BILL. Inspection today?

PAY. Ah, the Old Man crawls over the ship from arsehole to appetite any time he ain't got nothing else to do. You never know when till you see him.

KIN. What the devil he wants to inspect this hooker for, I can't figure. He's seen it before.

BUT. He ain't seen Billy.

BILL. What's the Captain like? On the *Rights of Man,* the captain . . .

JEN. You going to jaw some more about that rocking horse? I suppose *you* was at Spithead, too?

BILL. Spithead? Where is that?

JEN. A little party the Navy had a year ago. A mutiny, Baby, a mutiny. Know what that is?

BILL. Why did they mutiny?

O'DAN. Arra, it's easy to see you're new to the Navy.

JEN. Jimmy-Legs is ten good God-damn reasons for it, himself.

BILL. Who's Jimmy-Legs?

KIN. Master-at-Arms. We call him Jimmy-Legs.

BUT. Watch out for that one, Billy.

PAY. He's the devil himself between decks.

O'DAN. What d'you expect, the saints of heaven? Not in an English tub

BILL. Why don't you like the Master-at-Arms?

JEN. You'll find out soon enough, Baby.

BUT. Watch him, boy. Jenkins can tell you. He's had a time or two with Claggart.

JEN. Aye, and I'll have another one day before too long.

BUT. Sure, Jenkins. You look after Bill.

JEN. How old are you, kid? Sixteen?

BILL. I don't know, maybe . . . twenty.

JEN. He don't even know how old he is! My guess is, too young to know what his parts are for.

O'DAN. Is it anybody is that young?

KIN. Stow it, Jenkins. Come on, don't pay no attention to him. He's feeling ugly today.

JEN. Well now, ain't you getting holier than a bloody bishop. Let him talk up for himself, if he don't like it.

KIN. Stow it, I say. You got no reason to crawl over Bill. Let him be.

BILL. That's all right, Tom. I don't mind a joke. Black's the white of me eye, mates! (*All laugh except* JENKINS.)

JEN. Mama taught you pretty manners, huh? Oh! Ain't got no mama, you say? Well now, think what that makes you! (*Laughs.*)

BILL. Tell me what you mean, Mister Jenkins.

PAY. What's gnawing your arse, Jenkins? Can't you see the boy's trying to be friendly?

JEN. You forgetting who's leading seaman here? Come on, Baby, talk back, why don't you? Scared?

BILL. N-no. Why do you think I'd be scared, M-M-Mister Jenkins?

JEN. He stammers! What do you know! The little bastard's so scared he's stammering.

BILL. Don't call me that again.

JEN. Sounds good, ha? Sounds fine. I like the way it rolls out your mouth. Bastard Baby Budd . . .

(BILLY *strikes him.* JENKINS *staggers and falls, pulls a knife and gets up, lunging at* BILLY. PAYNE, BUTLER *and* KINCAID *get up and stand close to* BILLY, *silently protecting him.*)

JEN. Get away, God damn you! He's got to find out who gives orders here.

KIN. Not this time, Jenkins. Lay off.

O'DAN. Belay it. You're wearing me out, the pair of yous.

BUT. Put away the knife. (JENKINS *sees their determination and relaxes a little, uncertain what to do.*)

BILL. Will you shake hands? Or would you rather fight?

JEN. You little bas . . . (*Lunges forward.* BILLY *catches his arm and bends it, holding* JENKINS *cursing and powerless.*)

BILL. That's enough, mate. Pipe down and let us be.

O'DAN. Good lad! Save the great strength is in you, Jenkins, for fighting the devil is after your soul.

JEN. All right, all right. You can let me go now.

O'DAN. Leave him go, lad. I won't hurt him at all.

BILL. You're like Red Whiskers on the *Rights,* he liked to fight too. (*Freeing him.*) Will you shake hands, mate?

JEN. (*momentarily uncertain what to do*). Shake hands, is it? . . . Well, you beat me fair. You got guts, which is more than I give you credit for. (*They shake hands.*)

KIN. You're a hell of a peacemaker, Bill.

PAY. That's the only time I ever hear Jenkins eating his own words.

O'DAN. Ah, that's a terrible diet, would make any man puke.

JEN. Don't you be getting any wrong ideas. I'm still a match for you!

KIN. Better belay your mess gear, Bill.

JEN. Where you come from, Baby?

PAY. Stow it! Jimmy-Legs! (BILLY *goes on talking as* CLAGGART *enters.*)

BILL. I don't know, I guess from Portsmouth. I never lived ashore, that I can remember. Where do you come from? (*Drops a pot on deck.* CLAGGART *stands over him.*)

CLAG. Handsomely done, young fellow, handsomely done. And handsome is as handsome did it, too. You can wipe that up, Jenkins. (*To* BILLY.) What is your name?

BILL. Budd, sir. William Budd, ship *Rights of Man.*

CLAG. Your ship is *H.M.S. Indomitable* now.

BILL. Aye, sir.

CLAG. You look sturdy. What was your station aboard the merchant-man?

BILL. M-m-mizzentopman, sir.

CLAG. You like that station?

BILL. Aye, sir, well enough.

CLAG. How long have you been at sea?

BILL. Ten years, sir, near as I can tell.

CLAG. Education?

BILL. None, sir.

CLAG. So. You come aboard with nothing but your face to recommend you. Well, while beauty is always welcome, that alone may not avail us much against the French. There are other requirements in the service.

BILL. I'll learn quickly, sir.

CLAG. The sea's a taskmaster, young fellow. It salts the sweetness out of boyish faces. You cannot tell what motion lies asleep in that flat water. Down where the manta drifts, and the shark and ray, storms wait for a wind while all the surface dazzles.

BILL. I am a seaman, sir. I love the sea. I've hardly lived ashore.

CLAG. Then let the wind and sea have license to plunder at their will. As of today, a new maintopman swings between sky and water. (*He turns toward the ladder and notices the mess on deck.*) I thought I asked you to wipe that up, Jenkins.

JEN. That's the messboy's job.

CLAG. Clean up, Jenkins. (JENKINS *hesitates.*) That is an order. Turn to.

BILL. I'll give you a hand, Jenkins. Come on.

CLAG. Ah, there. See how helpful Billy is. Why can't you take a leaf from this innocent young David's book, Jenkins? (*Turns away.* JEN-KINS *accidentally brushes against him and receives a savage cut from* CLAGGART'S *rattan across his face.*) Watch what you're doing, man!

JEN. I swear . . . !

CLAG. Yes, what is it that you swear? Well, speak. Nothing at all to say? Then hear me: I have my methods with unruly tempers.

(*On deck there is a loud crescendo scream and a crash. Running foot-*

steps, shouts, voice calling for the SURGEON. *The men surge toward the ladder.*)

CLAG. Stand fast! (SQUEAK *enters down the hatchway, whispers to* CLAGGART.) All right, I know. (SQUEAK *comes down into the compartment and runs off.*)

JEN. It's Jackson! I knew it, by God, I told you so!

(*Men turn to stare at* CLAGGART *as several sailors enter down the companionway, bearing the body of* JACKSON, *inert and shattered. They carry him through the compartment and off to sick-bay.*)

SURG. (*as he moves through the compartment*). Clear the way, you men. Take him into the sick-bay, through here. Carry him gently. Easy, now. Easy. (*Exit.*)

JEN. (*pointing to* CLAGGART). He sent him back aloft. Killed him, he did!

O'DAN. Might as well have knifed him.

CLAG. Stand fast. Stop where you are. Your man Jackson is looked after.

O'DAN. (*in a low voice*). Then he's a dead man surely.

CLAG. Who spoke?

JEN. We'll have a showdown now! After him, mates! Cut into him!

(*The men move toward* CLAGGART *in a rush, drawing knives and cursing him, as* CAPTAIN VERE *appears in the companion hatchway.*)

VERE. Stand fast! Hold where you are. Master-at-Arms, what is the matter here?

(*The men stop in their tracks and stare at* VERE, *who comes part way down the ladder.*)

CLAG. These dogs are out of temper, sir.

VERE (*to men*). You will come to attention when I address you! Let me remind you that this ship is at war. This is a wartime cruise, and this vessel sails under the Articles of War. Volunteer or 'pressed man, veteran seaman or recruit, you are no longer citizens, but sailors: a crew that I shall work into a weapon. One lawless act, one spurt of rebel temper from any man in this ship, high or low, I will pay out in coin you know of. You have but two duties: to fight and to obey, and I will bend each contumacious spirit, each stiff-necked prideful soul of you, or crush the spirit in you if I must. Abide by the Articles of War and my commands, or they will cut you down. Now: choose. (*The men are silent.*) Very well. Master-at-Arms, this accident on deck, the sailor fallen from the yardarm. Do you know how it occurred?

CLAG. I do not, sir.

VERE. You are his messmates. Does any man of you know how this occurred? (*To* BUTLER.) You?

BUT. No, sir.

VERE. Jenkins, do you?

JEN. (*hesitates a moment.* CLAGGART *moves slightly, tapping his hand with the rattan*). No, sir.

VERE (notices the cut on JENKIN's *face*). What's this, what's this? Speak up, man. I want no random bloodshed aboard this ship.

JEN. I . . . fell, Captain. Fell, and . . . and cut my cheek.

VERE. I see. You fell. Master-at-Arms, you will excuse this man from duty till the Surgeon tends him.

CLAG. Aye, aye, sir.

VERE. We must not wound ourselves, draining the blood from enterprise that takes a whole man. (*He turns to go up the ladder and sees* BILLY.) Well. This is a new face. Who are you, boy?

CLAG. Maintopman 'pressed from the *Rights of Man* this morning, sir. William Budd.

VERE. Let him speak for himself. (BILLY *tries to speak but can only stammer incoherently.*) That's all right, boy, take your time. No need to be nervous.

BILL. I saw a man go aloft, sir, as I came on board just a while ago. He looked sick, sir, he did. This officer was there, too, he can tell you. (*To* CLAGGART.) Don't you remember, sir?

VERE. Did you send a sick man aloft, Master-at-Arms?

CLAG. I did not, sir.

VERE. Very well. (*To* BILLY.) Well, Budd. I hope you take to Navy life and duty without too much regret. We go to fight the French and shall need wits and hearts about us equal to the task.

BILL. I'll do my best, sir.

VERE. I'm sure you will. We are all here to do our several duties, and though they may seem petty from one aspect, still they must all be done. The Admiral himself looks small and idle to the man like you who can see him from the maintop, threading his pattern on the quarterdeck. The Navy's only life. (SURGEON *enters*.)

SURG. Captain—Jackson, the man who fell just now—he's dead, sir.

VERE (*after a pause*). Carry on, Master-at-Arms. (*He goes out up the companionway.* SURGEON *exits*.)

CLAG. You've made a good impression on the Captain, Billy Budd. You have a pleasant way with you. If you wish to make a good impression on me, you will need to curb your tongue. Jenkins, I thought you were ordered to sick-bay. Jump to it. And I suggest you change that shirt. See how fouled it is with a peculiar stain. Why can't you keep clean like Billy here? (*He strikes* JENKINS *viciously on the arm with his rattan, smiles at him, and exits up the ladder*.)

JEN. God damn his flaming soul! I can't stand it no more!

BILL. I don't see what you can do, mate. He didn't mean it when he hurt you then.

JEN. Listen, boy, I know Jimmy-Legs. He lives on hurting people. Stay away from him, and keep your mouth shut, if you don't want trouble.

O'DAN. Did you hear the lad speak up to the skipper?

PAY. Aye, you watch your tongue, Bill. Claggart will be after you for talking up like that.

KIN. He's a cool one, Billy is. None of us got the nerve.

BUT. It's nerve gets a man in trouble in this tub.

DANS. Jimmy-Legs is down on you already, Billy.

BILL. Down on me? Why he's friendly to me.

JEN. Claggart don't make no friends.

O'DAN. You seen Jackson when they brought him below. That's how friendly he gets. (*Bosun's pipe off*.)

DUN. (*off*). Relieve the watch!

KIN. First watch on the *Indomitable*, Bill. Better lay up to the mainmast and report. (*Exit*.)

BUT. Don't slip off the yardarm.

PAY. Watch your step.

BILL. Not me. You watch for me. Got to find the mainmast, and I'm in a hurry.

o'DAN. You'll never find your way in this old tub. I'll come along and show you. If anybody comes calling for O'Daniel while I'm out, take the message.

PAY. O'Daniel couldn't find his breeches if they wasn't buttoned on. You come with me. (BILLY *and* PAYNE *go off*.)

JEN. Poor bastard. I pity him, I do.

BUT. He's dead, ain't he? Better off than us.

JEN. Not Jackson. I mean the baby here. Billy.

BUT. We could have fared worse for a messmate.

JEN. Aye. He can take care of himself. Heave up the table.

Scene Two

In the early evening of the same day, the off-duty sections of the crew are mustered aft on the maindeck for JACKSON's *funeral. Above them* CAPTAIN VERE *stands uncovered at the forward break of the quarterdeck, reading the Committal Prayer. The westward sky is bright yellow and red, but fades into darkness as the scene progresses.*

The men are uncovered and stand at attention.

VERE. Unto Almighty God we commend the soul of our brother departed and we commit his body to the deep, in sure and certain hope of the resurrection unto Eternal Life, through our Lord Jesus Christ, at whose coming in glorious majesty to judge the world, the sea shall give up her dead, and the corruptible bodies of those who sleep in Him shall be changed and made like unto His glorious body according to the mighty working whereby He is able to subdue all things unto Himself. Amen.

MEN. Amen.

(*Short drum-roll followed by a muffled splash as* JACKSON's *body slips over the side. Then the bosun's pipe. Officers cover and march off*.)

CLAG. Ship's company: Cover! Petty officers, dismiss your divisions.

VOICE (*off*). Carpenters and gunners: Dismiss!

VOICE (*off*). Afterguardsmen: Dismiss!

VOICE (*off*). Fore, main, and mizzentopmen: Dismiss! (*The men break formation and go off, excepting* BUTLER, JENKINS, PAYNE, KINCAID *and* BILLY, *who gather near the ratlines, at the rail.*)

BUT. I suppose in this clear water you could see him go down for quite a way.

BILL. We're moving slow in this calm.

JEN. There'll be wind enough before dawn.

BUT. And that's the end of Enoch Jackson. Over the side he goes, and his mates forget him.

JEN. Whatever's happened to Jackson, he ain't worried none. He's got a hundred fathoms over him to keep him warm and cosy.

BILL. I'd rather be buried at sea than on the beach, when I come to die. Will you stand by the plank, Tom, so I'll shake a friendly hand before I sink? Oh! But it's dead I'll be then, come to think! (*All laugh.*)

PAY. Don't you worry none. By that time, you won't give a sailmaker's damn.

KIN. It's only living makes sense to me, anyhow.

BILL. Aye, I like to live. Even when it seems bad, there's a lot that's good in it.

JEN. Maybe for you, Bill. You wouldn't know trouble if it come up and spit in your eye.

BILL. Don't you try now, mate! You might miss, and I got a clean jumper on!

PAY. That's the way to be, if you ask me. There's always trouble, if you know where to look for it.

BUT. You don't have to see nothing if you close your eyes.

KIN. When I close my eyes I sleep sound as a drunk marine.

BILL. Aye, after I roll in my hammock, it's one, two, three, and I'm deep down under.

JEN. Well it's down under for me right now. Let's lay below.

KIN. Aye, we'll be on watch before long. Coming, Bill?

BILL. I think I'll stay and watch the water for a while. I like to watch the sea at night.

JEN. Aye. It's deep and silent, and it can drown a man before he knows it.

BILL. Sleep sound, mates. (*All but* JENKINS *go down the companion hatchway*.)

JEN. Billy: stay clear of Jimmy-Legs.

(JENKINS *exits down the hatchway.* BILLY *is left alone staring over the side until* CLAGGART *enters. He does not see* BILLY, *but stops near the quarterdeck ladder and gazes fixedly seaward*.)

BILL. Good evening, sir.

CLAG. (*startled, then subtly sarcastic*). Good evening.

BILL. Will it be all right if I stay topside a bit to watch the water?

CLAG. I suppose the Handsome Sailor may do many things forbidden to his messmates.

BILL. Yes, sir. The sea's calm tonight, isn't it? Calm and peaceful.

CLAG. The sea's deceitful, boy: calm above, and underneath, a world of gliding monsters preying on their fellows. Murderers, all of them. Only the sharpest teeth survive.

BILL. I'd like to know about such things, as you do, sir.

CLAG. You're an ingenuous sailor, Billy Budd. Is there, behind that youthful face, the wisdom pretty virtue has need of? Even the gods must know their rivals, boy; and Christ had first to recognize the ills before he cured 'em.

BILL. What, sir?

CLAG. Never mind. But tell me this: how have you stomach to stand here and talk to me? Are you so innocent and ignorant of what I am? You know my reputation. Jenkins and the rest are witnesses, and certainly you've heard them talking to me. Half of them would knife me in the back some night and do it gladly; Jenkins is thinking of it. Doubtless he'll try one day. How do you dare, then? Have you not intelligence enough to be afraid of me? To hate me as all the others do?

BILL. Why should I be afraid of you, sir? You speak to me friendly when we meet. I know some of the men . . . are fearful of you, sir, but I can't believe they're right about it.

CLAG. You're a fool, fellow. In time, you'll learn to fear me like the rest. Young you are, and scarcely used to the fit of your man's flesh.

BILL. I know they're wrong, sir. You aren't like they say. Nobody could be so.

CLAG. So . . . ? So what, boy? Vicious, did you mean to say, or brutal? But they aren't wrong, and you would see it, but for those blue eyes that light so kindly on your fellow men.

BILL. Oh, I've got no education, I know that. There must be a lot of things a man misses when he's ignorant. But learning's hard. Must be sort of lonely, too.

CLAG. What are you prating of, half-man, half-child? Your messmates crowd around, admire your yellow hair and your blue eyes, do tricks and favors for you out of love, and you talk about loneliness!

BILL. I just noticed the way you were looking off to leeward as I came up, sir. Kind of sad, you were looking.

CLAG. Not sadness, boy. Another feeling, more like . . . pleasure. That's it. I can feel it now, looking at you. A certain . . . pleasure.

BILL. (*flattered*). Thank you, sir.

CLAG. (*annoyed at* BILLY's *incomprehension*). Pah.

BILL. Just talking with you, sir, I can tell they're wrong about you. They're ignorant, like me.

CLAG. Compliment for compliment, eh, boy? Have you no heart for terror, fellow? You've seen this stick in use. Have you not got sense and spleen and liver to be scared, even to be cowardly?

BILL. No, sir, I guess not. I like talking to you, sir. But please, sir, tell me something.

CLAG. I wonder if I can. Well, ask it.

BILL. Why do you want us to believe you're cruel, and not really like everybody else?

CLAG. I think you are the only child alive who wouldn't understand if I explained; or else you'd not believe it.

BILL. Oh, I'd believe you, sir. There's much I could learn from you: I never knew a man like you before.

CLAG. (*slowly*). Do you—like me, Billy Budd?

BILL. You've always been most pleasant with me, sir.

CLAG. Have I?

BILL. Yes, sir. In the mess, the day I came aboard? And almost every day you have a pleasant word.

CLAG. And what I have said tonight, are these pleasant words?

BILL. Yes, sir. I was wondering . . . could I talk to you between watches, when you've nothing else to do?

CLAG. You're a plausible boy, Billy. Aye, the nights are long, and talking serves to pass them.

BILL. Thank you, sir. That would mean a lot to me.

CLAG. Perhaps to me as well. (*Drops his rattan.* BILLY *picks it up and hands it back to him.* CLAGGART *stares at it a moment, then at* BILLY.) No. No! Charm me, too, would you! Get away!

BILL. (*surprised and puzzled*). Aye, sir. (*He exits down the hatchway. After a pause in which* CLAGGART *recovers his self-control* SQUEAK *appears.*)

CLAG. (*without turning*). Come here. I thought I told you to put that new seaman Budd on report. Why was it not done?

SQ. I tried, Mister Claggart, sir. I couldn't find nothing out of place. Gear all stowed perfect.

CLAG. Then disarrange it. You know the practice. I want him on report.

SQ. Two of his messmates is once nearly caught me at it before.

CLAG. Then be more careful. Now get along and see you make out something. (SQUEAK *scurries off below decks as* VERE *comes into sight on the quarterdeck.*)

VERE. Master-at-Arms. What is that man doing above decks?

CLAG. Ship's corporal, sir. A routine report.

VERE. There is nothing in this ship of so routine a nature that I do not concern myself in it. Remember that.

CLAG. Aye, aye, sir. With your permission, sir. (*Exit.* VERE *walks along the deck and scans the sails as* SEYMOUR *enters.*)

SEY. Fine evening, sir.

VERE. Yes, a fine evening, Seymour. How is the glass?

SEY. Falling, I believe, sir. I think we'll toss a little before morning. Well, I suppose I should be in my cabin inspecting the deck logs.

VERE. Stay for a moment, Seymour. In the days and nights to come, you and I will not often have an opportunity to stand easy and talk.

SEY. Aye, sir. I expect the French will put us to our stations any hour now.

VERE. Are you impressed by omens, Seymour? This seaman we've just

buried: I think of him as an omen of some sort, a melancholy prologue to this voyage.

SEY. Aye, sir. Hard on the sailor, certainly, but that's the service. But
we've been lucky in other ways. An accident, now, that's unavoid-
able.

VERE. It was more than an accident, Seymour.

SEY. This maintop sailor? How do you mean, sir?

VERE. The man was sent aloft sick, by the Master-at-Arms, contrary to
my standing order. Budd, the new seaman, implied as much, and
the maintop watch confirmed it. The Master-at-Arms lied to me.

SEY. What are you going to do, sir? What action can you take? He's a
valuable man, one we can hardly do without as things are now.

VERE. I shall do nothing at present, only wait and observe him. No
court-martial could do more than strip him of his rank for such
misconduct. I will let him have his head until some act puts him
squarely counter to the law, then let the law consume him.

SEY. Why trouble the natural order to no purpose? Shouldn't we let
it be?

VERE. Must a man always shrug, let things alone and drift? Would to
God I could take this power of mine and break him now, smash
all the laws to powder and be a man again.

SEY. We must serve the law, sir, or give up the right and privilege of
service. It's how we live.

VERE. Live? Oh, you're right. Below this deck are men who at a call skip
on the hurling spars against the wind, at Beat-to-quarters run as
if they willed it. Yet each of us steps alone within this pattern,
this formal movement centered on itself. Men live and die, taken
by pattern, born to it, knowing nothing. No man can defy the
code we live by and not be broken by it.

SEY. You are the Captain, sir. You maintain that code.

VERE. Keep an order we cannot understand. That's true. The world
demands it: demands that at the back of every peacemaker there
be the gun, the gallows and the gaol. I talk of justice, and would
turn the law gentle for those who serve here; but a Claggart
stands in my shadow, for I need him. So the world goes, wanting
not justice, but order . . . to be let alone to hug its own iniquities.

Let a man work to windward of that law and he'll be hove down.
No hope for him, none. (*Enter* WYATT.)

WY. Eight o'clock report, sir. Ship inspected and all in order.

SEY. Very well, carry on. (WYATT *goes off*.) By your leave, sir. Good
night.

(*Exit.* VERE *remains, crosses to the hatch and looks down, then slowly
upward at the set of the sails.*)

Scene Three

The maindeck several nights later.

*Four bells is struck offstage. A sailor climbs wearily down the ratlines,
drops to the deck and goes below.* CLAGGART *stands by the larboard
rail.*

As BILLY *enters from below decks, he sees the Master-at-Arms.*

BILL. Hello, sir. (CLAGGART *looks at him without answering, then turns
and goes off forward. The* DANSKER *follows* BILLY *up onto the
deck.*) Well, that's all there is to tell, Dansker. I always lash my
hammock just so, and stow my gear same as all the others. They
don't get in trouble.

DANS. Mister Claggart is down upon you, Billy.

BILL. Jimmy-Legs? Why he calls me the sweet and pleasant fellow, they
tell me.

DANS. Does he so, Baby lad? Aye, a sweet voice has Mister Claggart.

BILL. For me he has. I seldom pass him but there comes a pleasant
word.

DANS. And that's because he's down upon you.

BILL. But he's my friend. I know he talks a little strange, but he's my
friend.

DANS. Nobody's friend is Jimmy-Legs. Yours the least of all, maybe. Lay
aloft, Baby. You'll be late to relieve your watch.

BILL. Aye, Dansker. (*He climbs up the ratlines out of sight. The*
DANSKER *watches him go.* CLAGGART *appears, but the* DANSKER *ignores him and goes off aft. As* JENKINS *comes into view climbing
down the ratlines,* CLAGGART *gestures off and fades into a shadowy
corner of the deck near the quarterdeck ladder.* SQUEAK *enters as*

JENKINS *drops to the deck, and intercepts him as he starts down the companionway.*)

SQ. It's all right, mate, slack off and stay a bit.

JEN. What do you want? I pick my own company.

SQ. So does I, mate, so does I. And if I may make so bold to say it, you'll be smarter to pick your company more careful.

JEN. If you got something to say to me, talk up, else I'll get below.

SQ. Don't be hasty, now, mate, don't be in a sweat. It's haste gets good men into trouble. What d'you think of our new hand here, Billy Boy? Mister Claggart's taken with him, too. Fine young fellow, ha?

JEN. Talk plain. What d'you mean?

SQ. I overheard him talking just this day. Would maybe surprise you some, what he had to say about yourself and a few other lads.

JEN. What?

SQ. Aoh, bit of talk about his messmates. He don't fancy us! Not like his feather boys aboard the merchantman.

JEN. You lying cut-throat, try something else! Billy's in my mess; since he come on board he's rare been out of my sight. You're lying, you bloody mark! I know you too well. You'll need to try some other way to get Bill into trouble. Get away, and don't come lying to me no more.

SQ. Aoh, so it's that friendly you are! Well, now, ain't that sweet! You're not smart, Jenkins. Remember, man: I tried to help you out. When you're feeling the cat between your shoulders . . .

JEN. (*seizing him*). Damn your lies! Get back to Jimmy-Legs and kiss his butt. And stay out of my way! (*Throws* SQUEAK *down and exits.* SQUEAK *watches him go.* CLAGGART *steps out of the shadows.*)

CLAG. I heard your little talk. You lack subtlety; but I'm the greater fool to use you in these matters. You're inept.

SQ. Aoh! Why don't you do it yourself, if you don't need me!

CLAG. I need nobody, least of all a rum-soaked footpad from the *Old Bailey*. If you wish to have free rein with your distasteful habits, mind your cockney manners! I stand between you and the flogging whip. Improve your style, or you stand tomorrow forenoon at the gratings!

SQ. I only meant as you could do it better, Mister Claggart, I wouldn't say nothing to . . .

CLAG. (*cuts him on the arm with his rattan*). Don't touch me!—Keep Budd in petty troubles, that you can do. Unlash his hammock. Keep him on report. In time I'll let you know what plans I have for him. Get aft! (SQUEAK, *eager to get away, scuttles aft as the* DANSKER *enters.*) Well, old man. Moon's in and out tonight. There's weather somewhere. (*The* DANSKER *turns down the night lamp over the cabin door and starts off.*) Stay and have a pipe.

DANS. I have the watch.

CLAG. You take your duties as seriously as ever.

DANS. Aye. They are all of life for an old seaman like me. (*Turns to go.*)

CLAG. You move away from me as though I were some kind of stalking beast. You avoid me, too.

DANS. Your word, John, "too."

CLAG. You know what I mean. The hands detest me. You are a hand, older than most, and older in your hatred, I have no doubt. But why, man? You at least should see me as I am, a man who knows how the world's made: made as I am.

DANS. How can I know what goes on in your head?

CLAG. The enigmatic Dansker. Come, it's dark, we can drop disguises when night serves to hold the disclosing soul apart.

DANS. You know who you remind me of . . . maintopman: Billy Budd.

CLAG. More enigmas! That sunny, smiling infant with no spleen nor knowledge in his head?

DANS. I'll leave you now.

CLAG. No, stay a while. This is a night for secrets and disclosures.

DANS. You have half the truth and Billy Budd the other. He can't see there's evil in the world, and you won't see the good.

CLAG. So. And I take it you come in between.

DANS. I keep outside. I am too old to stand between sky and water.

CLAG. And yet you hate me, too.

DANS. I hate an incomplete man.

CLAG. Damn all this talk. Hate me and have done. Let it alone, I say. Whatever else it is, this thing is Man, still!

DANS. I'll be off.

CLAG. Don't go. The moon's gone under. Let us talk this out. You are a wise man in your senile way.

DANS. Then take this for all my wisdom. You recognize the hatred of your shipmates as an honor paid to a soul they cannot understand. Your fine contempt for human love is nothing but regret.

CLAG. Stop there. I know the rest by heart. Nothing you say to me but clatters in my belly, watch on watch. Aye: when this arm moves out in gesture of love, it mocks me with a blow. Who lifts this arm? What officer commands this hireling flesh? Somewhere below the farthest marks and deeps, God anchors hearts, and his sea rusts mine hollow. The flukes break in the bottom, and I slack and stand, go in and out forever at God's humor. Look at this sea: for all her easy swell, who knows what bones, ribs and decay are fathomed at her base and move in her motion, so that on the flattest water, the very stricture of the dead can kill that beauty with a dance of death?—Here is a man. He holds, past fathom curves, drowned fleets of human agonies that gesture when the long tide pulls.

DANS. Aye, John. But you must know that other men are moved so. Look up some evening at the quarterdeck for another poor thoughtful devil like you, like me, pacing all night between his doubts.

CLAG. What, Vere? That fine-drawn manner doesn't deceive me. There's a whited sepulchre, like all soft-spoken charmers of this world.

DANS. You don't believe in anything besides yourself, eh John?

CLAG. I've said what I have said. I know myself, and look to that. You should try it. Go to your post, old man, and your ever-lasting duties. (CLAGGART *turns away.* BILLY *scrambles into view down the ratlines and calls out excitedly.*)

BILL. Quarterdeck ho!

RAT. (*coming forward to the forward break of the quarterdeck*). Sound off!

BILL. Strange sail one mile off the larboard beam!

CLAG. (*to* DANSKER). A Frenchman! Get to your station.

RAT. (*on the quarterdeck ladder*). Mister Duncan! Sound Beat-to-quarters! Clear for action!

DUN. (*offstage*). Aye aye, sir!

RAT. Gardiner! (*Enter* GARDINER.)

GARD. Sir?

RAT. Report to the Captain, strange sail on the larboard beam. Then send Payne to the wheel. (*Exit* GARDINER.) Master-at-Arms, send a man to the mast to relay lookout's reports. Inspect battle stations and report to me when they are fully manned.

CLAG. Aye aye, sir. (*Exits.*)

VOICE (*off*). She's a French frigate! Steering east by south! (*Enter* VERE *and* SEYMOUR.)

VERE. Prepare to make chase. Have your quartermaster steer small.

RAT. Aye aye, sir.

(*Enter the* DRUMMER *and sound Beat-to-quarters. Men run on, to gun stations, rigging, crossing stage and off.*)

SEY. She's too fast for us, sir. We'll never come up with her.

VERE. We are bound to try, though we were sure to fail. And we may smell powder before this chase is over.

CLAG. (*re-entering*). Battle stations fully manned, sir!

SEY. May we try a shot at her now?

VERE. She's drawing south. Yes, commence firing, Mr. Seymour.

SEY. Larboard battery, fire one!

DUN. Fire! (*Fire one gun.*)

VERE. Fire at will!

SEY. Fire at will!

(*Guns fire dissynchronously.*)

ACT TWO

Scene One

The quarterdeck and part of the maindeck a few minutes before 0800. A high wind. On the quarterdeck are Lieutenant WYATT, *Midshipman* REA *and the helmsman,* STOLL.

REA. I'm glad this watch is over. I'm tired.

WY. Make your entry in the log before your relief comes up. Bring it out here and I'll sign it.

REA. Aye, sir. What was our last position, do you remember?

WY. Thirteen ten west, forty-three forty north.

REA. And an easterly breeze.

WY. Aye, make it so. That'll make Ratcliffe happy. Last time he had an east wind, she blew his hat over the side. And put down "Running ground swell."

REA. Aye aye, sir. *(Exits.)*

WY. Helmsman, keep her close-hauled.

STOLL. I can't, sir. Too much cloth in the wind.

WY. Well hold her close as you can, and let the next watch reef sail if they like.

STOLL. Aye aye, sir. *(Enter RATCLIFFE.)*

WY. Morning, Johnny! You're on time!

RAT. What's the course?

WY. Steady south. Wind's easterly. Glass is dropping.

RAT. East wind? Damn it. *(Enter BYREN, the relief helmsman.)* By the way, you forgot to sign the order book.

WY. All right. Thanks.

STOLL. I've been relieved, sir. Byren has the helm.

WY. Very well. *(Exit STOLL.)* Who's mate of your watch?

RAT. The Admiralty midshipman. That lobcock Gardiner, hang him. *(Eight bells.)*

WY. Where the devil is he? It's eight. *(Enter REA and GARDINER separately, meeting.)*

RAT. There he comes. He looks happy. That means trouble for some poor devil. *(GARDINER snatches the log out of REA's hands and bounds up to the quarterdeck.)*

REA. I've been relieved, sir. Horatio, Lord Gardiner has the watch.

WY. Ah, Midshipman Gardiner. The backbone of the British Navy.

RAT. The backside, if you ask me.

WY. All right, Rea. You can turn in. *(REA exits.)*

RAT. Pity we lost that Frenchman last night. A little action would season the monotony of these interminable watches.

WY. Did you ever hear of a ship-of-the-line running down a frigate, even with the wind? Ah, it's a magnificent morning! Thickening overcast, heavy ground swell, a fresh levanter breeze, and you, Johnny, are the Pride of the Morning!

RAT. Mmmm. Has the skipper been on deck yet?

WY. Not since sunrise. He came up then and paced the deck and stared off east like a sleepwalker. Then went below again without a word.

RAT. He thinks too much.

WY. Well if you ever make captain, your crew won't have that to complain of, anyway. Am I relieved?

RAT. Yes, I relieve you. (*Tosses his cap to* WYATT.) Here. Take this below, will you?

WY. What? You'll be out of uniform, man. Mister Gardiner wouldn't approve of your standing watch without a hat, would you, Midshipman Gardiner?

GARD. Sir, the Articles state that officers on watch . . .

RAT. Well hang it, I lost twelve shillings the last time my hat went over the rail, and this is the only other one I've got. To hell with the Articles.

WY. Mind your language! It's downright mutinous. Well, don't expect me to stand your watches if you catch your death of cold. Good morning. (*Exit.*)

GARD. Midshipman Rea, sir, I don't like to say it, but his log entries are impossible.

RAT. Then enter yourself, Mister Gardiner. So are you.

GARD. Yes, sir. But I do think he ought to be told . . .

RAT. Go find the Captain and report to him the wind's abeam. Respectfully suggest we ought to take in topsails.

GARD. Aye aye, sir. (*Goes down stairs.*)

RAT. And don't forget to tell him I haven't got a hat.

GARD. What's that, sir?

RAT. Nothing, sir! You got my order. Dump your ballast and shove off.

GARD. I thought you spoke to me, sir.

RAT. I avoid that whenever possible. Move!

GARD. Yes, sir.

RAT. Ye gods, what a brat. Nothing off, helmsman. She's well enough thus.

BYR. Nothing off, sir.

GARD. (*nearly bumping into* VERE *as he emerges from cabin, followed by* SEYMOUR *and* HALLAM). Atten-tion!

RAT. Good morning, sir.

VERE. Morning, Mister Ratcliffe.

GARD. (*starting after* VERE, *bumps into* HALLAM). Damn it, man, watch what you're doing!

VERE. Midshipman Gardiner.

GARD. Sir?

VERE. How long, pray, have you been in this ship, or any ship?

GARD. This is my first cruise, sir.

VERE. Your first cruise. A wartime cruise as well. And you are a midshipman. A midshipman, Mister Gardiner, let me tell you, is neither fish, flesh, nor fowl, and certainly no seaman. You're a saltwater hermaphrodite, Mister Gardiner. And unless you have a mind to be generally known as Spit-kit Gardiner, I recommend more tolerance toward the men. Now, is that clear?

GARD. Aye aye, sir!

VERE. Very well, you may carry on.

RAT. We've a weather helm, sir, and bow seas.

VERE. Take in topsails, if you please, Mister Ratcliffe.

RAT. Aye aye, sir. Mister Duncan!

DUN. (*enters*). Aye, sir?

RAT. Douse your topsails and topgallants. Haul in the weather braces.

DUN. Aye aye, sir. (*Exit.*) Away aloft! Hands by topgallant sheets and halyards!

GARD. Aloft there! Keep fast the weather sheets till the yards are down da . . . if you please!

RAT. Get aloft yourself, Mister Gardiner, see they do it right, since you're not satisfied.

GARD. Sir, the Articles state that . . .

RAT. Did you hear me?

GARD. Aye aye, sir.   (*Exits up ratlines.*)

DUN. (*off*). Haul tort!

VERE. You disapprove of Gardiner, Mister Ratcliffe?

RAT. He seems to think he's the only midshipman aboard capable of doing anything properly. He's always looking at you as if your hat
weren't squared.

VERE. That is an unfortunate simile under the present circumstances.

RAT. (*caught*). Oh, I—er— Keep her close to the wind, helmsman. Don't
fall away!

DUN. (*off*). Let go topgallant bowlines!

VERE. I think Gardiner has had enough correction for one day. Call him
down to our level, Mister Ratcliffe.

RAT. Aye, sir. Mister Gardiner! You may come off your perch now!
(BILLY *descends rigging and starts offstage.*) What do you think
of our new man Budd, Captain?

SEY. That boy did a smart piece of work for us last night, sir. He's the
nimblest man on the tops I've ever watched. Wyatt wants him for
captain of the foretop.

VERE. Very well, let Budd take the post. He certainly deserves it for his
actions last night during the chase. I'll speak to him myself.

SEY. He'll like hearing it from you, sir.

VERE. Hallam, go call Budd, the lad moving forward there. (*Exit* HAL-
LAM. GARDINER *appears, looking sick.*) Well done, Gardiner. You
may lay below and draw an extra tot of rum. You look . . .
chilly.

GARD. Thank you, sir.   (*Exit.*)

SEY. By the way, sir, Budd has been on the Master-at-Arms' report once
or twice for some petty misdemeanor. Nothing serious. (*Steps
aside with* RATCLIFFE. BILLY *enters, followed by* HALLAM.)

BILL. You sent for me, sir?

VERE. Yes, Budd. Your division officer recommends you for a post of
more responsibility. He thinks you can perform duties of a higher
station, and so do I, after last night. So I've agreed that you shall
have Williams' place on the foretop.

BILL. But—Williams is captain of the foretop, sir.

VERE. The station calls for a younger man. Lieutenant Wyatt asked for
you, and the spirit you showed last night warrants it. That is a
real honor for a man so new on board.

BILL. The Navy's new to me, Captain, but I hardly know anything else but the sea and ships.

VERE. And how do you like us, now that the awesomeness has worn away a bit?

BILL. The Navy's a bustling world, sir. Bigger than the *Rights of Man,* and I get lost sometimes. But my mates lend me a hand. Why even Jimmy-Legs—beg pardon, sir, the Master-at-Arms, I mean— he's good to me, too.

VERE. The sea and the Navy exact a discipline, but it need not be a harsh one. In some ways I envy the man who dances across the tops and seems to rule the ship and sea below. Up there is a pleach of ropes for you to make a world of. Though winds have their way with tackle of your world, you live at ease against your strength and the round bole of the mast in your back. You are a king up there, while the water curds and frolics at the forefoot. I envy you that stance.

BILL. You can trust me, Captain.

VERE. I do, boy. Very well, that's all.

BILL. Aye aye, sir. Thank you, sir, thank you! (*Runs off.*)

VERE. Hallam, find the Master-at-Arms and bid him report to me.

HAL. Aye aye, sir. (*Exit.* SEYMOUR *joins* VERE.)

VERE. If I had a son, I'd hope for one like Budd.

SEY. Aye, sir. Fine boy. He's a force for order in this ship, certainly. I hope his charm's contagious.

VERE. One such is enough. Men cannot stand very much perfection. It's a disease that we stamp out at its first rash showing. (*Enter* CLAGGART. SEYMOUR *withdraws.*) Master-at-Arms, I want to make a change on the Watch, Quarter and Station Bill. I needn't have troubled you about it until later, but I am especially interested in this change.

CLAG. The time of day is indifferent to me, sir.

VERE. Williams, present captain of the foretop, is assigned to the after-guard. I am replacing him with Budd.

CLAG. William Budd, sir? You do not mean the so-called Handsome Sailor?

VERE. Aye, William Budd, the new seaman from the *Rights of Man*.

CLAG. I know him, sir.

VERE. Do you find anything unusual in this replacement?

CLAG. You must be aware, sir, that he is . . .

VERE. Well? That he is what? I know he's an able seaman.

CLAG. Nothing, sir. But I wondered if he were entirely trustworthy. He has been aboard such a brief time.

VERE. Long enough to prove himself to me, and to his shipmates.

CLAG. Very good, sir.

VERE. He is captain of the foretop. That is all.

CLAG. With your permission, sir. Will there not be some dissatisfaction among the foretopmen who have been aboard much longer than Budd?

VERE. Master-at-Arms: I concern myself with these matters. They are none of your function. Until such time as the senior topmen formally object to Budd for incapacity, he is captain of the foretop. Make it so on the Bill. (*Exit.*)

RAT. What are you waiting for, man? Light to dawn? Promotion? You got the order.

CLAG. With your permission, sir.

(*As* CLAGGART *goes off,* RATCLIFFE *spits over the rail.*)

Scene Two

Forward part of the deck. Night. Eight bells. A man descends the rigging and goes off. CLAGGART *enters, stands by the hatch for a moment, then exits forward.* BILLY *comes down off watch, drops to the deck and remains in shadow, leaning over the rail, looking seaward.* JENKINS *stealthily and silently comes up from below deck.*

BILL. Jenkins! What you doing topside . . . (JENKINS *puts his hand over* BILLY'S *mouth.*)

JEN. (*in a whisper*). Stow the noise! (*Releases* BILLY.)

BILL. You're after Mister Claggart, like you said you would!

JEN. Well? What about it? You try and stop me?

BILL. He knows, Jenkins! I tell you, he knows! He's ready for you!

JEN. Then by God, I'll oblige him! I been waiting up here every night, waiting for him to come by when it's dark. Now get away and let me do it!

BILL. No! I won't let you hang yourself!

JEN. I don't give a fiddler's damn what happens to me! Move out of my way, mate!

BILL. No! Give me the knife.

JEN. The knife's for Claggart. You're a nice boy, Bill, but I ain't playing with you. You get away below, quick. This game ain't for boys.

BILL. Damme, no, Jenkins! You'll hang yourself!

JEN. Take your hands off! The moon's under, I can do it now! Oh, sweet mother of God, leave me go!

BILL. No!

JEN. Yes, by God!

(JENKINS *strikes* BILLY; *struggle, in which* BILLY *wrests knife from* JENKINS, *and it falls on deck.* BILLY *knocks* JENKINS *down.*)

CLAG. (*offstage*). What's that noise? Stand where you are! (*Entering.*) You again! Well? Explain this pageant.

BILL. He . . . I had to hit him, sir. He struck at me.

CLAG. Mm. And drew that knife on you, too, no doubt.

BILL. Yes, sir.

CLAG. I have been waiting, forward there, for Jenkins. You intercepted him, I take it.

BILL. I didn't know you were looking for him, sir.

CLAG. You shouldn't meddle, my fine young friend, in matters that don't concern you! I was expecting him. (*Enter* DANSKER.) There, help the body up. I do not thank you, boy, for cheating me of the pleasure of his punishment.

WY. (*offstage*). What's the disturbance there? You, forward on the spardeck!

CLAG. Master-at-Arms reports all in order, sir!

WY. (*offstage*). Stand where you are.

CLAG. The sweet and pleasant fellow saved you, Jenkins. But I reserve you still for my own justice in due time. Say nothing to this officer. (*Enter* WYATT.)

WY. What's the matter, Master-at-Arms? It's an odd hour for star-gazing.

CLAG. A slight matter, sir. I found these two men together here on deck, contrary to the Captain's orders. I was sending them below when you called out.

WY. Oh, is that all. Carry on, then.

CLAG. Aye aye, sir. Now then, get below, both of you. (*Enter* VERE *followed by* HALLAM. *The* DANSKER *goes off.*) Atten-tion!

VERE. Wyatt, what's this mean?

WY. Two men on deck without permission, sir.

VERE. Is there no more to this? The story's lame, man. What occurred? (*Silence.*) Very well, then. Go along, both of you.

BILL. Aye aye, sir. Come along, mate.   (*Exits with* JENKINS.)

VERE. Your knife, Master-at-Arms?

CLAG. William Budd's, sir, I believe.

VERE. Return it to him.   (*Exits with* HALLAM *and* WYATT.)

(CLAGGART *raps rail with rattan.* SQUEAK *approaches warily.*)

CLAG. Listen carefully; you may make up for your late mistake if you do this smartly. Give Budd just time enough to get to sleep. At four bells wake him. Bring him to the lee forechains. You understand?

SQ. Mister Claggart, sir . . . we done enough to him. He's a good lad, Mister Claggart. Couldn't it be somebody else? Jenkins, maybe?

CLAG. So. He's softened your heart too, eh? Do as you're ordered, man, or I'll see your back laid raw with a flogging whip! Remember: I will be watching you. Bring him to the lee forechains. And when you're there . . .

SQ. Dansker. Moving forward.

CLAG. Step back, you fool. Wait for me.

(*Exit* SQUEAK. *The* DANSKER *enters.*)

DANS. Baby saved you, eh? And you are angry.

CLAG. Saved me, you say? From what? I've tried to tempt Jenkins to this blow, so as to break his toplofty spirit with his neck; and I am "saved" by that guileless idiot! He'd turn the other cheek to me, in Christian kindness! Well, there's a second pleasure in striking that same face twice. I can destroy him, too, if I choose to do it!

DANS. Crazy, crazy!

CLAG. All right, old man, call it madness then. Whatever its name, it will plunder the sweetness from that face, or it will kill us both.

DANS. You are afraid of him.

CLAG. Afraid? Of Budd? What nonsense is that?

DANS. He usurps the crew; they turn from hating you to loving him, and leave you impotent.

CLAG. That bastard innocent frighten me! That witless kindness that spills from him has neither force nor aim. Stand out from between us, or you founder together, sink in five hundred fathoms with him, if I want it so!

DANS. Aye, then, if you take that tack, let it be both of us. You expect me to sit by and watch your deliberate arm seize him and force him under?

CLAG. Why not? You have always done that. I thought your practice was to stay outside. What breeds the saintly knight errant in you?

DANS. I am old, but I have some manhood left.

CLAG. What can you do? You've drifted with the tide too long, old one. You are as involved as I am now.

DANS. So you may say. In this ship a man lives as he can, and finds a way to make life tolerable for himself. I did so. That was a fault. But no longer.

CLAG. Stand clear. You haven't courage to cross me.

DANS. Eh, I'm not afraid of you; I see your scheme.

CLAG. Damn your feeble, ineffectual eyes! (*Striking him; the* DANSKER *falls.*) You can see only what I let you see!

DANS. Say what you like. I see your scheme; so will Captain if need be.

CLAG. (*pulling him to his feet*). Take a warning for yourself, old man. And keep away! You are on watch, eh? Well, go back to sleep again, or I'll report you.

(DANSKER *exits.* CLAGGART *watches him go, then violently breaks his rattan and throws the pieces over the side.*)

Scene Three

Forward part of the main deck. Four bells. CLAGGART *stands with one hand on the rail, waiting. After a short pause, hearing a sound, he fades into shadow.* SQUEAK *enters, bending over and running.*

SQ. Hssssssssssst! (BILLY, *sleepy and rubbing his eyes, enters.*)

BILL. You brought me all the way up here, out of my hammock. Now what do you want?

SQ. I heard you're captain of the foretop, Bill. That right?

BILL. Aye. What's that to do with you?

SQ. Ah, now you can be more use to your shipmates then ever you was before.

BILL. What?

SQ. You was impressed, now, weren't you? Well, so was I. We're not the only impressed ones, Billy. There's a gang of us. Could you help . . . at a pinch?

BILL. What do you mean?

SQ. See here . . . (*Holds up two coins.*) Here's two gold guineas for you, Bill. Put in with us. Most of the men aboard are only waiting for a word, and they'll follow you. There's more for you where these come from. What d'you say? If you join us, Bill, there's not a man aboard won't come along! Are you with us? The ship'll be ours when we're ready to take it!

BILL. Damme, I don't know what you're driving at, but you had better go where you belong! (SQUEAK, *surprised, does not move.* BILLY *springs up.*) If you don't start, I'll toss you back over the rail! (SQUEAK *decamps.* BILLY *watches him and starts off himself.* DANSKER, *offstage, calls out.*)

DANS. Hallo, what's the matter? (*Enters.*) Ah, Beauty, is it you again? Something must have been the matter, for you stammered. (CLAGGART *appears and comes forward.*)

CLAG. You seem to favor the maindeck, Billy Budd. What brings you topside at this hour, man, against my orders and the Captain's?

BILL. I . . . found an afterguardsman in our part of the ship here, and I bid him be off where he belongs.

DANS. And is that all you did about it, boy?

BILL. Aye, Dansker, nothing more.

CLAG. A strange sort of hour to police the deck. Name the afterguardsman.

BILL. I . . . can't say, Mister Claggart. I couldn't see him clear enough.

DANS. Don't be a fool, speak up, accuse him.

CLAG. Well?

BILL. I can't say, sir.

CLAG. You refuse? Then get below, and stay where you belong.

BILL. Aye aye, sir. Good night, sir. Good night, Dansker. (*Exits.*)

CLAG. I'm glad you saw this mutinous behavior.

DANS. Your crazy brain squeezes out false conclusions. He has done nothing except find you out, though he's too innocent to know it.

CLAG. I am not hoodwinked by his weak excuse. What else would he be doing at this hour, but fanning rebel tempers like his own?

DANS. I stood in the shadows forward when your pander Squeak slipped by me, running from this place. You set him on, on purpose to trap Billy.

CLAG. And I will do that, old man. But you will say nothing about it; see you don't. (*Enter* VERE *followed by* HALLAM.)

VERE. Well, Master-at-Arms? You stand long watches.

CLAG. Sir. May I take the liberty of reserving my explanation for your private ear. I believe your interest in this matter would incline you to prefer some privacy.

VERE (*to* DANSKER *and* HALLAM). Leave us. Hallam, stand within hail. (DANSKER *and* HALLAM *go off.*) Well? What is it you wish to say, Master-at-Arms?

CLAG. During my rounds this night, I have seen enough to convince me that one man aboard, at least, is dangerous; especially in a ship which musters some who took a guilty part in the late serious uprisings . . .

VERE. You may spare a reference to that.

CLAG. Your pardon, sir. Quite lately I have begun to notice signs of some sort of movement secretly afoot, and prompted by the man in question. I thought myself not warranted, so long as this suspicion was only indistinct, in reporting it. But recently . . .

VERE. Come to the point, man.

CLAG. Sir, I deeply feel the cruel responsibility of making a report involving such serious consequences to the sailor mainly concerned. But God forbid, sir, that this ship should suffer the experience of the Nore.

VERE. Never mind that! You say there is one dangerous man. Name him.

CLAG. William Budd, the . . . captain of the foretop.

VERE. William Budd?

CLAG. The same, sir. But for all his youth and appealing manners, a secret, vicious lad.

VERE. How, vicious?

CLAG. He insinuates himself into the good will of his mates so that they will at least say a word for him, perhaps even take action with him, should it come to that. With your pardon, sir; you note but his fair face; under that there lies a man-trap.

VERE (*after a pause*). Master-at-Arms, I intend to test your accusation here and now. Hallam! (*Enter* HALLAM.)

HAL. Aye, sir.

VERE. Find Budd, the foretopman. Manage to tell him out of earshot that he is wanted here. Keep him in talk yourself. Go along.

HAL. Aye aye, sir. (*Exits.*)

VERE (*angry and perturbed*). Do you come to me with such a foggy tale, Master-at-Arms? As to William Budd, cite me an act, or spoken word of his, confirming what you here in general charge against him. Wait; weigh what you speak. Just now, and in this case, there is the yardarm end for false witness.

CLAG. I understand, sir. Tonight, when on my rounds, discovering Budd's hammock was unused, I combed the ship, and found him in conclave with several growlers; men, who, like himself, spread unrest and rebellion in the crew. They were collected here, near the lee forechains, and when I ordered them below, young Budd and others threatened me, and swore they'd drop me, and some officers they hate, overboard, some misty night. Should you, sir, desire substantial proof, it is not far.

(*Enter* HALLAM, *followed by* BILLY.)

VERE. Hallam, stand apart and see that we are not disturbed. (HALLAM *exits.*) And now, Master-at-Arms, tell this man to his face what you told me of him.

CLAG. (*moving near to* BILLY, *and looking directly at him*). Certainly, sir. I said this man, this William Budd, acting so out of angry resentment against impressment and his officers, against this ship, this Service, and the King, breeds in the crew a spirit of rebellion against the officers, the mates, and me, urging some outrage like the late revolt. I myself have seen and heard him speak with manifest malingerers and men who growl of mistreatment, harshness, unfair pay and similar complaints. I say this man threatened his officers with murder, and was bent tonight on urging other men to act concertedly in mutiny. I have nothing further to say, sir.

(BILLY *tries to speak, but can make only incoherent sounds. He seems to be in pain from the contortions of his face and the gurgling which is all he can effect for speech.*)

VERE. Speak, man, speak! Defend yourself! (*Remembering* BILLY'S *impediment, goes to him and puts a hand on his shoulder reassuringly.*) There is no hurry, boy. Take your time, take your time.

(*After agonized dumb gesturing and stammering, increased by* VERE'S *kindness,* BILLY'S *arm hits out at* CLAGGART. CLAGGART *staggers, falls, lies still.*)

VERE. Stand back, man! It was a lie, then! (BILLY, *shaking, only stares at the body.* VERE *raises the body to a sitting position. Since* CLAGGART *remains inert,* VERE *lowers him again slowly, then rises.* BILLY *tries again to speak, without success; he is crying and badly frightened.*) No need to speak now, Billy. Hallam! (*Enter* HALLAM.) Tell the Surgeon I wish to see him here at once. And bid Mister Seymour report to my cabin without delay. (*To* BILLY.) Retire to the stateroom aft. Remain there till I summon you. (BILLY *exits.* VERE *waits, turning once to stare at* CLAGGART'S *body. Enter the* SURGEON.) Surgeon, tell me how it is with him. (SURGEON *bends over* CLAGGART *briefly, then looks up in surprise.*) Come, we must dispatch. Go now. I shall presently call a drumhead court to try the man who out of God's own instinct dropped him there. Tell the lieutenants that a foretopman has, in an accidental fury, killed this man. Inform the Captain of Marines as well, and charge them to keep the matter to themselves. (SURGEON *exits*.) The divine judgment of Ananias! Struck dead by the Angel of God . . . and I must judge the Angel. Can I save him? Have I that choice?

ACT THREE

Scene One

CAPTAIN VERE'S *cabin, a quarter of an hour later.* VERE *and* SEYMOUR.

SEY. Budd beat a man to death! What had he done?

VERE. Lied again: lied to Budd's face, hoping to kill him by it. Oh, the boy was tempted to it past endurance.

SEY. False witness has its penalty, sir. Budd has set our justice right.

VERE. Aye, too right. This natural, right act, done in an instinct's fever of recognition, was late and fatal.

SEY. What are you going to do, Captain? Isn't this last lie of the Master-at-Arms the very act you were waiting for, so as to let the law destroy him, as you said? He should have suffered at the yardarm if Billy hadn't killed him.

VERE. Yes. He should. But by fair process of authority. Budd has prevented that, and turned the law against himself.

SEY. You can't condemn the boy for answering with his arm for lack of words! The motive was clearly justified.

VERE. Aye, but was the act? For God's sake try, try to convince me I am wrong!

SEY. This Master-at-Arms, you knew him for a liar, a vicious dog.

VERE. A dog's obeyed in office. Claggart was authority.

SEY. Then authority's an evil!

VERE. It often is. But it commands, and no man is its equal, not Billy, nor you, nor I. It will strike us down, and rightly, if we resist it.

SEY. Rightly! What power gives evil its authority? We should thank God the man's dead, and the world well rid of that particular devil.

VERE. Our life has ways to hedge its evil in. No one must go above them; even innocents. Laws of one kind or other shape our course from birth to death. These are the laws pronouncing Billy's guilt; Admiralty codes are merely shadows of them.

SEY. That's tyranny, not law, forcing conformity to wrongs, giving the victory to the devil himself!

VERE. I thought so once. But without this lawful tyranny, what should we have but worse tyranny of anarchy and chaos? So aboard this man-of-war. Oh, if I were a man alone, manhood would declare for Billy.

SEY. Then do it. Put your strength and your authority behind Budd, and let him go.

VERE. When I think I could have watched him grow in comely wholesomeness of manhood . . . all lost now. What could have been, quenched in evil, swept out by that undertow.

SEY. It's more than anyone can have to answer for, Captain; to his peers, or to his God. Let him go free and try on mortal flesh! Will you urge a noose for him, marked like a common felon, and that devil still to have his wish, killing the boy at last?

VERE. Can I do otherwise? I'd give my life to save his, if I could.

SEY. It's in your hands, Captain. Only you can help him now.

VERE. Billy, Billy. What have we done to you? (*Knock.*) Yes, come in. (*Enter* HALLAM.)

HAL. Lieutenants Ratcliffe and Wyatt, sir.

VERE. Let them come in. (*Enter* RATCLIFFE *and* WYATT.)

SEY. You both know why you've been summoned hither?

WY. Yes, sir.

RAT. Aye, sir, in a general sort of way.

SEY. Then take your chairs. Ratcliffe. You here, Wyatt. You are appointed members of a court-martial convened under extraordinary circumstances by Captain Vere. I am Senior Member, and I declare this court open. (WYATT, RATCLIFFE, *and* SEYMOUR *sit.* VERE *remains standing, apart.*) Sentry, bring the prisoner in. (HALLAM *salutes and exits.*) As you know, the Master-at-Arms has been killed by the foretopman, Budd. Whether by accident or by design, and whether the act shall carry the penalty of death or no, you are to decide. There is only one witness, Captain Vere. I shall call upon him to give his deposition as soon as the sentry brings in the prisoner. (*An uneasy silence.*)

WY. Budd wouldn't kill a minnow without good reason.

RAT. What did the . . .

SEY. I had rather you did not express an opinion until after you have heard the evidence. (*Another awkward silence.* HALLAM *finally enters with* BILLY.) Sentry, stand outside. (*Exit* HALLAM.) You may sit down.

BILL. Th-th-thank you, sir.

SEY. Captain: will you be good enough to give us your account?

VERE (*turning toward them*). I speak not as your Captain, but as witness before this court. The Master-at-Arms early this morning detailed to me an account of mutinous sentiments expressed by Budd, and in particular, spoke of overhearing a specific conversation last night on the mid-watch. He alleged that Budd offered him violence and threatened further violence against the officers.

WY. Budd a mutineer! That's absurd, he's the best-liked man . . .

RAT. Did the Master-at-Arms specify who the other malcontents were, sir?

VERE. He did not. He said merely that he was in possession of substantial proof of his accusation.

SEY. With your permission, sir . . . Budd, did you speak with anyone in the Master-at-Arms' hearing last night?

BILL. I . . . spoke a little . . . with the Dansker, sir.

WY. Who is the Dansker?

BILL. He's just called the Dansker, sir. He's always called so.

RAT. I know him. A mainmast sailor.

SEY. Sentry. (*Enter* HALLAM.)

HAL. Sir.

SEY. Do you know a mainmast sailor referred to as "the Dansker"?

HAL. Aye, sir.

SEY. Go on deck and find him. Let him know apart that he is wanted here, and arrange it so that none of the other people notice his withdrawing. See you do it tactfully. I want no curiosity aroused among the men.

HAL. Aye aye, sir.   (*Exits.*)

SEY. Please go on.

VERE. I sent at once for Budd. I ordered the Master-at-Arms to be present at this interview, to make his accusation to Budd's face.

RAT. May I ask what was the prisoner's reaction on being confronted by the Master-at-Arms?

VERE. I perceived no sign of uneasiness in his demeanor. I believe he smiled.

RAT. And for the Master-at-Arms?

VERE. When I directed him to repeat his accusation, he faced Budd and did so.

WY. Did Budd reply?

VERE. He tried to speak, but could not frame his words.

SEY. And then, sir?

VERE. He answered with blows, and his accuser fell. . . . It was apparent at once that the attack was fatal, but I summoned the Surgeon to verify the fact. (*Turns away.*)

SEY. (*to* BILLY). You have heard Captain Vere's account. Is it, or is it not, as he says?

BILL. Captain Vere tells the truth. It is just as Captain Vere says, but it is not as the Master-at-Arms said. I have eaten the King's bread, and I am true to the King.

VERE. I believe you, boy.

BILL. God knows . . . I . . . thank you, sir.

SEY. Was there any malice between you and the Master-at-Arms?

BILL. I bore no malice against the Master-at-Arms. I'm sorry he is dead. I did not mean to kill him. If I'd found my tongue, I would not have struck him. But he lied foully to my face, and I . . . had to say . . . something . . . and I could only say it . . . with a blow. God help me.

SEY. One question more—you tell us that what the Master-at-Arms said against you was a lie. Now, why should he have lied with such obvious malice, when you have declared that there was no malice between you? (BILLY *looks appealingly at* VERE.) Did you hear my question?

BILL. I . . . I . . .

VERE. The question you put to him comes naturally enough. But can he rightly answer it? Or anyone else, unless, indeed, it be he who lies within there. (*Knock and enter immediately* HALLAM.)

HAL. The mainmast man, sir.

SEY. Send him in. (HALLAM *nods off and the* DANSKER *enters.* HALLAM *withdraws, closing door.*) State your name and station.

DANS. I have no name. I'm called the Dansker, that's all I know. Mainmast man.

SEY. You have been summoned in secrecy to appear as a witness before this court, of which I am Senior Member. I may not at this time disclose to you the nature of the offense being tried. However, the offender is William Budd, foretopman. (*Pause.*) Do you consent to give this court your testimony, though ignorant of the case at trial, and further, to keep in strictest confidence all that passes here?

DANS. Aye.

SEY. (*pushes forward a Bible*). Do you so swear?

DANS. (*touching the Bible*). I do.

SEY. Then this is my question. In your opinion, is there malice between Budd and the Master-at-Arms?

DANS. Aye.

VERE (*wheeling around*). How!

SEY. Explain your statement.

DANS. How should he not have hated him?

SEY. Be plain, man. We do not deal in riddles here.

DANS. Master-at-Arms bore malice towards a grace he could not have. There was no reason for it.

RAT. In other words, this malice was one-sided?

DANS. Aye.

RAT. And you cannot explain how it arose?

DANS. Master-at-Arms hated Billy . . .

SEY. One moment. I notice that you have been using the past tense in your testimony. Why?

DANS. I look around and sense finality here.

WY. You cannot explain further the cause of Claggart's hate for Budd?

DANS. Master-at-Arms made his world in his own image. Pride was his demon, and he kept it strong by others' fear of him. Billy could not imagine such a nature, saw nothing but a lonely man, strange, but a man still, nothing to be feared. So Claggart, lest his world be proven false, planned Billy's death. The final reason is beyond my thinking.

VERE. Aye, that is thoughtfully put. There is a mystery in iniquity. But it seems to me, Seymour, that the point we seek here is hardly material.

SEY. Aye, sir. Very well, you may go.

DANS. One thing more. Since this Master-at-Arms first came on board from God knows where, I have seen his shadow lengthen along the deck, and being under it, I was afraid. Whatever happened here, I am in part to blame—more than this lad. (*To* BILLY.) I am an old man, Billy. You—try to—forgive me.   (*Exits.*)

SEY. Have you any further questions to put to the accused?

RAT. No.

WY. None.

SEY. William Budd, if you have anything further to say for yourself, say it now.

BILL. (*after glance at* VERE). I have said all, sir.

SEY. Sentry. (*Enter* HALLAM.) Remove the prisoner to the after compartment. (HALLAM *and* BILLY *exit. A long pause.*) Have you anything to say, Ratcliffe?

RAT. Yes, sir. Claggart was killed because Budd couldn't speak. In that sense, that he stammers, he's a cripple. You don't hang a man for that, for speaking the only way he could.

WY. If you condemn him, it's the same thing as condoning the apparent lie the Master-at-Arms clearly told. I'd have struck him, too. The boy is clearly innocent, struck him in self-defense.

RAT. Aye. I'm ready to acquit him now.

SEY. Good. Then we can reach a verdict at once.

VERE. Hitherto I have been a witness at this trial, no more. And I hesitate to interfere, except that at this clear crisis you ignore one fact we cannot close our eyes to.

SEY. With your pardon, sir, as Senior Member of this court, I must ask if you speak now as our commanding officer or as a private man.

VERE. As convening authority, Seymour. I summoned this court, and I must review its findings and approve them before passing them on to the Admiralty.

SEY. Aye, sir, that is your right.

VERE. No right. Which of us here has rights? It is my duty, and I must perform it. Budd has killed a man—his superior officer.

SEY. We have found a verdict, sir.

VERE. I know that, Seymour. Your verdict sets him free, and so would I wish to do. But are we free to choose as we would do if we were private citizens? The Admiralty has its code. Do you suppose it cares who Budd is? Who you and I are?

SEY. We don't forget that, sir. But surely Claggart's tales were simply lies. We've established that.

VERE. Aye. But the Nore and Spithead were brute facts, and must not come again. The men were starved out before, but if they should think we are afraid . . .

RAT. Captain, how could they? They certainly know Budd is no mutineer.

WY. Of course not. Since he came on board, he's done more to keep the crew in hand than any of us.

SEY. That's true. The men took naturally to him.

VERE. As officers we are concerned to keep this ship effective as a weapon. And the law says what we must do in such a case as this. Come now, you know the facts, and the Mutiny Act's provisions. At sea, in time of war, an impressed man strikes his superior officer, and the blow is fatal. The mere blow alone would hang him, at least according to the Act. Well then, the men on board know that as well as you and I. And we acquit him. They have sense, they know the proper penalty to follow, and yet it does not follow.

SEY. But they know Budd, sir, and Claggart too, I daresay. Would they not applaud the decision that frees Budd? They would thank us.

WY. String him to a yard, and they'll turn round and rescue him, and string us up instead!

RAT. Aye, that's a point. It's twice as dangerous to hang the boy as it would be to let him go. If there's a mutinous temper in the crew, condemning Budd would surely set it off.

VERE. That is possible. Whatever step we take, the risk is great; but it is ours. That is what makes us officers. Yet if in fear of what our office demands we shirk our duty, we only play at war, at being men. If by our lawful rigor mutiny comes, there is no blame for us. But if in fear, miscalled a kind of mercy, we pardon Budd against specific order, and then the crew revolts, how culpable and weak our verdict would appear! The men on board know what our case is, how we are haunted by the Spithead risings. Have they forgotten how the panic spread through England? No. Your clemency would be accounted fear, and they would say we flinch from practising a lawful rigor lest new outbreaks be provoked. What a shame to us! And what a deadly blow to discipline!

RAT. I concede that, sir. But this case is exceptional, and pity, if we are men, is bound to move us, Captain.

VERE. So am I moved. Yet we cannot have warm hearts betraying heads that should be cool. In such a case ashore, an upright judge does not allow the pleading tears of women to touch his nature. Here at sea, the heart, the female in a man, weeps like a woman. She must be ruled out, hard though it be. (*Pause.*) Still silent? Very well, I see that something in all your downcast faces seems to urge that not alone the heart moves hesitancy. Conscience, perhaps. The private conscience moves you.

WY. Aye, that's it, sir. How can we condemn this man and live at peace again within ourselves? We have our standards; ethics, if you like.

VERE. Challenge your scruples! They move as in a dusk. Come, do they import something like this: if we are bound to judge, regardless of palliating circumstances, the death of Claggart as the prisoner's deed, then does that deed appear a capital crime whereof the penalty is mortal? But can we adjudge to summary and shameful death a fellow creature innocent before God, and whom we feel to be so? Does that state the case rightly?

SEY. That is my feeling, sir.

VERE. You all feel, I am sure, that the boy in effect is innocent; that what he did was from an unhappy stricture of speech that made him speak with blows. And I believe that, too; believe as you do, that he struck his man down, tempted beyond endurance. Acquit him, then, you say, as innocent?

RAT. Exactly! Oh, I know the Articles prescribe death for what Budd has done, but that . . .

WY. Oh, stow the Articles! They don't account for such a case as this. You yourself say Budd is innocent.

VERE. In intent, Wyatt, in intent.

WY. Does that count for nothing? His whole attitude, his motive, count for nothing? If his intent . . .

VERE. The intent or non-intent of Budd is nothing to the purpose. In a court more merciful than martial it would extenuate, and shall, at the last Assizes, set him free. But here we have these alternatives only: condemn or let go.

SEY. But it seems to me we've got to consider the problem as a moral one, sir, despite the fact that we're not moralists. When Claggart told you his lie, the case immediately went beyond the scope of military justice.

VERE. I, too, feel that. But do these gold stripes across our arms attest that our allegiance is to Nature?

RAT. To our country, sir.

VERE. Aye, Ratcliffe; to the King. And though the sea, which is inviolate Nature primeval, though it be the element whereon we move and have our being as sailors, is our official duty hence to Nature? No. So little is that true that we resign our freedom when we put this on. And when war is declared, are we, the fighters commissioned to destroy, consulted first?

WY. Does that deny us the right to act like men? We're not trying a murderer, a dockside cut-throat!

VERE. The gold we wear shows that we serve the King, the Law. What does it matter that our acts are fatal to our manhood, if we serve as we are forced to serve? What bitter salt leagues move between our code and God's own judgments! We are conscripts, every one, upright in this uniform of flesh. There is no truce to war born in the womb. We fight at command.

WY. All I know is that I can't sit by and see Budd hanged!

VERE. I say we fight by order, by command of our superiors. And if our judgments approve the war, it is only coincidence. And so it is with all our acts. So now, would it be so much we ourselves who speak as judges here, as it would be martial law operating through us? For that law, and for its rigor, we are not responsible. Our duty lies in this: that we are servants only.

RAT. The Admiralty doesn't want service like that. What good would it do? Who'd profit by Budd's death?

WY. You want to make us murderers!

SEY. Wyatt! Control yourself!

VERE. What is this vessel that you serve in, Wyatt, an ark of peace? Go count her guns; then tell your conscience to lie quiet, if you can.

RAT. But that is war. This would be downright killing!

SEY. It's all war, Ratcliffe; war to the death, for all of us.

VERE. You see that, Seymour? That this war began before our time?

SEY. And will end long after it.

VERE. Here we have the Mutiny Act for justice. No child can own a closer tie to parent than can that Act to what it stems from: War. This is a wartime cruise and in this ship are Englishmen who fight against their wills, perhaps against their conscience, 'pressed by war into the service of the King. Though we as fellow creatures understand their lot, what does it matter to the officer, or to the enemy? The French will cut down conscripts in the same swath with volunteers, and we will do as much for them. War has no business with anything but surfaces. War's child, the Mutiny Act, is featured like the father.

RAT. Couldn't we mitigate the penalty if we convict him?

VERE. No, Ratcliffe. The penalty is prescribed.

RAT. I'd like to think it over, Captain. I'm not sure.

VERE. I repeat, then, that while we ponder and you hesitate over anxieties I confess to sharing, the enemy comes nearer. We must act, and quickly. The French close in on us; the crew will find out shortly what has happened. Our consciences are private matters, Ratcliffe. But we are public men, controlling life and death within this world at sea. Tell me whether or not in our positions we dare let our consciences take precedence of the code that makes us officers and calls this case to trial.

RAT. (*after a pause; quietly*). No, sir.

WY. Can you stand Budd's murder on your conscience?

SEY. Wyatt! Hold your tongue!

WY. (*jumping up*). I say let him go!

SEY. Sit down, sir!

VERE. Let him speak.

WY. I won't bear a hand to hang a man I know is innocent! My blood's not cold enough. I can't give the kind of judgment you want to force on us! I ask to be excused from sitting upon this court.

SEY. Do you know what you're saying? Sit down and hold your tongue, man!

VERE. The kind of judgment I ask of you is only this, Wyatt: that you recognize your function in this ship. I believe you know it quite as well as we, yet you rebel. Can't you see that you must first strip off the uniform you wear, and after that your flesh, before you can escape the case at issue here? Decide you must, Wyatt. Oh, you may be excused and wash your hands of it, but someone must decide. We are the law; law orders us to act, and shows us how. Do you imagine Seymour, or Ratcliffe here, or I, would not save this boy if we could see a way consistent with our duties? Acquit Budd if you can. God knows I wish I could. If in your mind as well as in your heart, you can say freely that his life is not forfeit to the law we serve, reason with us! Show us how to save him without putting aside our function. Or if you can't do that, teach us to put by our responsibility and not betray ourselves. Can you do this? Speak, man, speak! Show us how! Save him, Wyatt, and you save us all. (WYATT *slowly sits down.*) You recognize the logic of the choice I force upon you. But do not think me pitiless in thus demanding sentence on a luckless boy. I feel as you do for him. But even more, I think there is a grace of soul within him that shall forgive the law we bind him with, and pity us, stretched on the cross of choice. (*Turns away.*)

SEY. Well, gentlemen. Will you decide. (*Officers write their verdicts on paper before them, and hand them to* SEYMOUR, *who rises, draws his dirk and places it on the table, pointing forward.*) He is condemned, sir. Shall we appoint the dawn?

Scene Two

CAPTAIN VERE's *cabin, 0400. Ship's bell strikes offstage.* VERE *sitting alone at his desk. Knock at the door.*

VERE. Come in. (*Enter* SEYMOUR.) Oh, it's Seymour.

SEY. It's eight bells, Captain.

VERE. What's the hour of sunrise?

SEY. Four fifty-two, sir.

VERE. Eight bells. And one bell at four-thirty. Odd and even numbers caught between two hands. Budd shall not live to head the odd made even or wrong made right.—Call all hands to quarters at four-thirty.

SEY. Aye aye, Captain. (*Turns irresolutely.*)

VERE. The wind has slackened, I think. How is the glass?

SEY. It's risen slightly. Sea has flattened out.

VERE. Fair weather after foul . . . it's all nature, nature and law. How exigent are these Mediterranean climates of the heart, and temperate zones of mind!

SEY. Have you been here all night, sir?

VERE. All night, Seymour . . . all my life moving between dark and dark. It has been a long night, but day will be quick and deadly on the mainyard. D'you think, Seymour, a man can forgive a wrong done of the heart's own election?

SEY. Most people are decent enough. You can forgive them trespasses.

VERE. No, by God. There's wickedness alive. It's dead now in one man, but it's alive to feel and smell at night. . . Seymour, go below. Get Budd and bring him here.

SEY. But Captain . . .

VERE. Do as you're told. Get Budd and bring him here. (SEYMOUR *exits.* VERE *sits motionless for a few moments, then rises and goes to the cabin door.*) Sentry.

HAL. Yes, sir?

VERE. Who has the deck this watch?

HAL. Mister Ratcliffe, Captain.

VERE. Very well. (*Pause.*) Sentry!

HAL. Sir?

VERE. When Mister Seymour has returned, admit him right away.

HAL. Aye aye, Captain.

VERE. The wind's still sharp. You must be cold there, Hallam. Go to the leeward side. I'll be responsible.

HAL. Thank you, sir. This is the coldest hour now, just before sunrise.

VERE (*closes door, returns slowly to his desk*). The lamp holds steady when the vessel heels. Does the law hang straight in crooked lives? It burns, and shapes nothing but shadows here, plumb in the twisting cabin of the mind. (*Footsteps, voices.* VERE *turns to door. Enter* SEYMOUR, BILLY, *and* HALLAM.) Take off the manacles. (HALLAM *frees* BILLY.)

SEY. (*to* HALLAM). Outside, man. Bear a hand. (*Exits with* HALLAM.)

VERE. Sit down. No, it's better that I stand.

BILL. I was thinking, locked up below there . . . the Captain knows the rights of this. He'll save me if it's right. Then you sent for me. Is there hope for me, Captain?

VERE. Billy, what hope is there?

BILL. Tell me why. I only want to understand.

VERE. How young you still are, Billy! Oh, I can tell you this: nothing is lost of anything that happens. I have given you the judgment of the world . . . deadly constraint . . . a length of hemp and a yardarm. I have done this to you, no one else.

BILL. I can't get the rights of all that's happened.

VERE. There's not much right, Billy. Only necessity. You and Claggart broke man's compromise with good and evil, and both of you must pay the penalty.

BILL. Penalty? What for? Would anyone make laws just to be broken by fellows like me?

VERE. Aye, boy. You have learned this late. Most of us find out early and trim to a middle course.

BILL. Do you mean . . . it's better to be like that?

VERE. Better as this world goes. When a man is born, he takes a guilt upon him, I can't say how or why. And life takes its revenge on those who hurt its pride with innocence.

BILL. Do you think Claggart knew it would come to this?

VERE. He knew he would kill you, and he died to gain that end. But if you trust me, he'll not win entirely.

BILL. How could he hate me like that?

VERE. The world we breathe is love and hatred both, but hatred must not win the victory.

BILL. Claggart is dead. Now I'm to hang. Doesn't that show the law is wrong, when it can't choose between him and me?

VERE. Yes, it's all wrong, all wrong.

BILL. I don't know, Captain. I never was a hand to wonder about things, but now I think that maybe there's a kind of cruelty in people that's just as much a part of them as kindness, say, or honesty, or m-m-m . . . I can't find words, I guess, Captain.

VERE. There are no words. We are all prisoners of deadly forms that are made to break us to their measure. Nothing has power to over-come them, except forgiveness . . . Can you forgive what I have done?

BILL. I *can* trust you, can't I? *Can* you show me it's all right, my being . . .

VERE (*turns away; a long pause*). It's nearly dawn, lad. In the Spanish villages they're lighting fires.

BILL. I'm not afraid, sir. (*Steps toward* VERE.) It's getting light.

VERE. There's no time for either of us left. Go, take the morning. God knows you have the right to it. And when you are on the main-yard, think of me, and pray for those who must make choices. Hallam. (*Enter* HALLAM *in doorway*.) Take Budd into your charge. (BILLY *and* HALLAM *go out*.) Time has run out.

Scene Three

Main deck aft. Drum-to-formation. Crew forming up. WYATT, *Midship-men* GARDINER *and* REA.

WY. Bear a hand. Form the men up in ranks.

GARD. Aye, sir. All right, you! Close ranks! Move up, Stoll. That's better. Talbot, square your hat. Form up straight there, damn it! (*Drum. Men come to attention.*)

WY. Division commanders report!

VOICE (*off*). Carpenters and gunners, present or accounted for, sir!

VOICE (*off*). Marine Detachment, present or accounted for, sir!

VOICE (*off*). Afterguard, present or accounted for, sir!

GARD. Fore, main and mizzentopmen . . . one absentee!

WY. All hands will stand by to witness punishment! Stand easy.

VOICES (*off*). Stand easy! (WYATT *walks away from men. Murmur in ranks.*)

KIN. Where the devil is Billy? He wasn't in his hammock when they piped us up.

O'DAN. He'll be getting himself in trouble if he don't fall in.

KIN. Who the hell they punishing, and what for?

JEN. It's got to be flogging, or they wouldn't have us all up here.

KIN. Vere never flogs anybody. And there ain't no gratings up.

DANS. They flog men at noon. The early morning's for hanging.

KIN. Hanging! (*The word travels back.*) Who? What for?

O'DAN. The skipper, he don't confide in me no more.

KIN. I thought they waited till they got ashore before they hanged a man.

DANS. Not in wartime.

JEN. He goes up them ratlines, out on the yard, they slips a noose around his neck, and then he jumps and hangs himself.

O'DAN. They'd have the devil's work getting O'Daniel to jump.

KIN. It's jump, or get pushed.

JEN. Where's Claggart? God, you don't suppose it's Claggart! Oh, Judas, let it be that fishblooded nark!

KIN. Not him. He's too smart, he is.

JEN. Where is he, then? He ain't here.

DANS. He is here.

KIN. Where? I don't see him.

DANS. He is here.

KIN. Ah . . . you're balmy, old man.

(*Enter* VERE, SEYMOUR, RATCLIFFE *and the* SURGEON. *Drum sounds Attention.*)

WY. (*to* SEYMOUR). Ship's company present to witness execution, sir.

SEY. Very well. (*To* VERE.) Ship's company present to witness execution, sir. (VERE *nods*.)

SEY. (*to* WYATT). Lieutenant Wyatt, have the prisoner brought forward.

WY. Aye, aye, sir. (*Marches to wing*.) Sentries, bring forward the prisoner. (*Marches back to his post*.)

(*Enter* BILLY *with two sentries. Astonished murmur through the crew, who momentarily break ranks*.)

WY. No talking in ranks! (*Continued restless movement and murmurings*.) Form up!

GARD. You men are at attention!

WY. (*over subdued muttering*). You hear me? Silence in ranks!

(*Silence. Sentries lead* BILLY *to the foot of the ropes.* SEYMOUR *looks at* VERE, *who nods.* SEYMOUR *steps forward and reads*.)

SEY. Proceedings of the court-martial held aboard *H.M.S. Indomitable* on the eighth August, 1798. Convened under the authority of Edward Fairfax Vere, Senior Captain, Royal Navy, and composed of the First Officer, the Sailing Master, and the First Lieutenant of said vessel. In the case of William Budd, foretopman, Royal Navy. While attached and so serving in the aforesaid vessel, he did, on the eighth day of August, 1798, strike and kill his superior officer, one John Claggart, Master-at-Arms, Royal Navy.

(*Crew breaks out uneasily, astonished, talking excitedly*.)

JEN. Billy! Did you, boy?

VOICE. Good lad! *All*

VOICE. Serves him proper! *together*

KIN. Hi, Billy! Hurrah!

WY. Quiet! Silence, you men! Form up!

GARD. Stand at attention, hang you! Silence in the ranks!

WY. Do you hear? (*Excited muttering, low voices*.)

SEY. You will be silent and remain at strict attention until dismissed. (*Silence*.) . . . Master-at-Arms, Royal Navy. Therefore, the court sentences the aforementioned William Budd, foretopman, Royal Navy, to die by hanging on the first watch of the day following these proceedings. By authority of his Gracious Majesty George Rex and Alan Napier, Viscount Kelsey, First Sea Lord. Signed, Philip Seymour, Senior Member.

(*During the last phrases of the reading, the crew, upon hearing the sentence, breaks out again, some stepping forward, shouting; they are in an ugly temper.*)

VOICES. No he don't!
   Not if I know it!
   Hang the jemmies instead, I say!
   You ain't hanging Billy,   *All*
   Not Billy, you bloody swineheads!   *together*
   Not him, by Christ! damn your eyes!
   Let them dance on a rope's end!

WY. Stand back! Sentries, guard your prisoner, if you have to fire!

GARD. Stand back, you damned clods! Keep back!

SEY. (*steps forward*). Silence there! You will resume discipline instantly! Be warned. (*Waits a silent moment. Men stop in disordered formation.*) Stand back into ranks.

GARD. Form up again, quick about it now! (*There is a surly movement into irregular lines.*)

SEY. (*warily resuming procedure*). Prisoner, have you anything to say? (BILLY *shakes his head.*) If you have nothing to say, when the drum roll is sounded, you will proceed to carry out the sentence of this court. (*Signals to* WYATT.)

WY. Sound off!

(*Drum roll.* BILLY *turns and starts up the ropes.*)

VOICES. Get him! Now!
   Bill! Stay where you are, boy, don't do it!
   Wait, Billy! Wait!   *All*
   Rush the deck, mates! Don't let them do it! *together*
   We're here, Bill, don't you worry!

BILL. (*stops, turns forward, looks at* VERE, *and shouts out loud and clear, without trace of stammer*). God bless Captain Vere!

(*A second's pause;* VERE *is profoundly shaken;* BILLY *goes quickly up the ropes and out of sight. The crew moves back a step, is silent; officers and men in deep breathless quiet watch him out of sight and are staring overhead as the curtain falls.*)

Christopher Fry

► The London Mercury Theatre production of Christopher Fry's *A Phoenix Too Frequent* in 1946, followed by John Gielgud's production of *The Lady's Not for Burning* in 1949, brought to wide public attention a new and different dramatic talent. Nothing quite like it had been seen on the contemporary English stage. Ever since Ibsen and the "moderns" of his generation exploded the social problem play on the London stage of the 1890's, British drama had been generally solemn, occupied with expounding theses and exposing social evils. The theatre was a place for exhibiting slices of life in natural speech and for compelling the audience to consider the evils and maladjustments that existed around them. Without question new life and vitality were brought into the theatre by this realistic and didactic form of drama.

But drama of this type loses some of its force after a half-century of steady cultivation. English drama actually had reached its classic heights in quite a different tradition—that developed by Shakespeare and the Elizabethans. In this earlier tradition language shared interest with character and action, and the language took the form of poetry. It was accepted as fitting and proper that the poet should supply his naturally less articulate characters with diction ideally appropriate to their situation. Hamlet was expected to soliloquize in immortal poetry, just as

Juliet was expected to find incomparable phrases to express her ecstasy and her anguish.

This extended dimension of the stage is sacrificed for other values when the author aims to reproduce the speech of the street or the drawing room. As a result of the influence of Ibsen and his followers, the public had almost lost its ear for poetic diction on the stage. Dramatists, likewise, seemed to have lost the knack of combining poetry, action, and wit into good theatre.

Fry had this gift, Gielgud knew how to stage and interpret it, and the public responded. Critics welcomed "back into the theatre all the wealth of our literary heritage," and hailed Fry for releasing the theatre from its doldrums. In *The Lady's Not for Burning* they saw an exuberant and sustained flight of fancy about witchcraft in the early 15th century. It was bright and witty instead of solemn and tragic, and it was sprinkled with glittering passages of language:

> "For instance, Helen comes,
> Brushing the maggots from her eyes,
> And, clearing her throat of several thousand years,
> She says 'I loved . . .'; but cannot any longer
> Remember names. Sad Helen. Or Alexander, wearing
> His imperial cobwebs and breastplate of shining worms
> Wakens and looks for his glasses, to find the empire
> Which he knows he put beside his bed."

And the more delicate notes, as in Thomas's speech near the end of the play:

> "I've been cast adrift on a raft of melancholy.
> The night-wind passed me, like a sail across
> A blind man's eye. There it is,
> The interminable tumbling of the great grey
> Main of moonlight, washing over
> The little oyster-shell of this month of April . . ."

Fry was born in Bristol in 1907 and was educated at Bedford Modern School. He alternated in his earlier years between tutoring and schoolteaching and working in the theatre. He acted at Bath, he directed the Tunbridge Wells Repertory Players from 1934 to 1935, and he became director of the Oxford Playhouse in 1940.

During this period Fry was cultivating that talent which flowered after the war in a brilliant series of plays. He composed the lyrics and music for *She Shall Have Music,* produced in London at the Saville Theatre in 1935. He wrote a play in verse called *Siege* in 1937, which he did not produce or publish. He followed this with an experimental play called *The Boy with the Cart,* which received many amateur performances, and was published in 1939. He wrote *Thursday's Child* and *The Tower* as pageants, the latter for the Tewkesbury Festival; and *The Firstborn* which was broadcast over B.B.C. in 1947 and performed at the Edinburgh Festival in 1948. His *Thor, with Angels* was the Canterbury play for 1948, and his *A Sleep of Prisoners* was written for the Festival of Britain.

These were regarded as occasional pieces. But *The Lady's Not for Burning* was full-dress drama in the great tradition. It led Sir Laurence Olivier to commission Fry to do *Venus Observed,* which was ready in 1949. (It was first performed in New York on February 13, 1952.) Done in the same expansive spirit and style as *The Lady's Not for Burning,* it too was received with delight, though some critics felt that its poetry was too often self-conscious or self-imitative, and that its wit was too often labored or mere word hunting ("all I saw/Was the tip of a fin, which might have been finnan haddy"). These criticisms were minor tones in the wide chorus of praise for the eloquence and the inventiveness of a gifted writer.

Venus Observed has a diverting plot which serves adequately as a frame for the dramatic development in the comic spirit. It has clear and engaging characters and character development, well contrasted and well realized. The middle-aged Duke, not an unfamiliar figure in English plays and novels, is gay, worldly, and smoothly philosophical among his old loves and in urbane rivalry with his son for Perpetua. Fry gives him dexterously composed lines, colored with imagery and decorated with fancy, and they are unflagging in their zest. The All-Hallows Eve speech is a good example.

Fry lavishes still more insight and delicate eloquence on Perpetua, allowing her the pure music of words in the "lemon, amber, umber" passage, the tour-de-force of the endless sentence ("There isn't any reason why a sentence . . ."), and fragile insights set over against the casuistry of the Duke:

"Why are you so sure
That I must love you? The field is wide,
And everyone's heart is a great eccentric;
Its whole distinction is a madness."

Fry's work as a whole, and this play in particular, has indeed given language back to the theatre—in an age which had almost forgotten the sensuous pleasure of poetic diction and its intensifying of dramatic values.

VENUS
OBSERVED

Characters

THE DUKE OF ALTAIR
EDGAR, *his son*
HERBERT REEDBECK, *his agent*
DOMINIC, *Reedbeck's son*
ROSABEL FLEMING
JESSIE DILL
CAPTAIN FOX REDDLEMAN, *the Duke's butler*
BATES, *the Duke's footman*
HILDA TAYLOR-SNELL
PERPETUA, *Reedbeck's daughter*

Scenes

The Observatory Room at Stellmere Park, the Duke's mansion

The Temple of the Ancient Virtues, Stellmere Park

ACT ONE

*A room at the top of a mansion: once a bedroom, now an observatory.
When the curtain rises the* DUKE OF ALTAIR *is in argument with his
son* EDGAR. *Also present is* HERBERT REEDBECK, *the* DUKE'S *agent*

DUKE. Anyone would think I had made some extraordinary
Suggestion. But in fact how natural it is.
Aren't you my son?

ED. Yes, father, of course I am.

DUKE. Then it's up to you to choose who shall be your mother.
Does that seem to you improper, Reedbeck?

REED. No,
Your Grace; it's not, perhaps, always done,
But few parents consider their children as you do.
I don't dislike the plan at all.

ED. I sweat
With embarrassment.

DUKE. You have been
Too much with the horses. This, that I ask you to do,
Is an act of poetry, and a compliment
To the freshness of your mind. Why should you sweat?
Here they will be, three handsome women,
All of them at some time implicated
In the joyous routine of my life. (I could scarcely
Put it more delicately.) I wish to marry.
Who am I, in heaven's name, to decide
Which were my vintage years of love?
Good God, to differentiate between
The first bright blow on my sleeping flesh,
The big breasts of mid-morning,
And the high old dance of afternoon—
Value one against the other? Never, not I,
Till the eschatological rain shall lay my dust.
But you, dear boy, with your twenty-five impartial years,
Can perform the judgement of Paris,
Can savour, consider, and award the apple

With a cool hand. You will find an apple
Over there by the spectroscope.

ED.   But why must you marry?
Or, if that's an impertinence, why do I have to have
A mother? I've been able to grow to a sizable boy
Without one.

DUKE.   Why? Because I see no end
To the parcelling out of heaven in small beauties,
Year after year, flocks of girls, who look
So lately kissed by God
They come out on the world with lips shining,
Flocks and generations, until time
Seems like nothing so much
As a blinding snowstorm of virginity,
And a man, lost in the perpetual scurry of white,
Can only close his eyes
In a resignation of monogamy.

ED. Anyway, it would be an impossibly hasty
Judgement. Honour you as I may, I don't
See how I can do it.

DUKE.   If Paris had no trouble
Choosing between the tide-turning beauty,
Imponderable and sexed with eternity,
Of Aphrodite, Hera, and Athene,
Aren't you ashamed to make heavy weather of a choice
Between Hilda, and Rosabel, and Jessie?
And if you can't make up your mind about a woman
At first meeting, all hope of definition has gone;
Prejudice, delirium, or rage
Will cock their snooks, and the apple will go bad.
No, boy, no; go and water your horses
And come back and choose your mother.

ED.   At what time?

DUKE. What is it now?

REED.   Five past eleven.

DUKE.   They should
Be here. At eleven twenty-nine we're to have
The total eclipse of the sun, to which I've invited them.
The mouth of the moon has already begun to munch.
We shall all feel ourselves making a north-west passage
Through the sea of heaven, and darkness will cover
The face of the earth. In that moment
All women will be as one.

ED.   That's what I was going
To ask you. I don't want to play the heavy son,
But would you say you loved these women equally?

DUKE. Equality is a mortuary word. Just choose.
Shall I be happy on Tuesdays, Thursdays, and Saturdays,
Or on Mondays, Wednesdays, and Fridays? Some such difference
Is all that your choice involves.

(*Enter* CAPTAIN FOX REDDLEMAN, *a manservant. He looks like, and was
once, a lion tamer.*)

REDDLE.   'Scuse, your Grace:
But a telegram for our little friend Mr. Reedbeck.
A telegram, Mr. Reedbeck. B'Jason, four
Flights I've had to come up to bring it to you.
Please Jenny it's worth it. And the boy's waiting.

ED. Well, father, I don't know; with a certain sense
Of preconceiving myself, I may come back.
I shall do what I can for you; I only hope
You'll not live to regret the way my fancy
Takes you.   (*Exit* EDGAR.)

REED.   Oh! Would you ever think
Such a joy could happen to me, in the world as we know it?

REDDLE. I have to tell your Grace, in all decency
To the footman Bates, who I religiously despise,
If the fellow comes on duty with a bloody nose
'Tis my doing, and long may it bleed. And h'wot
About the boy below, Mr. Reedbeck? Any answer?

REED. No, no, Reddleman, only thanksgiving.
Oh, and I suppose a shilling, he'd like a shilling.

DUKE. And go gently with Bates, Reddleman, or else
    You'll drive him back to his old nervous habits
    Of biting his nails and burglary. Remember
    You're not a lion tamer now.

REDDLE.   And that
    Was a hit below—I'm wearing no belt—below
    The navel. Thank God I'm severed from my mother
    Or she would have felt it severely. I'd remind you
    'Twas fighting for king and country I lost me nerve,
    And b'Daniel, it's a sad job to be parted
    From the lords of the jungle.

DUKE.   I'm sorry, Reddleman;
    I wasn't meaning to hurt you.

REDDLE.   Well, go easy,
    Go easy with me, your Grace. Now, Mr. Reedbeck:
    Thanksgiving and a bob for the boy below:
    Very good.   (*Exit* REDDLEMAN.)

REED. A red-letter day for me, your Grace;
    Let me see: the twenty-ninth of October?

DUKE.   Yes;
    The leaves transfigured by the thought of death,
    The wind south-west, a blue sky buffaloed
    By cloud, the sun approaching its eclipse.

REED. You remember I have a daughter? I've spoken of her
    From time to time; I had the astounding fortune
    To beget her, as though I'd been chosen to release
    A rose from the world's rock; and then I had
    The misery to lose her, when her mother
    Left me for America, ten years ago.
    Well, now I'm holding in my hand a message
    Which says she's returning to me, returning today,
    No time of arrival, just bare and astonishing
    "Am in England hope to kiss you before lunch
    Perpetua." I can hardly believe it could happen,
    I can't believe so, not in the world as we know it.

DUKE. Go easy, Reedbeck, go easy with yourself.

REED. If she should come in time for the eclipse—

DUKE. Then, of course, she shall join us to see the eclipse.
It will be a change for her after America.
I'm going now, to dress. Subdue yourself, Reedbeck.
Otherwise you'll capsize in disappointment.
Expect the worst.   (*Exit the* DUKE.)

REED.   Not at all, oh, no, not at all,
No shadows of that sort. (*He hums to the telephone.*)
                                   Must warn my housekeeper.
"I galloped, Dirck galloped, we galloped all three . . ."
Oh, Mrs. Lendy, Mr. Reedbeck here; I have to ask you
To prepare a room for my daughter. I'm so glad
To hear you gasp. However, we must keep our heads,
Such as they are. Tell her to join us here
And ask to be shown to the Observatory Room.
There will be refreshment for her, and a total
Eclipse of the sun.

(*Enter* DOMINIC, REEDBECK's *son.*)

DOM.   I want to speak to you.
How long are we likely to be alone?

REED.   In a moment,
Dominic dear. You'll put her some flowers, Mrs. Lendy.
Are the Helianthus gone? Well, *uliginosum*.
You call them chrysanthemums, I think. And on her bed
The lilac linen sheets. Some time before lunch.
Good-bye. Oh, Dominic, my dear, dear boy,
Your sister's coming home!

DOM. (*silent, and then*).   That makes you happy.

REED. Oh, dear, it's one of your knock-the-bottom-
Out-of-everything mornings. Or do you mean
You've heard, and you know what's bringing her home?
I hope nothing's amiss?

DOM.   Not with her.

REED.   Well, then—

DOM. Do I say what I have to say *here*? Or do we go back
To the house? It isn't going to be pleasant.

REED. Of course it is.
There's nothing unpleasant that isn't going to be pleasant.
Perpetua's returning to me; the world
Is no longer depressed at the poles, and everything
Will be pleasant: the east wind, smoking fires,
Revolution, debility—

DOM. Jail?

REED. Yes, jail,
Solitary confinement, the cat-o'-nine-tails,
Your Aunt Florence—

DOM. Can you keep your feet
On sober earth for five difficult minutes
And talk responsibly? Why are we so rich?
I've asked you before; but you, a Duke's bailiff,
An agent: where did our money come from?

REED. Have you no capacity for delight?
Do for all our sakes be pleasant, dear boy.

DOM. You said our money came from legacies, you told me
From legacies!

REED. Just so; we've been very fortunate.
Your Uncle Hector, when he put on immortality
In Tasmania, increased, to a certain extent,
Our freedom from care; and old Lady Bright, my first
Employer, when she passed on, passed on
Herself to heaven and the rest to me; and then—

DOM. I have to ask for figures. My Uncle Hector
Died, leaving—?

REED. Don't let's talk of death.
I've a heart this morning as light as a nebula.
But you, you sombre boy, you can't even
Sputter up a few sparks when I tell you
Your sister's coming home!

DOM. Died, leaving—?

REED. Really,
How can I be expected to remember?

There was some music, certainly; the piano score
Of *The Quaker Girl;* and I recollect some ninepins;
And a small South American lizard called Faithful
Which died in quarantine. But Lady Bright—

DOM. You've stolen the money, haven't you: steadily
And consistently? O God, why ask? I know
Already. And thieved with so little subtlety
Anyone might know. Raised rents
But entered in your books at the old figure;
Sale of produce and timber, at prices higher
Than you've recorded. I've been ferreting,
Ever since an unmistakable innuendo
From Bates the footman.

REED.   Come now; Bates
Is a common burglar, and sees, of course,
His reflection in all about him. He was caught
Red-handed with the silver, and his Grace,
Being short of staff at the time, asked him to stay
And clean it.

DOM.   Bates is quite a decent fellow.
I've had a long talk to him. He used to suffer
From a pathological lust for climbing ladders
And had to rationalize it when he got
To the top. And now he's determined to be honest,
Even if it makes him ill, he says. But with you
It's unrelieved, wicked cupidity.
Of course I go down from Cambridge. I couldn't stay there
When any morning I might wake up and find
I'd become the son of a convict. We're both in
For misery now, and Perpetua comes home
Just in time to share it.

REED.   I wish I could explain
How very mistaken I'm sure you must be. Especially
On such a cheerful morning. It's really too bad.
We have the dark every twelve hours as it is
Without inventing more.

(*Enter* BATES: *he shows a trace of rough handling. He announces* MISS
ROSABEL FLEMING, *and withdraws.*)

ROSA. I expected to find the Duke here.

REED.   The competitors!
I'd forgotten them. You'll forgive me, madam, I hope;
You find me a little disjunct. His Grace
Will join us shortly. My name is Reedbeck.
This was my son.

ROSA.   Was your son?

REED.   There's no
Other tense for me now except the past,
Miss Belmont. You were Miss Belmont?

ROSA.   Rosabel Fleming.
I am still Rosabel Fleming.

DOM.   Please excuse me.
I'd like to know you, but I can't look anyone
Happily in the eye. I'm pleased to have met you. (*Exit* DOMINIC.)

ROSA. Is he in trouble?

REED.   The paradoxes of virtue
Have confused him. Won't you sit down, Miss Fleming?

ROSA. I begin to understand why the theatre
Gives me so little work.
That could scarcely have been called a splendid entrance,
Even by the most loving.

REED.   Go down from Cambridge.
Did you hear him say that? No, you were not here.
It let all the life out of me for a moment.
All the Latin I have myself, you know,
Is horticultural: *muscari comosum*
Monstrosum, and *scrophularia nodosa,*
Et cetera ad infinitum. But how I longed
As a boy for the groves and grooves of Academe.
Give me civilization, Miss Fleming; you can keep
Your progress.

ROSA.   This room, surely, is something new?

REED. The Observatory Room, giving upon

An uninterrupted sweep of the Surrey heavens;
At night the weeping stars; by day—

(*Enter* MRS. JESSIE DILL.)

JESS.   I'm sorry.
I thought it would be just his Grace. I'll go again.

REED. No, no, his Grace will be here. By day
The brandishing sun inciting the earth
To revolution and rotation—

JESS.   I'm Mrs. Dill.
It's my own fault the man hasn't announced me.
It seemed to me "All those stairs, for the poor young chap
Just to say Here's Jessie." He went on insisting,
Of course, but when we got to the second landing
He must have thought it was getting a bit undignified
Both of us coming up two steps at a time,
So he slid back down the banisters.
Surely I've met you before, dear?

ROSA.   Rosabel Fleming.

JESS. I should have remembered. I saw you, once upon a time,
Being very sweet in a play about Ophelia.
And this is a strange thing, too, being up here
In this room together. You'd hardly recognize it.
Well, I don't know, I should say that's a telescope.

ROSA. I think I must go. I hadn't understood
The Duke would have visitors. . . .

REED.   We were just talking
About this room when you came, Mrs. Dill. My name
Is Reedbeck. This was one of his Grace's
Bedrooms, as perhaps. . . . But now, as you see,
He prefers to regard the skies here, scavenging
Through the night for knowledge. He also uses
The room for experiments.

JESS.   He always did.

ROSA. I've decided not to stay. I only came in
For a moment, finding myself not far away.
If you'd be kind enough to tell him—

(*Enter the* DUKE.)

DUKE.   Good morning, Rosabel.
    Good morning, Jessie.

JESS.   Here he is, himself.
    He's the same boy, God bless him, not a day older,
    Even if he does have to use a telescope.

DUKE. Flattery, Jessie; for years the frost has lain
    On my stubble beard. The swallows and other such
    Migratory birds have left me months ago.

JESS. You must build yourself a nice fire.

DUKE.   No, Jessie;
    I have to consider my years and decline with the sun,
    Gracefully but gratefully decline.
    I have also to apologize for keeping you waiting.
    I was up all night with the universe again
    And slept late. Or is that not to be
    Forgiven? A silence broods on Rosabel.

ROSA. I was conscious of it. I was wondering
    What note to sound. I'm suddenly very uncertain
    Why I'm here.

DUKE.   For a total eclipse of the sun.
    Didn't I mention it to you in my letter?

ROSA. Is there some tradition that old friends should meet again
    During an eclipse? Or what other reason? Your birthday?
    No, you're a Sagittarian. This is only October.

DUKE. And the leaves are falling. What shall a robin do then,
    Poor thing?

JESS.   Sit in this barn, and keep himself warm,
    And tuck himself up alone in the east wing,
    Poor thing.

(*Enter* EDGAR.)

DUKE.   My son Edgar, Miss Rosabel Fleming.
    I introduce Rosabel first, Jessie, to give you
    Time to enjoy your joke. My son Edgar,
    Mrs. Dill.

JESS.   How lovely it is to meet you.

I've known your father, you know, ever since
I was ever so slim. Though, of course, properly speaking,
It was my husband who was really his friend.
I hope your father will allow me to say
His friend.

DUKE.   I'm delighted to let you say it.
I didn't know he had ever been alive
Or we might have said it before.

ED.   It's just as well
We understand my father.

ROSA.   And it's just as well
We don't all have to. It's a thing I have no love for,
To have to go groping along the corridors
Of someone else's mind, so that I shan't
Be hurt. No one has any right to ask it.

DUKE. We're not, I hope, in this mellow October light
Getting ill at ease? We're here this morning to watch
The sun annulled and renewed, and to sit affectionately
Over the year's dilapidation. "Mellow"
Is the keynote of the hour. We must be mellow,
Remembering we've been on the earth two million years,
Man and boy and Sterkfontein ape.

REED. (*singing abstractedly at the window*).
                    "You call me old
                    But I am still
            A chippy young chap on Chipperton Hill
                    And shall be, while
                    My flesh can cover
            The bones of a bona-fide lover.
            Heydilly, heydilly, hang me a sheep."

DUKE. Happy, happy Reedbeck. He has a daughter
Returning to him.

JESS.   And there he sits and purrs
As though the morning was a saucer of milk.

REED. I caught myself singing. I do beg your pardon.

ED. Sing away, Reedbeck. Bring her in with music.

This is wonderful news.

(BATES *at the door.*)

REED. Can this be—is it . . . ?

(BATES *announces, and enter,* MRS. TAYLOR-SNELL.)

DUKE. The exact Hilda. Punctuality

Was drawing its last breath. The sun has mooned

Away half its light already.

HIL.   A party, Hereward?

You didn't tell me.

DUKE.   I scarcely knew. And anyway

We shall all feel quite alone, except, perhaps, Jessie.

Mrs. Dill, Mrs. Taylor-Snell. There will only be

The appearance of people being near to us.

Miss Rosabel Fleming, Mrs. Taylor-Snell.

Reedbeck you know. You've disappointed him.

He hoped you would have been his daughter.

HIL. Did you ever propose it, Reedbeck?

REED.   You see before you

A creaking bough on which, at any moment,

A dear young daughter may alight.

DUKE. My extension in time: Edgar.

ED.   Five feet ten

Of my unlimited father.

HIL.   I have often

Expected to meet you.

ED.   I suppose so;

But until he's dead I'm really a redundancy.

I make him feel bifurcated.

JESS.   Wherever

Does he learn those terrible words?

ED.   I spend

Such a lot of my time in the stables.

DUKE (*to* BATES, *who has loitered by the door*). What is it, Bates?

BATES.   There are faces

As can be mauled about wiv, and there are faces

As can't be mauled about wiv. Mine can't
Be mauled about wiv. Memo, guvnor, to be 'anded
On to the proper quarters, and *you* know
What basket I refers to.
Will that be all, guvnor?

DUKE.   That will be all, Bates.

(*Exit* BATES. REEDBECK *throws open the window and leans out.*)

HIL. Be careful, Reedbeck! There really is such a thing
As the force of gravity.

REED.   Only the wind blowing
And the rattle of leaves. I hoped it would prove to be
Internal combustion.

DUKE (*aside to* EDGAR). I should have mentioned to you,
The case of Athene is minutely complicated
By a husband. But don't be deflected. He would still
Have the shooting over the estate. Nothing
Is insurmountable.

ED.   Except yourself,
I take you to mean. But it's all right;
I'm devoted to you.

HIL.   Why don't you give it up,
Reedbeck? There's no daughter there. How much
This house has aged, Hereward, since I saw it
Last. I was thinking so coming up the stairs.
It looks as though the walls have cried themselves
To sleep for nights on end. And the number of windows
Broken! I don't think you should throw nearly
So many stones. The spiders are larger, the jackdaws
Ruder, the servants more eccentric. You mustn't
Drift into Gothic, when your physique is so
Stubbornly Norman.

DUKE.   I see no point in trying
To make time look as though it were standing still
By renewing the face of it. I like to watch my own
Deft and reckless plunge into ancient history.

It assuages my lust for speed. Dark glasses for the ladies,
Reedbeck; tell them to look at the sun.

ED.   And to pray
For all small birds under the eye of the hawk.

JESS. I can remember, when I was a kid,
Being got out of bed and told I had to look
At something in the sky. I kept on saying
Oh, yes, mum, isn't it lovely, isn't it lovely?
It was a comet or a zeppelin or something,
But all I could see was the usual end
Of the Crystal Palace.

REED. (*handing glasses*). Look at the sun, Mrs. Dill.

JESS. And now I can't help feeling
As if I'd just been got out of bed again
To look at something I probably shan't see.

DUKE. That's the human predicament, in a nutshell.

ROSA. There's a kind of humour abroad this morning that seems to
Put me outside the party.

REED.   Look at the sun, Miss Fleming.

ROSA. Thank you.

ED.   I've such a feeling of pre-natal
Tension, it's more than a boy can bear. Father,
I'm going to make the decision now
And pin the future down for you.

HIL.   But will you
Find that easy? I couldn't help overhearing.
The future has the most uncertain temper.
After all you've said, Hereward, do you teach
Your child to tamper with time?

DUKE.   He had it to play with
When he was young; but he'll soon see
How it will rag him to death. Meanwhile, the eclipse.
Let me be your guide. Observe how Sol Salome
Almost hidden by the head of the Baptist moon
Dances her last few steps of fire.

HIL.   You're confusing
The sex of the sun.

DUKE.   It's the act itself: observe
The copulation of Jove, magnificent in
Mid air.

JESS.   The bulk of the moon, creeping on
And on. It makes me feel more solemn than I've ever
Felt before at eleven o'clock in the morning.

ED. No nice eclipse for you, Miss Fleming?

ROSA.   Why, yes,
It was what your father invited me to see.
I was far away for the moment.

ED.   Before you go
To the window, I wonder if you'd mind accepting this apple?

ROSA. No, thank you. I'll go and see what there is to be seen
Before it's too late.

ED.   Father, may I have your attention?
There, Miss Fleming, it will come in useful sometime.

DUKE. Daylight, you see, is shamming twilight. Nature
Is being made a fool of. Three or four stars, there,
You can see them wince, where only a moment earlier
Morning was all serene. The crows, with much
Misgiving, talk themselves into their trees. Even
The usually phlegmatic owls
Care a hoot or two. The bats from the barn
Make one flickering flight, and return to hang
Their heads. All of them tricked and fuddled
By the passing of a small cadaverous planet.

HIL. Yes, we understand the event perfectly.

JESS. Let him enjoy it. Space, ever and ever,
On and on. . . . Well, I don't know.

ED. Father, I don't know whether you have noticed:
A certain event has occurred.

DUKE.   Is now occurring.
We're crossing perceptibly into the dark.

Daylight differences are made subordinate
To the general shade.

ED. Father, for God's sake, look!
I am giving Miss Fleming an apple.

ROSA. You've already
Given me an apple.

DUKE. I observe you're plying
Rosabel with fruit. *Bis dat qui cito dat.*
We can now turn our attention again to the sun.

ED. So a revolutionary change begins
Without raising a hand's turn of the dust.
Ah, well; give me some dark glass.

HIL. What a shame
If that cloud spoils the climax for us.

REED. No,
It avoids, you see; it glides mercifully
And dexterously past. I hope and pray
The same will be true of the cloud that hangs over my own
Sunshine: but young men can be so ruthless,
So ruthless; it's terrible to think about.

DUKE. What now, Reedbeck?

REED. Ah, yes; to the cosmos it doesn't
Matter; I suppose I agree.

JESS. To think
We're in the shadow of old Lunabella.

DUKE. To think.

JESS. When she moves over will she see us
Coming out of her shadow? Are we really
As bright as a moon, from the moon's side of the question?

DUKE. We have a borrowed brilliance. At night
Among the knots and clusters and corner boys
Of the sky, among asteroids and cepheids,
With Sirius, Mercury, and Canis Major,
Among nebulae and magellanic cloud,
You shine, Jessie.

JESS. You're making me self-conscious.

DUKE. Here we're as dull as unwashed plates; out there
We shine. That's a consideration. Come
Close to paradise, and where's the lustre?
But still, at some remove, we shine, and truth
We hope is content to keep a distant prospect.
So you, Jessie, and the swamps of the equator,
Shine; the boring overplus of ocean,
The Walworth Road, the Parthenon, and Reedbeck
Shine; the dark tree with the nightingale
At heart, dockyards, the desert, the newly dead,
Minarets, gasometers, and even I
Fall into space in one not unattractive
Beam. To take us separately is to stare
At mud; only together, at long range,
We coalesce in light.

JESS.   I like to think I'm being
A ray of light to some nice young couple out there.
"There's the Great Bear," they'd say, and "Look,
There's old Jessie, tilted on her side
Just over the Charing Cross Hotel."

HIL.   You both
Chatter so. It's a moment for quiet. Who knows
If ever I'll see this again.

ED.   The end of our lord
The sun.

ROSA.   It's no good. I must get out into the air!
It's impossible to breathe up here!

DUKE.   What is it,
Rosabel? Claustrophobia on the brink
Of the free heavens? Come now, think of it
As the usual dipping of day's flag. You used
To love this room at night.

ROSA.   How do you know?
How can you tell who loves, or when or why they love,
You without a single beat of heart
Worth measuring? You sit up here all night

Looking at the stars, travelling farther and farther
Away from living people. I hate your telescope!
How can you know, and what, if you knew, can it mean,
What can the darkest bruise on the human mind
Mean, when nothing beats against you heavier
Than a fall of rain? And out you whip
Your impervious umbrella of satisfaction!
How you prink across every puddle, and laugh
To think that other men can drown.
You would never believe there are some affections
Which would rather have decent burial
Than this mocking perpetuation you offer them.
You're a devil, a devil, a devil, a devil!

DUKE.   Only
On one side of the family, Rosabel,
Please believe that.

ED. (*taking the apple from her hand*).
                          I beg your pardon; I think
I've made a mistake.

ROSA.   Now I must go. I've spoilt
The eclipse. For that I'm sorry.

DUKE.   It's frankly impossible
To spoil the eclipse.

REED.   It would be fanciful
No doubt to say that the moon has placed a penny
Not on the dead but on the living eye of the sun.

ED. Yes, Reedbeck, it would.

JESS.   Don't you be put down.
It's nice that anyone can say anything at all.

DUKE. So Rosabel believes when the cold spell comes
And we're compelled to enter this draughty time
And shuffle about in the slipshod leaves,
Leaves disbanded, leaves at a loose end,
And we know we're in for the drifting of the fall,
We should merely shiver and be silent: never speak
Of the climate of Eden, or the really magnificent

Foliage of the tree of knowledge,
Or the unforgettable hushed emerald
Of the coiling and fettering serpent:
Pretend we never knew it, because love
Quite naturally condescended
To the passing of time. But why should we, Rosabel?

HIL. But if what I gather to be true is true,
Though it's no business of mine,
I must say, Hereward, you certainly seem to have been
Coruscating on thin ice. I think
She has cause to be angry. I do think so.
You've behaved a great deal less than well.

DUKE. I've behaved according to my lights of love
Which were excellent and bright and much to be
Remembered. You have all of you been my moments
Of revelation. I wish I understood why
You want to behave like skeletons in my cupboard.

JESS. Not Jessie, alas; her weight is all against it.
But need we make Miss Fleming cry?

ED.   I'd like it,
Father, if Mrs. Dill would have this apple.

JESS. I'd like it, too; though it's prettier on the tree.

ROSA. Your moments of revelation! I only wonder
What we revealed. Certainly not
What goes on in other hearts than your own.
That's as remote to you as a seaside lodging-house
To a passing whale.

HIL.   Could she put it more fairly?

JESS. I remember seeing what was thought to be a whale
At somewhere like Tenby; at least, my father said
Look, there's a whale, Jessie; but all I saw
Was the tip of a fin which might have been finnan haddy
Or Father Neptune or an old forgotten
Channel swimmer.

REED.   Can you play with Leviathan
As with a bird? That's really quite the strangest

Of rhetorical questions. And when will my daughter come?

DUKE. Rosabel—

JESS.   We might as well never have changed the subject.

DUKE. Rosabel, why pick on me to be
The villain? I'm a Roman in a world
Of Romans, and all creation can recognize me
As genus Man. Old men, young men, virgins,
Viragoes, all walk hand in hand with me
In the green enclosure of insensibility.
An individual torment in Indo-China
Makes less noise in your ear than the drop of a fir cone.
So why do I have to be sensible
Of a heart which is fortunate enough to be
Four thousand miles nearer my way, someone,
Moreover, to whom I've already given pleasure
And the refuge of a bed, which I never gave
(Such is my frailty) to the Indo-Chinee?
Don't let's go mad with inconsistency.
Either everything shall be near, or everything
Shall be far. Allow me the wrong end of the telescope;
I like to conform.

JESS.   Mr. Reedbeck will propose
The vote of thanks.

REED.   I really think, a few moments ago,
I heard what could only have been a motor-car.

ROSA. Where have I got myself now? Into such
An embarrassment, if I could vanish I should vanish,
And even then transparently kick myself.
It was hopelessly stupid.

HIL.   Stupid, and what was called,
In the days when musk had a scent, indelicate.

DUKE. I shall plough up the orchard, Edgar;
It was never a great success.

(*The shadow lifts from the sun, and the light falls on* PERPETUA REED-
BECK.)

ED.   God be praised,
  The sun again.

REED.   My daughter, it's my daughter, Perpetua,
  My dear, my dear!

(PERPETUA *runs to him.*)

ROSA.   Where shall I hide a most
  Unhappy head?   (*Exit* ROSABEL.)

REED.   O my little sixpenny
  Ha'penny daughter, home again, home again,
  Home again!

HIL. (*thinking of* ROSABEL).
               Can she take care of herself, that woman?
                    (*She follows* ROSABEL.)

PER. Let me look at you. Every feature where I left it
  Ten years ago! I'd forgotten you were so beautiful.

REED. You mustn't spoil me, not so soon;
  I shall puff myself up and explode like a frog.

PER. Perhaps we should sing until we're used to it?
  Might that be the wise thing?

REED.   I should stop at every
  Note to listen to you. But, my dear,
  I must present you to his Grace. I'd forgotten
  We were not in heaven. Your Grace—this—
  This is—

DUKE.   Steady, Reedbeck.
  Let me dry your eyes. Dear man, these tears are something
  Remarkably like champagne.

REED.   No doubt they are.
  My dear daughter: his Grace the Duke of Altair.

DUKE. You have made your father as happy as if his heart
  Were breaking. And isn't it likely you're going to make
  Others happy as well? We have only autumn
  To offer you, England's moist and misty devotion,
  But spring may come in time to reconcile you
  If you'll wait so long.

PER.   I need no reconciling.
I was born and grew in this green and pleasant aquarium,
And I've spent four days on a wicked October sea
For love of recollected mildew
And my dear frog-father; only I'd scarcely expected
Quite so much impenetrable murk
In the middle of morning. Surely there must be something
Out of sorts about your daylight?

DUKE.   Nothing
Which time won't mend. But, first, let me introduce—
Ah, they've left us; Hilda and Rosabel
Have passed away with no last word. They always
Bore themselves with the true brevity of empires.
But here is Mrs. Dill, more universe
Than empire, less conquered but more embracing.

JESS. I'm very pleased to meet you. Your father loves you
With every word in the language.

DUKE.   And this, Miss Reedbeck,
Is my first youth, my younger days: The Marquis
Of Charlock.

ED.   You're a kind of legend with us here,
But the truth is better.

PER.   I'll tell you the truth:
I'm very happy this morning; I'm really out
Of prison.

REED.   Of prison, my darling? Why do you say
Of prison?

PER.   I mean, of course, the boat was a prison
And the frowning sea was Dartmoor.

DUKE.   To refresh you
There's wine in the bottle, cider from the wood,
Biscuits in the barrel; and there you can see
Our English sun, convalescent after passing
Through the valley of the shadow of the moon.

PER. So that was why I had to search my way
Up the stairs in gloom. How far off is the sun?

DUKE. The best part of ninety-three million miles.

PER. You would hardly think it could matter.

ED.   What will you drink,
Miss Reedbeck?

PER.   Something of England, the cider, presently.
I'm so at peace, though I still can feel
The lunge of the sea. Your floor isn't meant to sway?

DUKE. The floor is battering at your feet like Attila
With a horde of corybantic atoms,
And travelling at eighteen miles a second,
But it cannot be said to sway.

JESS.   That would be much
Too easy.

DUKE.   Our stability is a matter
For surprise.

REED.   I feel the terrible truth of that.
Even now, for example, when I see my Perpetua
Sitting like a girl on a swing on an Easter Monday
Under a Wedgwood sky, I can feel my heart—

PER. That's just what it's like, a girl on a swing.

REED.   My heart
Knocking most anxiously against the future,
As though afraid to be alone with the present time:
Ready, really, for almost any disaster
Rather than this unsteady tight-rope of joy
I'm walking on now. Are you ill, perhaps? Is that it?
Have you come home for your health?

PER.   I've come home to be home.
A pigeon's return—just so simple, Poppadillo.
I wanted to stand where I first grew, and to have
My roots and my branches all in one place together.
And that's no curious thing. Here, swinging
On my swing, with the Atlantic foam still racing
Under my eyelids, I seem at rest already.
And so I sent no word to say I was coming,

Because, in the sense that means the most,
I was here all the time.

ED.   And so you emerged
Like Venus from the sea.

PER.   But sicker.

REED.   What
Shall I do for my returning Mayflower
Suppose she is disappointed in the land
Her roots are in?

PER.   You needn't be afraid.
If this is still an island
Enclosed in a druid circle of stony sea,
As misty as it was that chilly Thursday
When I was born to the wilting of plovers
And the smell of a saturation of hops,
Then I'm safely and happily home.

JESS.   Here's to your happiness,
Dear; God save the King, and a mild winter.

REED. Your happiness, my dear.

ED.   Happiness, Miss Reedbeck.

DUKE. I should like you to offer Miss Reedbeck an apple, Edgar.

ED. Anything except an apple, father.
I will offer her
The cloudy peach, the bristling pineapple,
The dropsical pear, the sportive orange,
Apricot, sloe, King William, or a carillon
Of grapes, but not, as God's my judge, an apple.

DUKE. Then, as Paris abdicates, I must offer
The sweet round robin fruit myself—

(*He holds an apple up between his fingers.*)

The green sphere the myth of the world began in,
Which Melanion let fall, delaying
Mercurial Atalanta—

(PERPETUA *has whipped a very small pistol from a pig-skin holster at her belt. She shoots and shatters the apple. There is an incredulous, shaken silence.*)

PER. I—I'm terribly sorry. That was thoughtless of me.
    Perhaps you wanted to eat it.

DUKE.   There are others;
    Nature is pleased to give us more. And you
    Have been very good; you let me keep my fingers.

REED. Only by the mercy of God! My dear girl,
    My dear girl! What in the world possessed you?
    You might have been the death of him!

PER.   No, it was quite safe.
    To please, I always aim. But that, I agree,
    Is no excuse. It was dreadful, and shameful of me.
    I was thinking of something else, or else
    It would never have happened.

(*Enter* ROSABEL, *followed by* HILDA.)

ROSA.   What was it? We heard a sound
    Like a shot!

REED.   Good gracious, a *sound* like a shot!

HIL. Is no one hurt?

DUKE.   An apple came to grief
    As apples must.

ED.   One pip too many.

JESS.   And nobody
    Was more surprised than the Duke.

REED.   Oh, yes, I think so,
    I think my surprise can hardly have been bettered
    Except, no doubt, by the apple. And I'm still
    Anchored in amazement, I have to confess.

PER. I also have to confess; I see I must.
    I thought I could come back again to England
    And slip into this new beginning, silently.
    But now the pistol has gone off; the silence anyway
    Is well and truly broken, and so I'll explain,
    Though the explanation, I'm afraid, will seem
    As wild as the shot.

REED.   What can it be? Be quick
    And tell me.

PER.   I've lately been in prison. But not
For what we should call a crime.

REED.   They put you in prison
Without rhyme or reason?

PER.   There may have been
A little rhyme. I was thought to be unsafe
For democracy, because I broke, or shot,
Or burnt, a good many things, or rather—and this
Is the reason—a bad many things: the unsightly,
The gimcrack, the tedious, the hideous, the spurious,
The harmful. Not I alone, of course;
We were all students, and called ourselves
The Society for the Desecration
Of Ancient and Modern Monumental Errors.
We destroyed, or tried to destroy, whatever we loathed
As bad.

ROSA.   Whatever you loathed, you destroyed?
Why, that was admirable, superb, the most
Heavenly daring!

PER.   No, I think it was only
Exasperation. And then we went to prison.
And there I knew it was all no use.
The more we destroyed, the worse the bad sprang up.
And I thought and thought, What can I do for the world?
I was wearing the prison drab. My name was a number.
Inside or outside the prison, Perpetua
(I thought), you're no one, you're everybody's colour.
You must make good, before you break the bad,
Perpetua. And so I came home to England
Simply to trace myself, in my own way.

(*She offers the pistol to the* DUKE.)
I'd better surrender this. I only kept it
For a kind of memento. And I apologize
Again for destroying the apple. Still half at sea
As I am, it appeared to be, in a misty way,
Like a threat to my new-come freedom.

DUKE. I hope you will think so again, some other time.

ROSA. (*taking the pistol*). May I have it, to remind me of your story,
　　　To know there has been someone in the world
　　　Who dared to do such things! If only I
　　　Could be such a brave one, there might be
　　　Some justification for me.

DUKE (*taking it from her*).　　Caps for you,
　　　Dear Rosabel, not bullets. I'll have it
　　　Filled for your next big scene. (*A gong booms from below.*)

ED. Luncheon! Can we be supposed to eat
　　　On a day when the sun is drowned by the moon,
　　　And apples meet such a strange end?

DUKE. I see nothing strange. If we can move and talk
　　　Under the sun at all, we must have accepted
　　　The incredible as commonplace, long ago;
　　　And even the incredible must eat.
　　　Shall we go down?

　　　　　　　　　　　(THE CURTAIN FALLS ON ACT ONE)

ACT TWO

Scene One

*The Temple of the Ancient Virtues, beside the ducal lake, in the after-
noon.* DOMINIC *and* PERPETUA *are there.*

DOM. You haven't spoken for three and a half minutes.

　　　Four minutes. This is the most pregnant pause
　　　Since darkness was on the face of the deep. I suppose
　　　You think I shouldn't have told you.

PER.　　　　　　　　　　　　　　Oh, yes, you should.

DOM. It was better than leaving you in a fool's paradise,
　　　You must admit.

PER.　　　　　　　I could be twice as silent
　　　For seven times as long.

DOM.   Well, then you shall be.
I know myself how the shock stuns one.

PER.   No shock
At all. I was able to believe you at once.
Poppadillo has the most beguiling
Jackdaw look about him. But you think
He wouldn't be happy in prison?

DOM.   He wouldn't, but what
Difference does that make? Would you be able
To look anyone in the face, with a father jailed?

PER. Oh, yes, if he were comfortable. But I think
He might feel shut in. No, Dominic, I'm sure
You're right. If someone has to go to prison,
I must.

DOM. You? What can you possibly mean?

PER. You said I should have to, and now all I mean
Is Yes, quite so.

DOM.   Quite what is quite so, will you tell me?

PER. I heard you say, perhaps it might have been
Six minutes ago, if I made myself agreeable
The Duke (you said) being much in that mind at the moment
Might, with any luck, be inclined to marry me,
And no gentleman (you added) would incriminate
His father-in-law. And I agree with you,
And I see my carefree hours already numbered,
My freedom of choice and my individual day.
I'm no longer a woman after my own heart.
Broad cupid's arrows on my wedding veil.
But still, Dominic, for my father's sake
Not ours, I mean to try.

DOM.   God bless you, then,
And God speed you, and thank God I can breathe again.
And a coronet's no martyrdom, particularly
When it sits on a man whom women find easy to like.

PER. I wonder how many women have stood perplexed
And plagued in this temple, two whole centuries of them,

Looking out this way, on the same view
Of the metal rusting year. Lemon, amber,
Umber, bronze and brass, oxblood damson,
Crimson, scalding scarlet, black cedar,
And the willow's yellow fall to grace.

DOM. Do you have to be so melancholy? Everything
Is better now. Though there is still the anxiety
Whether you can prepossess him before he strikes.

PER. Oh, yes, there is that anxiety still.
Here comes the straying lamb who gave us life.

DOM. Don't pamper him. We have to make him realize
He's been sinning all this while.

PER.   He looks as worried
As though he knew it already.

(*Enter* REEDBECK, *out of breath.*)

REED.   So here—here—
You are. I wondered, missed you, but luckily caught
Sight of you going down through the trees. I lost
My hat on the way; it blew (oh, what a gasping old fellow)
Off, blew off; now upside down on the water
Among the *Alisma Plantago-aquatica*.
Didn't think I should have enough breath to say so.

PER. Try only breathing, for a time; that's always
Nice.

DOM. What was the hurry? Did you think I was going
To throw her in the water?

REED.   Among the *Alisma
Plantago-aquatica*. Has he been talking to you?
He's not as fond of me as either of us
Would like.

PER.   I've been hearing unimaginable
Things about you.

REED.   Yes, the imagination
Is a frail craft, soon capsizes, quite understand.
Now this, my dear, called sometimes the Temple
Of the Ancient Virtues, and at other times

The White Temple, both because it is white
And because it was designed by Martin White
In seventeen hundred and ninety-three, was erected
By the third Duke of Altair for his wife Claire
For her use when she played the part of the Delphic Oracle,
A way she had of informing the Duke of her pregnancy,
Which she did on twenty-seven separate occasions.

PER. Tell me why you've been cheating the Duke,
There's a good boy. What made you do it?

REED.   I hope
I've done nothing so monosyllabic as to cheat.
A spade is never so merely a spade as the word
Spade would imply.

DOM.   One's helpless to help him.

PER. Poppadillo, suppose I put it this way:
What made you supercherify with chousery
The Duke?

REED.   That might be said to—that perhaps
Is not an unfair expression. And I say in reply
The reason was the fading charm of the world.
The banquet of civilization is over—

PER.   Shall we call it
The groaning board?

REED.   You may call it what you will.
With a little wealth to do it I should like to perform
The grace after the meat, a last, gentlemanly,
Valedictory grace: a grace for departing grace
(Is that not rather good?):
The spacious lawns of life are being
Inevitably ploughed, and we don't know, we really
Don't know, what's going to be sown there.
Dignity has dropped upon all fours.
Indeed there's hardly to be seen
One intense perpendicular
In all the streets of men. Someone, you know,
Someone must keep alive that quality

Of living which separates us from the brutes;
And I have proposed it should be I.

DOM. It should be me.

REED.   Beloved boy,
It would be delightful if you thought so.

PER. I understand so far; I only wonder
Why the Duke has to be . . . out of pocket.

REED. I care so much for civilization,
Its patrician charm, its grave nobility;
He cares so little. Therefore certain eccentric
Means have had to be taken for splendid ends.
Church and State, in a way, agree
In justifying such a course of action.
A kind of casual taxation. I hope I explain
Quite clearly. It's true I have overlaid the Law
With a certain transposition; we might
Call this process Reedbequity. But what
A gain to the world.

DOM.   Do you hear that, Perpetua?
He even unblushingly gives our name
To his wicked practices!

PER.   Dominic wants us all
To be good. Perhaps if you had gone to the Duke
And explained all this, he would have eased the path
To Reedbequity without the bother of iniquity.
Don't you think he might?

REED.   My dear, I've never believed
In the equal distribution of property.
I only think it can have more beauty
In my hands than in his. But that would have been
A most impertinent thing to say to him.

PER. We must keep you from harm. Heydee,
I'm not to be myself, I see.
I'm sad to see myself go;
But I was only promise, after all,
And the world can't live on that.

REED. Have you something that worries you? I believe
  I've made you discontented with me, on a day
  Which should have turned out so glorious, and now
  I don't know *where* we are.

DOM.   It's only a step
  From where you are, father, to where you will be
  If we can't prevent it. You'll discover
  Civilization is sadly dwindled when
  You make your way to prison. Here's the Duke.
  Be cheerful, if you can, Perpetua.

PER.   My smile
  Will be like the glint of handcuffs, but he's very
  Welcome to it. Sing out a joke, Dominic,
  In your merry way.

DOM.   Ssh!

PER.   That's a most promising
  Start to a conversation. There must be a joke
  Lying about somewhere, even when the leaves are falling.

REED. Something about . . . when the leaves in Eden fell . . .

PER. Dear Poppadillo; thank you.

REED.   Was it at all
  Serviceable?

PER.   It had a kind of ancient virtue,
  Proper for this time and temple, yes.

(*Enter the* DUKE, *carrying a bow and quiver.*)

DUKE. May your little girl come out and play, Reedbeck?
  Daylight is short, and becoming always shorter.
  But there's the space for an arrow or two between
  Now and the sunset.

PER.   I've never handled a bow.
  How shall I manage?

DUKE.   Beautifully.
  The light will hang fire to see you; you might
  Even hear the flash of the foliage
  Where Artemis parts the leaves to patronize

And praise you; but take no notice, and watch what you're doing,
And do what I tell you.

PER.   Implicitly.

DUKE.   Take notice
Of the excellent marksmanship of the year, whose arrow
Singing from the April bow crossed over the width
Of summer straight for the gold, where now, if you look,
You will see it quivering.

PER.   The year has a world of experience.
But still, show me; and I'll try not to shame the shades
Of all the arching duchesses and ladies
Who played on these lawns before.

DUKE.   They'll arch the more,
Adoring what you do, feathering their shafts
And shooting until doomsday's Parthian shot.
Be confident; and, if you miss,
The fashion of the game will be to miss,
Until you change your mind and hit.

(*He begins to instruct her in the use of the bow, holding it with her,
and speaking low into her ear, so that* REEDBECK *and* DOMINIC *cannot hear.*)

And then, Perpetua, tonight
If a clear sky inclines you to it, and the heavens
Remain suspended, how would it be
If we trained the telescope on the infinite
And made what we could of what we could see of it?
Are you still as interested as you were
This morning?

PER.   Yes. I come from a city. The stars
Are new to me.

DUKE.   They shall answer you
By numbers. But we'll not tell the world
What we mean to do. There's a little tension today
Already, nerves perhaps not ready to accept
The quiet session of scientific study

You and I propose. So let's be as mute
As we're mutable, and avoid misapprehension.

PER. I—if so—if so—yes, very well.

DUKE. You can tell the world you need a long night of sleep.

PER. Yes, yes, I can. But here's the good afternoon light
Fading to waste unless we make use of it.

DUKE. I know that thought so well. Come on, then,
Let the trial begin.

PER.   Watch me, Poppadillo.
Come and judge what a huntress I should make,
What a rival for Artemis, and what chance Actaeon
Would have if I pursued him.   (*Exeunt the* DUKE *and* PERPETUA.)

REED.   She really makes me
Respectful of astrology; it must
Have been the arrangement of stars she was born under.
It couldn't have been all me and her mother. Why,
I couldn't even dream so beautifully,
Let alone propagate. It must have been
The state of the zodiac when she was conceived.
But even so, I was there, and that in itself
Is remarkable. What did you say to her, Dominic;
What did you say to her?

DOM.   I simply told her
You were crooked.

REED.   And then she said?

DOM.   She said
She was not surprised.

REED.   Oh. *I* should have been;
It would have seemed like a thunder clap to *me*.
But you've made her feel differently towards me,
You've sent me off on my own again. And what
Did she mean by "sad to see herself go," and "not
To be herself any more"? What made her say that?
Was something agreed between you?

DOM.   I made a point.

REED. What point, now what point?

DOM.   I made the suggestion
She might like to marry the Duke, and save you that way.

REED. You—said—such a—thing? You dared
To consider selling your sister? You,
Sprung from my loins, and so utterly
Unprincipled?

DOM.   That sounds most convincing,
Coming from you!

REED.   Poor litle girl, poor
Little girl. But I'll intervene—*inter venio,*
Yes—though I can't relieve her
Of her inhuman brother.

DOM.   Or her dishonest
Father.

REED. (*shaking him, in a sudden burst of rage*). You're a vain, vexing,
     incomprehensible,
Crimping, constipated duffer. What's your heart?
All plum duff! Why do I have to be
So inarticulate? God give me a few
Lithontriptical words! You grovelling little
Gobemouche!

DOM.   Stop it, father, stop it at once!

REED. You spigoted, bigoted, operculated prig!
(*Enter* JESSIE.)

JESS. Am I in the way? I came to write a letter.
(REEDBECK *releases* DOMINIC *suddenly, and* DOMINIC *trips and falls
     sprawling on the floor.*)

REED. I was having a word with my son.

JESS. (*to* DOMINIC).   How do you do?
Please don't bother to get up.

REED.   You're very welcome
To write your letter. I don't wish to shake him
Any more. But if you hadn't come in
I think I should have gone on shaking him
Until I couldn't see him.

JESS.   He would still

Have been there, of course. When my mother used to shake me
It always gave me hiccups, and then I was given
Peppermint on sugar to cure them. If only your son
Had hiccups, and you had peppermint and sugar,
Mr. Reedbeck, everything would seem different.

DOM. I have to leave you. I'm afraid my father
　　Must be feeling very chastened and confused.　(*Exit* DOMINIC.)

JESS. It was lovely exercise for both of you.

REED. It did no good; I've only shaken my own
　　Composure.

JESS.　　　　　　Sit down, Mr. Reedbeck, and let it settle.
　　I have to get a few lines off every day
　　To my father, eighty-seven. He can't read a word
　　Of my handwriting, and doesn't try, but he likes
　　The postman.

REED.　　　　　　Well, I'll leave you, then;
　　I won't stop and hinder you. I suppose
　　That action of mine, that sudden accession of rage,
　　Wasn't in the nicest mood of civilization?
　　And yet I don't at all feel like apologizing,
　　I don't feel at all like apologizing. Would you apologize?

JESS. I'm sorry, I was trying to think how to begin
　　So that Dad won't mind he can't read it.

REED. Well, I won't stop and hinder you now,
　　But I should be very upset if I proved to be
　　Nothing but a barbarian after all,
　　A barbarian dreaming of the higher excellences.
　　But I won't stop and hinder you.

(*Enter* HILDA.)

　　　　　　　　　　　　Mrs. Dill
　　Is trying to write a letter. We mustn't hinder her.

　　　　　　　　　　　　　　　　　(*Exit* REEDBECK.)

HIL. I see Hereward has made another backward
　　Flight into his heyday. It's a handsome thing
　　To see him so happy, but are we so happy for the girl?

JESS. Doesn't she like playing at bows and arrows?

HIL. She does, no doubt, but—May I interrupt you?

JESS.   I'm only

Writing a letter when nothing else occurs to me;
I like to talk.

HIL.   Because of the strange business
Of the eclipse this morning, and what went on,
We've been thrown into each other's confidence
Unexpectedly soon. And for my part
I think I'm thankful. I've always hidden more
Than was good for me, hoping in that way
To make my life seem pleasant to everyone,
But who should care? So I've lost the habit
Of daring to ask myself what I do, or why.
Why did I come here today, and what did I expect?
And why did he ever invite us here together?
I know him painstakingly enough
To be sure it was kindly meant; it couldn't have been
To watch our faces fall.

JESS.   I like being here
So much I never even wondered.

HIL.   There
Was still something in me to be hurt,
Which a little surprised me. And then
Reedbeck's daughter came, as though to show
How the years had gone by for us
But not for him, as though the old
Magician in his blood was bound to draw us
Into that revealing circle. But I sigh
For her, as once I sighed for myself; and, if
I knew how, I should tell her how lightly he flies.

JESS.   And then

You must tell her how nicely he alights.
That's important, too.
I should let them be, because be they will.

HIL. When I first met him, I remember, he seemed
At once to give my spirits a holiday,

Though (like a first holiday abroad) almost too unlike
The daily round of the roundabout life I led—
And lead still, O my heavens—which had, and has,
All the appearance of movement without covering
Any ground whatsoever. I know I have
No particular heights or depths myself;
No one who thought me ordinary or dull
Would be far wrong. But even I despair
For Roderic, my husband, who really is
The height of depth, if it doesn't sound unkind
To say so: not deep depth, but a level depth
Of dullness. Once he had worn away the sheen
Of his quite becoming boyhood, which made me fancy him,
There was nothing to be seen in Roderic
For mile after mile after mile, except
A few sheeplike thoughts nibbling through the pages
Of a shiny weekly, any number of dead pheasants,
Partridges, pigeons, jays, and hares,
An occasional signpost of extreme prejudice
Marked "No thoroughfare," and the flat horizon
Which is not so much an horizon
As a straight ruled line beyond which one doesn't look.

JESS. Keep him warm and fed. They bloom
    Once in seven years.

HIL.   Not Roderic.

(*Enter* EDGAR, *carrying a bow and quiver.*)

ED. Are either of you ladies any good
    At taking out a thorn? I took a look
    In a mirror for some reason or other, and there it was.
    A bramble slashed me when I was out riding yesterday.
    I've brought my own needle.

HIL.   Am I hurting you?

ED. Yes, but how nice of you. Isn't it strange?
    For the first time in my young life
    I'm jealous of my father. I though I'd better
    Mention it before I begin to brood.

HIL. Jealous of him, why?

ED. To me he's a man
Once and for all; once, once only,
And certainly for all. And any man
Who has to follow him (me, for instance)
Feels like the lag-last in a cloud of locusts:
By the time I come to a tree it's as bare
As a hat stand. Talent, conversation, wit,
Ease, and friendliness are all swallowed up
In advance. And just at present
I feel depressed about it.

HIL. Now, take heart.
You have those virtues, too. There's room for both of you.

ED. Not, I think, at the moment.

JESS. Do you mean
Only two can play at bows and arrows?

HIL. I think at the moment it's greatly important
There *should* be room for both of you. Suppose
You make a bid for it. Why not?
Nothing hinders you except weakness of hope,
And that's ridiculous. We'll go together.
Mrs. Dill wants to write a letter.

JESS. Never mind;
Everything writes itself in time.

(*Enter* BATES.)

BATES. It's Mrs. Taylor-Snell I'm looking for;
Oh, that's right, lady, you're here. I have
A message to give you, they said; prompto.
On the telephone it come. It's not so nice
As you might like to have it, but it's not so bad.
It seems there's been a bit of a accident,
And they'd be glad if you could make it convenient
To find your way back 'ome.

HIL. Roderic!

BATES. Whoever it is, missis, you're not to worry.
Your old man has got hisself throwed off his horse,

Hunting little rabbits and uvver breeders.
Now, now, lady, you never know,
It may only be a front toof a bit loose.

HIL. Didn't they say what the injury was?

BATES. Took a bit of a toss, come a bit of a purler,
What Jack and Jill done; don't you worry, lady.

HIL. I can't help worrying, dear Bates. (*To* JESSIE.) I'll go
Without saying good-bye to Hereward. There's no reason
Why anyone's afternoon should suffer,
Except mine; and later I'll telephone
And tell you what has happened.

JESS.   It's wretched for you,
It's really wretched for you; I'm awfully sorry.
What would you like me to do?

HIL.   Nothing, except
To forget I laughed at him. I have my car;
I can slip away easily.

ED.   I'll run on ahead
And get the car started for you.

HIL.   No.
Thank you, but I'd rather go quietly alone.
If you want to do something for me, put your shoulders
To your father, and make yourself your own success.
Good-bye.

ED.   Good-bye, good luck.

JESS.   I expect you'll find
It's something nice and simple like a collar-bone. (*Exit* HILDA.)
Oh, please God, make it a collar-bone. She turned
So pale and unhappy, poor lamb.

BATES. I wouldn't have anything happen to that one:
It's a pity we can't do something to oblige her.
But there's that uvver one, Fleming she says she's called:
Flaming nuisance, I reply: what about her,
Eh, miss? What's she doing snooping
About the east wing all the afternoon? I tell you,

Miss, I knows an undesirable character
When I see one; I've been one myself for years.

JESS. And look how we love you. So don't you have
    Nasty thoughts about Miss Fleming, who is not
    Undesirable at all. And go away
    Like a good boy, and let me write my letter.

BATES. I just fought you might like the opinion of a expert.

(*He begins wandering away.*)

    But don't let's say anyfing good about
    Captain Fussing Reddleman, lord of the kitchens.
    He can go and tame his lions on some uvver poor bastard's mug.
    I prefers to keep mine natural.   (*Exit* BATES.)

ED. I wonder if I should.

JESS.   If you should what?

ED. From here I think I could send an arrow right past him
    Into the target.

JESS.   If you think you can, then do.

(EDGAR *takes an arrow, fits it in his bow, and shoots. A distant cry of
    remonstrance from the* DUKE.)

ED. Oh, that was very beautiful. I enjoyed that
    Extremely.

JESS.   What did you do? Did I encourage you
    To be mischievous? I was thinking about my letter.
    You might have shot your father.

ED.   I jolly nearly
    Did. But my arrows, I never quite know why,
    Have a considerate way of going where
    I mean them to go, which was nearer the gold than his.
    He's probably shooting not so well
    To give Perpetua some encouragement.
    When I come to think of it, that shot of mine
    Was taking a very easy advantage.

JESS. I shouldn't say easy, twice the distance off.
    And as you didn't kill anybody, I may say
    I think it was splendid, and I think perhaps
    You should do it more often.

(*Enter the* DUKE.)

DUKE. What, by Saint Sebastian's groin,
>Do you think you're up to? Edgar, for goodness' sake!

ED. I was drawing a bow at a venture, father.

DUKE.   So
>I thought. But remember what damage was done to Sir Lancelot
>By an arrow in the buttocks. Did I beget you
>To be shot from behind?

ED.   I'm extremely sorry,
>But you took a step to the south.

DUKE.   Am I never to move?

ED. Oh, yes, father, but the other way, or any way
>Except between me and where I aim.

DUKE.   I hope
>I'm being patient. I had quite supposed
>The contest was between Miss Reedbeck and me.

ED. When all the time it was really between you
>And your loving son; or so my hackles tell me.

DUKE. Ah—! Now I see;
>Your days are starting to press upon me,
>You who were always so unassuming and easy.
>But not this time. No, I'm sorry,
>Not this time, Edgar.

ED.   It is this time.
>I'm sorry, too, but it is this time. You've had
>A long innings, and a summer of splendid outings,
>And now I must ask you, father, not to monopolize
>Every heart in the world any longer.

JESS.   Excuse me
>Worrying you, but how do you spell epidemic?
>Two *p*'s and two *m*'s?

ED.   I'd forgotten we weren't alone.

DUKE. We're alone with Jessie; nothing could be happier.
>One *p*, one *m*. If the generations join
>In a life-and-death struggle under your feet
>Don't let it, Jessie, disturb your spelling.

JESS. One *p*, one *m*. Quite enough, when you look at it.

DUKE. Now listen, Edgar, take nothing for granted,
    Not even my flair for breaking into love;
    You're apprehensive far too soon. The field,
    If not entirely yours, is not entirely mine:
    I am as innocently there
    As an old warhorse put out to grass:
    My equine equability is pastoral to a fault.

ED. But when you're grazing you're irresistible;
    Buttercups and daisies fall to your fetlocks in swathes;
    I've seen it happen. And between this morning's eclipse
    And this afternoon you've lost the autumnal look
    Which was such a comfort to me; I see you have
    The appearance of a very mild March day.
    And what does a boy do then?

DUKE.   Aren't you being
    Just a thought parricidal for a fine afternoon?

ED. Oh, God, I love you like the rest of them.
    I'm only asking you to forgo yourself
    This once, to suspend your animation
    For a few short months, for my sake.

DUKE.   Edgar,
    I mean to be a good father to you, but
    A good father must be a man. And what
    Is a man? Edgar, what is a man? O
    My man-child, what in the world is a man?
    Speaking for myself, I am precisely that question:
    I exist to know that I exist
    Interrogatively. But what gives birth
    To a question? A desire to be answered. A question
    Desires, as a man must desire, as I
    Desire. That, at least, you'll allow me.
    You wouldn't have your father merely rhetorical.

ED. Not at all, but—

DUKE.   But what is the mark of the question?
    What is the note of this interrogation?

Loneliness. The note, my son, is loneliness.
Over all the world
Men move unhoming, and eternally
Concerned: a swarm of bees who have lost their queen.
Nothing else is so ill at ease. We know
How patiently the toad suns on the stone,
How the indolent fish waves its tail in time
With the waving weed. If a pulse was in the stone,
And the stone grew moist, and the toad petrified,
Patience would still be as patient in the sun.
Or if the weed wove its way up river
To breed, and the fish waved green and still,
The water would never wonder: all
Is at one with the rest.
And the trees, when the weather is waking, quicken without
Question, their leaves assemble in a perfect faith
Of summer; and so with all the world's life,
Except ours. We can hear the lyric lark
Flaking its limit of heaven from a cloud,
And see the self-assimilated cat,
The adaptable chameleon, and the mole
Rubbing along companionably
With the obliging earth. But where, O Edgar,
Is an element compatible with *us?*

ED. Would you mind if I reminded you, father,
What we were talking about when you started talking?

DUKE. Thank you, but I know: your wish to remove me.
But if being alive is a question, heaven-bent
For an answer, and the question is a man's
Estrangement in a world
Where everything else conforms, how should I dare
To suspend myself for a day, or even an hour,
When that hour might ravish me
Into a complete, unsolitary life,
Where happiness leaves no room for the restless mind
And I, as unlaborious

As a laburnum tree, hang in caresses of gold.

ED. And what do I hang in?

DUKE.   You hang in abeyance, Edgar.
  If I should die, with the great question unanswered,
  I leave myself in you to ask it still.
  But this is all academic. The field is still open.

JESS. I always think "niece" is such a difficult word.

DUKE. *I* before *E*, except after *C*. And so,
  Edgar, let nothing dismay you—

JESS.   Except
  In the case of "neigh," that humorous noise of a horse.

(*Enter* PERPETUA.)

PER. Is archery all over? I went to the lake
  And tried to spear fish with an arrow, but I'm tired
  Of that.

DUKE.   Edgar, I'm nowhere to be seen;
  For all the personality I exert
  You might never have had a father; advance, advance,
  You son of a cipher.

PER.   Could we not all shoot together?

ED. Miss Reedbeck—

PER.   Perpetua.

ED.   Yes. Perpetua,
  This is All Hallowe'en. Tonight half England
  Will be dancing in memory of a world they don't remember.
  The sky will very likely be black with broomsticks.
  There's a dance on in the Old Woolmarket
  At Mordenbury. Will you come?

PER. (*glancing towards the* DUKE). All Hallowe'en.
  I should have liked it dearly, but tonight—

ED. You've made some other plan.

PER.   No, no.

ED. Then come. Meet England first among the wisps
  Of magic we still possess. Will you, Perpetua?

PER. If I dared to trust my eyes and my feet
  To be lively, so long after sunset,

I should say yes willingly. But I must and will
Sleep early. Four days on the see-saw sea,
And then such a wave of homecoming, have left me
Ready to rest. I'm so sorry to refuse.

ED. Well, I see you must, though I'm very sad you must.
But if later you should feel revived, or if
You found you could rest before dinner—

PER. It still has to be no, and still I'm sorry.

ED. I can well imagine how tired you are. You can let
Your sleep make you a Hallowe'en instead.
Dreams know where to look for deeper and stranger
Shadows than I do. Horses, it always seems
To me, are half a dream, even when
You have them under your hand, and when I *dream* them
They tremble and sweat, the caves of their nostrils blowing
Bright clouds of breath, a foaming sea
Breaks against their mouths, their flanks are smoking
Like Abel's fire to heaven, as though
A dreadful necessity had ridden them hard
Through the miles of my sleep, all the benighted way
From legend into life. And then in the morning
There they are in the stables, waiting to be blessed.

PER. Show me these wonders.

ED.   Now?

PER.   Yes, why not now?
All of us.

ED.   That goes for you, papa.

DUKE. Invisibly I come.

ED. (*glumly*).   Invisibility
Makes you look younger than ever.

                              (*Exeunt* PERPETUA *and* EDGAR.)

DUKE.   Jessie,
Will you make an end of dotting your *i*'s and join us?

JESS. Thank you, dear,
But I'd like to finish this letter to my father,
Even though he'll never read it.

DUKE.   Jessie, my love,
If he'll never read it, do you have to write so much?

JESS. Well, no, but he lives such a long way out of the village
I like to make it worth the postman's while.

(*Enter* ROSABEL.)

DUKE. Rosabel, where have you been mooning
All the long afternoon? Come with your friends
And look at horses. Edgar is showing Miss Reedbeck
Round the stables.

ROSA.   Yes, yes, I may follow you—
When do you mean to show her how to observe
The stars through your telescope? Is it tonight?

DUKE. No, not tonight; sometime, perhaps, or perhaps
Never; who can say?

ROSA.   But *you* will be there, I suppose.
Who is it that's mooning then? And all night long?
And making the world look small and apologetic
And as good as unpopulated? I hate your telescope!

DUKE. So you have said. Don't let it obsess you.
Look up, Mrs. Siddons, it's easy enough
To see over the top of a telescope. So try,
Or you'll soon make yourself ill. Anyway
I'm washing my hands of all the sky tonight,
And I'm going early to bed.   (*Exit the* DUKE.)

ROSA. (*to herself*).   So no one at all
Will be there. Now I know why all day long
Life has been tilting and driving me towards
Tonight. I'm not myself any more,
I am only the meaning of what comes after dark,
If I have the courage.

(*She remembers* JESSIE *and turns to her*.)
                          Obsessed, obsessed.
It's very true. One thought in my head,
Persevering like someone running on a race-track;
When it seems to be going it's coming again.
I wrestle with it, and hold it close,

I can't let it go, nor laugh it away. Is this
How men get driven to send history lurching on
To God knows where? Nothing matters
Except that he should be made to feel. He hurts
Whoever he touches. He has to be touched by fire
To make a human of him, and only a woman
Who loves him can dare to do it.

JESS.   Listen, love,
You'll be sending yourself silly. I always think
When someone knocks you down, it doesn't improve things
To knock yourself up. The way a thing is, is often
The way you happen to look at it. He's as kind
As anybody living, if you take a running jump.
And if you only had a stamp we could go together
And put this in the box.

ROSA.   I'm over-run
By the most curious thoughts. I believe I was kept
From quite succeeding in anything I set
My heart on, so that now I should give all
My heart to this, tonight. The girl Perpetua
Has the courage that makes a person come true.
Did you hear her say how she went to war on things
She hated? I think she came to show me
What it is I have to do; indeed, I can't do less!
And nothing less will do to open his eyes
On to the distances that separate him
From other people.

JESS.   Look at me: I've put Cumberland
When I mean Northants.

ROSA.   Tonight, no one is there.
You'll see, I shall send his Observatory
Where Nero's Rome has gone; I'll blaze a trail
That he can follow towards humanity!

JESS. Now I wonder who's the most likely person to have a stamp?

                                        (THE CURTAIN FALLS.)

Scene Two

The Observatory Room at night. The DUKE *is lying on a day-bed in the dark. Enter* PERPETUA. *The light from the corridor follows her a little way into the room. She stands uncertain. The* DUKE *speaks from the darkness.*

DUKE. And Endymion, when the moon had borne him
Fifty daughters, was rewarded with
An eternal siesta; his breast and belly rose
And fell like the sea; his breath played
All day with the motes of the dust,
While all about him suffered, withered, and crumbled
Into the dust his breath played with; only,
Between the slats of his perfect sleep
Came little slants of sun, and they were muddy
With the hard wading of humanity;
This made him change his position slightly,
And that stirred up the scent of the thyme which made
His unimpassioned bed.

PER.   It's rather frightening
When a dark room starts to speak.

DUKE.   My original
Syntax, like original sin, grows vastier
In the dark. Come in.

PER.   What does your legend mean?

DUKE. It means, Perpetua, we're all as well
As can be expected. Does anyone know you're here?

PER. No one.

DUKE.   They would think I meant to love you.
I wonder if I mean any such thing.
We'll make some light. Matches?

PER.   No.

DUKE. No, here are some. (*He lights an oil lamp.*)
                              This was the first

Astonishment of creation; after that
Came the frenzy of which you and I
Are the humble result. An access of starlight
And the fish began to swim; God gave way
To hallucinations; you and I again.
Would you like a drink?

PER.   Thank you. Tell me, as one
Hallucination to another, what
Happiness do you get up here with your telescope?

DUKE. I can't remember. That's a handsome moth
Come in to die, two petals, two tendrils,
And a flake of snow, meticulous, irrelevant,
Unwise. You came to see my stars. I have them
Here.

PER. I expect you can find your way about them
Even in the dark. Tell me who it is
We're trained on now.

DUKE.   Senator Saturn, white-
Hot with gravity. His moon, out of love
For his grey steel brow,
Streamed away her life into a circle
Of tormented arms. You see them there,
You see how they circle and never touch.
Saturn is alone, for all their circling round him.

PER. And alone so long. I'm looking at the same star
That shone alone in the wake of Noah's
Drifting ark as soon as the rain was over,
That shone on shining Charlemagne
Far away, and as clear
As the note of Roland's homing horn.
Alone so long, and now casually
Descending to us, on a Thursday midnight:
Saturn, who once glinted in the glass
Of Ariadne's mirror at the moment
When she died and melted out of Naxos.

DUKE. Ariadne died in childbirth. One

Life put the other out. It was Edgar's mode
Of entrance. Where in the sky shall we go to now?

PER. Wherever you may like to take me. I'm
A stranger here.

DUKE.   She died a girl in love,
And I went on in love without her
For longer than was fair. But this is not
Astronomy.

PER.   Astrology, then. You can't
Throw someone against the sky and not expect
A certain vapour of magic to condense
In moisture on their lashes. Let me believe
For a little while in man's ordeal by star
And tell me your own. I want to hear it.

DUKE. Isn't it a strange love, Perpetua,
That will never, can never, know what it was?
Death chose to interrupt us while we were still
Careening together high above the spires
Of common sense. And so what modulation
Would have come, how soon, how scaling down,
Is never to be known. And I can never tell
Whether a love, which was haled away
While it still was hale, was all and more
Of love than I could expect again: or if
The one twin-hearted permanence
Was waiting somewhere ahead. That has always
Perplexed me. What have I been doing, since
She died? Making do because the best
Was done? Or have I been turning head by head
To find the face which, willingly,
I should never let pass? For a long while now
I've been thinking the first, but today
The question seems to have sprung into life again.

PER. With your mind so full of inquiry, I'm surprised
You've had any time for love.

DUKE. It takes no time.
It's on us while we walk, or in mid-sentence,
A sudden hoarseness, enough to choke the sense.
Now isn't that so?

PER. Not so with me.

DUKE. You must try
To use longer sentences. Then you would certainly feel
The fumbling in the quiver behind every syllable
And so to the arrow string, like a sudden
Swerving parenthesis.

PER. Do you think I should?

DUKE. No doubt of it.

PER. There isn't any reason
Why a sentence, I suppose, once it begins,
Once it has risen to the lips at all
And finds itself happily wandering
Through shady vowels and over consonants
Where ink's been spilt like rivers or like blood
Flowing for the cause of some half-truth
Or a dogma now outmoded, shouldn't go
Endlessly moving in grave periphrasis
And phrase in linking phrase, with commas falling
As airily as lime flowers, intermittently,
Uninterrupting, scarcely troubling
The mild and fragile progress of the sense
Which trills trebling like a pebbled stream
Or lowers towards an oath-intoning ocean
Or with a careless and forgetful music
Looping and threading, tuning and entwining,
Flings a babel of bells, a carolling
Of such various vowels the ear can almost feel
The soul of sound when it lay in chaos yearning
For the tongue to be created: such a hymn
If not as lovely, then as interminable,
As restless, and as heartless, as the hymn
Which in the tower of heaven the muted spheres

With every rippling harp and windy horn
Played for incidental harmony
Over the mouldering rafters of the world,
Rafters which seldom care to ring, preferring
The functional death-watch beetle, stark, staccato,
Economical as a knuckle bone,
Strict, correct, but undelighting
Like a cleric jigging in the saturnalia,
The saturnalia we all must keep,
Green-growing and rash with life,
Our milchy, mortal, auroral, jovial,
Harsh, unedifying world,
Where every circle of grass can show a dragon
And every pool's as populous as Penge,
Where birds, with taffeta flying, scarf the air
On autumn evenings, and a sentence once
Begun goes on and on, there being no reason
To draw to any conclusion so long as breath
Shall last, except that breath
Can't last much longer.

DUKE.   Now point me out the comma
Where you loved me.

PER.   Not at any.

DUKE.   Let me see;
Was there a colon somewhere?

PER.   Perhaps one;
But if so we passed it without any trouble
Of any sort.

DUKE.   Never mind. There are sure
To be other sentences. The little god
Is older than he was, and moves more slowly.

PER. Even when he aims at you?

DUKE.   For me, I'm afraid,
He makes a special effort, shoots
Most generously, and then, poor boy, can't handle
A bow for several weeks.

PER.   Why are you so sure
    That I must love you? The field is wide,
    And everyone's heart is a great eccentric;
    Its whole distinction is a madness. Wildly
    Away from any mark it goes, making
    Anywhere the same gigantic mimicry of sunshine,
    No one else knows why. Be sure of nothing.

DUKE. Do you know what night this is?

PER.   All-Hallows Eve.

DUKE. All-Hallows Eve. If the earth is ever wise
    To magic, this is the night when magic's wisdom
    Comes rolling in across our sedate equation.
    All the closed hours unlock; the rigorous ground
    Grows as soft as the sea, exhaling
    The bloom of the dead everywhere. They almost
    Live again: as nearly, at least, as we
    Can brush on death. And through the night
    They trespass agreeably on our time of trespasses,
    Molesting the air in a pale, disinterested
    Way, until they thankfully notice
    The dark is paler, and sigh themselves out again;
    Though not before they've planted, as they go,
    A seed of chill which grows rapidly
    Into a rigid winter where the sun
    Can hardly raise himself to make a noon.
    But still, that's presently. What's more to our purpose
    Is that tonight the gravity of mirrors
    Is so potent it can draw the future
    Into the glass, and show shadows of husbands
    To girls who sit and comb their hair. Suppose
    You try it.

PER.   I'm two or three centuries
    Too late.

DUKE.   We know nothing yet.
    There's the mirror. In your bag no doubt
    A comb. And while you comb tradition says

You must eat an apple: though God knows why
Any apple should trust itself between your teeth
After this morning's little episode.
However, here's one intrepid to the core.

PER. How old is this mirror? The glass
Is very loath to let me in.

DUKE.   Eight duchesses
Have rested there in passing, before the glass
Began to cloud; and after that came three
Peering housekeepers, a chambermaid
Who, what with frequent tears and the ageing mirror,
Never saw her face; and me, who by
Much early study have overcome the need
To try.

PER. And I am the eight duchesses
And the three housekeepers and the chambermaid
Combing their hair. I am any girl: Perpetua
Perpetual, making no gesture I can call
My own, engraving theirs one lifetime deeper.
Midnight, the apple, and Perpetua
Combing her hair, as all the time she was.

(*The* DUKE *quietly crosses the room until his reflection falls into the*
mirror. PERPETUA's *attention is caught; she stares into the glass be-*
fore she turns suddenly to look at the DUKE.)
It seemed to be your son.

DUKE.   Perpetua,
You must play fair.

PER.   You must tell that to the mirror.
The reflection seemed to be Edgar.

DUKE.   Then the mirror
Is very penetrating. It has seen
How young, to all intents, I am.

PER.   I suppose so.
You think there's no magic.

DUKE.   That's as kind
As anything you've said. I think there *is*

Magic: an old dim-sighted mirror
And a shaded lamp for one genial moment
Raised me out of the falling leaves. A pity
The vision has gone. I'll agree to immortality
If immortality is to be always twenty-five
Seen by a man approaching fifty. The thought
Alone sends me begging to Olympus.
And you, being twenty-five, and looked upon
By me, together we make one golden flesh
For which both worlds, this and the next, will try
To outbid each other, and while the bidding mounts
We'll spend our love between them, disregarding
Both, until—

PER.   Until, next year,
I am twenty-six.

DUKE.   Which is twenty-five and one more.
I am the one.

PER.   It remains for me to love you.

DUKE. It has always been understood to be so easy.
Why ever should you not? Am I, before
God, too old? Consider the rocks
Of Arizona, and then consider me.
How recently the world has had the pleasure
Of pleasing, the opportunity of knowing me.
Age, after all, is only the accumulation
Of extensive childhood: what we were,
Never what we are. Don't deliver me
Up to my grey hairs.

PER.   Them I could certainly
Love. No, it's rather that I wonder
Whether you're not almost too young to be lived with.

DUKE. When we're married I shall age beside you; forgive me
Loitering now till you draw level.

PER. When we're married?

DUKE.   Are we to be formal?
Should I have asked you first?

PER.   Not if you have
     Some other way of knowing the answer. Have you?

DUKE. Perhaps I may pass that question back. Have I?

PER. Your Grace—

DUKE.   Somewhere I have a Christian name.

PER. Do you know anything against my father?

DUKE. In my heart, nothing.
     He loves me in his way, and that absolves him
     From any defect on earth. No doubt
     He'll have to stand in a corner of heaven with his face
     To a jasper wall, but here let him thrive.

PER.   You mean
     You know.

DUKE.   I know he wishes to make honey.
     Any bee would tell you, that's impossible
     If clover objects to rape.

PER.   So this is how
     You know I shall marry you: for Poppadillo's sake?

DUKE. This is how.

PER.   And perhaps it is going to feel
     Strange to you at first to know I am not.
     No, no, you're mistaken, and I was quite
     Mistaken, too! This isn't how I mean
     To lose my way, by force of circumstantial
     Evidence. When I lose my way I shall lose it
     In my own time, and by my own misguided
     Sense of direction.

DUKE.   Planting your own brambles,
     Digging your own pitfalls, willing your own
     Will-o'-the-wisps, designing
     Down to the last detail Perpetua's Folly.

PER. Without respect of persons. But do you mean
     You have sat perched up here, for months and years,
     Your eyes shrewdly glittering with starlight,
     Knowing that my father, fifty feet below,

Was being clever in your clover, and you said
Nothing?

DUKE.   We were being so happy together.
And if I had mentioned it, he would have felt
Obliged to discontinue, which would have been
Immensely sad. And, what is more,
Swarming stars and solitary Duke
Would have been unvisited tonight.

PER. How happy do you feel to know you tried
For a bride by this conspiracy of silence?

DUKE. How happy do you feel to know you were ready
To take a husband to make that silence absolute?

PER. I made no pretence of loving you. I was glad
When Edgar came to the mirror; I don't know why.

DUKE. I seem to have come to the end of myself
Sooner than I expected. So there's to be
No climax and adorable close
With ego agonistes crowned and smiling?
The strange charm of being alive breaks off
Abruptly, with nothing determined, nothing solved,
No absolute anything. I thought this time
The ends of the ring would join. But, no,
I'm back among the fragments.

PER.   Is this fair?

DUKE. How nature loves the incomplete. She knows
If she drew a conclusion it would finish her.
But, O God, for one round Amen!

PER.   That only
Comes on judgement day, and so,
As love won't live with judgement, Amen must wait
Show me one more star and I must go.

DUKE. I think they're falling.
While I love you without being loved they're sure
To be restive.

PER.   When they fall do they scorch the air
In passing? Is that what I can smell?

DUKE.   Or is it
    The smell of man being born to trouble? Or both
    The upward sparks and the downward stars together?

PER. Something *is* on fire. I can hear the flames
    Crunching on wood.

DUKE.   Have my almost mindless gardeners
    Been suddenly visited by imagination
    And lit us a Hallowe'en bonfire?

PER.   Why, look, the garden's
    Capering with light. The fire is underneath us—
    Look! It's the house, this wing of the house is on fire!

DUKE. Merciful heaven,
    Wouldn't you think my blood was warm enough
    To get us through a night without encouragement?

PER. Shall we be able to get away?

DUKE.   By all means.
    We'll leave the moths to perform whatever
    Immolation is necessary. A more
    Temperate life is better for us,
    And the cooler coast of the garden.

(*He throws open the door and looks on to the stairs.*)
    Well, here's a riproaring gauntlet to be run
    By a couple of God's children.

PER.   No! No, no!
    Not that way!

DUKE.   Which other? The only alternative
    To downward is upward, and how do you propose
    Two such wingless babes as we are—
    No, Perpetua; quickly, love, before
    The even chance is out of patience with us.

PER. No! There's no chance there. You can see
    There's no chance there. It's all in the fire,
    Every tread of the stairs. What shall we do?

(*She runs to the window and looks down.*)
    So far away, so far away.

DUKE.   Trust me;
    Try this way in my arms, Perpetua. Hope
    Is forlorn, but I'm sure very fond of us.
    We'll give her the benefit, shall we, and both be brave?

PER. Don't make me. I'd rather jump to the garden, and die
    Fair and broken. I'll make my own death
    As it suits me.

DUKE.   That as well? I'm sorry; you can have
    Your own way in everything else.

PER.   Please,
    Please, please, please.

DUKE.   Well, I see
    We've chosen. Hope has got tired of waiting
    And taken half the staircase with her. Now,
    We'll ring a rescue, and then indulge in the luxury
    Of having nothing to do but fold our hands.

(*He holds her beside him while he uses the telephone.*)
    Gently, my dear, you White Queen; nothing
    Has hurt us yet. A fire at Stellmere Park.
    Two people trapped: neither anxious to die.
    I suggest you should make remarkable speed.
    God bless you. They didn't wait for blessing.

PER. Aren't you desperate, too? Aren't you even afraid?

DUKE. Why, yes, yes, I have to be; I love myself,
    And I shall be sad to say good-bye to myself;
    There's no one like me, though so many better.
    Will you kiss the last of a singular man?

PER. Easily, oh, easily.

DUKE.   There's always a good thing left
    Even when the world would seem to be spent out.
    Do you think you love me?

PER.   Yes, I love you:
    Between the giddiness I love you.

DUKE.   May it also
    Be between my arms? I love my love
    With a death because it has no alteration

And no end. This concluding grace, Amen.
In the long world we're being shaken from
The star which, when it's rising, is called Venus,
Setting is Lucifer, the goddess
Graduating into demon, and what good
Is that for a man's immortal spirit? But you
And I, pursuing love no farther than this
Pure outcry of recognition,
Possess it most faithfully.

PER.   I only know—
Listen to the fire now, listen to it!
It means to let nothing escape. I only know
We go together into pain.

DUKE. Out of the world like snow. And so
The phoenix and the turtle did. •
Pain took them, too, and welded them
And melted them, and made a union
Of beauty born and beauty reft away,
And, when the air was empty, time was brimming,
And light was beating with one heart.

PER. I'm afraid of the fire, I'm afraid, I am so
Afraid of the fire.

(*The voice of* REDDLEMAN *is heard outside the door.*)

REDDLE. (*off*). Your Grace! All right, all right, your Grace!

DUKE. The voice of tomorrow morning, after all.
We're not to be allowed perfection, Perpetua.
The kind world intervenes.

(*Enter* REDDLEMAN.)

REDDLE. Ah, you poor sinners. I'm with you now;
Did you think I was never coming?

PER.   Never coming,
Never, never coming!

DUKE.   Quietly yet,
Fly up gently, we've still got far to go.
How do you propose to rescue us, Reddleman?
And how the hell did you get here?

REDDLE.   By me flair
  For elementary science. I thumbed a lift
  On the rising heat. And, by the blistering
  Of the blessed St. Laurence and the blessed St. Vincent,
  Shadrac, Meshac, Abednego, and all
  The sainted salamanders, I've got me nerve again;
  For there's the conflagration below, frumping
  And grouching like all the golden lads of lions
  I ever put me hand into the fire of!
  Didn't God make sinners of you and trap you here
  For the decent purpose of putting me back
  In the way of salvation?
DUKE.   And us, too, I hope.
  Can we go the way you came?
PER.   ·   God be kind,
  Be kind.
REDDLE. Have you any objection, now,
  To dropping from time to time into me arms
  From a great way off? 'Twould be to avoid the stairs,
  Themselves being gone entirely.
PER. Must it be that way?
REDDLE.   In the Captain's keeping,
  Via Leo, con brio, the way of the lions!
DUKE. He's got himself well up in the god class now,
  Perpetua: all we have to do is trust ourselves
  To the rope of his nerve, spit on our hands, and go.
(BATES *appears at the window.*)
BATES. Well, *you've* got yourselves in a picklin' walls-up
  And no mistake.
DUKE.   Are we to have all
  The guardian angels at a blow?
  You spoil us, Bates.
REDDLE.   He spoils me night of glory.
  Send him about his business, if you love me,
  Your Grace, for the love of God, send him
  About his business!

BATES.   Couldn't the Lord Lieutenant
     Even keep his nose out of this little job?
     Come on, miss; come and take a butcher's
     At the panorama; it's lovely outside 'ere.
PER. Oh, yes, yes!
REDDLE.   Monkeys, monkeys, monkeys!
DUKE. How do you think we're going to get down, Bates?
BATES. Well, I come up by the ladders, but according
     To the rules we have to slip down by the snakes. Still,
     Do what your fancy tells you, mate. I'm
     Not looking.
PER.   And I wish I hadn't looked, and I wish
     We were safe on the ground.
DUKE.   Think of something high
     Like Kanchenjunga. That very nearly takes us
     Down the ladder before we start.
REDDLE.   Your Grace,
     You're not so out of your mind as to go
     Out of the window? Encouraging robbery
     And violence, you are, to set your foot
     On a ladder propped up against your property
     Without permission, and in the middle of the night
     When no decent man would be lashing one ladder
     To another, and he in his shirt.
BATES.   You save 'em
     Wiv your trousers, go on, let's see you; save 'em wiv your trousers.
DUKE. Reddleman, by all means love your lions,
     But condescend to the snakes. Come on.
REDDLE. Where's a fine soul under heaven?
DUKE.   Not playing
     With fire, wherever else he may be.
BATES.   That's right, miss,
     Let me take you, miss; fink nuffing of it.
     Relax yourself, as though you was mink.
     Fink lovely foughts, miss, and you won't weigh nuffing.
     Wonder what stretch I'll have to do for abduction?

DUKE (*climbing through the window after them*). A beautiful room,
    Reddleman; worth a fortune
    In memories and astronomical equipment.
(*He disappears from view.* REDDLEMAN *leans out.*)
REDDLE. H'wot do you think the dear God gave me back
    Me nerve for? To come crawling after heathen
    Like spittle down a window? B'Jason,
    I've a better opinion of meself.
    Anyway, it makes me giddy and it's no position
    For any reasonable man to get himself into.
(*He crosses the room, throws open the door, and meets the glare of the
    fire.*)
    Tossing your mighty manes, roaring yellow murder!
    The Captain's not afraid!
(*Exit* REDDLEMAN. *The* DUKE *climbs back in at the window calling him,
    races across the room to the door, calls:*)
DUKE. Reddleman, you hell-raking maniac!
(*He picks up the half-eaten apple from the dressing table, calls to* RED-
    DLEMAN:)
    Who would have the heart to disappoint you?
(*He puts the apple between his teeth and follows* REDDLEMAN *the way
    of the stairs.*)

                        (THE CURTAIN FALLS ON ACT TWO)

ACT THREE

*The Temple of the Ancient Virtues, an hour or so later. The light from
    the burning house reflected in the lake.* ROSABEL *is sobbing in the
    dark. Enter* DOMINIC, *carrying two chairs and a stable lantern. He
    halts and listens to the sobbing.*

DOM. May I interrupt your unhappiness,
    Just to bring in one or two things? It's begun
    To rain. Everything's going to get wet.
    I wonder if you need cry quite so despairingly.

It makes me feel very awkward. I am not good
At comforting people, even when I know
Where to look for them. I'm Dominic Reedbeck . . .
How do you do? And where would you be?

ROSA.   Oh, no,
Don't look for me.

DOM.   I couldn't look for you;
I don't know who you are. Everyone
Is safe, you know; they're all accounted for,
Except Miss Fleming. Do you know where she is?

ROSA. No. No one must ever see her again.

DOM. Why not? Is she so badly burned? What is it,
Oh, what *is* it? I wish you'd help me to be helpful;
I find it so difficult.

ROSA.   I'm here. I wish
I were dead.

DOM.   I don't see how you can wish for something
You only know the name of. Now that it's raining
I won't be the only one coming in here. Perhaps
You should try to feel better. If I were you.

ROSA. They wouldn't look for me in hell.

DOM.   Oh, yes, they would.
It's the obvious place to look for anyone,
If you're speaking euphemistically.

ROSA. I'm grateful to you. So would anyone
In hell be. Your voice is very cold.
I want harshness. I want hatred.
If you would hate me it might help me to bear
To think of myself. You're going to find it easy.
It was I who started the fire. I did it
Deliberately.

DOM.   Perpetua was there.
The Duke was there. They might never have got away.

ROSA. But you haven't understood. You can't have understood.
It was I who did this unimaginable thing.

DOM. I was thinking of myself.

My sister was there because I sent her there.
Perhaps you were compelled to be the means
By which I was shown I had fallen into error.
If so, I must thank you. Thank you, Miss Fleming.

ROSA. You're mad! Do you think I hurled myself away
From all the decent world for your sake?
Hate me, hate me! Oh, why is it
You won't understand?

DOM.   I do understand. I know
Too well our preternatural aptitude
For sin. My father made it quite clear to me.

ROSA. Oh, what shall I do?

DOM.   There's Sergeant Harry Bullen,
The policeman from Swinford Magna. He's a very
Reasonable chap; I'm sure he'd arrest you
Willingly if you went and asked him.
And he's here, which is very convenient for you.

ROSA. Yes, where? Where is he?

DOM.   I saw him five minutes ago,
Coming head first down a ladder, to show the Duke
(As he said) that in the ordinary course of living
It makes little difference which way up you are.
He was joking, I think.

ROSA.   I'll find him, and give myself up.
Yes, up, out of this ditch of despair. No one
Need think of me again. I hardly remember
What I was like before today, but I think
I was an ordinary woman. No one
Else will remember. "She was always demented!"
It isn't true: never; until today
Struck me like a tornado, God knows from where.
But now I shall give myself up. Do I look
Plain and frightful? It could scarcely matter
Less. But, please God, help me avoid the Duke,
Wherever he may be.

(*Enter the* DUKE, *carrying things salvaged from the fire and over his
  shoulders a string of Chinese lanterns.*)

DUKE.   He's down at the Temple,
  I think, putting up some lanterns which he found
  In a box. You'll find him there, presumably
  Intent on some small ceremony of his own,
  Though fairly uncertain whether it's obsequies
  Or jubilation; he's in two hearts about it,
  And both weigh heavier than the one he had.
  God bless you, Rosabel; hold these; for a time
  We thought we had lost you.

ROSA.   Did you think so? Lost me?

DOM. You must tell him now. It will be much easier now;
  No postponing.   (*Exit* DOMINIC.)

DUKE. It's important that we should offset the smacking of the furies
  With a little decorous gaiety, with a show
  Of holier, if also homelier, flames.
  The lanterns, Rosabel. They'll be very pale
  Compared with the foment of wild flamboyant rose
  We have in the sky tonight; but never mind;
  Think what deeds of spring are done
  By the glow-worm light of a primrose.

ROSA. I started the fire.

DUKE.   How did you come to do that?
  A careless flash from your incendiary eyes,
  Perhaps.

ROSA.   You must believe me. I fired the wing,
  To destroy the observatory, to make you human,
  To bring you down to be among the rest of us,
  To make you understand the savage sorrows
  That go on below you. Today, this awful day,
  The violence of a long unhappiness rocked
  And fell, and buried me under itself at last.
  How vile it was I know. I know for life.
  But I didn't know you were there; believe me, I didn't
  Know any living soul was there!

DUKE. O,

O, O, O, Rosabel:
If you had only asked me first.
I could have told you no fire would be enough
To burn down heaven, and while it's there
I shall find some wide-eyed place where I can sit
And scrutinize the inscrutable, amazed
That we can live in such a condition of mystery
And not be exasperated out of our flesh,
As we might be, were it not that flesh
Is interesting, too.
Your fire was too small, Rosabel, though enough
To singe my butler into ecstasy,
And smoke tears into eyes unaccustomed to them,
Mine, I mean. So much I delighted in
Is now all of ash, like a dove's breast feathers
Drifting dismally about the garden.

ROSA. Time and I both know how to bring
Good things to a bad end, all
In the course of love. No wonder
"God be with you" has become "Good-bye,"
And every day that wishes our welfare says
Farewell. Tonight will go past, as a swan
Will pass like a recurring dream
On the light sleep of the lake,
And I shall be smoothed away in the wake of the swan;
But I can never return what I've lost you, or lose
What I gave, though the long steadiness of time
May long to make us well.

DUKE. So much I delighted in is all of ash.

(ROSABEL, *giving a moan almost too low to hear, goes out. Her place is taken by* PERPETUA, *but the* DUKE, *now hanging the lanterns, hasn't seen the change.*)

But the lost world of walls and stairs,
Where I could cosset ghosts for their melancholy
Charm, has let the daylight into me

With a straight left of love. So no remorse,
Rosabel. I love my love, and my love loves me.
Everything goes but everything comes.
We fall away into a future, and all
The seven seas, and the milky way
And morning, and evening, and hi-cockalorum are in it.
Nothing is with the past except the past.
So you can make merry with the world, Rosabel.
My greatful thanks.

PER. I have to make you understand.

DUKE.   I forgive you:
You can mine the lake so that it bursts
In a hundred and one torrential rainbows
Over the roof of the Carpenters' Arms; you can shatter
Conservatories into a deluge of crystal,
And shoot the cowman's nine insufferable
Children: I forgive you in advance.
I've achieved the rare, benevolent place
Where the irk of the lonely human state
Is quite unknown, and the fumbling fury
We call our life—It wasn't Rosabel
Who spoke then. It was surely Perpetua?

PER. I have to make you understand. You must
Be patient with me.

DUKE.   God so, it's the little firebird.
Are you rested? Lanterns, you see, to light our love.
I thought we could sit by the cinders
And toast our hearts, if Bates, as he was told to,
Brings the champagne.

PER.   You have to give me
Your best and gentlest attention. Be
At your most understanding. I need it, if I don't
Deserve it from you. Tonight, when we seemed
Closely, and only us of all the living
World, attended by a dragon breathing out
Almost certain death—

(*Enter* BATES, *with champagne and glasses in a basket, and carrying another lantern.*)

BATES.   That Captain Reddleman,
    As he likes to demean hisself to call hisself—
    Now you're not getting yourselves into anuvver
    Critical situation? You can scramble down
    Off of that one on your own
    Virgin initiative; I'm badgered if I'm going
    To throw anuvver expensive rescue party.

DUKE. Matches, Perpetua?

PER.   No.

BATES.   His illuminated
    Lordship Reddleman should ought to have
    His brain looked into. In and out, in and out,
    In and out of the burning building, like
    A perishing nigger in and out of a flaming
    Woodpile. And what he says about me's
    Enough to arrest a cock in the middle of his crow
    And bring a blush to his ruddy comb. It isn't
    The language I've been brought up to.

DUKE (*lighting the lanterns*).   The first astonishment
    Of creation; after that came the frenzy.

PER.   Let me
    Talk to you.

BATES.   Here's his incandescent majesty
    Coming now, wiv his head under the table.

(*Enter* REDDLEMAN, *carrying a table on his head.*)
    What's the matter, mate; lost your tit-fer?

REDDLE. There's no doubt at all your Grace has noticed
    There are some men are born too small in the soul
    To do gratifying deeds, and not sprain all decency.
    And 'tis the footman Bates
    Who's the diminuendo of all small souls.
    He's a demi-semi soul, and that's magnanimous.
    I have to put on me glasses, and then search

As though I was after looking for a louse
In Molly O'Magan's obster-eperous hair.
Would it be here you were wanting the table set up,
Your Grace?

DUKE. Put it where the wind won't blow;
It's blowing cold. And for Christmas' sake
Will you pair of immortals kiss each other
And come off the tiles?

BATES. I'd just like to know who give him permission
To go measuring my soul? I never done.
I've got it nicely laid away: spotless,
Wiv lavender.

REDDLE. 'Twas a mighty night of miracle,
With Cuchulain at me right hand, and Daniel at me left,
And the smallest soul in the world dashes it from me,
And he naked in his shirt.

DUKE. Ah, miracles, Reddleman,
Miracles; don't trust them. How far
Can a man journey on a miracle? It's better
To bounce your behind on any spavined hack
Than to straddle a flash of lightning.
Straighten your laurel wreaths, the couple of you,
And remember one another in your prayers.
It seems I have something else to listen to.

(*Enter* REEDBECK *and* DOMINIC.)

REED. Ah, here he is. I'm not what you thought me, your Grace.
I must tell you plainly I'm not at all what you thought me.

DUKE. No?

REED. No. If you ask these men to go, your Grace,
I shall be only too grieved to tell you what I am.

BATES (*to* REDDLEMAN). Nuffing to stay for, boy. I'll come and see you
Popping yourself in and out of the fire again.

REDDLE. Breakfast, your Grace, at what o'clock?

DUKE. The morning
Must wait, Reddleman. I have still
The rest of the night to consider. (*Exeunt* BATES *and* REDDLEMAN.)

PER. (*to* REEDBECK).   Darling,
    Not now. Any day or night of the year,
    There's always time, you can go together, and look
    At the pigs or the winter wheat, and talk your two
    Hearts out; but just this night, and for just
    These five minutes of this night, leave me
    To talk to him alone.

REED.   I've worked myself up,
    I've reached the pitch now; it would never do
    To put it—put it off; walked much too fast,
    Breath very short, and then heart very heavy,
    Imagination—disconcerting—too vivid: I see you
    Both up there, no amount of stars
    Any use, in dreadful danger, and who but me,
    I, whichever it is, responsible?

DOM. Please blame me for that. Do allow me
    To know which sin belongs to whom. We shall only
    Get confused, father, unless you keep strictly
    To your own wrong turning.

REED.   Extremely difficult
    To know where to stop, once you begin to believe
    You're not all you should be. Let me see,
    There was something worse Dominic said
    I had to confess to you.

PER.   He knows, he knows.
    So now, you poor worried Poppadillo, half
    Awash with sleep, you can go back
    To bed at once, or else I think I shall cry.

REED. But I don't quite know what you know he knows,
    And I think I'd better—

DUKE.   Drink, Reedbeck, I think
    You'd better drink. We have something to celebrate,
    You and I, which lights me more than the most
    Tower-toppling blaze that ever lit
    A city lane—

PER.   Oh, do let me speak to you!

REED. I've reached the pitch. I've worked myself up
       To the point of whatever the point was when I first
       Came in. But you're quite right, half awash, suddenly
       Woken up in alarm—

DOM.   Now, *think* a minute.

DUKE. Master Dominic: pass to your saintly father
       This glass of champagne.

REED.   Excuse me. But I know
       There's some good reason why I shall have to refuse.
       Now that my attention has been drawn
       To what must be a myopia in my moral vision—
       Must have been suffering from it all my life,
       I suppose: and tonight feels very latter-day;
       Wrath of God: here we are
       Looking such weak vessels and so temporary
       Among the four terrible elements
       (The rain and the firemen's hose remind me of the fourth)—
       What was I going to say? Yes, yes, I think
       It wouldn't be correct to drink with you before
       I give myself up to Sergeant Bullen.

DUKE.   Drink up,
       And keep your sins for some leisurely angel;
       They've nothing to do with me. Dominic,
       If what appear to be discrepancies
       In your father's books afflict you, let me tell you
       Though they seem unusual they're as much in order
       As Sergeant Bullen's collar and tie. There exists
       A document assigning to your father
       All those percentages from rents and sales
       Which you seem to have thought are misbegotten.

DOM. Do you mean you've noticed the discrepancies
       And legalized them?

DUKE.   My dear conscience-nudging,
       Parent-pesting, guilt-corroded child,
       If I may address you with so much affection,

The arrangement was perfect. It embarrassed
Neither of us. Take a drink to wash
Your conscience down. And one brimming for you,
A pale representation of my heart,
Perpetua.

PER.   It's too full, seriously,
Far too full. You've been good to my father.
Please will you put it down? I know my hand
Isn't steady enough to take it.

DUKE.   Then let me sip
Some away from the western rim
And leave the east for you.

REED.   Made it legal?

DUKE. There now. Shall we drink
To the babe born in the fire, the crowning of souls
In extremity? As long as we live, Perpetua,
We shall be able to tell how, at midnight,
We skated over death's high-lit ebony
And heard the dark ring a change of light,
While everywhere else the clocks
Were sounding the depths of a dark, unhappy end.
And then we shall be able to say
How an autumn duke—

PER.   —found that fear could seem
Like love to a silly girl, who now knows
It was fear and not love, wishes you to forgive her,
Wishes she could sink away with the night
Where she won't any more trouble you.

DUKE *(after a long pause, raising his glass)*. Then the toast is: Fear.

PER. I had to tell you.

DUKE.   Do I
Have to drink alone?

PER.   No. No. (*They all drink in silence.*)

DUKE. Do you think I can't forgive you? I forgive
Both of us for being born of the flesh,
Which means I forgive all tossing and turning,

All foundering, all not finding,
All irreconcilability,
All the friction of this great orphanage
Where no one knows his origin and no one
Comes to claim him. I forgive even
The unrevealing revelation of love
That lifts a lid purely
To close it, and leaves us knowing that greater things
Are close, but not to be disclosed
Though we die for them. I forgive
Everything, my most dear Perpetua,
Except that I wasn't born something less ambitious,
Such as a Muscovy duck.

REED.   I couldn't think
Of allowing such generosity. Legalized!
No, your Grace, I simply couldn't accept it.

DUKE. Reedbeck, my God! For how many years have you
Stood here? You must be very old by now.
I remember you well in happier times.

PER.   Poppadillo,
Why do we all have to get between someone else
And the sun? Keep me from doing this again.

REED. Whatever you say, my dear; though whatever you're saying
I really don't know. I'd like to help, but you're both
Talking in my sleep, evidently.

(*Enter* EDGAR, JESSIE, *and* HILDA.)

ED. That was a hideous mile or two of driving!
We saw the fire on the clouds, and guessed
It could only be here.

HIL.   I saw it from home, reflected
In my bedroom window. I tried to telephone
But I couldn't get through.

DUKE.   I must ask you, if you will,
To remember we've been appreciating this very
Minor act of God for more than two hours.
The earth has moved on roughly a hundred

And thirty thousand miles since then,
And histories have been much altered.
I hope the dance was a great success.

JESS.   Yes, lovely,
But it's doing myself a great kindness to be able
To sit down. Dancing all hours, and a couple of miles
Of apprehension makes All Hallowe'en
Into a marathon if a girl's not quite
As hale and hallow as once she was.
Is everybody safe?

DUKE.   Safe: I'll not say
"As houses," considering what goes on,
But as safe and suffering as health can be.

HIL. It's a fortunate thing that providence
Was in her friendly mood tonight
And kept you out of Galileo's lap.

DUKE. Not she. She saw two souls there, happily occupied
At the narrow end of the telescope,
Two star-loving minutiae, male and female,
Perpetua and my unoffending self:
And instantly shot out a vituperative
Tongue. And we were rescued by two
Heavenly agents, Bates and Reddleman.

REED. God bless them; I've never liked either of them,
But God bless them.

HIL.   And keep them in the heavenly business.

JESS. I'll kiss them for it presently. They must
Have got a bit above themselves
To rescue you from there.

ED.   And so
You meant to meet there, even this afternoon.
And the only comfort I had, all the way home,
Was that Perpetua was safely sleeping
Away in another house.

PER.   We meant to meet there,

And this afternoon we were lying to you,
And never was a lie less happy for everyone.

DUKE. I hear me whistling down the wind.

JESS.   We wouldn't
Like you to think we're setting up in competition,
But in our own small way we've met
With a catastrophe, too.

HIL.   Both our cars
Swung in at the gates together, and as our attention
Was all on the fire—

JESS.   Our wings aren't what they were,
As Lucifer said after his long day's fall.

DUKE. What's the matter with the Fates today; fidget, fidget;
Why can't they settle down to some useful spinning?
I forgot to ask you, Hilda (Jessie and Lucifer
Remind me), how is Roderic?

HIL.   Asleep when I left.
Two ribs broken, and a slight concussion,
Nothing worse. But that was enough to show me
How bad it is to see Roderic hurt, but how
Intolerable it would be to see Roderic
Maimed, or dying day by day; and I sat
Beside him and marvelled, and wondered how
So much could lie there in a human shell,
The long succession of life that led to him,
Uninterrupted from the time
Of time's aching infancy;
In the beginning was Roderic; and now
Haunting the same shell, were a childhood
And a manhood, half a hundred years
Of sights and sounds which once echoed and shone
And now may only exist in him. And though
He tries to be a copy of all his kind
How can he be? He is Roderic-phenomenon,
Roderic only, and at present Roderic in pain.

I felt I must tell you so. This afternoon
I made a cockshy of him, but this afternoon
I could no more truly see him than he, poor darling,
Can truly see half that there is to see.
I must get back home. I only wanted to be
Quite certain no one was hurt.

DUKE.   Rosabel
Is hurt.

ED.   But we saw her with Harry Bullen;
She seemed most vigorous, talking his helmet off;
He was mopping his head with a handkerchief.

DUKE.   Rosabel,
Why? With Harry Bullen? Why should she be?

DOM. Because she thought it was necessary
To her peace of mind. She has given herself up.

DUKE. And I give you up! How, by hell's grand canyon,
Do you know she has?

DOM.   She was really very unhappy;
I think I helped her to decide.

JESS.   But why?
Given herself up for lost, or what?

DUKE.   You strapping,
Ice-cold, donkey-witted douche of tasteless water!
I could willingly—Dominic, dear boy,
God would tell me He loves you, but then God
Is wonderfully accomplished, and to me
You seem less lovely, and for this good reason:
You think more of the sin than of the sinner.
Poor Rosabel. Where shall we find her?

HIL.   When
We saw them they were standing by the sundial.
What has she done?

DUKE.   Loved me beyond her strength.
We go and get her out of the arms of the law,
However attractive Bullen's arms may be.

Dear Rosabel! And after that we must find
Beds for ourselves away from the smell of smouldering
Memory. Bring along some of the lanterns.
Excellent, blessed Rosabel. Ros-a-bel!

(*He goes, calling her.* HILDA *follows him.*)

REED. (*to* JESSIE). Beds, yes, yes, beds, quite important.
There's one at least at my house if you'd care to oblige it,
Care to make use of it. No more sleep for me
Tonight; it wouldn't be wise; I've only just
Managed to digest the sleep I've had already.
In something of a fuddle.

JESS.   Dear, I'd get
Into anybody's bed tonight, and sleep
Without a murmur, even in the arms of Morpheus
If he'd give up his lute and let me. Where's the step?

(*She goes out,* REEDBECK *holding a lantern for her, and he follows her.*)

DOM. A fine rain raining still. Aren't you coming,
Perpetua?

PER.   I'll stay in the dry and rest.

DOM. I was hoping to talk to you, to tell you, to say
How responsible I feel for all that fear
And danger, I mean yours tonight. I expect
You think I was very much to blame.

PER.   No,
Dominic.

DOM.   They think I'm altogether wrong,
All the time. But I don't know how that can be.
And yet the whole of life is so unconsidering,
Bird, beast, and fish, and everything,
I wonder how the Creator came to be
Mixed up in such company. Do you think I'm wrong?

PER. No, Dominic.

DOM. (*with a sigh*). Ethics are very difficult.

(*He goes into the rain, leaving* PERPETUA *and* EDGAR. *They sit in silence
for a moment.*)

ED. Did you forget I was here?

PER.   I didn't forget.
But I wish I could forget, and I wish you had forgotten,
This afternoon's brazen lying.

ED.   I have forgotten.
Why should we remember this afternoon
When probably no one else does?

PER.   But am I sure
I want you to forget as incuriously as that?
I want your father not to be hurt by tonight,
I want you not to be hurt by this afternoon,
I want to be free to make my own way,
But I want to be remembered.

ED.   My memory
Is for nothing else. But, as it happens,
I hardly need it. Over and over again
I see you for the first time. I round
Some corner of my senses, and there, as though
The air had formed you out of a sudden thought,
I discover you. Any memory I had
Vanishes, to let you in so unannounced
My whole body stammers with surprise.
I imagine I love you. And I don't think
You can fairly object, when all you have to do
Is walk freely through my thoughts and round
My heart. You needn't even turn your head.

PER. Don't say this now. I'm still remembering
I can give pain, and that in itself is loss
Of liberty.

ED.   No, I just mentioned it in passing.

PER. No one is separate from another; how difficult
That is. I move, and the movement goes from life
To life all round me. And yet I have to be
Myself. And what is *my* freedom becomes
Another person's compulsion. What are we to make
Of this dilemma?

ED.   I haven't the sense to ask.
   Whatever the human mystery may be
   I am it.

PER. There's comfort in that.

ED.   Tell me:
   Do I seem to you to be only a sort
   Of postscript to my father?

PER.   No, Edgar,
   Across and across my heart, never at all.

ED. I begin to notice myself, too,
   I must say. Here the little parents come.

(*Enter the* DUKE *and* REEDBECK.)

   So now the house goes with a dragging wing.
   Are your spirits very heavy, father?

DUKE.   They ride;
   No, no, they ride well enough.

REED. (*to* PERPETUA).   Isn't it time
   My all night wanderer went to bed?

DUKE.   She will stay
   For a moment's peaceful conversation.

PER. I want to know about Rosabel. When Dominic said—

DUKE. I'll keep her story for a rainy day.

ED. And for now the rain has blown over. Shall we go
   And see how the last of the flames dance down
   To sleep among the ruins, Perpetua?

DUKE. Our peaceful conversation, Perpetua.

ED. Perpetua?

PER.   I'll find my way to bed.

ED. I shall take the liberty to light you there.
   Tomorrow, then, father.

DUKE.   Tomorrow to you.

PER. Tomorrow to us all, but not too soon.
   I need the soft pillows to make my peace
   Before I trust myself to another day tomorrow.

(*Exeunt* EDGAR *and* PERPETUA. REEDBECK *is almost asleep in a chair.*)

DUKE. Shall I be sorry for myself? In mortality's name
    I'll be sorry for myself. Branches and boughs,
    Brown hills, the valleys faint with brume,
    A burnish on the lake; mile by mile
    It's all a unison of ageing,
    The landscape's all in tune, in a falling cadence,
    All decaying. And nowhere does it have to hear
    The quips of spring, or, when so nearing its end,
    Have to bear the merry mirth of May.
    How fortunate to grow in the crow-footed woods,
    Eh, Reedbeck? But I see you're anxious to sleep.

REED. I? No, no; I'll never go to sleep
    Again tonight, much too disturbed.
    Don't know what to suggest I make of anything.
    I only hope a quiet dignity
    Will meet the case. Civilization is simply
    (If I had to define it) simply dignity,
    Simply simple dignity; but then
    Sons and daughters come into it, most lovable,
    Most difficult, and unexpected combustion,
    And so forth and so forth. Now le Roi Soleil,
    How many children did he have? One legitimate,
    Several illegitimate . . . le Duc de Maine,
    La Duchesse de Chartres. . . .

DUKE.   Shall I be happy for myself?
    In the name of existence I'll be happy for myself.
    Why, Reedbeck, how marvellous it is to moulder.
    Think how you would have felt when you were lying
    Grubbing in your mother's womb,
    With only a wall to look at,
    If you could have seen in your embryonic eye
    The realm of bryony, sloes, rose-hips,
    And a hedge's ruin, a golden desuetude,
    A countryside like a drowned angel
    Lying in shallow water, every thorn
    Tendering a tear. Think, Reedbeck,

Think of the wonder of such glimmering woe;
How in a field of milk-white haze the lost
Apollo glows and wanders towards noon;
The wind-blown webs are brighter,
The rolling apples warmer than the sun.
Heavens! you would have cried, the womb
Echoing round you: These are the heavens, and I,
Reedbeck, am stillborn. Would you not?

REED. (*waking slightly*). And la Duchesse de Condé, I think.

DUKE. So with ourselves; imagine: to have the sensation
Of nearness of sight, shortness of breath,
Palpitation, creaking in the joints,
Shootings, stabbings, lynching of the limbs,
A sudden illumination of lumbago.
What a rich world of sensation to achieve,
What infinite variety of being.
Is it not?

REED.   Dominic not fond . . .
Perpetua. . . .

DUKE.   Reedbeck, I have to tell you
I mean to marry. I can still remember,
In my ebbing way, how pleasant it is to love;
An ancient love can blow again, like summer
Visiting St. Martin. A breath will do it,
If the breath comes deep, and deep it has come.
You must give me your felicitations. I marry
Rosabel, when Rosabel
(After six months, I understand)
Is disengaged from custody.

(*Only deep breathing comes from* REEDBECK.)
Thank you, dear fellow. Rosabel
Would thank you, too, if she were here.
She and I, sharing two solitudes,
Will bear our spirits up to where not even
The nightingale can know,
Where the song is quiet, and quiet

Is the song. Tell me, Reedbeck, before
We leave each other in sleep, where would you say
The lonely moment is coaxing us to go?

(REEDBECK *gives a gentle near-whistling snore.*)

Well, yes, yes, quite so, my little one,
It comes to that in the end.

(THE CURTAIN FALLS FINALLY)

BIBLIOGRAPHY

STUDENTS' BIBLIOGRAPHY
OF MODERN DRAMA

ANDERSON, MAXWELL. *The Essence of Tragedy.* Washington, 1939.

ATKINSON, BROOKS. *Broadway Scrapbook.* New York, 1947.

BELL, AUBREY F. G. *Contemporary Spanish Literature.* New York, 1925.

BENTLEY, ERIC. *The Playwright as Thinker.* New York, 1946.

BLOCK, ANITA. *The Changing World in Plays and Theatre.* Boston, 1939.

BLUM, DANIEL. *A Pictorial History of the American Theatre, 1900-1950.* New York, 1950.

BRADBROOK, MURIEL C. *Ibsen, the Norwegian, A Revaluation.* London, 1946. (One of the best critical works on Ibsen.)

BROWN, JOHN MASON. *Two on the Aisle: Ten Years of the American Theatre in Performance.* New York, 1938.

Still Seeing Things. New York, 1950.

As They Appear. New York, 1952.

BYRNE, DAWSON. *The Story of Ireland's National Theatre: The Abbey Theatre, Dublin.* Dublin, 1929.

CHANDLER, FRANK W. *The Contemporary Drama of France.* Boston, 1921.

Modern Continental Playwrights. New York, 1931. (Excellent survey, with complete bibliographies.)

CHARQUES, RICHARD D. (ed.). *Footnotes to the Theatre.* London, 1938.

CLARK, BARRETT H. *Eugene O'Neill, The Man and His Plays,* Revised ed. New York, 1936, 1947.

A Study of the Modern Drama, New ed. New York, 1934.

European Theories of the Drama, Revised ed. with a Supplement on the American Drama. New York, 1947.

CLARK, BARRETT H., and GEORGE FREEDLEY (eds.). *A History of Modern Drama.* New York, 1947.

COLE, TOBY, and HELEN K. CHINOY (eds.). *Actors on Acting*. New York, 1949.

CUNLIFFE, JOHN W. *Modern English Playwrights*. New York, 1927.

DICKINSON, THOMAS H. *An Outline of Contemporary Drama*. Boston, 1927.
  The Contemporary Drama of England. Boston, 1931.
  (Ed.). *The Theater in a Changing Europe*. New York, 1937.

DOWNS, BRIAN W. *Ibsen: The Intellectual Background*. Cambridge, 1948.

DUKES, ASHLEY. *The Youngest Drama*. Chicago, 1924.

ELIOT, THOMAS STEARNS. *Poetry and Drama*. Cambridge, 1951.

ELOESSER, ARTHUR. *Modern German Literature*. New York, 1933.

FAY, W. G., and CATHERINE CARSWELL. *The Fays of the Abbey Theatre*. New York, 1935.

FERGUSSON, FRANCIS. *The Idea of a Theater*. Princeton, 1949.

FLANAGAN, HALLIE. *Shifting Scenes of the Modern European Theatre*. New York, 1928.

FLEXNER, ELEANOR. *American Playwrights: 1918-1938*. New York, 1938.

FREEDLEY, GEORGE, and JOHN A. REEVES. *A History of the Theatre*. New York, 1941.

GAGEY, EDMUND MC ADOO. *Revolution in American Drama*. New York, 1948.

GARDNER, HELEN. *The Art of T. S. Eliot*. New York, 1950.

GASSNER, JOHN. *Masters of the Drama*. New York, 1940.

GERHARDI, WILLIAM. *Anton Chekhov, A Critical Study*. New York, 1923.

GILDER, ROSAMOND. *A Theatre Library. A Bibliography of One Hundred Books Relating to the Theatre*. New York, 1932.

GORELIK, MORDECAI. *New Theatres for Old*. New York, 1940.

GREGORY, LADY. *Our Irish Theatre, A Chapter of Autobiography*. New York, 1913.

HAMILTON, CLAYTON MEEKER. *The Theory of the Theatre,* Consolidated ed. New York, 1939.

HUDSON, LYNTON. *Life and the Theatre*. London, 1949.

IRVINE, WILLIAM. *The Universe of G. B. S.* New York, 1949.

ISAACS, EDITH J. R. *The Negro in the American Theatre*. New York, 1947.

JAMES, HENRY. *The Scenic Art*. New Brunswick, 1948.

KOHT, HALVDAN. *The Life of Ibsen*. 2 vols. New York, 1931.

KOMMISSARZHEVSKI, THEODORE. *Myself and the Theatre*. New York, 1930.

KOSLOW, JULES. *The Green and the Red: Sean O'Casey . . . The Man and His Plays.* New York, 1950.

KRUTCH, JOSEPH WOOD. *The American Drama Since 1918.* New York, 1939.

LANGNER, LAWRENCE. *The Magic Curtain.* New York, 1951.

MAC CLINTOCK, LANDER. *The Contemporary Drama of Italy.* Boston, 1920.
The Age of Pirandello. Bloomington, 1951.

MC GILL, V. J. *August Strindberg, the Bedeviled Viking.* New York, 1930.

MALONE, ANDREW E. *The Irish Drama.* New York, 1929.

MANTLE, ROBERT BURNS. *Contemporary American Playwrights.* New York, 1938.

MATHIESSEN, F. O. *The Achievement of T. S. Eliot.* New York and London, 1947.

MARRIOTT, JAMES WILLIAM. *Modern Drama.* London, New York, 1934.

MAUGHAM, W. SOMERSET. *The Summing Up.* New York, 1938.

MILLER, ANNA IRENE. *The Independent Theatre in Europe, 1887 to the Present.* New York, 1931.

MILLETT, FRED B., and GERALD EADES BENTLEY. *The Art of the Drama.* New York, 1935.

MODERWELL, H. K. *The Theatre of To-day.* New York, 1927.

MOREHOUSE, WARD. *Matinee Tomorrow: Fifty Years of Our Theater.* New York, 1949.

NICOLL, ALLARDYCE. *British Drama,* 4th ed. revised. London, 1947.
World Drama: From Aeschylus to Anouilh. New York, 1950.

O'CASEY, SEAN. *The Flying Wasp.* London, 1937.
Inishfallen, Fare Thee Well. New York, 1949.
Rose and Crown. New York, 1952.

O'HARA, FRANK HURBURT. *Today in American Drama.* Chicago, 1939.

O'HARA, FRANK HURBURT, and MARGUERITTE H. BRO. *Invitation to the Theatre.* New York, 1951.

PEACOCK, RONALD. *The Poet in the Theatre.* New York, 1946.

PEARSON, HESKETH. *G. B. S.: A Full Length Portrait and a Postscript.* New York, 1950.

QUINN, ARTHUR HOBSON. *A History of the American Drama from the Civil War to the Present Day.* New York, 1937.

REYNOLDS, ERNEST. *Modern English Drama: A Survey of the Theatre from 1900.* London, 1949.

ROBINSON, LENNOX (ed.). *The Irish Theatre: Lectures Delivered during the Abbey Theatre Festival held in Dublin in August, 1938.* London, 1939.

SHAW, GEORGE BERNARD. *Bernard Shaw and Mrs. Patrick Campbell: Their Correspondence.* New York, 1952.

Selected Prose of Bernard Shaw. New York, 1952.

SKINNER, RICHARD DANA. *Eugene O'Neill, A Poet's Quest.* New York, 1935.

SMITH, HUGH ALLISON. *Main Currents of Modern French Drama.* New York, 1925.

SOBEL, BERNARD. *The Theatre Handbook and Digest of Plays,* 6th ed. New York, 1948.

STANFORD, DEREK. *Christopher Fry, An Appreciation.* London and New York, 1951.

STARKIE, WALTER. *Luigi Pirandello, 1867-1936.* New York, 1937.

STRONG, L. A. G. *Common Sense about Drama.* New York, 1937.

SUTTON, GRAHAM. *Some Contemporary Dramatists.* London, 1924.

SYMONS, ARTHUR. *The Symbolist Movement in Literature,* Revised ed. New York, 1919.

THOMPSON, ALAN REYNOLDS. *The Anatomy of Drama.* Berkeley, 1942.

TOLLER, ERNST. *I Was a German.* New York, 1934.

TOUMANOVA, PRINCESS NINA ANDRONIKOVA. *Anton Chekhov, The Voice of Twilight Russia.* New York, 1937.

VERNON, FRANK. *The Twentieth-Century Theatre.* London, 1924.

WARREN, L. A. *Modern Spanish Literature.* New York, 1929.

WAXMAN, SAMUEL MONTEFIORE. *Antoine and the Théâtre Libre.* Cambridge, 1926.

WILSON, NORMAN SCARLYN. *European Drama.* London, 1937.

WINSTEN, STEPHEN. *Days with Bernard Shaw.* New York, 1949.

WINTHER, SOPHUS KEITH. *Eugene O'Neill, A Critical Study.* New York, 1934.

YOUNG, STARK. *Immortal Shadows: A Book of Dramatic Criticism.* New York, 1948.

ZUCKER, A. E. *Ibsen, the Master Builder.* New York, 1929.